THE SCHWEPPES ROCK YEARBOOK

VOLUME NINE

EDITED BY LLOYD BRADLEY

Virgin

In-house editor
CAT LEDGER

Editor's assistant
ALISON TAYLOR

Cover by
MARCUS LYNCH

Design by
SUE WALLIKER at **MEKON DESIGN LTD**

Assisted by
LYNN PAULA RUSSELL and **SAM SULLIVAN**

THE ROCK YEARBOOK VOLUME 9

A Virgin Book
Published in 1988
by the Paperback Division of
WH Allen & Co Plc
44 Hill Street
London W1X 8LB

ISBN 0 86369 278 8

Typeset by Phoenix Photosetting, Chatham, Kent

Printed and bound in Great Britain by Scotprint, Musselburgh, Scotland

CONTRIBUTORS

★ **Lisa Anthony** once worked at *Smash Hits*, once worked at CBS Records and once or twice contributed to *Just 17*. A "mine" of information on snowshakers, Space "Adventure" and the Cutty Sark (very interesting tea clipper . . .). However, far more interesting is her cat Malley, who, early in 1985, snaffled Morrissey's hearing-aid causing everyone to shout at him very loudly indeed. This made him so utterly miserable he went off to found The Smiths. But none of this matters now because Lisa's in Australia. (Tells fibs.)

★ **John Bauldie** is a freelance writer who lives in Essex. At present he is attached to *Q* as a sub-editor, reviewer and hi-fi columnist. He also edits and publishes *The Telegraph*, a magazine about Bob Dylan, from which a "best of" selection, *All Across The Telegraph*, is available from quality booksellers everywhere. A former lecturer in English Literature and a Fellow Of The Royal Society Of Arts, he likes 10,000 Maniacs and Bolton Wanderers.

★ **Lloyd Bradley**, having survived an EMAP Metro Christmas party and gone "through the card" (including the legendary Kingsize Monster Doner and the more-than-substantial Double Shish) at Tufnell Park Kebabs, feels life holds little challenge. A little tea shoppe "somewhere on the South Coast" beckons. Meanwhile he writes for *Q*.

★ **Geoff Brown** has written books on Michael Jackson and Diana Ross, and commented on all aspects of black music, theatre and film in numerous papers and films. Currently the sports editor at *Time Out*, he still gets on the good foot at least once a day.

★ **Richard Cook** is the editor of *Wire*, Britain's jazz and new music magazine. He also broadcasts and writes elsewhere. The best thing about him is his wife, Lee Ellen.

★ **Ian Cranna** is a former contributor to *NME* from his hometown of Edinburgh, and a pioneering editor of *Smash Hits*. Having moved around several times since, at pop's mad hatter's tea party, these days he can be found scurrying between *Smash Hits*, *Q* (modern guide to music and more) and *Sounds*, hoping that some day someone will ask him to write the definitive history of House Music. File under: Old Enough To Know Better, Too Young To Care.

★ **Adrian Deevoy** single-handedly invented rock 'n' roll, on a roundabout in Basingstoke in the early fifties, but swapped it with some "dudes from Memphis" for a bag of conkers. After his death (in mysterious circumstances) cut short a "career in the movies", he went to work for *Q* as Staff Writer and whiles away his spare time trying to "vibe up" a Gilbert O'Sullivan revival.

★ **Fred Dellar** is a mine of information ("Fredfacts" – *NME*), a wordsmith *par excellence* (crossword compiler – *Smash Hits*) and a bit of a tease (puzzle pages – *Just 17*). As well as all this he still finds time to be the most genial fellow in music journalism and once co-wrote *The Hip*, possibly the best jazz book ever.

★ **Paul Du Noyer** is the assistant editor of *Q*, the self-styled "modern guide to music and more." His media career began as a part-time illustrator on the *Liverpool Catholic Pictorial*, drawing pictures of the Virgin Mary for children's colouring competitions. From here it was but a short step to reviewing punk rock concerts for the *New Musical Express*. One way or another, he feels he's paid his debt to society.

★ **Paul Elliott** divides his time between the clean air and sobriety of horticulture and the seedy excess of rock 'n' roll. In other words, he shovels shit at a garden centre for half his time and does much the same for *Sounds* on a weekly basis. Boring Arsenal supporter and midfield supremo with a left foot reminiscent of the godlike Liam "The Claw" Brady, Elliott is also contemplating a career in pro football having steered the mighty Forest Lodge to an emotional triumph in this year's inter-garden centre six-a-side league.

★ **Simon Garfield** is Deputy Editor of *Time Out*. He could have become Editor, but decided to have his first child, Benjamin, instead. He is the author of *Expensive Habits: The Dark Side Of The Music Industry*, and is currently writing a book about lunch.

★ **Andy Gill** spent far too many years working for the *NME*. He now writes for *The Independent* and *Q*, and edits the film, book and video sections for the latter. He lives in Ilford with 1 girlfriend, 2 cats and 82 Sun Ra LPs, and in his spare time contributes vocals to Andy & The Armchairs.

★ **Bill Graham** writes for the Irish rock magazine *Hot Press*. He is not to be confused with the Secretary of the Navy in President Fillmore's Administration.

★ **Chris Heath**: "Unkempt", "unshaven", "always off playing ping pong", "he writes quite a lot", "a bit of a groover" (???), "not very good at standing up", "Clark Datchler won't talk to him", "nobody can hear a word he says anyway" . . . just a few descriptions of the man by his loyal, caring "friends".

★ **Paolo Hewitt** is lean, wiry and the *NME*'s sage-like expert on all things funky – a taxing position that involves a great deal of "staying out 'til all hours". Occasional DJ partner to the aforementioned Lloyd Bradley, he believes he should have been included in the last Italian World Cup Squad, and in another life probably was.

★ **Tom Hibbert** of *Smash Hits*, *Q* and other "fine" titles is an English person with a pathetic devotion to Jack Palance, the bloke in *Man In A Suitcase* and other poor actors. His wife is far more impressive, having once kissed Elvis Presley on the lips and having been born just around the corner from Eric Brann of Iron Butterfly. (Eats toast.)

★ **Colin Irwin**: Apart from being Editor of "Britain's best-selling pop weekly" *Number One*, Irwin is a failed footballer with a peculiar obsession with pictures of old race-horses, kittens, Muhammad Ali and traditional folk music of all shapes and sizes. His BBC Radio 2 programme *Acoustic Roots* is now into its fourth series and he spent many years making the tea at *Melody Maker*. He is not Irish but would like to be.

★ **Gavin Martin**: Once described as the "Shirley Temple of rock journalism", this short, stroppy Son Of Ulster began writing for the *NME* at the age of 13, and is presently Media Editor of that magazine.

★ **Charles Shaar Murray** was born in 1831 in Bad Ass, Texas. The eldest of 27 children, he spent his first 120 years in a state of edgy anticipation waiting for Johnny Guitar Watson to make his first record. When this failed to go platinum, Murray decided in a fit of pique to opt for reincarnation as a British pop-culture pundit. He resides in London with his wife, two Stratocasters and a word processor, and lives in hope that Simon Garfield will be able to read his forthcoming book on Jimi Hendrix before qualifying for an old-age pension.

★ **Betty Page** disappeared in Florida in 1964, but mysteriously re-emerged in Mornington Crescent in 1986 to edit that venerable pop pickers' organ, the *Record Mirror*. She is the only human being in existence to simultaneously appreciate the talents of Go West and Rachmaninov, and when not "cracking the whip" over unruly freelances can be found in bijou Blackheath plotting her future career as astro-psychotherapist to the stars (sic). Collects distinctive items of latex leisurewear.

★ **Penny Reel** has been writing about reggae for some sixteen years, and for *Echoes* for ten. Previously with the *NME*, he can now be found in the company of *Sounds*.

★ **Cynthia Rose**, a native of Fort Worth, Texas, has worked on both *New Musical Express* and *The Dallas Morning News*. She founded and ran *deluxe* magazine in the States and now edits London weekly *City Limits*.

★ **Colin Shearman** spent the most miserable two years of his working life as a TV critic on *Time Out* and the happiest compiling *Q*'s Diary and absurdly easy pop trivia Quiz. He also used to write regularly for *The Guardian* Arts Page.

★ **David Sinclair** is rock critic of *The Times*, a contributor to *Q* and drummer with The Riding Hoods.

★ **Mat Snow**, along with Michael Jackson, Prince and Madonna, spent most of 1988 pretending not to be worried about saying goodbye to his twenties. Still hacking out a crust on the rock-face of life, he can at least claim the birth of his first book – sensationally titled *The Face Game* – as a foundation-stone on which might be built a reputation as immortal as that of, ooh, Woody Woodmansey's *U-Boat*. Meanwhile, he is still trying to sell the editors of *Q*, *Sounds*, *The Guardian*, *Sky* and *Time Out* his definitive Astrological Guide To Rock 'n' Roll.

★ **Chris Stapleton** worked in Sierra Leone from 1975–1984, acquiring a taste for palm wine, paldver sauce, Super Combo Kings and Zairean rumba. Since then he has contributed regularly to *Q* and *Blues & Soul* and, with Chris May, co-authored *African All-Stars*. He lives in North London with his wife Bryony and works as a sub-editor on a national daily.

★ **Caroline Sullivan** contributes to *Melody Maker*, *Jackie* and other post-modernist publications. She knows nothing about syllogism, situationism, deconstructivism or contextualism, but absolutely everything about The Bay City Rollers.

★ **Phil Sutcliffe**: Contributor to *Q*, *Time Out*, *Kaleidoscope*, *Running*. Has his moments.

★ **Karen Swayne** left the peace and quiet of the countryside for the bright lights of the big city and a job on the newly launched *No. 1*. After five years of asking pop stars their favourite colour and what their first snog was like she ended up as Film and Reviews Editor. She has just moved to New York for more of those bright lights and to be nearer Matt Dillon. Her favourite colour is black and her first snog was horrid.

★ **Richard Tipett** worked at IPC in Farringdon Street, but got bored of a) not knowing who his editor was from one day to the next and b) trying to find his way round the dimly-lit labyrinth of corridors. He left for the thrill-a-minute world of TV publications and osmosed into Features Editor of *Look-In*. Hobbies include hop imbibing (participant), motor-racing (non-participant) and worrying about the *TV Times* losing its franchise.

★ **John Tobler** remains concerned about the pathetic state of popular music, but has been saved from complete despair by the re-emergence of informative rock writing and the nostalgic value of CD and video in recalling the glories of the past. He is anxiously waiting for an artiste who he finds offensive, but who his children adore – it could be a long wait.

★ **Johnny Waller**: Born 1955. Still alive. Former computer-programmer who has contributed to *Sounds*, *Record Mirror*, *Time Out*, *Blitz* and *ZigZag* as self-opinionated enthusiast with genuine love for language and music – both exceedingly rare in rock journalism. Has discarded fleeting ambition of being one of those trendy bastards who always get invited on TV to analyse new youth cultures and is currently establishing his own syndication agency, S.I.N., to rival Reuters and Tass.

ACKNOWLEDGEMENTS

Well . . . another year, another *Rock Yearbook*.
Except, like practically every other year, it nearly wasn't. And wouldn't have been without a "lorra lorra" help from a "lorra lorra" people. Although it seems a little unfair to single out people for special praise, the following diamond geezer-type individuals more than deserve it:

Cat Ledger "for just being herself".
Alison Taylor for doing all sorts of things nobody else wanted to do with staggering efficiency and perpetual good humour.

Adrian Deevoy, John Bauldie, Ian Cranna and Mark Ellen for advice, assistance and the occasional "little chat".
John Tobler and Andy Gill for their invaluable help with the videos and books respectively.
And Stanley Morgan for the loan of the VCR.

Sue, Paula, Sam and the rest of the Mekon "posse", probably the most cheerful designers in Farringdon – or anywhere else in the world for that matter.

Adam Scott (LL Cool J/Public Enemy photos), Peter Lawrence (Folk photos), Richard Wooton (Country), Simon Hart and The Terrapin Trucking Co (The Grateful Dead), Titan Books (Batman), S.I.N. (Indie), Karen Swayne (Film feature), and Paul Elliot (Voivod), all of whom came through in a crisis to prevent an embarrassing amount of white spaces and red faces.
And the press officers of London's record and TV companies, without whose efficiency in dispatching photos and record sleeves there'd have been a great deal more.

Music Link for single-handedly organizing
The Schweppes Rock Yearbook Awards.

And, most importantly, Diana and Georgie for putting up with it all for the last six months.

In *It's A Wonderful Life* James Stewart maintained that the best-off fellow in town was the one who was "rich in friends". He had a point.

Goonight, Gobless anmineowyergoifyerdrivinome!

Lloyd Bradley

CONTENTS

6 EVENTS OF THE YEAR
Who did what, played where, sued who and ended up in chokey during the past 12 months.

18 THE YEAR IN MUSIC
What happened in rock, country, jazz, heavy metal, reggae, soul, world, dance, indie, folk, single and Ireland.

52 QUOTES OF THE YEAR
The business's big mouths open up, Terence Trent D'Arby fills two pages.

62 ACTS OF THE YEAR
Rick Astley, George Michael, T'Pau, The Pogues, LL Cool J, Terence Trent D'Arby, The Grateful Dead, Wet Wet Wet, Michael Jackson, and Whitesnake under the microscope.

82 THE YEAR IN ALBUMS
Short comments on the year's long players.

109 THE YEAR IN VIDEOS

120 FEATURES
Tom Hibbert watches TV adverts plunder the pop charts, Ian Cranna assesses Stock, Aitken & Waterman, Cynthia Rose thumbs through the current crop of " 'zines", Colin Shearman turns on to rock on the box, Lloyd Bradley goes all acoustic, John Bauldie finds his CD collection isn't all it should be, Karen Swayne wonders why pop stars "get into films", Simon Garfield follows the ZTT/Holly Johnson court case, Caroline Sullivan keeps up with the bouncing bimbettes and Paul Du Noyer ponders a tabloid creation called "Whacko Jacko".

140 THE SCHWEPPES AWARDS
Chaired by Martin Griffin, Music Link.

142 THANKS . . . BUT NO THANKS
The Yearbook's self-styled gurus applaud all that's laudable and take cheap shots at all that isn't.

146 THE YEAR IN BOOKS

158 IN MEMORIAM
Sadly missed participants in that big jam session in the sky.

162 THE YEAR'S BPI AND RIAA AWARDS

169 THE YEAR'S CHARTS
The UK and US Top 20, albums and singles, week by week.

196 REFERENCE
UK and US record companies, distributors, publishers, publications and music associations.

★ THE

AUGUST 1987

2 Alex Sadkin, producer best known for work with Grace Jones (*Warm Leatherette, Nightclubbing*), Simply Red (*Men And Women*), The Thompson Twins (*Quick Step, Side Kick*), Bob Marley (*Survival*) and Duran Duran (*Seven And The Ragged Tiger*), dies in a Miami hospital from injuries sustained in a car crash in Nassau the previous week.

4 'La Bamba', title song to a soon-to-be-released Ritchie Valens bio pic, performed by Los Lobos unseats Madonna's 'Who's That Girl' (another film title song) at number one in the UK singles charts. In the same week Michael Jackson's first new release in five years, 'I Just Can't Stop Loving You', enters at 18.

● **Kim Wilde In Sleazy Sex Romp Shocker! Accompanying the release of her 'Say You Really Want Me Single' is a promo video in which the pouting one writhes around, a trifle unenthusiastically, on a bed with four boxer-shorted hunks. Surprisingly, the video is banned, unsurprisingly the single gets nowhere.**

10 A New Jersey court finds soul singer Wilson Pickett guilty of possessing a shotgun with intent to endanger life, following his involvement in a fist-fight in a bar.

13 The Primitives are served a writ by their former booking agents, the Miles Copeland owned Prestige, for alleged breach of contract. The action concerns a benefit concert the group played at Guildford University for expenses only and the £400 booking fee the agency expected.

15 Madonna begins a UK "tour" at Leeds' Roundhay Park with three dates at Wembley Stadium (18, 19 and 20) to follow. The Leeds concert was hastily arranged after a fourth Wembley date was shelved following massive objections to the shows by Wembley residents and Brent council.

16 As millions mourn the tenth anniversary of Elvis' death, UK fan club members receive printed sheets of snappy answers for the purpose of countering any speculation that The King's drug intake was anything other than above board. Tasteful to the last, American tabloid "newspaper" the *National Enquirer* runs an "Elvis Is Alive" world exclusive.

18 Michael Jackson's single reaches number one. This decidedly slow ascent (it stalled at number three) may have owed something to the single's B side, 'Baby Be Mine', being already owned by some 40 million people as a track on *Thriller*.

20 Vocalist/guitarist Lindsay Buckingham quits Fleetwood Mac.

24 Donny Osmond takes time off from his Donny Osmond Entertainment Corporation, a TV and film company, to release his first single for ten years, 'I'm In It For Love'. Coinciding British TV appearances reveal the former pin-up not only to have started shaving but to have a acquired a worrying fondness for black leather.

25 Rap star Scott La Rock is shot dead in a New York street, believed to be the latest victim in the escalating Bronx/Brooklyn hip hop rivalry.

28 LWT launches *Night Network*, a "youth-oriented" confection of pop videos, gossip, live performance, pop videos, quiz shows, "cult" TV series and, er, pop videos transmitting between 1am and 4am at weekends. The tone is set by Nicholas Parsons, one of the presenters, posing for the press dressed as a Beastie Boy. TV stations north of Watford wisely refuse to have anything to do with it.

29 A severely jet-lagged Stevie Wonder steps "straight off a plane and onto the stage" (according to his press office) for a disappointing start to a week of concerts at the Wembley Arena, his first in the UK for three years. The shows got much better towards the end of the engagement.

Also . . .

● Unlikely couplings of the month were The Pet Shop Boys recording with Dusty Springfield ('What Have I Done To Deserve This'), The Fat Boys and The Beach Boys ('Wipe Out') and Yello and Shirley Bassey ('The Rhythm Divine').

● Ex-Beatles take the following courtroom action: George Harrison, Ringo Starr and Yoko Ono file a $40 million lawsuit against Capitol Records, claiming the delay in releasing Beatles CDs has cost them dearly in royalties; McCartney, Starr and Harrison filed a $15 million suit against sportswear giants Nike over a TV commercial; and Ono, Starr, McCartney and Harrison took action, for an "undisclosed amount", against Dave Clark for selling video compilations of Fabs' hits without permission – the former sixties pop star was marketing videos made from clips of *Ready Steady Go!*, of which he owns the rights.

● ZTT serve injunctions on Holly Johnson to prevent the former Frankie Goes To Hollywood singer from pursuing a solo career away from the label.

● Heublin Inc, an American liquor firm, boast a 200% increase in sales of their Brass Monkey ready-mixed cocktail. The falling-over qualities of the blended vodka, rum and citrus juices were glorified in a Beastie Boys' song of the same name.

YEAR

SEPTEMBER 1987

1 **After months of delay, *Bad* – Michael Jackson's follow-up album to *Thriller* – is released. The public responds with suitable enthusiasm: the LP enters the charts at number one; was certified double platinum (600,000 units) within a week; Gallup Poll returns show it to have outsold the entire UK Top 30 that week (one in four of every album bought).**

● In Los Angeles, charges of "distributing harmful matter to minors" are dropped against The Dead Kennedys' lead singer Jello Biafra. The incident concerned was the inclusion of the "Penis Landscape" poster by artist H. R. Geiger (who designed the original *Alien*) in the group's *Frankenchrist* album.

4 Hot on the heels of Morrissey, Smiths' drummer Mike Joyce quits the band claiming that his "present role within The Smiths has been fulfilled."

5 Ian Asbury spends a night in the cells in Vancouver, after a Cult show ends in a riot when fans and security staff fight pitch battles in the auditorium. Police arrested the singer following complaints from staff that he had assaulted them.

8 Rick Astley, self-confessed "fat, ugly northerner," begins a run of five weeks at number one with the Stock, Aitken & Waterman produced and written 'Never Gonna Give You Up'.

9 In Ottawa, Pink Floyd begin a ten-month sell-out tour of the US and Canada. The shows go ahead despite the group being locked in a courtroom battle with ex-member Roger Waters over the use of the name: Waters is claiming that without him the Floyd are no longer Floyd, therefore should not be allowed to pass themselves off as such.

10 Michael Jackson's world tour – announced as his last – begins at the Korakuen baseball stadium in Tokyo. Japanese ticket touts rise to the occasion by selling tickets for up to 17 times their face value – one was arrested offering his stock of 550 £26 tickets at £400 each.

11 Level 42's 'It's Over' becomes the first CD Video single to go on sale in the UK. It contains 20 minutes of music and 5 minutes of video which will remain unseen until CDV players reach the shops.

● Peter Tosh, founder member of The Wailers, is shot dead in his Kingston, Jamaica, home by a trio of armed robbers. Four other people, including Tosh's wife, were injured, one fatally. A week later former drugs dealer Dennis Lobban is charged with the murder.

14 In the wake of Mick Jagger's second solo album, Keith Richard announces his solo deal with Virgin. In spite of Jagger maintaining the group is merely "on hold", this move appears to signify the end of The Rolling Stones as Richard has often been quoted as saying he would never record solo while the group was still together.

16 Writers/producers Stock, Aitken & Waterman withdraw their High Court injunction against M/A/R/R/S that kept a remixed version of the group's 'Pump Up The Volume' single out of record shops for four days during the previous week. The court order concerns "samples" taken from SAW's 'Roadblock' and it is denied that the move was a "dirty tricks" campaign to prevent M/A/R/R/S knocking Rick Astley off the top spot.

17 Peter Gabriel's 'Sledgehammer' video soundly trounces all competition at the annual MTV Video Awards by carrying off 10 of the 20 trophies on offer: Best Video, Best Male Video, Best Concept Video, Best Performance, Best Special Effects, Best Art Direction, Best Editing, Best Director (Stephen Johnson), Most Experimental Video and The Van Gaird Special Award.

18 BBC's arts programme *Omnibus* screens a Bob Dylan special. The documentary reveals little about the great man other than his reluctance to give straight answers and his passable talent for portrait sketching.

24 The original Tom Robinson Band reforms to play a one-off reunion gig at London's 100 Club. The reason is the tenth anniversary of their first hit single '2–4–6–8 Motorway', the venue because that was where they were playing the day it entered the charts.

28 Record shop chains Virgin and HMV surprise nobody except mutant funk outfit Big Black, when they refuse to stock their thoughtfully-titled album *Songs About Fucking*.

30 Radio One celebrates 20 years on the air. The only DJ to survive two decades at the station is John Peel, whose determinedly "oddball" approach singled him out as the man least likely to stay too long.

Also . . .

● James Brown and Bobby Byrd begin legal actions against rappers Eric B & Rakim, over the latter's blatant appropriation of the Brown/Byrd-written 'I Know You Got Soul' for their hip-hop hit of the same name. In keeping with his cash-conscious reputation, Brown does not object to the single on artistic grounds, but merely wants a share of the writing royalties.

● The first bootleg CD appears. Titled *Castaways* it is a collection of Bruce Springsteen outtakes and live rarities such as 'Murder Incorporated', 'Frankie' and 'This Hard Town'. It reportedly is selling well at £50 upwards.

● Following their appearance as promotional giveaways, the first 3″ CD single reaches American shops when Frank Zappa puts out his evergreen 'Peaches En Regalia' in the format.

● The BBC announce they will be discontinuing the *Whistle Test* (*neé Old Grey*) rock show, but are unclear as to what, if anything, will replace it.

OCTOBER 1987

1 The government ignores advice from the BPI and shelves its controversial plans to impose a levy on blank cassette tapes. The decision is seen by many as a bid to stay in favour with young voters.

9 The New York Supreme Court dismisses the lawsuit filed against Boy George by the mother of Michael Rudetski, the musician who died from a heroin overdose at George's London home in 1986. The civil action alleged that George was responsible for the death due to his failure to get medical help, and the claim was reduced from $44 million to $20 million before the singer was cleared.

2 After a month's delay to let Jackson-mania die down, Bruce Springsteen's *Tunnel Of Love* album is released to critical acclaim and an instant number one chart position.

5 Ex-Smith Johnny Marr begins rehearsals with The Pretenders – he takes over on guitar from Robbie McIntosh – in preparation for the band supporting U2 on American tour dates.

7 Three weeks after slapping an injunction on 'Pump Up The Volume', SAW's Pete Waterman is served a writ by Blue Mountain Music, M/A/R/R/S's publishers. They claim that Waterman "appropriated" a large portion of 'Pump Up' and used it for 'My Love Is Guaranteed' by Sybil.

8 *The Roxy* bans The Beasties Boys' video for 'She's On It', a clip made up of live footage from their US tour. Producer Alastair Pirrie believes "the spectacle of a near-naked woman in a cage being prodded by a group of unpleasant looking youths with beer cans is not the sort of thing to be put out on the air when a lot of young children are watching." *TOTP* swiftly follows suit.

10 Texan Wanda Nicholls lodges an official complaint that David Bowie raped her and bit her on the legs and back, telling her "Now you've got AIDS." Bowie admits to knowing the woman, but dismisses the alleged incident, which supposedly took place at a party after his show in Dallas, as "publicity seeking." A Grand Jury sits to decide whether he has any charges to answer.

14 Jimmy Castor and John Pruitt of The Jimmy Castor Bunch file a $750,000 "breach of copyright" lawsuit against The Beastie Boys. The complaint concerns a snatch of TJCB's 1967 hit 'The Return Of Leroy (Part One)' cropping up on 'Hold It, Now Hit It', a track on the Beastie's *Licence To Ill* album.

15 The Bhundu Boys consider prosecuting the Grenfield Lodge Hotel in Leicester after they were refused entry on what appeared to be racial grounds. The manageress told tour manager Jody Boulting, prior to the group's arrival: "They are black . . . he [the manager] won't like that." The band were then turned away on the grounds there was no room, despite having booked four days previously.

16 Dave Robinson resigns as managing director of Stiff Records, the company he founded eleven years ago. Robinson, a seminal figure in the late-seventies "indie" scene – he signed Elvis Costello, Ian Dury, Nick Lowe and The Damned – was believed not to have got on too well with Jill Sinclair, MD of ZTT who bought the company in 1986.

● The Pogues, another Robinson signing, get the go-ahead from the company to start their own record label – Pogue Mahone, their original name – to release through the ZTT group.

18 LWT's *South Bank Show* screens its documentary on The Smiths. Filmed during the recording of *Strangeways*, it is updated to cover the fact the band split up nearly two months ago.

22 Echo And The Bunnymen dates for tonight and the following ten days are postponed to the New Year, after singer Ian McCulloch needed surgery on his leg. He tore calf muscles after being pulled off the stage by over-enthusiastic fans at one of the closing dates of the group's US tour.

23 Level 42, about the only survivors from the UK jazz/funk explosion of the early eighties, split up as the Gould brothers, Phil and Boon, leave over musical differences.

27 The Jesus And Mary Chain are thrown off *The Roxy* for refusing to "perform" (i.e. mime and pretend to play their instruments) during a rehearsal for 'Darklands'.

29 "Decades", Ron Wood's first ever British exhibition of the portrait painting and drawing skill that won him a place at Ealing Art College, opens in London. The portraits are of rock stars, celebrities and Wood's personal friends from over the last 20 years.

30 The Stranglers' record company withdraws the sleeve for their forthcoming single, 'All Day And All Of The Night'. Under the catalogue number VICE1, displaying a photo of Monica Coughlan and announcing "Jeff Mix" on the B side, it proved a bit much for Epic's legal department.

Also . . .

● The rumblings of serious discontent between Holly Johnson and ZTT Records beccme public. The ex-Frankie Goes To Hollywood singer claims the company will not let him record for an AIDS benefit album without a guarantee that they would own the rights to the recording.

● Clint Eastwood starts work as producer/director on his Charlie Parker biopic, *Bird*.

● With early anticipation of the Christmas rush, EMI, RCA, Polydor and CBS all introduce budget price CDs. Extensive portions of their back catalogues become available, in glorious digital clarity, for the paltry sum of £7.99.

NOVEMBER 1987

1 LL Cool J, Eric B & Rakim and Public Enemy begin a series of three shows at Hammersmith Odeon. Each night is marred by violence and crime outside the theatre, notably on the underground, resulting in a total of 16 arrests and 4 police officers injured.

6 George Michael releases *Faith*, his first recording since the demise of Wham! As expected, it enters the album charts at number one, but is prevented from becoming the week's best-selling CD by the Paul McCartney compilation *All The Best*.

8 Terence Trent D'Arby pulls out of a concert in Vienna scheduled for the following Tuesday, citing the former Nazi connections of Austrian President Kurt Waldheim. The promoter, while claiming to respect D'Arby's views, points out that D'Arby knew of the engagement months ago, before any tickets were sold, so therefore will still sue him.

10 Beastie Boy Adam Horovitz (Ad Rock) is acquitted, by Liverpool magistrates, of causing actual bodily harm to Joanne Clarke. The charges arose after The Beastie Boys' Liverpool concert ended in a riot and Ms Clarke was struck in the face by a beer can allegedly thrown from the stage.

11 The Grand Jury sitting on the Bowie rape case decide the singer has no charges to answer. A relieved Bowie – the charge carried a maximum sentence of 25 years in prison – pronounced that the incident had set the cause of genuine rape victims back 100 years.

13 U2 stop traffic throughout San Francisco's city centre when 20,000 fans turn up to their impromptu concert on the Justine Herman Plaza. Dubbed the "Save The Yuppies Show", Bono announces: "The business community is a bit short this week. [It was a couple of weeks after the stock market crash.] That's why I'm wearing this hat, we'll be passing it round later."

15 Jesus And Mary Chain vocalist Jim Reid is forcibly removed from the band's tour bus by police after a show in Toronto. Several members of the audience filed complaints that Reid had deliberately hit them with his microphone stand. Charged with assault, he is released on bail of $2,000 to appear in court in the New Year.

● Backseat passenger Ray "Pablo" Falconer is killed when the car driven by his brother, UB40 bass player Earl Falconer, crashes into a wall in Birmingham.

16 Former Clash drummer Topper Headon is jailed for 15 months at Maidstone Crown Court for supplying heroin to a man who later died.

● Madonna joins the current trend for selling the same songs twice as her *You Can Dance* album of remixes is released well in time for Christmas. Goodwill, however, is in short supply as the set barely scrapes past the million mark.

17 T'Pau's 'China In Your Hand' begins a run of five weeks at number one, while Nina Simone tops the indie singles chart with a re-release of her 1957 classic 'My Baby Just Cares For Me'.

18 Sly Stone is charged with possession of cocaine, for the second time this year. The drug was found on him when police entered his house to arrest him for non-payment of child support and found him "incoherent and violent".

22 Ivan Taressenko, chief drummer with Glastonbury stars The Mutoid Waste Company, dies in hospital, a victim of the Kings Cross Fire.

23 'Pump Up The Volume' stars M/A/R/R/S – a collaboration between AR Kane and Colourbox – break up following a string of well-reported rows between each other and their record label 4AD.

27 Durutti Column reveal an extreme case of techno-mania when they release the cassette version of their new *The Guitar And Other Machines* on Digital Audio Tape. Commercial potential is thought to be limited as DAT players are not officially available in this country.

28 Michael Jackson's Wembley dates are announced (two shows only at this stage) and ticket demand – personal, postal and telephonic – tops 1.5 million, enough to fill the stadium for almost 20 shows.

Also . . .

● Word emerges from The Revolution – a UK-based, unofficial Prince information service – that the Paisley Park keeper will be releasing his second album of the year. It is to come out in a black sleeve, with a black label, no credits and no advertising on 7 December. No official acknowledgement is forthcoming from WEA and the saga of *The Black Album* begins.

● Reverend Jesse Jackson follows Neil Kinnock in a bid for pop stardom – the Labour leader appeared in a Tracey Ullman video. The then US Presidential candidate gives his wholehearted support to the single 'A.F.R.I.C.A.', by New York rap crew Stetsasonic, which takes its hook-line from a sampled segment of one of his speeches, after they send him a demo for final approval.

● Three of Michael Jackson's eight Australian shows are cancelled, apparently due to poor advance ticket sales.

● Bookmakers William Hill announce Rick Astley's forthcoming release, 'When I Fall In Love', 7–4 favourite for the Christmas number one.

DECEMBER 1987

1 The US Supreme Court rejects the appeal by a Kentucky schoolteacher concerning her sacking for screening Pink Floyd's film *The Wall* to her class. The court decides that in subjecting minors to the film's "bad language and inherent sexual content" she had "abdicated her function as an educator". Amazingly, "diabolical acting" wasn't mentioned.

● The Pogues' 'Fairy Tale Of New York' enters the charts at number 32. It is not banned by the BBC, in spite of the lyric *"you scumbag, you maggot/ you cheap lousy faggot/merry Christmas, let's hope it's your last"*, and becomes second favourite for Christmas number one, 5–1 behind Rick Astley.

2 Luc Havan, the Florida nightclub owner accused of aggravated battery after beating record producer Jaco Pastorius to death in September, has his charge altered to second-degree murder.

5 The Jesus And Mary Chain are banned from appearing on the US version of *TOTP*. As the names of acts are flashed on the screen by way of introducing their performance, the CBS TV network anticipates complaints of blasphemy. They want the band to be billed as The JAMC, which Reid and Co won't agree to.

7 The rumoured release date for Prince's so-called *Black* album arrives, and his record company comprehensively deny that such a record is or ever has been on their schedules. However, during the days before Christmas, excellently reproduced bootleg cassettes of previously unheard Prince material – complete with track listings – are circulating freely. Some music papers go as far as to review it as *The Black Album*.

3 Run DMC's management company, Rush Productions – half-owned by Run's older brother Russell Simmons – sues Profile, the group's record company, for $7 million in alleged unpaid royalties on the *Raisin' Hell* album. The action is widely perceived as a clumsy attempt to get Run DMC, the biggest selling rap group in the world, away from Profile and on to the Rush-owned Def Jam label (home of The Beastie Boys and LL Cool J). Profile countersues for $4 million, claiming that Run DMC broke their contract by stopping work on their new LP.

8 One more Michael Jackson show is added to Wembley Stadium. It is instantly sold out due to excess ticket demand from the first two.

9 With 14 shopping days left, CBS Records introduce the first picture compact discs. Michael Jackson's *Bad*, Springsteen's *The Tunnel Of Love, The Hardline According To Terence Trent D'Arby* and George Michael's *Faith* make the ideal gift for the pop fan who *truly* has everything!

10 Abba stars Agnetha Faltskog and Bjorn Ulvaeus are prosecuted for tax evasion in Sweden. It is alleged that, due to their failing to declare stocks and shares owned in 1985, they are some £600,000 in arrears. Faced with the possibility of a large fine and/or a jail sentence they resolve to fight the case.

11 An extended edition of the BBC's *Arena* devotes itself to the much acclaimed Talking Heads concert film, *Stop Making Sense*.

12·13 Simply Red's two sold-out shows at London's Wembley Arena are cancelled, as vocalist Mick Hucknall is taken ill with flu.

14 A story breaks that Janice Long is not going to return to Radio One after having her baby. The rumours are hotly denied, but subsequently turn out to be true.

15 Two more Michael Jackson shows, both sell outs, are added, setting a new venue record of five full houses (72,000 per concert). The previous best stood at four nights each for Springsteen, Madonna and Genesis.

17 Carol Decker contracting a throat infection means T'Pau have to cancel three nights of their UK tour.

18 Warner Brothers Records in the US admit that operations were called to a halt earlier in the month after several hundred copies of a new Prince album were pressed, but claim they didn't have a definite release date for it. It also transpires that the WEA UK sales team had been taking orders for the album (catalogue number WX147), even though the company was denying it existed. Meanwhile Prince's *Sign 'O' The Times* concert film takes over $1 million at the box office on its first weekend of US release.

22 The Pet Shop Boys' 'Always On My Mind' comes from nowhere to take the Christmas number one spot. The Pogues are at number two, and Rick Astley is beaten to number three by Mel (Smith) & Kim (Wilde)'s 'Rockin' Around The Christmas Tree' (the latter had its video censored following complaints over a scene featuring Mel Smith in a fridge).

31 *Whistle Test*, axed by the BBC during the summer, returns for an all-night special to see in the New Year.

Also . . .

● George Martin, best known for his production work on The Beatles, receives a CBE in the New Year's honours list.

● A row breaks out between the Vatican and the good burghers of Pacentro in Italy, home town to Madonna's grandparents before they emigrated to the US at the turn of the century. The town, eager to exploit its tourist potential, wants to erect a statue of the pop star, clad, traditionally, in basque and fishnets. The church believes such a sight is likely to "corrupt the morals of the town's fine young people."

JANUARY 1988

1 Communard Jimmy Somerville is attacked and beaten up in the early hours, while enjoying a New Year's pub-crawl in East London. Contrary to press reports, the assault is believed to be an attempted mugging rather than a personal attack. His two assailants were so drunk Somerville was not badly hurt.

4 Billy Idol refuses MTV permission to broadcast his 'Hot In The City' video, claiming the cable channel's cutting of nine scenes "eliminated every scrap of meaning" from the clip. Among these "meaningful" events were semi-naked girls cavorting around with phallic-looking crucifixes.

7 The Housemartins call it a day and split up. They leave behind them enough recorded material to take them up to the third anniversary of their 1985 debut single 'Flag Day', claiming it was always their plan to limit the group's lifespan to three years, regardless of success achieved.

8 Tickets for George Michael's first British solo shows – two dates at Earls Court in June – go on sale, and, unsurprisingly, are instantly sold out. Two more London and seven nationwide dates are added by the end of the month.

11 'So Emotional' gives Whitney Houston her sixth consecutive number one single in America, a feat only previously achieved by The Beatles and The Bee Gees.

14 In celebration of the tenth anniversary of the group's last live show, a Sex Pistols Convention is held at London's 100 Club. Guests include Glen Matlock and Wally Nightingale – this far from household name, it transpires, is actually the guitarist Malcom McLaren fired to make room for one J. Rotten.

14·15·16
Magma, an obscure and often quite odd French jazz/rock band who enjoyed a certain cult following in the seventies, play three nights at London's Bloomsbury Theatre. The shows are the first venture for Interesting Promotions, a company owned and run by world snooker champion Steve Davis, who sensibly admits "I'm not really after making money out of this."

15 While Krush enjoy a Top Five hit with their 'House Arrest' single, their manager, former *NME* writer Amrik Rai, appears on LWT's *The London Programme* admitting he paid London pirate radio stations hundreds of pounds to ensure blanket airplay for the record on its release. "It was," he boasted "worth every penny."

18 Former Frankie Goes To Hollywood singer Holly Johnson begins his High Court struggle to free himself from an injunction served by ZTT Records, which prevents him pursuing a solo career with another company. He is claiming his ZTT contract is unenforceable and within restraint of trade.

19 The Sugarcubes react unconventionally when *The Chart Show* demands they censor the video for their 'Cold Sweat' single before it is aired. The offending scenes – during which it is implied, by a flashing knife blade intercut with shots of, er, bacon, that singer Einar is having his throat cut – are removed, but the band insist on replacing them with shots of frolicking monkeys. The bemused *Chart Show* producer agrees.

20 Radio 1 silences its DJs for "More Music Day", a bold experiment to find out if people really do want the attendant chatter. However, the interruption of the music only for news, traffic and weather bulletins, is declared "not such a good idea" after the carefully monitored listener response results in complaints from two-thirds of callers.

25 The Armoury Show announce an official split. Founder members Richard Jobson and Russell Webb had been drifting apart for some time as Jobson concentrated increasingly on TV, radio and modelling work. Both will stay signed to EMI on solo contracts.

30·31 After a five-year split, Pere Ubu re-form and play two shows at London's Institute Of Contemporary Arts. A new album is also on the cards for late spring.

16 Tina Turner's *Break Every Rule* tour breaks the attendance record for rock concerts by a single act when she performs in front of 180,200 people at Rio's Americana Stadium. The show is also broadcast live, by satellite, to the US and Japan, reaching an estimated TV audience of 26 million.

Also . . .

- Bill *"Ghostbusters"* Murray begins directing an update of *A Christmas Carol*, which, confusingly, includes screen roles for Miles Davis, Larry Carlton and David Sanborn.
- The Sex Pistols' *Never Mind The Bollocks* album goes gold in the US, a mere eleven years after it was first released.
- Pollstar, a US information service for rock promoters, releases figures for the previous year's biggest-grossing tours: U2 $35 million; Bon Jovi $28 million; Pink Floyd and The Grateful Dead $27 million each; David Bowie $22 million; Mötley Crüe $21 million; Whitney Houston $20 million. The best average earner was Bowie, whose total came from only 45 shows.
- After separation of nearly three years, Darryl Hall and John Oates start work on a joint project for release in early spring.
- Adam Horovitz begins a co-starring role in *Lunatic*, a film described as "a teenage *One Flew Over The Cuckoo's Nest*," directed by Hugh Hudson and starring Donald Sutherland. Mike Diamond sets up his own interior design company, Pod, and Adam Yauch is spending a lot of time skiing, yet The Beastie Boys deny they have split up and the record company talks of a new album for August.

FEBRUARY 1988

1 The Cars, whose million-selling single 'Drive' became an unofficial theme song for Live Aid, announce they have split up as the group's two leaders, Rick Okasek and Benjamin Orr, both want to go solo.

2 Tiffany's 'I Think We're Alone Now' takes over from Belinda Carlisle's 'Heaven Is A Place On Earth' at number one. This heralds a succession of teenage girls in the UK Top Ten – 'I Should Be So Lucky' is only two weeks off the top.

4 Chuck Eddy, a US rock critic, serves The Beastie Boys a $500,000 lawsuit for "commercial appropriation of his image." Apparently, when on assignment to cover part of the Beasties' tour last year, the threesome crept into his hotel room and threw a bucket of water over him. Eddy took the "joke" well, until he watched a retailed video of Beastie Boys promo clips linked with scenes from their home movies. The group had filmed the water incident and put it on to the tape.

5 Former Stiff Records owner Dave Robinson accepts undisclosed damages from *The Daily Telegraph* following his libel action against the paper. Robinson had sued after an article alleged that Island Records – for whom he was MD – ran into financial trouble due to his gross mismanagement.

8 The Who get back together to perform at the BPI awards ceremony at the Albert Hall. This reunion is considered so important that, when the televised event gets behind schedule, Rick Astley is prevented from taking the stage to pick up his Best Single Of 1987 award (for 'Never Gonna Give You Up') so the group can still squeeze in their three numbers.

● Minneapolis rockers Hüsker Dü finally announce their split, after a long period of internal turmoil. The official reasons are "philosophical and creative differences", but drummer Grant Hart's escalating unreliability is thought to have much to do with it.

15 Morrissey releases his first solo single, 'Suedehead', and it enters the charts at number five – a higher first placing than anything The Smiths ever put out.

10 Holly Johnson wins his court battle against ZTT Records, and is freed from his contract – which the judge referred to as "nonsensical" and "unreasonable restraint" – and can start work recording his solo album for MCA. In a later settlement, it is decided that ZTT shall pay all the case's estimated £300,000 costs.

11 Ticketless Butthole Surfers fans riot at the group's show at London's Mean Fiddler. Police are called to restore order after ticket-holders are attacked as they approach the venue, and a mob tries to batter down the auditorium's fire escape doors.

12 Was (Not Was) play a one-off UK show at London's Town & Country Club. In spite of the band enjoying a considerable critical and commercial following in this country for several years, this is their first-ever UK appearance.

16 Thames TV move pop show *The Roxy* to a 12.30am slot, due to poor ratings. Two weeks later, the Network Controllers Committee opts not to recommission the show after the present series ends in March.

17 Channel 4 launches *The Late Shift*, a series of three-hour programmes made up of documentaries about, and concert footage of, acts such as Lou Reed, Pink Floyd, Marvin Gaye and Art Pepper. Presented by Vivienne Goldman and Charlie Gillett, it aims to "take a more serious approach to the presentation of pop music."

22 Jesus And Mary Chain singer Jim Reid, charged with assaulting fans with a microphone stand during the group's Canadian tour last November, is cleared by a Toronto court after apologizing and donating £500 to the Salvation Army, the judge's favourite charity.

24 Bananarama (holders of the record for most hits by an unchanged girl group) announce a new line-up: Siobhan "Mrs Dave Stewart" Fahey has been replaced by Jaquie O'Sullivan, previously lead singer with The Shillelagh Sisters and a long-time friend of the trio.

26 Bon Jovi and Mötley Crüe manager Doc McGhee faces a possible five years in prison after pleading guilty to a charge, dated from 1982, of smuggling 20 tons of marijuana (street value $10 million) into the US.

29 As a taster for the upcoming album *The Story Of The Clash Vol 1*, 'I Fought The Law' is released as a single.

Also . . .

● Co-director Bob Geldof starts the cameras turning in Dublin on *Cowboys*, the feature film he co-wrote. Sounding not a million miles removed from 'Rat Trap', the plot concerns a young factory worker who is determined to be a pop star.

● *Money* magazine publishes a list of Britain's biggest earners. Richard Branson tops the music business entrants with a staggering £130 million, Paul McCartney weighs in next at £79 million, then Elton John (£42 million) and Mark Knopfler stands at equal 19th (with Benny Hill and Dudley Moore) with just £10 million to his name.

● George Clinton signs to Prince's Paisley Park label after his proposed deal with Virgin falls through. Collaborations between the two generations of funkateer are believed to be unlikely. Meanwhile white label copies of *The Black Album* are changing hands in Los Angeles record shops for $400, despite WEA statements that all copies pressed have been destroyed.

● The Beatles win their courtroom battle with Nike, and the sportswear company withdraw its TV advert featuring the original recording of 'Revolution'. The Fabs sued for $15 million last July, after Nike acquired the rights from Michael Jackson who owns The Beatles' back catalogue. It is not known if the ex-group received any financial settlement.

MARCH 1988

2 Amid much furrowing of brows by critics, musicians and executives, Paul Simon strolls off with the Record Of The Year "Grammy" for *Graceland*, at the American music business awards in Los Angeles. Much the same as he did last year for exactly the same album. U2 collect Album Of The Year for *The Joshua Tree* and no one is particularly surprised when Michael Jackson (winner of a record eight categories in 1984) goes home empty-handed.

3 Run DMC comprehensively lose their legal battle to leave Profile Records. Not only do the group withdraw their accusation that the company did not "accurately or completely account to them" to the tune of $7 million in back royalties, but they agree to pay Profile's estimated $500,000 legal costs *and* sign a new contract holding them to the label for *ten* albums – effectively until the turn of the millenium.

6 German radio DJ Ruth Rockensachaub plays Prince's *Black Album*, from a vinyl pressing and in its entirety, on her show which broadcasts all over Germany and parts of Switzerland and Austria. As there was no reaction from WEA she plays it again on Wednesday. On Thursday the station receives a telex from the record company warning of a £3,500 fine if she does it again. The incident adds weight to the rumours that, instead of following a company directive and destroying all finished copies, employees at WEA's German pressing plant were sneaking them out.

7 Camden's favourite sons, Madness, reappear with the single 'I Pronounce You'. Now trimmed down to a four-piece – Suggs, Lee Thompson, Chris Foreman and Carl Smith – they have gained a definite article to become The Madness, and claim not to be "nutty" at all.

● "Outrageous" singer/actor Harris Glenn Milstead, known to the world as Divine, is found dead in bed in a Los Angeles hotel room.

8 At a lavish press conference, Pepsi Cola unveil plans for a new series of all-action TV commericals, starring an all- (among other things) skiing, parachuting, flying Michael Jackson. His fee of $10 million is said to be "well above average for stunt work."

10 *Time Out*, a London listings magazine, escapes prosecution under the Marine Broadcasting (Offences) Act 1967 on a legal technicality. In what was to be a test-case in a new government initiative to crack down on pirate radio, the magazine was charged with illegally assisting Radio Caroline and Lazer 558 by publishing their frequencies and programme details. Finding against *Time Out* would have made any future media examinations of pirate radio's sudden growth virtually impossible.

● Andy Gibb, younger brother of Bee Gees Robin, Barry and Maurice, dies in an Oxfordshire hospital from a heart attack.

14 Grace Slick announces she is quitting Starship with the words: "I'm shifting in other directions. I'm 48. How long can I jump around on stage?"

17 Responding to pressure concerning live music licence renewals, Hammersmith Odeon's parent company, Rank Leisure, give Hammersmith and Fulham Council the go-ahead to "advise" the theatre's management as to which bands should be allowed to appear. Moves to vet the Odeon's bills began after disturbances outside the LL Cool J shows last year, and what appears to be a blanket ban on rap acts is the first manifestation.

● Aswad's 'Don't Turn Around' reaches number one in the singles charts. It is the first record by a black reggae band to do that since Musical Youth's 'Pass The Dutchie' in October 1982 and the first time Aswad have made the Top Ten in 14 years of recording.

21 It is announced that UB40's bass player Earl Falconer will face charges of driving with excess alcohol in his blood and causing death by dangerous driving. The charges relate to the crash last November in which his brother Ray was killed.

22 Mick Jagger plays his first solo concert at Tokyo's 48,000-seater Korakuen baseball stadium, backed by little-known American musicians. It is the first of eight Japanese dates, and no plans are revealed to play anywhere else.

29 A play called *Speed The Plow* opens in New York; it's about the Hollywood film industry and stars Madonna. Apparently, she's quite good in it.

Also . . .

● A Fuji film commercial is broadcast in the US featuring Bon Jovi, standing in a swimming-pool and peforming 'Living On A Prayer'. The director responsible for this masterpiece is none other than Jimmy "Little Jimmy" Osmond.

● Eddie "The Eagle" Edwards, the unsuccessful Olympic ski-jumper turned cult figure, attempts to cash in on his post-Calgary celebrity by recording the truly dreadful single 'Fly, Eddie, Fly'. It gets about as far in the charts as he did off the slope – practically nowhere.

● The number of CD players purchased in the UK passes the magic million mark – eight per cent of all households – while figures for discs sold are given as 19 million.

● The second biggest draw on the US tour circuit, behind Michael Jackson, is the "Rat Pack" reunion show: Frank Sinatra, Sammy Davis Jnr and Dean Martin (combined age 204). Their 40-date tour sold out in hours, to the tune of slightly more than $20 million.

APRIL 1988

2 The *South Bank Show* presents *Ken Russell's ABC Of British Music.* This special, directed by Russell, visually interprets the best and worst of British music over the last century "from Elgar to The Beatles" using video clips (his own and other people's), specially filmed scenarios and live footage. Before it is screened, a clip shot by Russell to accompany The Pogues' 'Ballad Of The Gentleman Soldier' has scenes showing the murder of British soldier removed.

4 After 25 years, the Crossroads Motel – or the King's Oak Country Hotel as it metamorphosed into – closes its doors for the final time. A nation mourns.

5 James Brown turns himself in to South Carolina police after a warrant is issued for his arrest following complaints made by his wife that he beat her up and took five shots at her while she hid in a car. The "Godfather Of Soul" is charged with assault with intent to commit murder and aggravated assault and battery. He is bailed for $15,000 to appear in court in June.

7 After 13 years away, Barry White returns to the UK and begins a brief tour. So fondly is he remembered, he sells out the Royal Albert Hall for two nights, then revels in nostalgia as he only performs one number less than ten years old.

● Alice Cooper's well-worn gallows gag – in which he simulates hanging himself on stage – goes badly wrong during his Wembley concert. The safety rope snaps, leaving Cooper dangling by his neck for several seconds before a roadie rushes on and cuts him down.

9 BBC2 screens a "fly-on-the-wall" documentary, filmed in Paris during the recording of Talking Heads' *Naked* album.

12 James Brown's wife, Adrienne, is arrested at an airport in Georgia, after being found in possession of a quantity of PCP (the illegal drug Angel Dust). She claims to have been set up in an attempt to discredit her case against her husband.

14 Sixteen-year-old starlet Tiffany applies to a California court for "legal adult status" in the latest move in a battle between her manager and her mother. Mum, Mrs Janie Williams, sought to re-negotiate a two-year-old, seven-album contract that gives manager, George Tobin, half her daughter's royalties (estimated so far as $3 million) and complete control over "musical direction and presentation." Tiff wanted her mother to have no say in her career, so left home to live with an aunt. Her mother filed a missing persons' report and had the chart-topper officially listed a runaway. The judge asks for one month to decide whether Tiffany is mature enough to make her own choices.

15 Reggae drummer Sly Dunbar sets up his drum kit in a New York courtroom as a $3 million lawsuit brought by composer Patrick Alley against CBS and Mick Jagger continues – Alley alleges that Jagger's hit 'Just Another Night' was a steal from one of his compositions. Dunbar, who played on Jagger's recording, drums along with both records to prove they are substantially different in structure. The case is later thrown out.

20 *Moonwalk*, Michael Jackson's official biography – written by the boy himself, and edited by Jackie Onassis – goes on sale in the UK. Anybody hoping to find any form of insight into Jackson's life is sorely disappointed.

23 The row between The Pogues and LWT's *Friday Night Live*, over the alleged censorship of their song 'Birmingham Six' on the show (the band were faded out early to make way for a commercial break) becomes public when *Right To Reply* includes the missing minutes and a letter from *FNL*'s producer Geoff Posner. Posner states that if the political content of the song bothered them they would never have allowed the group to perform any of it. Pogues' manager, Frank Murray, remains unhappy with this explanation, claiming "there seemed to be a couple of minutes spare at the end, which the comedians had to fill with ad-libs."

25 Months of speculation are ended when Bruce Springsteen's "Tunnel Of Love Express" UK tour dates are announced. The three dates sell out immediately and more are promised.

● Thomas Dolby "premières" his new album, *Aliens Ate My Buick*, and new group, The Lost Toy People, in a one-off show at London's Town & Country Club.

● Prince releases 'Alphabet St', the first single from an album called *Lovesexy* that will see the light of day next month. Although his record company, WEA, admit to the album's existence, they will not say if it contains any material from the aborted *Black Album*.

26 'Theme From S-Xpress' by S-Xpress on Rhythm King and *The Innocents* by Erasure on Mute are at number one in the national singles and album charts respectively. It is the first time both charts have been topped simultaneously by releases on independent labels.

Also . . .

● By reaching number one in the American charts, Michael Jackson's 'Man In The Mirror' achieves a record for *Bad* that even *Thriller* couldn't manage: four number one singles from the same album. The feat is equalled two weeks later, when Whitney Houston's 'Where Do Broken Hearts Go?' becomes her fourth number one from *Whitney*.

● Sonny Bono is elected mayor of Palm Springs, an upmarket Californian resort town. Like his fellow celebrity mayor, Clint Eastwood, Bono decided to run following continued frustration with the local planning department over a proposed extension for the restaurant he owns.

● The editing of over 300 hours of previously unheard John Lennon material into a series of 52 hour-long radio broadcasts begins in the US. The tapes – including 24 Lennon songs, material by The Quarrymen, countless versions of 'Strawberry Fields Forever' and interviews – were made public after Yoko Ono decided "John's music belongs to the world."

MAY 1988

2 Sacked Cult drummer Les Warner announces that the group deliberately misled him over his status as a member – he never had a contract – and that he is suing them to the tune of £20,000. The amount, he claims, is money he believes to be owing to him for his work with the group and compensation for loss of future earnings.

3 Kim Wilde is named as the opening act for Michael Jackson on all of his UK dates. The official story behind this surprise selection is that it was Jackson's personal invitation; apparently, he was lost in admiration for the pouting songstress after she reached number one in the US with her cover version of The Supremes' 'You Keep Me Hanging On'.

5 The IRS blocks the sale of Grace Jones's luxury Manhattan apartment, claiming that she owes over $1 million in back taxes. The move comes just weeks after the singer-cum-actress was forced to close her New York restaurant, La Vie En Rose, due to lack of custom.

6 *Wired*, a new TV rock show aimed at a more mature audience and produced by ex-*Tube* supremo Malcom Gerrie, is launched on Channel 4.

8 Plans for Run DMC to include British dates as part of a European tour in autumn are put in jeopardy after Wembley Arena refuses to allow three shows there. In spite of Run DMC's previous London shows ('86 and '87) being trouble-free, the venue states that they had "checked with the local authorities and police of venues where rap has been staged and unfortunately it would appear that in staging the concerts here we would be jeopardizing our community relations programme."

9 Prince's *Lovesexy* album is released, featuring one track from *The Black Album*, 'When 2 R in Love'. The LP is not without its own controversy, though, as the cover features a completely naked Prince and large numbers of record shops (mostly in the US) refuse to either stock or display it.

12 George Michael calls off five British tour dates in June and July following doctor's orders that he must rest his throat.

13 Mötley Crüe's manager Don McGhee is sentenced to five years in prison after pleading guilty to drug-smuggling charges. However, the jail sentence is suspended for five years on the condition he sets up and funds a drug rehabilitation centre and performs 3,000 hours of community service working there. Earlier in the week, Mötley Crüe were sued for $2.2 million and $400,000 after two fans were injured by fireworks at the band's 1985 show in Huntsville, Alabama. Robert Miller lost an eye and David Wright suffered damage to his mouth.

14 Led Zeppelin re-form – with John Bonham's son Jason on drums – and perform at Atlantic Records' 40th anniversary show at New York's Madison Square Garden. However, as Robert Plant and Jimmy Page both have active solo careers, the group maintains that, like their Live Aid appearance, this is a strictly one-off reunion. Also together, again just for the occasion, are Crosby, Stills, Nash & Young.

16 The Fields Of The Nephilim are held by police after their show in Nottingham following the discovery of a suspicious-looking bag of white powder at their hotel. Its contents are subsequently "sent to forensic for analysis," and the band released from custody after it is proved to be nothing more sinister than flour used in their stage make-up.

17 The double A-sided 'She's Leaving Home'/ 'With A Little Help From My Friends' by Billy Bragg/Wet Wet Wet gets to number one. The songs are taken from the *Sgt Pepper Knew My Father* album, a collection of Beatles' covers performed by representatives from the next generation of musicians and put together by the *NME*. Both the single and album are on sale in aid of the Childline charity.

19 The House Of Lords finally settles the four-year-old Amstrad vs BPI case by ruling that the electronics firm was not encouraging law-breaking by marketing a home hi-fi system with twin cassette decks and a high-speed copying facility. They state however that Amstrad's advertising for the equipment was "cynical" and "deplorable" and recommends that the copyright laws be "amended or repealed."

22 More charges are brought against James Brown after police were called to his South Carolina home following another incident with his wife. Brown was apprehended attempting to get away and subsequently charged with possession of illegal drugs, possession of an illegal firearm (seven grammes of PCP and an unlicensed revolver were reportedly found in his car), assaulting a police officer, resisting arrest and failing to stop for police.

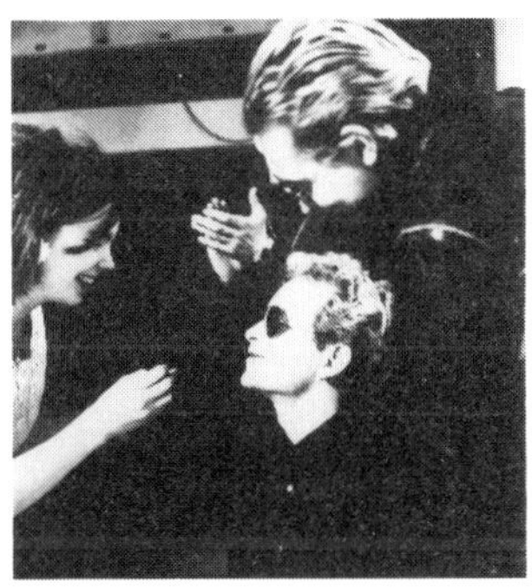

23 The Sugarcubes are forced to cancel six US concerts – their first visit to America – after the US Embassy turned down their application for both work permits and visitors' visas with no explanation.

28 Two members of Sinead O'Connor's touring band – drummer Mike Joyce and guitarist Frank Hepburn – are injured in a fight with security staff at a Dutch nightclub. The incident forces the cancellation of the band's two Irish shows.

29 The International AIDS Day concert at Wembley Arena does not go ahead. The last minute cancellation – only ten days before the event – was because advance ticket sales had reached a mere 1,000 (11 per cent of the venue's capacity). Organizers put this lack of support down to the absence of the established crowd-pullers needed to bolster such participants as Holly Johnson, Aztec Camera, The Communards and Roger Daltry. The ticket prices were £19.50.

Also . . .

● **The oddest offer of the month – if not of the year – comes when Australian novelty company The Trend Connection attempts to strike a deal with Mick Jagger: $20 million for his ashes. Apparently the company wants to put them into egg-timers – 1,000 to sell at $1 million each. Jagger's office describe the bid as "preposterous" and confess to treating it with "a pinch of salt."**

● Spandau Ballet brothers, the former Anna Scher Theatre members Gary and Martin Kemp, reveal plans to portray the notorious London gangsters Ron and Reg Kray in a forthcoming feature film.

● George Michael's *Faith* album tops the US black music charts.

JUNE 1988

1 The IBA force Amnesty International to alter greatly their Harry Enfield-written and performed radio advert for the upcoming Festival Of Youth. Objections occur because the watchdog organization finds the term "buggerallmoney", the name of one of Enfield's TV characters, "too crude" and believe that the advert should be purely factual rather than humorous.

3 James Brown, still facing charges of trying to kill his wife, files for divorce.

5 The Pet Shop Boys give a rare live performance at the anti-Section 28 concert, *Before The Act*, at London's Piccadilly Theatre. The only pop group on the bill, they perform 'It's A Sin' and 'One More Chance'.

7 Just days after the company's 40th birthday celebrations, Atlantic Records agrees to recalculate the royalty rate for 35 of their early artists, stars like Solomon Burke, Wilson Pickett and Ruth Brown whose huge hits got the company started. They also set up a $1.5 million dollar trust fund to provide tax-free grants for their pioneering artistes, to prevent them from dying in poverty like Jackie Wilson or Big Joe Turner.

8 In an unexplained and rather baffling turn of events, all charges against James Brown are dropped in return for the singer performing a "community concert" in Atlanta, Georgia.

10 Marvenco – a tiny Californian record label – wins its ten-year legal battle to release *Elvis – The Beginning*, an album of Elvis Presley's first recorded concert. The show took place in Houston in 1955, before "The King" ever appeared on TV, and was attended by less than 200 people.

11 The Nelson Mandela 70th Birthday Party at Wembley Stadium proves to be a rock concert of Live Aid proportions. It is broadcast live on BBC2 and to 40 different countries, and an estimated audience of a billion watch performances by, among others, Whitney Houston, Phil Collins, Dire Straits, George Michael, Peter Gabriel, The Bee Gees, Harry Belafonte, Midge Ure, Eurythmics, Ashford & Simpson, Al Green, Mick Hucknall, Aswad and Stevie Wonder. Predictably, voices are raised from a posse of right-wing MPs protesting about publicity for terrorism, while American television operates a six-hour delay on transmission so that all political references can be edited out.

11-12 The Fall provide all the live music for the world première of Michael Clarke's ballet *I Am Curious Orange*, at the Municipal Theatre in Amsterdam. The group plan to rejoin the production when it opens at the Edinburgh Festival in August and, in September, for a three-week residency at London's Sadlers Wells.

13 To commemorate their 20th anniversary, Jethro Tull release a 65-track box-set album, containing, as well as their better-known work, rare Tull material and previously unreleased recordings. The celebrations continue at the group's sold-out Wembley Arena show on the 19th.

● After months of postponement, Bob Dylan releases *Down In The Groove*, his 33rd album. The set features such luminaries as Jerry Garcia, Mark Knopfler, Eric Clapton and Ron Wood.

16 The US Embassy partially relents and grants The Sugarcubes visitors' visas for entry into America. Although this does not permit their cancelled performances, the group are now able to do press and promotion.

14 Gary Glitter is once again at the top of the British singles charts, lending his considerable presence to the promotion of the best-selling 'Doctorin' The Tardis' – a funked-up blending of his 'Rock 'n' Roll (Pt 1)' and the *Doctor Who* theme tune by The Timelords.

18-19 Attendance at Amnesty International's Festival Of Youth at Milton Keynes Bowl is so low – 10,000 on Saturday, 12,000 on Sunday – the event makes a loss.

22 Dennis Lobban, convicted of the murder of Peter Tosh, is sentenced to hang by a Jamaican court. The trial continues for two other men charged in connection with the incident.

24 UB40 bass player Earl Falconer is sent to prison for 6 months, with a further 12 suspended, after admitting to causing his brother's death in a car accident last November.

27 The Fat Boys file a $5 million lawsuit against the Miller beer company, following a TV commercial featuring three equally overweight rappers, clad in Fat Boys-style Davy Crockett hats and delivering a "Fat Boys derived rap" extolling the virtues of Miller's brew.

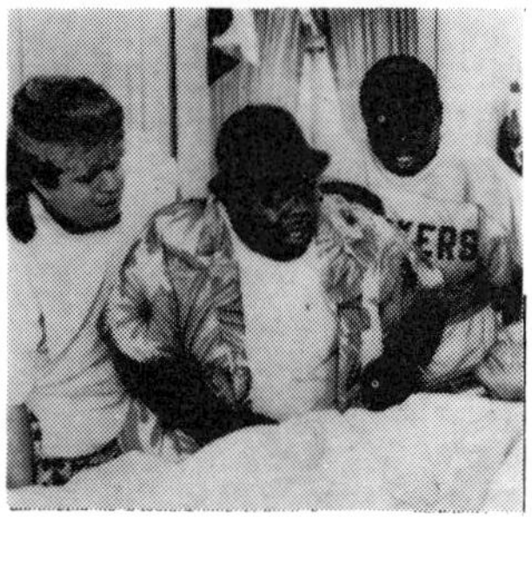

28 Tracy Chapman's self-titled debut album gets to number one in the charts. Its success is believed to be a direct result of her appearance at the Nelson Mandela concert – the LP sold 12,000 copies in the UK during the following Monday.

Also . . .

● After having an offer of $75 million turned down early last year, MCA try to buy Motown again. Their improved offer ($80 million) is again rejected by Berry Gordy. Days later, Solar Records boss Dick Griffey announces that he will go up to $100 million to buy the label.

● Virgin sells its smaller, High Street shops to the Our Price chain for £23 million so that the company can concentrate on its mega-store outlets. The move gives Our Price, a subsidiary of WH Smith, a 22 per cent share of the UK's record retail business.

● The two Alabama teenagers who sued Mötley Crüe for a total of $2.6 million, after being injured by the group's special effects at a show three years ago, settle out of court for $200,000.

JULY 1988

1 Mild Man Of Pop In Love Nest Rumpus! Brenda Richie, long-serving wife of Motown recording star Lionel, is charged with assault, resisting arrest, trespassing, battery, disturbing the peace and vandalism after breaking into the apartment of Diane Alexander – Richie's girlfriend – and attacking her and the the singer. Richie, whose press interviews are famous for his unequivocally endorsing marital fidelity and his wholehearted condemnations of "rock 'n' roll lifestyles", had sloped off before the police arrived.

2 UB40 commence a European tour with Leroy Bushall deputizing for the jailed Earl Falconer.

4 David Bowie, presumably mindless to increasing critical and public indifference to his screen career, announces a new film project. He is to star in and co-produce *The Delinquents*, a musical love story set in Australia of the fifties. With the memory of Mick Jagger in *Ned Kelly* still horribly fresh, it is hoped he will not attempt the "strine" accent.

● As 'Dirty Diana' reaches the top of the US singles charts, Michael Jackson sets a new record: five number one singles ('Bad', 'I Just Can't Stop Loving You', 'The Way You Make Me Feel' and 'Man In The Mirror') from the same album (*Bad*).

6 MCA buys Motown after arriving at a figure of $61 million. This price, somewhat lower than was originally being negotiated, does not include either Jobete Publishing or Motown's film interests. The arrangement also ends speculation as to Stevie Wonder's future with the company: he has a clause in his contract allowing him to leave if the company was ever sold, and after lengthy discussions with MCA arrived at satisfactory terms.

9 A US radio executive offers $2 million to anyone who can bring Elvis Presley to station WDAF in Kansas City by 14 August. A far from minor stipulation is that the aforementioned "King" must be very much alive.

11 Epic Records censors the sleeve for The Godfathers' new single "Cause I Said So'. The company objected to a painting of Margaret Thatcher adorned with a black, toothbrush-type moustache and the song title in Gothic script. They blacked out the picture and left the lettering, and the band maintains it "makes no sense at all now".

14 Michael Jackson steps onto a British stage, his first UK appearance as a solo artiste, in front of a capacity crowd at Wembley Stadium. It is the first date on a tour that, by the time he leaves on 11 September, will have played to close on three-quarters of a million people, for a box-office total of £13 million. Included in this are the biggest concert by a single artiste (Aintree racecourse) and seven nights at Wembley Stadium (the promotor claims ticket demand could've sold out two more with no further advertising, but the venue had used up 1988's quota of live music licences).

15 MTV ban the video for Neil Young's 'This Note's For You' single on the grounds that it is offensive. Among the scenes objected to was a Michael Jackson lookalike performing a Pepsi-type commercial during which his hair catches fire, and is extinguished by a quick-thinking Whitney Houston double with a can of Coke.

18 Nico, one-time Velvet Underground vocalist, fashion model, Andy Warhol associate and acknowledged originator of "Goth" style and dirge-like Euro-style vocal technique, dies in Ibiza following a brain haemorrhage. The 49-year-old former-Christa Paffgen collapsed while cycling.

● Following the last-minute cancellation of Ozzy Osbourne's Nottingham Rock City Show, sections of the capacity crowd go on the rampage through the venue, destroying property and fighting with security. Police are called to restore order and make four arrests.

19 Music publishers acting for Abba's Bjorn and Benny open negotiations with Harry Enfield concerning payments owing for the comedian's appropriation of slabs of their 1974 single 'Money, Money, Money' for his hit 'Loadsamoney'.

20 Following a series of "creative differences", Microdisney split. While stressing that the break-up had nothing to do with the group being dropped by Virgin following the less-than-satisfactory sales of their *39 Minutes* album, vocalist Cathal Coughlan claims to be already working on a solo album that will be "very different to Microdisney".

21 It is announced that Elton John will star opposite Glenda Jackson in a Ken Russell-directed film adaptation of D H Lawrence's *The Rainbow*. Both have worked with Russell before, John in *Tommy* and Jackson in *Women In Love*.

22 Legal representatives of George Harrison, Paul McCartney and the John Lennon estate are awarded a High court injunction to prevent Charly Records releasing a CD of their first audition tapes. This move will no doubt save certain former Decca Records employees from any more painful memories: the tapes, recorded on New Year's Day 1962, were commissioned by the label who, after hearing them, promptly turned the group down.

25 As if throwing down some musical (or possibly sartorial) gauntlet, Prince opens at Wembley Arena just two days after the end of Michael Jackson's first stint there. Unsurprisingly, the UK press devotes many column inches to comparing the two and, *most* surprisingly, His Royal Shortness comes off best.

29 Boy George's US entry visa is withheld by immigration officials, who are waiting for a detailed medical dossier on the singer from his lawyer. The US Embassy claims that no decision can be reached regarding his visa application until the medical reports have been examined.

Also . . .

● Madonna lands the role of Evita Peron in the forthcoming big screen version of *Evita*, to be directed by Oliver Stone. The singer beat off competition of the Streisand/Elaine Paige/Greta Scacchi calibre.

● Chas Chandler, formerly Jimi Hendrix's manager, announces his discovery of three boxes of Hendrix tapes containing 15 unreleased tracks left over from the *Axis Bold As Love* and *Are You Experienced* sessions, and original multi-tracks of those albums. He claims he always knew the tapes were there, but, not wanting any part of the "circus" that surrounded the guitarist's death, left them in storage.

● Electronics firm Tandy claim to have developed a system that could put recordable and erasable CD technology "in the shops within two years" and at a price comparable with cassette tapes and tape decks.

● With characteristic vagueness, Echo & The Bunnymen "appear to have split up."

YEAR IN ROCK

Who'd have thought it? Two decades on from the Summer Of Love – as commercially landmarked by the CD *Sergeant Pepper* 20 years after its vinyl release on 1 June 1967 – and what might the biggest grossing live act in the United States be? None other than extremely old ultra-hippies **The Grateful Dead**, far more rich and famous than they ever were in the days when they "spoke" for a generation. As the title of their hit single 'A Touch Of Grey' implied, they carried it off with a slightly bemused grace.

But Jerry Garcia would certainly have felt some rapport with the key event of June '88, the Nelson Mandela 70th Birthday Celebration staged at Wembley Stadium and relayed live to a billion TV screens around the world. Lamenting the demise of rebellious fine young nastiness in rock 'n' roll, Rochdale sage Andy Kershaw observed that "worthiness and *caution*" have become its dominant characteristic, expressed in ventures like the Prince's Trust concerts (backing royalty yet!). But Dire

The Grateful Dead: Old, rich, famous and slightly bemused

Straits, Whitney Houston, George Michael, Phil Collins, Simple Minds, Sting, Eurythmics and squads of others coming out against South Africa's apartheid system and for a white-haired black man who has languished in jail for 26 years proved genuinely controversial.

Right-wing MPs argued fiercely that it was "unbalanced" of the BBC to broadcast the show – without, presumably, offering South Africa an equal ten hours of airtime to defend racism. The Beeb went ahead, but later proposed changes in their staff guidelines which would compel them to take a six-of-one-half-a-dozen-of-the-other "objective" line on racial discrimination and, by implication, apartheid. This was hardly an intended effect of the Mandela concert but, to their surprise perhaps, with the scoundrel times decreeing that even the mildest campaign for common decency could be deemed outrageous by the authorities, the cossetted pop plutocracy were back in the front line.

New life for The Dead was one of the less predictable benefits of a rock/pop scene which, on both sides of the Atlantic, continued to prove that there are worse predicaments than a state of flux. Without an all-consuming mass movement to call the tune – despite the insistence of rap and house or the polite enquiries from New Age and World Music – the emphasis was on singers and bands, the key question being "Do you actually *like* these people?" In the nature of things, even the greatest hit-makers still displeased most of the people most of the time.

David Coverdale walks very large dog

American tours can make millions, while in the UK they're an act of charity to faithful fans and thus less and less common

George Michael was a fair f'rinstance. The British certainly didn't cold-shoulder his new maturity *sans* Ridgeley, but there was an element of pull-the-other-one-George in the home crowd's reaction. No Wham! whammy in America though. The man went mega. Five consecutive number ones pulled off *Faith*, equalling a record held by The Beatles and The Beach Boys. The album performed like a thoroughbred, cantering back to the top of the chart repeatedly and still there six months after release. With his world tour colossal, Michael looked a good bet to survive even the malice of the British tabloid press (who had him pencilled in as the next candidate for crucifixion after Boy George and Elton John).

But not a lot of people know that one artist from this side of the Atlantic was outstripping Michael, and even U2 – **David Coverdale**. In the guise of **Whitesnake**, he completed an odyssey begun when Deep Purple broke up in 1976. Since then, with the crazed intensity of an Ancient Mariner, or at least Indiana Jones, he had set out to redeem himself. His awesome persistence and perspiration were rewarded when the eponymous *Whitesnake* album (a *"1987"* was added in the UK), out two weeks after *The Joshua Tree*, sold a million more – quintuple to quadruple platinum.

Imagine this though: in the summer of '87, with the album at number four, Whitesnake were *still* in the support slot on an interminable tour with Mötley Crüe, though *Billboard* did suggest that they were "ripe for headline status". Coverdale was approaching 40 and had been on the road for 16 years. Well, by Christmas it actually happened and he was last reported putting up the "standing room only" stickers in Long Beach, Calif, or Boise, Idaho, or Cheboygan, NY – wherever 20,000 souls gather together for some macho emoting. Coverdale's career strikes me as an epic flawed by commercial obsession which means that he rarely permits himself the chance to live up to his ability as one of the great white blues singers extant.

A couple of all-new names made it with less need to invest in Right Guard. **Terence Trent D'Arby**, dread-locked black American, reversed the Coverdale pattern by breaking in Britain first. Improbably handsome and laden with style, his debut album, *The Hardline According To . . .* entered the UK charts at number one in July '87, and loped back up again with each single. In the States it was a far longer haul, but finally in May 'Wishing Well' went to number one and the LP, 28 weeks after release, was at number three behind *Faith* and *Dirty Dancing*. Despite the mercurial rise, D'Arby had a still presence which persuaded you of depth and durability to come.

The same could not be said for **T'Pau**, *the* one-off sensation of the year in Britain. It began with them playing to three dogs and a man at that revered London sweat-box, the Marquee. But, with a much-changed line-up behind singer **Carol Decker**,

Madonna and lips (and elbow)

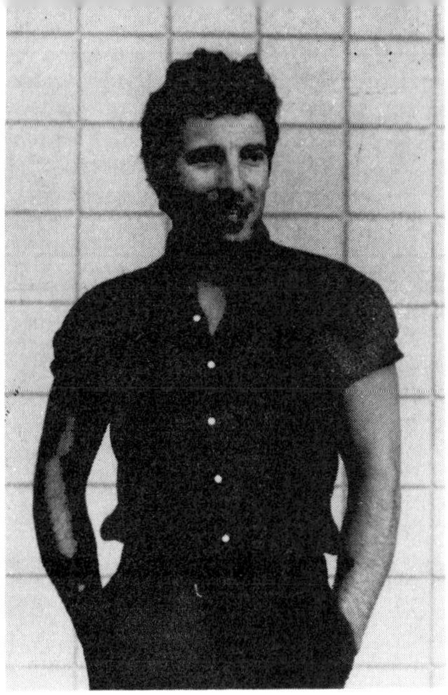

Bruce Springsteen modelling for "Boss at C&A"

the unutterably turgid 'China In Your Hand' was all-conquering pre-Christmas, and their *Bridge Of Spies* album lumbered on to triple platinum. They even laid the foundations of a putative career in America. If T'Pau is pop music call me mom.

But, as a personal corrective on the basis that this business of the majority loathing what a lot of people like is the difference of opinion that puts the horse-racing into musical taste, the following are honourable mentions for artists I like who did all right, touched hearts, rocked out, and rotted few brain cells: **The Pogues** (rollicking Irish-American culture clash on *If I Should Fall From Grace With God*), **Eurythmics** (scorching cold *Savage* joining *Touch* as a classic), **Black** and **Johnny Hates Jazz** (the soft edge of *Wonderful Life* and *Turn Back The Clock*), **Talking Heads** (*Naked* a shot of adrenalin as ever). When there's no Movement, more than ever you need such people to keep you moving.

Of course, even when they both like you, the British and American markets behave very differently. In the UK a big hit album will often go straight to number one and be out of the Top Ten within a month; in the US the climb is slower, but then sales sustain and spread over months. Likewise American tours can make millions while in the UK they're an act of charity to faithful fans, uncertainly written off against promotion and thus less and less common. Within these criteria a row of legendary names were big winners – though there were cautionary tales too, discouraging complacency.

Bruce Springsteen, who ranks with, say, Conrad and Cézanne in my artistic pantheon, recovered from the somewhat ill-conceived live box-set with the withering *Tunnel Of Love*. No anthems for Reagan to misappropriate this time, but an aching view of relationships which may have been closer to home than was originally understood as, a few months later, his marriage did seem to be breaking up. It did well, if outsold by more cheery

U2 in "Just *one* grammy?" rumpus

items, and on stage, as confirmed at Wembley Stadium in June '88, Springsteen and the E Street Band remained the most compelling rock 'n' roll experience available.

Tina Turner: Went out in "a blaze of glory"

Pre-Christmas, Bruce mates **U2** and the rather unconnected **Madonna** concluded their respective *Joshua Tree* and *True Blue* global campaign marathons with yet more chocka 50,000-seaters. **Tina Turner** temporarily retired in a deserved and superbly orchestrated blaze of glory from The World's Hugest Gig Ever in Rio, 16 January 1988. That,

Bon Jovi celebrate octuple platinum in the dressing-up box

typical of her American tour, she had drawn only 7,000 (60 per cent of capacity) in Birmingham, Alabama the previous month thus passed unnoticed – as did her *Live In Europe* album.

Just below the summit, as Whitesnake exemplified, the **Bon Jovi** octuple-platinum pension plan had been studied diligently: **Def Leppard** (one-armed drummer), **Heart** (cleavage) and **Dave Lee Roth** (hairy chest) brought their distinctive qualities to bear on reaping riches in the States while in Britain they all had hit singles and were probably disappointed on the album front. Remarkably, **Boston**, dire precursors of all this thumping mediocrity, went back on the road in America and moved tickets on the U2 scale without releasing a record.

It should be noted though that those untrammelled souls who play the way they do because they like it were not precluded from prosperity. Glamour-free **Chris Rea**'s *Dancing With Strangers* was a solid triumph in Britain as were American guitar band **REM**'s *Document*

Chris Rea attempts to disprove his "glamour free" image

The image of Sabrina desperately struggling to unbutton her jacket so that the TV cameras could peer down her cleavage looked rather demeaned and pathetic

(self-styled "crunchy and angular") and straight-shooting **John Cougar Mellencamp**'s *The Lonesome Jubilee* in their homeland and Aussie **INXS**'s cool-tough *Kick* everywhere. **Sting**'s further adventures into jazz-rocking with *Nothing Like The Sun* scored heavily and on-stage his easy charm and terrific band were irresistible. The weatherman said the only clouds on Sting's horizon had been formed by the condensed hot air occasionally issuing from his lips in interview situations.

Of the newer bloods coping with the launch or aftermath of That Crucial Second Album, **The Pet Shop Boys** had a brilliant sequence of Brit hits with the *Actually* singles, while **Erasure**, current silver medallists

"It must've sold more than three copies – Grandma Bowie bought four!"

among synth-duos, made *Top Of The Pops* as regularly as ever, but the mundanity of *The Innocents* hinted that Vince Clarke's hopalong mind might well be on the next band already. Meanwhile the diverse, erstwhile highly commercial, talents of **Paul Young**, **Howard Jones**, **Nik Kershaw** and **Spandau Ballet** lay fallow and the year's most extravagant legal wrangle constituted the last rites over the **Frankie Goes To Hollywood/ ZTT** masterplan.

While the above were coining it, the 12 months saw a number of favourite suns sink rather briskly in the west. The second album from a Stones-free **Mick Jagger** was universally acclaimed a travesty; **Paul McCartney**'s *All The Best* hits album – its US peak was in the sixties – confirmed that his solo career had not been all that collectable (the alleged collaboration with **Elvis Costello**, though, offered hope that an infusion of Lennon-like bile might be the re-making of him); there were vast, if not capacity, turnouts for **Bowie**'s *Glass Spider Tour*, but this proved to be for old times' sake and the spectacular set, as the mundane *Never Let Me Down* LP, stiffed.

On the other hand, when **Pink Floyd** bounded free of the legal restraints former fountainhead **Roger Waters** sought to impose on them, they struck oil. *A Momentary Lapse Of Reason* shipped tons everywhere, their awesome concert reputation and a $10 million investment in staging saw them chalk up some stupendous takes through the winter (such as 146,000 people paying $2,825,860 on three nights in Toronto). This must have been bitter gall for Waters who, outside of a face-saving Madison Square Garden sell-out, could drum up few takers for his elaborate *Radio KAOS* concept.

While other middle-aged scions of legendary bands like **Robert Plant** and **Robbie Robertson** held their heads up artistically and commercially, the most delightfully surprising comeback of 1987/88 belonged to movie mogul **George Harrison**. 'Got My Mind Set On You' and its self-mocking video carried *Cloud Nine* to insouciant platinum on both sides of the Atlantic. One senses that he's not in any rush to produce the follow-up. However, after a five-year hiatus, Sgt

Robert Plant looks "legendary"

George Harrison yearns for a collarless suit

Pepper peers **Fleetwood Mac** were so fired up by their *Tango In The Night* reunion that they overcame **Lindsey Buckingham**'s departure, replacing him with two new boys, hit the road in America and Europe, and vowed to go straight back into the studio. Their row of single smashes in Britain restored a youthful spring to the step of many a Beatles generation punter.

In the absence of a New Wave to claim rock for youth, as Elvis, The Beatles and The Sex Pistols had, many of the above codgers provided a tapestry of lived-in and still imaginative music. But there *was* a totally teenage sound emanating from Britain. Not so much a style as a production value, the brand-name on it was **Stock Aitken & Waterman**. As mixmaster-come-entrepreneur, Waterman, in particular, was Svengali to a troupe of bimbettes and one young man, who bounced up and down and sang to machine rhythms with lusty lungs and all the feeling of a British Telecom dial-a-recipe. Oddly enough, the only decent track the trio allowed out of their hit factory was their own bone-shaking dance classic 'Roadblock' – they wouldn't chance such tough stuff on their juvenile leads.

They already had **Bananarama** and a fully clad **Samantha Fox** in the charts on a regular basis (both prospered in America too) and during the year they came up with **Kylie Minogue**, star of the lame Australian TV soap *Neighbours*. She grinned and skipped her way to mind-numbing chart-toppers with 'I Should Be So Lucky' and 'Got To Be Certain'. But SAW's real champion turned out to be the lone lad in the stable, **Rick Astley**. The UK was a pushover for his bathroom "soul", and even allowed him a Top Ten entry with his copy of Nat "King" Cole's 'When I Fall In Love'. Astonishing, though, was the US capitulation that confirmed Astley as an international phenomenon: consecutive number one singles with 'Never Gonna Give You Up' and 'Together Forever' while his LP, *Whenever You Need Somebody*, went gold and headed for the Top Ten.

"Our" Sam

"Their" Tiff

In the absence of a New Wave to claim rock for youth, many old codgers provided a tapestry of lived-in and imaginative music

"C'mon Rog, make our day!" Pink Floyd react to unconfirmed Waters sighting

There again, perhaps the American reaction to him wasn't so outlandish in the light of their own bimbettes' onward march . **Tiffany** had been rampant, if that's the word for a toothy stick of a 16 year old, and where she led others followed. Britain loved the whole gang of them – in a way Astley was only fair exchange. Early February in the UK saw her at number one with **Kylie Minogue** two, **Taylor Dayne** four, **Debbie Gibson** seven and **Belinda Carlisle** slipping from the top to 13 with 'Heaven Is A Place On Earth'. Carlisle was a slightly different case, but indicative in that, on leaving the Go-Gos, she had realized that if she posed as a cutesy-pie juve airhead the market force might be with her.

At times, this surfeit of dross seemed like some strange craving to stow white female pop singers back in the toy girl/sex object closet whence they had emerged via the efforts of artists like Chrissie Hynde, Kate Bush and Annie Lennox (black women have generally been given more respect). When the UK year closed with the image of Italy's **Sabrina**, miming at Montreux, desperately struggling to unbutton her leather jacket so that the TV cameras could peer down her cleavage, pop looked rather demeaned and pathetic.

However, the advent of Astley did not mean that the other young white

Wet Wet Wet, casual, but, er, casual

The Christians play hide the big guy's sunglasses

soulsters who emerged as contenders during the year deserved the offhand dismissals they often attracted. **The Christians** and **Wet Wet Wet** were both very competent and dedicated bands, strong melodic writers and excellent harmony singers, yet the former were lauded by most critics and the latter scorned – as far as I could see the determining factors were Gary Christian's shaven head and Marti Pellow's perma-grin. But the real critic victims, the enjoyable **Curiosity Killed The Cat**, seemed to worry themselves out of fame and fortune into neurosis. In regard to soul credibility, sharp suits were the only concern of the British year's final new sensations, **Bros**, but at least there were hints of spunk in their second single, 'Drop The Boy', after their jaw-slackening debut with 'When Will I Be Famous'.

When it came to repositories of rubbish the ageing hacks who contributed to the two *Dirty Dancing* movie soundtracks were probably more culpable than ten Tiffanys and, for this, the first edition was rewarded with six million sales in America alone. How could this be? In part, soundtracks were the equivalent of the hits compilations which have held sway in the British charts for years. But they are an element of a far more insidious marketing package in which the film promotes the single which promotes the album which promotes the film . . .

Conversely, the remix album was a device which began to establish itself in the UK when the US record industry couldn't see it at all. In Britain **The Pet Shop Boys**' *Disco* went platinum, **Janet Jackson**'s *Control* gold, and **Level 42**'s freebie lashed on to *Running In The Family* gave sales of a flagging album a final boost. But it was only when **Madonna** came up with the *You Can Dance* remixes that the risk was taken in America and it sold a million, though that may have been deemed a minor humiliation rather than a fair return.

Still, reassurance could be gleaned from the constancy, and steadily growing audience, of sundry talented survivors from creative times in the late seventies and early eighties, people who hoed their own row regardless and found themselves pan-Atlantic going concerns: **Squeeze**, **New Order**, **Echo & The Bunnymen**, **The Cure**, **OMD**, **Depeche Mode**, and **The Smiths/ Morrissey** all had a good year.

And the summer was starting to feel like the real thing, with **Fairground Attraction**'s 'Perfect' a suntan smash in the golden days tradition of Mungo Jerry, The Kinks and The Beach Boys. It set the ice-lolly mood for the biggest-ever British season of open-air thrashes – a record 12 dates at Wembley Stadium including the Mandela fest, Springsteen and Jacko, Amnesty International's weekend at Milton Keynes, plus the dinosaurs of Castle Donington. If powerful people like Harvey Goldsmith thought the sun would shine, then most assuredly it would. In fact, on reflection, everything was for the best in the best of all possible musical worlds . . .

PHIL SUTCLIFFE

Squeeze's mixed reaction to "Pan-Atlantic going concern-dom"

YEAR IN COUNTRY

Route 88 stars (L to R): Kristine Arnold (Sweethearts Of The Rodeo), Randy Travis, Janis Gill (Sweethearts), K. T. Oslin, Michael Jackson, k. d. lang (rear), Lyle Lovett

It was a year when country music's influence infected the work of mainstream stars from U2 (singer Bono duetted with Johnny Cash and they played with The Judds) to Bruce Springsteen (his *Tunnel Of Love* album had the simple honest approach which is a country staple). Appropriately, the new music coming out of Nashville continued to develop and expand as well. Rather than clinging to old world values, performers like Lyle Lovett, Nanci Griffith and Rosanne Cash showed they had the sophistication and imagination to bring the music into the modern world without sacrificing their integrity.

Here in Britain something unthinkable two or three years ago happened, a shrewdly packaged collection of artists promoted under the Route 88 banner played a sell-out series of dates. The market for *country nouveau* with its deep-seated reliance on the art of songwriting, ringing purity, emphatic truths and high cries was proven indisputably.

Country music is being desegregated, appealing as much to cosmopolitan city dwellers as it does to an imaginary, antiquated rural audience

The Route 88 artists were nothing if not a diverse bunch. **Lyle Lovett**, promoting his second album *Pontiac*, combined wry eloquent love songs with some deeply troubled, even murderous epics and looked like a macabre freakshow, his gaunt face and curious hair curls matching the cool acerbity of his singing and subject-matter. Former Canadian performance artiste **k. d. lang** came magnificently into her own with *Shadowland*, a lavishly-styled revitalization of some of country's more grandiloquent moments. Recorded with Owen Bradley, the veteran producer who'd made his name with the legendary Patsy Cline, the album had the reach and atmosphere to suggest a country opera. Lang's exuberant stageshow and her own immaculate retro-cowgirl chic complemented the record admirably.

Route 88 brought formidable talents like Lovett and k. d. lang along with pleasing new quirks and distinctive stylists. The Californian sister duo **Sweethearts Of The Rodeo** dropped the schmaltz and gloop of their first album in favour of straightforward acoustic punch on the follow-up, *One Time One Night* (which included adventurous covers of Los Lobos and Beatles tunes) making them "this year's Judds". There was **K. T. Oslin** who, having previously made her name and money in haemorrhoid commercials (true!), released *80s Ladies*, a fashionable collection of hard-headed

A wryly eloquent Lyle Lovett

odes to professional feminism. Just to underline the diversity of talent Route 88 had on offer, the line-up included stalwart Western swingers **Asleep At The Wheel** and progressive bluegrass team **New Grass Revival**.

But any new movement or development needs a star, a figurehead to keep the charts, awards men and accountants happy. And in 1988 that figure was a plain-talking, clean-living, square-jawed Southern boy, possessed with endless reserves of genuine charm and untiring patience for fans and autograph hunters. Ladies and Gentlemen . . . **Randy Travis**. At 28, Travis would be a pop music veteran, but in country he's a mere stripling. However, his debut album *Storms Of Life* showed he was very much an old head on young shoulders. Perhaps drawing on the hard times and crises of his teenage years (now omitted from his publicity biography) he captured the indefinable quality of world-weary remorse peculiar to the greatest honky tonk singers. Certainly his second album *Always And Forever* was lighter in subject-matter, and Travis was marketed as a kind of crossover heart-throb: he was presented as having the sort of loyalty for fans and propriety which appeals to the old brigade of country devotees, and the sort of credibility and talent which attracts the disparate New Country fans.

It worked. With *Always And Forever* Randy went from being a star to being a phenomenon, the most eligible bachelor in town, the guy most likely to open a museum or celebrity shop. Travis is a new country music icon who, unlike the veteran icons, will not test fans to the limit by swamping the market with product (in the past it wasn't unusual for George Jones or Willie Nelson to release four or five records a year, resulting in an all-too-apparent strain on resources). In common with many of country music's most celebrated male stars, Travis has a protective, almost maternal force behind him: one Libby Hatcher who, in true American dream style, plucked him from dishwashing in a Nashville

The now-schmaltz-and-gloop-free Sweethearts Of The Rodeo

Former dishwasher Randy Travis

steakhouse to make him a star.

Hatcher guards Travis from outside prying and awkward questions about his past. There are vague rumours about teenage delinquency in his native South Carolina – borne out by 'Good Intentions', one of Randy's own compositions and the toughest song on his second album. It's a prize example of how the sensationalistic gossip pop press operate in this country, and the respectful way Nashville writers treat their subject-matter that Randy's not yet been treated to a muck-raking exposé in the US, thus Fleet Street has little to go on.

But it would be wrong to think events in country were limited to those artistes taking part in Route 88. **Steve Earle**, the Springsteen-style Texan country rocker who had long written for other people before becoming a star in his own right with 1985's *Guitar Town*, saw his earlier career being revived by two of Britain's prime country influenced outfits: **The Proclaimers** incorporate two Earle songs into their show, and the Texan cemented a mutual admiration with The Pogues when he recorded his song 'Johnny Come Lately' with them. In town to produce English group The Bible, Earle played a one-off acoustic show at London's Mean Fiddler with an impressive collection of new songs that show him to be moving back to the directness and drive of that first album, after the disappointing stadium-oriented *Exit O* set.

Nanci Griffith, another Texan, but one with a sweet ringing voice, patterned frocks and the headstrong spirit of Loretta Lynn, sold out a week-long stint of shows and shifted copious amounts of her *Little Love Affairs* album. The latter was a high-class soap opera, plaintive thumbnail sketches dealing with love's trials and tristes. In Ireland she became something of a megastar, with only new local favourites Hothouse Flowers able to budge her off the top of the charts.

Rosanne Cash, daughter of Johnny, may be unwilling to play either the celebrity interview game or live shows, but her *King's Record Shop* was a stand out country record of '88. The opening track 'Rosie Strike Back' was a rare, unflinching look at the reality behind many a country cheating song, and was adopted by an American Battered Wives group as its national slogan. The record also included a charming reworking of a tune her father made famous, 'Tennessee Flat Top Box', and the brooding duet with John Hiatt 'The Way We Make A Broken Heart'.

If Randy Travis had captured the new middle America heartland, the rest of the new country audience, attracted to the likes of Lyle, Rosanne, The Sweethearts, the excellent **Highway 101**, the superlative spartan bluegrass team **The O'Kanes** and temptress of twang **Rosie Flores** aren't so easy to pin down in the sprawling demographics that make up the US charts. This can only be A Good Thing. It means country is being desegregated, appealing as much to cosmopolitan city dwellers as it does to an imaginary, antiquated rural audience. The new performers attract what could loosely be called a college audience in the US, and here it's people attuned to the overall roots music revival of recent years.

The performers themselves provide a one-on-one warmth, character and individuality increasingly absent from mainstream American music, where much seems to become homogenized. Country has a tradition of respect for such traits, and its solid bond with the past, its inherent feeling of community and its regard for elders is another attractive factor amidst the turmoil and ephemerality of the pop world.

London's annual Wembley Festival underlined the scope of the big amorphous market they call country. There **Willie Nelson** and **Merle Haggard** vied for affections with **Daniel O'Donnell**, the Barry McGuigan-styled golden boy of Anglo-Irish country crossover. Later in the year there were well-attended shows by the daunting American legend **Johnny Cash** (reborn on stage and record) and the part-Cherokee Texan songstress **Rattlesnake Annie** who sang country songs from native America's forgotten past.

There's new consciences, pin-ups, heart-throbs, the old frontiersmen still stalking their territory, new tough-minded ladies and incisive, revealing writers . . . About the only thing country music didn't offer in 1988 was a teenage starlet to equal Tanya Tucker in the early eighties or current pop stars Kylie, Tiffany and Debbie. However, the way things are going it can only be a matter of time 'til the breach is filled.

GAVIN MARTIN

YEAR IN JAZZ

Andy Sheppard: Player of the Year

Well, no, nothing much happened, really. Things don't "happen" in jazz much, not the way they're supposed to in pop music. Even Wynton Marsalis hasn't said all that much in the last 12 months. After the heady period we went through a couple of years ago, when the industry realized that people still played saxophones and trumpets as well as guitars, jazz has settled a little more comfortably into its steady disintegration. Most of the people who are playing contemporary jazz aren't too bothered by the term, or if it survives or not. They're just working away at their corner of a music which has spread out too far and wide to hold on to a corporate identity.

If 1986–87 was a year of consolidation, then 1987–88 saw that settling-down get perhaps a shade *too* quiet. In the UK, the most notable event was probably National Jazz Month, held in October '87 to prove that the music was alive and well on these shores at least. It made its point, crowned by *Wire*'s British Jazz awards on 1 November, but the workmanlike low profile that jazz subsists on here reasserted itself quickly enough.

The disappointing thing has been the lack of follow-through on the part of live venues, broadcasting media and the record business itself, after the original talk of a "jazz boom" began. Two years ago, it felt as if a substantial audience for jazz stood undecided in the wings, waiting for major marketing to give it the necessary push. That option hasn't been taken up with any confidence, except by Island's Antilles label, still the most audacious outpost as far as putting jazz into British record shops is concerned. Other attempts, by Virgin, EG and EMI, seemed too cautious to have any effect. **Loose Tubes**, for instance, finally got an album out on a major label (*Open Letter*, EG), but its promotion and impact seemed modest.

Most young musicians are still scratching around for some kind of deal; or even some place to play. London suffered from its usual dearth of decent venues, a bizarre situation, with only John Dabner's splendid Jazz Cafe in Newington Green going for a regular, hardcore policy of live jazz. It was the so-called provinces that set the example, fostering small but healthy local scenes: Sheffield, Leeds, Oxford and Edinburgh are some of the cities that can be proud of their local jazz.

Most of the best music is still coming out of America. Plenty of Americans are still bemused by talk of a "jazz revival" over here, and the question they most frequently ask, with wide eyes, is – do people really *dance* to jazz in Britain? But the American record industry is tuning up for jazz again. MCA have charged up the jazz side of their operation, with strong signings like **Jack DeJohnette** and **Henry Butler**; RCA through their offshoot Novus label, are putting out records by such major players as **Steve Lacy** and **Adam Macowicz**; Blue Note are steadily getting all their old classics on to compact disc (like everyone else),

Dianne Reeves: A "newish" face

and putting a lot of faith behind such newish faces as singer **Dianne Reeves**; Columbia have hired Bob Thiele, the great Impulse producer of the sixties, who's signing in names like **Ornette Coleman** and **David Murray**. And though musician-owned labels are going through a quieter time, an important independent like Giovanni Bonandrini's Black Saint/Soul Note operation is making tremendous waves in the US jazz market, showing a greater alacrity than any of the big boys in recording the most significant American jazzmen (Bonandrini says, with a laugh, that his distributors complain that he puts out too many records).

It's true that there are more records than ever for a besieged jazz consumer to deal with. The all-conquering advance of the CD has sped up the transfer of enormous back-catalogues to silver disc; the determination of European labels such as Splasc(h) (Italy) and CMP (Germany) to break into global markets has meant a vast influx of albums by unfamiliar names for would-be consumers. It's the paradox of jazz that, though it has to struggle constantly for attention, it is documented with fanatical intensity. Even Derek Bailey's Incus, the most noble and long-standing of musician-run independents, began putting out compact discs in 1988.

One way to summarize the year is to select five names who've done outstanding work in the music, for jazz has always been about individuals making a personal path through a collective music. One: **Andy Sheppard**, West Country saxophonist, arguably the most significant British player of the past year. His Antilles album *Andy Sheppard*, grabbed almost as much attention as **Courtney Pine**'s debut (and *his* second LP, *Destiny's Song And The Image Of Pursuance*, did pretty well too); and Sheppard's good-natured demeanour and hard-hitting synthesis of post-bop and free tenor styles has become a tonic.

Two: **Bill Frisell**, the Clark Kent of the guitar. Bill's painfully self-effacing personality is sometimes at odds with a style that sews together a crackling, violent electric sound with a limpid and mysterious manner on ballads. With his strangely vocalized method on the instrument, he's a guitarist who can fit into almost any context – the model for a late-eighties musician. Frisell had a very prolific year, doing sessions with Marianne Faithfull and Mathilde Santing as well as solo gigs, a fine record with his new band (*Lookout For Hope*, ECM), work with Marc Johnson's and Paul Bley's groups and various guest star roles.

Americans are still bemused by talk of a "jazz revival" over here, the question most ask is, Do people really *dance* to jazz in Britain?

Three: **John Scofield**, who is Frisell's guitar partner in Marc Johnson's **Bass Desires**. Sco is more of a straight-ahead player, a veteran of Miles Davis's early-eighties bands, but he's grown into the role of group leader with quiet authority and his current group is peerless. They stunned audiences on two British tours in the last 12 months, and Scofield's latest LP (*Loud Jazz*, Gramavision) is a hot record even within the constraints of the studio.

Four: **Andrew Hill**. The return of this pianist and composer to public duty is long overdue. Hill's albums of the early sixties were always connoisseurs' records, full of dark, troubled but exhilarating music, and two marvellous sessions for Soul Note – *Shades* and *Verona Rag* – saw him still in command of his old powers, sounding as modern as ever without resorting to mere rhetoric. His failure to make a British tour was the most disappointing non-event of the year.

And five: **Edward Vesala**. Even if hardly anybody is familar with the music of this Finnish drummer, bandleader and composer, it didn't prevent him from making one of the great records of recent years with *Lumi* (ECM). With his immensely resourceful group, **Sound And Fury**, Vesala drew on the many areas open to a contemporary player with good ears – jazz and folk musics, rhythms from many countries, Western harmony and Eastern linearity – and threaded them through his own enigmatic vision. The results are unforgettable.

Maybe it's with such music, in such a refined and personal synthesis, that jazz will move on. Even progress. Meanwhile, the saddest part of the year was the large number of names from the jazz past who passed on. In particular, two of the best-loved figures in the music, **Gil Evans** and **Chet Baker**, will be much missed.
RICHARD COOK

Arranger Gil Evans: Will be sadly missed

YEAR IN HEAVY METAL

"An armour-plated raging beast
That's born of steel and leather
It will survive against all odds
Stampeding on for ever"
'Heavy Metal' – Judas Priest

A brutally thrilling Queensryche

It's hard to believe that such a song could exist in the late eighties – and from mature (i.e. 35-year-old), overt leather fetishists at that! But then, as Priest camply insist, that's heavy metal; big but crass and too safe to be threatening. Or, at least, that's half the story.

Fortunately, for every old legend that's gasping, toothless, on its last legs (the laughing-stock that is Black Sabbath and the sly commercial concern that is Deep Purple spring to mind), there's another experienced act that still has its wits, its balls and its integrity about it (say, AC/DC or Aerosmith). For every New Wave Of British Heavy Metal survivor that's lost its way (Saxon) there's one making great records and great stacks of money (Def Leppard). For every dull, goofed concept album (Iron Maiden's *Seventh Son Of A Seventh Son*) there's a brutal thriller (Queensryche's *Operation: Mindcrime*).

Without growing fat on self-congratulatory technical indulgence, Queensryche have emerged as one of the great guitar bands

A fresh, weird and wild Voivod

For every sex-obsessed, sweet-talking second-hand riff salesmen (Zodiac Mindwarp) there's a band experimenting with odd and original ideas (Voivod). For every bunch of clock-watching mercenary hacks (Whitesnake) there's a hot new act playing out of love rather than greed (Wolfsbane).

And for every dullard (Dio) there's a diamond (Dave Lee Roth).

Metal hasn't done so badly over the past year. Although famed more for its stubborn conservatism than for any spirit of adventure or thirst for invention, every year it throws up its wild cards and surprises.

This year's freshest, weirdest and wildest vibes came via Montreal, Canada, from a French-speaking post-thrash metal quartet, **Voivod**. *Dimension Hatross* is their fourth and finest album; difficult, probing, somewhat psychedelic, unique and eccentric and with a reach and power matched only by its sheer unpredictability. Its scope is vast, its surges as breathtaking as any basic speed metal rattle, although Voivod aren't tied down to the standard snare-heavy formats. Guitarist Piggy is the most imaginative this side of Steve Vai and the LP's concept is a bizarre sci-fi trip with parallels in modern society.

Yes, *Dimension Hatross* ranks with the works of Celtic Frost and Metallica as a classic of eighties metal.

And incredibly, this isn't the only great metal concept LP of 1988. Where **Iron Maiden**'s *Seventh Son* dawdles through a heavy, misty mid-

Living Colour headily brewing funk and metal

seventies good vs. evil scenario, **Queensryche**'s *Operation: Mindcrime* buries the notion that all concept albums are puffed up with crusty whimsy and amateurish fiction.

Lyrically, *Mindcrime* is raw and contemporary, a tale of attempted revolution and social decay. The music has equal bite. Without growing fat on self-congratulatory technical indulgence, Queensryche have emerged as one of the great guitar bands, and with a producer as giving as Peter Collins, their imagination runs wild. The result is a spectacular and innovative triumph founded on great songs, showing Queensryche to be way out on their own.

One of the subtler hard rock records of the year was *Out Of The Silent Planet*, the debut from Texan trio **King's X**. Rich in depth, cool, stealth, wristy Zeppelin-redolent riffing and dark melodies, its songs are strong and simple and, with the fluid vocal of tall black bassist Doug Pinnick, always distinctive.

The term "Black Metal" was coined some years ago by Geordie ghouls Venom, but recently it's been redefined by New York's **Living Colour**. All-black and toting a heady brew of metal and funk, they will have a struggle

David "Diamond" Lee Roth

Heart charted

overcoming the inherent and subliminal racism in heavy metal (only Jimi Hendrix and Phil Lynott have done so in 20 years!). But even if that staunch ignorance doesn't yield, Living Colour's potential crossover audience is still huge. Bigger, certainly, than that awaiting LA's **Faith No More**. This kooky, twisting ten-legged rhythmic metal machine scored a novelty hit with 'We Care A Lot' from their second LP *Introduce Yourself*, but they shouldn't expect too many more if their music is to continue clattering wildly off the beaten track, a barbed hybrid of

Def Leppard "gleam in megabuck splendour"

hipshake and headbang.

There's nothing convoluted, however, about **Wolfsbane**, the hottest thing to hit British metal since the brilliant but ill-fated Diamond Head. Mixing the coarser excesses of Van Halen, AC/DC and Motorhead into a lewd ragbag of hot, greasy, horny heavy metal, the Tamworth quartet are already holding five aces: a pile of great songs; a deal with Def Jam; a souped-up rhythm section; a teen guitar killer; and the loudest frontman east of David Lee Roth, the unshaven and unhinged **Blaze Bayley**.

It was **Roth** himself who made the most entertaining, fun record of the year with *Skyscraper*, the ninth in a run of classics that stretches unbroken back to '78 and *Van Halen*. *Skyscraper* isn't metal shy ('Hot Dog And A Shake', for example, is a frantic blowout in a hurry for a good time with guitarist Steve Vai wigging out at the controls), yet it still finds time for quiet reflection, and makes grabs at jazz and swing and a strange kind of funk.

Over 12 albums, Canadian trio **Rush**'s music has continued to grow, restless and creative. The sleek, crisp and melodic *Hold Your Fire* is (*Power Windows* aside) their most emotive record yet. **AC/DC** returned with another round of hard-assed metal boogie, *Blow Up Your Video*. Although they remain the ultimate in conservatism, they are strong, intoxicating and pure in their own way.

Napalm God **Zodiac Mindwarp** and his ham-bitchin' **Love Reaction** spat out their debut major label long-player, *Tattooed Beat Messiah*, which in spite of Top 20 cock-rocker 'Prime Mover' was too trashy for its own good; a big sound but little else. LA glam goons **Poison** made the same mistake: *Open Up And Say Ahhh!* is a dumb gas that's fun for as long as it takes to realize that there's only two or three songs worth holding on to.

Still, Poison got into the charts, as did **Heart**, **Magnum**, **Kiss** and **David Coverdale**'s hired guns, **Whitesnake**. The fairytale of the year, though, was the **Def Leppard** story. With Rick Allen doing the seemingly impossible, drumming with one arm (the other was lost in a car smash) and employing incredible foot technique on a custom-made kit, the *Hysteria* LP was three nail-biting years in the making and a classic for its pains.

Laden with hits and gleaming in the megabuck splendour of Mutt Lange's rich production, *Hysteria* hit the peak of the British LP listings on its release, and after years of near exile, Def Leppard at last became a household name in their own backyard.

Rush look "sleek, crisp and melodic"

Megadeth remains a paradox. Their music, an acidic, exacting and idiosyncratic speed metal mutation, is the kind of streamlined and exhilarating noise that's attracted new kudos to metal over the past five years. Conversation, however, isn't a plus. Muddled and bullish, singer/guitarist Dave Mustaine is the Mega mouthpiece and a fool with it. Although the music is effectively bullshit-free, as long as Mustaine's clouded head isn't the group will hold little sway beyond their existing fans.

Other quality speed metal came from def Bay Area thrashers **Exodus** and **Testament**, frighteningly manic Germans **Kreator**, Arizona's **Flotsam & Jetsam**, Nottingham's **Sabbat** and extraordinarily vicious Canadians **Sacrifice**.

Good hardcore, though, was a little harder to come by. **Gang Green**, **DRI**, **Circle Jerks**, **Crumbsuckers** (all from the US) and Brighton's **Virus** (although still a shade green) were among the best. Hulking, close-cropped New Yorker **Billy Milano** and his band **MOD**'s *MOD For USA* debut grabbed all the publicity, though. Milano pleaded that the album's racist, sexist and homophobic jibes were all rich parody. It was, however, artless and unfunny, and Milano is now rethinking MOD's game-plan.

The ultimate slow metal band also emerged partially from its cult shroud. Like Swans playing Dio, Sweden's **Candlemass** go through their second LP, *Nightfall*, at a crawl, neo-classical grandeur with its feet in concrete. Next to that, **Head of David**'s grisly *Dustbowl* and **Pentagram**'s doomy *Day Of Reckoning* seem almost sprightly.

And for laughs, we were treated to

Van Halen play it for laughs

AC/DC demonstrate the "hard-assed metal boogie"

Van Halen singer **Sammy Hagar**'s haircut (the image of the Wizard of Oz's lion and far more amusing than VH's *OU812* LP); **Ted Nugent**'s customary, haggard penis dementia; **Iron Maiden**'s potty megametal fable; the **Mötley Crüe** doppelganger scam (Matthew Trippe, a very stupid man, claimed to have stood in for bassist Nikki Sixx when the "real" Sixx, Frank Farrano, was in jail some years back); and, best of all, the **Kingdom Come** sensation – when the mighty **Led Zeppelin** re-formed (with departed drummer John Bonham's son Jason on the old man's stool) to help in the Atlantic label's 40th anniversary celebrations, many had been under the impression that Zeppelin had regrouped earlier in the year, when in fact what they'd heard was the Mega-Zep grunge of LA's Kingdom Come.

Not all that glitters is gold.

PAUL ELLIOTT

MOD's Billy Milano pleaded that the album's racist, sexist, and homophobic jibes were all rich parody. It was, however, artless and unfunny

Megadeth: Limited appeal as long as David Mustaine (second left) remains their "mouthpiece"

YEAR IN REGGAE

The doyen of the dance-hall **Frankie Paul** maintained his astonishing prolificacy and popularity during the year in most certain terms, scoring his biggest hit to date in the process. His pairing with Jamaica's premier producer Prince Jammy had already been responsible for a couple of moderate sellers in 'Cover Your Mouth' and 'Cool Now King Jammy's' for Shelley's UK Live & Love outlet, when in July the Count released a third 'Sara', followed almost simultaneously by an LP of the same title. Within a month both single and album had attained pole position in their respective charts as published by the weekly *Echoes*: the single for a consecutive eight weeks duration and the album for some three months solid. A follow-up *Get Ready* on the same label released in September, while never achieving the same keen excitement as *Sara*, nonetheless contrived to enjoy lengthy chart activity on its own account, maintaining a consistent Top Five position for another five months, well into the following year.

The success of these was the signal (in case any was needed!) for a flurry of Frankie Paul releases, even if his ensuing productions that year – a further Jammy production 'Posse Come Run' (set to the rock steady 'Baba Boom' rhythm), a version of 'Laugh It Off' on pre-release, 'One In A Million' and 'Endless Dreams' for the Three Kings triumvirate and a duet with **Pinchers** on 'Nutting No Deh' – failed to register.

The LP *Sara* was only dislodged from atop the chart towards Christmas by another set from the same artiste *Give Me That Feeling*, this time for producer Harry Mudie, at which juncture Frankie Paul had yet a further two sets in the same chart, *Rub-A-Dub Market* for Prince Jazzbo's Ujama set-up and his Vena sessions courtesy of Fattis Burrell, *Warning*.

During 1988 the floodgates burst and a slew of new titles were unleashed on the market, leading one critic to remark that the singer merited some kind of special mention in the *Guinness Book Of (Frankie Paul) Records*. During January he scored another Top Five hit with 'Leave It To Me' for M&R, a Top Ten hit with 'Game Of Love' and a Top Twenty hit with 'Fiona' and also issued his latest Jammy production on Live & Love, 'Casanova', which went Top Ten the following month. An album also titled *Casanova* was to top the charts later in May. Also released in February were pres like 'Bad Man Pickney', 'Agony' on Ujama and 'Nah Have No Glamnity' (Exterminator), plus two further discos 'PFP Calibre' for Redman, a Top Twenty hit, and 'How I Love You' on the Black People imprint. In March he had two Top Ten entries for hitmaker Germain with 'Come To Me' and 'Tell Me That You Love Me', and a minor hit with 'We've Only Just Begun', plus a further two Redman pres, 'Shine On' and 'Dirty Bungle', as well as 'For Your Eyes Only' (Vena), 'Through The Years' (Blue Trac) and 'Moving Up' (Techniques). April brought pres such as 'What About Us' for Tapper Zukie, 'Forward Up' for Techniques and another Redman title 'Slow Down' which gave him another Top Ten hit when it was released on disco the following month. And June realized such as 'Love Been Taken' for Youth Promotion, 'Never Gonna Give You Up' for Tapper Zukie, pres like 'Shame Them' and 'Through The Fire' and issue of the Jammy side 'I Know The Score' taken from the *Sara* album.

Frankie Paul's follow-up, *Get Ready*, while never achieving the same keen excitement as *Sara*, nonetheless contrived to maintain a Top Five position for another five months

The astonishingly prolific Frankie Paul

In addition to *Sara*, the latter half of 1987 was dominated by just a few titles greatly exceeding everything else in popularity. From May to July 'Don't Touch My Style' by **Joseph Cotton** topped the reggae singles charts for a consecutive seven weeks. Cotton was previously Jah Walton who recorded the notorious 'Teacher White' back in the seventies. Under his nomenclature he developed a humorous *labrish* for a series of releases delivered in the manner of Lovindeer's 'Babylon Boops', achieving a second chart-topper with his follow-up to 'Style', 'Half Slim'. Other brisk Joseph Cotton sellers were the witty 'Ragamuffin Roll Call' towards the end of the year and 'Carry Me Go Married' and 'Fit And Ready' during 1988.

Another huge hit was **Freddie McGregor**'s 'Just Don't Wanna Be Lonely', which topped the *Echoes* chart for five consecutive weeks during August and also crossed over into the national listing. His follow-up, 'That Girl', was denied the top spot only by the dominance of 'Sara'. But ironically the most consistently popular reggae record of 1987 was from an artiste whose involvement in the music dates back to the ska era and Freddie McGregor's erstwhile, senior partner in The Clarendonians, **Ernest Wilson**. Wilson's 'Promise Me' for Techniques remained in the upper regions of the chart for months and may even have been the year's biggest seller in the field.

Of the newer artistes, Jammy protégé **Chuck Turner** – described by one reviewer as "the George Michael of reggae" – made a name for himself with a series of light, catchy dancehall tunes. His first hit was the minor 'Run Around Girl' and this was followed by the enduring 'Tears', another chart entry of incredible longevity, plus further releases during 1987 such as the two Brixton Promotion titles 'Through The Fire' and 'No Love'. In 1988 he scored his first Top Ten hit with 'One The Hard Way' for Jammy and continued to maintain his popularity on further releases like 'Youthman Struggling' and 'Another Love Song'.

But if anyone was going to challenge Frankie Paul in 1988, then newcomer **Courtney Melody** looked the likeliest contender. His first hit in 1987 was also the title that catapulted him to dancehall notoriety, 'Bad Boy' recorded

Aswad: First pop hit reached number one

Freddie McGregor: Crossed over

for Techniques. It entered the charts in November 1987 and went on to become one of the crucial hits of the Christmas season, maintaining a Top Ten position well into the spring of the following year. In March his debut album *Ninja Showcase* was issued, followed the same month by the inevitable batch of ensuing releases: 'Pressure Dem', a duet with **Danny Dread** entitled 'Call Me' and 'Ninja Me Ninja' for King Tubby's Firehouse imprint. In March he had pres like 'Jump Reggae Music' and one of the most popular sound system raves duetting 'Protection' with newcomer **Ninjaman**. Other releases up to the middle of the year included 'Put It Down' for Harry J, 'Loving Woman' for King Tubby, plus two Ujama titles 'Down Presser' and 'Cook Food'. In June he scored another chart hit with 'Call

Maxi Priest: Lasting mainstream success?

Me', the same month as his second album, *Bad Boy*, made serious inroads into the LP listings.

On the home front, Ariwa's recording artiste **John McClean** had the Christmas top spot with 'If I Give My Heart To You', a position he maintained for a consecutive ten weeks, scoring big also with his follow-up, 'Say You'. And **Aswad** finally overcame years of public indifference for a crossover hit with 'Don't Turn Around' – their first national hit, reaching the coveted top spot – and also topping the reggae chart in the process. Also enjoying what looks to be lasting mainstream success is **Maxi Priest**, whose breezy cover of Robert Palmer's 'Some Guys Have All The Luck', taken from his huge-selling *Maxi* album, took him onto *TOTP*, and **Lee Perry**'s collaboration with **Adrian Sherwood**, *Time Boom X De Devil Dead*, didn't show sales figures worthy of its media fanfare.

Novelty of the year was comment on the (non-)activity of the 'Dibbi Dibbi Girl', as originally expressed by **Peter Metro & Sister Charmaine**, and given answer by one **Bruce Lee** with his recording, also entitled 'Dibbi Dibbi Girl', and **Tippa Lee** with 'Dibbi Dibbi Sound' for a saga that continues still . . .

PENNY REEL

Lee Perry: Feted by the media

YEAR IN SOUL

Dearly beloved. Twelve months have passed since last we gathered here. They've been . . . well, not bad. But they sure haven't been particularly great. Only the most generous soul brother or sister would call it a vintage year. The music's best-selling artists have presented us with work that not even their mothers or fathers would insist were masterpieces. Talent attempting to consolidate itself has failed to do so satisfactorily (yet), while freshly emerging acts have hardly rocked one back in one's socks with breathtaking beats or awesome melodies.

Even in a sphere so expressive, inventive and constantly capable of reinventing and refreshing itself, it is inevitable that from time to time the music seems to instinctively pause and take stock. To call time out. That's what has been happening in soul. You don't agree? Well, if it were not so the two buzz names which have continually recurred this year would not be those of soul veterans **James Brown** and **George Clinton**. Their influence on the current music scene shows soul's innate good sense in knowing when to return to the root for succour.

The overall effect on the year of an artistically largely dormant Brown has been remarkable. His name is used by any number of young samplers, house or hip hop acts as a totem of cool, a trait which stretches back beyond Afrika Bambaataa some years ago, into the seventies when Brown's standing in the commercial marketplace was at a low ebb but his music was always monitored by his peers.

James Brown with Cold Cut

George Clinton looking influential

No wonder the DMC Annual DJ Convention made an award to James Brown for his "timeless contribution to the music industry". Wild thing was he turned up to receive it

A new album, produced with the **Full Force** team, was still some months away from completion but still his sound seemed everywhere. Urban and Charly, two of several labels dedicated to the diligent excavation of soul mines long since boarded up, re-packaged the music of Brown's seventies acolytes such as saxophonist **Maceo Parker**, his trombonist **Fred Wesley**, band **The JBs** and singer **Lynn Collins**. More significant to contemporary taste was the use of Brown cuts by samplers. He was sampled more often than Bollinger at a bubbly tasting. Best value was the follow-up to 'She's The One', 'The Payback Mix (Cold-Cut Style)' courtesy of Doctorin' The House guys. A virtual mini-album. No wonder the Disco Mix Club at the DMC Annual DJ Convention and World Mixing Championships made an award for his "timeless contribution to the music industry". Wild thing was, he turned up to receive it.

George Clinton's influence during the past year has not been quite so all-pervasive as Brown's. But Dr Funkenstein – whose **Parliament/ Funkadelic** sides are surely next in line for regurgitation on a massive scale in a vast array of styles (more than just pinching 'One Nation') – acts like a vapour that seeps into the pores. As an artist, Brown is separate, not exactly aloof but more inclined to plough his own furrow. If there is input from the outside, Brown assimilates it thoroughly before using it. Clinton, by contrast, has been far more gregarious since the end of his Parliafunkadelicment dynasty. Perhaps financial necessity has dictated that he should hop into the studio with anyone who offers cash in return for the secret of *The One* more often than he'd wish, but I think he also just enjoys working with as diverse a range of folks as possible. He's pepped as many sides of funk as Heinz have squeezed types of food into a can. Take, for example, this year's *The Light*, by our friend **Afrika Bambaataa** again. Clinton stamps his mark on three tracks – 'Clean Up Your Act', 'Zouk Your Body' and 'World

Racial War' – and they're clearly the pick of the record.

Brown and Clinton contrived to be such major influences on the dancefloors – and airwaves – without releasing major records partly thanks to the inadvertent connivance of several major acts whose new work did not live up to expectations. In most cases it was hardly a surprise. Who, apart from the singer/songwriter himself, expected **Michael Jackson**'s *Bad* to be as successful as *Thriller*? Certainly a marketing department whose optimism was of certifiable proportions would have been required to project 40 million-plus sales for *Bad*.

Artistically, however, there were grounds for expecting *Bad* to do good. Jackson and his producer **Quincy Jones** have rarely been wrong when making decisions about how best to capture the young pop singer's best side. This was achieved only on a small percentage of *Bad* – the gospel-tinge of 'Man In The Mirror', the pop skip 'n' jump of 'The Way You Make Me Feel' and the punch of 'Bad' itself – most of the tracks are not notable additions to his cannon. Nor was *Moonwalk*, his autobiography, a less than revealing quick read. Even the snaps were a disappointment. It sold, of course, like the publishing equivalent of *Thriller*. Tickets for the *Bad* tour sold wildly too, which probably proved the greatest consolation to an artist who considers the stage to be his "real" home.

Bambaataa, sprinkled with Clinton "fairydust"

Prince, better in *Black*?

Previously the hot ticket had been for **Prince**'s *Sign 'O' The Times* tour, which sadly never reached Britain. I say sadly because the show I caught in Milan was one of two concerts from '87 which I will cherish and use as a loadstone against which to judge others in the late eighties. The film of the tour doesn't quite capture the atmosphere of the shows – I don't think celluloid, or vinyl, could – but it's a decent enough document of the event.

Less laudable were Prince's records. *Lovesexy* was an album which sounded as though it had been dashed off, a series of drafts and sketches in the manner of an artist keeping his hand in between major projects. Own 'Alphabet St' and 'Dance On', and you have all that was essential on the album. It begged many questions. If Warner Bros, the distributors of his Paisley Park label, had pulled the plug

Alexander O'Neal: The man with no neck

Stevie Wonder, no longer compulsive

on *Black* – the studio work which preceded *Lovesexy* – was this quick filler Prince's way of thumbing his nose at them? *Black* certainly had many more interesting ideas than were apparent on *Lovesexy* and it also delivered a far greater rhythmic clout. But if Warners found *Black* too risqué for current moral imperatives and wanted a marshmallow record, then Prince surely gave them one.

What of Prince's former confederates? In the last year, **Jesse Johnson** has produced his best LP. This may not be saying a great deal but at least the second side of *Every Shade Of Love* showed that when he simply stuck to the task of making catchy pop–soul tracks he did himself justice. **Morris Day**, on the other hand, seemed a trifle confused as to his direction and ultimate destination on *Daydreaming* (jaunty funk remains his forte) and his live shows were not much more than his *Purple Rain* persona revisited.

But **Alexander O'Neal**, produced by **Jimmy Jam & Terry Lewis**, took advantage of the absence of new work by **Luther Vandross** to establish himself as the soul balladeer of the year in terms of mass popularity. The up-tempo tracks on *Hearsay* have stood the test, but without Monte Moir's pen the slower stuff on the album's second side lacked substance if not sentiment. (Moir had begun

Barry White models wash 'n' wear beard

producing in his own right, one of the first projects being the duo **Deja**.) O'Neal visited Britain twice in the year and his shows proved him to be a much more accomplished and comfortable performer than had previously been the case.

Prince and friends are the Minnesota clan, The Ohio Bunch is personified by **Roger Troutman** and his brothers. Roger's *Unlimited* album with the sexy

The O'Jays visit Scotch House

single 'I Want To Be Your Man' proved him to be one of the most interesting and versatile writers, producers and performers of his age. He'll go on to great things in the manner of Cameo's Larry Blackmon.

None of the foregoing lost ground in the year. We shall pass briefly over **Bobby Womack** whose *The Last Soul Man* was a witheringly awful LP. His reputation was scarcely rescued by live performances which fundamentally differed not a shred from those of three or more years previously. Perhaps we expect too much too often from the great talents of black music. For instance, **Stevie Wonder**'s *Characters* was in no way a bad record when compared to the common realm of releases and there is still no pain involved in the playing of it. But the old compulsion to play his newest record at least once a day for six weeks after release has gone.

The sense of disappointment on the part of the music's major, established stars' new offerings would perhaps be less acute if there was not a dearth of exceptional new voices coming through. Quantity? Sure there's that, but it is no substitute for quality. Still, **Will Downing**, **Tony Terry**, **Miles Jaye** and **Broomfield** all made promising noises and are clearly artists to follow in the future. Jaye wrote some of the better songs

Will Downing: Promising noise

on **Teddy Pendergrass**'s *Joy*. TP's once magnificent voice is, understandably, muted still. Muted, too, is perhaps the best description of the reunion between **David Ruffin** and **Eddie Kendricks**, the marvellously symbiotic singers whose complementary styles made **The Temptations** the best vocal group of the sixties. The Temps, still going if not always strong, were themselves reunited with the third great solo singer to have graced their ranks – though **Dennis Edward**'s reappearance was less than orgasmic.

A better monument to the great soul vocal groups of the sixties and seventies has been provided this year by the wonderful **O'Jays**. *Let Me Touch You*, their best album in several years, was testament enough to their enduring strength: their long-overdue return to

Aretha: Breathtaking gospel

The same old brothers Johnson

Regina "Party Girl" Belle

Jean Carne, back after lengthy hair 'n' nail growing sabbatical

Mica Paris: Soul from the heart

The sense of disappointment on the part of soul's established stars would perhaps be less acute if there was not a dearth of exceptional new voices coming through

the London stage (in the company of lead singer Eddie Levert's sprogs in the trio **Levert**) proved them to be in as good voice out of the studio as in it.

Has it *really* been so much the year of the old-timer? Well, **Barry White**'s 'Sho' You Right' was as hard-driving as any record in the past 12 months and even the **Brothers Johnson** were no longer prefixed by 'whatever happened to' when they released *Kickin'*. Sounded just like the Bros J of old, which a dozen years on from *Look Out For No 1* might not be a good thing.

In normal circumstances one of the year's best soul performances might be included elsewhere. **Aretha Franklin**'s breathtaking gospel singing on *One Lord, One Faith, One Baptism*, recorded at the New Bethel Baptist Church in Detroit, transcends the labels by which we find our way around the marketplace. But it sure ain't pop music. The material is standard gospel fare, the spirit with which it is sung is very far from standard. Even the speeches and invocations by the several Reverend Fathers who appear on the record have a great deal more *soul* than so many of those pitching for a berth on *Billboard*'s top black albums chart. Like, for example, *Whitney* of **Houston** fame and **Brenda Russell**'s *Get Here*. One a big pop seller, the other a much-vaunted debut, but both very superficial LA confections.

The records of **Angela Winbush** and **Joyce Sims** encourage confidence in their futures, and it was good to see **Betty Wright** with her own label, Ms B, and **Jean Carne** up where she belongs with *You're A Part Of Me*. But the larger portion of women soul vocalists seem in need of a stronger sense of purpose and direction. But then they can't all be Anita Baker and it is, I suppose, too much to expect a chit of a thing like **Shanice Wilson** to sound other than she does, i.e. a big fan of Janet Jackson and Five Star. But with **Regina Belle**, **The Weather Girls**, **Gladys Knight**, **Stephanie Mills** and **Evelyn King** all making reasons to smile and shimmy, the party girls aren't flagging just yet.

Joyce Sims: A bright future and no clothes

As I write this the top black albums according to *Billboard* are by **Terence Trent D'Arby** and **George Michael**. Now you've stopped laughing, this if nothing else speaks volumes for the state of "soul" in the United States. Just wait until the first boxed sets celebrating the blue-eyed funk of **Stock, Aitken & Waterman** productions roll off the presses: a Trivial Pursuit-style game of spot-the-hook/riff/influence on the collected works of Princess, Latoya Jackson, Rick Astley, Mel & Kim (not forgetting those two great cultural ambassadors, Mandy Smith and Samantha Fox) will doubtlessly accompany the set.

A more lasting impression, it is to be hoped, will be made by some of the real singers emerging from the British gospel scene. Those likeliest to make American ears quiver soonest are **John Francis**, **Lavine Hudson**, **Beverly Wint**, **Mica Paris**, **Heather Small** of **Hot House** and **The Wade Brothers**. Their soul comes from the heart – much of the soul elsewhere this year has come from clinical business decisions and records based on the ideas of others.

GEOFF BROWN

YEAR IN WORLD

Britain has long toyed with world music. A brief dalliance with sitars in the sixties and the rise of Osibisa and Afro-rock in the seventies suggested that public tastes were never quite as comatose, nor parochial, as they are sometimes painted. But was the public ready for a full, mainstream blast of non-western music?

One positive sign came in May 1987 when 'Im Nin 'Alu', an updated Yemenite folk song from Israeli singer **Ofra Haza** reached 15 in the singles charts. The song had received an early publicity boost when it was sampled on Coldcut's remix of Erik B and Rakim's 'Paid in Full'. A novelty hit, maybe, but that did little to deter WEA from snapping her up. Other signs came from world music sleuths who confirmed that by mid-July Dave Lee Travis had slotted tracks from Malian singer **Salif Keita** onto his Radio 1 show; that Anne Nightingale and Steve Wright had given the thumbs up to **Mahlathini** and **The Mahotella Queens** from Soweto and that **Mory Kante**, a Guinean traditional musician lately given to mega-polished Paris funk excursions, had received similar treatment.

Hugh Masekela signed to a major label

These are small signals of what could be a more vigorous shake-up as the range and force of world music makes itself felt. Western musicians, from **Peter Gabriel** to **Paul Simon**, **Stevie Wonder**, **Talking Heads**, **Jellybean**, **Jimmy Cliff** and **Ziggy Marley** have led rock, soul and reggae towards the African sound. Tours by **Shirati Jazz**, from Kenya, **Celina Gonzalez** from Cuba, and Mali's **Ali Farka Toure** further spread the message. While the WOMAD festivals showed that it was possible to listen to British Rockers alongside Himalayan dulcimer players, Zambian dance bands and devotional singers from Pakistan with no sense of incongruity. The road from Barking to Bamako shed a few thousand miles when **Billy Bragg** and kora player **Jali Musa Jawara** shared the bill at the Crossing The Border festival.

And naturally the record industry fuelled this new interest. Late in 1987, eleven independent companies launched a combined promotion to push world music into record stores and sitting rooms, and the flow of music has been prodigious. Among the highlights: albums of Kenyan benga from World Circuit records, Zairean soukous, Hungarian and Balkan folk from Hannibal, Urdu love songs from Triple Earth, South African mbaqanga from Earthworks, Malian roots and West African kora music from Sterns and Rogue respectively. Globestyle released several albums of hot Latin music, the hottest coming from Cuban émigré **Rolando La Serie**.

The ripples spread to the larger companies. In a blur of cheque books, Island signed **Salif Keita**, **Arrow**, the Trinidadian soca star, and Zairean keyboards player **Ray Lema** to its new tropical label, Mango. Virgin took on **Youssou N'Dour** and signed a deal with Earthworks which resulted in compilations from Zaire, the French-speaking Caribbean and South Africa along with *Thokozile*, an album from Mahlathini – the lion-voiced Soweto "groaner" – and The Mahotella Queens.

Apart from Ofra Haza, WEA's roster included **The Bhundu Boys**, **Miriam Makeba** and **Hugh Masekela**. London released *Akwaba Beach* from the kora player **Mory Kante** and *Haiti* from **David Rudder** – touted with some justification as the Bob Marley of soca; EMI put out *Third World Child* and *Shadow Man* from **Savuka**, a South African band led by guitarist **Johnny Clegg**.

As the dust settled, certain trends became clear. One was the attraction of the voice. "Islamic vocals" provided a useful umbrella term for singers like

Salif Keita found favour with Dave Lee Travis

Ofra Haza reached number 15

further spines. Rai music, the Algerian hit sound distinguished by roughhouse vocals, violins, synths and increasingly tight, bass-heavy productions, continued its rise with the British debut from **Cheb Mami**, *The Prince of Rai*. Factory put out the classic 'N'Sel Fik' from **Fadela And Sahraoui**.

The club scene was dominated by the new global free-for-all: Antillean zouk, Latin salsa and music from Zaire and Cameroon cutting the greatest dash – and borrowing freely from each other. Production standards improved as tropical artistes took the formal devices of funk – loud bass lines and programmed drums – and gave them a celebratory southern twist. Much of the best stuff came from Paris, which has a huge community of African and Antillean artists with producers to match. The best known is **Ibrahima Sylla**, whose Syllart Productions created sophisticated modern sounds for **Les Quatre Etoiles**, Malian **Nahawa Doumbia** and Senegalese artiste **Baaba Maal**. Thanks to a deal with Sterns, the best Syllart material is now readily available in Britain.

Eleven independent companies launched a combined promotion to push world music into record shops and sitting rooms, and the flow has been prodigious

David Rudder: The Bob Marley of soca?

Salif Keita, Youssou N'Dour and Nusrat Fateh Ali Khan, whose complexity, timbre and stratospheric range reflected age-old traditions and gigantic new talents. The Balkan singers, pure, eery and vibrato-free, found a fashionable new audience as Hannibal's *Balkana – The Music Of Bulgaria* built on the success of the 1986 4AD album *Le Mystère Des Voix Bulgares* which shifted over 30,000 copies. A tour of Balkan artists, including the amazing **Trio Bulgarka**, sent shivers down

Paris became the crossroads of the new black music, a focal point in the African diaspora. Zouk bands like **Kassay** blended their Antillean roots music with elements from Africa and Latin America. Zairean artists like **Sam Mangwana** moved from soukous to biguine and beyond. A global spirit hung over the classy, multi-track studios where even a moderately polished zouk album could cost £60,000 to record. The city saw some phenomenal hits: Mory Kante crashing the charts with his single 'Ye Ke Ye Ke' and album *Akwabw Beach* – on stage, this being Paris, he swapped his flowing traditional gown for a chic white suite. Savuka enjoyed even greater success with *Third World Child*, *Shadow Man* and the single 'Asimbonanga'.

Johnny Clegg (centre) with Savuka

Mory Kante on Steve Wright's playlist

In Britain, however, the charts have proved more resistant to world music. Interest in South African music grew with the summer '88 tour from Mahlathini and The Mahotella Queens; the Zimbabwe vogue, with albums and tours from The Bhundu Boys, **Lovemore Majaivana**, the splendid **Devera Ngwena** and a Discafrique compilation *Goodbye Sandra*, while DJs like John Peel, Charlie Gillett and Andy Kershaw constituted a steady trickle in the opposite direction.

Such forays could be seen as superfluous given the amount of world music already in Britain. African bands, from **Taxi Pata Pata** to **Dade Krama**, pulled the crowds. The Balkan-influenced **3Mustaphas3**, pulled crowds and legs. Birmingham-born **Najma Akhtar** recorded *Qareeb*, a classic album of Urdu ghazals or love songs. The bhangra beat, the Asian community's fusion of Punjab folk and western disco, flowered into compilations whose assertive titles (*Bhangra Now, Bhangra Fever, Bhangra Power*) underlined the fact that bhangra was arguably Britain's top-selling independent music: it just sold in the wrong shops to hit the Gallup charts, that's all.

The fact that world music slots neatly into most western categories suggests that the current interest will continue. Kora musicians like **Dembo Konte** and **Kausu Kuyateh** attract a strong folk roots following. Likewise Salif Keita, although *Soro* has a spacy enough sound for the New Age market. Bhundu Boys' gigs attracted pogo dancers, for heaven's sake. African and Asian musicians turned to house and hip hop, with the **Joi Bangla Crew** producing a Bengali spin 'n' scratch, **X-Boys** infusing a house version of 'Not Fade Away' with shades of African percussion and xylophone and **M/A/R/R/S** cutting an Afro–Acid remix of Mory Kante's 'Ye Ke Ke Ke'.

If you were looking for the world, Britain in 1988 seemed a reasonable place to start.

CHRIS STAPLETON

YEAR IN DANCE

It is right and fitting that last year this very space was taken up by Mark Moore, a DJ who 12 months later would find himself in the UK Top Ten with his record and group, both entitled S-Express. For if the year had any notable trends, the rise and rise of the DJ as a recording artist was one of its strongest.

The groundbreaker was 'Pump Up The Volume' by **M/A/R/R/S**, a weird amalgamation of club DJs Dave Dorrell and C. J. Macintosh meeting cult indie musicians, Colourbox and A. R. Kane, and providing an irresistible dance groove over which they inserted familiar bits and pieces from other records. The creation of such a record relied on one particular machine – the sampler. A new invention that allows musicians, DJs and just about anyone with an ounce of sense, to feed into it any part of a record, and reproduce it perfectly, for use on their own recordings. No more frustrating hours spent over a guitar or instrument, trying to figure out someone else's tune or rhythm. Let the sampler do your stealing. And for the DJ, with boxes crammed full of rare vinyl, the sampler was a godsend.

Record companies, ever eager to follow trends and not create them, realized that DJ records could be made for as little as £500 and acted accordingly. Soon **Bomb The Bass**'s 'Beat Dis', **S-Express**'s 'S-Express', and **L.A. Mix**'s 'Check This Out', were soaring up the charts.

Of course, all this sampling was making some people ill. Notably, **Stock, Aitken & Waterman**, Britain's most successful producers, who burst the balloon by threatening court action against M/A/R/R/S for lifting a segment from their 'Roadblock' single. The case was settled out of court but the good and worthy judges of the high courts have still to bring in the verdict on the legality of sampling. When they do, it will have reverberations for many, especially in the hip hop community, who, even as we speak, are still rifling through their old **James Brown** records for rhythms and riffs to steal. **Spoonie Gee**'s 'The Godfather', **Big Daddy Kane**'s 'Raw', **Kid 'N' Play**'s 'Do This My Way' and **Sweet Tee**'s 'It's Like That Y'All', were just four examples of artistes and producers lifting from the Godfather's seminal recordings.

Brown responded in two ways. He instructed his lawyers to grab the royalties he felt were due to him, despite the fact that these very same sonic thieves had boosted his popularity to an all-time high. Then he walked into a studio with New York outfit, **Full Force**, and produced his best LP this decade in *I'm Real*. Ironically enough, on tracks such as 'Static', the Godfather can be found screaming over samples of his own drumbeats, as the wheel came full circle.

No matter. The record proved to be a commercial as well as artistic success, a celebration which was severely marred when the local police force nailed him for allegedly beating up his wife in a severe and brutal fashion, possession of narcotics and illegal firearms, and assaulting an officer. The charges were subsequently brought to court where Brown found himself in front of a very lenient judge. He was given a minimal fine and ordered to play a concert for charity, a quality which seems conspicuous by its absence in Brown's household.

Meanwhile, hip hop went from strength to strength. Despite the media's reluctance to embrace this art form, acts such as **LL Cool J**, **Run DMC**, and relative newcomers **Eric B & Rakim**, all sold more healthy amounts of records. In fact, when the latter moved from Island to MCA Records, nearly a million pounds passed into their bank account. The acceptable face of rap came with hip hop's answer to The Marx Bros, the huge, in every sense of the word, **Fat Boys**, who specialized in boosting the

Full Force with James Brown

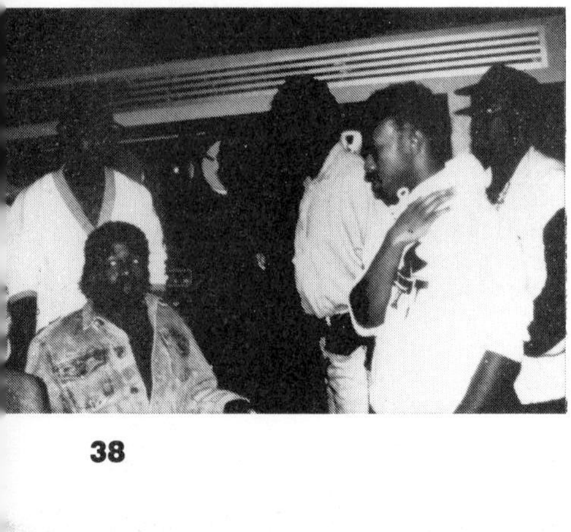

Big Daddy Kane: "Borrowed" from James Brown

M/A/R/R/S: A groundbreaking single and court case

funk quotient of old Chubby Checker and Beach Boys records.

However, to achieve major chart success it seemed that rap had to follow the Fats and either dampen its ardour or mix with white music forms to find any significant chart placings. At the time of writing, Run DMC's biggest-selling single is still their collaboration with Aerosmith from 1986, 'Walk This Way' LL Cool J's only major single success came with 'I Need Love', a soft, rap ballad which was routinely booed down when he tried to perform it in London. It took the enchanting sound of Ofra Haza's voice on the Coldcut remix of Eric B & Rakim's 'Paid In Full', to place them in the British Top Ten, and despite the critical acclaims showered down on **KRS One**'s brilliant debut LP, he still remains very much an underground item.

Only **Public Enemy**, with their aggressive rhetoric about separatism, revamping of Malcolm X's politics and open support for Louis Farrakahn, America's biggest Muslim leader, caused any true ripples. And they proved to be pretty confused as their demands for separate black states in America to be formed, with millions of dollars paid to the black community as compensation for 400 years of racism, didn't quite square with their righteous condemnation of apartheid in South Africa.

Yet there was no denying their musical competence. On their second LP, *It Takes A Nation Of Millions To Hold Us Back*, tracks such as 'Don't Believe The Hype' and 'Night Of The Living Bassheads' were state of the art hip hop, fiery and inventive enough to establish them as major leaders in the rap pack.

Despite advance orders of more than two million, Run DMC's long awaited *Tougher Than Leather* LP was a major artistic disappointment. Another rap soundtrack – to the controversial Dennis Hopper film *Colors*, concerning LA street gangs – featured **Roxanne Shante**, **Ice T** and even old funkster **Rick James**, and came through as one of the rap LPs of the year. And its New York label, Cold Chillin', with producer **Marley Marl** at the helm, just failed to become the new Def Jam as its artists, such as the aforementioned Roxanne Shante, Big Daddy Kane, **MC Shan** and **Biz Markie**, all made substantial gains.

Rap's advances were due, in no small part, to the increasing involvement of the major companies in the music. Buoyed by the success of such multi-million-selling acts as The Beastie Boys and LL Cool J on the CBS licensed Def Jam, WEA licensed itself to Cold Chillin', Atlantic Records took on First Priority, whilst MCA picked up Uptown. Inevitably, a certain tension developed. Rap is fast-moving music – one week's "sound" is next week's dustbin. To compete, records have to come out at exactly the right time or find themselves automatically dated. The independent's ability to move speedily contrasted heavily with the slow pace of the majors who take so much more time over their releases, with the result that **Rob Base And DJ E–Z Rock**, could rush out in double-quick time their 'It Takes Two' single, using the break from Lyn Collins' 'Think', whilst Marley Marl had to wait two months at least for his version of it, on Roxanne Shante's 'Go On Girl', to see the light of day. The result? A top 20 hit for Base and E–Z Rock, and a major setback for Marl,

James Brown as himself

The Fat Boys and a, comparatively, not so Chubby Checker

James Brown's celebration was severely marred when the police nailed him for, allegedly, brutally beating up his wife, possession of narcotics and illegal firearms

Public Enemy's Flavour Flav

who had established himself as the rap producer of the year, when he appeared simply to be imitating.

His main contender for this title was one **Hurby Lovebug** who masterminded, amongst other things, **Salt 'N' Pepa**'s second LP, *A Salt With A Deadly Pepa*, which yielded their massive-selling 'Push It' single. Hurby also produced his own LP, *The House That Rap Built*, made up of promising new acts.

And talking of house, Britain finally capitulated and totally embraced the music, or to be more specific, Acid House, a wild mixture of heavy percussion with off-beat synthesizers and quirky melodies providing the record's hypnotic qualities.

The popularity of this music dates back to a vacation four British DJs took in Ibiza last year. Impressed by the reaction local DJs got from certain off-beat records – Pete Wylie's 'Sinful' or The Thrashing Doves's 'Jesus On A Payroll' – along with the much wilder house tracks ('Acid'), one of them, Danny Rampling, set up his own version on his return to London.

The Schoom Club quickly became *the* hotspot by mixing obscure Acid House with well known "Balearic Beats", as records such as the above, popular on the holiday islands, were termed.

One of the main men behind this music's move from the cult clubs to a much wider audience was **Todd Terry**, a shy, retiring 21 year old. Recording under different pseudonyms, records such as 'A Day In The Life' by Black Riot, 'Can You Dance?' by Royal Party and 'Alright, Alright' by the Masters Of Work, were all his own handiwork, and their massive success in clubs all over Britain led to the current interest in the music from larger record labels.

Across the Atlantic, apart from house centres such as Chicago and Detroit,

Derrick May: Detroit "techno" houseman

most Americans couldn't understand the fuss generated by this type of music. In New York, for instance, house is still seen by many as a minority music, made for and by gays. However, that doesn't seem to hinder its development: Detroit, in the guise of such artists and producers as **Derrick May** and his Rhythim Is Rhythim project, attempted to shed their Motown image by creating a harsher, more industrial sound, which, when aligned to a strident house beat, was dubbed Techno.

Hopefully the news that no less a figure than Prince has asked house supremo Marshall Jefferson to work with him will not only open up some intriguing musical possibilities, but contribute greatly towards the future acceptance of house by mainstream America.

One of the most impressive dance music trends is a new generation of British artistes emerging straight out of the clubs and into the charts, **Mica Paris** and **The Pasadenas** being prime examples. On the home-grown hip hop front, **Derek B** leads the way. First located on the independent Music Of Life label, he soon moved to Phonogram when singles of his, such as 'Good Groove', started hitting the Top Ten. With the added promotional clout, his debut LP, *Bullet From A Gun*, entered the LP charts at number eleven, proving Derek B, former clothes shop salesman and Club DJ, at home anyway, a match for anything America had to offer. Behind him, **The Cookie Crew**, a female rap duo from Peckham, scored heavily with their collaboration with **The Beatmasters**, and were soon being chased by the likes of **The Wee Papa Girl Rappers**, the Public Enemy produced **She Rockers**, **M.C.Duke**, **The Demon Boyz** and **Hi-Jack**.

Rare Groove, the unearthing and revering of obscure seventies funk, carried on unabated, as a small section of its followers started adopting the dress of the time. Three groups dominated the action: **The Brothers International**, **Push**, and **The Brand New Heavies**, all strong live attractions, and all talking, somewhat bafflingly, about "going back to go forward". The majors such as RCA, Polydor and Arista, along with enterprising independents such as Charly and Westside, all weighed in with Rare Groove compilations of varying quality.

National radio's continuing inability to reflect, not only the demand for rare groove but all aspects of dance music, has, over the last year, led to an unprecedented growth of the pirate radio network. Illegal stations such as Kiss, LWR, and hundreds of others, all commanded huge audiences and all made stars out of DJs such as Norman Jay of Jazzi B. The latter, with his partner, also made a DJ record – but with a difference: it featured a female lead singer. Enlisting the undiscovered vocal talent of one **Rose Windrush**, **Soul II Soul** came up with 'Fairplay', a more than credible slice of British dance music which compared heavily with new American talent such as **Johnny Kemp** or **Tony Terry**.

The man of the moment, though, is **Keith Sweat** whose debut LP firmly established his credentials and gave an insight into the current strength of the dance scene: he enlisted the help of top rap producer Teddy Riley to make sure he got it right, then, as it sold in the thousands, Sweat refused to quit his high-flying job on Wall Street. Perhaps he knew something we didn't. Perhaps he figured that with so much creativity happening in so many areas of dance music, from Acid House to Rare Groove, Funk to Hip Hop, he'd better bide his time. And he should have plenty of that, because the perfect beat has never looked less like stopping than it does now.

PAOLO HEWITT

Derek B psyches himself up to take on US rap

YEAR IN INDIE

The Sugarcubes: Playful, Icelandic and not quite enough ears

The Sugarcubes have signed a multi-million dollar deal in America, yet in the UK remain loyal to One Little Indian and are thus the perfect incarnation of indie rock in 1988

The main question is not "What happened on the independent scene?", but rather "What *was* the independent scene?" during the last 12 months.

If the music industry's definition depends on the means of production and distribution remaining in the hands of truly independent operators, "indie rock" will include such commercial heavyweights as Erasure, New Order, Depeche Mode and even Kylie Minogue. If, by comparison, the term refers to a musical attitude, then surely such major label artistes as The Beastie Boys, The Primitives and Gaye Bykers On Acid must stand up and be counted.

An inconvenient blurring of guidelines, but what they all have in common is that they are all high profile, all available to anyone in practically any High Street record store. Away from that are the true inheritors of "The Spirit Of '77", the bands, labels and records that exist – for the main part – away from the constant media attention, blanket advertising and costly promo videos. Music that attracts fervently loyal followings – who regard themselves as somehow more informed and open-minded than their *TOTP*-devoted counterparts – by word of mouth and crudely-fashioned, fly-posted handbills. And it's just as mixed a bag as the regular Gallup Top 20.

Over the last 12 months, the trends have moved towards increasingly rough-and-ready guitar-based rock, which often seems to be a direct descendant of skiffle. On closer inspection though, the discerning fan can detect influences as diverse as rockabilly, funk, poetry and sixties-style psychedelia. Among the leading acts to forge new designs from old elements are: **The Wedding Present** (whose *Tommy* compilation captured their early intensity); **Close Lobsters** (their *Foxheads Stalk This Land* earned rave reviews); **The House Of Love** (the Creation label's hottest new talent); **The Woodentops** (reached new heights with the *Wooden Foot Cops On The Highway* album); **Fields Of The Nephrilim** (new wave desperados who burst through with the abrasive *Dawnrazor* album and 'Moonchild' single); and old favourite **The Jazz Butcher** (the, er, delightful *Fishcoteque* LP).

In recent years, the ultimate "indie" band have been **The Smiths**: their surprise signing to EMI and sudden, subsequent disintegration changed all that. But as **Morrissey** began a solo career with *Viva Hate*, **The Sugarcubes** were unleashed on an unsuspecting world.

Although these playful Icelandic demons have now signed a multi-million dollar American deal with Elektra, in England they remain loyal to the One Little Indian company and are thus the perfect incarnation of indie rock in 1988. Certainly the UK music press has grasped their elemental blend of mystery and melody to their ink-stained bosom, featuring elfin vocalist Bjork on their front covers with shocking regularity.

But such an uncompromising group as The Sugarcubes – or indeed The Smiths or New Order – are hardly

A Wedding Present

indicative of the health of the indie scene in general: in contrast, they are obvious (though exhilarating) exceptions to the apparent rule of fuzzy guitars, monotone vocals and unimaginative tunes speeding along the fast lane to nowhere and boredom.

So what have been the most important trends in the independent market? Certainly the surprise of the year was the hijacking of the indie scene by disco music: the return of the Hi-NRG songstress (once defined by Donna Summer's best work) in the unlikely shape of **Kylie Minogue** and the reborn **Hazell Dean** has been almost solely due to the astute skills of the **Stock, Aitken & Waterman** partnership. In particular, the success of Minogue's 'I Should Be So Lucky' was due partly to SAW's mind-numbingly hypnotic repetitiveness but also to a commercial technique which ensured the record maximum radio play: not being BPI members, her record label, PWL, didn't ask for royalties, so Radio One and all its rivals could play 'Lucky' all day for free!

But as the charts became less and less dominated by straight "rock", both indie artists and labels have explored areas of dancefloor music other than disco. UK hip hop, house and soul have all begun to break through: surprise hits by new artists such as **Eric B & Rakim**, **Cookie Crew**, **Derek B**, **S-Express** and **Bomb The Bass** consolidated the lo-budget, hi-tech success that was M/A/R/R/S's innovative 'Pump Up The Volume'. Then came a single that married the brash glam-rock stomp of an early seventies hit with the eerie theme tune from a classic children's TV show!

'Doctorin' The Tardis' by **The Timelords** was an irrepressible piece of dance-floor junk. Welding together the basic mindless stack-heeled mantra of Gary Glitter's 'Rock 'n' Roll (Part 1)' with the electronic sound-effects counter-melody of the *Dr Who* theme, it was the British equivalent of 'Una Paloma Blanca' – a summer hit bought by people who like to go to dodgy discos and drink too much.

In a way, it's surprising that no one had thought of such an idiotic hybrid before. Can we now expect a hip hop version of the *Blue Peter* theme or find the BBC commissioning The Sugarcubes to compose the tune for a new series of *Playschool*?

In fact, hybrid may be the way ahead. When no one has any brand-new ideas (most of the time, unfortunately) the options are either to recycle old ideas – hence the huge success of the Strange Fruit compilation EPs of radio sessions featuring old favourites like **The Cure** and **The Buzzcocks** and the charting of **New Order**'s 'Blue Monday '88' – or combine a variety of styles. Already the westernized style of Indian music called Bhangra has been mixed with house in the hope of discovering The Next Big Thing. In fact, Bhangra music itself is already a big seller, but since the leading bands tend to sell their records through specialist Indian shops only and play sell-out concerts that attract only Asian music-lovers, it's difficult for them to achieve the serious media attention which would be required to "cross over".

M/A/R/R/S: Innovative

Close Lobsters contemplate a return to the seabed

Happily, though, the live circuit is flourishing. Groups such as Depeche Mode and New Order can now comfortably sell out Wembley Arena, while in the clubs a flurry of new bands seems to spring up weekly. Currently flush with club success are the exotically named **Junior Manson Slags** (no record deal yet) and **Stitched-Back Foot Airmen**, a group whose composed versatility was shown on the *Seven Eggtiming Greats* album and the recent 'Costa Del Sol' EP.

Following the demise of the Time Box, the main London showcase for emerging acts remains Panic Station (Monday night at Camden Town's Dingwalls). At the venue's anniversary show in May, a capacity crowd was treated to sweat-soaked appearances by such future luminaries as **Blue Aeroplanes** (a set worthy of their stunning *Spitting Out Miracles* LP), **The Flatmates**, **The Darling Buds** and **The Chesterfields**.

Last year's buzzwords of "grebo" – as typified by the fierce, unwashed attack of Crazyhead, Gaye Bykers On Acid, Loop and Pop Will Eat Itself – and "shambling" (the so-called "anorak bands" like Brilliant Corners, Flatmates, Close Lobsters, etc.) have become largely redundant as the bands involved begin to evolve and adapt.

As ever, the most interesting artistes were those who actually confounded any categorization at all – especially **Wire**, **Danielle Dax**, **Head** and **Nick Cave**. My tips for indie success in '89? Oh, a shot in the dark for Depeche Mode, New Order and Erasure . . . plus perhaps a Slaughter & The Dogs revival?

JOHNNY WALLER

YEAR IN FOLK

"Tell me," they used to ask me at the sort of parties you'd spend your time studying the rubber plant, "what exactly *is* folk music?" And out would come the finest cliché in the book: "It's *all* folk music . . . as Louis Armstrong used to say (or Woody Guthrie or Ledbelly or Big Bill Broonzy or the bloke in the pub round the corner depending on the culture of the audience) . . . it's all folk music 'cos I ain't never heard no horse sing!" Cue cheap laughs. Cue, too, a very bad old joke that's never rung so true. For this was the year a young singer-songwriter from Barking topped the charts singing a Beatles song one minute and brought the house down at a bona fide folk festival the next (this between jaunts to Eastern Europe).

Yeah, so let's hear it for **Billy Bragg**, but let's hear it too for **Salif Keita**, whose album *Soro* beat all-comers in the *Folk Roots* poll. And let's hear it for another African whose virtuosity borders on genius, **Ali Farka Toure** from Mali, who was to be found at another folk festival dazzling the audience shoulder to shoulder with Britain's own most durable folk legend **Martin Carthy**.

And let's hear it for **The Pogues** who, in a year that saw the demise of Ireland's finest band De Dannan, took their own highly individual brand of sentimental bar-room ballads to a new level of acceptance (their Christmas number one – well it *should* have been – 'Fairytale Of New York' could have been lifted from any Irish ballroom in the last 50 years). And let's hear it for **King Edward II & The Red Hot Polkas**, Rod Stradling's instinctive and visionary English country dance band who not only added a couple of members of eccentric rockers **The Mekons** to their ranks, but started nosing around in reggae circles and wound up working with reggae cult hero **The Mad Professor**.

And what about our two finest unaccompanied groups, **The Watersons** and **Swan Arcade** joining forces under the umbrella of **Blue Murder** to produce some thundering gospel? Or the ethnic music of Bulgaria being trailed around Europe to ecstatic reactions under the name of Balkana, even to a spot on *Wogan*? Or a Yemenite singer called **Ofra Haza** singing a traditional song in her native tongue all about selling brides to rich men and watching it get sampled all the way into the charts by rappers **Eric B & Rakim**? And even more extraordinary, Ofra herself getting a hit in her own right with that same song 'Im Nin Alu' over a thumping disco beat!

The "Barking bard" Billy Bragg

Has the folk world gone mad, or has it at last found sanity? For as the edges become blurred to the point of complete indecipherability, the music gets ever more unpredictable. In this, surely the most exciting age for the genre since those pioneering days in the sixties, who would dare to draw demarcation lines about what is and what isn't folk music?

Is it the blessed **Natalie Merchant** and her **10,000 Maniacs** with their modern-day social commentaries about child abuse? Is it the singing restauranteuse **June Tabor** singing, as magnificently morose as ever, a Natalie Merchant song ('Verdi Cries')? Is it the wonderful Yorkshire/South Moluccan band **The Deighton Family** singing Cliff Richard's 'Travelling Light' in Barnsley accents? Is it elfin-like **Marta Sebestyen** and **Muzsikas** from Hungary enchanting everyone with their native music?

Or is it another bunch of rock heart-throbs, **Hothouse Flowers** from Dublin telling the world their biggest inspiration is the long-dead father of modern-day Irish folk music, Sean O'Riada . . . and liberally using the uillean pipes to prove it? And can you say with any real degree of certainty that it's not **Fairground Attraction**, who topped the charts with a pleasant little ditty called 'Perfect' and have a lead singer called **Eddi Reader**, who used to sing – quite spectacularly – barrelhouse blues round the folk clubs?

Several years ago the colourful Geordie singer **Bob Davenport** – a man not averse to a bit of controversy – put a few noses out of joint by accusing the existing folk circuit of racism. This naturally brought howls of protest from all concerned, but he was right. He didn't actually mean that folkies went round Brixton shouting "nigger" at the inhabitants – and "chauvinistic" might have been a more appropriate, if less intoxicating word – but the only black artists to be found regularly on the British folk circuit at the time were **Johnny Silvo** and **Cliff** of **The Spinners**, while there was little apparent interest in black folk music, be it indigenous or African. Davenport might equally well have attacked the lack of empathy with any non-British or American folk music, for apart from the odd freak like Brittany's **Alan Stivell** (who could be filed under Celtic so it was all right) there has always been an appalling lack of awareness of music emerging from beyond these islands.

Which is why the current explosion is just so damn thrilling. **Taxi Pata Pata** bringing the house down at last summer's Bracknell Festival; Palm Wine guitarist and singer **S. E. Rogie** from

Nanci Griffith

Sierra Leone being rescued from obscurity, in the manner of Ted Hawkins, by the irrepressible Andy Kershaw, godlike DJ of this parish; **Blowzabella** belting out pipes and all sorts with a blinding array of musics of all ethnic shapes and sizes; **Flaco Jimenez** from San Antone lending his inimitable Tex-Mex accordion once more to Ry Cooder's otherwise disappointing band this year . . . the memories are unyielding.

We're calling it "roots music", now, of course, "folk" being one of those anti-social sort of words, like AIDS or Tories. And if it means we can groove to the broad-ranging likes of **Nanci Griffith**, **Sweet Honey In The Rock**, **The Easy Club** and **Vin Garbutt** and *still* get pigeonholed, then who's complaining?

Fuelled all the way by *Folk Roots* magazine in cahoots with Kershaw's excellent Radio 1 show, the roots revolution is fast changing the entire public conception of what used to be folk music. A few years ago would anyone have given the earthy young American singer-songwriter **Tracy Chapman** a second glance? No, she'd have been dismissed as a Joan Armatrading apologist; yet here she is being hailed – rightly – by the pop press of all things, as a sensitive and inspirational new talent. Nor should it be interpreted that this revolution is

The Deighton Family

Fuelled by *Folk Roots* magazine and Andy Kershaw's Radio 1 show, the roots revolution is fast changing the entire public conception of what used to be folk music

King Edward II & The Red Hot Polkas

devoted to sweeping away the existing folk club network. The folk clubs have habitually given sanctuary to some damaging, retrogressive attitudes, but their basic values as an outlet for emerging talent, an alternative to the ludicrous gloss of showbiz, and as a haven for musical honesty and integrity, remain as sound as they ever were.

And there's no reason, either, why folk clubs themselves shouldn't flourish in the wake of this new dawn. **Clive Gregson** – once Stiff Records' great white hope – has become a somewhat unlikely darling of the folk clubs in the last year, in the company of his rather more picturesque singing partner **Christine Collister**; while confident singer-songwriter **Pete Morton** and wondrous Northumbrian piper **Kathryn Tickell** have joined the staple diet of the folk circuit.

De Dannan finally had one row too many, but in their place we had the . . . ahem . . . supergroup **Patrick St** (Andy Irvine, Kevin Burke, Artie McGlynn and Jackie Daly) emerging as a real tour de force), a reappearance from **Relativity** (the occasional alliance between members of the **Bothy Band** and **Silly Wizard**), and even the great Irish singer **Len Graham** formed a band, **Skylark**. Yes, all this and the maestro himself, **Donal Lunny**, got himself a new group together to indulge his passion for creating a new rhythmic-based sound.

Oh, and the best album of the year came from an Irishman too. His name is **Davey Spillane**, a piper inspired by the Celtic boom of the seventies and who sprang to fame with Moving Hearts. His album, *Atlantic Bridge*, took the uillean pipes into new territories, blending the temperamental old instrument with rock, blues and country (**Jerry Douglas** and **Bela Fleck** were among the guest musicians) and the whole thing is a triumphant monument to the roots explosion.

10,000 Maniacs

That, and the odd little **June Tabor/Andy Cronshaw** experiment apart, the records of the year were compilations. The splendid *Woody Lives* to mark the 20th anniversary of **Woody Guthrie**'s death, which further marked **Rory McLeod** as one of *the* inspirational figures in the current herd; a delightfully shambling selection put together by **Andy Kershaw** under the wryly modest title *Great Moments In Vinyl History*; the story of the English folk dance revival (*Tap Roots*) and another trailblazing selection from the Cooking Vinyl label, *Hot Cookies*.

If they could just get someone to give these records decent titles then we'd be *really* rocking!

COLIN IRWIN

YEAR IN SINGLES

The Pet Shop Boys and Dusty Springfield

If you believed the statistics bandied around by prophets of doom, this could easily have been an obituary for that beleagured little piece of black vinyl known affectionately as The Single. But despite great debates that "the single format is dead", onslaughts from its modern equivalents – the CD and cassingle – and the news that during the last year singles sales dipped by 6 per cent to their lowest for 15 years, the 45 has survived and is thriving.

This downturn, curiously enough, has meant the most varied Top 100s in years, as it was easier for bands to break the charts – a "soft" patch opened up opportunities for the new as well as the strictly secondhand: records which earlier bombed their base in a tougher chart environment got a better run on re-release; as fans of established acts waited for the albums, the fresh talent, whose singles weren't seen as mere loss leaders for LPs, provided some very pleasing successes; club DJs – literally – putting together records in their bedrooms were going Top Five; the charts groaned with oldies like Eric Clapton, Starship and Fleetwood Mac, who for years couldn't get themselves arrested; suddenly a crop of teenagers appeared – 19-year-old Bros! 19-year-old Kylie Minogue! 18-year-old Elisa Fiorillo! 18-year-old Glenn Medeiros! 17-year-old Debbie Gibson! 16-year-old Tiffany! And 15-year-old Vanessa Paradis! It was as if all the rules had been taken away.

It seems incredible now, but prior to 8 August 1987 the name Rick Astley would not have registered the slightest glimmer of recognition

There were, however, five rather talented and blessed teenagers-at-heart, a duo and a trio, who, in paying no heed whatsoever to all this talk of downturning market trends, brought an otherwise absent degree of consistency to the charts. The duo, **The Pet Shop Boys**, came, tested the water with a number one record, perfected their deadpan, understated, thoughtfully bittersweet Europop, looked a bit miserable, and they conquered. Now they're one of the most successful pairs of all time, with four number one hits, well able to conquer the success tallies of Wham! and The Everly Brothers.

They never put a foot wrong. The Catholic guilt anthem 'It's A Sin' struck a chord in schoolboys ancient and modern and stayed at number one for three weeks in July, 18 months after their debut chart-topper 'West End Girls'. A mere month later, they were back with their gorgeous collaboration with sixties songstress **Dusty Springfield**, 'What Have I Done To Deserve This?', which would certainly have reached the pole position had it not been for a certain freckly bombshell from Newton-Le-Willows, of whom more later. 'Rent' followed in October, but it was left to their idiosyncratic version of Elvis Presley's

From left: Matt Aitken, Pete Waterman, Mike Stock

Bananarama: Four more hits

'Always On My Mind' to score them numero uno mk III, and the Christmas top slot to boot. The unflappable pair wafted back in April to claim their fourth with 'Heart'. Where will it all end, and would we want it to anyway?

And then there was the trio **Stock, Aitken & Waterman,** now legendary writers/producers/remixers/starmakers, who positively bulldozed their progeny up the charts with alarming regularity. And wasted no opportunity in putting two fingers up at a music business that was bent on booing them at every awards ceremony.

Between July and September of 1987, songs written and/or produced by SAW accounted for 9.82 per cent of all singles sold in the UK. SAW wrote and produced five singles in the 25 July chart, including their very own "rare groove" 45, 'Roadblock', which caused a host of snobbish DJs a great deal of needle when they realized it wasn't an obscure seventies import. SAW spent the rest of the year merrily getting up people's noses and setting themselves the ridiculous target of ten Top Ten singles in a year. No problem . . .

And so to the SAW Hit Factory Roll Of Honour. It seems incredible now, but prior to 8 August 1987 the name **Rick Astley** would not have registered the slightest glimmer of recognition. Those in the know forebodingly warned that this Astley chap was "potentially the most important artist to emerge from the SAW stable." This 21-year-old former truck driver and studio tea-boy came out of nowhere with a voice like Luther Vandross crossed with Jeffrey Osborne, and a debut single 'Never Gonna Give You Up' which launched into the chart at 32, took three weeks to get to number one and doggedly stuck there for five more, becoming the best-selling single of 1987.

But how could he follow this? Well, 'Whenever You Need Somebody' emerged in October '87, eventually running out of steam at number three in the face of stiff competition. In December a battle royal was fought between kingpins Rick and The Pet Shop Boys. Back in the summer, Rick's debut had prevented the Boys from claiming their third number one. They gained sweet revenge when 'Always On My Mind' left Rick's faithful reproduction of Nat "King" Cole's 'When I Fall In Love' stuck at number two, hindered in its inexorable progress to the top by a strategic re-release of the original. His fourth single, 'Together Forever', also stuck at number two and was, ironically, stitched up by Stock, Aitken & Waterman's female secret weapon, Aussie soap star **Kylie Minogue** and her blockbusting UK chart debut, 'I Should Be So Lucky' – five weeks up top in February and March.

Aah, Kylie – the perfect formula. Forget *EastEnders* – last year's obsession – along came *Neighbours*, hooked a nation, and launched Ms M into a singing career with a little help from the SAW-cy trio. Well, she was a darn sight prettier than Nick Berry, a cutesome 19, and she could sing a bit – even if some radio stations went so far as to play a slowed-down version of her hit ditty in order to "prove" she was really a speeded up Rick Astley. Still, Kylie had the last laugh as she went on to invade most of the civilized world with her simplistic, catchy hi-NRG romp. Its universal appeal could perhaps be understood only after hearing its 100th play on the radio, by which time it had been reduced to something of a mantra. And to dismiss any notions of novelty value, she was back the following May with the equally bouncy 'Got To Be Certain', which comfortably eased its way to the top end of the chart.

Kylie "Prettier Than Wicksie" Minogue

Ms M wasn't the only young woman to benefit from the SAW mill. Ex-musical actress **Sinitta** had been looking like a one-hit wonder after her 'So Macho' escapade, but proved us all wrong by steaming back with the endearingly camp 'Toy Boy' (peaked at four in August), consolidating her success with 'GTO' and the coy 'Cross My Broken Heart'. Another hi-NRG starlet given the SAW fairydust treatment was **Hazell Dean**, her career resurrected with the robust 'Who's Leaving Who?' in March. No doubt **Mel & Kim** would've been right up there with them had Mel not tragically been taken seriously ill with cancer of the spine. This meant that between 'FLM', a Top Tenner in July, and 'That's The Way It Is', a Top Tenner in February, there was an uneasy and unhappy silence while Mel was struggling with her illness. Then the spectacularly successful **Bananarama** surfed into the record books on the coat-tails of SAW with four consecutive Top 20 singles, thus clocking up 14 hits in total, making them the most successful girl group ever – with one line-up. Only The Supremes could boast more hits (24), but with several different members involved.

Madonna takes a little rest

One woman who had absolutely nothing to do with Stock, Aitken & Waterman was, of course, **Madonna**. Taking a little rest from being queen of all she surveyed during the last year, claiming a brief number one in July with 'Who's That Girl', theme tune from the critically savaged film of the same name in which she starred, returning again in September and December with two more singles taken from the soundtrack. Even Queens of Pop have to have a creative lull and it looked like she was rounding up her troops, for no sooner had we welcomed in 1988 than the invasion of the gurlies was upon the singles chart. They came mysteriously out of nowhere, an alien force invading a hitherto male dominated arena – a bunch of wannabees who wennandidit.

Perhaps unfair to tar **Belinda Carlisle** with the bimbo brush, since she had a solid pop record with The Go-Go's, but she kicked off a flush of female success in January with her number one 'Heaven Is A Place On Earth'. But her crown was summarily swiped by a real upstart – 16-year-old shopping-mall teenybop bratpacker **Tiffany**, wailing her naive way through a cover version of 'I Think We're Alone Now'. She was followed in turn at number one by the aforementioned Ms Minogue. At least 17-year-old American popsicle **Debbie Gibson** wrote her own material. After a false start in September with 'Only In My Dreams' bombing out at 54, she hit the Top Five in January with the insufferably jolly 'Shake Your Love', which paved the way for a re-release of the former to crash into the Top 20.

And just when you thought they couldn't get any younger along came **Vanessa Paradis**, pouting 15-year-old chanteuse, with 'Joe Le Taxi', sung entirely in French. But let's hear it for the rest of the girls, of all ages: **Taylor Dayne**, **Samantha Fox**, **Taja Sevelle**, **Pebbles**, **Elisa Fiorillo**, **Natalie Cole**, **Cher**, **Joyce Sims**, **Brenda Russell**, **Kim Wilde**, and homegrown newcomers **Sinead O'Connor** and **Mica Paris**, all making worthwhile inroads in the chart.

Yes, teenagers were back in the charts in force, and new acts breaking in at every opportunity, taking advantage of lower singles sales to sneak up the hit parade. Many of these campaign victories were finally scored after records had been released twice and even three times. **Danny Wilson** certainly never lost faith in the fine 'Mary's Prayer'. It was first released early in 1987, bombing at 86. They had another go in August, and reached 42. But the jackpot was hit in April '88, when it went all the way to number three. Once a good song, always a good song, or something. It was a similar story for duo **Climie Fisher**, whose 'Love Changes Everything' was released in August '87 to little effect. Their clever working of a fashionable hip-hop theme into 'Rise To The Occasion' did the trick for them, letting 'Love Changes' back on

Tiffany: A-wailing in the shopping malls

the track in March to reach number two. Similar persistence was shown by **Was (Not Was)**, **Deacon Blue** and **Icehouse**, whose 'Crazy' was released twice but never quite made it.

But, by sticking with it way beyond the call of duty, **T'Pau** surpassed any of them. Nobody wanted to know about 'Heart And Soul' until it was a hit in America, then it went Top Five here. They followed up with an epic, swirly ballad by the name of 'China In Your Hand', and it stayed swirling away atop the chart masthead for five weeks, stunning even lead songstress Carol Decker, who reckoned it never really warranted such a dramatic reaction.

Still, it set T'Pau up as premier pop rockers, allowing them to cheekily re-release a live version of their second chart flop 'Intimate Strangers', changing the title to 'Sex Talk'. Hmm, raunchy.

The "if at first you don't succeed . . ." dictum also applied to 1988's teen pop phenomenon **Bros**. In September '87 they tried the old "Bootleg Mix" scam in the clubs with 'I Owe You Nothing', but DJs were never going to believe it was a rare groove, and it flagged at number 80. They tried again in November with 'When Will I Be Famous?', and that was cheeky enough to do it, being held off the top spot by 'China In Your Hand' mania. 'Drop The Boy' nearly made it all the way in March, then, on re-release, 'I Owe You Nothing' bounded effortlessly to number one.

So who else really consolidated their chart position during the last year? **Johnny Hates Jazz** certainly did – no shattered dreams for these boys, with a solid performance and three Top 20 hits. **Terence Trent D'Arby** was busy bolstering his world-beating arrogance (and domination of the LP chart) with three sizeable singles, including the sublime 'Sign Your Name'. Colin Vearncombe, aka **Black**, scored two Top Tenners before fading. But happiest bunch of all must be **Heart**, who, after 14 hits in their native America, had their first UK hit with 'Alone' in July, and promptly followed up with four more. Scots soulsters **Wet Wet Wet** made

Would be rare groovers Bros

In September Bros tried the old "Bootleg Mix" scam in the clubs with 'I Owe You Nothing', but DJs were never going to believe it was a rare groove, and it flagged at number 80

T'Pau: Nobody wanted to know

more than a splash. Kicking off with 'Sweet Little Mystery' in July, they had three hits under their belts by the time they became top boys in May with the Beatles' 'With A Little Help From My Friends', a single double A-sided with **Billy Bragg**'s version of 'She's Leaving Home', recorded in aid of the Childline charity.

It was a mixed year for the more familiar names. **Whitney Houston** didn't quite repeat her staggering American success here, but managed four in the Top 20. **Luther Vandross** never seemed to be out of the chart – five singles of his, including the much-released 'Give Me The Reason' – figured in the listings. Rock dinosaurs **Fleetwood Mac** put on their pop sensibility hats and 'Little Lies' and 'Everywhere' earned them well deserved Top Five hits.

Even **Michael Jackson** failed to make a Madonna-esque clean sweep with the first singles off his mega album *Bad*. 'I Just Can't Stop Loving You', a sickly duet with Siedah Garrett, managed two weeks at number one in August, but was promptly toppled by the Astley Effect, and the following trio of 45s failed to match this performance, largely because most people had quite sensibly dashed off to invest in the long-player.

The Communards had the year's biggest seller

The Communards, who recorded last year's biggest-selling single, had their greatest success with yet another cover version, 'Never Can Say Goodbye', but performed respectably with two of their own songs. Other, traditionally "albums artistes" such as **Eurythmics**, **Simply Red**, **Prince**, and **U2** had little more than sporadic showings in the Top 30. Even **George Michael** couldn't be guaranteed

Five Star: The hit machine stalled

Cliff reached his half century

number one singles any more. 'Faith' made it to number two, but 'Father Figure' and the sublime ballad 'One More Try' fared much better in America.

Last year's hit machine **Five Star** had a quiet year by their standards. They released four singles, but didn't make the Top Ten. Norwegian chart champs **A-ha** had an even quieter one, with only two singles, including the Bond film theme 'Living Daylights', which got to number five in July '87. Likewise **The Beastie Boys** who, after a rather noisy year, were quiet after 'Girls' failed to broach the Top 40 in October.

In the "old stalwarts" department, you could always rely on **Shakin' Stevens** to have a hit. He had three, as did **Cliff**, whose 'My Pretty One' was his 50th Top Ten solo hit. **Eddy Grant** and **Billy Ocean**, no spring chickens themselves, seemed to dominate the airwaves in January and February with their respective monsters 'Give Me Hope Jo'Anna' and 'Get Outta My Dreams, Get Into My Car'.

The ultimate novelty "house" record, 'Doctorin' The Tardis', mixed Gary Glitter with the *Doctor Who* theme and got to number one in June

Bands with their roots in the indie tradition came up with some pretty impressive results: stand up **Depeche Mode**, **The Jesus And Mary Chain**, **The Pogues**, **Lloyd Cole**, **The Cure**, **Erasure**, and of course, Manchester's joint finest, **The Smiths** and **New Order**. After three singles in the Top 40, the shock announcement was made that The Smiths were no more, but **Morrissey** returned as a solo artist, his single 'Suedehead' outdoing any of The Smiths' singles by going straight in at number five. New Order were doing reasonable business until the world went crazy over their remix of the legendary 'Blue Monday', which further boosted its lead as the biggest ever selling 12-inch record, getting to number three in May.

Sadly, last year's giantkillers **The Housemartins** decided to duck out altogether, but only after three more singles, two of which went Top 20. A strange move, considering the success enjoyed by **The Sugarcubes**, **REM**, **The Proclaimers**, **The Wedding Present** and **The Primitives** was largely due to a market they pioneered.

A brief salute should be made to the sub-section marked Goths, Grebos, Post-Hippies and Led Zeppelin Fans, comprising the varied talents of **Sisters Of Mercy**, **The Mission**, **All About Eve**, **Zodiac Mindwarp**, **The Cult**, **Pop Will Eat Itself** and **Fields Of The Nephilim**. Devoted live audiences

Morrissey, a Smith no more

The Housemartins split up

assured relatively high chart placings for a largely non-pop noise, **Sisters Of Mercy** coming out tops with their 'This Corrosion' single astonishingly reaching number two in October.

Talking of Led Zep, it was a good year for heavy rock and metal. For sustained effort, first place went to **Def Leppard**, with **AC/DC**, **Whitesnake** and **Mötley Crüe** a close second. **Iron Maiden** fans were out in force in March, sending their 'Can I Play With Madness' single in at number four. Thrash metal had its turn too, with **Metallica**, **Anthrax** and **Megadeth** being loud and proud in the Top 75.

Stock, Aitken & Waterman weren't the only demons of the dancefloor in the chart either. Dance music's domination of the listings during much of 1988 came from a variety of sources. Rap (even hardcore) was prominently represented by **LL Cool J**, **Eric B & Rakim**, **Run DMC**, **Public Enemy**, **Salt 'N' Pepa**, **Mantronix**, plus our very own **Derek B** and **Wee Papa Girl Rappers**. There was a seemingly insatiable thirst for records with "house" in the title. It started off with 'House Nation' by the **Housemaster Boyz** in September, building up to 'House Arrest' by **Krush** in December, 'Rok Da House' by **Beatmasters And The Cookie Crew** and 'This Brutal House' by **Nitro Deluxe** in January, to perhaps the ultimate house record, 'Doctorin' The House' by **Coldcut**, in February, and the ultimate novelty "house" record 'Doctorin' The Tardis' – mixing Gary Glitter with the *Doctor Who* theme and getting to number one in June.

Simon "Bass" Harris

The advent of the DJ as pop star, armed only with a couple of turntables and a bunch of samples, provided some exciting 12-inch throbbers, and a few copyright problems. It all started back in September, when the ubiquitous **M/A/R/R/S** took their seminal 'Pump Up The Volume' to number one. Other successes were clocked up by **Bomb The Bass**, whose 'Beat Dis' debuted at five in February; **Simon Harris** with 'Bass (How Low Can You Go)', 'It Takes Two' by **Rob Base And DJ E-Z Rock**, 'Check This Out' by **LA Mix**, and, decked in flares and platforms, **S-Express** and their 'Theme From' matched M/A/R/R/S' two weeks at number one in April. And that's just a, for want of a better word, sample.

Film soundtracks again provided a launch-pad for singles chart success. *Who's That Girl* and *The Living Daylights* helped out Madonna and A-ha, and the names **Abigail Mead** and **Nigel Goulding** would never have figured in the Top Five without the benefit of *Full Metal Jacket*. *Dirty Dancing* launched the career of **Patrick Swayze**, and **Los Lobos** owed a debt of gratitude to Ritchie Valens, whose 'La Bamba' song (from the biopic of the same name) gave them a number one in August.

Prefab Sprout: Late jackpot winners

A chart review wouldn't be the same without a welter of cover versions, and this year was no exception. Rick Astley, The Pet Shop Boys and The Communards, as already mentioned, saw no crime in the cover, neither did, among others, **Alison Moyet** ('Love Letters'), **The Stranglers** ('All Day And All Of The Night'), **Billy Idol** ('Mony Mony').

Comebacks were made by a variety of artistes long absent from the chart. Back, back, back came **Barry White**, **James Brown** and **Scritti Politti**. But most impressive relaunches were undertaken by **George Harrison** ('Got My Mind Set On You' reached two in October) and **The Bee Gees**, who buried the ghost of 'Saturday Night Fever' by reaching number one with 'You Win Again' and staying alive for four weeks.

But there was a plethora of what might be termed Very Pleasing Successes during the year. Hoorah for **Jellybean**, who with the help of three guest vocalists, clocked up four Top 20 hits. Well done **Voice Of The Beehive**, steadily improving their track-record through the year, as did **The Christians**, **INXS**, and **Jermaine Stewart**. And, at long last, the jackpot was scored by **Then Jerico** ('The Motive'), **Prefab Sprout** (King Of Rock 'n' Roll), the **Hothouse Flowers** ('Don't Go'), and **The Adventures** ('Broken Land').

Biggest hoorahs, though, go to **Fairground Attraction**, who broke dance music's stranglehold on the upper reaches of the chart with their first single, the pure, simple, perfectly-formed 'Perfect', a shining number one in May. And the indefatigable **Aswad** who, after 14 years in the business, proved reggae was a commercial force, getting to number one with 'Don't Turn Around'.

A fond mention must go to the ones that got away. Despite such a fresh and invigorating chart atmosphere, wouldn't it've been lovely if **The Wonder Stuff** had done wonders with 'Give Give Give Me More More More', or **Then Jerico** with 'Muscle Deep', or perhaps **Wendy & Lisa** with 'Waterfall', **Head** with 'Sin Bin' and **So** with 'Are You Sure?'.

Predictions are always subject to the whims of fate, but chart futures will hopefully be assured to Elisa Fiorillo, Steven Dante, The Adventures, Derek B, Sinead O'Connor, Prefab Sprout, Julia Fordham, Roachford and Mica Paris. For as long as the singles chart remains a shop window for the album chart, there'll always be special offers, one-offs and new lines. And that can only be a healthy trend.

BETTY PAGE

Fairground Attraction: "Pure, simple, perfectly formed"

YEAR IN IRELAND

Inevitably, the year in Ireland began and ended with **U2**. Last Christmas they returned home after a triumphant world tour in the wake of *The Joshua Tree*. But instead of taking the traditional superstar sabbatical, they immediately began beavering away on new songs to complement the live tracks of a double album that would accompany their film of the 1987 tour, *Rattle And Hum*.

In the wake of this success, the group have changed both internal and international perceptions of Irish music. In a country demoralized by unemployment, youth emigration and government cuts, the public were eager to cheer new heroes whether they be sportsmen like Stephen Roche or Jack Charlton's soccer squad, or musicians like U2 who represented a new Irish modernity. Taking their cue, the Irish national press belatedly followed their UK counterparts in recognizing popular music as a circulation builder.

Throughout 1987, London A&R men cluttered Irish venues as they competed to sign Emerald Isle hopefuls – in the elusive quest for the new U2. The attention flattered all the young groups labouring in the rehearsal rooms clustered around Dublin's Temple Bar neighbourhood, but both bands and talent scouts often forgot that the act with the closest personal ties to U2 had been their absolute opposites: those cracked Dada exhibitionists **The Virgin Prunes**. In searching for clones they often missed the clues to substance – many were chosen, but in 1988 only **Sinead O'Connor** and **Hothouse Flowers** made an unqualified advance.

Former Eurovision Song Contestants Hothouse Flowers

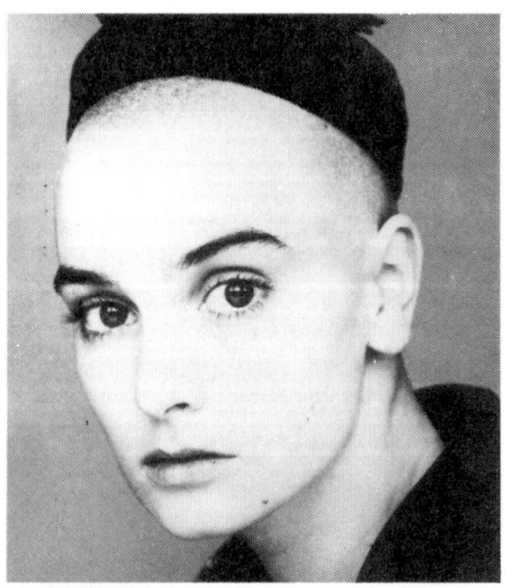

Sinead O'Connor: "A sexually candid, agonized and irate adolescence"

The "mongrel and multi-cultural" Pogues

O'Connor's success was the more controversial surprise. Perceptively plucked from an obscure Dublin band, Ton Ton Macoute, the teenager was almost smuggled out of Dublin to mature for two years in London before her first album *The Lion And The Cobra* was released with little fanfare in late '87. To idle ears it could sound like just more bawling Celtic romance, but this featherweight packed more punch than Barry McGuigan. Her vocals could scald, chill and celebrate, while her lyrics – often more withering than 'Wuthering Heights' – detailed a sexually candid, agonized and often irate adolescence. A blend that meant *The Lion . . .* was one of those albums that gained stature with each hearing.

The combination of a successful single, 'Mandinka', her striking beauty-and-the-baldhead image and increasing readiness to provide controversial editorial copy shot O'Connor out of the ruck. But her anti-Bono jibes and sympathy for the IRA caused Dublin brows to knit in puzzled offence. Stormy petrels would seek stormy weather, and O'Connor didn't care to show much solidarity with a Dublin she'd increasingly disclaimed since her departure.

She went on to flirt with hip hop, but Hothouse Flowers were much more traditional Celtic soul men. Association with the tragically unhip Eurovision Song Contest through a video funded by the European Community seemed a hazardous hype, but the calculated risk was justified when their rousing, piano-driven single, 'Don't Go', cracked both British and Continental charts. But their album, *People*, was uneven. The Flowers had a manifesto of Celtic mystique and leader Liam O'Maonlai possessed the chops and the charisma, but whether they yet have the songs and the insight to sustain their ascent is an issue for next year's edition.

The Flowers' rootsy emotionalism also mirrored prevailing Irish values: especially an attachment to white rock that was unmoved by the UK vogue for hip hop and sampling. This could indicate a cultural conservatism that gave priority to "authentic" tradition-bound forms of emotion. But it was also due to the economics of a small, album-oriented market where the Irish wing of PolyGram, to save vinyl, released only the full-length version of Grandmaster Flash's *The Message*;

Cactus World News

Stump: Humorous and "awkwardly ambling"

where singles, least of all small quantities of 12" independent imports, have rarely been commercial, particularly after Irish excise duties have been paid.

Instead, Ireland stuck to its acoustic roots and became the European beach-head for New Country, with Texan **Nanci Griffith** actually topping the album charts, even gaining sufficient celebrity to warble a radio advert for Tipperary Spring Water. With local veterans **The Flesh Cowboys** also packing out venues, country gained from the Irish taste for a well-made song with a strong storyline.

But then folk music has also been an integral component of the tightly-knit Irish music scene. Unlike England, it has never been marginalized and the same people who buy Michael Jackson records also purchase **Christy Moore**'s album. But with Moore recuperating from a mild heart attack, an unexpected champion emerged in **Van Morrison** whose own sort of homecoming, *Irish Heartbeat*, recorded in a fortnight with senior traditional troupe The Chieftans, was the most marvellously heartening surprise of the year. And if a Glasgow Celtic fan like Ray Houghton could play for Ireland's soccer team, **The Pogues** were equally adopted as a home-team, though their eclectic borrowings on the *If I Should Fall From Grace With God* album owed more to England's own roots revival and the mongrel, multi-cultural experience of North London.

Indeed, between the rovers in London and the tax exiles at home – Def Leppard, Elvis Costello and The Waterboys were all familiar Dublin figures – it was becoming increasingly difficult to define the Irish musical community. The younger bands might attract media attention, but the New Year saw a cross-breeding between outsiders like Costello, The Pogues and The Waterboys, folk musicians like Moore and **Donal Lunny**, singers like **Mary Coughlan** and **Mary Black** and Nashville-based exiles like **Maura O'Connell** and guitarist **Philip Donelly**, whose importance cannot yet be accurately judged.

That Petrol Emotion: The sole northern band of substance

Meanwhile, in London, long-lost veteran **Rory Gallagher** made a gutsy comeback with his *Defender* album on Demon. And two other Cork-derived outfits enjoyed contrasting fortunes: **Stump**'s "fierce pancake" of Flann O'Brien-style humour and awkwardly-ambling rhythms found favour with Ensign, while **Microdisney** – critics' pets without an obvious commercial consistency – were, sadly, dropped by Virgin and then split up.

But Virgin did capture **That Petrol Emotion** from Polydor, the sole Northern band of substance. Petrol stood apart not only because their musical ambition took the Derry blare of their guitars to places other more commercially-minded Irish bands feared to tread, but there was also the tragic fact that Dublin's growth as an industry centre hadn't stimulated any new energies in the six counties. Where once there was regular traffic between Dublin and Belfast, there was now an unconscious mental border. If Dublin had organized in the shadow of U2, Ulster bands looked unavailingly to London, with troubadour **Andy White** the only Northern figure to shrug off the province's apathy.

Contrast that dismal prospect with Dublin activity where it was becoming impossible to keep track of all the acts recording or releasing albums: **Aslan** and **Tuesday Blue** (EMI); **In Tua Nua** and **Something Happens!** (Virgin); **Light A Big Fire** (Siren); **The Fountainhead** (China/Polydor); **Cactus World News** (MCA); **Cry Before Dawn** (CBS); **A House** (blanco y negro/WEA); **The Stars Of Heaven** (Rough Trade); and **Gavin Friday** (Island). Not forgetting others like **Blue In Heaven**, **The Real Wild West**, **The Golden Horde**, **Paul Cleary And The Partisans** and **Princess Tinymeat**, who all have realistic hopes of entering the charmed circle.

But most were still in the limbo of development – names on contracts, but hardly household figures. Looking to both Europe and America, these Irish bands were generally out of step with both UK "pop playmates" and the indie scene's extremes of experimentation. Generalization is impossible, but the Irish bands were more attuned to American models of success: unremitting touring and the rock rhetoric of loudly-coloured guitars and unembarrassed emotion. Only The Stars Of Heaven with their discreet country-rock and Gavin Friday who'd journeyed to New York to record a cabaret-flavoured album with Marianne Faithfull's producer, Hal Willner, found any virtue in being fastidious.

So despite U2, Sinead O'Connor and Hothouse Flowers, 1988 was a period of uncertain transition. Ten years ago, Irish rock was far off the beaten track; now it is flooded with record company advances. But the record-buying jury is still out. Only 1989 will know its verdict.
BILL GRAHAM

Tragically, Dublin's growth hadn't stimulated any new energies in the six counties. Where once there was regular traffic between Dublin and Belfast, there was now an unconscious mental border

QUOTES OF THE YEAR

"In America, our record company is run by a pile of complete egocentrics, and they'd say to us, Listen, you don't know anything about America, you don't know how America works, trust us. So I trusted them and ended up looking like a complete slut."

CAROL DECKER, T'PAU

"I went on a skiing holiday with some friends and this guy turned up who was the vilest, most nightmare person you can imagine. So we decided to give him my membership to The Limelight."

KIM WILDE

"If Morrissey's a genius then what's he doing in a fucking pop group?"

SHANE MACGOWAN, THE POGUES

"I'm used to being called a raving madman, but it's different for Patricia . . . it's all very well being the idiot, but being the idiot's lieutenant is no fun at all."

ANDREW ELDRITCH, SISTERS OF MERCY

"I like Cameo – but I'm not sure if it's just for the codpiece Larry Blackmon wears."

BRYAN FERRY

"American cleaning-women are so efficient. If it says 'do not disturb' on your door, they don't. You could be lying in there dead for three weeks, but they won't disturb you."

JOE ELLIOTT, DEF LEPPARD

"I'm irritated that the world that we live in, and its culture and society, can build and maintain Madonna."

NATALIE MERCHANT, 10,000 MANIACS

"I won't get divorced. Not only could I lose my wife but I could lose all my money too."

LIONEL RICHIE

"My hangovers have got worse as I've gotten older."

SUZANNE VEGA

"All I can think in interviews is, Please God don't let me say anything dorky."

TIFFANY

"We chose Steve Lillywhite to produce our album because he wasn't as fat and sweaty as our previous producer."

SHANE MacGOWAN, THE POGUES

"I don't mind that we've moved into the yuppie market. Being a yuppie is better than being one of those people who wear baseball caps and try and pretend they live on the street."

MICK HUCKNALL

"We did 'Roadblock' just to show someone who works in our company that we could make a trendy record."

MIKE STOCK

"The one dilemma of living here is giving so much money to a government I disapprove of. Every year there's another Cruise missile with my name on it."

GEORGE MICHAEL

"I don't really like 'Hi Hi Hi', to me it's a bit flared trousers."

PAUL McCARTNEY

"Last Halloween I had a party where we had a seance. We tried to contact Liberace and Sid Vicious."

DEBBIE GIBSON

"Sadly, I've become one of the most boring sods I've ever met."

STAN HOUSEMARTIN

"People want you to stay the way you were in 1971 just because that was when they were 20, were having fun and weren't divorced yet."

LOUDON WAINWRIGHT

"I started drinking at the age of 15, which is when I stopped growing up emotionally."

GILSON LAVIS, SQUEEZE

"The hats have served us well, but we've had enough of them now – they make you sweat and the dye runs and leaves lines round your head."

KIM APPLEBY, MEL & KIM

"I'm 45 years old. I've nearly died a few times. I didn't even plan on living this long, so all this shit is add-on stuff."

JERRY GARCIA, THE GRATEFUL DEAD

"I think music should be heard in cars. I think that's where it's best. Not all cars though – some cars shouldn't be *allowed* to have music in."

BILL CARTER,
THE SCREAMING BLUE MESSIAHS

"The punks hated us for Knebworth, and quite rightly so. But we couldn't go playing the Nottingham Boat Club just to prove to people in long overcoats that we were OK."

ROBERT PLANT

"We were victims of seventies self-indulgence."

KEVIN GODLEY

"We won't go on Saturday morning television anymore, because they make fools of you."

NEIL TENNANT,
THE PET SHOP BOYS

"I'm going to go on stage in jeans, because last time I went on in my mini-dresses and everything, and was asking for trouble."

PATSY KENSIT

"The 'Anfield Rap' was the hardest project I'll ever do because I was dealing with footballers who have, surprisingly, no sense of rhythm at all."

DEREK B

"One company, I can't remember which one, put in a bid for us without even hearing the tape. Then, after they'd heard it, they said they didn't want us."

HARRY PRIESTMAN, THE CHRISTIANS

"If The Undertones had had the opportunity to sell out, they probably would have taken it."

FEARGAL SHARKEY

"We don't call ourselves pop stars, we call ourselves career women."

PEPSI,
PEPSI AND SHIRLIE

"If someone had told me that they would dance to Yemenite songs in discotheques like The Palladium in New York, I would not have believed them."

OFRA HAZA

"I've met Bono many times and he's told me several jokes, none of which have been very funny."

MIKE PETERS, THE ALARM

“When we heard we were going to Muscle Shoals to record with a lot of celebrated guests, I had these nightmare visions of people like Percy Sledge clustered round a microphone trying to edge each other out. It wouldn't have done our music any good.”

MARK PRINGLE, HOT HOUSE

“There's nothing like putting up a good shelf or laying a decent bit of carpet.”

EDDI READER, FAIRGROUND ATTRACTION

“With some people, your real life is an intrusion into their fantasy.”

BRUCE SPRINGSTEEN

“When people hear somebody like me they're confused, they forget that black people in America have a tradition in folk music and a history.”

TRACY CHAPMAN

“Our songs are written in Icelandic and translated into English – and then re-translated into nonsense by the critics.”

BJÖRK, THE SUGARCUBES

“In my opinion it's everyone else that's mad.”

MARK E SMITH, THE FALL

“I never swore as a kid, but when I came into the industry it seemed that every other word I heard was the one that began with ‘F’ and I picked it up, I'm afraid to say.”

CLIFF RICHARD

“If I took off my sunglasses, everyone would see I was lying through my teeth.”

GEORGE MICHAEL

“Sean Penn asked me *never* to see *Shanghai Surprise*. He said, As a friend, don't watch it. So I never will.”

CHRISSIE HYNDE

“I was thinking of our set list, and the subject matters are quite depressing, but when you're dancing to them you'd never know.”

TRACEY, VOICE OF THE BEEHIVE

“All rock 'n' roll is about having a good time and getting laid, it'd be stupid to pretend otherwise.”

LEMMY

“My friendship with David Bowie seems to be over. I don't know what I've done to upset him, but when I turned up for a pre-arranged interview with him he just walked past me and said, You're a fat shit.”

JONATHAN KING

“When people recognize me they're generally very pleasant. If they're not, they call you a wanker or something like that. But I can deal with that, I'm from Newcastle.”

STING

“People wouldn't look twice at me if I wasn't in the pop charts.”

RICK ASTLEY

“People don't realize how hard we work.”

SHIRLIE, PEPSI & SHIRLIE

“I always used to see the neighbours outside riding their bikes and I felt a bit weird because that's what I wanted to do, but I had to stay in . . . dancing.”

DELROY PEARSON, FIVE STAR

“Michael Jackson – he's a great singer but he's not the most masculine guy, is he?”

ALEXANDER O'NEAL

“I'm surprised I'm still here – didn't pull a garage job: car in the garage, engine running, radio on, going to sleep. You get suicidal for the longest time. I ain't shaved today.”

RUN, RUN DMC

“In this songwriting racket you have to put it all in one bite. Just make it simple and interesting and you've got a goer. You can't just lay it down like a boiled egg on a plate. Somehow it's got to be fried up. It's got to be flipped over and fried . . . even poached. Anything but scrambled.”

JOE STRUMMER

“It's pretty dumb to write off CDs as belonging to yuppies, they should belong to everyone and the price should come down to a point where there are no social connotations involved.”

PETER GABRIEL

“Marilyn Monroe was a victim and I'm not. That's why there's really no comparison.”

MADONNA

“I might take up landscape gardening: a patch of soil, a few seeds and some barbed wire – somehow that's very 1988.”

MORRISSEY

“We're one of *the* most stylish groups around, but it must be stressed that style is not *just* about wearing clothes.”

MARTIN FRY, ABC

“I've been in *2000 AD*, and it's like getting the OBE, Billy Bragg got upset that I got there before he did.”

HANK WANGFORD

“I get on with everybody.”

BRYAN ADAMS

“I ate before Michael and I'll eat after Michael.”

FRANK DILEO,
MICHAEL JACKSON'S MANAGER

“If I start feeling like an idiot, that's when some of my best ideas come.”

DAVID BYRNE

“We're more rock 'n' roll than Def Leppard. We're more rock 'n' roll than anybody.”

PAL, A-HA

“BBC England? What's that, a college radio station?”

FLAVOUR FLAV,
PUBLIC ENEMY

“If you listen to the lyrics of our songs, some of them are pretty bloody clever!”

SARAH FLETCHER, THE FLATMATES

“We used to meet producers and they'd ask, Who do you want to sound like? *Strange* question, we wanna sound like *Wet Wet Wet*! So now we tell them we want to sound like a tin of baked beans.”

GRAEME CLARK, WET WET WET

"I'll always be able to scream on pitch. I'll always be able to scream wicked. And if they don't like it they can shove it."

"If I saw him now [Michael Jackson] I'd probably hug him and say Thanks, because without him I'd probably be stealing stereos out of people's cars."

"I'll be around in a year's time whether I'm singing or plucking chicken feathers and stuffing them into cotton pillows."

"I think I'll have another tattoo after lunch – it will say – I love mum."

"You have to be careful in this business, or you can become a monster."

"I like to bonk, but no more than anyone else. It's sad that the newspapers are trying to make me the superstud of 1987."

"Coming between people's marriages can get you killed."

"I wear my girlfriend's knickers – not the frilly kind, just the basic cotton ones from Marks & Spencer."

"I don't want to be thought of as this year's Whitney Houston."

"I'm not afraid of AIDS. There are a lot of doctors in the medical community who will tell you that AIDS has been exaggerated. The risk to a healthy heterosexual like myself is not great. I like having fun."

QUOTES OF THE YEAR

"I'm young – what am I supposed to think about except music and art and sex."

"To my mind America is the most racist, sexist, homophobic, violent society in the so-called free world."

"I've got a compact disc player – you may think that it makes me sound like a yuppie. But if you're in bed with someone and you don't want to get up and turn over the LP, you just slip on a disc for 72 minutes."

"I'm really embarrassed when fans gush."

CONTINUING THE "HARD" LINE ACC

"In ten years time I'll probably be mad. I do feel as if I'm going in that direction, because I'm a romantic and as such I'm basically fucked up. Yes, I should imagine that in ten years' time I'll be completely insane."

"I think happiness is a very overrated emotion."

"I do have some very strange thoughts – still, all geniuses are mad aren't they?"

"Even if I never make another record after this album I'll know it was a brilliant album and that's all that matters to me."

"Take Whitney Houston – after a month of waking up next to her life would get very boring."

"It's terrible really, I even get bored with beautiful women, I've gone out with some extremely beautiful women and yet most of them are crushingly boring."

"I had a job writing in a weekly newspaper but after a while that got boring because I realized the people I was interviewing were far less interesting than me and I didn't see why I should be talking to them."

"I may say a lot of strange and incomprehensible things as far as other people are concerned, but that is the way of all brilliance."

“Success is about being able to open my big mouth and say exactly what I want.”

ORDING TO TERENCE TRENT D'ARBY

“I look at writing and recording like going to the toilet.”

“My grandmother used to say, If you want to create a monster take a young man and give him confidence.”

“A lot of the people I've been compared to are dead.”

“Terence Trent D'Arby is a really complex person.”

“Look . . . fair enough, yes, I was hyped. Plain and simple.”

“The press think they have more power than they actually have.”

“I admit I'm arrogant but not that arrogant – my arrogance is cool.”

“I think I'm a GENIUS. Point fucking blank.”

“Sex will be my downfall. I love . . . I love . . . I love women.”

“I've delivered the goods, and fuck anybody who doesn't agree with me.”

“I care passionately about South Africa – but I'd be lying if I said I cared more about South Africa than I do about my art and sex.”

“I sit in my very plain flat in Kentish Town, in London, and read books and listen to music and practice being an enigma.”

“I met Muhammad Ali in 1980, when he was really tubby. A drop of his sweat fell on my nose and I thought: Please God preserve this.”

“Have I got a girlfriend? Will it make me more accessible if I say I haven't?”

“I'm trying to prove that you can sell records, be a massive crossover success without chopping off your dick!”

“I've been here three times. The first time I was an Ethiopian pirate around 6BC. Then I was a painter in the 18th Century. The last time I was here I was a very talented but unsuccessful country and western singer.”

“I've always been blessed or cursed with perception.”

“I do think I went into the army with ten marbles and came out with eight and a half.”

“I have sex more times than I wash my hair.”

“I am a true soul genius and, unlike certain other singers, 100 per cent man.”

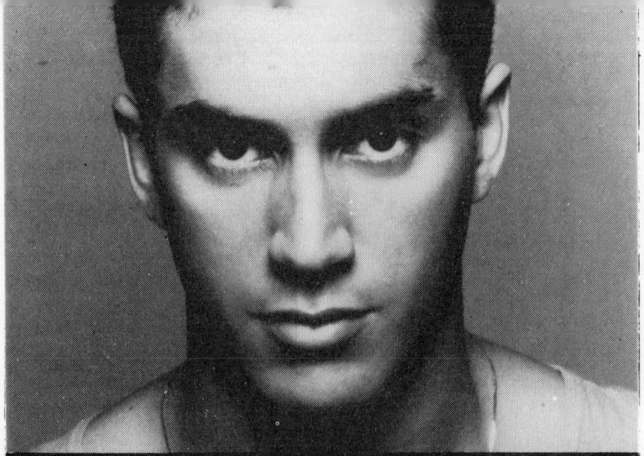

“The New York hip hop scene is dying away because the people in it aren’t branching out, they’re not crossing over. Most of it sounds the same because most of them use the same samples.”

MANTRONIK

“Why do interviewers always ask us about a Satanic connection just because of one mention in one song. I’ll tell you, it’s because the home of Satanism is London, England, and they wanna find out what cult we’re in, so they can buddy up to us, so they can exchange child-killing stories.”

GIBBY, THE BUTTHOLE SURFERS

“At the Marquee, the sweat was just pouring off me and there was this girl at the front who reached out and wiped my arm and then licked the sweat off her hands. It was wild.”

BRYAN ADAMS

“Everybody dreams of getting hold of an autograph hunter and shouting WHY DON’T YOU LEAVE ME ALONE YOU LITTLE BASTARD!!!!”

PAUL HEATON, THE HOUSEMARTINS

“My wife left me because of the band and everything – but fuck it, I’d have left the bitch anyway.”

ALEC JOHN SUCH, BON JOVI

“I often pass a mirror and I glance in it slightly but don’t recognize myself at all.”

MORRISSEY

“I thought that the WEA Aztec Camera was somehow morally inferior to the Rough Trade Aztec Camera.”

RODDY FRAME

“People became obsessed with whether Bono and I were having a thing, then me and Adam Clayton. Eventually Bono said he’d organize a picture of me and U2 in bed together just to straighten things out.”

MAIRE NI BHRAONAIN, CLANNAD

“The music business does not revolve around heavy metal bullshit.”

MICHELLE SHOCKED

“It’s *not* a joke. It’s my idea of good fun, but it’s not a joke.”

MARK MOORE, S-EXPRESS

“I’d probably have hated us if I hadn’t actually been in the band.”

ROSS SOUP DRAGON

“So there we were all blacked up and wearing Donny Osmond suits with Marshall stacks and this absolutely massive clapometer plugged in behind us. I’m singing into this plugged-in cucumber and the bassist’s got one stuffed down his trousers. Why? To test people’s preconceptions . . . and because we’re really bloody stupid.”

MARY MARY, GAYE BYKERS ON ACID

“It’s a bit frustrating, because we wanted to have a flawless career and we don’t have that now.”

LLOYD COLE

“People don’t tell me that I’m beautiful very much, not in those words.”

LEMMY

“Don’t expect me to pick up the pieces again and put everyone together again and make it whole because I can’t be bothered anymore.”

MICK JAGGER

“I think The Sex Pistols were the worst thing that’s ever happened.”

CLIFF RICHARD

“I’ve been told on many occasions that when I lose it my mouth hangs open to one side. Rather attractively too, I might add.”

JOE STRUMMER

“Would I beat up a journalist again? Yeah, like I said, I’m only human.”

KEVIN ROWLAND

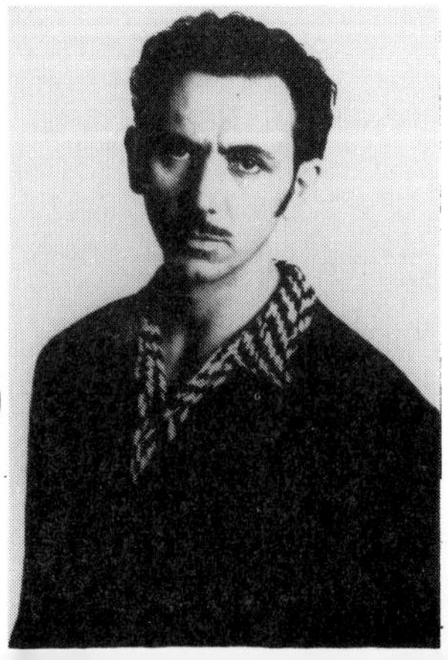

"Your metabolism is built around gigs. At nine o'clock, which is gig time, your whole body goes into overdrive. When we're not touring I just go down the pub at nine and start singing along with the juke-box or talking really loudly and then I won't be able to sleep until two in the morning."

FISH

"I've said a lot of things in my time, and 90 per cent of them are bollocks."

PAUL WELLER

"A cat can't have as many lives as I've gone through in the past few years."

GARY GLITTER

"I'm more angry now than I ever was . . . I think."

DAVID BYRNE

"Everything I wanted I had to work for. I sold oriental carpets, I was a waiter, I was even a pimp for two weeks. It made me strong."

LENNY WOLF, KINGDOM COME

"For some time, my parents have been saying I belong on the end of a rope."

DAVID LEE ROTH

"I'm the closest I've been to Paul for the last ten or twelve years. I still love him and I'm going to continue my friendship regardless of his attitude, because I don't have time to screw around."

GEORGE HARRISON

"I saw a Hue & Cry bootleg on some guy's market stall the other week. I was going to take it off him, because legally you can. But I decided to let it drop because he was an awfully big bloke."

GREGORY KANE, HUE & CRY

"I've got people who want to kill me and people who want to make love to me, just so they can sell their stories to the newspapers."

BONO

"I certainly can't see any similarities between me and Sade. I don't think she was ever a joiner by trade."

THOMAS LANG

"I never want to become fashionable, just contemporary, thank you very much."

JIMMY PAGE

"There are still a few of us around that seem to give a shit, people like me and Joe [Strummer]. We're sort of almost like the last cowboys now."

MICK JONES

"My last *NME* interview was pathetic. I had a drink and joked with the guy about politics. Then he took my obviously sarcastic comments and made a fool of me. If I'd known he was going to put a knife in my back, I would have dropped the bastard there and then."

FISH

"It's easier now than ever before for girls to hold a high chart position and hold mass media attention, yet they're doing absolutely nothing of any value with that power except building up their bank balances and buying designer clothes."

WENDY JAMES,
TRANSVISION VAMP

“There's nothing wrong with a bunch of 14-year-old girls screaming their heads off, but it puts you off the performance . . . you wonder if they're listening.”

BEN VOLPELIERE-PIERROT, CURIOSITY KILLED THE CAT

“I used to be compared with Helen Terry, but that was simply because we were a couple of fat birds.”

ALISON MOYET

“There's a challenge within the group, that if Ian Anderson gets back in the charts – with or without Jethro Tull – then we'll split up.”

NICK, WESTWORLD

“We don't need much make-up because we're young.”

CRAIG LOGAN, BROS

“I think Conservatism in this country is going to backfire heavily. I think it already has, with all those people taking drugs in suburbia and going to clubs and taking Ecstasy. That's all to do with the lax political climate.”

BOY GEORGE

“I think plants respond to talking. I'm getting really hippyish now, but I think they do. If they could talk back to me they'd probably say, Clark, you're one helluva guy.”

CLARK DATCHLER, JOHNNY HATES JAZZ

“I was in a fish store yesterday, thinking about buying some goldfish. But I didn't feel like carrying a tank and a bag of fish – I needed someone to get them for me.”

LL COOL J

“'Paid In Full' we put together in half an hour. Right there on the spot. Rakim's brother hit me with a bassline, I stuck a drumbeat on it, went out and drank a soda, came back and Rakim had the words ready to roll. Simple as that, but that don't mean it gotta *sound* simple.”

ERIC B

“Once I worked for a jeweller for six months. When I left, I stole a gold watch because I figured they weren't going to give me one for long service.”

TOM WAITS

“It's all about image, nothing to do with music or talent or any of those things I suffer greatly from.”

JOHN LYDON

“I could definitely challenge The Beastie Boys to a hotel room smashing contest. I've been at it far too long for them, they're beginners. When I hear Terence Trent D'Arby has smashed up a hotel room, I just think, Ha ha ha, that'll cost you!”

ROD STEWART

“We showed up to do *The Tube* in Newcastle and we were on right after Erasure who had a real nice stage-set. Then we looked across at our set and there were two maracas crossed above this Mexican cantina with swinging doors. Even without trying to be malicious people do these things.”

LOUIE PEREZ, LOS LOBOS

“When I have a new guy in the band, it takes a month just to put him at his ease and let him realize I'm just a normal guy.”

OZZY OSBOURNE

“I want to be promoted as a madman whose influences come from trees, wind, earth, birds, fire and water, stamping my muddy boots all over EMI's well-tended carpets. I'm the last dustbinman. Every record I've ever made is complete garbage. Especially the new one.”

LEE SCRATCH PERRY

“It's not everyone else being crap that makes us look good, it's us being good that makes everyone else look crap.”

CARL McCOY, FIELDS OF THE NEPHILIM

“We was going to do this anti-crack song with Michael Jackson. So we had dinner with Mikey and Quincey, patted his llama, played with his monkeys and talked a lot about the deal. But nothing's come of it yet.”

JAM MASTER JAY, RUN DMC

“When I die I’m going to have my coffin stuffed full of money and, as the wee thing goes towards the furnace, I want my friends to run up and grab as much as they can.”

JIMMY SOMERVILLE

“I’ve only ever worn a suit once, when I tried to get a job before I was in the band.”

JOEY RAMONE

“There’s a lot more to life than being in Brussels on a grey day with a gig to do.”

MARK KNOPFLER

“You have to be careful, because if your wig’s too big you’ll look like a dwarf.”

FRED SCHNEIDER, THE B52s

“I used to spend around 50 hours a week drinking, which is incredibly time-consuming.”

CHRISTY MOORE

“The worst thing anybody could say about Age Of Chance is that we’re interesting.”

GEOFF T, AGE OF CHANCE

“I can’t understand why nobody else has realized that Michael and Janet Jackson are one and the same person.”

MICK JONES

“Calypso songs were like the newspaper for the small man. And at that point we had colonial government that wasn’t really able to deal with that sort of thing – there was even a time when calypsonians had to register their songs at the police station every day.”

DAVID RUDDER

“Mrs Thatcher’s like a really big pop star, isn’t she?”

MICK TALBOT, THE STYLE COUNCIL

“Everywhere Bros go they’ve got screaming girls running after them. Are we jealous? Nah! We’ve got screaming old women running after us.”

DRUMMIE, ASWAD

“Pop music today doesn’t have much to say, that’s why everyone was so keen to do the Mandela concert.”

JERRY DAMMERS

“I am, how you say, a womanly woman. I have certain charms and I like to wear clothes that will display them. I will not hide myself. People know when Sabrina is around.”

SABRINA

“If you have some degree of integrity, it’s unbearable to live with an identity that’s just slapped on you by someone else and isn’t really representative of you.”

ANNIE LENNOX

“I think a little depression is valuable for writing, and sometimes it comes on me very strong. Freud said that, but then he had cocaine.”

LEONARD COHEN

“Francis Rossi once said he had a complete set of Quo records at home and a complete set of Quo cassettes in his car. God, that’s like drinking your own urine.”

JEAN JAQUES BURNEL, THE STRANGLERS

“Bruce Springsteen? Oh, he’s great, but he needs his hair styled.”

JAMES BROWN

“Everyone thinks I’m Mr Nice Guy, but I’d love to play a Rambo-like character in a film.”

SHAKIN’ STEVENS

"People thought I'd lost my nut when I told them he was going to be the biggest pop star. If you could have seen this kid then, how skinny he was and pale. That was when he was making the tea. I'm sure some people thought we'd lost our marbles."

That's Pete Waterman – architect of the Stock, Aitken & Waterman dynasty – talking, trumpeting with his usual bravado and bluff arrogance. Partly it's the spiel he likes to shower everywhere, a picture of himself as a mixture of the alchemist – "I can make *anything* a hit"

ACTS OF THE YEAR

RICK ASTLEY

– and the guru – "I can predict a star a million others will turn down." Partly though he's telling the truth. If Rick Astley as "the boy next door" was an image Waterman planned – those casual clothes, the unostentatious suits, etc., etc., then it was also one that wasn't far from the truth. In other words it worked because Rick Astley really *was* the boy next door. Even after a string of hits he was still modest, unassuming, polite charming, shy and easily embarrassed. *Really.*

It didn't always go down too well. Those journalists who expect liberal sprinklings of fairy dust on their pop stars, who expect and respect star quality in terms of extrovert extravagance, pronounced him boring. Others, however, were mightily relieved. How nice it was to meet such a pleasant ordinary chap. He simply wasn't the sort of person who stood out.

Let me give you an example. For a year before his first record was released he made tea and helped out – as his early publicity blared again and again – at PWL studios, supposedly being groomed for stardom. Quite predictably the rest of the PWL roster – Bananarama, Sinitta and Mel & Kim and so on – were regularly asked what he'd been like. A typical first answer was "um", a typical second one was "er" and a typical third one was "um, er, nice". The honest ones put it another way: they didn't really remember him.

They weren't the only ones. On the Saturday night of the Ferry Aid recording a journalist stayed up for a few hours drinking with a PWL engineer, a cable TV presenter and Rick. A few months later, as 'Never Gonna Give You Up' was nearing the end of its long, long stay at the top of the charts, the journalist and Astley met again by accident. It was Astley who had to insist over a period of half an hour, first politely then less so, that they'd met before and finally had to recall the time and place before the journalist, crippled with embarrassment, recalled Rick as the fourth person present.

But then that was, perhaps, how Rick Astley was. A normal bloke, from a town in Derbyshire that no one had ever heard of. A father who ran a garden centre and who was delightfully uncool enough to celebrate his son's success by wearing a "I'm Rick Astley's dad" T-shirt. An adolescence during which he'd been naff enough to make a tiled copy of the first Level 42 album cover in pottery classes, along with a flying teapot inspired by the obscure imagery of tragic hippie band Gong. A childhood punctuated by stupid bicycle accidents and daft hobbies like collecting bottles. A girlfriend who was the same person he'd fancied at school and who he'd finally got together with at the cricket club disco, not to the strains of some achingly trendy fifties bossa nova tune but to Soft Cell's 'Tainted Love'. A bloke who is still more likely to play you – and sing along with – The Smiths in his car rather than some unavailable soul import. Someone who became such a muso in his late teens that when bands came on *The Tube* (his favourite music programme – it was *live*, you see) he could usually, at a glance, spot the make of every instrument and amplifier they were using. A pop star who'd wince uncomfortably when you called him one, a pop star unselfconscious and honest enough to reveal all of the above details, simply because they're true.

The twist to the whole normal bloke theory was, of course, The Voice. It was such a deep, soulful thing that it seemed almost impossible that it could come out of such a scrawny body. The word went round when 'Never Gonna Give You Up' first entered the charts – many people have since suggested that Stock, Aitken & Waterman planted the idea – that The Voice was actually Luther Vandross. A preposterous idea – for one thing, if you were going to create a puppet frontman you wouldn't choose Rick Astley, would you? – but it caught hold, eventually doing Rick a considerable favour. After all, if the voice *was* Rick Astley and not Luther Vandross, then Rick Astley can sing *just as well.* (It is, incidentally, his voice as it sings in the flesh; no clever tricks.) The final twist was the Kylie Minogue story – when her 'I Should Be So Lucky' steamed up the charts it was suggested, and again widely believed, that Kylie's vocals were actually Rick Astley's sped up. By that time Rick Astley, the voice that could effortlessly flip from the ersatz soul of his disco hits to the mature over-the-top balladry of 'When I Fall In Love', was an image firmly fixed in the public imagination.

Consequently a nation quietly sick of pop stars with skyscraper egos and preposterous clothes had no trouble at all warming to Astley. The exceptions were the tabloid press. Imagine their grief – a Mr Clean who really did seem to be clean. They dug nevertheless, but with little success. The best they could find was Rick's old band FBI who he'd abandoned after being approached by Pete Waterman, but Rick's old mates rather spoilt the game by offering only a sprinkling of resentment and a mountain of best wishes and personal tributes.

The only other obvious story was the puppet one. Stock, Aitken & Waterman pull strings, dopey Rick responds. Even that wouldn't stick as Rick seemed quite clear about his career, his management (separate from Stock, Aitken & Waterman) and his financial deal. However, it seems there was more to the SAW/Astley relationship. Pete Waterman often blurted on about Rick being "like a son" – more than just another musical project – and the evidence, which neither of them has made much noise about, seems to bear that out. For months Rick Astley lived in Pete Waterman's flat. Waterman also, according to his partners, got so involved that his judgement – usually the world's best "Woolworths ears" – concerning Rick's music went completely wibbly. 'Never Gonna Give You Up' was recorded in December 1986 – it stayed on the shelf for over six months before Waterman realized it was any cop. Anyway, it just didn't make sense to suggest that Stock, Aitken & Waterman were taking him for a ride. Why, if that were the case, would they let Rick write four songs (and take a corresponding proportion of the publishing royalties) for an album that would sell largely on the basis of *their* songs?

In the end, to the press's obvious relief, at least a couple of Rick Astley stories turned up. The first, the BPI awards fiasco, was one of the British record industry's greatest own goals: faced with an overrunning programme, Rick Astley, after having been announced as the winner of the year's Best Single award for 'Never Gonna Give You Up', was left stranded in darkness on the stage, without his award; behind him The Who, deemed more important (the next day the buck was passed furiously back and forth as to who decided this) struck up the lacklustre first chords of 'Who Are You?'. The next day we were told Rick had blubbed his way to sleep. *That*, he cheerfully explained over the next week, was rubbish but he had been miffed. Oddly, the affair probably boosted his popularity just when he needed it – the British public may be slothlike in responding to any of the larger evils in the world but there's a tremendous well of sympathy and support open to anyone who is the victim of injustice on our TV screens.

The press's only other "coup" was the story that Rick had got so exhausted he needed to take some unscheduled holiday to recuperate. It wasn't the breakdown they blew it into but it helped fill a few pages. (It's also perhaps the start of a worrying trend – the same thing happened to Johnny Hates Jazz's Clark Datchler.) Unfortunately for the press the story fizzled out. Rick Astley returned. No recluse's beard, no dark glasses fetish, no mad dog stare, just the same polite easily embarrassed . . .

The most annoying thing for the press must have been that, while sticking two fingers up at the myth they try to peddle that without their "support" your days are numbered, the records continued selling – in Pete Waterman's cute term, "by the shed-full". 'Never Gonna Give You Up' was the best-selling British single of 1987. The three follow-ups ('Whenever You Need Somebody', 'When I Fall In Love' and 'Together Forever') reached numbers three, two and two respectively. In America, it was much the same story.

The cynics of course reached for their usual final round of ammunition when faced with such undeniable success: will it last? Perhaps not, but I suspect it will. There's The Voice, for one thing. And he's smart enough. As Pete Waterman says (and he's supposed to be the heartless manipulator, remember) of Rick's pre-success apprenticeship: "He's had fifteen years experience crammed into a year, which no other British pop star has ever had the benefit of seeing." In other words, he's seen pop stars go mad at the sight of success, has seen them do everything wrong and trounce sourly off to obscurity.

"He's an ordinary guy with a wonderful voice," goes Waterman's catalogue description. "He's not pretty. He looks ordinary and that's his appeal to people. He's totally unaffected by it all. He still blushes when someone asks for his autograph, and it's not put on."

It was Waterman who presumably suggested the basic personality that Rick Astley was to present in his songs – the dependable, sincere romantic, the lover who stays when other lovers might have gone away, the boy who would make you forget all the other boys because this boy wasn't fooling. It's these simple – *brilliantly* simple – emotional scenarios that Stock, Aitken & Waterman excel at painting, but Rick Astley adds more to them than any of their other acts. The public has spotted this: have you noticed that whenever people launch into one of those anti-Stock, Aitken & Waterman rants (one of the great popular British pastimes in 1987 and 1988) they usually politely exclude Rick – murmuring "good voice" or something like that – as if he alone is an innocent caught up in the fighting?

Pete Waterman again:

"When I hear Rick Astley singing 'Never Gonna Give You Up' I get goosebumps. I think, 'Is *this* one of my songs?' I can't listen to 'When I Fall In Love' without a lump in my throat." When he first saw the 'When I Fall In Love' video – a cheesy affair shot in the Scandinavian snow – he burst into tears in front of a group of friends. "The feeling I get when I hear Rick Astley singing, I couldn't pay for that. People go on a big dipper or on Concorde because it's what they've always wanted to do, they get a big high and that's it. Listen to Rick Astley and you get a lifetime of thrills every time he sings a song of yours."

That, of course, isn't an experience that many people can share but it's an emotion many will probably agree with – not your serious rock academics of course, just people, normal people. A great voice; simple, trite, brilliant songs ('Don't Say Goodbye', perhaps his best moment, hasn't even been released as a single); urgent rhythms . . . the boy-next-door-turned-star . . . shazam!

Pete Waterman does, of course, have one more, almost scientific explanation for all this. Let's return to PWL studios where we find Stock, Aitken & Waterman, fresh from writing a few more hits, discussing this very issue over a cup of coffee. Pete Waterman: "The knicker elastic goes. *Seriously*. When I first heard Rick Astley's voice I turned round to my girlfriend and said 'There'll be a lot of wet knickers when they hear this guy's voice.' That's what he does to women. He's so low, he's *warm*. It's like the womb situation, isn't it?"

A nation quietly sick of pop stars with skyscraper egos and preposterous clothes had no trouble at all warming to Rick Astley

Mike Stock and Matt Aitken, less prone to such gushing outbursts, glance at each other. There's an awkward pause. "It could be," murmurs Mike Stock, politely but dubiously. "I mean, er . . ." he searches for the words, "I haven't really analysed all this too closely." Rick Astley, fortunately enough, is elsewhere. He's easily embarrassed, is Rick.

CHRIS HEATH

GEORGE MICHAEL

"In a sense, I think what I'm really aiming for is to become a star of a different proportion." Even disregarding the designer tan, photogenic stubble and ludicrously expensive wardrobe, it's easy to understand why George Michael purports to such lofty heights.

In the two years since the demise of Wham!, he's not only been able to keep his head above water in the same fast-moving rapids as Prince, Bruce Springsteen and Michael Jackson but he has also gone on to a couple of unique pop achievements: his first solo album *Faith* reached number one in the US charts on no less than three separate occasions; and he became the first white artist of the eighties to get an LP to the top of the American black charts. As well as this, a little over three-quarters of a million people bought tickets for his recent world tour and it's been a long time since the LP passed the ten million sales mark worldwide.

The former Giorgios Kyracos Panayiotou, the overweight myopic from the unremarkable London suburb of Bushey, has spectacularly launched his solo career, fulfilled his ambition from Wham!'s early days – to "still be writing catchy, derivative pop songs in five years' time" – and is now several times a millionaire. Yet all is far from perfect in his view of life: while he has no truck with the record-buying public, he is involved in a conflict that his spiralling success can only exacerbate – with himself.

In spite of sounding almost arrogantly certain that his music is good enough to "blanket the planet", alongside Prince and Madonna, he believes he has yet to fall into step with them. In the interviews that launched the European leg of his tour, he dwelt on the fact that whereas other members of The Big League are *exactly* the people they portray themselves as, he has to become someone else in order to work. That his images of the world's top pop stars are woefully distorted serves to underline the insecurity brought on by his joining them. He'll never be like them he claims, he just doesn't think he's "vivid" enough.

This stems back to schooldays, when Michael lived in awe of classmate Andrew Ridgeley. Ridgeley, it has been told, always had a clique of people around him, was chased by girls and was self-confident enough not to give a damn about much. Michael befriended him in the hope that some of this style would rub off. Throughout the Wham! era, Ridgeley would appear to be slightly to the fore in publicity shots, his smile looking a little easier.

Now on his own, the underlying theme of *Faith*'s visuals is "Lookit me Ma, I'm a big boy now!" The near-naked posturing of 'I Want Your Sex', the biker-style tough of 'Faith', the lingering one-camera study of 'One More Try' all give the impression Michael is trying hard to convince himself of his blossoming from an ugly duckling into macho sex god. Indeed, the whole work is as much an exercise in soul-baring as it is in entertainment.

Since 1985, when Michael took 'Careless Whisper' – considered by many to be his finest work – as a solo number, his desire to be "taken seriously" was never in doubt. The song's lyric indicated a leaning towards deeply personal statements. The catalyst for the creation of *Faith*, it has been admitted, was a failed relationship in 1986 – Michael won't be drawn further on the subject and has never admitted who the heartbreaker was – and its subject matter was his life since the end of Wham!: two years during which, he believes, heartache and mistrust were his main emotions.

This readjustment had one main aim: to re-create George Michael, Pop Star, not just the young bucko with the shuttlecock thrust down his shorts

The broken love affair sank him into a huge booze-ridden depression – the actual Wham! split was provoked by this emotional distress; maybe if he'd been more secure he'd have felt no need to shake things up. At the time, he just wanted a fresh start, now claiming,

"I didn't want to be a star any more, because I was feeling sorry for myself." He drank and fought his way around the world, carefully avoiding London because he didn't want his family and friends to see him in that state. It was now, he feels, that he developed this character that wasn't him, and was loathe to get back into music where so many people would take it as real.

Eventually, he poured his heart out to Andrew Ridgeley and the ideas for *Faith* took shape. At the same time as working on the album, he entered into a stable (and subsequently long-lasting) relationship with Asian/American club DJ Kathy Jeung. She provided two vital ingredients for his newly-established life: company when his demanding love of self means he periodically shuts out the rest of the world; and objective analysis of his career – a familiar Michael complaint is that everybody close enough to offer opinions has a vested interest (i.e. he pays their wages).

This process of readjustment had one main aim: to re-create George Michael, Pop Star. To become more "real" and not just the publicist's dream image of a young bucko with a shuttlecock poking from his shorts.

To this end, the moodier feel of *Faith* worked brilliantly, completely crossing over in the States. But his fans in Britain are still divided into two camps: those who appreciate what he does as an artiste and those who still view him as a bedroom pin-up (albeit a "hunkier" one than before). Self-worshipper that he is, this stigma bothers him a great deal – he's been quoted as saying there's nothing he'd like more than for people in England to realize there's been a change, but sees no immediate solution to the problem.

What he will do though is stick at it. He sees himself as one of the main pop writers of the eighties, and aims, in the next decade, to write material that becomes something "historical". It is contentious claims like this that reveal the root of George Michael's insecurity – as his opinion of, and standards set for, himself continue to rise they will always stay just out of reach, leaving him perpetually frustrated.

Even if he doesn't reach these iconic levels, there is little to dispute George Michael as a pop music phenomenon of the last five years. The solo tour proved as much by grossing in the region of £35 million. (A necessary income when you consider a tiny part of the outlay included five leather jackets costing no less than £1,200 each, 15 Gaultier suits – a snip at £1,000 a throw – and 25 pairs of, relatively cheap, Levi 501s.)

The tour's receipts and *Faith*'s sales show that while two may be company, one, quite clearly, is not a lonely number. He's taken a deep, career-oriented breath and survived where others have failed: Mick Jagger is a pertinent example of a singer who confidently stepped out by himself, only to retreat shamefacedly into the security of band fellowship. But Michael is dissatisfied with that. In believing that *Faith* was far removed from Wham!'s lightweight confections, he expected a different audience, one that didn't scream nearly so much. To make the show appear more adult he "overcompensated in the raunch department" and appeared anything other than grown-up.

What he really ought to be worrying about though, is "Can it last?" If he has nothing to prove regarding his solo performances, can he find the motivation to play live? Without the benefit of further emotional crises, can he continue to make soul-stirring rock 'n' roll? If his recent round of interviews is anything to go by, maybe he doesn't want to. "My show isn't rock 'n' roll," he bluntly stated. "That's not what I'm about. I don't play rock 'n' roll. Far from it."

Can it be that this "historical" music for the nineties will be a film score or TV theme?

RICHARD TIPPET

T'PAU

Just as T'Pau's debut album, *Bridge Of Spies*, touched the magical one million sales mark, Carol Decker, the group's flame-haired singer, still couldn't quite put her finger on why the group had become so successful. "I haven't really had time to stop and think about it," she told *Q* magazine at the beginning of 1988. "We're not an image band. I think people like that. And I think they like our honesty and our sense of humour. Also – and this sounds quite unusual these days – I think th[illegible]ust actually like the music." [illegible]e, Carol Decker would be the [illegible] to mention it but the [illegible]ason for T'Pau's rapid and [illegible]ssing success is Carol Decker herself.

Musically, T'Pau weren't offering anything disturbingly new when they arrived in late 1987. Their first single, 'Heart And Soul', failed initially in Britain and it was only after it had enjoyed a healthy spell in the American charts that it was re-released here. Their sound was that of the prototypical modern rock group comprising "raunchy" guitars, big drums and layered synthesizers. The members of the band looked as though they had been assembled from "eighties rock star" identikit files. But Carol Decker was T'Pau's trump.

Critics and public alike warmed immediately to the singer – the former invariably using the words "feisty", "ballsy" and "fiery". A concert review in *The Independent* transformed midway into a lengthy thesis on Carol Decker's popularity. It concluded that people of all ages and both sexes relate to her because she swears, tells jokes and shows her knickers on stage yet retains an alluring sexiness. She combines, quite effortlessly, a tomboyish charm with a womanly wisdom and can therefore appeal as big sister, good mate or object of desire. While marketing departments in '88 were busy stirring up underage excitement with Tiffany, Vanessa Paradis and Kylie Minogue, Carol Decker blew in and cleaned up because she was so obviously devoid of contrivance. You got the impression that if Carol Decker was, as all the other formularized bimbettes have been billed, "the girl next door", then you wouldn't be forced to move house.

T'Pau formed shortly after Carol Decker met up with Ronnie Rogers in 1982. They immediately became songwriting partners and soon after that became, and are to this day, partners of the romantic variety. Prior to their fateful meeting they had been playing with varying degrees of success in separate groups in their native Wellington, Shropshire. Audiences then comprised largely of enthusiastic but undiscerning young farmers, "the green welly brigade" as Carol Decker puts it.

They took their name from a Vulcan stateswoman in *Star Trek* who, it has since been established amid mild controversy, indulged in some form of affair with Mr Spock's dad.

As they evidently weren't a group of pretty boys or pouting producer prodigies, T'Pau realized that they were going to have to take the traditional, long and unscenic, route to success. This meant two years of touring, building a large and faithful following. It was during this period of bedsits and Transits that Carol Decker learned how to cope with an audience of lagered-up letches offering the time-honoured "witticisms" that almost every female singer has to contend with.

"It was good training. I can handle any sort of heckling now although the situations arise less and less now. The thing is they're all so predictable and they're so easy to put down with a quick one-liner."

Unfortunately, at a concert in Germany, a remark from a soldier in the audience caused Carol to lose her sense of humour and, with it, her temper. She lunged into the crowd and physically set about the astounded squaddie, intent on causing severe and hopefully permanent damage. The message came across very clearly: Carol Decker would not stand for sexist abuse in any form.

The press took to Carol as she gave an honest, down-to-earth interview. If something or someone got her goat she would explain why in graphic detail. Similarly, if journalists "stitched her up" or betrayed her trust she would confront them about it. If she was questioned about an obscure political issue she would inform her interviewer that she knew nothing about the subject and ask why they couldn't just have a normal conversation. She unashamedly told the staunchly left-wing *NME* that she had voted SDP in the general election and in her explanation charmed her interviewer to the extent that the issue was dropped.

The high chart position of 'Heart And Soul' and the direction in which the group's sound was progressing pointed T'Pau towards America where the pickings were rich and the audiences large, appreciative and less fashion-conscious than the British. The band were always more than aware that the music they were making would not be competing with the assorted derivatives of funk that vied for position on the turntables of London's painfully fashionable clubs.

They chose Roy Thomas Baker to produce their album. Although Baker was English he had lived in Los Angeles and understood the American market

having produced numerous albums for Queen and The Cars.

Bridge Of Spies was critically well-received. Although no claims to greatness or references to sliced bread were made and a few reviewers remarked upon Carol Decker's tendency to scream on the rockier numbers, all conceded that it was a stirling performance. Some even had the foresight to predict great things in America – exactly where T'Pau were heading.

They embarked on a gruelling tour of the USA and Canada supporting gravel-gargling Canadian rocker Brian Adams. It quickly came to the point where T'Pau were receiving as good if not better a reception than the headlining act and upon their return to Britain they were all but stealing the show.

The turning-point in T'Pau's career came when they released 'China In Your Hand' – the massive, smoochy rock ballad from *Bridge Of Spies*. The song allowed Carol Decker to flex her not inconsiderable vocal range and the band to "rock out", which they did to great effect. The single shot to number one and remained there for five weeks. They later performed the song live at the music industry's annual BPI Awards to a near-standing ovation. Prior to this, *Bridge Of Spies* knocked Paul McCartney's *All The Best* off the top of the album charts.

After five years of being broke – Carol and Ronnie could often be found, in the early days of T'Pau, sitting under blankets to save on heating bills and eating nothing but vegetable soup – the money began to trickle in. The couple decided to buy a home in London and even allowed themselves a few indulgences. "We haven't got great wodges of royalty money yet," laughs Carol, "although we're getting money from TV appearances and money from the record company so we're comfortable. It's great to have a few quid. Although I must admit I spend it at a terrifying rate. It mainly goes on make-up, which I buy pounds of, and clothes. I have to change my clothes a lot – you know, mix and match like Lady Diana – because your fans get bored if they see you in the same clothes. I've started having clothes made for me now which is an extravagance I've always fancied."

Fame, thus far, for Carol Decker and T'Pau has been highly enjoyable if something of a blur. She admits that relaxing has become a rare luxury. "When I get the chance I like to swim or have a drink but not both at the same time! I'm a bit of a wino, and I've developed a liking for champagne. I find the drinking is less time-consuming than swimming so I tend to concentrate on that!"

You got the impression that if Carol Decker was – as all the other formularized bimbettes have been billed – "the girl next door", then you wouldn't be forced to move house

Ronnie Rogers has made the wise move of keeping a day-to-day log-book of events that documents the band's rise to fame. They have promised themselves that whenever they have enough time they will take stock, read the diary and try to work out exactly why they were such a success in 1988.

ADRIAN DEEVOY

ACTS OF THE YEAR

THE POGUES

Saint Patrick's Day 1988 and The Pogues are in the middle of a week-long stint at London's Town & Country Club. They've just spent a month in Australia, before that they were in Europe, before that America and, to be truthful, the demands of this energy-sapping schedule are beginning to show. However, such considerations as monitor trouble, feedback, broken strings and dodgy tuning may be important for those who like to sit and hear pristine reproductions of what they play on their stereo, but for the crowd here, it's about as worrying as (yet) another spilled drink.

They stand and scream and stomp and rage and bang their glasses through songs of love, war, hate, anger, redemption and retribution, but there's never a feeling it's going to turn violent. It's a proud, joyful experience and, a rare thing in the current climate of accountant-dominated, image-hyped Britpop, it's a celebration of The Triumph Of The Underdog. But then, The Pogues are no orthodox band, and theirs is no orthodox success story.

A look at the stage at the culmination of a night's performance confirms this first point. Aside from the regular roguish-looking, eight-man line-up – which includes a self-taught accordion player, a traditional Irish music veteran, a roadie turned bassist and a dole queue reject assuming the role of "Poetic Genius" – there's the stalwart punk trouper Joe Strummer, an ample helping of Two Tone-era Specials and a brass section . . . 23 people in all, the members of the band choosing to play from amongst the audience are supplanted with energetically dancing stage invaders.

Clearly, such an unlikely set of heroes didn't spring from nowhere. True, 1988 started with The Pogues' bitter Broadway/Irish duet battle 'Fairytale In New York' high in the charts, its acrimonious words echoing those of many couples during the "Season Of Goodwill". But such widespread public recognition came only after six years of taking knocks, repairing holes and generally honing the outfit.

Shane MacGowan – known as Shane O'Hooligan in his teenage grab at stardom with punkabilly firebrands The Nips – together with sparring partner, the beer-tray-bashing, tin-whistle-blowing Spider Stacey (formerly a member of short-lived punk combo The Millwall Chainsaws), hatched the idea for the group in the early years of this decade. Severely dissatisfied with the limitations of what was known as "the standard rock format" and the transient, throwaway nature of most pop music, the pair fell back – probably quite literally – on the Irish traditional music loved by MacGowan's parents.

Combing the squatlands of north London, they recruited a motley bunch of reprobates, responsible musicians and runaways. At first they called themselves Pogue Mahone, but following the reaction of those sensitive types at Broadcasting House – they discovered that, translated from Gaelic, it meant "kiss my arse" – threw Mahone away. MacGowan had flushed out his adolescent longings in his Nips songs; now, with The Pogues, he could inject his punk fire and vigour into old Irish traditions and bring them into step with the times. Songs like 'Dark Streets Of London', the first Pogues single, was a direct follow-on from such Irish standards as 'Poor Paddy', a black comedy about migration and exploitation in "the land o'er the seas". 'Streets' had the same theme, but it applied as much to the thousands of kids who crossed the north/south divide in the early eighties as it did to those, like MacGowan, who'd crossed the Irish Sea.

Red Roses For Me, the group's first album in 1984, couldn't have been further removed from the predominate frippery of mainstream popular music. While fellow Londoners like Spandau Ballet were intent on romanticizing their city, selling it as a vision of The Good Life, MacGowan originals like 'Transmetropolitan' ripped back the façade to lay bare a few ugly truths.

Recruiting Dubliner Phil Chevron (on guitar) and producer Elvis Costello, the second album, *Rum, Sodomy And The Lash*, built on the strengths and themes of *Roses*. Songs like 'A Pair Of Brown Eyes', 'Sally MacLennane' and 'The Sick Bed Of Cuchulainn' confirmed that Shane MacGowan – utilizing third-person narrative, historical conceits, Irish balladry and mythology – had a unique vision in his songs. Critics assumed he had a preoccupation with death, but really his obsession was with life: life as it is lived, loved and ended. The group's version of Eric Bogle's 'Waltzing Matilda' was a haunting, timeless blast at the horrible waste of war – be it the Somme or the Falklands – while MacGowan's own 'Old Main Drag' turned the despondency of 'Dark Streets Of London' into abject despair and abuse.

MacGowan would sometimes snarl and harangue the audience between songs, but mostly he just scratched his head like Stan Laurel looking lost and puzzled by his elevation to stardom

Observers grilled MacGowan on the meanings and intent behind his songs. Naturally, he shrunk away. He became increasingly obstreperous and fuelled himself with masses of drink in the fashion of his prime Irish influences, singer Luke Kelly and writer Brendan Behan. On stage he was by turns a comical and troubled-looking figure. Sometimes he'd snarl and harangue the audience between songs, but mostly he just scratched his head like Stan Laurel looking lost and puzzled by his elevation to stardom.

A long delay ensued between the second and the triumphant third album. A contractual wrangle put an embargo on new releases, broken only by the 'Poguetry In Motion' EP (their first Top 30 hit) and a pairing with The Dubliners hospitalized after being knocked down by a taxi. Happily, he was soon released; apparently he was asked to leave after a bunch of friends and colleagues convened an impromptu party in his ward.

They continued to build a rambunctious, diehard audience through a constant touring schedule. Eastern inflections, and New Orleans Cajun. Sartorially speaking though, they remained the easiest emulated group on the block – all it took was a visit to the Oxfam shop and the off-licence and anyone could be a Pogue.

The only dark cloud on the horizon is that the wear and tear caused by constant touring might do the band

for their mentors' and fellow gargle merchants' 25th anniversary recording 'The Irish Rover' (number one in Ireland, Top Ten in the UK). Taking advantage of the break they ventured into "acting", appearing as the caffeine-addicted, fairly deranged McMahone family in Alex Cox's mutant spaghetti western *Straight To Hell*.

During this time, they lost bassist Cait O'Riordan, who left to live with producer Elvis Costello – long-time roadie Darryl Hunt took over her instrument – and gained Irish veteran mandolin player Terry Wood, who added a delicacy and authenticity to their rapidly improving attack. Naturally, it gave cause for concern when MacGowan contracted pneumonia, and more worrying still when he was

U2 were so taken with them, that The Pogues were invited to support them on a large slice of their world tour. This move into stadium rock changed them not one iota – MacGowan still looked worried, people still fell over and the audience screams and shouts just became louder.

Success with *If I Should Fall From Grace With God* was inevitable. 'Fairytale' had shown their appeal crossed generations, and now – travel having introduced them to other musics possessed of the same tradition and energy as theirs – they were mixing in opera, country, Spanish flamenco,

irreparable damage. While instances of such rare medical complaints as banjo wristbone, accordian muscle ache and guitarist finger block are dealt with as they occur, the air of fatality that haunts MacGowan's songs seems to hover over him too. Even his natural resilience and hardy metabolism must have its limits. In an interview with *Q* magazine he hinted that the band was very much a finite arrangement. If it is, it would not be untypical of MacGowan's contrary methods just to pack it all in without explanation. Until then, if indeed he does, The Pogues and their audience can feel gratified as having made up one of the few truly cross-cultural phenomena of the eighties.

GAVIN MARTIN

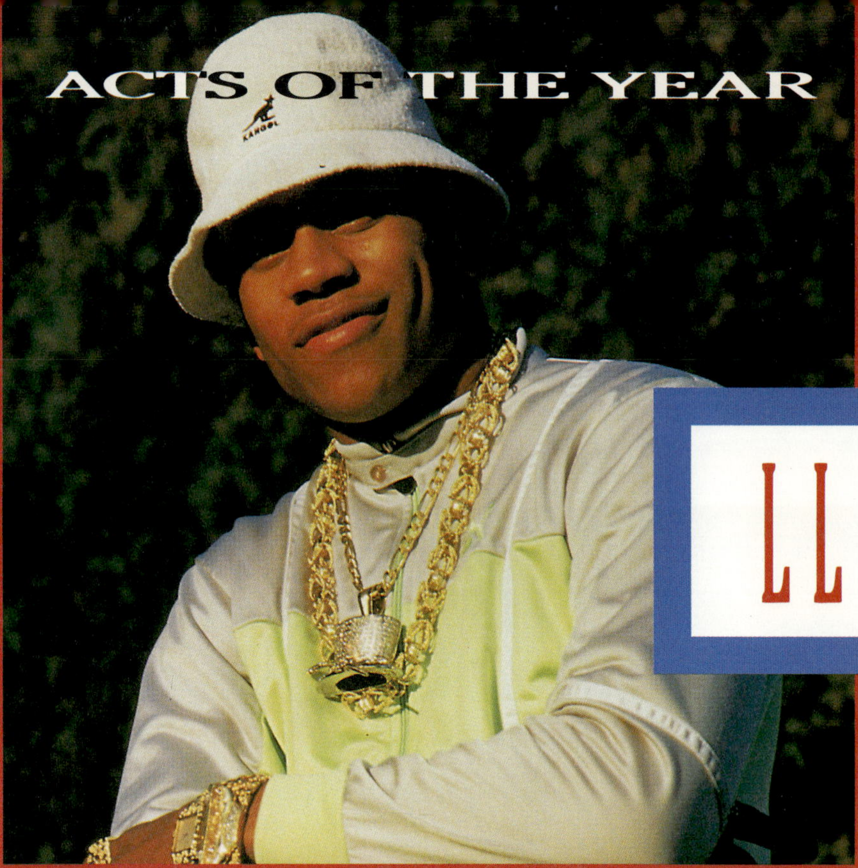

LL COOL J ★

Two DJs, working in tandem, build up the volume as they furiously scratch-mix 'The Theme From 2001'. Above the set, the six-foot high letters 'LL' are flashing faster and brighter. Slowly, a massive ghetto-blaster is lowered from the rafters, LEDs pulsing and VU meters twitching. As it touches down, the tape eject door opens and out bounds LL Cool J, the self-proclaimed "legend in leather".

From start to finish, this entrance has taken nearly seven minutes and the noise in the auditorium has increased from a low rumble to a level at which it threatens serious damage to Hammersmith Odeon's substructure. And nobody – least of all the far-from-shabby support acts Eric B & Rakim and Public Enemy – is left in any doubt as to who is headlining the show. More than that, though, the crowd's excitement, whipped up further by a combination of subtle pacing, special effects and bone-crunching hip hop beats, establishes LL Cool J as, currently, rap music's main attraction. Such a standing is further consolidated by the worldwide sales of last year's *Bigger And Deffer* passing three million and peaking at number seven in the US pop charts.

And it adds up to nothing short of what the former James Todd Smith deserves. For behind the bluster and gold chains that is rap music's stock in trade, is an intelligent, thoughtful, hard-working young man: "hard as hell" may be how LL Cool J chooses to describe himself, but a bonehead he certainly is not. Also, he is deadly serious about rap, viewing it as a bona fide form, not just some mutant strain of street funk or a means to a quick buck, thus affording it the same commercial and artistic considerations as any aspiring young pop star.

Born in 1968 in Queens, NYC, rap quickly became a dominating influence on his life – long before any records were made it was a force in New York's black neighbourhoods, and J cites such pre-Sugarhill figures as DJ Hollywood, Cool Herc and Double Trouble as adolescent reference points. In keeping with the DIY spirit of the times – in those days, anyone with the nerve to try, and the flair to entertain, could chance their luck at parties, playgrounds or street corners – J picked up a microphone anywhere he could, from the age of nine onwards.

Six years and a considerable local reputation later, he was experimenting with his mother's stereo, crudely quick-mixing backing tapes for his ever-growing stockpile of rhymes. Naturally enough, a stream of rough-and-ready demo tapes starring his re-invention of himself as LL Cool J (Ladies Love Cool James) began arriving at every record company in the city whether they were signing rap artistes or not. To an outfit they turned him down, but, in a back-handed testament to his musical vision, when a reason was given it was, invariably, because what he was attempting – to mix basic beat box tracks with other music forms – was "too different" from the hip hop sounds of the day.

Undeterred, he approached two young New Yorkers with a similarly broad outlook, a stable of talent under their management wing and ideas for forming their own record label. Russell Simmons and Rick Rubin, as Rush Productions/Management, represented Run DMC (Simmons is Run's older brother), The (then fledgling) Beastie Boys, Whodini and T La Rock, and were in the process of setting up Def Jam Records to develop their fusions of hip hop and slick soul (Whodini), heavy metal (Run DMC) and snot-nosed punk (The Beasties). Not tied down to any previous contracts, LL Cool J was free to provide their first release; 'I Need A Beat' came out at the end of 1984 and, made for less than $700 and selling over 120,000, it put the company immediately into the black. A balance sheet that attracted such interest from the major labels that, a year later, Def Jam signed a pressing and distribution deal with CBS worth over a million dollars before they had so much as released an album.

Fittingly, the company's first long-player was LL Cool J's *Radio*, and, just as appropriately, it sold 500,000 in a matter of weeks to earn Def Jam their first gold disc.

Since then, the company has grown and diversified into bedroom soul (Oran "Juice" Jones), thrash metal (Slayer), films (*Tougher Than Leather*), film scores (*Less Than Zero*) and multi-platinum notoriety (The Beastie Boys' *Licence To Ill* album and tour). And LL Cool J's development has followed similar lines: *Bigger And Deffer* was the label's first album to be produced without assistance from either Simmons

Singled out for special treatment was 'I Need Love'; favoured adjectives included "limp", "puerile" and "slushy". And, regardless of the paying customers' obvious delight, concert reviews were similarly unenthusiastic about the level of showmanship involved, believing it somehow undermined rap's ghetto "traditions". "Would have been more at home in a heavy metal show," scribbled one outraged critic; "all the excesses of stadium rock," fumed another.

What they failed to realize was that, in viewing rap as a valid music –

"Hard as hell" may be how he chooses to describe himself, but a bonehead he certainly is not

standing alongside heavy metal and taking its place in the stadiums – J believes the fans were entitled to the type of shows that entails. He feels that rap's still essentially black, working-class audience pay money to escape everyday life, not see it duplicated on stage. A point that is largely lost on thrill-seekers who arrive in search of an evening's danger – kept at arm's length of course. Also, by introducing a series of accepted pop clichés he, and others, have taken rap to a much wider audience and so escaped the initial patronage.

Criticism centres on the fact that he brags about being tough but isn't really as he's New Man-ish enough to record love songs. Unlike the disturbing amount of rappers, who, on stage and in interviews, let it be known that they are perpetually ready for confrontation – probably armed to the teeth as well – and are readily accepted as being more "committed" to life, music and the struggle, he is treated with scorn. It's much the same as the reggae stars of ten years ago, who couldn't get themselves taken seriously by the music press unless they played pure roots dub and ranted about revolution.

The tabloid furore that surrounded events outside his recent London shows – confrontations between youths and police and a series of robberies on tube trains in the area – provided an opportunity for him to unequivocally state his case on rap music and the would-be hard men it attracts: "That wasn't down to the music, that was down to those kids – they were going to meet *somewhere* to do battle. But it gets reported as being part of rap, which not only attracts more trouble but gives people – journalists – who don't understand it the wrong idea.

"Bragging, playing up your name, is the foundation of rap. It's the only way you can get the fans to remember you, but it's what you do with your name afterwards that counts. Too many rappers out there have nothing else to say so they step up the way they talk about themselves from how bad they are to how they're killers, just to impress the audience. All they're killing is the music – and a lot of people who should know better are encouraging it."

Although obviously upset by what is happening to hip hop as a whole, he is confident enough not to let personal criticisms bother him. Indeed, no doubt taking comfort in his widespread audience (including, thanks to his ballads, a huge female following – a rare thing in rap), it appears to be a challenge he is rising to: in between the final track and the run-out groove on *Bigger And Deffer*, backed by raucous, mocking laughter, he hoots *"Ha! Another album – you didn't think I could do it again! The joke's on you, suckers!"* And he's more than a little bit right.

LLOYD BRADLEY

or Rubin; it takes on board such diverse influences as doo-wop ('The Do Wop'), balladeering bedroom soul ('I Need Love' – a Top Ten pop hit) and rock 'n' roll ('Go Cut Creator Go'); and it could yet become the label's biggest seller – *Licence To Ill* has tailed right off after reaching four million, whereas *Bigger And Deffer* is still going strong.

Of course, all this has not been without its setbacks. In the wake of his success, LL Cool J has had to endure an excessive amount of sniping from both fellow rap performers and sections of the press, the latter notably in the UK and initially supportive of the entire Def Jam roster. His crimes, it seems, are little more than he wants to sell records and doesn't suffer fools gladly.

As regards his "brother" artistes, their attitude is certainly due to that well-known, green-eyed monster. The favoured form of attack is that, underneath the groin-tugging, chest-beating surface, LL Cool J is a bit of a wimp. "He lives in *Queens*, with his *grandmother*," spluttered one. Remarkably, in interview situations, J does little to counter such charges, choosing instead to agree – he *likes* the fairly middle-class suburb of Queens, and feels *comfortable* at his gran's. And will quietly point out that such would-be detractors usually have nothing to offer other than their own fanciful notions of "street cred", to impressionable white middle-class journalists. The very writers who appeared to adjust their attitudes towards LL Cool J as soon as he started having hits.

ACTS OF THE YEAR

TERENCE TRENT D'ARBY

It is possible, though rather unlikely, that Billy Ocean thinks he's a genius. After all, he sells more records in the States than any black artist other than Michael Jackson – with three US number one singles in the last four years, he's left the likes of Whitney Houston, George Benson and Prince gasping in his wake. More startlingly, he does all this without sharing his deepest and most intimate thoughts and opinions with the press; when it comes to the "oxygen of publicity", Ocean scarcely needs to breathe at all. Not only has he never announced that he is a genius, but he's never announced anything at all. There is no *Hardline According to Billy Ocean*, he just carries on making records which vast numbers of people find irresistibly listenable and danceable, and keeps himself firmly and happily to himself.

Terence Trent D'Arby probably thinks Billy Ocean is a sell-out. Ocean, after all, sells records; Terence sells Terence. Not that he doesn't sell records as well: *Introducing The Hardline According To* . . . is, at the time of writing, scooting merrily towards its first million in the US and has long passed that point in the UK. However, the main purpose of the exercise is that we should all love Terence . . . or, at any rate, not be unaware of Terence or – worst of all – indifferent to Terence. His ultimate ambition, it would seem, is to be able to tell the entire world to fuck off while it sobs, broken-hearted, on its collective knees, arms outstretched imploringly, begging *please* Terence *pleeeeaase*.

To this end, Terence has mastered the art of the rock and roll interview. Not for him the strenuous mask-juggling and enigma-building of vintage Dylan or Bowie, or the pregnant silences of a Prince or a Jacko. Similarly not for him the down-home-Sunday-afternoon-carwashing-Mr-Normal routines beloved of Mark Knopfler or Phil Collins, let alone the cheerful insolence of the early Beatles or the giggly bitchiness of Boy George before the fall. Terence favours the combative sneer and verbal terrorism of early Mick Jagger and Johnny Rotten, the scornful dismissals of those few rivals he will actually acknowledge that he has. He talks in headlines. He's *good copy*, unlike, say, George Michael and Simon Le Bon, who have never, to my knowledge, said anything interesting in their lives. He knows that rock journalists, by and large, will take a performer on face value if they are capable of supplying a ready-made theoretical framework for what they do, and at the moment the only pop star who does it better is Morrissey. "Rock and roll," he says, "is attitude."

And that's what *The Hardline* is: attitude. Terence's radicalism – or pretensions to same, if you prefer – is barely detectable in his music or his show, which are efficient if derivative assemblies of bits and pieces drawn from the collective pop unconscious, and far less innovative and challenging than the eye-popping, ear-bashing collages and cut-ups which, say, Prince and Cameo scratch-mix out of many of the same ingredients. Terence, for all his fulminating against white yuppies and the black bourgeoisie, is smack dab in the middle of the new mainstream. He is thus reduced to expressing his "attitude" by bad-mouthing every successful black American act as "emasculated" (compared with his own unimpeachable virility, that is), getting spotted in "compromising" situations with Paula Yates, being difficult with Columbia Records' US publicity department and refusing to show up for a *Rolling Stone* photo session because the guitar he wanted to pose with had been left in Philadelphia. Basic brattishness, in other words, with a smattering of ideological veneer.

Still, it's a hard, competitive world out there and everybody needs a hustle if they're going to make the difficult transition from being a talent to becoming a star. Terence is undoubtedly a talent – he can knock out good tunes, sing in a variety of well-established styles and string a series of athletic hot moves together smoothly enough to pass as a great dancer – and he's undeniably extremely pretty; all of which adds up to something considerably more durable and impressive than Curiosity Killed The Wet Bros or whoever is about to replace them on bedroom walls. However, major – as opposed to transitory – stardom is a very different matter. It's something which transcends the simple statistics of record sales: in the seventies, the music business's most closely-guarded secrets included the remarkably poor sales figures of David Bowie and The Rolling Stones. Both were amongst the most controversial celebrities of the time, but Led Zeppelin outsold The Stones five to one and Bowie's four-million-selling *Let's Dance* (1983) was the biggest success of his career. Bowie and The Stones were icons; others who shifted far more units were merely successful.

Terence will not be satisfied with mere success; it's iconic status that he's after. To satisfy *that* particular urge, though, he's going to have to do something that's sufficiently distinctive for others to want to copy. He's going to have to become a Prince, a Madonna, a Jacko or a Bruce; as soon as you hear certain records on the radio, you can tell immediately that someone is attempting to clone those worthies' achievements. Madonna, for example, is virtually the sole begetter of the horde of disposable bimbettes clogging up the charts at the moment: her work doesn't need the press – gutter or rock – to explain or justify it. You only need to hear her records or watch her videos to understand exactly why it's radical – her interviews are fairly tedious affairs and add very little to the work itself. Similarly, no one needed to read the newspapers or, indeed, do anything more than listen to the records to twig that The Sex Pistols were running a genuinely dangerous Hardline. Terence, by contrast, needs his "attitude" and his explanations to communicate why he is more radical than a veteran soul-rock hackette like Tina Turner. He's stroppy off-stage and knows a lot more about politics than she does, but the performances themselves say little more and – in the case of the early Turner comeback records which were also produced by Terence's studio mentor Martyn Ware – occasionally even less.

If anybody attempts to copy Terence Trent D'Arby, it's hard to see where they could possibly start. They could borrow his vocal inflections, but they could just as well go to source and rip them off from Al Green, Stevie Wonder, Smokey Robinson, Bobby Womack or Sam Cooke. They could steal his dance moves – or go directly to old film of James Brown, Jackie Wilson, Joe Tex, Prince or Michael Jackson. They could painstakingly study his unique approach to songwriting – except that he does not, on currently available evidence, at any rate, have one. They could hire a tight, versatile band, but there are so many competent under-employed players available that anyone with sufficient available funds to pay decent wages could form such a group by next week.

On the other hand, they could cop Terence's attitude. They could wear a lot of black leather and spiky stuff off-stage and slick suits on. They could announce "I'm trying to prove that you can be a massive crossover success without chopping off your dick!" and play sulky punk-rock bad boy all over the place. They could claim to be a genius before pulling back with a disarming smile and admitting that it was just an attention-getting device all along, all a "bit of a wind-up". If the professed radicalism was more than mere smoke and mirrors, they would then have to acknowledge that, sooner or later, there's going to have to be a Hardline and an "attitude" in the lyrics, the grooves and the music as well as in the presentation and the self-referential mythologization. And if they had the requisite amount of talent and as much front as Harrods, they could then hope, one day, to sell nearly as many records as Billy Ocean.

CHARLES SHAAR MURRAY

Terence, for all his fulminating against white yuppies and the black bourgeoisie, is smack dab in the middle of the new mainstream

THE GRATEFUL DEAD

"We're ready for anything now. It just took a while, that's all. It's like The Grateful Dead are the slowest-rising rock 'n' roll band in the world." Jerry Garcia, the band's benign, bear-like, 45-year-old patriarch, speaking in 1987 on the eve of the release of *In The Dark* – The Grateful Dead's first studio LP in seven years – can hardly have anticipated what was to happen in the subsequent weeks. His shambling, unfashionably tie-dyed, throwback band had suddenly and bewilderingly become one of the hottest acts of the year.

There have been few more remarkable stories of rock 'n' roll survival and regeneration than that of The Grateful Dead. Born of San Francisco's acid-soaked and idealistic mid-sixties, The Dead's music could not be defined by such categories as blues or rock or psychedelia, rooted though it was in all of them, and more. With their hippy creed of co-operation and harmony, and with a communion with their audience, the intensity of whose allegiance and devotion was unusual for those or any other times, The Dead came to embody something of the spirit of the age. In 1966 they were the free-tripping house band for Ken Kesey's Acid Tests – early multi-dimensional experiments in the communal taking of the not-yet-outlawed LSD; in 1967 they lived in and played on the scarf-and-miracle streets of San Francisco's Haight-Ashbury district; in July 1969 they helped celebrate the triumph of Woodstock, but a few weeks later they played at Altamont – the dark and frightening free concert whose chaos and violence devasted most of the illusions dreamed up in the preceding dappled and drowsy years.

Phil Lesh

Brent Mydland

Mickey Hart, Billy Kreutzman

As times grew darker and colder in the "progressive" seventies, The Dead maintained themselves by playing live sets which, with their meandering improvisations and protean structures, were always different, always unpredictable and could last for hours at a time. They attracted a travelling tribe of devotees for whom Dead-watching became a way of life. Ever-increasing numbers of "Deadheads" would follow the band from town to town, often paying their way by manufacturing and selling tie-dyed Dead T-shirts or headbands, hustling tickets or simply camping outside the concert grounds and dancing to the music, without necessarily needing to see the band. They were an extended nomadic family, both self-sufficient and mutually supportive. Their lives were focused upon and directed by The Dead's concerts.

For more than a decade it was the Deadhead's unshakeable fidelity which maintained the band, who were – as far as the TV-watching, radio-listening, record-buying public were concerned – just about invisible. And The Dead repaid the fans' faith by making them feel that they were a part of the set-up. Concert tapers, for example, looked upon with disgust or hatred by most other artists, were not only tolerated but specially catered for by having "tapers' sections" reserved for them.

Through the 1970s, the band's audience continued to grow. Stadium concerts drew enormous crowds – many of them teenagers for whom Woodstock wasn't even a fond memory, and the strength of numbers of this young audience is always to be

Jerry Garcia

Bob Weir

Garcia, probably quite seriously, stated that the band might well have to consider playing "some really weird and horrible stuff", just to cut back the crowds to a more manageable size

admitted in evidence against those who assert that The Dead trade solely in nostalgia. Their continued popularity may, perhaps, be partly explained because the disappointingly dreary decade had little else which offered the sense of community and belonging at the heart of The Dead's attraction. The curious community of Deadheads have subsequently been kept strong and involved by a sustaining subculture of information exchanges, fan magazines, tape archivists, Dead historians, telephone hotlines and a dedicated computer database.

In 1986, a series of concerts (including a number of dates with Bob Dylan and Tom Petty & The Heartbreakers) saw The Grateful Dead become one of the summer's top attractions. In July of that year Jerry Garcia, whose presiding genius is a focal point for the fans' assiduous attentions – and who had only recently been plucked from the "black hole" (his words) of heroin addiction – collapsed in a diabetic coma and was, for five days, near death. Curiously, Garcia's subsequent against-all-odds recovery coincided with the beginning of a new era in The Dead's history which no one would have predicted.

Early in 1987, while The Dead were working on a long-planned concert video (*So Far*) and beginning rehearsals for a new, long overdue studio LP, Robert Hunter – a lyric writer who has worked for The Dead for the past 19 years – handed Garcia the words to a new song: "When it seems like this night could last for ever/And there's nothing left to do but count the years . . ./I will walk alone by the black muddy river/And believe in a dream of my own." Hunter told *Rolling Stone*'s Mikal Gilmore: "'Black Muddy River' is about the perspective of age and making a decision about the necessity of living in spite of a rough time, and the ravages of anything else that's going to come at you. When I wrote it, I was writing about how I felt about being 45 years old, and what I'd been through. And then, when I was done with it, obviously it was for The Dead."

The song, with its keynotes of optimism and survival, set the tone for the new record. *In The Dark* achieved for The Grateful Dead a coherence that they hadn't managed in the studio since the two justly celebrated 1970 LPs, *Workingman's Dead* and *American Beauty*. It's a product *of* maturity *about* maturity, a consideration of life from the vantage point of experience and a looking forward still, while acknowledging the worth of what's gone before. Unexpectedly, *In The Dark* became a major commercial success. In the summer of 1987 The Grateful Dead were one of the top-grossing acts in the USA, playing huge stadiums and again co-headlining at a number of shows with Dylan and Petty. A single from the LP, the dance-along, sing-along 'Touch Of Grey' with its catchily optimistic chorus – "I will get by/I will survive" – was a Top Ten hit. Its clever promotional video, in which a bunch of skilfully animated puppet skeletons took the parts of the elderly Dead bopping out a concert version of the song, was a high-rotation video-hit on MTV.

The unanticipated scale of the new-found success threw up a series of curious paradoxes and predicaments for the band. Opposed as they were to what LP co-producer John Cutler referred to as "the shallowness of the MTV generation", suddenly The Dead were MTV heroes; the band who, in 22 years, had never come (or even wanted to come) close to the charts had a summertime smash hit. Dead publicist Dennis McNally told *Q* magazine that when he came to break the news to Jerry Garcia that the single had gone Top Ten, Garcia "was genuinely disturbed". And finally The Dead's audience, already numerous and loyal enough to have made the band the most financially successful group in rock history, was swollen yet further by new battalions of young Deadheads. This dramatic influx of followers prompted Garcia, probably quite seriously, to state that they might well have to consider playing "some really weird and horrible stuff", just to cut back the crowds to a more manageable size.

Nevertheless, there can be little doubt that The Grateful Dead have enjoyed this (for them) strangest of trips. With Jerry Garcia more affable and clear-witted than he's been in a decade, and with the band as happy and as outgoing as they've been since they started out in 1965, the year has been just fine. As Garcia said to Mikal Gilmore as *In The Dark* was about to be released: "It's like we have a new beginning. It's more fun now than it's ever been."

JOHN BAULDIE

WET WET WET

In a million record collections, four young men, in similar pose and Ivy League attire, have turned their faces self-consciously away from the camera. Identical yet different. These boys-next-door bursting with underdog provincial pride, ring a hazy bell in the record industry's collective memory . . .

Perhaps, at last, another Beatles. . . ?

Well, not quite. But in Wet Wet Wet you certainly have one Ringo, two Georges and Macca's upturned thumbs; in short, the front cover of the band's debut album, *Popped In Souled Out*, portrays a Fab Four *sans* hippy-dippiness, radical chic and all the other unpalatable stuff. An industry dream, you might think, an obvious marketing ploy to pull in the teenies with user-friendly faces and zit-free American-style dance music with a cheeky non-London accent – just like the Moptops a quarter-century ago.

But look closer and you see no visible strings. And, as if to send up the soberly-suited family-entertainment combo on the front, the back cover shows Wet Wet Wet off-duty in T-shirts, plimmies and guitars brandished at crazy angles just like those sweaty old stills from the Cavern Club.

Could it be that Wet Wet Wet, for all their seemingly contrived ultra-commercial appeal, are somehow *for real*?

Like Liverpool, the Glasgow satellite town of Clydebank is long past its heyday. Recession has closed down the John Brown shipyard and the Singer sewing-machine factory; the clock-on hooters have been silent since the mid-sixties when the foursome were born. The sons of a taxi driver, tiler, school cleaner, joiner and shorthand typist, the only showbiz in the Wets' collective family-tree was Mrs McLoughlin, a former nightclub singer who donated her Yugoslavian maiden name – Pellow – to her irrepressible ham of a boy Martin.

By their own admission "really bad footballers" and "a fairly thick bunch", Clydebank High School had little to offer young Marti, Graeme Clark, Neil Mitchell and Tom Cunningham. Indeed, like so many before, their worlds revolved round rock 'n' roll: The Ramones (Graeme), Status Quo (Tom), ABC (Neil) and Spandau Ballet (a New Romantic Marti). It was Graeme who organized Tom and Neil to form the band which, in the finest DIY tradition, rehearsed in his parents' kitchen after he'd saved up £20 to buy his bass and Tom's drums; Neil couldn't afford a keyboard so he hummed parts.

After their lusty re-hash of The Clash songbook got them booed off at school concerts, they opted to write their own material.

Meanwhile, after a spell working in a sausage factory, then as a painter and decorator, Marti found himself unemployed. However, he was remembered by the trio for his brilliant classroom mimicry of Michael Jackson; they phoned him one day with a simple request: "C'mon, gie' us a wee blast." He did, he enjoyed it and ended up singing to Mrs Clark's cooker on a regular basis.

So far, so cute – and also as authentic a bunch of hopefuls as ever tried to make the best of meagre resources (dead-end jobs to finance a cheapo £150 demo tape), a shifting identity (Magazine as a main influence giving way to Costello and Squeeze), and a stupid name (Vortex Motion). Clearly, greatness – or even goodness – was not just around the corner. But, in tune with Scotland's tradition of Saturday night fever, the group's music was evolving towards popularist, danceable ersatz Americal soul. The sort made intellectually hip by, among others, Scritti Politti, providers of the group's new name: "*his face is wet, wet with tears*" is from their song 'Getting, Having And Holding'. The extra "wet"

They remain unfashionably laddish and never stop grinning, a billion girls are baying for their bodies and you could take them home to mum (who has probably bought their album too)

was added to stand out from the then-current vogue for double-barrelled names – Duran Duran, Talk Talk and so on.

So it was the band lined up their second-ever gig, at Glasgow's Night Moves club. "They were," says the promoter, "abysmal." Nonetheless, Elliot Davis saw promise, and so signed Wet Wet Wet to his own pet scheme – a Glasgow-based independent record label called The Precious Organization, itself the consequence of failure. Elliot had previously managed a local pop-soul outfit called Sunset Gun, but they had broken up between the pincers of a major record company's high sales expectations and the public's refusal to oblige. He visualized Precious as a mini-company that could talk the music business's language, make use of their marketing and distribution muscle, yet at the same time shield its acts from artistic interference.

A fine notion, but in practice Precious proved itself as little more than a glorified management company. Despite their strenuous efforts to keep at bay the "creative input" of Phonogram Records – for whom the Wets signed after a furious "bidding war" between no fewer than nine majors – The Precious Organization could not prevent the Wets' career from being stalled for two unnecessary years and an equally unnecessary £600,000.

Their first, self-produced efforts were rejected, so upon Phonogram's insistence, the band didn't follow their own inclination to be produced by an old-time soul alchemist such as Thom Bell or Willie Mitchell, instead going into the studio with two highly-rated commercial hotshots in succession, to little satisfactory avail. Thus, months later, Wet Wet Wet had become deeply indebted to their record company yet had nothing to show for it. At least now Phonogram had no creditable objection to the band flying out to Memphis to record with Willie Mitchell.

Not only was this a horizon-widening experience for the group, but under the veteran Mitchell's tutelage, they learned how to psych up a performance. Yet upon their return Phonogram rejected the Memphis sessions tapes as not right for today's pop market. Here lies a conflict of taste; I've heard them, and the characteristic Mitchell bass pulse and the warmth of sound seems incontestably commercial. On the other hand, Phonogram and Precious finally worked out a compromise – using remixes of the band's original 1985 material and new numbers produced by Michael Baker – which were immediately and consistently successful from the band's first single, 'Wishing I Was Lucky', in March 1987.

Though in the end it has all worked out well, Precious and the Wets would have done well to consider Phonogram's track record with Scottish pop–soul groups: their 1984 signing Friends Again had foundered after internal tensions had become exacerbated by Phonogram's pressure to come up with a hit album; the spin-off act Love & Money has never sounded at home with a high-tech production sheen; and as for Hipsway, to date they haven't followed up 1986's brief glory.

So far, the high spot in this remarkably buoyant career has been their self-produced hit version of The Beatles' 'With A Little Help From My Friends'. Not only did it top the singles chart, but it was an appropriately selected benefit record for Childline. Although it is certain this recording was done out of the band's proven sense of charity – they have also played live for various Glasgow causes, plus CND and Red Wedge – it was a timely swipe against music-press pontificating about their breadhead, teenybop image.

Ah yes, the breadhead teenybop image. Nothing caused more glee in some quarters, as the Wet bandwagon gathered steam, than the revelation that Van Morrison had sought the advice of m'learned friends after the similarity between the lyrics to 'Sense Of Wonder' and the Wets' second hit single, 'Sweet Little Mystery', was drawn to his attention. The band changed the offending verse. The Wets got off more lightly with their third single, 'Angel Eyes', when they explained in advance to Squeeze that they were "paying tribute" in its lyric to 'Heartbreaking World'.

The sound of sharpening claws that greeted news of the "Magpies of Pop" episodes testifies to the resentment many males (but seldom females) bear towards a fresh-faced success story in pop, especially where no ironic campness can be discerned. They can't stand it that the band all still live with their parents in Clydebank, that they remain unfashionably laddish and never stop grinning, that a billion girls are baying for their bodies, and – horror of horrors! – you could take them home to mum (who has probably bought their album too).

However inoffensive their image, Wet Wet Wet have succeeded where many more militantly "independent"-minded groups from The Clash onwards have failed. Not without tribulations, they have prevailed over record company wisdom while retaining their unity, integrity and quality. Though the criminally unreleased Memphis sessions remain a casualty of this classic band-label marriage of convenience, Wet Wet Wet's account with Phonogram now stands in the black, though *Popped In Souled Out* had to sell a million to do it. From now on they are at last working for themselves, and the promise which Marti has made to those who might follow their example is: "We're doing something totally unique. We've set up an indie label in Glasgow, and that is a label which is gonna be beneficial to Glasgow in the next ten years. We *are* Precious; we started it along with our manager (Elliot Davis), and that's gonna help new bands, new talent to come up. We're trying to change the attitude of London record companies that there is no life North of Watford."

MAT SNOW

MICHAEL JACKSON

"This is a great honour. Thank you, Mr Enrico and Pepsi Associates. Ladies and gentlemen, thank you."

Here we have, in its entirety, Michael Jackson's last major public statement. The occasion: a press conference announcing his ten million dollar plus contract to endorse Pepsi Cola (a carbonated beverage he would never himself drink). The year: 1986. Two years later and there's another Pepsi press bash in New York; 500 journalists arrive to witness the unveiling of Michael's latest series of glossy, super-slick commercials for the noted fizzy pop. Michael is there in the flesh – but this time he is less "forthcoming". To the assembled multitude he says precisely nothing, he merely blinks into the crowds of flashing cameras. And then he is gone. Not that anyone really expected anything more. Michael Jackson had long ago become the greatest enigma, the most unapproachable character, on the stage of contemporary entertainment.

Never one to engage in light repartee with reporters, Michael had struck himself dumb. You might get a few words – bland words – from Mr Enrico, the Pepsi man, if you were lucky; Frank Dileo, Michael's manager, might partake of conversation and Quincy Jones, Michael's producer and musical collaborator, might be willing to tell you something you already knew – Michael's a really talented guy, you know. But Michael? Don't be daft. Michael Jackson's not talking. Michael Jackson is the superstar on highest and Michael's not talking.

Jackson's first album after breaking with Motown – *Off The Wall* in 1979 – sold six million copies, thus making him a solo artiste of respectable proportions. Nothing more. But *Thriller*, three years later, sold . . . what? 35 million copies? 40 million? Whatever, it was, as everyone now knows, the most successful LP of all time and little Michael had become a "phenomenon". After *Thriller* – and wasn't it strange, the retraction that appeared on the 'Thriller' video (all ghouls, spooks, zombies, cats' eyes and Vincent Price) divorcing Michael from any belief in the occult, heaven forfend? – the rest was silence.

Apart from celebrity shenanigans at the White House, the Pepsi hair scare scenario, the Jacksons' controversial Victory tour (controversial = overpriced tickets, wonky ticket allocation, dodgy staging and the much publicised fact that Michael was a reluctant participant in the whole affair anyway), and *Captain Eo* (the film he made for Disneyworld and the closest, perhaps, that he would come to his overwhelming ambition to be something cute and fantastical on the silver screen, just like his beloved E.T.), the rest was silence. Punctuated loudly and brutally and with tiresome regularity by the low-life tabloids and their rumour-mongering antics. It would take an age – half a decade – for Michael Jackson to follow up *Thriller* – but as *the* prime target celebrity, he was never out of the "news". How we became grimly fascinated by this singing, prancing tot who had never, we were led to believe, never really grown up. Oh, those Rumours – a succession of weird tales of the bizarre boy, sagas of quirks that were to give birth to a media-manufactured pop star nickname more widely used even than "Elvis The Pelvis" or "The Fab Four". Wacko Jacko. Who can forget those stories? The facelifts, the skin-lightening treatments, the female hormones ingested to keep the voice on high and the hair in trim . . . the shrine built in his home to his one love Elizabeth Taylor . . . the proposals of marriage to his other one love Diana Ross . . . the nights spent sleeping in a hyperbaric oxygen chamber in the hopes of living to be 150 years old . . . the facemask donned on his rare ventures into the real world in the hopes of warding off unfriendly bacteria . . . the one million dollars he offered in vain for the remains of the Elephant Man . . . the tuxedos and the skateboard lessons for his pet chimp Bubbles . . . You had to laugh, didn't you?

Sales of *Bad*, in comparison with *Thriller*, were "modest" – it's only shifted 16 million so far. Michael was, reportedly, "upset"

Though Bubbles, at least, was fact. The Jackson pet – part of an extensive and exotic menagerie – did exist and really was, it seems, treated as a member of the family. To be exploited in 1987 when Michael struck a lucrative deal with the Ideal toy company and launched Michael's pets – a range of soft, plush toys which were promoted thus:

"LOUIE THE LLAMA . . . He's somewhat rare and truly unique, a pet you'll love and want to keep.

MUSCLES THE SNAKE . . . He may seem sly and sneaky and mean, but he's the nicest snake you've ever seen.

BUBBLES THE CHIMP . . . Michael Jackson likes to carry this pet, for holding Bubbles is as lucky as you can get."

And so on.

Michael remained mum about all the Rumours. It was left up to Frank Dileo to sate public curiosity and tell the world, via the press, the true state of his charge's mental state.

The oxygen chamber? Well, yes, Michael *did* on occasion take refuge in such a tent. "I'm on the record as saying I hate it, and I do," said Frank.

The attempted purchase of the bones of John Merrick? Well, yes, Michael *had* tried to strike a bargain for the Elephant Man's skeleton and had been greatly peeved to be turned down. Michael was a great admirer of the Elephant Man, you see. Michael could "relate to" Merrick's plight . . .

The face mask? Well, yes, Michael *did* don this sensible protective garment quite often . . .

The only thing that was ever denied outright was the matter of the facial alterations. Skin-lightening treatments? Poppycock. Well, yes, he *had* had his nose done – but that's what people *do* in Hollywood – and, oh, yes, he *had* had a Kirk Douglas-styled cleft fashioned into his chin. But *really* that was it.

Michael whacko? Absolutely not.

The week that the new LP, *Bad*, came out – finally – the popular press could talk of little else. This wasn't just a mere trifling record, it was an EVENT. The video of the title track, a lavish and lengthy concoction, directed by Martin Scorsese in which Michael is transformed from timid egghead to streetwise kid with a leather fist (and from black and white to colour), was "premièred", amid much blaring of trumpets, on Channel 4 and MTV and networks the globe over. An EVENT. Had any LP in musical history arrived with such a fanfare? It was said that Jackson was desperate to exceed the sales of *Thriller* with this one. It was reported (erroneously, according to Dileo) that he had the words "100 Million" – indicating his sales target – written on a mirror in his home. But even Jackson could not, surely, have been surprised when the backlash, albeit minor, came. They said it was not on a par with *Thriller* – and really it was not. Despite Jones's triumphant production and Michael's impeccable singing there was no disguising the fact that the songs lacked the epic qualities of a 'Billie Jean', a 'Beat It' or a 'Thriller'. They said that the 'Bad' video was, well, a bit weedy – and really it was: a pale imitation of the street gang logic and dancing machismo of 'Beat It'. In 1984, Jackson had received an unprecedented eight Grammy awards for *Thriller*. In 1988, he missed out on the Album of the Year award – U2 bagged that with *The Joshua Tree* – and on everything else, too. No Grammies for Michael – and Michael was, reportedly, "disappointed". Meanwhile, sales of *Bad*, in comparison with *Thriller*, were "modest" – it's only shifted 16 million so far, for goodness sake! – and Michael was, reportedly, "upset". Dileo was more philosophical: "What happens if *Bad* doesn't match *Thriller* but ends up selling 25 million and becomes the *second* largest album of all time? he asked *Rolling Stone*. "What are people going to say to that? That we're *losers*?"

Michael Jackson arrived in Japan in September 1987 for the first leg of a world tour. Bubbles flew out on a separate plane. They spoke of hi-tech pyrotechnics, spectacular disappearing tricks and Michael's new crowd-pleasing wheeze of grabbing his crotch at every available moment. The Michael Jackson show was a victorious spectacle, a show – in embryo – that would eventually (re)establish the boy as the world's greatest, most breathtaking entertainer. This tour, however, would be his last. Dileo confirmed that. And then the young man would go into films – a *Peter Pan*, an *E.T. II* or whatever.

And, in the meantime, there was the autobiography, *Moonwalk*, published in the spring of 1988 with an introduction by Jackie O. Here were showbiz platitudes and toytown prose aplenty as Michael (and his editor) skated over all controversy, intrigue and insight. "To me, nothing is more important than making people happy," wrote Michael. "I'm a vegetarian, so fortunately fresh fruits and vegetables are a favourite of mine," wrote Michael. "Once, by coincidence, I wore a black glove to the American Music Awards ceremony, which happened to fall on Martin Luther King Jr's birthday. Funny how things happen sometimes," wrote Michael. Elsewhere he spent much time railing against the behaviour of his public. How dare people be so interested in his private life? How dare they ask him if he goes to the lavatory just like everybody else? I'm just an ordinary guy, for crying out loud, although "I believe I'm one of the loneliest people in the world."

Moonwalk brought us no closer to understanding the seemingly fragile figure that is Michael Jackson – and for all his protestations of "ordinariness", a man of such wealth, a man of such talent, a man who cages himself off from the world, a man who lives like *that*, is *not* like you or me. His is a loneliness of his own making.

Moonwalk romped to the top of the book bestsellers charts. But that goes without saying . . .
TOM HIBBERT

ACTS OF THE YEAR

WHITESNAKE

A group which has taken ten years to reach multi-platinum status is likely to have one or two skeletons lurking in the cupboard. But in the process of steering Whitesnake into the first division of international rock acts, David Coverdale has left behind him enough rattling bones to fill an attic.

The album which finally cracked it worldwide for the preening, hair-moussed vocalist was *Whitesnake 1987*, but it did so against the odds. It was the first Whitesnake product to see the light of day since 1984's *Slide It In*, and although Coverdale *always* describes the making of his albums as a nightmare of one sort or another, *Whitesnake 1987* does seem to have been produced under considerable duress. On the eve of recording, drummer Cozy Powell left to replace Carl Palmer as the P in ELP. After much prevarication Aynsley Dunbar was drafted in as Powell's replacement. Then guitarist John Sykes flew off to attend the funeral of his old Thin Lizzy colleague Phil Lynott and was some time away. Coverdale later complained bitterly of how long it took to get the guitar tracks done. He also commented darkly about the time taken to get Dunbar's drum tracks recorded.

Work then ground to a halt while the singer underwent major surgery to relieve an infection which had caused flooding of the sinuses. While he convalesced, a second producer, Keith Olsen, was drafted in when the original, Mike Stone, objected to the ever-extending schedule for the sessions. Costs spiralled, tempers frayed and by the time work was completed Coverdale had fired the entire group: Dunbar, who had never really joined in the first place, Sykes, who had co-written most of the songs, and long-suffering bassist Neil Murray, who knew only that he had been cut off the payroll and wasn't even sent a copy of the album.

Initially then, there wasn't a band in existence to promote *Whitesnake 1987* which was released on 31 March to a chorus of unsympathetic reviews. Undeterred, Coverdale set about recruiting a "dream" line-up of musicians to provide a "group presence" for a video which was to be made in Los Angeles to promote the first single, 'Still Of The Night'. What he came up with was a neo-supergroup of skilled heavy rock players with various features in common: skinny waists, pipe-cleaner legs, a thick mass of hair on top and, with one exception, about ten years younger-looking than the boss.

They were a Dutchman, Adrian Vandenberg (guitar; ex-solo act); an Irishman, Vivian Campbell (guitar; ex-Dio); a Puerto Rican, Rudy Sarzo (bass; ex-Quiet Riot); and a Texan, Tommy Aldridge (drums; ex-Ozzy Osbourne). It was an extraordinary irony that this multinational quartet of convenience, and its bronzed, windswept leader, was later to receive a BPI nomination for Best British Group of 1987 along with The Bee Gees, Level 42 and The Pet Shop Boys (who won the award).

Among the dry ice and exposed flesh of that first video shoot there was apparently a meeting of musical minds and Coverdale's dream line-up became his new touring unit, initially supporting (and disgracing) the dismal Mötley Crüe and subsequently headlining in its own right, as the album outsold all expectations. In the American chart, where Coverdale's only previous success had been a number 40 placing for *Slide It In*, *Whitesnake 1987* stayed in the Top Ten for nearly six months. 'Here I Go Again' was a number one single and the follow-up 'Is This Love' made second place.

In Britain the new-look Snakes became a familiar sight on *Top Of The Pops* enjoying hits with 'Still Of The Night' (number 16), 'Is This Love' (9) and 'Here I Go Again' (9). By June 1988, worldwide sales of *Whitesnake 1987* were nearing 6·5 million.

All of which was eloquent testament

to the staying power and some would say overweening ego of one David Coverdale, the son of a steel-worker, born in September 1951 in Saltburn-on-Sea, Yorkshire. At the start of 1973, young Coverdale was a complete unknown, working in a clothes shop in Redcar and singing in semi-pro bands, such as The Fabulosa Brothers, in the evenings. Nevertheless, on hearing that Ian Gillan had left Deep Purple, he decided to apply for the post and sent an unsolicited tape to the group. "I was conceited enough to think I might stand a chance," he said. "When I actually got the job I couldn't speak." Later that same year, one of his first dates with Purple was at The California Jam, where the band headlined before an estimated audience of 750,000.

Although, when Coverdale joined, Deep Purple was at the peak of its popularity, the group was already past its best. Within two years the first of many acrimonious personnel changes occurred when Ritchie Blackmore left to form Rainbow, and less than a year after that the band disintegrated. Coverdale recorded two solo albums *Whitesnake* (1977) and *Northwinds* (1978), neither of which made the slightest commercial impact, and although he relished the control which solo status afforded him, he nevertheless recognized the need to get out on the road with a band.

Thus, the first Whitesnake line-up which included bassist Neil Murray and guitarists Micky Moody and Bernie Marsden was recruited in January 1978. To list in detail the serpentine twists and turns that have occurred in the Whitesnake roll-call since then would be an exercise of tortuous and tedious complexity, but the best known and most durable of the early line-ups incorporated Murray, Moody and Marsden together with ex-Deep Purple cronies Ian Paice (drums) and Jon Lord (keyboards). With variations of this band in tow until 1981, Coverdale built a sturdy reputation in Britain with a steady run of chart albums and singles, the most notable successes being a Top 20 hit with 'Fool For Your Loving' in 1980 and a number two album, *Come And Get It*, released in 1981.

This was the period when the so-called New Wave Of British Heavy Metal was in its primacy. Coverdale and his boys, though too seasoned a bunch of campaigners to fit comfortably into this young, gung-ho class of spandex warriors, were vigorously championed by *Sounds* and its newly-established offshoot, *Kerrang!* They swept forward on an upsurge of interest in hard rock along with groups like Iron Maiden and Def Leppard.

Coverdale's music was and, with some minor adjustments for the Bon Jovi era, still is a continuation of the progressive blues–rock tradition that predominated in the early seventies. His style of singing is based on that of the two classic heavy-mannered rock prototypes, Paul Rodgers and Robert Plant. In the early days the balance was towards Paul Rodgers' intrinsically bluesy grunt-and-strut school of singing, but as Whitesnake progressed into the eighties and Coverdale's curls grew ever longer and more beautifully tangled he modified his approach on songs like 'Slow And Easy' and 'Still Of The Night' in favour of the Robert Plant style of shake, shimmy and shriek. A memorable pair of pictures in a music paper showed Robert Plant with the caption "I come from the land of the ice and snow" and directly opposite an almost identical-looking picture of Coverdale accompanied by the words, "That's funny, so do I."

At the end of a British tour in August 1983, Whitesnake headlined Castle Donington, the premier event in the HM calendar. It was a curious fact that the sound that year was uniformly bad for all the support acts, including ZZ Top, yet perfectly adjusted for Whitesnake. Coverdale denied that it was a stitch-up, and argued that he had hired the best PA available for everyone else while admitting that as headlining act he had exercised his prerogative not to let the other bands use the delay towers and the quad sound "because they cost me £80,000."

Initially, there wasn't a band in existence to promote *Whitesnake 1987*. Undeterred, Coverdale set about recruiting a "dream" line-up to provide group presence for a video

Since then, no line-up of Whitesnake that has recorded an album has survived intact to tour that album. 1982's *Saints An' Sinners* did not list the musicians, but Cozy Powell arrived around then along with guitarist Mel Galley and Colin Hodgkinson, who replaced Neil Murray on bass. Galley co-wrote half the tracks on 1984's *Slide It In* – "Mel Galley's and my writing is a marriage made in heaven," Coverdale gushed at the time – but following an accident that left Galley with a severely broken wrist, the marriage was dissolved, and the guitar department was turned over to cheeky blond flash-fingers John Sykes for the making of *1987*.

Moody, Marsden, Paice, Sykes, Hodgkinson (replaced by his predecessor Neil Murray), Galley, Murray (twice), Dunbar, sundry managers and producers, the list of sackings stretches on, while Cozy Powell and Jon Lord remain the only two musicians known to have left Whitesnake with dignity and on their own terms. Commenting, in 1985, on the extraordinarily high turnover of personnel Coverdale said: "Whenever it's been down to me asking people to leave . . . it's not because I don't like them any more or that I've fallen out with them, it's because I don't think they're contributing enough to the band any more. Or that I've got nothing to learn from them any more."

So will the current "dream" line-up, as yet unrecorded, survive long enough to make a Whitesnake album? "These guys are terrific," Coverdale was reported as saying in the 12 March 1988 issue of *Kerrang!*. "Everybody's getting on not only musically but privately too. And from what I understand after talking to myself this morning, I'm not firing anybody in the near future."

DAVID SINCLAIR

YEAR IN ALBUMS

A

ABC
Alphabet City (Neutron)
You never expected it, never believed they could fly back so gracefully so high. That they could and they have is one of those delicious miracles that makes it all worthwhile.
Melody Maker

The welcome return of Martin Fry, romantically sitting on thorns, heart bleeding all over the shop . . . ABC have made the finest record of their careers.
Record Mirror

Fry sings as though he takes all this nonsense seriously.
NME

AC/DC
Blow Up Your Video (Atlantic)
Some hints on how to enjoy this LP:
1) Give your brain the evening off.
Smash Hits

Short trouser rock with more bristles than brain cells.
Record Mirror

How can a bunch of blokes who are all under five feet tall produce such a colossal noise?
Q

ACT
Laughter, Tears And Rage (ZTT)
Your record is good for sleeping too. Is that what you want? It's certainly no good for sleeping with. It's as sexy as Nick Owen. Or a pigeon.
Melody Maker

JOHN ADAMS
The Chairman Dances (Nonesuch Digital)
Adams and cohorts look through the telescope the wrong end and make minimalistic meanderings quake with vivid possibilities. May the force be halfway up your trouser leg.
Melody Maker

If Mr Adams is playing with a full deck, he's taken pains to include both jokers.
Q

THE ADVENTURES
The Sea Of Love (Elektra)
The only possible motion to this is a simultaneous lifting of the left heel and dropping of the right shoulder.
NME

ANTHONY ADVERSE
The Redshoes (el)
He even has a line about a mazurka. I mean, really, a mazurka?!
Sounds

It's precious, it's camp, you can't dance to it and you'd be hard pushed to have sex with it.
NME

AEROSMITH
Permanent Vacation (Geffen)
A record that's more than just a means of clearing up a few bills.
Sounds

Sounds like the band have been on a 24-hour lager frenzy session.
Record Mirror

AGE OF CHANCE
One Thousand Years Of Trouble (Virgin)
They may be angry but they sure know how to boogie.
Sounds

AGNOSTIC FRONT
Liberty And Justice For . . . (Rough Justice)
Quite what the vocalist has in his mouth to ensure incomprehensible rantings I'm not sure, but a box of eggs is the best bet.
Melody Maker

a;GRUMH . . .
Black Vinyl Under Cover (Play It Again Sam)
I cannot imagine this music being played in any context outside state subsidized radio.
Q

A-HA
Stay On These Roads (WEA)
Life is sad and so is Pal Waaktaar.
NME

Their previous effortless grasp of the English language seems to be floundering.
Record Mirror

THE ALARM
Eye Of The Hurricane (IRS)
The Alarm are Welsh. And lately they've decided to rediscover their Celtic "roots" and that, apparently, is what this LP is all about. So if you're wondering what lines like "the rebecca ride at dawn petticoat ghost and torn" are all about, it's probably something to do with Wales.
Smash Hits

Try deciphering it for yourselves.
Melody Maker

ALIEN SEX FIEND
Here Cum Germs (Plague/Anagram)
Alien Sex Fiend still call their songs names like 'Death' which shows an obvious talent for words.
Sounds

I was ready to slate the Fiends until I saw the photos inside the LP, where they smile and joke and have written captions like "Nik doing his camel impression". And then they seemed so nice, so friendly that I just decided to let them off.
NME

ALL ABOUT EVE
All About Eve (Mercury)
The lyrics have very long hair indeed.
Smash Hits

AMERICAN MUSIC CLUB
Engine (Zippo)
If only American Music Club wasn't such a naff name.
NME

ANGST
Mystery Spot (SST Records)
As an optimistic high school band auditioning for the first time for a night's work in the local lounge, they'd be hard pushed to get the gig.
Q

ISABELLE ANTENA
Hoping For Love (Les Disques Du Crepuscule)
One should always expect great things for a record which has "Made In Benelux"

stamped down the spine.
Melody Maker

AR KANE
1969 (Rough Trade)
The 'Up Home!' EP took their ice floe lission to its ultimate cloud nebula state of amorphous enormity, on *1969* they've stepped back from the full drench to locate a new sense of empty expanse, limpid and indistinct.
Melody Maker

JOAN ARMATRADING
The Shouting Stage (A&M)
The sheer excellence of these songs points to a slight professional coldness at the core. Why do these unremittingly intimate accounts of her love life all too often lack the privacy that would make them truly beguiling?
Q

THE ART OF NOISE
In No Sense? Nonsense (China)
The Art Of Noise's main fault is that they are not really very entertaining.
Q

ASLAN
Feel No Shame (EMI)
Most of it, however, is just parasitic of the soft white underbelly of U2.
Record Mirror

Located, if not stranded, somewhere in the singalong suburbs of U2.
Q

For a bunch who are so anxious to dispel any comparisons with a certain other Irish rock band Aslan often don't help their own cause or claims.
Sounds

It's true that Aslan are Irish and it's also a fact that their first album carries a small child's face on its sleeve, but that's the end of the much-hyped link with U2.
NME

THE ASSOCIATION
Golden Heebie Jeebies (Edsel)
The Association never quite became druggy enough to crack the hippie market, nor straight enough for barbershop quartet fame. They were trapped in a ba ba ba shop quartet with a sitar.
NME

RICK ASTLEY
Whenever You Need Somebody (RCA)
Straightforward, deliriously catchy dance music.
Smash Hits

Crystal clear production over dead dull tunes.
Record Mirror

An entirely valid tactic, but not one to hold interest over the course of 40 minutes spent in a sedentary position.
Q

I just hope he gets enough to get a decent haircut.
Sounds

Churning out sewage, churning out effluent, SAW are fouling the air. Rick's just their little helper.
Melody Maker

To slag Rick off is to slag off all that is good and true and earnest.
NME

ASWAD
Distant Thunder (Island)
Aswad seems to be one of those bands of infinite duration, shedding albums as others shed toenail clippings.
NME

Spiffing things to watch out for are a backing rhythm on the splendid 'The Message' which appears to be played on a domestic washing machine.
Smash Hits

'Don't Turn Around' may be their first number one, but I doubt if it's their last.
Record Mirror

Ignore it.
Melody Maker

AZTEC CAMERA
Love (WEA)
The sound of white boy melancholy and yearning for requited romance that lacks either objection or ecstasy, the emotional extremes by which one must inevitably judge anyone who sings in the soul genre.
Q

B

DEREK B
Bullet From A Gun (Tuff Audio)
Nimmo. Guyler. Jameson. Hatton. Few names evoke the stuffiness of England – this land of Cornish pasties, bridge tournaments and village fetes – more readily than "Derek".
Melody Maker

BAD NEWS
Bootleg (EMI)
Why did The Comic Strip agree to perform this material? Have they no pride?
NME

The sleeve photo is the best joke by a mile.
Q

A 17-week-long demented axe grinding geetar solo from the hand of a bevvy of Megadeth-ites is preferable to this mindless, jokeless useless load of old tosh.
Smash Hits

Sit back and get your laughing gear around *Bootleg.*
Record Mirror

BALKANA
The Music Of Bulgaria (Hannibal)
Not liking rock is one thing, but there are limits to how far you have to go to avoid it.
Q

BANANARAMA
Wow! (London)
So, can the all-writing, all-producing, all-conquering team of Stock, Aitken & Waterman succeed in injecting some real life into non-singing, non-dancing determinedly ordinary Bananarama? Answer – well, a bit.
Q

They have no pretensions toward anything other than dancing round their plassy bags and making loads of loot.
Sounds

It's a shame they used up a good title like *Wow!* Someone could've made a record called that.
Melody Maker

Terry Hall has a lot to answer for.
NME

BAND OF SUSANS
Hope Against Hope
(Further/Blast First)
Since this album was recorded, two or three Susans have left, which can only be tragic news.
Sounds

BAR-B-Q KILLERS
Comely (Fundamental)
It's more like music to scrape the enamel off the bath to.
Sounds

BASIA
Time And Tide (Portrait)
She sounds the most fun you can have with your clothes on.
Sounds

THE BATHERS
Unusual Places To Die
(Go! Discs)
If The Bathers' singer-songwriter Chris Thompson has ever bust his corsets to Monty Python's 'Summarise Proust in 15 Seconds' sketch, then it certainly doesn't show.
Sounds

BAUHAUS
In The Flat Field (4AD)
The CD itself is, naturally, matt black.
Melody Maker

BEAT FARMERS
The Pursuit Of Happiness
(Curb)
A gloomy buffalo sits on the sleeve, embedded in the middle of the road and cruelly apt.
NME

BEE GEES
ESP (WEA)
The Bee Gees are special, I'm sure you'll agree – one of pop's truly great groups.
NME

Few people know that the CIA are planning to cripple Iran by playing this album on special loudspeakers secretly parachuted into the country.
Record Mirror

On 'This Is Your Life' Baz even attempts a rap, ferchrissakes.
Sounds

REGINA BELLE
All By Myself (CBS)
All By Myself is the album that reaches the parts *Whitney* (the album) missed by a mile. If its release has caused any sleepless nights in the Houston household, they are entirely justified.
Q

THE BELOVED
Where It Is (Flim Flam)
It's not such a good thing for a devout Beloved fan (if there is such a thing).
Record Mirror

PAT BENATAR
Best Shots (Chrysalis)
One of the charming things about Pat Benatar is that she still looks like a newscaster.
NME

CHUCK BERRY
Hail! Hail! Rock 'n' Roll (MCA)
Keith Richard – who stole most of Berry's licks as a youngster – handles most of the guitar duties, while Chuck shouts "Go Keef go", mixes up his lyrics and forgets the names of some of his famous friends.
Record Mirror

CINDY LEE BERRYHILL
Who's Gonna Save The World (New Routes)
Lee. An enigmatic little word, yet . . . strangely compelling. Where would Ricki Jones, Jamie Curtis and Jeffrey Pierce be without it? Could Harvey Oswald have been as sharp a shooter? Really makes you think.
Melody Maker

BFG
Fathoms (Attica)
My guess is that BFG stands for Bathroom Fixated Goths.
Melody Maker

BHUNDU BOYS
True Jit (WEA)
The Bhundu Boys are getting there – they'll be on *Top Of The Pops* by this time next year, or I'll eat a kebab.
Sounds

They know Britain better than most bands who were born here, and it's the space and place of our sense of them, as a group, as bodies, the shock of the sound of their music here, the power of their presence, that fleshes out their importance.
That's the politics.
NME

BIG AUDIO DYNAMITE
Tighten Up Volume 88 (CBS)
A shambling bag of half-ideas and rhyming couplets that you wouldn't put your name to even if you were a poet and didn't know it.
Sounds

By now Jones is obviously used to getting mauled by the critics.
NME

BIG BLACK
Songs About Fucking
(Blast First)
An anathema against the curse of current pop, harsh realism in a world of holocaustic nuclear madness.
NME

My God, Holmes. We're too late. They're dead from the neck up.
Melody Maker

THE BIG EASY
Original Soundtrack (Island)
This week's offer: a free holiday in the Bayou to anyone who can understand more than ten per cent of the lyrics.
Q

BIG PIG
Bonk (A&M)
Bonk could be likened to the experience of having sex in a vat of porridge. Interesting but hard going.
NME

BLACK
Wonderful Life (A&M)
Yes, Liverpool is still a good place to come from.
Q

When relentless gloom-mongering like this became a hit, when you're confronted with it on Capital Radio all the lifelong day it's hard to bear.
Melody Maker

It beats the pants off Johnny Hates Jazz.
Record Mirror

BLOOD UNCLES
Libertine (Virgin)
The Blood Uncles are surprisingly eloquent.
Record Mirror

Libertine is the work of charlatans and poseurs.
NME

It's a rare album that is so genuinely successful in its bid to achieve this kind of rampant psychotic unpleasantness.
Q

Truly a sign of the times.
Sounds

BLUE MERCEDES
Rich And Famous (MCA)
Can it be that they really are trendy and I am merely getting old?
Sounds

BLYTH POWER
The Barman And Other Stories (Midnight)
An album for train spotters by train spotters.
Melody Maker

Just in case you're worried that Blyth Power's train-spotting obsession is waning, 'City Of Morpeth' is an ode to a mail train.
Sounds

Blyth Power at their best at last.
NME

THE BODINES
Played (Magnet)
In fact the entire office pleaded on bended knees for this record to be removed from the record player.
Record Mirror

Glossop's unlikely chart candidates will become extremely popular indeed.
NME

THE BOMB PARTY
Liberace Rising (Workers Playtime)
In preference to the normal practice of numbering sides we have a spanking side and a rubber side.
Record Mirror

BOURGEOIS TAGG
YoYo (Island)
Clearly the eyeballs of "Brent Bourgeois" and "Larry Tagg" should be fed to rats for bringing our fine industry into disrepute.
NME

BILLY BRAGG
Help Save The Youth Of America (Go!Discs/PolyGram)
I get the feeling that most Bragg fans are the sort that the man himself can't stand, the drunken sods at the back bellowing out the rock 'n' roll songs.
Melody Maker

LAURA BRANAGAN
Touch (Atlantic)
A record that gives you the feeling of being dragged around a field for ten minutes by a rampaging buffalo.
Melody Maker

BRANIAC 5
World Inside (Reckless)
It sounds like Hawkwind with a limited supply of drugs.
NME

THE BRILLIANT CORNERS
Somebody Up There Likes Me (Revolver)
You see here the shadow of a man, dumbfounded, almost raving over a Brilliant Corners LP. Tomorrow he will be seeking medical advice.
NME

BROS
Push (CBS)
Bros don't go on about how they are serious musicians desperate to be recognized as such by the likes of the *NME*.
Record Mirror

This album is an insult to 12 year olds.
NME

Their upstart snottiness reminds me of the young Generation X.
Sounds

I remember when pop music meant jerking off to pictures of Marc Bolan and duffing up Bay City Rollers fans in lunch breaks. Being 13 was never as vapid as this. If it had been, we would all be traffic wardens by now.
Melody Maker

JAMES BROWN
I'm Real (Polydor)
More of a statement about Full Force than Brown himself, but doubtless he will take full credit for the work. A small price to pay for the most compulsive, deeply funky album so far this year.
Q

SAM BROWN
Stop! (A&M)
'Wrap me up' is a good example as she casts her intestines to the four winds.
Sounds

Her sleeve notes suggest that someone once thought her songs were "pieces of doggy poo!"
Record Mirror

CARMINA BURANA
The Apocryphal Dances (Midnight Chime)
I have met this shy black-clad quartet, and can report that they still haven't got over the death of Ian Curtis.
Q

This band deserve to be violently shaken.
Melody Maker

JONATHAN BUTLER
Jonathan Butler (Jive)
If you really enjoy listening to a full four sides of "woah woah ooh baby, you're my everything ooh, no no no", this could be the LP you're looking for and you're probably a bit off your head.
Smash Hits

BUTTHOLE SURFERS
Hairway to Steven (First Blast)
The tracks are marked only by symbols – mostly obscene.
Melody Maker

C

CABARET VOLTAIRE
Code (EMI)
The longer they go on the more difficult it becomes to write about Cabaret Voltaire.
Melody Maker

CAMEO
She's Strange (Club)
If Larry Blackmon thought the girl in the title track was strange, then their British record company's behaviour made her look like a Girl Guide.
NME

CAMPER VAN BEETHOVEN
Our Beloved Revolutionary Sweetheart (Virgin)
This is the group that once sent out a press release that was unnaturally keen to report their singer was nearly bitten by a dog while walking home from work.
Melody Maker

Sentimentality, however, is not the reason to buy these seven tracks by these silly buggers from Santa Cruz.
Q

IRENE CARA
Carasmatic (Elektra)
She's still doing the kind of songs that have New York cab drivers spontaneously boogieing behind closing credits.
Q

THE CARDIACS
A Little Man And A House And The Whole Wide Window (The Alphabet Business Concern)
The Cardiacs have telescoped the entire dregs of the early seventies into one album.
NME

This has rather a lot to do with the kind of twaddle you talk when you stay up late for the first time.
Melody Maker

CARMEL
Everybody's Got A Little Soul (London)
We don't like Carmel in this country because nobody has told us to.
NME

THE CARS
Door To Door (Elektra)
Anyone with a passable voice and access to a bath could come up with a Cars album in a couple of minutes.
NME

ROSANNE CASH
King's Record Shop (CBS)
"Who's Johnny Cash?" The reply might be "Oh, he's Rosanne's dad."
NME

CASSANDRA COMPLEX
Feel The Width
(Play It Again Sam)
Meaningful? I nearly choked on one of Rod's conceptualized patterns.
NME

Clearly working on a pretty advanced level.
Melody Maker

EUGENE CHADBOURNE
Camper Van Chadbourne
(Fundamental Music)
Silly noises by silly people. If you wear your jeans back to front, if you eat bananas with their skins on, if you mistake lamp posts for milkmen you'll enjoy this.
Sounds

Devote your life to listening to his back catalogue.
Melody Maker

TRACY CHAPMAN
Tracy Chapman (Elektra)
I believe in Tracy Chapman.
Sounds

The fuss is featherweight.
Melody Maker

CHEAP TRICK
Luxury (Epic)
This album is so cynical it makes Stock, Aitken & Waterman seem naïve.
Sounds

CHER
Cher (Geffen)
It's worthy of a Ken Russell video with Rick Wakeman plinking away at a bank of synths while trolls, elves, pixies and the odd hobbit gambol around.
Sounds

THE CHESTERFIELDS
Westward Ho!
(The Subway Organization)
Subversion in a romper suit; they'll never pull it off.
Melody Maker

They use words like FRESH! POP! and THRILL! on their album covers when they really should be using Z's (as in The Chesterfieldzzzzzzzzzz).
NME

THE CHRISTIANS
The Christians (Island)
The bloke who writes the songs is called Henry.
Smash Hits

Christian lyrics do not aspire to the heights of Keats, Tennyson or even the great Neil Tennant, but they nevertheless fail to irritate and are perfectly OK really.
NME

CHROME MOLLY
Angst (IRS)
Angst is easily more fun than a Rubik's Cube.
NME

THE CHRYSANTHEMUMS
Is That A Fish On Your Shoulder Or Are You Just Pleased To See Me
(Eggs Plant)
You warm to a record with a name like this.
Q

CLANNAD
Sirius (RCA)
Clannad should get back to basics; a fiddle, a flute and a washboard at the very most.
Sounds

THE CLASH
The Story Of The Clash Part 1 (CBS)
Punk's Not Dead Pal!! (Except it is really).
Smash Hits

This collection is seriously flawed, but if it wasn't it wouldn't be a Clash record.
Q

LEONARD COHEN
I'm Your Man (CBS)
Only a peeled banana solemnly clasped alerts you to the possibility that we may be in for a more than usually amusing Cohen experience.
Sounds

Leonard is neither grim nor gloomy.
NME

Leonard Cohen: Gives you that feeling like your "dog just died."
Q

NAT "KING" COLE
The Capitol Years (Capitol)
He was tall, black and one helluva piano player.
NME

LLOYD COLE AND THE COMMOTIONS
Mainstream (Polydor)
Naturally, it's the least mainstream thing he's done.
Melody Maker

Mainstream is just that.
Record Mirror

THE COMMUNARDS
Red (London)
Some of the most depressing music to emerge in 1987.
NME

A blissfully creative and caring relief from all those heavy macho guitars.
Smash Hits

THE CONDITIONZ
Head (Primal Lunch)
The nation won't exactly be mourning the fact that this Conditionz LP is an undisputed let-down, but frankly, I'm gutted.
NME

THE COOLIES
Doug (DB US Import)
It tells of the rise and fall of a skinhead ne'er-do-well who strikes it rich after beating up a gay chef, stealing his notebook and then publishing the stolen recipes in a best-selling cookbook.
NME

ALICE COOPER
Raise Your Fist And Yell (MCA)
With titles like 'Chop Chop Chop' and 'Time To Kill', and lyrics that speak of decapitation and impalement, it's obvious that his attitudes haven't changed since he started offending parents and elders in the seventies.
Q

HUGH CORNWELL
Wolf (Virgin)
When you're hot you're hot; when you're not you're not.
NME

ELVIS COSTELLO
Out Of Our Idiot (Demon X Fiend)
The man would love to write songs as moving as those that inspired him.
Sounds

A sack of moonrocks for the title alone.
Melody Maker

THE CROSS
Shove It (Virgin)
One night last autumn, Queen's "superstar drummer" Roger Taylor found himself with nothing to do. This well-packaged, well-produced, pompous trash is the result.
Record Mirror

It's difficult to imagine how pathetic this is without actually having heard it . . . Stop it, Rog. Stop it now. You stupid, stupid man.
Melody Maker

A nifty little debut and, I'm sure, the start of a fruitful new era in Roger Taylor's career.
Sounds

D

THE DAMNED
Mindless, Directionless Energy – Live At the Lyceum 1981 (ID)
True fact: I actually saw this concert, and it was appalling. It hasn't "mellowed" with age – in fact, it's got worse.
Smash Hits

The Damned will continue regardless of mere humanity.
NME

MORRIS DAY
Daydreaming (WEA)
Doesn't even sound like Prince on a bad night, when he can't find a clean pair of heels and there isn't a glass of Babycham in the house.
Sounds

TAYLOR DAYNE
Tell It To My Heart (Arista)
In a world free from financial pressures people like Taylor Dayne wouldn't make albums at all.
Record Mirror

A dance LP that doesn't owe a smidgen of thanks to Stock, Aitken & Waterman! Is that a bad thing? No it isn't, but neither is it completely good.
Smash Hits

DEAD CAN DANCE
Within The Realm Of A Dying Sun (4AD)
File under ground.
NME

See it as your challenge for the month.
Q

THE dBs
The Sound Of Magic (IRS)
You couldn't help thinking that were the dBs to finally split, it might be a musical mercy killing.
Sounds

THE DEEP FREEZE MICE
War, Famine, Death, Pestilence and Miss Timberlake (Cordelia)
Isn't it odd to think that the greatest pyschedelic pop LP of the eighties was recorded in a garden shed on a Leicester allotment?
NME

DEF LEPPARD
Hysteria (Bludgeon Riffola)
So Leppard haven't lost their balls. They've simply come to realize there are moments when they're best tucked quietly away.
Sounds

THE DEL-LORDS
Based On A True Story (Enigma)
Guys with an absolute conviction in the power of real rock 'n' roll.
Sounds

A US Import sticker reminds us "their second album got the highest possible rating from Sounds (UK)." It boasts "Their third is in your hands . . ." Don't you think that's just asking for trouble?
NME

DEPECHE MODE
Music For The Masses (Mute)
The "Mode" make very dubious puffing noises as though they were blowing up a paddling pool.
Smash Hits

What I want to know is are Depeche Mode pervs?
NME

Let's just hope they don't start going to Sunday School.
Melody Maker

DIAMANDA GALAS
You Must Be Certain Of The Devil (Mute)
You're probably not going to like this. It's not catchy, it's not tuneful, it's not "fun". In fact it sounds like Hell on Earth.
Record Mirror

Interpretation seems irrelevant.
Melody Maker

DIO
Dream Evil (Vertigo)
When the lyrics work in tandem with the music, the results can be striking.
Q

Two members of RM's staff threw themselves off a tall building rather than review this and I don't blame them.
Record Mirror

DOG FACED HERMANS
Human's Fly (Calculas)
More fun putting lighted matches under my fingernails than listening to this dirge.
NME

Everything. It has everything.
Melody Maker

DOLPHIN BROTHERS
Catch The Fall (Virgin)
I blame the parents. On this evidence it's clear that Mr & Mrs Dolphin sent their boys to piano lessons when they could have been more usefully employed listening to T Rex records.
NME

THE DREAM ACADEMY
Remembrance Days (blanco y negro)
One for opening eyes.
Melody Maker

More soporific than an overdose of sleeping pills.
Record Mirror

DUBSEX
Push! (Ugly Man)
This is the worst.
Sounds

Hear Dub Sex.
NME

E

EARTH WIND & FIRE
Touch The World (CBS)
Earth Wind & Fire In No Pyramid Shock!
NME

The real issues raised by *Touch The World* are where have Earth Wind & Fire been that they don't appear to have heard any contemporary music?
Q

ECHO CITY
Songs From The Black Country (Rough Trade)
Echo City spend half their time installing huge lengths of plastic pipe and metal bars all over the country, and the rest trying to get other people to play it, supplying the hard bits themselves. The result is this LP, and a fine thing it is.
NME

DUANE EDDY
Duane Eddy (Capitol)
Duane Eddy has assembled a lot of hacks like Paul McCartney, Art Of Noise, Jeff Lynne and Ry Cooder to make his record for him. They've cocked it up naturally.
Melody Maker

E*I*E*I*O*
That Love Thing (Demon/ Frontier)
After the anonymity of their debut, E*I*E*I*O* have at least decided who they want to be. There's no good news involved, however: they want to be Huey Lewis.
NME

ELECTRO HIPPIES
The Only Good Punk . . . Is A Dead One (Peaceville)
While you've been reading this review the Electro Hippies have played another 13 songs.
NME

ERASURE
The Innocents (Mute)
"Soul I hear you calling," he wails, "Oh baby please give a little respect to me!" Maybe it's the lack of pretence, maybe it's the leotard, but Erasure can get away with such utterings while top "soul bands" like Wet Wet Wet and Hue & Cry fall flat on their smug faces.
NME

Nothing apart from a rusty six-inch nail scraped thrice across the vinyl, can disguise the simpleton delineated roles, the clean space in the mix for Bell's sobs, the neat, even numbered backing from Clark. And to think Depeche Mode were worried when he left.
Melody Maker

Why can't I like Erasure?
Sounds

RANDY ERWIN
Cowboy Rhythm (Heartland)
One's first urge on hearing this is to laugh at it. Then *with* it and then to finally admit this guy can sure yodel, and furthermore that he should yodel.
Melody Maker

Yodelayheehoo, what the hell does that mean?
Record Mirror

Heck, the first track, 'She's All Wet' has hardly any yodelling at all!
Sounds

THE ESSENCE
A Monument Of Trust (Midnight Music)
This has just got to be Robert Smith perpetuating some unfathomable practical joke.
Sounds

★

EURYTHMICS
Savage (RCA)
Ah me. Annie Lennox and Dave Stewart. What an odd couple they are and what a jolly odd LP this is.
Smash Hits

It's so attractive and so nasty.
Q

EVERYTHING BUT THE GIRL
Idlewild (blanco y negro)
One to roll about on the bedroom floor to. The crumbliest, flakiest of releases.
Record Mirror

How on earth can Tracey sing such a weedily pretentious couplet as "So here we are in Italy/With a sonnet and a dictionary" with such a po-faced voice?
Smash Hits

Pretty mega in the wee small hours of the morning bracket.
NME

Music for young single schoolteachers only.
Melody Maker

EXHIBIT B
Play Dead (Pentagon)
Wanders round like it's just fallen out of some dodgy Bistro or student's union bar wearing a pair of smelly Green Flash tennis shoes and a lifetime's supply of Clearasil.
Sounds

EXPOSÉ
Exposure (Arista)
Arista should have sent out warnings with each and every review copy bearing the legend, "Do not play this record straight after the new Chic/Sister Sledge one with the terrible sleeve and 16 trembling beauties within and not even within the same week if your memory is up to anything." They didn't.
Melody Maker

F

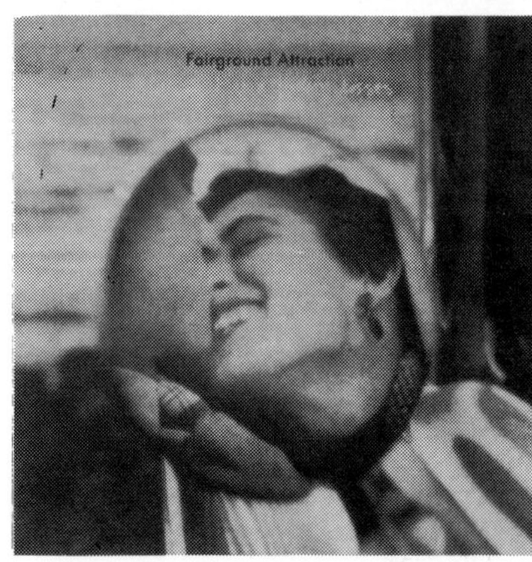

FAIRGROUND ATTRACTION
The First Of A Million Kisses (RCA)
I met a bloke from RCA the other day, and he still seemed to be nursing a vague disbelief that 'Perfect' was within kissing distance of the nation's number one.
Sounds

If they are "pop" it is along the same channels as the Goombay Dance Band or The Darts. I'm sure Gloria Hunniford plays it to death.
Melody Maker

Statements such as "Abble diddl-e wa do ay" ('Clare') succeed with loopy authority.
NME

FAITH NO MORE
Introduce Yourself (London)
What they didn't tell you of course was that Michael Ryan had this on the Walkman as he strode up the High Street that afternoon.
Melody Maker

TAV FALCO
Panther Burns (New Rose)
There are eight songs here and six are excellent; the remaining two are only very, very good . . . one of the last humans alive who understands rock 'n' roll.
Sounds

THE FALL
The Frenz Experiment (Beggars Banquet)
Quite good really, if you don't mind people who can't sing.
Smash Hits

It's all part of a tentative move towards the mainstream.
Q

We're talking industrial strength weird.
NME

And that's weird in its original sense of supernatural rather than its colloquial meaning of queer or incomprehensible.
Sounds

FAT BOYS
Crushin' (Urban)
Gone are the admirable paeans to baked beans and apple crumble, in their stead are . . .
Melody Maker

. . . self-mocking ironies about the sexual battlefield that reveal The Fat Boys to be a lot wittier than many more fashionable rappers.
Q

Perhaps they should have been born as Barry White in triplicate.
NME

FELT
Gold Mine Trash (Cherry Red)
Rhythms that lay you down and start massaging every inch of your body until you're so relaxed, so happy, so contented that you just want to turn circles.
NME

FELT
The Pictorial Jackson Review (Creation)
Barking mad and blithering onward. All the way round the bend.
Melody Maker

He is a strange fellow – obsessed with frozen food and air freshener – the kind of recluse the pop world needs . . . Recommended for deckchair listening.
Record Mirror

BRYAN FERRY
Bete Noir (Virgin)
It's difficult to imagine a more tasteful pop object than Bryan Ferry.
NME

Music that's as easily beautiful yet as distant as the Himalayan mountains.
Record Mirror

Rather like a Siamese cat wrapping itself around you, but contemplating scratching your eyes out.
Smash Hits

FISH CAKE SHAKE
Do The Heart Beat (Probe Plus)
The voice is coming right from the bottom of a deep sea diver's boots.
Melody Maker

FIREHOSE
"if 'n" (SST)
Nope, I haven't got a clue what it means either but it had me wondering for hours.
NME

CLIMIE FISHER
Everything (EMI)
In olden days Simon Climie and Rob Fisher would have remained a faceless pair knocking out off-the-peg songs for other brighter personalities to make their own.
Q

In my more persecuted moments I imagine that things like this are sent as divine examination.
Melody Maker

I'd written the first part of this review before playing the record.
Sounds

FISHER-Z
Reveal (Arista)
Never mind as if punk never happened, this is a world where ABC never happened, where Spandau Ballet changed the face of rock and where Magnet Records called the shots.
NME

FIVE STAR
Between The Lines (Tent)
Let's face it 'Somewhere Somebody' is just like falling in love, the way it goes oops and the way it goes aaaah and the way it goes phew.
Melody Maker

The really burning question of the whole LP: just where did such a supposedly sheltered child learn to laugh like that and do her parents know about it?
Q

Wood Green shopping city has been committed to vinyl.
NME

★

THE FLAMING MUSSOLINIS
Charmed Life (Epic)
They should either work with Stock, Aitken and Litigation, or go barking mad on drugs.
NME

DAN FOGELBERG
Exiles (Full Moon/Epic)
In the fifties or eighties anyone with a name like Fogelberg would've been renamed Danny Vengeance or Danny Torrent. But Fogelberg's roots are in the early seventies with The Eagles, which is a hell of a place to have your roots, and he was probably christened Danny Torrent and changed it to Fogelberg.
NME

THE FOLK DEVILS
Goodnight Irony (Situation Two)
Folk Devils? Nah. More like wee little demons twittering around on the edge of your consciousness.
NME

To hear people balk, talk and squawk about The Folk Devils with fear in their eyes, you'd sometimes think that here we had a bunch of rabid psychopaths with immunity from restraint, which wouldn't be too far from the truth.
Melody Maker

JULIA FORDHAM
Julia Fordham (Circa)
It's very commercial in a stale pink marshmallow sort of way, I can't see it appealing to many *Melody Maker* readers.
Melody Maker

She might just end up in the ranks of Joan Armatrading.
Sounds

THE FOUNTAINHEAD
Voice Of Reason (China Records)
The 'I's have been dotted and the 'T's most definitely crossed.
Sounds

The Fountainhead are Simple Minds on Valium.
NME

SAMANTHA FOX
Samantha Fox (Jive)
This LP will sell millions of copies, our Sammy will marry the boy next door and there'll always be an England. Ain't life grand!
Smash Hits

FRA LIPPO LIPPI
Light And Shade (Virgin)
I like this record, yet if I were Peruvian then I'd like it a whole lot better.
Sounds

FRANK CHICKENS
Get Chickenized
(Flying Lecords)
More songs about urban neurosis in Tokyo, the Japanese obsession with Western hamburger culture and the subordination of women in Japanese society. It doesn't read like a bag of fun but it is.
Q

You always know where you are with Frank Chickens, even if that somewhere is really nowhere, you always feel you've been someplace. But where? Hard to say.
Sounds

FREIWILLIGE SELBSTKONTROLLE
FSK In Dixieland (Ediesta)
With the aid of my German 'O' Level, I can pronounce the name of this band and impress my friends. Beyond that I'm as much in the dark as anyone else.
Sounds

FSK
Continental Breakfast
(Ediesta)
Some of the bits to which I have most rolled around on the floor while rubbing myself all over include a country/hillbilly dirge whose roughly-translated title is 'In Praise Of Cybernetics'.
Melody Maker

FRENCH, FRITH, KAISER, THOMPSON
Live, Love, Larf & Loaf
(Demon Records)
The first Cubist record of the week from some extremely Cubist people. John French is the original drummer with Captain Beefheart. Fred Frith is founder of famed British weirdos Henry Cow. Henry Kaiser is seemingly in a world of his own and he plays the guitar with the kind of impatience usually reserved for live gerbils on hotplates. Richard Thompson is a founder member of Fairport Convention so you'll know all about him. Previously, according to the sleeve-notes, this album has been issued in Borneo. Why?
Melody Maker

Wild Wrinklies strike back!
Record Mirror

FULL FORCE
Guess Who's Coming To The Crib (CBS)
Full Force are knobheads because they've penned some of my very favourite pop songs over the last year or two – 'I Wonder If I Can Take You Home', 'Private Property', 'Head To Toe' and 'Playing With Fire' – and they've *given them all away*.
Melody Maker

G

GANG GREEN
Another Wasted Night
(Funhouse)
"I drink Budweiser religiously," bawls Chris Doherty on the title track, giving us an insight into one half of Gang Green's gospel. The other half is skateboarding. And despite having practically no musical ability, they promote both activities with relish.
Sounds

ART GARFUNKEL
Lefty (CBS)
Then there's the track 'King Of Tonga' about the smirking monarch whose sole social duty is to deflower all the island's virgins. Disgusting.
NME

GAYE BYKERS ON ACID
Drill Your Own Hole (Virgin)
INNOVATIVE! DANGEROUS! SEXY! Well blow me down but would you believe that NOT ONE of these adjectives could be applied to this LP?
NME

Oh why didn't their mothers drown them at birth?
Record Mirror

DEBBIE GIBSON
Out Of The Blue (Atlantic)
Once you get past the rather worrying warning on the sleeve – "I would like to thank Billy Joel whom I have never met, but remains an inspiration to me always" – the songs are more like Madonna than anything else.
Smash Hits

GLASGOW
Zero Four One (Zero Four One)
If I see another sodding review which sneeringly quotes a soul singer's "Thanks To God" – a searing target for satire, no doubt, but an aged one – or expresses surprise at the mediocrity of a HM band's lyrics (as opposed presumably to the wit and genius of most HM band lyrics), I shall visit all the schools in the country and kill every child who expresses an interest in writing about pop for money.
NME

GLASS TIGER
Diamond Sun (Manhattan)
The prototype for Ian Faith, manager-figure in *Spinal Tap*, was Glass Tiger's manager, Derek Sutton.
Melody Maker

GARY GLITTER
C'mon . . . C'mon – The Gary Glitter Party Album (Telstar)
This is a crap record, naturally. But Gary's patent inability to hold a tune and the hopelessness of the band don't really matter.
Record Mirror

GILLAN GLOVER
Accidentally On Purpose
(Virgin)
These are the men who one million years ago practically invented heavy metal as we know it today.
Smash Hits

In some corner of Hell the bastard scum who invented heavy metal will one day receive their due punishment; they'll have to play their crap music for ever.
NME

GODFATHERS
Birth, School, Work, Death
(Epic)
They remind me of a schoolboy I once knew who claimed to be related to Henry Winkler. The Fonz. His failures, which were manifold, were transformed (he hoped) by his braggadocio "I might do it crap but I do it cool." No one was convinced, but there was a germ to admire.
Melody Maker

LOUISE GOFFIN
This Is The Place (WEA)
Offspring of Carole King and Gerry Goffin, who penned many a classic in the sixties and seventies.
Record Mirror

By now Louise Goffin must be tired of reading that she is the daughter of songwriting partners Gerry Goffin and Carole King.
NME

Her parents don't mean a doodly-squat to a journalist fledgling such as myself, although anyone whose surname rhymes with coffin and boffin and do you come here often? automatically gets the sympathy vote.
Melody Maker

GORE
Mean Man's Dream
(Ediesta/Red Rhino)
Imagine the deadest, most inhuman moments in Black Sabbath, Black Flag, Butthole Surfers, Killing Joke, Swans. Imagine if someone collated all this bludgeoning sludge, this scatomatic churning, into a seamless cycle of butchery without end or purpose. That's the sound of Gore.
Melody Maker

GRATEFUL DEAD
In The Dark (Arista)
A nasty shock for those who've dug the hole, selected the casket and have just been waiting for the Dead to drop in.
Sounds

The seven year itch has done them good. They've enjoyed a rest and now they've woken up to find themselves almost fashionable again.
Q

AL GREEN
Greatest Hits: Vol 2 (Hi)
Al Green hushes the words "since you've been gone," in the love-sick 'Oh Me Oh My (Dreams In My Arms)', and you almost suffocate with the truth.
Melody Maker

NANCI GRIFFITH
Little Love Affairs (MCA)
Nanci Griffith gives us dreams. Fluffy clouds of goodness and badness.
Melody Maker

Cline could've hardly told it better.
NME

She leaves the likes of Dwight Yoakam drowning in their shallow puddles of beer.
Record Mirror

GUADALCANAL DIARY
2×4 (Elektra)
This album does little to change my impression that 2×4 refers to a big lump of wood.
NME

GUANA BATZ
Rough Edges (ID)
Available on CD? How many Guana Batz fans own CD players?
NME

GUNS 'N' ROSES
Appetite For Destruction
(Geffen)
"Contains lyrics which some people may find offensive." Thus bleats the teasing sticker that's been stuck on the end of this cartoon monster's snout. What kind of people? The kind of codger that G 'n' R might offend are all relegated to walking frames.
NME

H

SAMMY HAGAR
Sammy Hagar (Geffen)
Of course, the way to do it is to whack on the headphones, crank up the sound, and pretend you actually are Sammy Hagar – bending every riff out of the tennis racquet, squeezing every lick out of the broom.
NME

HALF MAN HALF BISCUIT
Back In The DHSS
(Probe Plus CD)
Half Man Half Biscuit on CD? Okay, so you don't expect to find lo-fi punk groups on such a medium, but for the purposes of history, longevity and all that they probably deserve it.
Melody Maker

DARYL HALL AND JOHN OATES
Ooh Yeah! (Arista)
Their appreciation of the soul tradition combines well with their studio suss.
NME

Since Daryl Hall and John Oates re-invented themselves in the mid-seventies, their handling of all things soulful has never been less than convincing.
Q

JAN HAMMER
Escape From TV (MCA)
On TV this is fine, but on vinyl . . . flowery aural wallpaper.
Q

THE HAPPY END
Resolution (Cooking Vinyl)
As songs for swinging socialists go this is both an enjoyable and happily non-sermonizing collection.
Q

There's more genuine politics in The Pogues or The Band Of Holy Joy.
NME

HAPPY FLOWERS
My Skin Covers My Body
(Homestead)
They don't like the sun because they say it burns, they're bored when it's raining, they want to eat ice-cream, not food that is good for them, they hate the girls in their class, especially Jenny, because she wanted a kiss at recess, and they throw an unparalleled paddy when Mommy brings home a baby instead of a puppy.
Melody Maker

GEORGE HARRISON
Cloud Nine (WEA)
George Harrison was most definitely the nicest Beatle.
NME

He was the oddest of the Beatles.
Q

The boy The Beatles called in to make up the numbers.
Melody Maker

George Harrison used to be a complete and utter hippie. Only people who used to be complete hippies would call their LP *Cloud Nine*, come up with some long and ponderous songs like 'Just For Today' and 'Breath Away From Heaven' and waffle on (in 'This Is Love') about how all the world's problems would be solved if we all loved one another and everything. But he also used to be a Beatle.
Smash Hits

JERRY HARRISON
Casual Gods (Fontana)
The sort of thing that Jerry Harrison does to fill in the time while David Byrne is out wearing his grass suits, dealing with the stuff that's too dumb for people to have bothered formulating opinions on.
Melody Maker

TED HAWKINS
Dock Of The Bay – The Venice Beach Tapes II
(American Activities)
Just about everyone knows about Ted Hawkins these days – he's the man who looks like Ritchie Havens and sings like Sam Cooke might have after swallowing a cup of crushed glass.
Sounds

HAWKWIND
Xenon Codex (GWR)
A studio album. Their first in three years. It's not that they split up or anything it's just that they like to sleep for long periods. A bit like the *Blue Peter* tortoise.
Sounds

OFRA HAZA
Yemenite Songs (Globestyle)
If you thought 'Im Nin' Alu' was totally brilliant you'll like this, but if you thought it was a funny woman wailing you probably, er, won't.
Smash Hits

No one complains about not being able to understand Cocteau Twins lyrics.
Record Mirror

HEAD
Tales Of Ordinary Madness
(Virgin)
The loopy celebration of a misplaced maleness that says it's going out for a pint of milk and ends up playing football in the park with the lads for the rest of the morning.
Melody Maker

Head have all the faded glamour of an alcoholic ex-movie star caking her face with panstick in an effort to postpone her inevitable demise.
Record Mirror

HEAVENLY BODIES
Celestial (Third Mind)
It has a habit of leaving me in strange physical positions. It contradicts me and maddens me. I applaud its nerve and leave myself open, and highly impressed. Smart sleeve too.
Melody Maker

THE HELLCATS
Cherry Mansion (New Rose)
I believe that at least one of The Hellcats has ridden pillion with Tav Falco, which accounts for some of the authenticity infused into this rock and roll.
NME

THE HEPBURNS
The Magic Of The Hepburns
(Cherry Red)
The Alarm they are not. At last something sensible and stupid and serious has come out of Wales.
NME

The record begins with 'I'll Be Back Before The Milkman', a brief shimmering melancholy joy which captures the essence of a useful dawn better than almost any pop song in history.
Melody Maker

HOTHOUSE FLOWERS
People (London)
What an extraordinary tale this is! Bloke gets "discovered" by Bono, forms group, they release two singles, go on Eurovision Song Contest, get zero points, become pop stars and release an LP which goes straight to the top of the Irish charts. But is it any good? Yes it is, actually.
Smash Hits

THE HOUSE OF LOVE
The House Of Love (Creation)
I haven't got to grips with the words yet, but I imagine they're about the moments so precious they make you terribly aware of mortality.
Melody Maker

THE HOUSEMARTINS
The People Who Grinned Themselves To Death
(Go! Discs)
I go to the window and shout to the world outside, "This record is brilliant!" Because it is.
NME

The Housemartins are not a nice group. Their second album confirms that behind the smokescreen of their fab four football/fun loving boy next door image lurks the most critical and discontented group in the charts.
Record Mirror

About how horrible Mrs Thatcher is, how silly pop stars and trendy people who wear black all the time are, how wicked people who tear up our cities and carve up the countryside are etc. etc. etc.
Smash Hits

THE HOUSEMARTINS
Now That's What I Call Quite Good (Go! Discs)
They came, they saw, they thought "Pthrthrthr! I'm off." And they left (Sniffle).
Smash Hits

LAVINE HUDSON
Intervention (Virgin)
It's a cat-walk on exacting imagination (or truth, if you happen to be an *NME*-reader and a believer that's indulgently graceful without having to seem unrealistic).
NME

Abso-bloody-lutely excellent.
Melody Maker

ROBIN HYTCHCOCK & THE EGYPTIANS
Globe Of Frogs (A&M)
Regular as a cock's crow. And just as dreaded. A sod you want to shoot, or at the very least throw a boot at.
NME

His brand of bouncy psychedelic pop grows on you like a jolly giant toadstool.
Q

I LUDICROUS
It's Like Something Else
(Kaleidoscope Sound)
They want to make a film dedicated to all those who never made it, in which every time someone gets shot the screen goes black for five minutes.
Melody Maker

I Ludicrous have got their priorities sorted. They know there's no hope for any of us. They know humanity is fatally flawed and life, like Manchester United, Spurs and all Scottish goalkeepers, is completely and utterly Ludicrous.
Sounds

ICE T
Rhyme Pays (Sire)
When not engaging in unsufferably active sexual intercourse with a variety of women, turning down pleading requests for help from Gucci and Ronald Reagan, or killing people, Ice T likes to hang around with a man called MC Fosterior – surely a first for rap music – and tell you about his quite amazing personal wealth.
NME

BILLY IDOL
Idol Songs: 11 Of The Best
(Chrysalis)
He is a punk. Yes, even now.
Melody Maker

IGGY AND THE STOOGES
Metallic 2xKO (Jungle)
A pity that he failed to fling some abuse towards his band. They certainly deserved it.
NME

At one point Iggy's heard to mumble "it ain't too easy bein' in the Stooges sometimes." Too true, especially when there's a heavy duty crew of bikers in the crowd just itchin' to bust his head.
Sounds

IRON MAIDEN
Seventh Son Of A Seventh Son (EMI)
They choose not to write songs about foxy chicks, Chevrolets, rock 'n' roll etc., but opt for "weightier" topics usually about the world of mythology. And they've really gone for it this time. This is a "concept" album, i.e. the whole thing is a bit of a story all about this bloke who, because he's the seventh son of a seventh son, has special occult powers and the forces of good and evil have to battle it out for possession of his soul. In other words it's a load of pretentious old guff. And the music's not much better.
Smash Hits

IT BITES
Once Around The World
(Virgin)
A heavy wager on the finished product coming packaged in one of those cosmic Roger Dean sleeves with a hulking great spaceship hovering over some spooky planet.
NME

J

MICHAEL JACKSON
Bad (Epic)
Four hundred years in the making. Five million musicians, stylists and associates credited, "Michael Jackson's heartbeat recording by Dr Eric Chevlen in the Synclavier." No expense spared.
Smash Hits

Important words: Woo! Hee-hey! Aaow! A-acha-acha! Ooh! China-Chika! Uhh! mpenziwe! Na-nah! Dah! Root-do-do!
Melody Maker

The earth won't move but floors will shake. And to this day nobody goes "Aaow!" like Michael Jackson.
Q

MICK JAGGER
Primitive Cool (CBS)
We find it impossible to take seriously anyone capable of prancing around in front of 100,000 people wearing a lime-green polyester tracksuit and scarlet shinpads. It doesn't matter how good their songs are, how serious their lyric or whether 20 years ago they were Satan – it always comes back to those shinpads.
Melody Maker

THE JAZZ BUTCHER
Fishcotheque (Creation)
The Jazz Butcher (real name Pat Fish) has always suffered from the common assumption that he's professionally whacky.
Q

'Get it Wrong', however, is funny, a playful, waltzing tale of broken love with witty lyrics: "One mistake and it all gets bitchy/Start listening to records by Lionel Richie."
Sounds

JAZZY JEFF AND THE FRESH PRINCE
He's The DJ I'm The Rapper
(Jive)
By teenagers, for teenagers, a nice record – inoffensive, decent and friendly.
NME

JELLYBEAN
Just Visiting This Planet
(Chrysalis)
The overall effect is that of the playlist from the sort of disco that gives out free tickets outside foreign language schools.
Q

BILLY JENKINS AND THE VOICE OF GOD COLLECTIVE
Scratches Of Spain
(This Sliced Slice)
Imagine arriving in Benidorm. The man next to you on the coach has already lost his dentures while throwing up duty-free tequila, you reach the half-built hotel, tuck into paella and chips and sit back for the cabaret. Oh no, it's Billy Jenkins.
Q

THE JESUS AND MARY CHAIN
Darklands (blanco y negro)
If 'Psychocandy' was teen angst then this is mid-twenties resignation.
Record Mirror

The Jesus And Mary Chain – still the greatest fun there is in a Lou Reed T-shirt, pondering the leap from the edge of the world.
Melody Maker

JIM JIMINEE
Welcome To Hawaii
(Cat and Mouse)
Sleeve of the year so far. All the Jiminees disguised as an encyclopaedia sales team standing on Bognor beach squinting. Why's the album called *Welcome To Hawaii* then? Because they've got exotic garlands round their necks that's why.
NME

RICHARD JOBSON
Sixteen Years Of Alcohol
(Les Disques du Crepuscule)
The record packaging, like an After Eight, spells sophistication; just as the book included with it, and its Cocteauesque drawings, cry culture.
Melody Maker

ELTON JOHN
Live In Australia With The Melbourne Symphony Orchestra (Rocket)
Of interest to committed fans and people who like "classy" sleeve designs, hysterical sleeve notes and pictures of Elton dressed as Mozart.
Smash Hits

JOHNNY HATES JAZZ
Turn Back The Clock (Virgin)
JHJ make the sort of noises indicative of childhoods spent being chosen last for pick up games of rounders.
Sounds

An immaculate pop record.
NME

STEVE JONES
Mercy (MCA)
Sex Pistols with Dire Straits producer shock horror.
Record Mirror

JUDAS PRIEST
Ram It Down (CBS)
As Kenneth Williams might have said, "Carry On Judas Priest."
Sounds

THE JUSTIFIED ANCIENTS OF MU MU
Who Killed The Jams? (Jams)
Bill Drummond, his mind doubtless wonderfully concentrated by the cost of litigation invited by his unauthorized samplings on the first Justified Ancients Of Mu Mu album, decides to concentrate on re-writing famous songs rather than pirating performances.
Q

K

KANDA BONGO MAN
Amour Fou/Crazy Love (Hannibal)
Kanda Bongo's chubby, gap-tooth smile matches his stage name. He just added "man" to the moniker he was born with and turned into a star.
NME

SALIF KEITA
Soro (Sterns)
Last year he didn't even have the money to get home, and he didn't have a record deal, and he didn't have a band. All he had was a philosophical attitude, and the most beautiful voice in the world.
NME

KILLING JOKE
Outside The Gate (EG/Virgin)
Rooted in the madness of the world as opposed to the turbulence within Jazz's cranium.
Record Mirror

PAUL KING
Joy (CBS)
It's really like Bananarama singing 'Anarchy In The UK'.
Record Mirror

You won't believe me but this is a good record.
Melody Maker

KOOL MOE DEE
How Ya Like Me Now (Jive)
This is the kind of thing that goes down a storm at South London youth clubs.
Sounds

L

LA GUNS
LA Guns (Vertigo)
While there is a potentially wild imagination, a fresh enthusiasm, at play on this album, it's entirely stifled by LA Guns' perplexing fixation with prehistoric riffs.
Melody Maker

ANNABEL LAMB
Brides (RCA)
Annabel hasn't moved on, simply deeper. With a blindfold on, which is a tragic waste.
Melody Maker

Odious in the extreme. The sort of stuff Sting would make a black and white video to.
Sounds

k.d. lang
Shadowland (Sire)
When her voice and the gliding steel guitar chase each other ever upward, you could forgive her anything.
Melody Maker

THOMAS LANG
Scallywag Jazz (Epic)
A peaceful album, but in places there's too little of the scallywag and too much of the snoozy jazzzzz.
NME

How can these women sing such sad songs when they're obviously having so much fun?
NME

HUGO LARGO
Drum (Land)
They call it electrified chamber music. I call it extra-terrestrial Country & Western.
Sounds

More than half an hour of this would be too much pleasure to endure.
Melody Maker

THE LEATHER NUN
Steel Construction (Wire)
A strange attempt to remake a silly sort of mid-period Lou Reed record. Personally, I think they should stick to demolishing Abba.
Record Mirror

LEGENDARY PINK DOTS
Any Day Now (Play It Again Sam)
Legendary Pink Dots have discovered that if you borrow a church organ from any pre-synthesizer age horror movie, add it to the backing track from *Doctor Who* and then transpose it into a couple of songs, you'll finish up with one of the most tedious albums ever made.
Sounds

LEVERT
The Big Throwdown (Atlantic)
This amounts to something close to a vacuous version of Vandross. In addition, I personally find it embarrassing for men of this age to be imploring "don't you think it's time we made love?"
Melody Maker

THE LILAC TIME
The Lilac Time (Fontana)
All this slushy melody and honeycomb harmony. All this dusty, crusty bedsit colour. Delightful. Just what we need.
Melody Maker

LIME SPIDERS
Volatile (Virgin)
I'd hazard with some conviction that Lime Spiders would be absolutely hyper-phenomenal dynamite live in a grotty basement after 68 manly pints.
Melody Maker

LIVING COLOUR
Vivid (Epic)
They've set themselves up as a black Led Zeppelin, a bundle of contradictions about to change things for ever.
NME

Imagine Cameo jamming with The Red Hot Chilli Peppers and you're halfway there.
Record Mirror

The first significant response to the challenge Prince has been posing throughout the eighties.
Sounds

Living Colour are better as a concept than as a band.
Melody Maker

RICHARD LLOYD
Real Time (Celluloid)
Indicative of his most pungent moments.
Melody Maker

A performance which indicates his time has definitely come.
Sounds

JOHNNY LOGAN
Hold Me Now (Epic)
The fact that he's seen fit to do a cover version of 10cc's 'I'm Not In Love' and roped in Paul Hardcastle to perform a rather lame "production job" is a good example of the underlying naffness of the whole project.
Smash Hits

JULIE LONDON
Feeling Good (Liberty)
Everybody should have an LP like this in their collection. Why? Because this is diamonds and fur coats and money and gold rings. The essentials.
NME

LOOP
Heaven's End (Head)
Heaven's End is designed to fiddle with your preconceptions: it spits like the mid-seventies, it looks like the late-sixties and it has decided to shoot its load all over the eighties.
Record Mirror

THE LORDS OF THE NEW CHURCH
Live At The Spit (Illegal)
If this was an episode of *Spinal Tap*, it would be hilarious. But as it is reality it's actually quite horrific.
NME

LOVE AND ROCKETS
Earth, Sun, Moon (Beggars Banquet)
One massive apocalyptical explosion generating 60 minutes of the purest, most beautiful Bowie/Bolan permutations you could ever imagine.
NME

An enjoyable pot-addled trip back into psychedelic folkiness.
Q

LYLE LOVETT
Pontiac (MCA)
Beautifully played and produced, *Pontiac* is country that cuts through the corn with a scalpel.
Q

An uneven collection that far too often slips into the murky waters of misogyny – a new tune for the same old country song.
NME

NICK LOWE
Pinker And Prouder Than Previous (Demon Fiend)
The bimbo explosion currently sweeping the nation's charts is merely a stop-gap until Nick Lowe finds the time to claim the Top 40, the bars, the stadia and, yes, even the shopping malls as his own by right.
Sounds

A waste of talent and a waste of money. Your money.
Melody Maker

THE LUCY SHOW
Mania (Big Time)
Juddering, streamlined musical beats, rampant with possibility.
Q

Cool melodic exchanges between the guitars and vocals.
Melody Maker

LUDUS
Nue Au Soleil (Les Disques Du Crepuscule)
A queer musical series of yoga postures for the guitar – a lot of sticking of knees behind ears.
Record Mirror

These songs resemble the torrid rages and flailing manias of an irrational, impetuous child.
Melody Maker

LYDIA LUNCH
Honeymoon In Red (Widowspeak)
The sound of dying America.
NME

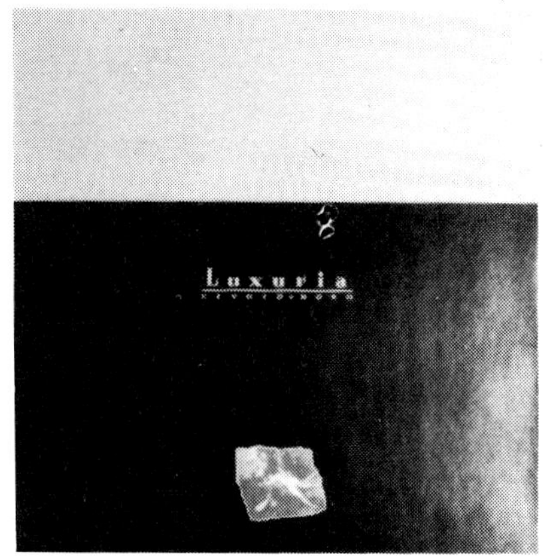

LUXURIA
Unanswerable Lust (Beggars Banquet)
Howie is back, and – thank heavens – he's still as arrogant, miserable and twisted as ever.
Q

The light of laughter still pours from Devoto, uplifting and making tolerable his disturbing honesty.
NME

Devoto has always been a cheeky rock maverick.
Sounds

A fairly poor and repetitive Magazine album and is a catalogue of uproarious philosophical allusions.
Melody Maker

M

MADAME X
Madame X (Atlantic)
If you take this album to a party, be sure you take some condoms too.
Melody Maker

THE MADNESS
The Madness (Virgin)
The sound of loadsaconscience.
Sounds

Chas now calls himself Cathal. As if that made any difference.
Melody Maker

MADONNA
You Can Dance (Sire)
Recommended for serious party boppers only.
Record Mirror

She knows she's leading you on, but you'll never catch up.
NME

Hopefully after the disappointing *Who's That Girl* soundtrack Madonna will remember that it was brilliant records like this that made her brilliant in the first place.
Smash Hits

MANFRED MANN'S EARTHBAND
Masque (Ten Records)
You'd be surprised how many people have confessed to being introduced to Bruce Springsteen via Manfred's version of 'Blinded By The Light'.
Sounds

MANTRONIX
In Full Effect (Ten Records)
Their records are like chemistry sets. A little of this blue stuff, a phial of that, add a little heat . . . there it is! Music!
Sounds

MARDEN HILL
Casaquez (El)
The worst record of all time apart from *Naked* by Talking Heads, and El Records can quote me on that at £250 per sentence.
Melody Maker

A world where *The Avengers'* John Steed forever seems to be creative controller and Emma Peel works the A&R Department.
Record Mirror

TEENA MARIE
Naked To The World (Epic)
The wild white girl of Motown (rtd) links up with Rick James again and reminds us of a whole slew of things we were forgetting about late seventies R&B.
NME

Off her trolley in an artistically magnificent and funkily righteous way.
Melody Maker

MEAT PUPPETS
Heuvos (SST)
The best album of 1974.
NME

MEGADETH
So Far, So Good . . . So What! (Capitol)
True, it's an intensely ugly noise, but at least there's a suggestion that they don't take themselves too seriously.
Record Mirror

The gruesome noise of corpses in the machinery.
Melody Maker

THE MEKONS
New York (Roir)
A testament to human courage and dignity in the face of complete drunken ineptitude.
Record Mirror

THE MEMBRANES
Kiss Ass Godhead (Glass)
Stomping around the seafronts of the EEC in their big floppy boots, The Membranes are the UK's Grateful Dead. Well, sort of.
NME

MENTAL AS ANYTHING
Mouth To Mouth (Epic)
Most Aussie groups tend to be dodgy at times: Mental As Anything are no exception.
Smash Hits

It's bound to do well in Finland. They like a good time over there I've heard.
Sounds

THE MICE
Scooter
(What Goes On Records)
It occasionally sounds like The Who at their most virulent, but who cares? When the Mice get going, the tough get out of the way.
Record Mirror

A scouring brush made of gold.
NME

GEORGE MICHAEL
Faith (Epic)
So why do we say "Oh George Michael . . . can't say I like him but I respect him. He's a craftsman, he's good at his job"? Do we say "That milkman's a bloody genius, he's good at his job" or "I reckon that lollypop lady's a genius because she get's the kids across the road okay"? No, we don't. So it's high time we stopped praising efficiency as if it were inspiration.
Melody Maker

THE MIGHTY LEMON DROPS
World Without End
(Blue Guitar)
If you play this LP loud enough your corpuscles might indeed be coiled.
Smash Hits

MINIMAL COMPACT
The Figure One Cuts
(Crammed Discs)
A refined way to get very depressed.
Sounds

★

ENNIO MORRICONE
Film Music 1966–1987
(Virgin)
Just about essential. Not to say that it's the perfect Morricone collection, just recognizing there's nothing else in this particular league.
NME

VAN MORRISON
Poetic Champions Compose
(Mercury)
A collection of deep devotion and powerful inspiration.
NME

A patchy, uneven affair, Morrison leaving the work half-undone.
Melody Maker

And who else could get away with name-dropping folks like Plato and Socrates in a mere song?
Record Mirror

VAN MORRISON AND THE CHIEFTAINS
Irish Heartbeat (Mercury)
Morrison's most thrilling stylistic manoeuvre since his 1980 masterpiece *Common One.*
Sounds

Pure glory.
Melody Maker

MORRISSEY
Viva Hate (HMV)
Those Morrissey disciples who blub away in their bedrooms or whatever it is you're supposed to do to Morrissey's more miserable offerings will find songs like 'Everyday Is Like Sunday' and 'Late Night, "Maudlin Street' very "poignant" and "touching".
Smash Hits

The King's crown may have slipped but it refuses to fall.
Sounds

N

NAPALM DEATH
Scum (Earache Records)
Occasionally it's groovy, but generally it's a mess.
Sounds

And on the cover the dreadful warning: "28 songs of intense, maniac and savage brutal hardcore trash"! This isn't essentially accurate.
Melody Maker

Writing as a wimp this is too much for me.
NME

TYKA NELSON
Royal Blue (Cooltempo)
But is she, ahem, *that* sister? You know the one he wrote so affectionately about on the *Dirty Mind* album.
Sounds

THE NEW DANCE ORCHESTRA
The Light Programme (Geffen)
A conscious attempt to produce a *Dark Side Of The Moon* hi-fi test for the eighties.
Q

NEW ORDER
Substance (Factory)
It starts out with the wonderful jangly guitars and haunting melody of 'Ceremony' and then wobbles all over the place.
Smash Hits

New Order chop, dice and disembowel with psychotic finesse. This, the world now knows, is why New Order are great and Siouxsie and The Banshees sort of aren't.
Melody Maker

As long as there's New Order there's a choice.
Record Mirror

PIETER NOOTEN/MICHAEL BROOK
Sleeps With The Fishes (4AD)
If God ever chooses a soundtrack for heaven it'll be this.
Record Mirror

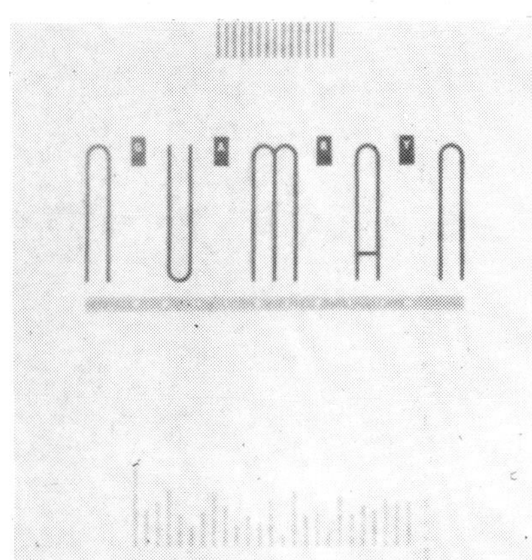

GARY NUMAN
Exhibition (Beggars Banquet)
He wanted so much to be taken seriously, but he always looked daft in his funny hats and his plastic catsuits, and he had a voice like David Bowie holding his nose very hard.
Smash Hits

O

SINEAD O'CONNOR
The Lion And The Cobra (Chrysalis)
Sinead could write 40 verses about Christina Onassis and still make it sound like some swishy-skirted Gaelic folk-rock song.
NME

'I Want Your (Hands On Me)' is the best title Sam Fox has never seen fit to use.
Melody Maker

THE O'KANES
Tired Of Running (CBS)
These boys sound mighty mournful like the dog just died, or the finance company repossessed the car, or the wife's just left for another woman.
Sounds

ALEXANDER O'NEAL
Hearsay (Tabu)
It's a sort of concept album (maan) with the songs following a problematic relationship during the course of a party at Alex's place (cue tinkling glasses and catty gossip).
Smash Hits

ORCHESTRAL MANOEUVRES IN THE DARK
The Best Of OMD (Virgin)
Two of the nicest blokes you could meet, with a very silly name for the last ten years.
Smash Hits

ORIGINAL SOUNDTRACK
Hearts Of Fire (CBS)
Even Eric Clapton's contributions cannot disguise Dylan's fall from grace.
Sounds

OUTLOOK
Outloud (WEA)
Whether he's making it or shaping it, Nile Rodgers' knack for producing music that fills dancefloors is undeniable.
NME

Don't be fooled by the sticker on this appalling album cover which reads "Outlook features Nile Rodgers" – it's an evil trap!
Record Mirror

THE OYSTER BAND
Wild Blue Yonder (Cooking Vinyl)
Forget your Hey Nonny Morris Men. This is folk music of burning wicker men, and bloodied maypoles in the shopping malls.
Melody Maker

Folk music need never be boring again.
Q

P

RAY PARKER JNR
After Dark (WEA)
An album memorable only for highlighting the difference between what Parker believes he can do and what he is actually capable of.
Q

PARTNERS IN GRIME
Ivor Biggun (Dead Badger)
The high point of the album was reviewing it without playing it, then selling it.
NME

DOLLY PARTON
Rainbow (CBS)
Dolly has indeed ascended to Soap Opera heaven, right up there with Joan and Princess Di.
Melody Maker

Signed up to a deal where she must deliver one rock and country LP every year. This is the sort of idea that crapheads like. Yet not even crapheads could approve of this stinking album.
NME

HERMENTO PASCAL AND GROUP
Hermento Pascal And Group (Brasil Universo)
There is apparently no instrument he can't play and nothing that doesn't count as an instrument, whether it's barrel organ pipes or children shouting their names (he once used a live piglet on stage to produce a squealing sound effect). Side two indeed features a chorus of squeaking chickens.
Q

PEBBLES
Pebbles (MCA)
A compromise between the company's desire to sell and one woman's good intentions . . . Pebbles pouts and poses for the camera and hopes you'll be able to read between the lines.
NME

I believe in Pebbles.
Record Mirror

PEPSI & SHIRLIE
All Right Now (Polydor)
The music is either slow or fast. If you're soft you can cry to it. If you're hard you can dance to it. The tunes you can remember and, well I never, the singers actually wrote some of the songs and are really singing on them. Put that in your precious pop pipe and smoke it.
NME

Top Shop here we come!
Q

PET SHOP BOYS
Actually (Parlophone)
"S.H.O.P.P.I.N.G., we're shopping." It's almost a camp Kraftwerk and will no doubt be dismissed by dullards who refuse to believe that The Pet Shop Boys know about being funny.
Melody Maker

The Pet Shop Boys are elegantly unique and dead funny, and you should love them for it.
Sounds

1987's most intelligent, bittersweet mainstream pop album.
Q

Weak and disappointing. Do you really want to know why Neil is yawning? Because he's patronizing you in your role as a consumer . . . What a creep.
NME

COURTNEY PINE
Destiny's Song And The Image Of Pursuance (Antilles)
Hell, by jazz standards he ain't even born yet.
Record Mirror

THE PINK FAIRIES
Kill 'Em And Eat 'Em (Demon Fiend)
Students of the Keith Moon percussion technique.
Sounds

Old rockers never die, but their songwriting sure loses its flavour on the bed post overnight.
Q

PINK FLOYD
A Momentary Lapse Of Reason (EMI)
The main question is whether this constitutes a valid Pink Floyd album without the participation of their erstwhile leader. And the answer is that it does. Superficially at least, and that's probably as far down as most people can be bothered to get in 1987.
Sounds

A Momentary Lapse Of Reason does sound like a Pink Floyd album.
Q

THE PIXIES
Come On Pilgrim (4AD)
Words like "dainty" and "childlike" are not applicable round these parts.
Q

Lots of strange psychological disturbances.
NME

"Where is my mind?" smirks huggable Black Francis, and you can't help but rattle your jewellery.
Melody Maker

THE POGUES
If I Should Fall From Grace With God
(Pogue Mahone Records)
Movement and life ooze from its grooves like the pus from one of Shane MacGowan's yellowheads.
Record Mirror

No longer based on traditional Irish music, but the words all seem to be about the same old Poguey things like dying, drinking and winning lots of money on the horses.
Smash Hits

THE POINTER SISTERS
Serious Slammin' (RCA)
The first thing to do when you've got to review an album like this which is going to be exactly the same as ten thousand other albums, is to look at the credits and find the funny dedications in between the ones to God, Jesus Christ, loving and talented parents, and He from whom all blessings flow. The best one is Ruth Pointer's sincere "thank you" to "my dearest friend Max Difray, who deals with my hair, even when it's turned into a dead dog."
Melody Maker

POISON
Open Up And Say . . .Ahhhh!
(Enigma/Capitol)
Next to Poison you realize just how sophisticated Mötley Crüe really are, while W.A.S.P. begin to look positively existential.
Q

IGGY POP
Instinct (A&M)
A dodgy fagged-out old rocker.
Record Mirror

It's a bit like meeting God down the pub.
Melody Maker

POP WILL EAT ITSELF
Box Frenzy (Chapter 22)
I don't think this band have tried too hard to conceal their crappiness.
Sounds

PREFAB SPROUT
From Langley Park To Memphis (CBS/Kitchenware)
Quite why the melodic and crafted *Langley Park* is a truly delicious record is making me

scratch my bonce like a koala with sunstroke.
Melody Maker

Praise must be lavished on arranger Thomas Dolby who has, once again, decorated McAloon's interior with stunning designs.
Sounds

Thomas Dolby's production – he can't leave a simple song alone.
NME

ELVIS PRESLEY
The All-Time Greatest Hits
(RCA)
Play these records and you will instantly turn into a wriggling tadpole of dementedness, you will weep with the mention of it and you will think to yourself "what a bloody genius!" You will not be wrong.
Smash Hits

THE PRETENDERS
The Singles (WEA)
Chrissie swells into motherhood, becoming the new Carly Simon for the eighties.
Record Mirror

MAXI PRIEST
Maxi (Ten Records)
A solid reggae feel.
Sounds

A droopy reggaefied drizzle.
Smash Hits

I'm not altogether sure this is a reggae album.
Record Mirror

PRINCE
Lovesexy (Paisley Park)
The one thing he is wearing on the cover is a crucifix on a chain; on the inner sleeve "Lovesexy" is defined as "The feeling U get when U fall in love not with a girl or a boy but with the heavens above" and lots of the songs seem to be as much about loving God as about making love to other people (though he seems quite partial to both).
Smash Hits

Maybe he should spend a little less time in the studio and a touch more out in the street before he ends up playing with his own concepts instead of other people's flesh.
Q

PSEUDO ECHO
Love An Adventure (RCA)
What can you say of an LP on which the one outstanding moment is the moronically infectious metallic thrashing of Lipps Inc's dancefloor chartbuster, 'Funkytown'?
Q

The dumper beckons.
Smash Hits

PUBLIC IMAGE LIMITED
Happy? (Virgin)
No longer fierce, nor funny, nor fine. Just one long-time dying whine.
NME

Q

QUEENSRYCHE
Operation Mindcrime
(EMI Manhattan)
Dwelling with relish, it often seems, on pain, fear, misery and degradation. It gropes a trough of human suffering and offers up little in the way of hope or relief.
Sounds

R

JESSE RAE
The Thistle (WEA)
You spend 364 days trying your best to show the uncaring uninquisitive English of the South East that the Scots are not just a bunch of haggis-bashing, och-aye-the-noo retards and then come down a bunch of football fans or, worse, Jesse Rae.
Q

THE RAILWAY CHILDREN
Recurrence (Virgin)
Nothing silly, nothing vulgar, not a note out of place – nothing, in fact, to suggest that The Railway Children like a good laugh or get drunk or feel like screaming, indeed do anything other than go to art school and design dull album sleeves.
Sounds

The kind of record a group would make just after their second double album.
Melody Maker

THE RAINMAKERS
Tornado (Mercury)
Twisted tales and fantastic voyages, provocative religious imagery and detached views of love . . . proof that there's hope for America yet.
Q

THE RAMONES
Halfway To Sanity
(Beggars Banquet)
Never have so few chords been played so often so brilliantly.
Sounds

THE RAMONES
Ramone Mania (Sire)
The Ramones make The Clash seem like A-ha, Gabba Gabba Hey.
Record Mirror

These hoarse songs are perfect pop because a crowbar couldn't shift 'em.
Melody Maker

ALAN RANKINE
She Loves Me Not (Virgin)
The lights are on . . . but nobody's home.
Sounds

RATTLESNAKE ANNIE
Rattlesnake Annie (CBS)
Folk, blues and country meet in Rattlesnake Annie's voice like some well-balanced stew.
Q

RAYMONDE
Raymonde (Blue Guitar)
Even Morrissey et al might be astounded at the sort of homage this group appears to pay to them.
Q

RAZORCUTS
Storyteller (Creation)
40 minutes of diluted pop charm by grown men who are trying too hard to sound like they've just had puberty thrust upon them.
Sounds

CHRIS REA
Dancing With Strangers
(Magnet)
Pleasantly wistful old-time rock, for people who think that Robert Palmer is too modern, Dire Straits too mega and Marillion too pissed.
Record Mirror

THE RED HOT CHILLI PEPPERS
The Uplift Mofo Party Plan
(EMI)
The harsh, howling bastard son of steaming white funk, pale-faced rap with the aesthetics of go-for-broke hardcore chucked in for good measure.
Sounds

So this is where all the funk went . . . the bass bending ludicrousness of George Clinton melts, ecstatically, into Prince's spunk-funk.
Melody Maker

RED LORRY YELLOW LORRY
Nothing Wrong (Situation Two)
This "album" consists of one song played 11 times.
Melody Maker

DIANNE REEVES
Dianne Reeves (Blue Note)
While her acrobatic range shows a depth of emotion, her sense of phasing, from abandoned scat to smoky ballads, is never short of impressive.
Q

R.E.M.
Document (IRS)
R.E.M. successfully mix current issues with past musical styles: The Byrds, Neil Young and Bob Dylan regularly crop up. A flawed masterpiece.
Record Mirror

They have made a more conventional record, true, but only more conventional to them.
NME

A bit like being hit by an avalanche.
Melody Maker

RENALDO AND THE LOAF
The Elbow Is Taboo
(Some Bizzare)
Yup, we're talking weird here.
Record Mirror

THE REPLACEMENTS
Sorry Ma, Forgot To Take Out The Trash (What Goes On)
This 18-track cornucopia of early Replacements hate-flail will steamroll your head.
Sounds

The sound of Middle America's children gone mad, strung out on drugs and bad dreams, on the rampage, clumsy, violent, hopes for the future sprawled desolate across the tracks.
Melody Maker

THE RHYTHM SISTERS
Road To Roundhay Pier
(Red Rhino)
A curious mixture of bluegrass bitterness and Boots cosmetic kits.
Sounds

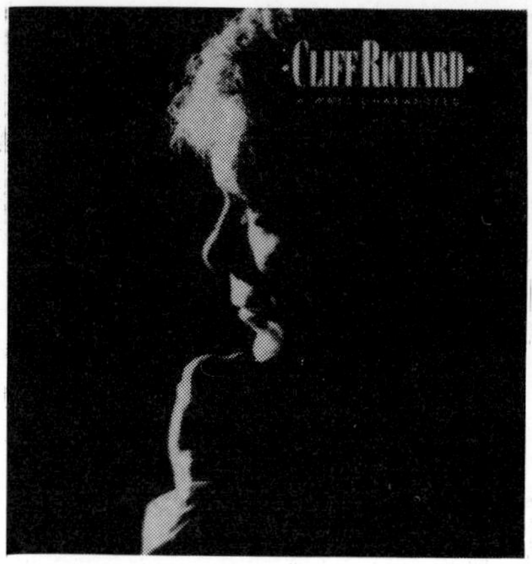

CLIFF RICHARD
Always Guaranteed (EMI)
Hopelessly out of his depth, you can imagine him sweating as he strings together those trite dance steps in a frantic bid to keep up.
Q

JONATHAN RICHMAN AND THE MODERN LOVERS
Modern Lovers 88 (Demon)
Jonathan Richman Makes Dance Record Shock!
Melody Maker

He's 37 going on 11.
NME

ROBBIE ROBERTSON
Fallen Angel (Geffen)
A tarnished jewel, a record that glows intermittently with his particular craft.
NME

Space does not permit a full description of Robertson's variety, drive, emotional impact or sexiness.
Sounds

ROBBIE ROBERTSON
Robbie Robertson (Geffen)
A long, intensely detailed landscape of contemporary rock.
Sounds

TOM ROBINSON
The Collection 1977–1987
(EMI)
Robinson's geniality and humanity shines through, even on the duffers.
NME

ROGER
Unlimited! (Reprise)
Roger is a historian of funk who sets out to show that the distance between Sam Cooke and LL Cool J is not so great.
NME

LINDA RONSTADT
Canciones De Mi Padre (Elektra)
A bit hokey, but flagging careers have been revived by dafter ploys than this one.
Q

DAVID LEE ROTH
Skyscraper (Warner Bros)
David Lee Roth's music is probably all the positive therapy most people will ever need.
Sounds

Rather like spending an hour with a neurotic child.
Q

What a prat.
Melody Maker

KEVIN ROWLAND
The Wanderer (Mercury)
An album of robust, romantic, healthily inebriated neo-classic songs: the word "baby" occurs 72 times, the term "middle class bitch" only once.
Record Mirror

Rowland's most confident, cohesive LP. Not his best, but probably his most emotional.
Melody Maker

This complacent Kevin Rowland is a disaster in creative terms.
NME

Naturally, no one expected him to continue whipping his body for the sake of his soul.
Sounds

He'll probably never be a pop star again but at least he's never boring.
Smash Hits

DAVID RUDDER AND CHARLES ROOTS
This Is Soca (London)
If calypso is the life-blood of carnival, then David Rudder is undisputed king of its festivities.
NME

RUFFIN AND KENDRICKS
Ruffin and Kendricks (RCA)
Give these men some proper songs immediately.
NME

RUN DMC
Tougher Than Leather (London)
Will do serious damage to your record player and good neighbourly relations . . . in every sense, Run DMC kick ass.
Sounds

Way ahead of the competition.
Record Mirror

The Ramones of rap, playing with the limits, seeing how far they can go.
NME

Run DMC are simply thrashing around with clumsy obesity. This album is as soft as their stomachs.
Melody Maker

TODD RUNGREN
Anthology (Raw Power)
If Rungren ever has anything approaching a major hit, it will be totally by accident.
NME

BRENDA RUSSELL
Get Here (A&M)
Brenda Russell's reputation as a soul singer is nowhere bigger than in Sweden.
Q

RUSH
Hold Your Fire (Vertigo)
Each work is a progression from the last.
Q

They keep getting better.
Sounds

Locked in a timewarp.
NME

S

SADE
Stronger Than Pride (Epic)
She's now an artist's impression of herself.
NME

Is it boring? Well of course it is. Relentlessly so.
Sounds

Sade always has been crap.
Melody Maker

SALT 'N' PEPA
Hot, Cool And Vicious (Champion)
A smiling, teasing strut straight down the centre of those hard bitten rap boulevards.
Sounds

CARLOS SANTANA
Blues For Salvador (CBS)
Carlos has stopped stumbling nowhere and, has at last, let his guitar speak for itself.
NME

SAVAGE REPUBLIC
Tragic Figures (Fundamental)
A Californian nightmare carving their vindictive initials onto traditional rock's tombstone.
Sounds

SAXON
Destiny (EMI)
Sounds suspiciously like the purr of a clapped out rusty scooter rather than the roar of a gleaming chrome Harley Davidson powerslave.
Record Mirror

SCARLET FANTASTIC
24 Hrs (Arista)
A ridiculous indulgence, a jaded Hollywood bauble, founded only its own say-so.
Sounds

BRINSLEY SCHWARZ
Please Don't Ever Change (Edsel)
Edsel's wilful desire to ruin what fond memories anyone might have of Brinsley Schwartz is a cruel, bastard thing.
NME

THE SCIENTISTS
The Human Jukebox (Karbon)
If they were applying for a grant I'd not even listen to their plea.
NME

THE SCREAMING BLUE MESSIAHS
Bikini Red (WEA)
All the essential requirements for survival in the modern world.
Q

The Screaming Blue Messiahs have never been quite this close to the edge before.
Sounds

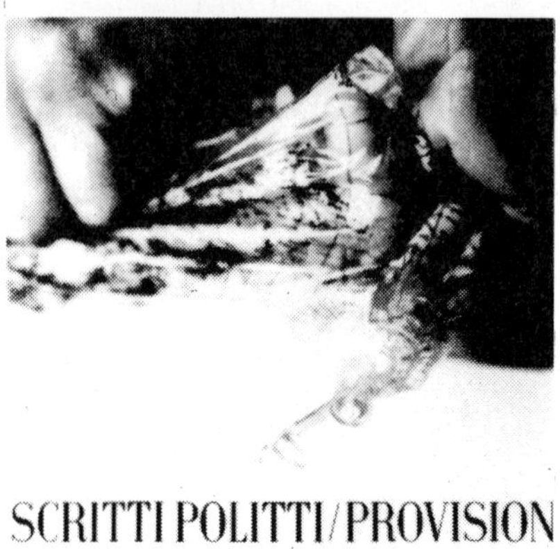

SCRITTI POLITTI
Provision (Virgin)
The aural equivalent of three months holiday in the Bahamas.
Record Mirror

The Scritti sound seems to have frozen into an archaic irrelevancy.
Melody Maker

SHAKIN' STEVENS
Let's Boogie (Epic)
The greatest living Welshman.
Melody Maker

SHALAMAR
Circumstantial Evidence (MCA)
The name has been rented out to three exploitative mulattos who mistake crass licentiousness for an inspired heart.
Melody Maker

SHAM 69
Angels With Dirty Faces (Receiver Records)
It only takes one prick to make a band, and in this case we're considering Jimmy Pursey.
Melody Maker

FEARGAL SHARKEY
Wish (Virgin)
Forget the fancy threads next time you go shopping, how about some songs?
Sounds

Flat on its back in a warm bed of pound notes.
Melody Maker

CYBILL SHEPHERD
Mad About The Boy (Les Disques Du Crepuscule)
Economy class Billie Holiday.
Melody Maker

ANDY SHEPPARD
Andy Sheppard (Antilles)
As different as it is possible to be from the by-the-yard jazzy soul arrangements that pollute most chart stuff at the moment.
NME

THE SHRUBS
Take Me Aside For A Midnight Harangue (Ron Johnson)
At best it's a Ubu-ist delirium of language, an avalanche of charm without purpose.
Melody Maker

JOYCE SIMS
Come Into My Life (London)
Stick to the single.
Q

SINITTA
Sinitta! (Fanfare)
The Christmas party record for wallies of all ages.
Record Mirror

THE SISTERS OF MERCY
Floodland (Merciful Release)
It thinks it has a lot to say about water and submission to sex, but is merely the sound of drowning.
NME

THE SKINNY BOYS
Skinny And Proud (Jive)
US hip hop seems to be entering a creative malaise . . . I mean, who really cares if people prefer to look anorexic?
NME

LYNYRD SKYNYRD
Legend (MCA)
Playing 'Freebird', Skynyrd were utterly horrible. Playing anything else they're merely a competent bar-room boogie band.
NME

SLAYER
Live – Undead (Road Runner)
Caught here in a retrospectively noisy 1984 tour, Slayer bring you the sound of Thora Hird negotiating a sewage outlet against her will.
Melody Maker

THE SMITHEREENS
Green Thoughts (Enigma)
The Smithereens are a pop music metaphor for hyper-realism.
Sounds

THE SMITHS
Strangeways, Here We Come (Rough Trade)
It reads like a suicide note and explains just why everything had to stop.
Sounds

Really just more of the same, torn between Morrissey's puerile urge to antagonize convention and outrage the public, and his more intellectual aspirations to actually achieve something positive.
Melody Maker

A masterpiece in terms of poetic, pop and emotional power.
NME

SNAKEFINGER'S VESTAL VIRGINS
Night Of Desirable Objects (Red Rhino)
Enjoy this album for its eccentric good humour, its amiable confusion of musical genres and its total lack of taste.
Q

THE SOFT BOYS
Live At The Portland Arms (Glass Fish)
A splendid insight into Robyn Hitchcock's youth and a still useful companion piece to his more recent escapades.
Sounds

SON OF SAM
Rich And Famous (Rouska)
Loads of barbed wire glamour and ideological grooviness, this is a record of no great significance whatsoever.
NME

THE SOS BAND
1980–1987: The Hit Mixes (Tabu)
A large number of these records I'd describe as "girl's tunes."
NME

THE SOUP DRAGONS
This Is Our Art (Sire)
There's no comparison between the *now* Soupies and the tatty little charmers they once were.
NME

Proves that life after the indie Top Five need not automatically mean detrimental big-label compromise.
Sounds

SPAGNA
Call Me (CBS)
If Spagna's 'Call Me' drove you round the twist this year, you'll be disgusted to learn that the girl with no nose has released a whole album of the song.
Melody Maker

RONNIE SPECTOR
Unfinished Business (CBS)
Nothing like The Ronettes.
Q

SPK
Digitalis, Ambigua, Gold And Poison (Nettwerk)
As bands whose name refers to excising parts of the male genitalia go, SPK are pretty dull.
Sounds

RICK SPRINGFIELD
Rock Of Life (RCA)
Naturally enough, there's not a single spark of innovation.
Sounds

BRUCE SPRINGSTEEN
Tunnel Of Love (CBS)
If *Born In The USA* was Springsteen's Goliath, then *Tunnel Of Love* is certainly his David.
Sounds

A chastened, harsh and often surprisingly humble record.
Melody Maker

Pop music is all about simple tunes and Springsteen's are worth every last cent of his billions.
NME

Maybe getting married has sent him all squiffy in the head.
Smash Hits

THE SQUARES
Enjoy Yourself . . . And Others (Boat)
Clearly made with very little cash.
Sounds

SQUEEZE
Babylon And On (A&M)
Expertly performed yuppie oriented R&B.
Record Mirror

A band for teachers who can't yet afford their first compact disc.
Melody Maker

In their own way they're building a career as substantial and durable as, say, Randy Newman.
Q

STATUS QUO
Ain't Complaining (Vertigo)
They almost succeed in being interesting.
Smash Hits

MARTIN STEPHENSON AND THE DAINTEES
Gladsome, Humour And Blue (London)
A wealth of quirky, quality, warm songs.
NME

I can see this album being played in every bedsit in the land.
Melody Maker

JERMAINE STEWART
Say It Again (Siren)
A sad symptom of the ever-expanding airhead soul scene.
Sounds

Camp as a row of tents.
NME

ROD STEWART
Out Of Order (Warner Bros)
An awful lot of this sounds like U2.
Melody Maker

The usual nonsense.
NME

Whatever the state-of-the-art backing, you can't disguise the fact that it's Rod, hollering away and talking through his cock.
Sounds

STING
. . . Nothing Like The Sun (A&M)
Has the makings of a very good single LP, but sticking out a double album of this stuff is pushing it just a little.
Record Mirror

Another exercise in tasteful music making.
Sounds

The most pretentious record I've ever encountered.
Melody Maker

THE STOOGES
Rubber Legs (Fan Club)
Loud, lusty and almost unbearably frightening.
Melody Maker

RICHARD STRANGE AND THE ENGINE ROOM
Going Gone (Interphon)
The perfect solution for those who think "intelligent pop" is a contradiction in terms.
NME

THE STRANGLERS
All Live And All Of The Night (Epic)
As live albums go, it's a respectable stab at capturing the growth of The Stranglers from their "One, two, three go!" era to their strange emergence as new age musicians.
Record Mirror

JOE STRUMMER
Original Soundtrack From *Walker* (Virgin)
If the movie turns out to be rubbish it certainly won't be Joe Strummer's fault.
Q

Sees Strummer's fascination with the ethnic reach its zenith . . . proves that Strummer didn't need to be Syd Barrett to preserve his myth.
Melody Maker

STUMP
A Fierce Pancake (Ensign)
A mixture of *Monty Python* and *The Owl And The Pussycat* set to a cra-zee soundtrack of twanging guitars and cardboard box banging.
Record Mirror

THE STYLE COUNCIL
Confessions Of A Pop Group (Polydor)
The best LP The Council have ever made and it's still retarded.
NME

A hollow, humourless sham of a record by a couple of yobs with nob pretensions.
Sounds

Some rather pious, mannered "soul" style music.
Smash Hits

Weller's entire career has been a history of ill-advised haircuts and lamentable musical gestures.
Melody Maker

THE SUGARCUBES
Life's Too Good (One Little Indian)
The Cubes are a continuation of that brilliant experiment engaged in by The Slits before dressing like a pillock became all important.
NME

They're not just weirdos; they're also capable of producing entertaining and excitingly original rock music.
Smash Hits

Unique in that almost every claim ever made for a great LP is true of *Life's Too Good*.
Melody Maker

SUICIDAL TENDENCIES
Suicidal Tendencies (Virgin)
Unless you've got a gap in your Dead Kennedy's collection, ignore this.
Record Mirror

ANDY SUMMERS
XYZ (MCA)
No muso is ever a good songwriter and half the trouble with musos is you can't tell them this.
NME

SUPERTRAMP
Free As A Bird (A&M)
An immoral waste of resources.
NME

THE SWANS
Children Of God (Product Inc)
Four sides of Swansmusic could be taken as overkill, but then few have ever listened to The Swans for light relief.
Q

KEITH SWEAT
Make It Last Forever (Elektra)
The most accomplished debut from a male soul artist since *Alexander O'Neal* . . . oozes class, confidence and control.
NME

SWEET HONEY IN THE ROCK
Breaths . . . The Beat Of (Cooking Vinyl)
Instruments could only adulterate their sweet and pure *a cappella.*
NME

SWEETHEARTS OF THE RODEO
Sweethearts Of The Rodeo (CBS)
A sprightly collection of tunes that would not disturb a southern Holiday Inn on Saturday night.
Q

Route 88's second division.
Sounds

DAVID SYLVIAN AND HOLGER CZUKAY
Plight & Premonition (Virgin)
Precious, pompous, pale, passive, almost perfunctory, pious, plain, pointless . . .
Melody Maker

We had it coming.
NME

T

TACKHEAD
Tackhead Tape Time (Tackhead)
They scour the bottom of the aspirin box in the quest for the hardest possible dance beat.
NME

TALKING HEADS
Naked (EMI)
A cosmopolitan kiln where an exotic mixture of soul, Caribbean, African, Latin and Western pop are baked into glossy hardness, with occasional colours of cajun and blues flashed across them.
Sounds

Wildly giddy, terrifyingly mundane and very nearly perfect.
Melody Maker

It's great that the Heads have the freedom to create the sort of record they want, but it's dull to listen to.
Record Mirror

TANKARD
Chemical Invasion (Noise)
Sod *Clutching At Straws*, this is *real* heavy drinking stuff: thrash metal's answer to Slade and Chas & Dave.
Sounds

THE JAMES TAYLOR QUARTET
The Money Spider (Re-elect The President)
The kind of boys who would've hung around in milk bars in the early sixties brandishing Calibri cigarette lighters, only they hadn't been born.
Q

TOT TAYLOR
My Blue Period (London)
Flaunts his unhealthy fixation for Cole Porter and Frank Sinatra across two sides of soul-sucking plastic.
Q

T-BONE BURNETT
The Talking Animals (CBS)
Listening to this humorist, humanist and amused observer of human folly is like having a slightly demented cousin regale you with a succession of infinitely convoluted, infinitely intruiging yarns.
NME

THE TEMPTATIONS
Together Again (Motown)
At worst soporific, at best . . . pleasantly soporific.
NME

10 cc/GODLEY & CREME
Changing Faces – The Best Of . . . (Polydor)
The fact that there is currently no one around quite like 10 cc may be a considerable relief to many people.
Record Mirror

Possibly the only group ever to benefit from involvement with Jonathan King.
NME

10,000 MANIACS
In My Tribe (Elektra)
12 songs that ring with both accessibility and credibility: songs with melodic tunes, atmosphere and poetic words.
Sounds

A consistency of tone and purpose they've not achieved before.
Q

TEST DEPT.
A Good Night Out (Some Bizzare)
Perfectly mirrors spiritual decay in post-welfare state Britain and as such defines the field upon which the battle for modern music and politics rests.
NME

TEST DEPT.
Terra Firma (Sub Rosa)
Too much said, too little explained. Hardly the firm ground we were expecting.
NME

THESE IMMORTAL SOULS
Get Lost Don't Lie (Mute)
More downward aspirants melodramatizing their feelings of despondency and dispossession.
Q

THEY MIGHT BE GIANTS
They Might Be Giants (Rough Trade)
Boasts song titles like 'Youth Culture Killed My Dog', 'Alienation's For The Rich' and 'Nothing's Gonna Change My Clothes' and matches them with lyrics just as funny.
Q

THIN WHITE ROPE
Bottom Feeders (Zippo)
Capable heirs to Creedence Clearwater Revival's dark rock 'n' country carnival.
Q

THIRD WORLD
Hold On To Your Love (CBS)
The album to re-establish Third World's primacy and confirm them as one of the few reggae groups ready and able to address the post-Marley challenge.
Q

13TH FLOOR ELEVATORS
The Psychedelic Sounds Of The 13th Floor Elevators
(Decal)
22 years on everyone knows about the Elevators, but still few have heard them. This time don't miss out.
Melody Maker

THIRTEEN MOONS
Origins (Wire)
Billy Bragg's enthusiasm for such an apparently humourless bunch is rather puzzling.
Q

GEORGE THOROGOOD AND THE DESTROYERS
Born To Be Bad (Manhattan)
Deliberately gives the impression that its songs were recorded in one no-expense-incurred late night session.
Q

He'll keep a lot of drunks very happy.
Sounds

3MUSTAPHAS3
Shopping (Globestyle)
They breed fabulous hybrids of Central European, North African, Middle Eastern and Western pops.
NME

A charming album from the United Nations house band.
Sounds

Peerless lunacy from these Creole Albanians.
Record Mirror

THREE WIZE MEN
GB Boyz (Rhythm King)
At last, a new starting point for British rap.
NME

THROWING MUSES
House Tornado (4AD)
Music for the Mad Hatter's tea party.
Record Mirror

If someone said "This is depressing, take it off", late at night, I'd understand and comply.
Melody Maker

TIFFANY
Tiffany (MCA)
About one more half-hit should see the end of this particular "phenomenon"
Smash Hits

Its phenomenon conceals the fact that nothing's happening.
Melody Maker

In ten years' time she'll be falling out of your copy of the *TV Times* on a piece of card advertising C&A clothes.
Sounds

TIMBUK 3
Eden Alley (IRS)
The unexpected success story of new country.
Melody Maker

PETER TOSH
No Nuclear War (Parlophone)
His spirit, troubled, committed, proud and occasionally generous, lives on, even in this shadowed, distended collection.
NME

TOTO
The Seventh One (CBS)
No cigar for guessing what the eighth one will be like.
Melody Maker

T'PAU
Bridge Of Spies (Siren)
The sound inhabits a hitherto no-go area somewhere in between Heart and Lena Zavaroni.
Sounds

Don't buy this record expecting to find a few more versions of 'Heart And Soul', because there aren't any.
NME

Hot on the heels of 'Heart And Soul', T'Pau unleash a collection of several thinly disguised reworkings of the same.
Record Mirror

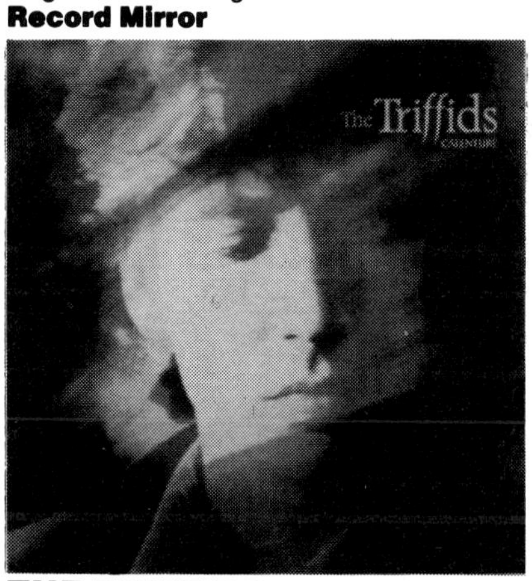

THE TRIFFIDS
Calenture (Island)
A loud, almost blaring album. A classic of its kind, baroque, overflowing with exaggerated emotions, epic gestures.
Melody Maker

I found myself wishing the drama would let up from time to time.
NME

THE TRIO BULGARKA
The Forest Is Crying
(Hannibal)
These three voices soar over peaks and harmonies so close you can imagine a huge electric pylon humming solitarily and mysteriously in a wide open plain.
Melody Maker

JETHRO TULL
On The Crest Of A Knave
(Chrysalis)
The entire album oozes pathos.
Q

TINA TURNER
Tina Live In Europe (Capitol)
Purely and unashamedly a grab at the purse strings of the very loyal and the very gullible.
Sounds

TUXEDOMOON
Pinheads On The Move
(Crammed Discs)
Perfectly illustrates the subterranean channels between street rhetoric and the performance-art/sound-lab culture.
Melody Maker

TWISTED SISTER
Love Is For Suckers (Atlantic)
Extols a Sladean let's-get-drunk-and-have-fun philosophy with self-deprecating humour and rugged music that remains strong rather than heavy.
Q

BONNIE TYLER
Hide Your Heart (CBS)
The most fascinating thing about Bonnie Tyler Inc is the total absence of authenticity, of sincerety.
Sounds

UB40
The Best of UB40 Vol 1
(DEP International)
There's a full discography showing just how many good tunes had to be left out.
Smash Hits

A back catalogue worth listening to.
Record Mirror

THE UNDIVIDED
The Original Undivided (Mango)
The Undivided prove as adept as ever at translating the horn-dominated sounds of ska into a reggae context that has a timeless quality all its own.
Sounds

UNSEEN TERROR
Human Error (Earache)
A wild test of stamina, this music for lunatics. I went and made a cup of tea straight afterwards and the kettle had a musical majesty previously unnoticed.
Melody Maker

UT
In Gut's House (Blast First)
Nasty girls making a dirty noise, wailing like she-devils over a harrowing backdrop of drums, guitars and violins.
Record Mirror

These women could be shopping-mall psycho-killers.
Melody Maker

Unreasonably adult music.
NME

UTFO
Lethal (Select)
UTFO scratch and sample Prince and Marvin Gaye to a set of rhythms with precious little regard for neighbours or migraine sufferers.
NME

V

RITCHIE VALENS
Greatest Hits (RCA)
You've seen the movie: now check out the real thing.
Melody Maker

THE VALENTINE BROTHERS
Picture This (EMI America)
A picture of mainstream, flab-free soul with an extra cutting edge.
Q

VAN DER GRAAF GENERATOR
Now And Then (Magnum)
A motley collection of seventies cop show-type instrumentals, awful fake jazz and one other nice Hammill song.
NME

VAN HALEN
OU812 (Warner Bros)
Proof enough that there is life after David Lee Roth.
Sounds

Get a copy and somehow the days won't seem so long.
Record Mirror

TOWNES VAN ZANDT
At My Window (Heartland)
These ten songs are as enduring a mixture of folk and country as only Townes could consistently craft.
Q

THE BEN VAUGHN COMBO
Beautiful Thing (Enigma)
Reveals him to be closer to the Barron Knights.
Q

THE VERLAINES
Juvenilia (Flying Nun)
A flaring and snot-nosed sound, something an artistic and knowingly precocious adolescent would scream at the world outside.
Melody Maker

THE VIBRATORS
Recharged (FM Records)
A concerted attempt to recapture some of the gloss and energy of old, and as much as I'd love to say it's paid off, I can't.
Record Mirror

VICIOUS RUMOURS
The Sickest Men In Town (Link)
It's time they addressed themselves to the very real problem of having made a ludicrously poor LP.
NME

VIEW FROM THE HILL
In Time (NME)
You might call it finely-crafted, delicate, quivering with nuance. I call it lethargic and lackadaisical.
Melody Maker

THE VIRGIN PRUNES
Heresie (Baby)
This project is all about madness, incomprehension and non-understanding.
NME

VIRUS
Force Recon (Metalworks)
A slab of gnarled and grisly Nuclear Metal.
Sounds

VISIONS OF CHANGE
Visions Of Change (Firefly)
More filler than thriller.
NME

VOICE FARM
Voice Farm (Ralph)
Totally sexless – all boink and no bonk.
NME

VOICE OF THE BEEHIVE
Let It Bee (London)
Not just a highly promising debut LP, but one that screams for attention with a bloody great grin on its face.
Record Mirror

An impossibly rich album.
Sounds

This is serious singer-songwriter stuff in a ra-ra skirt, Suzanne Vega marketed, for fashionability's sake, as Bananarama.
Melody Maker

VOIVOD
Dimension Hatross (Noise)
Organized chaos, disorientating by design.
Sounds

Rides roughshod over metal's rhythmic formalities . . . offers a paranoid vision of technology gone mad.
NME

VOLCANO SUNS
Bumper Crop (Homestead)
Volcano Suns have the ability to stretch straight across the spectrum of sound, from splintering shards of thrash guitar to piano-drenched harmony.
NME

Takes the "indie guitar" no higher or lower, further or sweeter.
Melody Maker

VOW WOW
Vow Wow V (Arista)
Their style is copped straight from Deep Purple with the songs cut to more compact 1980s length.
NME

W

TOM WAITS
Frank's Wild Years (Island)
Subtitled "Un Operachi Romantico In Two Acts" – whatever that means.
NME

It provides the ideal soundtrack for a drunken joyride in a Cadillac.
Record Mirror

Life may be a bummer but with Tom it's never dull.
Sounds

WAS (NOT WAS)
What Up Dog? (Phonogram)
There is a thin line that treads between sheer genius and out and out dementia. This is a bit of both.
Smash Hits

Weird (but not that weird).
Record Mirror

W.A.S.P.
Live . . . In The Raw (Capitol)
If W.A.S.P. are out to sting you with their wit, I raise my glass of cow's vomit to them with half-hearted disgust. If they are out to frighten, shock and preach devil worship then I must stop eating small furry animals because Hell sounds like a really boring place.
NME

JODY WATLEY
Jody Watley (MCA)
Pure laughing gravy.
Sounds

DARRYL WAY WITH OPUS 20
The Human Condition (Venture)
Classical lovers will be irritated, pop fans confused, jazz buffs bored, rock fans comatose.
Q

THE WEATHER GIRLS
The Weather Girls (CBS)
Impetus enough to squeeze into a red sequinned backless number, bang the tambourine and . . . thrash it, babe.
NME

WE FREE KINGS
Hell On Earth And Rosy Cross (DDT)
Hell On Earth is a perilous descent down a worm-rotted helter skelter; arrival at the bottom brings relief and an irrational urge to climb straight back up to the top and suffer the experience once again.
NME

THE WEDDING PRESENT
George Best (Reception)
Pet Shop Boys sing "I love you, you pay my rent", but The Wedding Present are the thorn to remind you of the loved one that moved out in the middle of the night, leaving you with no furniture and a £600 phone bill.
Sounds

WENDY & LISA
Wendy & Lisa (Virgin)
More candyfloss than highbrow.
Q

A love affair on vinyl.
Sounds

WESTWORLD
Rockulator (RCA)
Westworld have an annoyingly high opinion of themselves.
Smash Hits

So far you've only wasted five minutes, don't waste five pounds.
Sounds

WET WET WET
Popped In Souled Out (Phonogram)
Marti Pellow whiles away his hours hoping for the critical acclaim he covets.
Sounds

Huge lumps of it were made by the band for the band.
NME

Their debut album sparkles with a superior pop (if not heart-wrenching soul).
Q

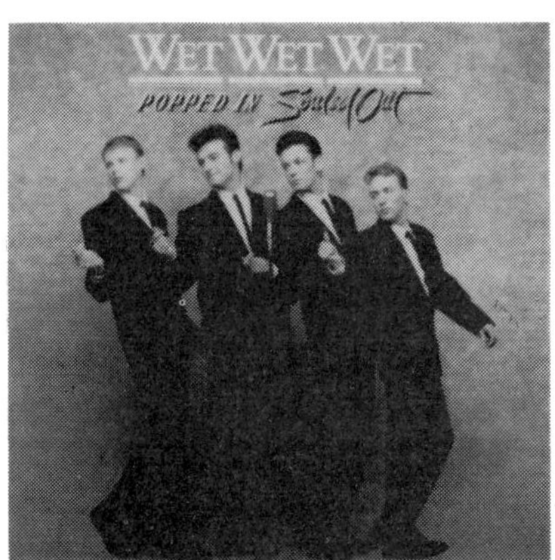

ANDY WHITE
Kiss The Big Stone (Decca)
Hark gentle people, Andy White has gone electric!
Sounds

It's not even that he's repressing anger. It sounds as if he's got none left to give.
Melody Maker

BARRY WHITE
The Right Night And Barry White (Breakout)
From the bowels of the earth a huge profound rumble. It sends tremors through your ankles, fondles the underside of the floorboards, and finally bursts through, like some benign, sensuous earthquake.
Sounds

The new Barry White largely concerns himself with that rum act that Mae West described as "emotion in motion".
Melody Maker

It's straight up to the master bedroom for a prolonged "sensual" romp on the bearskin rug.
Q

THE WHO
Who's Better, Who's Best? (Polydor)
Sorely illustrates their demise, charting the course of their fine pop thrash, through their pompous epic phase, to the days spent living off past glories.
Record Mirror

WHODINI
Open Sesame (Jive)
Don't expect to see Whodini make the hip hop first XI; they're most likely to be found in the pavilion making the sandwiches.
Sounds

KIM WILDE
Another Step (MCA)
She sells sexual imagery openly and calls it adult. Well, a few years ago the whole world did want to get into bed with Kim Wilde and now it just wants her autograph.
Melody Maker

Six months ago any interview with Kim Wilde would best have been conducted in a kiddies' playground, but these days in bed would be fine.
NME

SHANICE WILSON
Discovery (A&M)
Remember Janet Jackson's *Control* LP from 1986? Shanice Wilson's producer does.
Record Mirror

STEVE WINWOOD
Roll With It (Virgin)
Never less than solid, while this is mellow, refined and commercial, it's also totally lacking in even a smidgeon of SURPRISE.
NME

Aimed bullseye straight for the mainstream American adult market.
Sounds

WIRE
A Bell Is A Cup Until It's Struck (Mute)
For the first time in years it's not inconceivable for them to have a hit, a proper one, the sort that gets played on the radio. And for the first time in years you get the feeling that that's exactly what they want.
Melody Maker

Wire used to play pop and go pop! Now they're very odd. What does it mean? Who cares?
NME

BOBBY WOMACK
The Last Soul Man (MCA)
Calling your album something like that is a brave move, especially if one considers the Liverpudlian argot; however, Bobby Womack – armed with a voice like rusty engines and the worst glasses ever – has more claim to the title than most.
NME

We shouldn't make too much of the irony of the title.
Sounds

STEVIE WONDER
Characters (Motown)
An album of great scope and invention, his best since 1980's *Hotter Than July*.
Sounds

Far removed from the soppy cabaret-style artiste he has threatened to turn into over the last three years.
Q

Characters is Wonder rediscovering his talent and repaying us handsomely for the lax form he's shown in the past.
NME

I guess we'll just have to accept that, with a few exceptions, he now only makes pleasant MOR music.
Record Mirror

THE WOODENTOPS
Wooden Foot Cops On The Highway (Rough Trade)
The sort of record a group would make once they had blown their main chance.
Melody Maker

PETE WYLIE
Sinful (Siren)
If this album starts a revolution, I'll eat my copy of The Alarm's *Marching On* (with picture sleeve).
Sounds

Too much oxygen at birth.
Melody Maker

X

X
Live At The Whiskey A GoGo On The Fabulous Sunset Strip (Elektra)
Thinking of throwing your own party? Here's your soundtrack.
Sounds

Double live albums of this calibre are the vinyl equivalent of an elephants' graveyard.
NME

The X memorial album.
Melody Maker

Y

YARGO
Bodybeat (Bodybeat)
Not so much a song, more a workout towards zen orgasm.
NME

YEAH JAZZ
Six Lane Ends (Cherry Red)
Largely tales of woe and girls called Sharon, a formula which served Morrissey well, but which needs to be applied with more wit than Yeah Jazz can muster.
NME

YES
Big Generator (Atco)
Big Generator is five bowls of muesli looking for a spoon.
NME

A lyric sheet of pure gobbledygook which wouldn't get a CSE English pass.
Q

YO LA TENGO
Ride The Tiger (Shigaku)
Yo La Tengo is Spanish for "I have it here". Not yet they haven't.
Sounds

NEIL YOUNG AND THE BLUE NOTES
This Note's For You (Reprise)
Oblivious, unemotive and pretty grim, Neil. You're wasting your voice.
Sounds

He and his Bluenotes groove, dig and blues-hammer in such an effective and enjoyable manner that they take the resulting album into "Record Of The Year" territory.
NME

At the very least you've got to admire the grizzled old bastard's sheer persistence.
Melody Maker

Z

ZODIAC MINDWARP AND THE LOVE REACTION
Tattooed Beat Messiah (Mercury)
Zodiac has now, of course, become a complete impostor. I can imagine him in striped pyjamas at bedtime, soaking his feet in front of the weather forecast, while at the same time, this album is urging us to think of him as a tattooed beat messiah, a love dictator, a living detonator, the king of flies, a stormbringer, the wild one, the love commando, a hell-hound, a dirty dog, a gunsmoke lover, a dangerous stranger . . .
Melody Maker

Zodiac is extremely good-looking and the whole thing's an absolute stormer. Good grief, who'd have believed it?!!
Smash Hits

YEAR IN VIDEO

It has, it seems, not been a vintage year for that thing they call the pop video. Nevertheless, John Tobler manages to pick five winners, while a panel of so-called experts pronounce on the rest.

n last year's volume, Dessa Fox bewailed the fact that video was becoming tired, and while it would be pleasant to suggest that the last 12 months have seen a VHS-shaped phoenix rising from the ashes of a bonfire of Duran Duran promos shot on Mars, such a mirage has not occurred. Along with interesting mainstream music, ludicrous promo video budget has become a thing of the past and, having observed the generally revivalist nature of the vast majority of the year's more listenable music, one is forced to ask whether the "creative" promo clip may be an endangered species.

Inevitably, packages of the "Video Hits LP" type will enjoy brief success on a "flavour of the month" basis, but such items will only be of real interest as nostalgia in years to come. Thus, as the *Now* and *Hits* series (which accompany TV-advertised audio compilations) come out, they swiftly appear to be unwelcome reminders of the diseased state of popular music: just as the proverbial silk purse will not magically emerge from a sow's ear, so even the most mind-boggling video will not transform a mundane song into a joy for ever.

Since the price of music videos has, in the majority of cases, fallen to below ten pounds (demonstrating that market forces have had their say), it is comparable to the CD in cost as well as being the ideal medium for the retrospective compilation. Indeed, the two formats are often cross-marketed, although video always remains the poor relation.

This packaging together of all the clips (or the most memorable thereof) from an act's career has been embraced by the industry as the only way forward at a time when TV audiences are declining, and the vast majority of commercially successful videos have

Having observed the general revivalist nature of the vast majority of the year's more listenable music, one is forced to ask whether the "creative" promo clip may be an endangered species

been of this type. However, the results can be as diverse as the subject acts: while a genuinely exciting tape such as The Who's *Who's Better, Who's Best* stands a chance of enduring as well as U2's *Live Under A Blood Red Sky* – released in 1983 and still a regular feature of the Music Video Top 20 – *Best Of OMD*'s sales are reflecting the fact that it is only watchable by devout fans.

As far as big-selling acts on video are concerned, there can be little doubt that Queen – who provided the unforgettable 'Bohemian Rhapsody' video – are the most popular (another comment on the embarrassing condition of rock and pop in general in the late-eighties). Currently, there are at least five separate visual records of their art available, all of which remain commercially buoyant.

It is, of course, essential that any act which is the subject of a video compilation should have had a career lasting a reasonable time; it not only limits the contenders, but prevents many five-minute wonders who may appear on a *Now* or *Hits* compilation getting ideas above their station. It also means that long-lasting names from the past can find themselves as obvious choices, a good example being The Doors, whose video, *Dance On Fire* is a fine historic document of the life and times of an act we are unlikely to see bettered this century.

The Doors with *Live At The Hollywood Bowl*, also feature among a number tapes of vintage concerts which have made their mark this year: *Van Morrison In Ireland*, Marillion's *Live From Lorelei*, *Eurythmics Live*, Tina Turner's *Rio '88*. And now that companies are finally acquiring the rights for home video for feature movies like Led Zeppelin's *The Song Remains The Same*, Frank Zappa's *200 Motels* and the star-packed *The Last Waltz*, the next year could see an upturn in what has sadly become a rather turgid business. It would be far more of a pleasure to select next year's Top Five from innumerable contenders than to have the obvious sticking out like a beacon – with CD having reawoken the public's taste-buds to the glories of the past, the end of the 1980s (a decade which few will recall with any great pleasure, musically or otherwise) will hopefully compensate with similarly fascinating videos.

By now, this isn't simple nostalgia, it's almost history: popular music was at a zenith, both commercially and in terms of popularity, during the years between The Beatles and The Sex Pistols, and future generations cannot but be amazed by the glories of the past. Of course, there's always the chance that things might improve, as they can hardly deteriorate, but even if they don't – yet – there'll be plenty of worthwhile mouldy oldies around for our kids.

QUEEN. Magic Years Volumes 1, 2 & 3

(***Picture Music International,*** *60 mins each*)
With more successful (commercially and often artistically) videos under their collective belts/cod pieces than any other act, Queen's history is further documented here in a trilogy of tapes which include a good deal of previously rare footage. While the results aren't perfect – heavy-duty concentration is sometimes necessary for appreciation – this ambitious enterprise is simultaneously ground-breaking and somewhat unfulfilled, leaving space for future documentary innovation.

PETER GABRIEL. CV

(***Virgin Vision,*** *40 mins*)
The compilation of promotional videos is as popular and obvious a method of producing commercially viable product as the live gig souvenir tape, and has the added benefit of being comparatively cheap to assemble – the major costs are related to each single at the time of release. The point that often seems to be missed (and is indeed ignored here) is the value of chronology; this enables the viewer to recognize progress and changes of direction, although the reason for this is no doubt connected with the supposedly inferior quality of earlier clips. Gabriel's masterly collection, which includes 'Sledgehammer' and two impressive and different versions of 'Don't Give Up' with Kate Bush, almost atones for his absence from the two-volume Genesis compilation. An infinitely rewatchable tape.

TOP 5

ELVIS PRESLEY. Elvis '56: In The Beginning

(***Virgin Vision,*** *60 mins*)
Combining rare TV footage of early performances on shows hosted by Ed Sullivan and The Dorsey Brothers and previously unseen home-movie-type films with contemporary photographs taken by Alfred Wertheimer, and a soundtrack of his still unequalled pre-US Army recordings, this documentary is, quite simply, better than anything else released during the year. By observing 1956, probably Elvis's greatest year, it is possible to see why the "establishment" saw him as dangerous – the shy, boyish hillbilly charm is all there, yet something much darker is clearly visible just below the surface. A vital video which should be seen by everyone captivated by the magic of rock 'n' roll.

T'PAU. View From A Bridge

(***Virgin Vision,*** *20 mins*)
In a year which produced fewer charismatic new stars than any since 1954, Carol Decker of T'Pau was a diamond in an ocean of sewage. Had this been any other year, her striking voice and (usually) memorable songs would have been rivalled by others, but her only serious competition in terms of reasonable material came from Bon Jovi's *Slippery When Wet* compilation released by Channel 5. Decker and Bon Jovi both aspire to more traditional musical values rather than being studio-bound puppets manipulated by technology-crazy producers.

GRATEFUL DEAD. The Grateful Dead Movie

(***Hendring,*** *137 minutes*)
This tape retails for roughly three times the price of virtually all other music videos, which must have made it a risky proposition for Hendring, although The Dead's re-emergence with the *In The Dark* album certainly improved its chances. Spoken of in hushed terms by Deadheads ever since its preparation in 1976, this will enjoy a longer shelf life than most of this year's releases, although it must be stressed that this will not appeal to everyone – a legendary, if sometimes self-indulgent, hippie band playing seemingly interminably isn't obvious fodder for the upwardly mobile. However, its value as a nostalgic relic of simpler and happier times past will guarantee its position as a long-term favourite among the middle-aged.
JOHN TOBLER

VIDEO

ANITA BAKER. One Night Of Rapture

(***Elektra Entertainment,*** *55 mins*)

Anita Baker's singing on record is little short of ecstasy, and the sterling sound quality on this cassette gives even more than that. In a live "situation", she shows a talent for improvisation and note bending and sustaining that seem severely limited by the studio's confines. At a Washington DC show, she swoops, swings and swoons her way through the entire *Rapture* album, to melt even the iciest of hearts. However, Anita Baker being interviewed and "goofing around" during rehearsals is, to say the least, a bit of a pain. For a total of around 15 minutes, she attempts to inject a bit of "personality" into the proceedings, and ends up doing serious damage to what might have been one of the best tapes of the year. *(DD)*

CHUCK BERRY. Chuck Berry

(***Channel 5,*** *60 mins*)

"What song was I singing?" howls the venerable sleazeball, emerging from a blizzard of solos during 'Let It Rock', about halfway through this 1982 concert at LA's Roxy Theatre. The compilers of the tape don't seem to know either: the song is listed as 'Around And Around', and the versions of 'Promised Land' and 'Memphis' which follow appear on the sleeve as 'Birmingham' and 'Marie' respectively, while 'Carol' and 'Sweet Little Rock And Roller' aren't listed at all, which gives you an idea of how much care has gone into this thing. About the same amount as taken by Uncle Chuck himself: does he think that he somehow makes more money by giving the audience a shoddy show? Guest star Tina Turner (post-Ike, pre-comeback and desperate for whatever exposure she can get) keeps a nervous this-can't-be-happening grin plastered over her mug while trying to find a harmony line for 'Rock And Roll Music' that won't clash with Chuck's non-melody, and the band keep their heads down and go *chunka-chunka-chunka*. In other words, an utterly inadequate account of what made Chuck Berry great, and a fairly representative one of why he hasn't been great for a quarter of a century. Keep your money in your pocket until Taylor Hackford's *Hail! Hail! Rock And Roll* is released on video. *(CSM)*

BITING TONGUES. Wall Of Surf

(***Ikon,*** *32 mins*)

Manchester band Biting Tongues – a loose aggregate of musicians who combine irregularly to create a jazz-based avant-garde kinda indie noise – have managed to produce a colourful, challenging sequence of shifting styles. Sure, sometimes the visuals and soundtrack seem somewhat at odds and occasionally the band lack a sharp enough idea of how to present themselves: are they serious young musicians, mere video extras or the central personalities for the whole venture? But each musical segment (I hesitate to use the term "song") lasts around eight minutes and features enough ideas – both visual and musical – to prevent the attention from wandering too much. In fact, after the hesitant use of black-and-white stills photography in 'P.T.G. 2', the images suddenly explode into a kaleidoscope of vaguely psychedelic colour, culminating in a stunning executed scene where the vocalist whirls a blazing orb of fire around his head, the sparks literally flying everywhere. After such a highlight, 'Trouble Hand' and 'Compressor' are extended work-outs that constantly avoid dead-ends with relentless rhythms and blaring brass routines that fail to recapture that mood of exhilaration. *(JW)*

BON JOVI. Slippery When Wet

(***Channel 5,*** *41 mins*)

Arguably the Zeppelin of today, Bon Jovi's leader, Jon of that ilk, has Plant-style hair and throat and, between songs, comes across as an almost believable regular guy, despite poncing about on a trapeze-ish thing in stadium shows (as we see in Japan and presumably the US). Almost the Cliff & The Shads of the 1990s, but a bit dirtier, Bon Jovi's album of the same title was a 12 million seller, and it's not hard to see why, as songs with good hook-lines like 'Living On A Prayer' (included twice) and 'You Give Love A Bad Name', not to mention 'Never Say Goodbye' and 'Wanted (Dead Or Alive)' are very nearly respectable. The acceptable face of aluminium, maybe, but a video that's hard to dislike, and its retail price of two quid higher than the average means Channel 5 know it too. *(JT)*

JAMES BROWN. Music Biography 1956–1976

(***Virgin Music Video,*** *57 mins*)

"100% music video, no interview footage" it says on the cover, a bit like those smug notices you get on tinned food "no artificial flavouring or sweetening". In spite of such consideration, though, the video is a long way from being as wholesome as it might have been. You know something's wrong when the first track listed – v. rare album track 'The Boss' from the 1973 *Black Caesar* soundtrack – is cut ridiculously short. This journey through James Brown's hits, hairstyles and varying degrees of funkiness – well, 'Get Up Offa That Thing' wasn't very good , was it? – shows the by now standard bias towards early footage. Although the skinny-suited, rubber-legged dancing is dead good and the silly jumper worn in the *Ski Party* clip is a hoot, it's mostly been seen so much it's getting stale. It would've been nice to have seen more care taken with the selection of the five post-Sex Machine numbers, instead of slapping on those galloped through, well under par live clips seen here. *(LB)*

CREAM. Farewell Concert

(*Channel 5,* *50 mins*)

To suggest that the music of Cream – that short-lived but immensely influential triumvirate of Eric Clapton, Jack Bruce and Ginger Baker – has aged rather poorly is an understatement of thermo-nuclear proportions. This muzzily-recorded and fuzzily-filmed memento of the November 1968 Albert Hall concerts which climaxed their stormy career was directed by Tony Palmer and saddled with an excruciatingly pompous commentary by – of all people – Patrick Allen, and it features six numbers plus interviews with each of the trio. Jack Bruce sings as if he is not only suffering from an acute migraine but is on a mission from God to share it with the world, Baker's poly-rhythmic embellishments clutter rather than expand the beat and Clapton runs out of B.B. King licks somewhat sooner than B.B. himself would have done. 'Sunshine Of Your Love', 'White Room', 'Spoonful', 'I'm So Glad', 'Politician' and 'Toad' are pulped to the consistency of lumpy porridge before an exceptionally reverential audience who – if not actually stoned to the eyeballs – are definitely in some kind of altered state of consciousness. Invaluable research material for anybody currently preparing a dissertation on the pathetic fallacies of the late-sixties "rock-as-art" delusion, but not exactly overlong on entertainment value. *(CSM)*

DEPECHE MODE. Strange

(*Mute Film,* *30 mins*)

Filmed by Anton Corbijn in grainy monochrome in which only the enigmatic emblem of a loudhailer is chroma-keyed into colour, Depeche Mode work hard to shed the last traces of their Basildon roots in favour of some vaguely pan-European image such as Jean Luc Godard might recognize. With his customary flare, Corbijn drops his people into the middle of unsettling landscapes, the better to express their alienation and angst. And when it is presumed we tire of the boys' homely faces, a spot of rubber lingerie and existential crumpet both stresses the fetishistic undercurrent of Mode's recent tunes and signals some unspecified artistic sophistication. Good-looking but inconsequential, this conceit showcases a couple of good songs, including 'Never Let Me Down Again'. *(MS)*

DURAN DURAN. Working For The Skin Trade

(*Picture Music International,* *57 mins*)

You could always count on the Durans, back when, to provide a good squeal when it came to video time – all that spurious, Le Bon-engendered symbolism (what did the inverted umbrellas in 'Union of the Snake' mean?) was in a class of its own. This one, though, is mildly disappointing, because it's merely a straightforward concert document, filmed post-Taylors (though I can be no more specific as to time and place), and features the erstwhile heart-throbs lumbering through some of their dullest material. Le Bon's teen-god status has been eclipsed by younger guns like Bros and he knows it, seemingly – his performance is contained, almost low-key. The band clump through six singles – the late-period ones – and three album tracks (the latter including the notorious 'Chauffeur', for which Le Bon dons a peaked cap. Home, Simon!), any inherent sparkle in the music quashed by the Durans' lumpen "funkiness". And no 'Reflex'!! *(CS)*

EURYTHMICS. Savage

(*Virgin Music Video,* *52 mins*)

Accompanying visuals to the entire *Savage* album, and a pertinent reminder of one of the biggest hurdles facing CDV should it ever get off the starting-blocks in this country: coming up with televisual interpretations of every track on an album – even when the music is as inspired as this – will overtax even the most fertile imagination. Although this tape gives Annie plenty of scope to rummage about in the dressing-up box, the frumpy housewife or nylon-look-wigged, cleavage-exposing siren are firm favourites, the videos are so inconsequential they end up distracting from the music rather than enhancing it. In fact, the only ones that work are 'I Need A Man' (straight performance) and (partly) 'I've Got A Lover (Back In Japan)' (partly straight performance). *(DB)*

FIVE STAR. Between The Lines

(*Picture Music International,* *60 mins*)

Have Five Star, barely out of their collective teens, peaked already? Evidence offered up by this film, recorded at Wembley during last year's *Children Of The Night* (if you please) tour, when compared with 1986's fresh, gawkily vibrant shows would suggest some radical rethinking is needed *chez* Pearson. Camera close-ups capture that look of played-out boredom (often confused with "professionalism") on the quintet's faces, and on the Arena's huge stage, they space out so far their formation dancing doesn't quite come off – like the spangly cat-suits it looks a bit naff. Also, and this shows up badly in the *Between The Lines* songs, now the fresh-from-Romford audacity has been smoothed away there doesn't seem to be much that's special underneath. Deniece yells "aw-*right!*" and "wooh!" a great deal, but it's not enough to cover up the fact that the best stuff (from the first album) is crammed into a pretty formless medley. And they didn't even bring mum and dad on for a bow at the end. *(DB)*

GAYE BYKERS ON ACID. Drill Your Own Hole

(*Virgin Music Video,* *60 mins*)

In which quite possibly the only group to be directly influenced by The Edgar Broughton Band go on a *Magical Mystery Tour* on a budget of about £2.50 a minute. The computer game-plan to wealth-and-fame is the creaky storyline which binds together a few songs and much larking about. What we learn is that though the Bykers ape *The Young Ones* in general demeanour, nose-picking is about as rude as it gets. These Leicester lads are pussycats in grebo glad-rags. A few good jokes are over-stretched, and some absolute duds slip through the net, which is much as one would expect. One for the fans. *(MS)*

HEART. If Looks Could Kill

(*Picture Music International,* *30 mins*)

Out-T'Pau-ing T'Pau for over a decade now, Heart's world is an MTV Valhalla of dry ice, teased wigs, upstretched arms and soft-focus close-ups. Including the clips for 'What About Love', 'These Dreams' and 'Alone', this is rock balladry fit to bust, though 'Nothin' At All' bookends the guitar-solo-on-the-fire-escape trick with a little sisterly horseplay, two Grace Slicks for the price of one. *(MS)*

JIMI HENDRIX. Jimi Plays Monterey

(*Virgin Music Video,* *50 mins*)

According to Papa John Phillips's narration, Hendrix and Pete Townshend had a dreadful row backstage about who would follow who. After a flip of a coin, The Who were on first and Hendrix reportedly stood on a chair to announce that if he had to follow them he was "going to pull all the stops out and blow everybody away." He was as good as his word. This, the 1967 Monterey Pop Festival and his first appearance in America after finding fame in London, is probably the best performance he ever gave. Judging from his more-than-merely-wonky onstage announcements, there were a considerable amount of "controlled substances" involved, but stoned as the proverbial bat or not he scorches through such numbers as 'Wild Thing', 'Hey Joe', 'The Wind Cries Mary' and 'The Killing Floor' in a fashion that other "axe-men" take mind-altering drugs just to dream about. So spectacular a set is this that you pay no attention to Mitchell and Redding struggling to keep up (a battle they lose more than once) and you forget to play spot the dead rock legend. *(LB)*

HUNTERS AND COLLECTORS. The Way To Go Out

(*Ikon,* *40 mins*)

Where harsh Western industrialization meets Aboriginal tribal rhythms – like a cross between Devo and Test Department playing INXS's greatest hits – Hunters & Collectors are a hard-driving Melbourne bar band with a no-fuss, no-frills attitude. Song titles like 'Lumps Of Lead', 'Judas Sheep' and 'The Unbeliever' betray their solid, aggressive approach ('The Slab' even sounds like early Stranglers!) which can occasionally become oppressively earnest. Most of *The Way . . .* is a live show filmed in Australia in 1984, with rough vocals, bad stage lighting and minimal glamour or drama from the band. And the brief inter-song instrumental interludes – accompanied by images of urban life and bush scenery – are mere contemporary distractions providing little meaningful illumination. But – like the group themselves – it has a raw charm based on a sense of admirable determination married to an adventurous musical naivety. *(JW)*

INXS. The Swing And Other Stories

(*Channel 5,* *58 mins*)

Never the most inspiring band in the world – why is it that so much Australian rock 'n' roll is content to remain a poor relation of the American stadium bands? – the eleven music clips might just have got away with it had they been left to themselves. But they haven't. Inserted in between them is "documentary footage" and "interviews with each of the group's six members." What they should really be described as is "boring, contrived backstage horseplay" and "see the band answer questions that wouldn't tax a three-year-old;" it is so lumpen the never-better-than-average music seems exciting and comes as welcome relief. Perhaps that was the idea. *(LB)*

IRON MAIDEN. 12 Wasted Years

(*Hendring,* *50 mins*)

The unremarkable story of five unassuming lads who started off – somewhat unfashionably at the peak of punk – playing either suspiciously juvenile swords-and-sorcery epics or unpleasantly sexist ditties ('Charlotte The Harlot', indeed) in the backrooms of pubs and ended up doing something not entirely dissimilar 12 years later on the world's stadium circuit. For Maiden disciples there is an endless stream of live footage and interminable interviews with everyone associated with the band; the singer who jumped or was pushed shortly before the band made it mega feigns indifference; the group's designer, responsible for major contributions to the arts such as Eddie (The Maiden's monster mascot) and the vile things that are Iron Maiden record sleeves, reveals that "he just does" the artwork and blinding flashes of inspiration are few and far between; singer Bruce Dickinson and bassist Steve Harris fail to convince anyone that they are interesting blokes underneath it all while manager Rod Smallwood just seems to grin all the way through. Chances are, dear viewer, you will not. (*AD*)

MICHAEL JACKSON. The Legend Continues . . .

(*Optimum/Motown Productions,* *54 mins*)

"The little fella in front is incredible." Introducing an early Jackson 5 TV appearance, Ed Sullivan summed up the life and times of Michael Jackson pretty well. It's quite eerie to watch some of this stuff; there's Michael with a pink fedora aged eleven (and, in home-movie clips and the

Jackson 5's Motown audition, even younger) and he's already displaying total control and confidence, not just over all his vocal mannerisms but over the audience. Raised as a superstar he seemed to find a home on the stage straight away.

Gathering a collection of Jackson rarities and oddities (like an early Frank Sinatra skit) and coupling them with his historic later appearances (including up-to-the-minute footage from his '88 world tour), *The Legend Continues* couldn't really be anything but prime-time entertainment. As it is, it goes some of the way to contextualizing Michael's greatness. Among the celeb interviews (including much cooing admiration from screen goddesses Katharine Hepburn, Liz Taylor and Sophia Loren) is Gene Kelly who puts him in the lineage of song-and-dance men which includes Fred Astaire, Gene himself and the also-featured Sammy Davis Jr. Footage of James Brown and Jackie Wilson spells out Michael's much loved soul roots. The video bottles out from going further into the world of Hollywood style surgery, how Jackson has built on child fame where so many before him burned out and the dynastic rivalries of the Jackson clan.

But the clips speak for themselves which is why it's a crime bordering on sacrilege that the makers of *The Legend Continues* have chosen to split up Jackson's set-piece performance of 'Billie Jean' on the Motown 25th Anniversary Show – probably the single greatest showbusiness routine of our lifetime – with a series of understandably enthusiastic comments from the likes of Martin Scorsese. But, like the man said, it's still incredible. A rare treat. *(GM)*

JOHN AND YOKO. (Sandor Stern) Mark McGann, Kim Mayori

(***Sony,*** *145 mins*)

"The complete story" of John and Yoko, played out against carefully constructed lookalike backdrops by actors who don't even seem to want to look like, or sound like, the characters they're playing. Thus pretty, slim, American-voiced Hawaiian Kim Mayori, with hopelessly drawn-on eyebrows, doesn't begin to resemble the very weird Yoko who won John's art; thus the four mop-tops are truer to their sobriquet here than they should be, have nothing like scouse voices, and resemble nobody you've ever seen before. (The red-eyed sourpuss who looks like he's going to nut you any minute is, you discover, peace-loving Hari Georgeson.) The tale is traced faithfully enough, though for an especially long time when you already know both the storyline and the ending, but the characters are just so ridiculous that you can't help falling about, even at times when you should be reduced to tears. *(JB)*

LIAISONS DANGEREUSES. Liaisons Dangereuses

(***Ikon,*** *30 mins*)

Visually, the only variety comes in shades of red, blue and green stage lighting. Musically, they recall the black Euro-disco style of D.A.F., Kraftwerk and early Simple Minds – throbbing synths, pulsing bass cycles and urgently intoned vocals about love, decay, truth and beauty. At least, that's my best guess, since they're all delivered in a mixture of French and Spanish. There are no song introductions, no stage announcements, no concession to the audience at all; it's as though this electronic three-piece – two Germans and a French/Belgian vocalist – existed in a vacuum. However, aficionados will find 'Dias Cortas' and 'Mystere Dans Le Brouilliard' especially mesmeric, even riveting. To the uncommitted though, it will appear eerily repetitive and lacking in melodic warmth. *(JW)*

MADONNA. Ciao Italia: Live From Italy

(***Warner Video,*** *100 mins*)

A film shot on Madonna's 1987 world tour for Italian television, quite simply it shows what all the fuss concerning "that girl" is about: she is a masterful performer, up there with Prince and way ahead of Michael Jackson. I say this because unlike Jackson, who appeared to be putting on an exhibition rather than a rock show, the clearest thing to come over on this film is Madonna's obvious enjoyment. Her voice was by now feeling the effects of touring, but it doesn't matter as she flirts with the crowd, the camera and (bordering on the obscene) her band and performs every song you want to hear. It is very fitting that, while encoring with 'La Isla Bonita', she has difficulty stopping herself grinning during what is a pretty sad song. Enough said; if you buy just one concert film in your whole life, it ought to be *Ciao Italia.* *(DB)*

BOB MARLEY. One Love Peace Concert

(***Hendring,*** *90 mins*)

Not quite prosecutable under the Trade Descriptions Act, this tape stretches the boundaries of creative titling to the absolute limit. Instead of an hour and a half of Marley live, you get 90 minutes of the 1978 One Love Peace Concert – a show organized by Marley to bring together the two rival Jamaican Prime Ministerial candidates, in a bid to halt the sectarian violence during the run-up to the election. Marley himself performs five numbers. That said, there's enough here to keep the average reggae fan more than happy: Dennis Brown ('Whip Dem Jah'), Peter Tosh ('Get Up Stand Up'), U-Roy ('I'm A Rebel'), Judy Mowat ('Black Woman') and the (still) charming Althea & Donna ('Uptown Top Ranking' – what else?). The spirit of the occasion manages to overcome even the dodgy sound quality and indifferent approach to camera-work. *(LB)*

HUGH MASEKELA. Notice To Quit (A Portrait Of South Africa)

(***Hendring,*** *52 mins*)

Worthy as it is in principle, *Notice To Quit* trips itself up somewhat by trying to do too much at one go. It mixes transcripts of speeches by jailed South African freedom fighters, newsreel footage from The Cape and dub-type poetry supplied by the International Defence Aid Fund For South Africa, with a mere four Masekela numbers. Having seen Masekela in concert several times, it does him a severe injustice, as his onstage explanations, his beautiful band, his poignant songs and his haunting, almost verbal trumpet is enough to let you know what's going on in a way anybody can understand and nobody can ignore. Here, 'Stimela (The Coal Train)' does exactly that. Also, what no amount of radically intended footage can hope to achieve is capture the resilience of spirit, the hope and the love of life that is in itself an act of supreme defiance. 'The Joke Of Life', 'Motlaepula The Rainmaker' and 'Don't Go Lose It Baby', respectively, say it all. Perhaps next time the well-meaning souls who put this together will avoid the temptation to put their own interpretation on things. *(LB)*

JONI MITCHELL. Refuge Of The Roads

(*Hendring,* *60 mins*)

A self-directed 1984 video which offers an hour's worth of concert footage – in which Joni performs songs mostly from the late-seventies and early-eighties – interspersed with brief clips of film footage. Some of the non-concert stuff is vaguely "relevant" to the songs which it either prefaces or interrupts – thus we see Charlie Mingus before 'God Must Be A Boogie Man' or wild horses galloping along to 'Wild Things Run Fast' – some is home-movie sketches of Joni and her husband (bass player Larry Klein) fooling around to no particular purpose. A bit over-arty in this respect, but the songs are slickly delivered, and the cut-in footage is often welcome, for there's not very much happening on stage to demand attention. Then again, some of the songs don't need any distracting illustration – most notably 'Chinese Café'/'Unchained Melody', one of Joni Mitchell's best songs, which mixes wistful nostalgia with an unsettling awareness of the inevitable processes of time. *(JB)*

ALEXANDER O'NEAL. The Voice On Video

(*CBS/Fox,* *23 mins*)

This hits collection concentrates on the interaction between O'Neal and a selection of "foxy" ladies, with slow-burning stares and heavy-lidded sensuality predominating. Well, what did you expect? O'Neal isn't, after all, the subtlest of Romeos and the Theophilous P. Wildebeeste brand of smoochy soul isn't the subtlest of genres. However, what would seem ludicrously overblown in, say, a real-life situation works perfectly in this context because film softens the edges of those leers, rendering them quite irresistible. We get the hits from the prodigiously successful *Hearsay* album (two of which in particular, 'Fake' and 'Criticize', reveal a simmering bitterness that quite belies the sepia-toned gloss of the visuals), and more. The young lay-deez in the house will love it. *(CS)*

PRINCE AND THE REVOLUTION. Live

(*Channel 5,* *120 mins*)

Recorded on the US leg of the world tour of three years ago, the one that brought about the acrimonious end of The Revolution as Prince's backing band, this two hours of purple preening is really only one for the fans. Although among the 19 numbers is enough well-known material to satisfy the casual Prince-watcher – an almost 20-minute-long 'Purple Rain', an 8-minute 'When Doves Cry', and the less dauntingly-timed (approx 5 mins) 'Little Red Corvette', 'Let's Go Crazy', '1999' and 'Take Me With U' – it can be quite hard to watch. This is because, presumably in an effort to capture the flavour of the affair, it is filmed exactly as the audience would view it and the stuff that makes Prince's concerts so exciting – copious quantities of smoke and dry ice and far from all-encompassing lighting – tend to get in the way. At times it's difficult to see what is actually going on, which is a great shame because the choreography's dazzling, the costumes, er, interesting and Prince himself looks like he's thoroughly enjoying himself, confident in the knowledge that he was then, and indeed now, one of the most spectacular live acts working. *(LB)*

SONNY ROLLINS. Saxophone Colossus

(*Virgin Music Video,* *79 mins*)

An apt title. In two vastly different concert settings, Rollins proves himself to be exactly that, a colossus among the current field of free-form tenormen, and when talking to the camera reveals a character and articulacy on much the same scale. One show takes place in a former rock quarry that has been spectacularly transformed into a sculpture park; backed by his quartet, Rollins appears to dwarf the massive structures as he stands, feet apart, blowing with the strength, joy and passion that has made him the world's best improviser. The other performance, with the Nippon Symphony Orchestra, is a much softer, seemingly more disciplined approach that shows off the love-affair with his instrument that he talks about, quite seriously, in front of his wife (she, a remarkably understanding woman, feels this is infinitely preferable to his chasing other women). A jazz film should have an appeal far beyond the already converted, and could teach the average rock video director a thing or two about both concert filming and what makes interesting interview footage. *(LB)*

RUN DMC. The Video

(*Channel 5,* *25 mins*)

Five singles taken from Run DMC's first three albums, that – even leaving aside their appropriation of heavy metal-type guitars – are enough to explain how the group cracked the

notoriously narrow-minded MTV playlists and shot themselves to pop credibility: they did what so few hip hop or hard funk outfits have done, they put together witty, eminently watchable videos. The ironic humour seen in 'Walk This Way' – rap being sneered at but winning folks over in the end is a simplified analogy of their trouble with MTV – was present long before that single, as it shows up in the visuals for 'Kings Of Rock' and 'Rock Box'. 'It's Tricky' is a playlet about two con men who, remarkably in this sort of thing, make the group look like "suckers" in the end. And 'You Talk Too Much' is a surreal stroll through torn-up newspaper. Of course, the chaps don't smile too much, and the ideas and executions aren't of the Peter Gabriel standard, but it proves beyond doubt that there's no need for hip hop to neglect what it looks like. *(LB)*

CARLY SIMON. Coming Around Again

(*Channel 5,* *60 mins*)

Carly Simon's 1987 LP, *Coming Around Again*, was a marvellous record – full of melody and maturity, a celebration of marriage and recognition that amidst the perils and problems that inevitably beset any sexual relationship, the value of fidelity and the truth of love are worth singing about. So Carly sings, in this entertaining concert film, to a gathering of family, friends and townsfolk, on the picturesque quayside of Gay Head, Massachusetts. The only unfortunate thing is that, throughout the proceedings, a strong wind threatens to blow Carly and her classy band into the harbour. The wind not only fusses her hair, it certainly must have ruined the sound recording – and some technical jiggery-pokery (dare one suggest re-recording?) must have gone on in the studio later to make it sound OK. Thankfully, it sounds better than OK. Most of the songs on the record are here, supplemented by a spare sprinkling of other "hits" (including 'You're So Vain'), and Carly looks just fine too, prancing and dancing in the over-enthusiastic breeze. *(JB)*

TALKING HEADS. Storytelling Giant

(*Picture Music International,* *52 mins*)

This Talking Heads video collection is linked not by interviews with David Byrne, Tina Weymouth, Jerry Harrison or Chris Frantz, but with real-life talking heads: everyday folks describing their dreams or recounting personal anecdotes. The subtext is obvious: the vids themselves are simply scenes from American life – tales of ordinary madness – a conceit well in line with Byrne's obvious fascination with the ostensibly banal, which reached its fullest flowering with his feature-length movie *True Stories*, wherein two of these videos ('Wild Wild Life' and 'Love For Sale') first appeared. On the majority of *Storytelling Giant*, Byrne himself takes credit as writer, producer, director, choreographer or various permutations thereof, but it would be an oversimplification to suggest that the degree of his participation is an automatic index of superiority: the home-movie concept of 'Naive Melody (This Must Be The Place)' takes the whole beauty-of banality notion so far that it becomes almost insulting, and Jim Blashfield's animation of 'And She Was' provides one of the most powerful moments in the entire set. However, Talking Heads are still one of the most resourceful bands in the rock mainstream, and Byrne could have made an excellent living as a video-maker without ever having picked up a guitar or written a song himself. 'Once In A Lifetime', 'Burning Down The House' and 'Road To Nowhere' are still as fresh, startling and thought-provoking as ever, and if there's a group with a more impressive video CV than this, I can't wait to see it. *(CSM)*

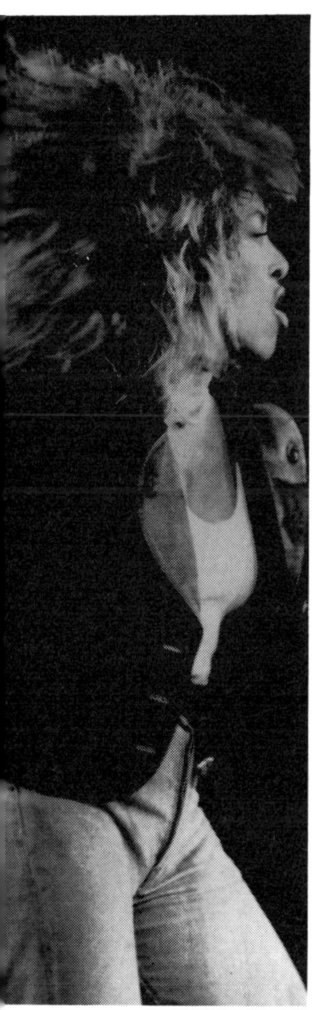

TERENCE TRENT D'ARBY. The Hardline According To . . .

(*CBS/Fox,* *63 mins*)

A live show of Terence performing his best-selling album interspersed with a profile of the man and his band. The film may be made by Malcolm Gerrie (of Channel 4's *The Tube* and *Wired* fame) but it's hardly an investigation or contextualization of the Brit soul star who's enjoyed an unquestioning, nay, obsequious reception by the British media. As with every D'Arby media venture, he stage-manages the whole performance. From the feigned opening interruption of Terence's early morning lie-in, to his outlandish bullshitting, to the "sensitive artiste" voice-overs as he walks by the river, to his group's cynical criticisms of their leader – it's all terribly *clever*, dryly humorous and a little fake. Just how much these qualities spill over to his, uhmm, *art* (Question: "What is art, Terry?" Answer "Whatever you can get away with"), is hard to tell. The camera-work is geared more to pick out the various mannerisms Terence has co-opted from Soul's Hall of Fame than to draw you into his performance. And the use of various camera speeds, some out of synch footage and much split-screen shots hinders rather than captures the momentum and excitement of the funkiest ego maniac on the block. A curio item for *Hardline* fans nonetheless. *(GM)*

TINA TURNER. Wild Lady Of Rock.

(*Hendring,* *60 mins*)

TINA TURNER. Rio '88

(*PolyGram Music Video,* *75 mins*)

These two shows illustrate one of the eighties most astounding career transformations. It's the story of how little Annie Mae Bullock went from being a crude bawling stereotype, parodying her glory days as one of the sixties' great R&B performers, to become the lion lunged First Lady of eighties synth soul – The Thighs That Shook The World, no less.

Wild Lady Of Rock captures our Tina at the fag end of the seventies in a poorly recorded performance at a seemingly lifeless Hammersmith Odeon. It's an undistinguished performance at best, and at worst it's a reminder of her strait-jacketed relationship with former partner/ husband Ike Turner. Tina was on her own but the shadow of Ike was still there in the laborious routines, the dull thud of a bar band at rock bottom, tired self-parody and strained choreography. It's all calculated to present a base, lowest common-denominator bitch-on-heat persona. Her penchant for covering contemporary rockers reaches a nadir on Rod Stewart's 'Hot Legs'; what should be good humoured and self mocking is merely gnarled desperation. It's all a little sad.

Switch to 16 January 1988 – the place is The Maracana Stadium in downtown Rio, the world's biggest football ground. A record-breaking audience of 180,200 Brazilians at carnival fever pitch are gathered to watch Tina's hip-shaking entry on a palm leaf-bordered float. The sound of a hundred samba percussionists rents the night air. The entrance is that of prize-fighting champion, it could be Muhammad Ali after a comeback. When she finally gets to the stage she'll be joined by a full complement of ostrich feather-crowned dancers; fireworks explode at suitable moments during the set and on a frame high over the stadium her name appears. Not in lights but, suitably considering the heat and inexhaustible energy she generates, in flames.

The event is extraordinary for two reasons. One, it's taking place in the impoverished, Third World surrounds of Brazil and, secondly, it centres on a lady who less than ten years before was considered a no-hoper on the world stage. Rio '88 doesn't concern itself with such matters – Brazil is featured in a brief opening montage of helicopters and police cordons, the whole city is apparently geared to Getting Tina To The Show On Time, and the introductory text implies that her star has been in the ascendant ever since she first stepped on stage. But the show is pretty phenomenal in itself: a testament to the li'l lady's guts and determination and a judicious management who have helped shape a set which broadens her emotional range with the likes of 'What's Love Got To Do With It' and a ballad rearrangement of The Beatles' 'Help'.

In truth Tina herself hasn't changed much, it's just that everything has been shaped to bring out the best in the vivacious personality. The lights, the action (the dancing calculated to bring out maximum audience participation), and the sound (a glossy synth-laden update of the styles she first enjoyed success with and the panoramic sweep of modern soul). It's all slightly camp, sassy, mockingly outrageous, typically, totally, Tina. And of course the video allows you superior sound quality (digital stereo actually) and a much better seat than the guy with the sombrero and hot-dog in the 100th row. *(GM)*

TOOLS YOU CAN TRUST. The Tools For Better Labour

(*Ikon,* *36 mins*)

Somewhere between The Fall and The Gang Of Four, Manchester quartet Tools You Can Trust are a jagged edge both musically and politically. Merging socialist slogans with catchy choruses, insistent songs like 'Show Your Teeth', 'A Brutal Light' and 'Can Of Worms' are intercut with deadpan diatribes about exploitative bosses and whinging bands in the indie scene. The promo video for 'Say It Low' replaces the grainy docu-drama monochrome approach with a warm orange glow for a delightful set-piece that resembles a family album photo in format, slowly presenting the band in a much more human, almost friendly, light. In general though, the bass-heavy, twin-drummer attack of the music reveals a deeply-bedded industrial background. Spitting venom, shooting out rare sparks of optimism, this is a darkly urgent soundtrack for Northern degeneration/regeneration. Like an old furnace, Tools You Can Trust are bold and ugly, yet blazing with energy. *(JW)*

VARIOUS ARTISTS. Girls, Girls, Girls

(*Wienerworld,* *52 mins*)

There's enough frolicking jailbait here to induce heart-failure in any post-pubescent male, plus – presumably included for respectability's sake – a handful of slightly more matronly "girls" to soothe the fevered brow. The rapacious Fairlights of Stock, Aitken & Waterman account for fully a third of the 15 tracks here (Kylie, Sinitta, Mel and Kim, Mandy Smith and Bananarama, to be precise – and I bet SAW are kicking themselves for not getting their paws on Sabrina first), while the rest represent a seemingly arbitrary trawl through the past year's Top 40, e.g., Hazell Dean, Taylor Dayne, Joyce Sims. Gall and wormwood to any rad-fem, this compilation is long on skin, gloss and sauce – the unexpurgated Sabrina vid, 'Boys', in which our heroine's breasts gradually unfetter themselves from the cruel confines of a white bikini, makes you wonder what our pop kids are coming to these days. No redeeming social value, but vastly entertaining. *(CS)*

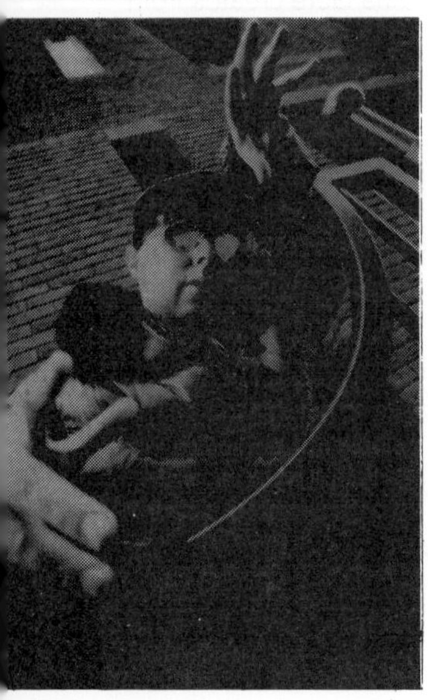

VARIOUS ARTISTS. Jack The Video

(*Wienerworld,* *52 mins*)

As the title implies, a collection of 15 house music-style hits. I say "style", because they're not all house (acid, deep, brutal or whatever) in the strictest sense of the word, and just as the records employ different time signatures, so the visuals vary in use of clichés and entertainment value. Worth the price of admission are The Art Of Noise's 'Dragnet' (a cheeky send-up of the Dan Ackroyd film), Two Men A Drum Machine And A Trumpet (deadpan lunacy worthy of their name), The Theme From S-Express (a perfectly captured mid-seventies gross-out) and 'Doctorin' The House' and 'How Low Can You Go' (both concentrate on good dancers dancing well). However, just as the music frequently lacks inspiration so do the "cut-ups" of black-and-white films and cartoons, and the obsessions with speeded-up footage shot from moving cars or subway trains, which unfortunately seems to take up much too much time to put this tape on the average pop fan's shopping list. *(LB)*

VARIOUS ARTISTS. Now That's What I Call Music 10

(*Picture Music International,* *60 mins*)

Peaking at 1.2 million, *Now 10* the album has been the biggest seller of the series so far. Quite why that is is beyond me, as the likes of Heart ('Alone'), Whitesnake ('Here I Go Again'), Cliff ('My Pretty One') and Level 42 ('It's Over') are hardly "soul stirring", and T'Pau ('China In Your Hand') is almost offensive in its awfulness. However, the video compilation has some magic moments: the gut-busting camp of Fred & Monty's 'Barcelona', the relentless use of fairy-tale cliché in Cliff's filmette, joyous scenes from *La Bamba* to go with Los Lobos's title track and an exuberant display of dancing from Jimmy Somerville in 'Never Can Say Goodbye'; and one major disappointment – the hideous human-type cat model of Nina Simone in 'My Baby Just Cares For Me'. *(DB)*

VARIOUS ARTISTS. Now That's What I Call Music 11

(*Picture Music International,* *58 mins*)

The stand-out track on this is Morrissey's 'Suedehead'. Not because it's any good, exactly the opposite in fact as, with all that footage of our hero mooning about at James Dean's grave and playing silly billies on a tractor, it illustrates perfectly why he's been so loathe to make videos in the past. Other than that, all of note among the Whitesnakes ('Give Me All Your Love'), T'Paus ('Valentine') and Johnny Hates Jazzes ('Turn Back The Clock') is the faintly disturbing looking spectacle of Elton John dressed up as a periwigged Palace of Versailles dandy (or something) to perform 'Candle In The Wind', Jermaine Stewart's fascinatingly awful dress sense ('Say It Again'), Climie Fisher pervily stalking some foxtress washerwoman ('Rise To The Occasion') and Morris Minor And The Majors' 'Stutter Rap', which is vaguely funny on the first couple of plays. *(DB)*

VARIOUS ARTISTS. Now That's What I Call Music 12

(*Picture Music International,* *58 mins*)

Now you're talking! *Anything* that features *anything* to do with Gary Glitter gets my vote. And although the sublimely cretinous 'Doctorin' The Tardis' doesn't include Big Gazza on the video, what you get instead is – and you may find this hard to believe – Daleks that look even more ropey than the one they made from egg boxes on *Blue Peter*. A worthy substitute. Other than that, *Now 12* runs pretty true to form: Bananarama dance round imaginary handbags ('I Want You Back'), Iron Maiden flirt with Hammer Horror-type shenanakins ('Can I Play With Madness?'), Morrissey's clip is expectedly angst-ridden ('Every Day Is Like Sunday'), Natalie Cole cavorts about in a mini-skirt ('Pink Cadillac'), Maxi Priest is wistful ('Wild World') and Sabrina's fabled white bikini remains in charge ('Boys'). *(DB)*

VARIOUS ARTISTS. This Was Rock

(*Channel 5,* *90 mins*)

This was rock? Well, in a sense it was (Chuck Berry – who also introduces each segment – plus the mighty Bo Diddley and a very young and spotty bunch of Rolling Stones), but it was also soul (Marvin Gaye, Ike & Tina Turner, Ray Charles, *Jaaaaaaames Braaooowwwwn*, Smokey Robinson & The Miracles) and pop (The Ronettes, The Supremes, Gerry & The Pacemakers and Lesley Gore). Drawn from *The T.A.M.I. Show* and *The T.N.T. Show* (two all-star California wing-dings from '64 and '65 respectively), this delirious whirl of energy, audacity and good humour is a quintessential sixties mix where highlights are the rule rather than the exception. SEE! (as the old movie trailers used to promise) Marvin Gaye as a young heart-throb smirking his way through 'Hitch Hike'! SEE the extraordinary suburban psychodrama Gore creates from 'You Don't Own Me' and 'Judy's Turn To Cry'! SEE Tina and Jaaaames bringing down the house with their rough 'n' greasy soul-revue showpersonship (though Brown's definitive collapse scene on 'Prisoner Of Love' has been omitted from this version)! SEE The Miracles and The Supremes demonstrating classic Motown choreography! SEE The Stones defending their somewhat questionable place at the top of the bill with sheer *attitude*! Beyond a shadow of doubt, this is what legends are made from, and it's a pleasure to see these icons back when they were earning their titles. It's a cert that anybody wanting to check Chuck, Tina, Jaaaames or Jagger at their finest would rather see 'em then than now. *(CSM)*

WHITESNAKE. Trilogy

(*Picture Music International,* *27 mins*)

Whitesnake ("the snake", to aficionados, I suppose) are highly enjoyable, as far as showbizzy heavy metalists go, singer David Coverdale's a likeable rapscallion and the four (hence the title *Trilogy*?) songs here are their best shots. The collection's *raison d'être*, however, seems to be the chronicling of the budding romance 'twixt Coverdale and a leggy poutstrel called Tawny Kitaen. Each clip is generously intercut with snatches of the lovebirds gambolling around the video-set backlot and engaging in heavy snog-up situations on the back seat of a parked car. Whether these constitute the "out-takes too hot ever to have been shown on TV," as promised on the wrapper, I couldn't say. Anyway, once you've become thoroughly conversant with Coverdale's seduction technique, the music itself – 'Still Of The Night', 'Here I Go Again', 'Is This Love?' and 'Give Me All Your Love' – will unsteam your glasses. *(CS)*

WOULD YOU BUY A CAR FROM THIS SONG?

Want to sell your product and you can't get a pop star to push it for you? Then get the next best thing, a pop song. Tom Hibbert mourns the demise of advertising "jingles".

As the offspring of a pair of Ovaltineys – members of that bizarre and sinister pre- and post-war children's cult coached and indoctrinated into singing the praises of a malty bedtime beverage in jolly and piping tones: "We are the Ovaltineys, happy girls and boys!!" – I was brought up to revere and respect the advertising jingle. Many was the time that, overtaken by euphoria behind the school bike sheds or somewhere else, I would burst into a jubilant snatch of "Light up the sky with Standard Fireworks!" or "Buy some for Lulu!!" (which was, I recall, the Rowntree's Fruit Gum refrain before they introduced the rather more annoying "Don't forget the Fruit Gums, mum!").

Then I grew up a bit and cruised the streets with my adolescent chums singing verses in harmony from the touching and surreal Toblerone ad – "Made from tri-ang-ul-ar almonds from tri-ang-ul-ar trees/And tri-ang-ul-ar honey from tri-ang-ul-ar bees/Oh, mister confectioner please, give me Toblerone" – or, when we'd been at the sherry cup, the bracing Orbit anthem: "Get into Orbit, Orbit, Orbit, Orbit sugar-free gum, for that clear minty taste that's good for your teeth – and that ain't bad!" . . . "They're mighty meaty matey!" (Wall's Pork Sausages), "Mum, muuum, Julian's been *wounded*!" (Germolene), "E for B and Georgie Best" (eggs) and poor old Malcolm and his malfunctioning nose (" 'Course you can, Malcolm!") in the Vicks Sinex classics – all these trills and more stick in my mind to this day. Showing, I suggest, the effectiveness of old-style jingle advertising; one remembers the product, one remembers the tune, one even remembers the words – "The hands that do dishes can be soft as your face with mild green Fairy Liquid" – for goodness sake.

But now in the eighties those jingle jolly days, sadly, are gone. Oh, occasionally a gem surfaces – "Do the Shake-and-Vac and put the freshness back, do the Shake-and-Vac and put the freshness back" (featuring mad and manic lady torturing carpet with vacuum cleaner in one hand and proprietary brand of shag-pile revitalizing powder in the other) – but more often (*too* often) these days, television advertisements are shot over with established pop and rock songs from the archives. Either in original version or with words rearranged to include brand-name references and plaudits. And the latter ruse is not unique to the eighties – it had been tested, on occasion, earlier: witness Christie's 1970 number one hit 'Yellow River' – "Yellow river! Yellow river! Is in my mind it's the place I love" – that was altered cunningly half a decade later into a tribute to . . . "Yellow Pages! Yellow Pages! (dum-dum-di-dum . . . something or other)." But it's a ruse that crops up with increasing and irritating regularity in our brave new pop music-literate consumer society.

See those potato heads, each one a carbon copy of little Jimmy Somerville, bursting from the turf to squeal "We want to be . . . Smith's Crisps! . . . We want to be . . . Smith's Crisps . . ." to the tune of Susan Maugham's dreadful old "chestnut", spirit of '62, 'Bobby's Girl' . . . And poor old Adam Ant: his bubblegum gem 'Apollo 9' is now reduced to a puff for Whitbread beer. (Whatever happened to the highly singable ". . . Whitbread Trophy Bitter! The pint that thinks it's a QUART"? . . .)

Why trouble oneself with the "hassle" of hiring jingle writers when one can simply purchase the rights to some old song and achieve product recognition in a trice?

The former ruse, meanwhile – original songs from the archives with the original lyrics by the original artistes (or retouched by sessioneers so sly you

Roy Orbison (left) and Billy Idol take a break from flogging hair colour and nuts

can hardly tell the difference) – is very much an invention of the eighties. "In the midnight hour – more, more, more" sneers Billy Idol (well, it's not Billy Idol, actually, but it's a fair impression); "Why settle for less?" enquires the oily voice-over. Billy's 'Rebel Yell' is thus used in an attempt to sell more (get it?) KP nuts. Such things are happening all the time, while the redundant jingle writer cries into his (Whitbread) beer.

Pop and rock music, it seems, have now come of age and grown respectable. Originally designed as an affront to "grown-ups", pop has now been around so long that no one can be bothered to be offended any more. Live Aid – lots of rock persons being caring before the viewing billions – helped a lot to make the "kids" music safe. We all know these songs; recognition, it is felt, will assist us to recognize too whatever product it is they're trying to flog us on the screens. So why trouble oneself with the "hassle" of hiring jingle writers when one can simply purchase the rights to some old song and achieve product recognition in a trice? "Ba ba ba ba ba ba, I feel free" croons Jack Bruce as the swish motor car whisks down the scenic route to the strains of a revamped Cream classic . . .

Rock videos and glossy telly ads are now being created by the same directors and creative teams: the images are becoming interchangeable – so why not the soundtrack type too? There's this girl in a shower rubbing her back down with Imperial Leather Shower – that's some kind of silky skin moisturizer or something (the precise intentions of the product are never made entirely clear) – while her boyfriend gets disgruntled waiting for her in the restaurant and The Kinks (well, it's not actually The Kinks but you'd have to be quite alert to spot the difference) go "So tired, tired of waiting, tired of waiting for you-ou-ou . . ."

And they've discovered the "youth market". Okay, so almost all school leavers are on the dole or serving time on some spurious "job creation" scheme and being paid a pittance these days, but there's still a pretty pocket of Thatcher Youth with sizeable wads of disposable income to fritter away on fab new products – fizzy beer and trendy trouserwear and enticing banking facilities. Look at the grim youth with the modern haircut and the designer trainers as he approaches his local National Westminster Bank and "presses for action". Blimey! Lights flash, camera angles go wonky and The Who's 'Pinball Wizard' comes blaring out of the breeze blocks. Who could ask for more? After that, our callow hero will probably nip, with his new-found wealth, down the Wimpy where the friendly staff will be happy to greet him with a perky dance routine and their revised rendition of The Drifters' 'Come On Over To My Place' . . . "Come on over to our place! Hey YOU! We're having a Wimpy! ! ! ! ! ! !" (Meanwhile, his parents are back home tucking into the fry-up they have prepared deliciously in their Silver Stone non-stick pan – you know, the one they rushed out to buy after witnessing the delightful commercial in which an animated fried egg attempts to crawl up said pan's slippery-smooth surface whilst The McCoys – for it is they! – go "Hang on Sloopy, Sloopy hang on" in the foreground . . .)

When that celebrated tanned "hunk" Nick Kamen sauntered into the launderette and dropped his trousers to Marvin Gaye, he set standards for others to follow. The success of the trousers, the re-released record and even the "star" Kamen himself, was quite astonishing. Levis got quite carried away, going in to soft porn with Percy Sledge and that nymphet wriggling into some denims on a bed. There was no going back.

Roy Orbison's 'Oh Pretty Woman' will sell you Poly Colour (stuff to stick in your hair), Bachman-Turner-Overdrive's 'You Ain't Seen Nothing Yet' will flog you wacky paints, Status Quo's 'Whatever You Want' shifts dodgy magazines . . . even Desmond Dekker is not averse to a spot of commerce: that tiresome sun in shades who warbles about some supposedly health-enhancing margarine to the tune of 'Israelites' . . .

Pity the poor jingle writer. Consigned to the ghetto of local commercial radio with his "Superflush! Superflush!" and "The Direct Bargain Centre has great bargains for your home" (a truly reluctant tune, this one), he stands scant chance of survival in the late eighties. The "creative" manager from the advertising agency goes home to his Art Deco cocktail cabinet and his remote-controlled compact disc player and relaxes to some old-time tunes. "Ah," he thinks, taking another sip at his Rusty Nail, "'Layla' by Derek And The Dominoes. Just the ticket for that new automobile contract. Let's make an offer in the morning." So he does. But don't think it's cheap. Jingles come cheaper by far.

The Quo shift "dodgy magazines"

The Clash cost too much

For the final appearance of George The Bear in a Hofmeister lager ad, they got hold of Little Richard's 'Tutti Frutti'. A snip at £25,000. Some bright spark thought that The Hollies' 'He Ain't Heavy He's My Brother' would make a splendid soundtrack for a Miller Lite ad. Cost: £24,000. Yet more peculiar: The Clash's 'Rebel Waltz' (from *Sandinista*) was selected as ideal backing for a Carvel decongestant campaign – but in this case even the agency had to baulk at the asking price: £1,000 per week of the commercial's run. If only they had approached a jingle writer in the first place, they could have devised an *ace* campaign. Why, even as I write this, I feel a rather catchy jinglette coming on . . . "Car-vel! Car-vel! It's a decongestant mar-vel!!!" Rather good, don't you think? Yours for a fiver . . .

So. Bring back the advertising jingle forthwith and leave the old pop songs to moulder with dignity in the archives and our memories. *Please.*

PROFITS WITHOUT HONOUR

★

An ex-Mecca Ballroom DJ, a cruise liner guitarist and a hotel band musician join forces to become 1987/88's most successful hit-makers. Ian Cranna examines the continuing rise of Stock Aitken & Waterman.

Although Stock Aitken & Waterman were not among the chosen few to be garlanded as Act Of The Year in this book, there is a very strong case for just such a recognition. It's called 31 number one hits and 35 million records sold around the world. (And that was just 1987.) For theirs was the sound that dominated the charts, dancefloors and airwaves of Britain with its instantly recognizable bouncy, chattering dance rhythms and chirpy, catchy pop tunes, no matter who the chosen vocalist – Mel & Kim, Rick Astley, Kylie Minogue, Bananarama, Hazell Dean, Sinitta, Samantha Fox . . .

The high priests of hip hated them, of course. Bland and mindless, sneered the elitists from their ivory towers (while silently cursing them for reaching just the people *they* wanted to reach). Now had Stock Aitken & Waterman been black and American, one can't help feeling it would have been a very different story and they would have been lionized as the voice of new realism or some such. Yet even here Stock Aitken & Waterman had the last laugh when they had copies of their seventies-style funk instrumental 'Roadblock' pressed up on white labels and imported from New York into the ultra-hip Rare Groove club scene. So good and so convincing was their forgery that some DJs even went around claiming to have copies of the seventies original!

Mike Stock (right), Matt Aitken (left), Peter Waterman (centre): Pedigree naffness

Had Stock Aitken & Waterman been black and American, one can't help feeling they would have been lionized as the voice of new realism

But why the sudden rise to massive prominence of this obscure trio, none of whom will ever see 30 again? On one hand, Stock Aitken & Waterman can be seen as part of the rise of that very eighties phenomenon – the creator-producer. With the rise of increasingly sophisticated keyboard technology and the increased accessibility of such products, one person operating alone in their proverbial bedroom can now produce highly professional techno-dance records. Witness, for example, the creative sampling technique which has brought hits for smart young club DJs like Tim Simenon (Bomb The Bass) and Mark Moore (S-Express), or the way the sound of House music has largely been taken over in Britain by white kids who already had the right electronic equipment.

Yet Stock Aitken & Waterman are no advocates of the help-yourself technique of sampling. They have complained loudly about preserving the "integrity" of the performance and even gone so far as to take legal action against M/A/R/R/S for pirating one of their productions. More to the point, Stock Aitken & Waterman are in fact the direct descendants of a much earlier phenomenon – the silent songwriter. Appreciation of this now endangered species has declined dramatically since the advent of The Beatles. When the lovable, down-to-earth mop-tops wrote their own songs so everybody else thought they could write songs too: before you could say "pass the joss-stick" there was a moral obligation to "write your own material" – regardless of whether you had any talent for this or not. From there, things progressed to the point at which if you performed someone else's songs you were "selling out to the establishment, man" – another useless sacred cow of the white hippy seventies which has still to be put to rest.

Where Stock Aitken & Waterman really belong is among the production lines of pop – Brill Building, Motown, Philadelphia International – all of which, curiously enough, are looked on as some kind of Golden Era by the very people who sneer at Stock Aitken & Waterman. It is an honourable tradition still carried on today among the black music sector in America where there is still a much closer adherence to the older values. Take, for example, the work of Chic in the seventies or the miracle-working Jam/Lewis team today, with other up-and-coming writer-production teams like the Calloway brothers or LA & Babyface waiting in the wings.

Nor is the factory connotation too strong an image. It is one that Stock Aitken & Waterman happily use themselves. Nor is there anything necessarily wrong with such a way of working. What if 'Never Gonna Give You Up' *did* only take three and a half minutes to write? What that

Bananarama: Outsold The Supremes

demonstrates is a real gift, a natural talent – something borne out by the fact that it was the best-selling British single of 1987. If it's really so simple, why don't more people do it? There is no natural law – only another self-denying hippy hangover – stating that popular music must be art, or that to be valid a piece of music has to be agonized over for hours in some gloomy garret.

And is there any *real* difference between what Stock Aitken & Waterman do with Bananarama or Rick Astley and what The Pet Shop Boys have done with Dusty Springfield or Patsy Kensit (sor-*ree* – Eighth Wonder)? The only difference is in the eye of the beholder. The Pet Shop Boys understand full well the value of presentation and play the game of appearances to win. Stock Aitken & Waterman, on the other hand, are uncomfortably honest in their opinions about what they do and calling an industry an industry. This is dangerous talk to the crusading image-makers and Stock Aitken & Waterman have paid the full price by being branded as deeply unfashionable by those who seek to preserve the myth of "rebel music" as they fondly imagine it.

"We've taken pop music back to the people who buy records, not the journalists who preach to people," enthused Pete Waterman to *Smash Hits*. "If Stock Aitken & Waterman do anything, we make music for people, for

Mel and Kim: Full of sound practical advice

people to buy. What a *big* crime that is! We *entertain* people. We write songs about life as we see it and as the kids see it."

While "the kids" responded to this simple, honest approach by buying their records by the shed-full (to use one of

. . . Kylie from Ramsey St . . .

the trio's own favourite terms), there remains the nagging doubt – compounded by their use of phrases like "listening with Woolworths ears" – that "entertainment" can cover a multitude of talentless sins, and with it the corollary that somehow Stock Aitken & Waterman are aiming for the lowest common denominator.

Indeed, if you were so minded, you could put together from their collective history a pedigree of naffness that would give any TV soap opera pause for thought. Waterman (now 40) – the ideas man and commercial ears of the operation – had not only been a DJ for the terminally unhip ballroom and nightclub chain Mecca but even worked

SAW's "magic touch" took Sam from page 3 . . .

. . . Sinitta (here with TV presenter Gaz Top) from West End musicals . . .

for a record company in both A&R and marketing. He had also worked with successful producer Pete Collins (Musical Youth, Nik Kershaw, Loose Ends, etc.) before parting company with him over their move to California – "the sun really got to me brain." Of the other two – who take care of the musical side of things – Matt Aitken (31) had played guitar on ocean liners (very Black Lace!) while Mike Stock (36) had played in posh hotel "function" bands and even scored the ultimate naff accolade, appearing in a band called Dodge who came *last* on TV "talent" show *Opportunity Knocks*.

It was after a chance meeting that Waterman was impressed by a song the other two had written called 'The Upstroke'. "What Pete *actually* said," Mike Stock recalled to *Smash Hits*, "was 'Stick with me boys, and I'll show you how to make a hit record.' Which we thought was completely arrogant, because we'd been trying for *years*." But they teamed up and 'The Upstroke' duly hit the lower regions of the British charts as performed by Agents Aren't Aeroplanes (a kind of female Frankie Goes To Hollywood) and championed by, of all people, John Peel (which the trio now find both flattering and amusing). But the team had yet to find that magic touch – they even wrote the Cyprus entry for the Eurovision Song Contest and came 18th!

The turning-point came when Waterman played the other two (who were still being "too clever") a demo of 'You Think You're A Man'. "It was," Stock remembers, "everything a well-tempered musician who's been practising for 20 years like me thought was naff. It was simple to the point of being puerile." It was also a Top 20 hit for Divine and the light began to dawn. Then came Dead Or Alive who wanted to sound like Divine and thus was born their first number one production, the brilliant dance–pop of 'You Spin Me Round'. Other records with left-field talents followed though the hits didn't (although in the case of Brilliant they certainly deserved to) before the dam broke with their own creation Mel & Kim.

Now there may seem to be in this pedigree of naffness more of a throwback to the seventies teenybop creations of Mickie Most and Chapman/Chinn (Mud, Sweet etc.) than a claim to the more exalted company of Gamble/Huff, etc. Yet the work of Stock Aitken & Waterman does not depend on the pubescent fantasies of teenage girls (though Rick Astley's fresh-faced looks certainly didn't hurt) – otherwise why work with so many female vocalists? And even the most cursory examination of the evidence shows that the Stock Aitken & Waterman Hit Factory is no British Leyland of pop.

You could put together, from their collective history, a pedigree of naffness that would give any TV soap opera pause for thought

. . . and Rick from the tearoom, to sell records by "the shed-full"

Firstly and most importantly, their compositions show not just mere craftsmanship but a perfect understanding of what makes a great pop record: the uplifting cross-rhythms of dance, the dynamism of supporting arrangements, a gift for memorable tune and the essential of keeping things simple.

Secondly, they are careful to tailor their material to fit the natural personalities of the acts they work with. For the laughing, exuberant East End sisters Mel and Kim Appleby they created the image of strong, independent girls giving their advice to less experienced friends in trouble. Their touchstone for a happy life of *Fun, Love And Money* and the counsel that if you dance you'll feel a whole lot better may not reach new heights of inspiration but for sound practical advice it takes some beating. And when coupled with a near-flawless album of jaunty dance–pop it was as effective a piece of total image creation as you could wish to see. For simple, boyish Rick Astley they created a series of uncomplicated songs of love and devotion that struck a chord in a million hearts and minds. Girls next door Bananarama may not have the glamour of The Supremes but they've sold more records.

Nor is Stock Aitken & Waterman's care and attention restricted to the recording studio. They did their bit for Ferry Aid. They were careful to steer their protégés clear of the more destructive aspects of the music industry. They thank their staff nicely and are quietly nurturing the next generation of studio talent in mixers Phil Harding and Pete Hammond. Indeed far from being the archetypal throw-it-out-and-see-if-it-sticks merchants, Stock Aitken & Waterman seem to be motivated by a genuine love of pop music rather than money.

Stock Aitken & Waterman will never feature highly in the taste or style ratings but then they have no pretensions to doing so, and it will be their downfall should they try to do so. Just as Neil Tennant of The Pet Shop Boys remarked that the public will always like high energy, so there will always be room for a good, honest pop song. The secret of Stock Aitken & Waterman's success is merely that they do it so well.

★ POLARIZING THE PRINT ★

The circulations of *Q* and *Smash Hits* are soaring, at the expense of the more established music press. Cynthia Rose nips round the newsagent and finds this rise mirrored by growing numbers of determinedly non-mainstream, but increasingly popular music and music related magazines.

Throughout 1988, television and advertising continued to homogenize global perceptions of "pop" – and to reshape the markets which consume it. From cable TV to satellite broadcast, feature films to advertising (keen to exploit the yuppie romance with Motown and vintage blues); from US TV's *Entertainment Tonight* to UK TV's Channel Four chat shows, all manner of media took to plundering pop fandom's central core: its cult of information.

The bigger budgets and undeniable clout of television (compare the value of 15 seconds' free "editorial time" to the thousands that must be paid for comparable commercial slots) have hit pop publishing hard. Once the world's most famous, the UK's weekly music press now displays a nearly-total disarray. Led by editors chosen not for their expertise in a shifting marketplace, but for visibility in "official" circles, or from within labyrinthine publishing houses like IPC.

The traditional giants – *New Musical Express, Melody Maker, Sounds* – simply roll on with no particular focus or destination clear in their sights. And, in a year which saw weekly breakthroughs for British-based, UK-made black music (not to mention UK-sited triumph for international artistes ranging from Tracy Chapman to Malathini to Michelle Shocked), they were regularly reduced to cover stories involving the likes of Iron Maiden and Pink Floyd. Plummeting circulation statistics show their predicament.

Nor has the so-called "style press" been well-placed to exploit the fickle climate of late-eighties taste. Having courted international bucks in the form of display advertising and distribution, organs like *The Face* are now crippled by formats, expectations and ad schedules which originate abroad. Up-and-comers of past years (such as *Blitz* and *i-D*) soldier on. But they remain condemned by lack of nerve, imagination and house graphic skills to dwell forever in the fading shadow of *The Face*.

New aspirants to the leisure press – like Scotland's outsize monthly, *Cut*, or America's resurrected *Spin* – convey the redundancy of the now-fossilized style-mag format. Their "preview" and "intro" sections look bitty and unappetizing; the feature slots old and tired (in 1988 – *Joe Strummer and Mick Jones*?); the quickie colour pieces (Latin hip hop! acid house! Miami deco!) indefensibly shallow and bland. Particularly since, today, the UK pop fan's eye can easily shift to a new range of publications. And all of them address specific aspects of his taste without passing comment on it as a whole.

Widely diverse in distribution and skills, these organs share little other than specificity. Some are frankly fanzines (football monthly *When Saturday Comes*, cartoon skate-zine *Sketchy*). Others have clearly ambitious, capitalistic aims: like would-be glossies *Soul Underground* and *Straight No Chaser*. But all wrestle with genuine 1980s passions, from jazz through to skateboarding, rap to cricket, fashion to hardcore sounds. And, though they vary in polish and price, all issue from just that impulse mainstream publications now lack – response to the actual marketplace within which pop is made and sold.

Even while struggling to use them as tipsheets, Britain's mainstream pundits persist in characterising such magazines' public as cultists and their market as an "underground". Yet were these czars possessed of real reporting skills, TV schedules and music-press policy would recognize in this new, fragmented press the shape of pop culture to come. Certainly current market research supports a thesis that youth demographics and spending trends have now broken down along lines of separate and individual tastes. The Mintel Company's 1988 *Youth Lifestyles Report*, for instance, reached one main conclusion: that, within Britain, "youth culture" as an entity has now "ceased to exist". "We found," reiterates one Mintel spokesman, "that now things are highly fragmented and almost tribal. And that kids are much more like young adults, mini-versions of their parents' peer groups. When it comes to music, money and style, each group makes their own, discrete choice."

Official success in addressing even a changed market, though, still means a format: like *Smash Hits* (with its 650,000 circulation); or like *Q*, the first music publication to win PPA's UK Magazine Of The Year Award. More than doubling its two-year circulation projections (from 38,000 to 78,000) in 1988, *Q*'s statistics provide the British magazine establishment with a blueprint and parameters for "progress". Lost on the souls that inhabit its ivory towers is the fact that *Smash Hits* and *Q* succeeded because they broke new ground, and anything that attempts to ape them won't. In 1989, IPC even plan to launch a direct competitor to *Q*, the ludicrously titled *McCoy* – with *NME* lifer Roy Carr in the editor's chair.

All will, however, eventually hit the wall of potential redundancy which has always loomed before the music press (how *many* Madonna analyses can one LP or tour sustain?). But alternative reads like *Soul Underground* (70p),

Sticky Wicket (50p), *Straight No Chaser* (£1), *When Saturday Comes* (40p), and *Skate Muties From The Fifth Dimension* (50p) have already scaled it to reach another side. Developed out of specific enthusiasms for skateboarding fever through London's late-eighties infatuation with pirate radio, they remain topical, responsive and energetic.

Take the case of skateboard mags. These have sprung from an international youth sports scene estimated to include 20 million fans worldwide. Its participants are accustomed to bonding through music and communicating via print. But, traditionally, their market has been dominated by two American publications: *Thrasher* (the scene's rough, streetwise voice) and *Transworld Skateboarding* (heftier and slick).

Thrasher appeared in 1980, the self-promotional brainchild of Independent Trucks, a division of US company Ermico – who manufacture skateboard axles. Written in florid, skateboarding slanguage and rife with gonzoid, go-for-it pep, it has managed to unify skaters and hardcore music-lovers around the world. (Circulation has also bounded – from 16,000 to almost 300,000.) According to house artist/Music Editor Brian "Pushead" Schroeder, the only secret is "attitude".

Both skate glossies run regular music columns and lavish features; they treat pop obsessions as the very stuff of life. As a consequence, their readers become participants: keeping letters pages lively, seizing on special offers, deluging the magazine with tapes, tips and international news. In Britain, the strongest such publications remain street-sheets manufactured by fans – magazines like *Sketchy, Bomber Terrorzine* and *Skate Muties*. But mainstream attempts to found a British *Thrasher* are certainly being made. Felix Dennis (whose poster-mag empire was founded on "radical" sixties organ *Oz*) resurrected a seventies skate-scene publication called *Skateboard!*, a package he has since ceded to Advanced Publishing. And Higginson Publications have put together a similar periodical, *Skate Action*.

Since 1986, London's entertainment world has also enjoyed a growing "underground" music sphere. Prodded into being by the capital's roster of pirate radio stations (now some 30 separate set-ups), it has been shaped and enlarged by waves of vinyl bootlegging and by phenomena such as "warehouse parties". (One-time-only, pay-at-the-door affairs in derelict buildings, publicized by word of mouth.)

The facility for playing, as opposed to merely commenting on, all sorts of music has given the pirate stations a clear lead over the pop press. But, despite sporadic attempts at radio journalism *per se* (interviews with visiting stars; KISS-FM's programme "The Word"), it's not an advantage illegal broadcasters have been able to exploit. What their musical choices have done is bring black musics like gospel, soul, jazz and fusion, dancehall reggae and hip hop a better, wider hearing within London and the UK. Not to mention making possible a roster of fresh reads.

Previous British street-mag movements have boasted brand-new graphic perceptions, but not the street-sheets of '88. Most design-conscious is *Straight No Chaser*, an artefact of London's new jazz and Latin-listening scene. Devised by DJ Paul Bradshaw and ex-*NME* Editor Neil Spencer (currently calling the shots for *The Face*'s stablemate *Arena*), its desktop design is the work of Andy Martin – another *NME* grad. But it offers merely a marriage of previous styles: imbuing Al McDowell's initial *i-D* format with the classic forties and fifties austerity Paul Elliman brought to jazz journal *Wire*.

The traditional giants – *New Musical Express, Melody Maker, Sounds* – simply roll on with no clear destination in their sights. Organs like *The Face* are now crippled by formats, expectations and ad schedules which originate abroad

Take *Soul Underground*: which sold its first 370 copies in October 1987. One year later, this would-be slick publication boasts regular advertising (sold by pirate station KISS-FM), mainstream distribution (by Comag in the UK, Trash & Vaudeville abroad), and a steady print run it likes to claim is near 6,000. It was started by freelance photographer David Lubich, new to London from student days "Up North". His founding partner was Darren Reynolds, a then-London Transport employee and full-time nightclub habitué. Reynolds' input lasted through summer '88, augmented by news and gossip which came from KISS-FM's impressive roster of "name" DJs. "First and foremost," Lubich concedes, "kids buy us for that news." By November of '88, *Soul Underground* hopes to be printing 40-page issues each month.

Though *Straight No Chaser* has clearly been extrapolated from the slim, serious *Wire*, its studious freshness has turned the trick against that publication. Even a longtime *Wire* salespoint like London record shop Honest Jon's report June sales of *Chaser* dwarfing the jazz mag's new issue by 50 to 1.

Dominated by demographics and almighty advertising cash, official media outlets grow less and less responsive to the burning concerns of youth. In America, this has given new life to grassroots print: "alternative" weeklies like the *Phoenix New Times, Dallas Observer, Seattle Weekly, Chicago Reader* and *LA Weekly*. Most are freesheets, subsisting on classified lonelyhearts ("the personals"), dining and entertainment ads. But all are part of a definite chain which now stretches from coast to coast. United to a degree by soft-left, pro-environment politics, what this new network really provides is a scrupulous attention to local issues and art. Plus it remains committed to staying globally *au courant* – treating international trends via video, vinyl and film.

Print has always served pop best by making it part of an ongoing context. And it is the guerilla thrills inherent in that function (rather than the reflections of "name" critics or "qualified" commentators) which sum up what's missing from today's mainstream pop publications. A fervent local champion like the *Dallas Observer*'s Clay McNear or an acerbic scene satirist like *Sketchy*'s Paul Brown will never enjoy global renown or MTV acclaim. Yet theirs were the words that made pop print worth reading, and chuckling over, in '88.

ARE THESE PEOPLE NECESSARY?

Rock on the box? There's never been so much of it. Colin Shearman, however, is still reaching for the off switch, as these new-style presentations insist on old-style presenters.

At the press launch for *The Chart Show* in 1986, the Controller of Channel 4, Paul Bonner, came over to the programme's youthful commissioning editor, John Cummins, and told him that he liked the programme but something would have to be done about those awful graphics. Surely they were much too small to read and not on the screen long enough either? Bonner seemed totally unconvinced by Cummins' explanation that, when dealing with the computer generation, this was far from the case.

Funnily enough, at the time Bonner seemed to be right and Cummins wrong, although by the following year *The Chart Show* had become the most successful pop programme on TV . . . mainly because it turned every rule upside down. It puts an awful lot of information on the screen when, of course, everyone knows pop fans are much too stupid to understand anything more complicated than Simon Bates saying: "And now let's meet this week's Top Ten!" It plays minority taste records from the indie, dance and HM charts. It eschews live music for video clips whereas *the* golden rule of pop shows states that live music is television's trump card – despite common sense telling you that the sound quality coming out of most TVs makes a sixties Dansette sound like the latest in laser technology. But most of all – and for this we should be very thankful indeed – it had no presenters.

The show's original producers, Jill Sinclair and Keith McMillan, realized that since *Max Headroom* any presenter would end up a parody of themselves. And, in any case, graphics could do the job just as well as any DJ with a spiky haircut and an insincere voice – also, they were less demanding when it came to expense accounts and made the show move faster. Surprisingly though – when you consider that nearly all this year's pop shows (*Network 7*, *The Roxy*, *Night Network*) have aped *The Chart Show*'s graphics, fast-moving approach or, more negatively, its totally unoriginal editorial content – none of them have learned the lesson about presenters.

Lenore Pemberton and Tim Graham (*Wired*)

David "No Longer A Kid" Jensen

Paul "Once A Window Cleaner" Nolan

Kevin "Nice Suit" Sharkey

So when *The Roxy* set up shop in summer 1987 as a rival to *TOTP*, the producers came up with the novel idea of having presenters just like . . . those on *TOTP*! But at least they were younger. David Jensen may be a kid no longer but he could still give most of the Radio 1 crew a run for their pensions. They also recruited from Ireland a soft-spoken but smartly dressed DJ called Kevin Sharkey ("Nice suit, shame about the DJ" commented pop mag, *Number One*).

ITV's greater involvement in the pop market – their sudden decision to launch a chart show after 30 years of hesitation plus the appearance of *Night Network* in August 1987 – was partly a wish to make more money. From their experience with *The Tube*, advertisers had finally realized that rock programmes get through to audiences for very specific products: soft drinks, jeans, shampoo, etc. But they were also worried that their increasing failure to attract younger viewers meant ITV's overall share of the market was declining – and pop shows were the obvious way of remedying the situation.

The head of teenage programmes at Tyne Tees, Andrea Wonfor, had been feeding these ideas into the ears of the various network channel controllers for some time in the hope they'd give her the go-ahead to produce an ITV rival to *Top Of The Pops*. And her pilot show, which she'd worked on for two years, looked likely to win the tender until the roof fell in at Tyne Tees. A number of demoralizing financial cut-backs – in one instance *The Tube* was refused permission to fly to Chicago to do a feature on house music – coupled with a run of rather childish moral warnings from the IBA – such as that surrounding Jools Holland's famous four-letter slip of the tongue in a tea-time trailer for *The Tube* – sparked off some serious backstage rows which eventually led to Wonfor, *Tube* producer Malcolm Gerrie and several other leading lights leaving the station, thus splitting up the most experienced pop production team in Europe.

Wonfor then re-submitted her pilot as an independent producer. It was undoubtedly the best of the dozen or so applications considered by the Network Controllers Committee but the regional ITV companies, wanting the work for one of their own number, ganged up to announce they simply wouldn't show the programme if it came from an independent. Tyne Tees managing director David Reay, who wanted the show badly because he'd just lost *The Tube* in the wake of Gerrie's resignation, added the *coup de grâce* by threatening to sack over 60 staff if they didn't get the contract.

As a result, the show went to Tyne Tees' now fairly inexperienced production team who, under all sorts of pressure to keep up the ratings, quickly abandoned their radical plans – features, new bands – and tried to make the show look as much like *TOTP* as possible. For the second series – as falling ratings created behind-the-scenes panic – the ageing Jensen was "promoted" off screen to associate producer and, still failing to learn from the chart show, a number of younger presenters were chosen for the fans to identify with: a particularly untalented window-cleaner called Paul Nolan, who'd risen to fame after appearing as a contestant on *Blind Date* and underage bride Emma "Wild Child" Ridley, most famous for appearing in her underwear on the front page of the *Sunday Mirror* against the headlines "This Girl Is Only 14!". You could have written everything they both knew about pop music on one side of a compact disc sleeve. When you think this was the year that a real, enthusiastic and knowledgeable music fan like Andy Kershaw won a Sony award for the quality of his broadcasting, you can't help wondering whether, in addition to all their other problems, the producers of *The Roxy* were entertaining some sort of death-wish as well.

You can't help wondering whether, in addition to all their problems, the producers of *The Roxy* were entertaining some sort of death-wish as well

Streetwise cousin to *The Roxy*, *Network 7*, on the other hand, was smart enough to learn a few lessons from *The Chart Show*. This tabloid magazine show lifted the graphics idea wholesale and then somehow persuaded everyone they'd thought of it themselves. During its mix of political, musical and general interest features, additional – but not always accurate – snippets of information would cross the lower part of the screen in the wide expanse between trendy presenter Magenta De Vine's knee and the hem of her mini-skirt. They also developed *The Chart Show*'s fast-moving style to an absurdly patronizing degree so that its features on joining the army or the ethics of the death penalty were on and off the screen while you blinked. At the end of the day, like most of the shows produced in this 12-month period, this was designer club TV which put all its effort into the style and left the content to rather inadequately look after itself. Like the worst tabloids – which it was obviously aping – the show was trivial, absorbing and instantly forgettable. Possibly the worst insult one can pay it is that Radio 1 DJ Simon Bates could be heard telling his mid-morning listeners how wonderful it all was.

It did, however, bring its ageing producer, Janet Street-Porter, to the attention of the BBC who took her on at an enormous salary to revitalize their youth programmes. Not surprisingly for someone who'd just invented a show almost bankrupt in editorial innovation, she hit upon the brilliantly lazy idea of bunging together a load of old programmes and passing them off as an "exciting new concept" called *Def II* (an appropriate title for the show since it's meaningless) . . . a jumble of old children's hour clips, some old films and a not terribly good soul show. Andy Pandy videos may go down well at Ms Street-Porter's dinner parties but do kids of 14 really want to re-live their parents' youth? The ratings suggest not. The only element which really worked was *Open To Question*, an already successful question and answer show – pulled in under the *Def II* umbrella – in which fairly left-wing sixth-formers give public figures a hard time, and is as far removed from the patronizing short attention span of *Network 7* as you could possibly imagine.

Malcolm Gerrie: Britain's most adventurous pop producer

Which brings us, finally, to *Wired* – the white-hot hope for TV pop shows which, while improving by leaps and bounds at press time, still hasn't completely found its feet. The only programme not to rip off ideas from *The Chart Show*, it opts for "magazine style", with a few lengthy features from London and New York (which makes it easier to sell in the US) intercut with music. It's aimed at the generation who grew up with *The Tube*. Its credentials are impeccable: produced by Britain's most adventurous pop producer, Malcolm Gerrie and directed by his old Tube sidekick, Jonathan Hewes; and its very first programme had the first of many musical coups when it caught Tracy Chapman in performance, before the Mandela benefit sent her debut album rocking up the charts.

But, for a show which sets out to be a TV version of *Q* magazine, it doesn't quite dig deep enough. This is because we're talking real journalism here, not pop paper pyrogenics, and – despite its impeccable production staff – its journalists often aren't sharp enough. In a feature on New York rappers, Public Enemy, in the first programme a researcher who'd championed the band in *NME* came to the conclusion after travelling around with them for a while that they probably were as anti-semitic as people say and probably weren't playing with a full deck either. An honest and personal piece about his change of mind would have had journalistic depth, given a sense of what the group were like as people and how their music was actually inseparable from their ideas and personalities. Instead we had just the usual pop show piece cutting from performance to interview, which never made any real attempt to confront the group with the implications of their naive belief in violent revolution.

Two enthusiastic hip-hoorays for *Wired*, then, in a year during which you couldn't help otherwise thinking that the only way to improve pop on television would be to line every production team up against a wall and shoot the lot of them.

★ TUNES YOU CAN TRUST ★

Without a good computer you had no chance of pop success, or so it's seemed. Yet beyond the circuitry, gadgetry and studio wizardry is a return to "traditional values". Lloyd Bradley investigates the techno-backlash.

At the time of writing, Tracy Chapman is enjoying her third week at number one in the UK album charts. The popular, if somewhat glib, explanation as to how come an utterly unknown, pretty dour black girl – she is bereft of all the usual trappings: micro mini-skirt, weave-on hairdo and make-up by Dulux, and doesn't appear to be a very good dancer – could achieve such celebrity, concerns the massive audience she reached when by appearing at the Nelson Mandela Concert. However, the simple fact that neither The Fat Boys or Eric Clapton, both on the same bill, look like topping any recognized charts tends to imply there's more to it than that.

Tracy Chapman's success, in fact, represents the sharp end of a kind of anti-techno backlash that, during the past 12 months, has been quietly chipping away at studio craft as the most important facet of pop music. Apparently "synthed out", artistes, writers (song and press), record companies and, most importantly, record buyers have been increasingly turning away from brash electronics-based performances towards a gentler, more human sound. "Real" songs, played on "real" instruments.

Long before Chapman – armed with nothing more "late-eighties" than an acoustic guitar, an LP of mild-mannered compositions and a wardrobe even Annie Hall would reject – headed for platinum, the evidence was mounting. While Stock, Aitken & Waterman's studio wizardry metamorphosed tea-boys, topless models and wonky soap-opera actresses into passable facsimiles of pop stars, 10,000 Maniacs reaped critical acclaim from the spiky folk seeds they sowed three years ago when they collaborated with ex-Fairport Convention producer Joe Boyd. While any "B-Boy" or "Fly Girl" with a ha'porth of nous and a reasonable record collection was using a budget-price sampler to knock up a Top Ten hit while sitting on their bed, Fairground Attraction eschewed the bass synth for the traditional Mexican guitaron and went to number one with 'Perfect'. In the quest for perfection, Michael Jackson's stage show was sampled, Synclaviered and computer-controlled to the degree that actually pausing to talk to the crowd was ruled out, yet London touts charged much the same prices for tickets for The Pogues' beery multi-cultural folk/rock extravaganza. And the likes of Randy Travis, k.d. lang and Lyle Lovett meant you could admit a penchant for country music without being pointed at in the street.

"The ease and lack of expense with which people can nick anybody's bits of music has led to it becoming so widespread that everything's starting to sound derivative. It's lost its impact." – Simon Edwards, Fairground Attraction

Simon Edwards, Fairground Attraction's guitaron player, believes that in becoming so accessible, sampling and attendant studio technology dug its own grave. "The ease and lack of expense with which people can nick anybody's bits of music has led to it becoming so widespread that everything's starting to sound derivative. First, people were just thinking, Oh, another sampling record, now they're realizing that underneath it all the actual *songs* aren't there."

Mark E Nevin, the group's guitarist and main songwriter, although mildly astounded by his band's success – a Top Ten album as well as the number one single – believes such a consumer reaction to rampant technology in music was inevitable and part of a much more all-encompassing dissatisfaction.

"Cars, clothes, what magazines you read . . . everything has become laid down as accessories to a certain *lifestyle*. It's become so you're pressured into feeling inadequate if you don't conform . . . you're almost made to feel unfashionable if you want to be a human being . . . you're kind of encouraged to be a walking Filofax. It's all so contrived and, underneath it all, people aren't happy. Music is one of the first areas where the change of attitude is manifesting itself simply because buying records is relatively inexpensive and if there's something there to be listened to, as opposed to just being heard, it can have quite an effect.

Danny Wilson, The Pogues and The Proclaimers all adhere to this line, airing sentiments concluding that after a couple of years dancing to a "pretty uptight" computerized soundtrack, people are keen to relax. The consensus of opinion is that record companies are wholeheartedly supporting such groups because it is what the public appears to want, and they are not breaking new ground for humanitarian reasons.

Remarkably, the last word on how such almost *olde worlde* values can be applied to 1988 comes from record producer Nicky Graham. He maintains, like Fairground Attraction, that having been virtually starved of traditional pop music values recently, record buyers are not only ripe to hear "the real thing" again, but can recognize it when it's served up.

However, unlike the above mentioned, he believes that rather than simply sit alongside techno-based stuff, bygone ideals can be happily married to modern methods. He has a point: sitting for lengthy spells at his piano and employing the time-honoured verse/chorus/verse/chorus system, he painstakingly composed the Bros album.

★ DIGITAL INACCURACY ★

If the publicity was to be believed, CD was supposed to transport the listener to new heights of aural enjoyment. Only all too often, this isn't the case. John Bauldie roots out some huge-selling, less-than-perfect examples.

After years of active service, you've retired your vinyl copy of Springsteen's *Born To Run*, and laid out over a tenner for a CD replacement. Hands atremble, you slide in the drawer, crank up the amp, press Play and let "The Boss" blow you away with previously unattainable digital clarity. Only it doesn't sound too healthy. No better than your knackered old album in fact. What do you do: upgrade your entire hi-fi? Move to a house with an acoustically more satisfying living-room? Get your ears syringed?

What you could've done, if you were in America, was taken it back to the shop. There, sales staff would have relieved you of the offending article and discreetly slipped you a new one: the same packaging, the same catalogue number, but much better sound quality. The CD had, it seems, been botched. Newly mastered substitutes were quietly distributed and Columbia instructed that replacements should be offered to any disgruntled customers who asked. It was a very public admission that all was not as it should be in the much-hyped world of CD. What made this red-faced confession a little easier for the company was their excuse: it wasn't their fault. The first batches of the disc were pressed in Japan by an independent factory, with inferior materials and sloppy quality control. The later, made-in-the-USA edition, was of "the expected standard".

Jethro Tull's *Aqualung* left something to be desired...

...as did Clapton's *461 Ocean Boulevard*

The *Born To Run* CD (which sold, in its imperfect form, in vast quantities to unsuspecting purchasers) is a far from unique case. Not-so-proud owners of CD versions of Cream's *Disraeli Gears*, Eric Clapton's *461 Ocean Boulevard*, Fleetwood Mac's *Rumours*, Jethro Tull's *Aqualung* and James Brown's *The Godfather Of Soul – The Best Of James Brown* will by now probably be knowingly nodding their heads. So will some U2 fans who don't like what they hear when they play *The Joshua Tree* CD. Neither did the band, it seems, when they first heard it. Soon afterwards U2 made some changes in the equalization of the sound on the CD to "brighten it up". The work was done in New York and new, improved CDs can be identified only by an "RE-1" mark in the centre ring matrix numbers. Which means, of course, that thousands of U2 fans have a CD that the band don't like the sound of.

Usually, the blame for faults on CDs lies with the record company concerned. Remastering – the transfer of the music from the original analogue tapes to the digital tape required to make a CD – is full of potential hazards. Remastering from copies of the original master tapes (or copies of copies) rather than from the original studio masters will always result in poor sound quality. As each analogue copy is another generation removed from the original recording, the quality of recorded sound decreases and the tape noise increases, giving the remastering engineer less to work with but more to do. It is not uncommon for original master tapes to have been lost – the likelihood of this happening to an act's early recordings is considerable as at the time of recording few would suspect that they were party to the Birth Of A Legend and consequently accorded the tapes scant respect.

However, the fuzzy-sounding European CD issues of Clapton's *Slowhand* and *461 Ocean Boulevard* and Cream's *Disraeli Gears* can't be attributed to ages-ago negligence; they were remastered from (copied) production masters filed in Hamburg, while the original tapes were known to be in a vault in New Jersey. And purchasers of two Byrds CDs, *Greatest Hits* and *Original Singles Vol. 1*, were dismayed to hear wavery and muffled sounds coming from the speakers. It turned out that CBS had no multi-track

U2 didn't like the first *Joshua Tree* discs

Springsteen's *Born To Run* was exchanged...

master tapes of Byrds material and had not only used old and decrepit two-track tapes, but had played them on a machine which had an unstable tape transport. The results were appalling.

But even the use of the original masters does not guarantee a good finished product. Sloppy remastering can cause all sorts of problems, the most common of which occur when, in the removal of the tape's surface noise, some of the music – particularly both ends of the sonic spectrum – is wiped out too, resulting in a flat, jumbled finished product where nothing stands out like it should. John Lennon's *Imagine*, his *Shaved Fish* compilation and Fleetwood Mac's *Rumours* (another CD which sold in its original form in massive quantities) were distinctly lacklustre CDs and prime examples of ham-fisted engineering. Both were subsequently re-remastered and re-issued following complaints (in *Rumours*' case the objections came from Ken Caillat, the album's co-producer) but with little trouble taken to inform an unsuspecting public.

Disintegrating master tapes often present major difficulties to remastering engineers. Tapes can begin to fall apart because of bad storage, over-use or just plain old age. According to Capitol Records engineer Larry Walsh, the Beach Boys' albums *Endless Summer* and *Spirit Of America* suffered from two of these conditions. "During the sixties and seventies the tapes got beat up pretty badly as not enough care was being taken over their storage. Also people had been using the actual masters to make personal cassette copies and things. When we came to remaster, the masters had been across tape heads something like a zillion times and we were left with a bunch of ends and pieces to put together and work with."

...Fleetwood Mac's *Rumours* should've been...

Occasionally, or only occasionally admitted to, a wrong decision rather than a technical hitch will lead to a CD being withdrawn. Early copies of Bob Dylan's *Blonde On Blonde* had several seconds shaved off the endings of certain songs – most noticeably 'Just Like A Woman' and 'Sad-Eyed Lady Of The Lowlands' – in a move to accommodate the double album on a single CD. The total playing time of the *Blonde On Blonde* vinyl was, however, well within the CD limit of 75 minutes, but it seems the company decided to err on the side of caution without taking a track off completely. In a curiously botched effort to right this particular wrong, CBS put out a new improved version, with complete 'Sad-Eyed Lady Of The Lowlands' but with no change to the other tracks. Now a third version is being remastered. "It's been a learning experience for us," said CBS's US marketing manager John Tavenner, glumly.

Dylan's *Blonde On Blonde* was "shaved"

CD is still flying high on the widely accepted myth that all CDs sound better than any vinyl – after all, no one likes to admit they've just wasted £10.99

... Beach Boys tapes had disintegrated

Although obviously at fault here and with dreadful Byrds botch-ups, CBS haven't felt obliged to offer any recompense – indeed they haven't even informed unlucky buyers, probably the keenest fans who bought the discs immediately after release. Other companies too are equally tight-lipped: Polydor slipped new, improved pressings of the Clapton and Cream CDs into the shops unannounced; Island never breathed a word about *The Joshua Tree*; Elektra replaced all the Doors CDs with considerably better-sounding discs – even altering the catalogue numbers – but they didn't tell anyone other than the dealers; Warner Bros refused to take up Ken Caillat's suggestion that they put a sticker on the second generation *Rumours* CD telling buyers, as the co-producer put it, "This wasn't the same piece of junk that was out before."

It's all a matter of customer confidence. CD, a relatively new medium, is still flying high on the widely accepted myth that all CDs sound better than any vinyl albums – after all, no one likes to admit they've just wasted £10.99. Nothing would debunk that quicker than a stampede of disgruntled punters, so record companies choose not to make public their more high-profile cock-ups. Disturbingly, they'll defend to the bitter end their right to offload less than satisfactory product. When questioned (by the independently published American newsletter *International CD Exchange*) on how he felt he could justify a lack of consumer protection on duff batches of discs, Hale Milgrim, Elektra's marketing vice-president, bluntly stated, "Does this happen when we make a better grade of vinyl, or come up with better cassette shells or better tape? What do you do whenever there's better technology than one, two or three years ago? We're trying to take care of our mistakes of the past and get it proper now."

But weren't we led to believe they'd "got it proper" when the format was launched? Wasn't that how they justified the ridiculously inflated prices?

THE CAMERA NEVER LIES

★

Pop stars on the silver screen? It's increasingly popular among those wishing to somehow consolidate their "art", yet, as Karen Swayne discovers, it usually ends in tears.

It's getting to be a standard interview question, "Do you see yourself getting into acting?" asks the journalist, to which the artist replies "Yeah, it's something I'd like to do in the future. But it'd have to be the right part." The plain fact of the matter is, of course, there'll *never* be "the right part". And if this sounds a little brutal, cast your mind back over the years and remember how, when respected larynxes and the big screen come together, the phrase "complete and utter berk" is always hovering somewhere in the mid-distance . . .

It all started harmlessly enough with the Rat Pack (Sinatra, Davis, Martin, *et al*) making amusing little home movies full of in-jokes and knowing winks. At least they had enough style not to take themselves too seriously and the guys got to do what they were good at – sing. Likewise Elvis Presley. He may have churned out some appalling cinematic garbage, but at least he could be relied on at some point – however contrived – to pick up a guitar and strum and swivel and sing. He did what was expected of him, and even when he was "acting", the homespun charm transferred neatly onto celluloid.

Prince struggles to convey "snigger-inducing" angst

Then came The Beatles. Their Scouse wit and lovable personalities were well enough ingrained in the public consciousness for films like *Help* and *A Hard Day's Night* to work. Scripts that taxed the Fabs no further than being their cheeky-chappie-selves in between the songs were a crucial factor. Prince took this tried-and-tested formula into the eighties with his quasi-autobiographical *Purple Rain*. Not a lot of laughs as His Royal Shortness showed the world a facts-meets-fantasy account of his struggle to fame and fortune, but the plentiful performance footage was genuinely exciting. In the absence of Prince on-stage in the flesh, so to speak, it kept many a fan content.

If the occasional cringe-inducing "emotional" scene in *Purple Rain* could be overlooked, his next screen adventure, *Under A Cherry Moon*, offered no such respite. Forced to watch their hero struggling to convey trauma and angst by fluttering his eyelashes and pouting meaningfully at the camera, even Prince's most devoted followers were hard-pushed to do anything other than snigger. Now on video, it's a firm favourite with the over-refreshed late-night crowd. (As is *Straight To Hell*, Alex Cox's confused attempt to make a "punk spaghetti Western" with the likes of Joe Strummer and The Pogues. The film only makes sense if the viewer is as drunk as the cast obviously were.)

Being used to total control in the recording studio, the Paisley Park-keeper demanded the same privilege on the set. As he discovered, godlike genius on record does not an Ingmar Bergman or a Robert De Niro make – a fact that fellow platinum-status artists Sting, David Bowie and Madonna must, by now, be just as painfully aware.

Madonna started reasonably enough in *Desperately Seeking Susan*, but as all it involved was playing herself it left her woefully unprepared for the role of Gloria Tatlock, the virginal missionary in *Shanghai Surprise*. "None too convincing" would be an overly-charitable description of this dictionary-definition miscasting. By the time *Who's That Girl* came out, even the hordes of

Madonna accepts criticism gracefully

easily gratified Wannabes had lost patience, and news that the film was a stinker – largely due to the star's horrendous overacting – spread with a speed that indicated Maddy's fans had a network BT would kill for. Unsurprisingly, the Marilyn Monroe comparisons stopped overnight.

Sting and Bowie too. Initially merely extending their on-stage personae to the screen – Sting's rigor mortis as the cool "ace face" mod in *Quadrophenia* and Bowie's other-worldliness in *The Man Who Fell To Earth* – they retained their dignity, then they both attempted to make their mark on the world of "serious" movies. The equally serious question of "Does their work conjure up images of great thespians adding a new dimension to the world of dramatic art?" has to be answered with a resounding "No, not really." Bowie creaked his way round a POW camp for *Merry Christmas Mr Lawrence* looking every inch the pop star he is, then who can forget that unfortunate fright wig in *Labyrinth*. Sting minced painfully through *Dune* clad in what looked like a tin-foil girdle, then hammed it up remorselessly in *Plenty* and *The Bride*.

Like The Pet Shop Boys in *It Couldn't Happen Here*, their very own *Magical Mystery Tour* (which leans heavily on

Bowie in terrifying fright-wig scare

vintage *Monty Python*), whatever charisma pop stars have gets kind of lost on the film set as soon as they start to act. And the only exception to the rule that they should just play themselves is Bob Dylan: never one of life's party people, he even failed to convince when playing a miserable old goat in the ill-fated *Hearts of Fire*.

So, secure in the knowledge that these characters continue to turn out the films they do because there's nobody within earshot with the guts to tell them they stink, why on earth should they want to do it in the first place?

Cash is not an issue. The average hit album will make its star much richer than the average hit movie. And anyway, all the above-named offenders already have more money than you or I could shake a stick at. The primary reason is they do it because they've been asked to. Movie moguls watch them shifting records by the million and it doesn't take a mathematical genius to work out that if you can get a fair percentage of those bums onto cinema seats you've got a ready-made audience and a nice little earner. Thus there is no shortage of offers "in the pipeline" and this may account for the damaging absence of a firm directorial hand in these films.

Promo videos have a lot to answer for at this stage. Three minutes miming their latest hit while looking distraught as a leggy lovely leaves them, or pretending to be terrorists while a leggy lovely sips champagne, or walking from one end of a yacht to the other while a leggy lovely looks on, have convinced some singers they're Oscar-winning material. What they tend to forget is that their public adores them for their toe-tapping toons, not for their personal interpretations of Method acting.

Once the offer's "on the table", the ego of the performer comes into play. Pop music still isn't taken seriously as an art form and, alongside the screams and adulation, most musicians, especially those a bit long in the tooth, crave respect. Movies, it seems, are accepted as "grown-up culture", infinitely more appropriate to a man with kids at boarding school and a home in Switzerland, than cavorting about with a guitar. That far more column inches in the "quality" newspapers are devoted to discussing films and film folk than they are to pop, is testament to this.

Of course, the swoon factor does still come into it. Once, young stars like Paul Newman and Clint Eastwood set young hearts a-flutter, yet with the advancing of years they are still allowed to woo and win a more mature female following. Pop idols, thanks to such a necessarily narrow target audience, cannot fail to fall from grace as time goes by.

Movies tend to last a lot longer too. Nothing hurts the used-to-be-very-famous more than being just that, and films tend to greatly outlast most albums. Whereas film buffs will continue to gather for Bogart or Keaton or Orson Welles festivals, only a handful of pop performers survive the passing of their era with such sustained interest. Equally, it is hard to imagine BBC2 turning Saturday afternoons over to a short season of Duran Duran concerts in the same way as they would accommodate the films of Kenneth More – even if the whole band died.

In the multi-media late-eighties, where every film aimed at anyone under pensionable age has a pulsating and intrusive rock soundtrack, things can only get worse: Bananarama were reportedly leafing through scripts in search of a "comedy" vehicle; Jermaine Jackson – the *really* strange one – will soon debut in a sci-fi movie called *Voyage Of The Rock Aliens*; portly Homburg hat-wearing rappers Run DMC have played two portly, Homburg hat-wearing rappers in the thriller *Tougher Than Leather*; Patsy Kensit will soon be seen in a religious "epic" entitled *The Countrymen Of God*; and Phil Collins has expanded his Cockney wide-boy cameo on *Miami Vice* to star as Great Train Robber Buster Edwards.

Lowe (left) and Tennant (right) take on Barbara Windsor (centre) in charisma contest

But it's not all doom and gloom. We have been spared the general release of Bangle Susannah Hoffs in *The All Nighter*, judged by one critic to have needed to improve considerably before it would be awful. The world would be an emptier place without Mick Jagger's excruciating "Australian" accent in *Ned Kelly*, or Grace Jones howling like a banshee in *Conan The Barbarian* or Cliff whooping it up with Una Stubbs on that double-decker bus in *Summer Holiday*. And we've still got Gary and Martin Kemp as the Kray twins and Andrew Ridgeley's entire screen career to look forward to.

Grace hunts for prehistoric contact lens

Godlike genius in the recording studio does not an Ingmar Bergman or a Robert De Niro make, a fact that Sting, Bowie and Madonna must, by now, be painfully aware

A SUITABLY SPECTACULAR FINALE

★ ★

ZTT/Frankie Goes To Hollywood was *the* perfect pop partnership of the eighties; its success pointed to a new dawn for independent record labels. Simon Garfield watched it submerge itself in a sea of good old-fashioned acrimony.

It was May 1987, and Paul Morley was making a point at a ZTT board meeting in Ladbroke Grove. Morley, then a ZTT director and – since his writing days at *NME* – a man aware of the power of bad press, had scanned the recent cuttings on his label's relationships with Propaganda and Das Psych-Oh Rangers and observed that "ZTT is now perceived as a bully label."

Frankie Goes To Hollywood as were

Faced with such a pedigree of exploitation, who can blame new artists for signing now and deciphering all the niggly clawback clauses later?

Eight months on at the High Court in the Strand, and Morley is nowhere to be seen. But his observations have seldom been more prophetic. In some eyes, the bully label had turned into a grisly ogre, a baffling high-walled maze of super-tech studio gadgetry and exploitative business practice. This was Holly Johnson's view, an opinion he raised throughout his three-week attempt to free himself from all ZTT ties and win back what he regarded as excessive recording costs deducted from the royalties he earned with Frankie Goes To Hollywood. And having toured the ZTT studios and turned a nose up at all manner of trivial pop diversions, it became – in essence at least – the view of Mr Justice Whitford, who let Johnson go to MCA with considerable funds in his pocket.

The popular press loved the saga. Not so much because it exercised the great, famous pop stars getting their own back on their publishing and record companies, but because it repainted a reassuringly venal and depraved pop world picture. The case covered homosexuality, bags of used fivers, drunken envy among spoiled adolescents, and an element that readers with even the slimmest knowledge of modern-day recording techniques were well aware of – that and these days rather trendy, rite of not all the sounds on every record were made by good-looking cover stars playing old-fashioned instruments.

For ZTT, the courtroom events marked not just the end of its relationship with Johnson, but also the close of a unique and ever-tumultuous first period in the label's history. Why bother to paraphrase the last decade of British pop in terms of CBS, PolyGram and Virgin or George Michael, Dire Straits and Boy George, when you could do it in terms of just one small independent company?

From its inception in 1983 to the court case in January 1988, ZTT had everything: entrepreneurship; sound creative judgement; inspired marketing; dramatic, shooting success; bullish financial takeovers; harsh boardroom tussles; and then a protracted downward spiral, bereft of most of the above. There was a human-interest angle: the two ZTT directors, businesswoman Jill Sinclair and record producer Trevor Horn, were married and had kids; Sinclair even wrote long workmanlike letters attempting to narrow the chasm between herself and Horn's parents. And then there was the legal angle: the severing of ties, rarely amicably, with signings The Art Of Noise, Propaganda, Andrew Poppy and Das Psych-Oh Rangers, and even a row with their distributors Island Records.

It's a perfect parabolic parable: massive success, massive failure and now, at the time of writing in June 1988, what looks like an upward swing with The Pogues and Nasty Rox Inc. How can this happen? Isn't success supposed to breed success and failure to breed failure?

For Jill Sinclair, the answer is rooted in experience: "It's very hard when you're a small licensed label, and you're very successful, to keep everyone happy. When you have great success, you think all you need to do is to make good records, but there's a lot more to it than that. We in our naivety did not realize the problems that small labels can get into with things like recording

Jill and Trevor: They seemed to control everything

costs. Those experiences have been very painful. Running a record label is so hard."

For music business solicitor Brian Carr, the answer has something to do with ZTT contracts. Acting for Propaganda in their successful attempt to leave ZTT in 1987, he discovered there was no limit to the amount Trevor Horn could charge for his efforts as producer. In theory this could mean that even a successful artist might never see any net earnings, such would be the debt to the recording process. "Normally a company exercises some control over expenditure in the studio," says Carr, "and in this case there was no control over Trevor's expenditure. The agreement entered into by the group [contained] no way in which one could obtain control . . . There's no use saying, as I think was said, that Trevor's not prepared to work to a budget, that's just being irresponsible."

Another ZTT act, bombastic Das Psych-Oh Rangers, signed to the label on the express understanding that they would *not* be produced by Trevor Horn, but soon found themselves part of the common ZTT dilemma. Horn and Sinclair seemed to control everything. They had signed the band, were producing the band, were using their own studios and were able to charge their own rates and work at their own pace, secure in the knowledge that any royalties due to their artistes would first have to pay their ZTT bills.

Additionally, the ZTT producers would receive royalties on each record sold, and the company's publishing arm, Perfect Songs, would take a large cut from all earnings accruing from every song in their catalogue. Frankie Goes To Hollywood – produced by Horn, engineered by an in-house ZTT engineer, recorded at ZTT's Sarm Studios and initially published by Perfect Songs on a 60/40 split – were locked into the lucrative Horn/Sinclair circle for every penny they made bar touring receipts and T-shirt sales (the latter of which cost them a royalty for use of company copyrighted artwork).

The terms of Holly Johnson's employment with his record and publishing companies were exposed fully in the courtroom. The band received perhaps half of the royalties a group with their success could expect (only 8 per cent of retail price on album sales at home, 6 per cent abroad; 4.5 per cent on single sales at home, 3.2 abroad). Technically they could be held to ZTT indefinitely, with no guaranteed release dates for any of their recordings. Publishing terms were similarly ungenerous.

There was nothing illegal in any of this, nor was there anything terribly novel – even in the wised-up late eighties it was clear that George Michael, Annie Lennox, Elton John and Joan Armatrading had all learnt little from the experiences of The Beatles, Stones and hosts of other shamelessly exploited artists.

In freeing Johnson, Mr Justice Whitford found the recording contract to be unreasonable, nonsensical, and unfair in that it detailed no way of limiting what were seen as excessive recording costs.

Johnson claimed afterwards that it was "a great day for musicians everywhere", and forecast wide-reaching implications for the music industry. In effect, the implications are likely to be small. The publicity generated by the case may direct more artistes towards good solicitors, but Frankie Goes To Hollywood themselves sought legal advice before signing. If anything, it may improve an artiste's case during any contractual renegotiation that follows commercial success.

It's a depressing detail of music business life, but it is exactly that – a *business*. Faced with such a pedigree of exploitation, not least in black music, who can blame new artists for signing now and deciphering all the niggly clawback clauses later?

Six months after the court hearing, Holly Johnson had recorded two tracks for his first solo album for MCA, and looked back on the trial as one of the worst experiences of his life. "The press aspect was dreadful," he claims. "Using the first days' evidence they tried to discredit me both as a performer and as an individual. I felt a bit like an empty shell afterwards. I wish I hadn't gone through the wear and tear. This probably sounds like idealistic twaddle, but it was worth it because you have to fight for what you believe. It's such a shame I was in the courts rather than in the charts."

Holly Johnson: "They tried to discredit me as an individual"

OVER THE HILL AT NINETEEN?

Gurlies . . . Bimbettes . . . Mild Childs . . . call them what you will, but there's no escaping the glut of training bras and dental braces clogging up the charts. Caroline Sullivan considers how "the kids" now mean exactly that.

Precociousness is rarely a pretty spectacle. If anyone begs to differ, history offers up a plethora of noxious examples to support this contention. Who, for example, could forget the sight of ten-year-old Tatum O'Neal in her eensy tuxedo, accepting her Oscar for *Paper Moon*? (Or, for that matter, Tatum of the same era in a strapless formal number that had clearly received radical structural alteration to accommodate an infant chest?) More timelessly, what about Shirley Temple lisping her way, curls akimbo, through 'The Good Ship Lollipop'? No, it's not pretty, but, unlike so many maladies currently afflicting society, at least the phenomenon of the prepubescent adult is neither new nor AIDS-related.

But is that any consolation in the face of the worst wave of precociousness to assail the music business since Eater recruited a 13-year-old drummer? Probably not.

In the music biz, "young" has always been equated with "saleable". It can have escaped no fan's notice that, during the past year, "young" has been subjected to the strictest of interpretations – some lag of a rock star in his mid-twenties can no longer be described as youthful because the Bimbettes have arrived to show him the real meaning of the word.

Bimbettes, Mild (as opposed to Wild) Children, little brats – call them what you like, but Tiffany, Debbie, Vanessa, Shanice, Pebbles and the supporting cast of junior-high popettes have been the big news of 1988. The Bimbettes possess varying degrees of musical ability, business smarts and perv appeal – the sole common thread, apart from age, is a vigorously-simmering ambitiousness that belies the sweetness of the adolescently-unformed faces. It's almost unseemly, really, such worldly levels of aspiration in people who, by rights, ought to be worrying about blind dates, not tour dates. Yet there it is – small girls in rock are a big-bucks proposition.

Most of the credit/blame can, of course, be levelled at Tiffany (surname: Darwisch), a 16-year-old native of Norwalk, Oklahoma, who recorded a blisteringly-banal version of Tommy James's 'I Think We're Alone Now' and – genius move – promoted the record by performing it in shopping malls. In one fell swoop, she reached her target audience, similarly young women (interestingly, most adult men are less than drooly over all that virginal nubility, disproving the theory that this phenom is a reaction against sexual awareness and AIDS), *and* facilitated the purchase of her single by playing literally at point-of-sale. A *brilliant* marketing strategy.

Hot on her pixie-booted heels came Debbie Gibson, whose creative instinct had been avidly fermenting in the basement recording studio of her Long Island, New York home. And then Shanice Wilson (14), Ana (13), Vanessa Paradis (15), Sabrina (19) . . .

Debbie is generally recognized as the most gifted of the gang, a plaudit attributable to the fact that she, alone among the Bimbettes, writes her own material. Evidently, she's been at it since she was five (first tune: 'Know Your Classroom'), so it's not surprising that she should have developed a knack for knocking out a pert pop song. But had her album, *Out Of The Blue*, been released by an older artiste, i.e. one who didn't benefit from the novelty value of age, the consensus would probably be that here was a medium talent and a dullish LP. Still, as we're continually reminded, Debbie's just 17 . . .

Two points will be noted at this juncture: most Bimbettes are American and none are British. Britain has its young girls who have made records, but most of them – Mandy Smith, Emma Ridley – were famous for something else before they decided to try their hands at pop. Their hearts aren't really in it, not the way Tiffany's and Debbie's are. There are undoubtedly many thousands of British girls who long to be Tiff-style stars, but the survival of the genre Bimbette depends upon its conferring stardom only on the freshest, most innocent-appearing candidates, the type fans can *relate* to, not aspire to. The average English 16 year old looks – usually is – more knowing than her American counterpart. Remember Samantha Fox at 16? (Junior songstress Sabrina, whose 38″ bosom was front-page news in the *Sun* last spring, is very much an anomaly.)

The Bimbettes possess varying degrees of musical ability, business smarts and perv appeal – the sole common thread, apart from age, is a vigorously-simmering ambitiousness

Three years ago, it was a different story. Every American teenage girl was determined to be Madonna, or die trying. The clothes! Those lengths of black lace arranged over training bras, the fishnet gloves on tiny hands – will we ever see its salacious like again? How did Wannabes transform into Actuality Ams (Actually Am a Star in My Own Right, that is)?

As soon as one of their own number had made it, teenagers suddenly saw Madonna as remote . . . married . . . old, and Tiff as Everygirl: the (excruciatingly-ordinary) embodiment of their fantasies. Anyone can look like

Kylie and curious organic headgear

Madonna being a role model

Tiffany and (the subliminal message goes) if *she* can make it, with her lack of any discernable star quality, anyone can.

The fact that Tiffany ever got her paws on a recording studio to begin with is a typical example of the American Dream going at full tilt. Schooled from toddlerhood, in the traditional USA way, to go for it, Tiffany went for it. Unencumbered by the crippling reserve that would hinder a Brit would-be Bimb, she committed her squeal to vinyl and started touring the malls. Success was inevitable, wasn't it?

What happens when a Mild Child gets long in the tooth? Has a real-life love affair that instils in her the desire to sing the blues like Big Mama Thornton? Learns to drink beer and drive? With a sprite like, say, Vanessa Paradis (whose 'Joe Le Taxi' is generally acknowledged to be the most proficient of the gurlie releases), whose entire raison d'être appears to be – to judge by her label's promotional campaign – her age. The Sell By date is writ large and unmistakable. With Debbie, on the other hand, turning 18 may not spell the end of the road – career longevity, at least in America, seems to be in store. Debbie is already doing cosmetics endorsements and she'll no doubt osmose gracefully into the sort of stadium-filling rock chick Americans love.

The Bimbette trend is no more a passing fancy than TV stars making records is – both are eighties manifestations and unlikely to go away no matter how fervently we wish they would. This appears truer in America than in the UK: as the Yanks see it, they've tapped into a hitherto unexploited goldmine of creativity, the issue of age proving almost irrelevant. If the artist is talented ("talent", naturally, being a relative matter, related to units shifted), they say, it doesn't matter how old she is. Expect younger and younger signings, and audiences that will accept a 12-year-old star with the same equanimity they'd display toward a veteran of 25.

In Britain, where fads change like Duran Duran's blondes used to, the tabloids will get bored with leering about gymslip pop stars, and your Bananaramas and Kim Wildes will reclaim the column inches.

You can infer all sorts of things from the advent of the Bimbettes. Are young audiences rebelling against the idea of parent-figures like Fleetwood Mac again dominating the charts? Is it all a music industry plot to subvert pubescent morals? Whatever the case, scores of record company VPs will thank heaven for little girls for a long while to come.

Tiffany tries the dental brace as earring approach . . .

. . . while Shanice works on her pout . . .

. . . while the toothsome Miss Gibson "chills" out

"THE TRUTH, THE WHOLE TRUTH AND ANYTHING BUT THE TRUTH"

Somewhere up there, above the clouds, there are derelict satellites; used up, broken down, long abandoned, they're left to circle the earth, forgotten. It's not worth anyone's time to bring them down again. And in the same way, there are Michael Jackson stories: circulating uselessly, repeated endlessly. And nobody even bothers to deny them.

Just like their mechanical counterparts out in space, the Michael Jackson stories trace their futile orbit through a rarified atmosphere – it's not the oxygen of publicity that ensures their survival, but the vacuum of complete non-communication. It seems that Michael's pronouncements to the world will never amount to more than murmured platitudes: "Thank you. You're wonderful. I love you. Goodnight. Thank you." He's even published a 283-page autobiography this year, *Moonwalk*, that winds up saying almost nothing of any consequence. Patiently we await some further enlightenment, but we might as well be standing by for a few short words from the smiling lips of the Mona Lisa.

Yet here is a silence that isn't merely golden, it's multi-platinum. Michael doesn't talk, because Michael doesn't need to talk. Some have called his latest album, *Bad*, a failure since it hasn't matched its predecessor *Thriller*, the best-selling record of all time at 40 million. But with *Bad*'s sales standing, at time of writing, around 14 million (and likely many more after his global tour), there can scarcely be a "successful" musician in the world who wouldn't relish a failure on the Jackson scale.

Between the superstar's reticence on the one hand, and the vast degree of publicity on the other, lies that vacuum. The media abhors it, and rushes to fill it – and nowhere more enthusiastically than in Britain, home to half-a-dozen tabloid papers whose thirst for non-news seems unquenchable. When historians come to record, for example, the sum of the *Sun*'s enrichment of the English language (a task that may not detain them *too* long) then the phrase "*Whacko Jacko*" will figure prominently – second only, perhaps, to "*Gotcha!*".

Where do the stories come from? There's a theory that Jackson's camp creates them. Michael's said the weirdo image hurts him; maybe it does, but it gets him

When historians come to record the sum of the *Sun*'s enrichment of the English language, the phrase "Whacko Jacko" will figure prominently – second only, perhaps, to "Gotcha!"

Pop idol Michael Jackson has been outrageously misunderstood.
Today

Zany superstar Michael Jackson is building his own Disneyland funfair – in his back garden. And he will buy toys worth £27 MILLION to put in it.
The Sun

He's getting his kicks watching surgeons perform plastic surgery on burns victims. He's "obsessed" by plastic surgery and, heaven forbid, wants to become a surgeon himself.
Peterborough Evening Telegraph

Michael Jackson's zany pets are causing havoc in his £8 million mansion. The other day Michael's boa constrictor made a meal out of his beloved macaw.
The Star

STAR JACKO ISN'T WHACKO!
The Sun

Jackson's compulsive quest for eternal youth has led him to a string of extensive face operations – some of which have gone wrong and brought him only pain and unhappiness.
Daily Mirror

SEXY KAREN LOSES JACKO TO A CHIMP:
Michael, 28, was heartbroken when blonde Karen Faye walked out after just three months. Karen later confessed to a friend "Playing second fiddle to a chimp isn't my idea of fun."
The Sun

Jacko followers believe he's spent up to a million dollars on cosmetic surgery in a bid to look more like his childhood idol Diana Ross.
The Star

At 29 Michael Jackson says he's still a virgin . . . and sex is definitely OUT. But Jacko is interested in having a child – offering more than £1 million to a suitable mother willing to have his sperm-bank baby.
Daily Mirror

He wants to look like his sister.
Daily Mirror

Mr Whacko intends to build a replica of Buckingham Palace to live in – and has even written to the Queen to ask permission for his architects to look at the plans.
The Sun

Animal-mad Michael Jackson is sending his pet chimp Bubbles bonkers. And the little ape could end up killing Whacko Jacko. An "animal expert" warns in *The Star*

Whacko Jacko, 30, has acquired TV footage of the Princess [of Wales] playing the piano. Now the strange singer wants to superimpose his own image onto the film to make it look as if he is playing a duet along with Diana.
The Sun

Who'll have my baby? asks Jacko.
The People

Reading about Michael Jackson is a national obsession, and therefore demands a steady flow of material. But can one man be *that* interesting? Paul Du Noyer strolls, metaphorically, down Fleet Street and discovers there's lies, damned lies and "Whacko Jacko" stories.

column inches. Stunts like the face masks, and lying inside his "hyperbaric chamber", could just conceivably suggest a mischievous talent for the imagination-grabbing wind-up. But the infamous obsessions with Disneyland characters, and the lavishly reported friendships with snakes and llamas and Bubbles the chimpanzee . . . these speak more of a man bewildered by reality, estranged from humankind.

Whatever their origins, Jacko tales have prospered. "Animal mad Michael Jackson is sending his pet chimp bonkers," claimed the *Star* last March. "And the little ape could soon end up killing him." Their source: a "top animal expert."

"Sexy Karen loses Jacko to a chimp" announced the *Sun*. "Playing second fiddle to a chimp isn't my idea of fun," explained this 25-year-old blonde, as she made her exit from Michael's life and her entrance into the cutting files. "Who'll have my baby?" he later enquired – in, of all places, the *People*. Interested applicants were advised, by the *Daily Mirror*, that he "says he's still a virgin, but he's offering more than £1 million to a suitable mother willing to have his sperm-bank baby."

"Jacko followers believe he's spent up to a million dollars on cosmetic surgery in a bid to look like his childhood idol Diana Ross," chimed the *Star*. But the *Mirror* begged to differ: "He wants to look like his sister."

On this point, at least, Jackson's people have hit back. Cosmetic surgery – to make him look younger, more feminine, more white – is the matter they're most at pains to contest. That's probably because it's the rumour that most of us find easiest to credit, given Michael's ten-year transition from pleasant black adolescent to moody Venusian humanoid. "It's bullshit. The man has had two operations in his life," his manager Frank Dileo told me, rather forcefully. "One to fix his nose, and one to put a cleft in his chin. Everybody in the world strives to look better. There's not a person in Hollywood hasn't had a nose job." Jackson himself attributes the other changes to his vegetarian diet and better photography.

By April this year, anyhow, the papers were falling back on the only new Whacko story they could find – namely, of course, "Star Jacko isn't whacko." Silly us, we should have known all along. "One of the world's leading psychologists" obliged the newsdesk of

Today with a medical opinion: "If he were to consult me on a professional basis, I would have to send him away without treatment. There is nothing for me to treat."

Hold that front page! Nothing to treat! But hang on . . . wouldn't that mean "nothing to write about"? It just might. As the Jacko stories started drying up, more than one Wapping editor had reason to be grateful for Frank Bough.

Somewhere underneath all this there is Michael Jackson the artiste. His stage show, by now unveiled across four continents, has reaffirmed his supreme abilities as a live performer. His music will delight for years to come – when satellites have burned out or plunged into the ocean, and press cuttings have yellowed, curled and crumbled. But he will always have cause to ponder the line in his best song, 'Billie Jean': *"Be careful what you do, cos the lie becomes the truth."*

Goodnight, Michael. You're wonderful. We love you.

THE *Schweppes* ROCK YEARBOOK AWARDS

With entirely characteristic generosity, we wanted to give something to everybody who's sung, played, produced, broadcast, written about or even just plain listened to pop music during the last 12 months. Let's face it, it's been that kind of year. Unfortunately, though, there aren't enough lovingly-inscribed, handsomely-framed certificates on the face of this planet. So, after wrestling with the economics of the "situation": above-mentioned, highly desirable and totally unique items to the winners; condolences to the runners-up; and to everybody else a thought – it's not the winning that counts . . .

The *Schweppes Awards* panel may be hard, but they're so fair it's painful.

Lloyd Bradley

PANEL OF JUDGES

Lloyd Bradley
(Editor, *The Schweppes Rock Yearbook*)

Paul Ciani
(Producer/Director, *Top Of The Pops*)

Junior
(Artiste/Songwriter)

Janice Long
(DJ, Radio Radio)

Peter Powell
(DJ, Radio 1)

Charles Shaar Murray
(Contributor, *The Schweppes Rock Yearbook*)

Siouxsie
(Artiste/Songwriter)

SINGLE

'Perfect' –
Fairground Attraction
'Don't Turn Around' – Aswad
'Everyday Is Like Sunday' –
Morrissey
'The Rhythm Divine' –
Shirley Bassey/Yello

ALBUM

Savage – Eurythmics
Faith – George Michael
Bigger & Deffer – LL Cool J

VIDEO

How Men Are – Aztec Camera
Pump Up The Volume – M/A/R/R/S
Little Lies, Big Love – Adele Bertei

FEMALE SINGER

Tracy Chapman
Whitney Houston
Sinead O'Connor

MALE SINGER

Michael Jackson
Terence Trent D'Arby

GROUP

Wet Wet Wet
Aswad
Jesus & Mary Chain

MOST PROMISING NEW ACT

Bros
Hothouse Flowers
Lyle Lovett

PRODUCER

Stock, Aitken & Waterman
Steve Lillywhite

COVER VERSION

'Breakfast In Bed' –
UB40/Chrissie Hynde

TV PROGRAMME

Top Of The Pops
The Story Teller

LIVE SHOW/ EVENT

The Mandela Birthday Concert
Michael Jackson Live

CONTRIBUTION

Jerry Dammers/Elephant House for Mandela Day
Q magazine

NEWS STORY

Michael Jackson . . . Elephant Man . . . Bubbles . . . Immigration
ZTT/Holly Johnson

QUOTE

"Fair enough I was hyped."
Terence Trent D'Arby

CLUB RECORD

'Pump Up The Volume' –
M/A/R/R/S

SAMPLE

Prince's 'Oh Yeah' sampled by Derek B

Harry Enfield: Loadsalaughs.

Tina Turner for calling it a day before looking completely ridiculous. The downside, however, is probably "a career in the movies".

THANKS...

Michael Jackson for getting out of his fantasies and back on stage.

Fairground Attraction: Perfect? As near as dammit.

The Late Shift: An intelligent approach to interesting films.

Bob Geldof for *not* making another record.

George Harrison: One of the most understated comebacks ever. 'When We Was Fab' *indeed*!

CD singles: Excellent value (24 minutes for less than a fiver), exceptional sound quality and they don't take up very much space.

The suit: An acceptable fashion statement again.

Kevin Rowland: Never a dull moment when "our Kev" airs his views on life and his ludicrous sense of sartorial style – a halfway decent album too.

Album Sleeve Of The Year: A wind-up or what?

New Country: Nashville realized there was a life outside its city limits and the world responded enthusiastically.

Phillip Schofield: for proving kids' television need not be childish.

Prince Charles: A continuing source of inspiration for old hippies everywhere – is he behind the Tull's re-emergence?

Mel Appleby: For dealing with tabloid revelations surrounding her recent illness with dignity and resilient good humour.

Jeremy Isaacs: For five of the most refreshing years in British television.

The Caped Crusader and Boy Wonder back on the Batphone.

Michael Jackson's new face: As terrifying a sight as his new trousers.

Def II for imagining that Magenta De Vine holds some sway over "the kids".

Bros: Why on earth should they be famous?

George Michael's a-bumping and a-grinding on stage: Eyewitness reports claim he looked as mystified as the audience at what he was attempting to portray.

. . . BUT NO THANKS

S-Express: There's always someone out there daft enough to copy them.

Ben Elton for getting visibly rattled as Harry Enfield stole his show.

Puffball skirts: Were they a joke?

Worst Album Sleeve Of The Year: Even in the highly competitive field of heavy metal bad taste this is an abomination.

Footballers making records: Particularly worrying was 'The Anfield Rap', as it sounded more at home in discos than on the terraces.

Bob Dylan's Wembley shows: As boring as *Hearts Of Fire*.

Neighbours and its *EastEnders*-style capacity to turn wonky actresses into pop stars.

Disturbingly sexist pop videos: Prime offenders are The Pet Shop Boys ('Always On My Mind', 'Heart'), Tin Drum ('Cosmetics') and Climie Fisher ('Rise To The Occasion').

Rock Star: As an insight into the music business this "literary work" is paralleled only by Barrie Keeffe's *No Excuses*.

Tim Graham: This seemingly ill-informed fashion victim is the one dark cloud on *Wired*'s otherwise sunny horizon.

Inexpensive keyboard samplers: It's impossible to stop them falling into the wrong hands.

Inflated concert ticket prices: Acceptable maybe for four hours of Springsteen or the spectacle of Michael Jackson, but *£9.50 for Will Downing?*

Public Enemy for appearing to condone violence, racism and homophobia then squealing when the press and public aren't 100 per cent supportive.

Tabloid pop columnists and their somewhat confused notions about morals.

COMPILED BY LLOYD BRADLEY, ADRIAN DEEVOY AND SUE WALLIKER

YEAR IN BOOKS

Although more publishers are recognizing the commercial potential of works of quality, they seem to be financing them with an increased turnover of cheapo cut 'n' paste jobbies. An ecology-minded Andy Gill dwells on the fate of the rain forests.

It shouldn't happen to a tree, really. When you consider that in decades past our foliaged friends might at least have had the honour of being sacrificed for *War & Peace* or *Crime & Punishment*, the knowledge that entire forests are felled to furnish us with a year's Rock Books ought to give the likes of Omnibus Press pause for thought.

Omnibus are masters of the quickie cash-in, for virtually any pop phenomenon that demonstrates either a certain staying power or a hardcore cult audience for whom reason (and thrift) flies out the window where their heroes are concerned. We're talking here about the likes of The Smiths and Echo & The Bunnymen, both of whom have been immortalized in biographical hackworks this year (the former a revised version, updated to include their demise), and especially that old standby of the merchandiser, Ye Sexe Pistoles, about whom surely there can be precious little left to cut and paste. Or so one might think. One would, of course, be mistaken: like the Motown back catalogue, there are always new ways of repackaging old Pistols tat – Lee Woods' *Sex Pistols Day By Day* is just that, a diary of their rakish progress, whilst Dave Thomas's *Johnny Rotten In His Own Words* is little better than theft, being an accumulation of published quotes from Lydon and others – mainly journalists, whose work appears, on this showing, to be outside the copyright laws which apply to other printed works.

The signs are, however, that Omnibus won't have this market all to themselves in future, as Sidgwick & Jackson muscle in with throwaway softbacks on the likes of Springsteen and Jackson, blotting a copybook which this year produced respectable, well-researched biographies of such as Peter Gabriel and Paul Simon.

The biography is the real meat-and-potatoes of rock books, of course, and this year saw several of note, particularly Eamon Dunphy's controversial U2 tome *The Unforgettable Fire*, and Barney Hoskyns' idiosyncratic *Prince – Imp Of The Perverse*, which made up in speculative insight for what it lacked in revelation. Purely by dint of the extravagant behaviour of its subject, however, all rock biographies pale somewhat in comparison to Charles White's *Life & Times Of Little Richard*, which received a welcome paperback publication this year. Doubtless Albert Goldman's *Lennon* biography (about to be published at the time of writing) will do its damnedest to reach similar sizzling, soaraway (©*The Sun*) heights; God knows, the Beatle-book industry – which this year featured anodyne offerings from such as press secretary Alistair Taylor and John's sister Julia Baird – could do with a kick up its collectively sycophantic arse.

One horrifying new trend of 1988 was the outbreak of the Rock Autobiography. Among the likes of Michael Jackson, Joan Baez and Miriam Makeba, only Chuck Berry demonstrated any ability to make the language reflect the person

One horrifying new trend of 1988 was the widespread outbreak of the rock autobiography, as everyone from Michael Jackson and Chuck Berry to Joan Baez and Miriam Makeba strove personfully to demonstrate how (a) bubble-headed, (b) ornery, (c) self-regarding, or (d) right on they are/were. Unfortunately, only Chuck demonstrated any ability to make the language reflect the person – and since the person could reasonably be considered mean-spirited, chip-shouldered and suspicious, this didn't make for too pleasant reading.

As far as reference works were concerned, the only one worth mentioning was Chris Stapleton & Chris May's exhaustive *African All-Stars*, which told you more than you ever wanted to know about all manner of African musics, with copious social and historical details thrown in to aid comprehension of this fastest-growing of regional musics.

There were quite a few oddities in 1988, too: Steve Turner's *Hungry For Heaven* considered the Christian urge in pop music (a new way to tap the U2 market); Harry Shapiro's *Waiting For The Man* attempted to chart the confluence of drugs and music; Johnny Rogan's *Starmakers & Svengalis* dealt with that fascinating breed, the rock manager; and Greil Marcus's anthology of Lester Bang's writings, *Psychotic Reactions & Carburetor Dung*, in attempting to do its subject justice, did him the injustice of including, alongside the good stuff, some crappy, half-witted (and previously unpublished) pieces. Talking of which, Nick Cave this year published his first slim volume of poems and lyrics, *King Ink*.

For an idea of the varied strengths of the Rock Book, however, you should turn to the following, all of which any self-respecting tree would be delighted to die for:

WHAM! CONFIDENTIAL: DEATH OF A SUPERGROUP

Johnny Rogan (*Omnibus*)

Remarkably, even more so given the subject-matter, Omnibus have published a book that a) takes more than 20 minutes to read (and probably took more than that to write) and b) is worth the effort. This book detailing Wham!'s brief, spectacular career is quite amazing in both the proximity of the observations – either Rogan himself or people he talked to were very close to the duo every step of the way – and the conclusions drawn from actions and events that go a long way to explain them. By giving you a front-row seat to the early days, China, the drinking, the South African affair, the sexual identity crisis, the post-teenage rich kids yobbishness and so on, you finish the book with a vivid picture of all that goes with (too) rapidly achieved stardom. The only question left to ask is not why did it all go wrong, but why didn't it all go wrong much sooner.

■

BRANSON: THE INSIDE STORY

Mick Brown (*Michael Joseph*)

In spite of this being set against a background of the music business, it isn't really a music or music-business story. However, the subject's far-reaching effect on pop music and the fact that it's a rattling good tale humorously and engagingly told, is enough to include it here. Far from the popular image of Branson as the shrewd mogal with an ear for what the pop-buying public wanted, Brown introduces us to an old hippie who lost and made several fortunes yet never seemed quite sure what he was doing. A grown man with a ludicrous collection of pullovers who relies on a mixture of little-boy-lost charm and sheer brass neck rather than wheeler-dealer smarts to get himself out of trouble. Immensely readable stuff.

■

TOP 5

STORMY WEATHER

Linda Dahl (*Quartet*)

The subject of *Stormy Weather* is women in, and their contribution to, jazz during the last half-century. Up until now, writers have so negected this area that the casual observer would be forgiven for thinking that the music is some kind of men's club that grudgingly acknowledges the ocassional freak of nature such as Billie Holiday, Ella Fitzgerald or Betty Carter. In documenting the massive part women from Ma Rainey to Sarah Vaughn have played in this field, Dahl goes a long way to redressing the balance and serves it up through anecdotes and personal reflections that illustrate the sheer enjoyment they got from it. A book that is at all times warm, witty, informative and never less than readable.

■

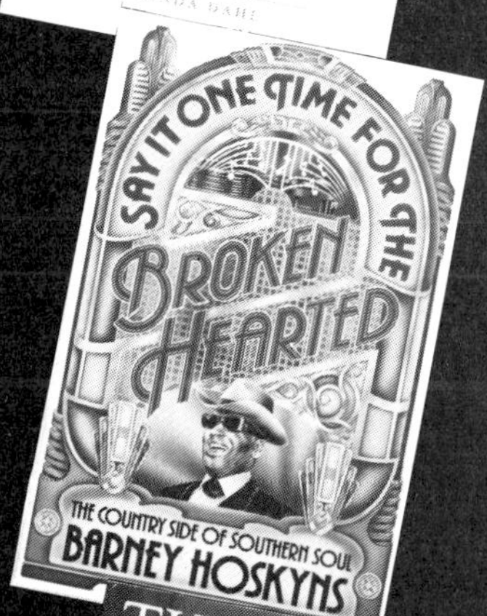

SAY IT ONE TIME FOR THE BROKENHEARTED

Barney Hoskyns (*Fontana*)

The notion of redneck country music and juke joint R&B having anything at all in common is pretty far fetched. The image of them getting into bed with each other is downright ridiculous, or it was until Barney Hoskyns spent a year in the deep South researching this fascinating book. In presenting a detailed picture of the music business South of the Mason/Dixon line in the sixties it shows how the two styles not only came from the same roots, and therefore owed each other a great deal, but were continuously cross-fertilizing and helping each other out. And it does this without feeling the need to write any sociological-type essays.

■

THE BOY IN THE BUBBLE

Patrick Humphries (*Sidgwick & Jackson*)

Although this book goes from the crew-cut Tom and Jerry (Simon & Garfunkel's first stage name) days of the late fifties, through to last year, it sensibly concentrates on the post-duo time, with two chapters devoted to *Graceland*, the recording, the controversy and the aftermath. Although this was written without Simon's co-operation, and therefore can shed no first-hand information on the affair, its mixture of intelligent analysis and thorough research makes up for that, putting it into the context of Simon's history and beliefs and the mood in South Africa at the time. This is equally true of the rest of the book. The lack of horse's-mouth type comment is adequately compensated for by the narrative's interaction of Simon and his surroundings, so whether it's the drippy folkie/hippie scene, stardom as a world-acclaimed lyricist or crossing over into "tasteful" after-dinner rock, the text is never the less than full-bodied. A vastly superior scissors-and-paste job, compellingly interesting and often drily amusing.

BOOKS BIOGRAPHIES

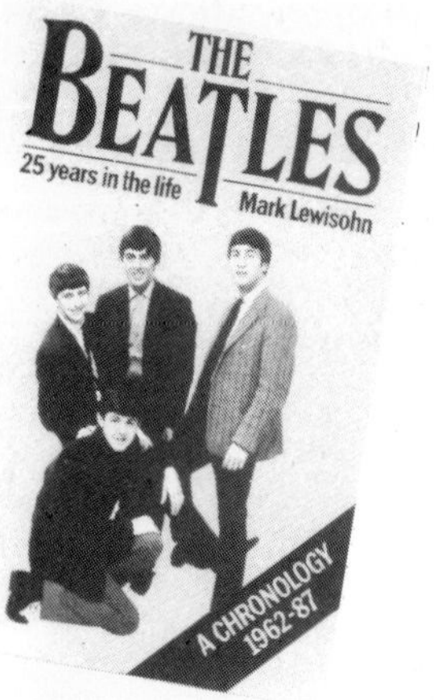

THE BEATLES: 25 YEARS IN THE LIFE

Mark Lewisohn (*Sidgwick & Jackson*)

As it announces on the cover, this is a *chronology* not a biography. Beginning in October 1972 and continuing through to October 1987 – it follows the progress of the surviving Beatles in areas other than music and keeps abreast of Yoko's exhumations of Lennon material – *25 Years In The Life* documents everything of importance in diary form: 1963, 25 August: ABC Theatre, Blackpool. 26 Odeon Cinema, Southport. Paul McCartney is disqualified from driving for one year and fined £31 for speeding in Wallasey. It is his third conviction of the year. And so on.

Assuming all information is correct, and it ought to be as Lewisohn is news editor of *The Beatles Book* magazine, this is a valuable reference book. Other than that it probably has limited appeal outside people who own every other Beatles book in existence. (*LB*)

THE LENNON COMPANION

Edited by Elizabeth Thomson & David Gutman (*Macmillan*)

Rather an imaginative concept for a "rock book" – a collection of essays and articles, some reprinted from newspapers, magazines and books, others commissioned for this volume, about the subject, John Lennon. Contributors include Tom Wolfe, Noël Coward, Kenneth Tynan, David Frost, Joshua Rifkin, Richard Crossman, Bernard Levin and George Melly, a list which should indicate that the cross-section of commentators covers a broad range and is usually veering towards the intelligent (if not necessarily well-informed) rather than the banal. Including the celebrated Maureen Cleave article about The Beatles being more popular than Jesus, and William Mann's intellectualizations of the group from *The Times*, this is probably not for the faint-hearted, but a stimulating read for anyone who wants confirmation that The Beatles, and especially John Lennon, were something rather extraordinary. A good book for a transatlantic flight. (*JT*)

YESTERDAY: THE BEATLES REMEMBERED

Alistair Taylor with Martin Roberts (*Sidgwick & Jackson*)

Unlike several other "insider" Beatle books, this fairly lightweight, but still adequate, volume of reminiscences by Brian Epstein's personal assistant (who became known as "Mr Fixit") seems unlikely to provoke any ire from Fabs or their widows. Containing no devastating revelations, but gently making the odd point (e.g. when Taylor was fired from Apple, which he helped to run after Epstein's death, he was unable to talk to any of his previous employers, who left the clearing out of Apple to a hatchet man), this is not the book for a Beatle beginner, but certainly qualifies as a prime candidate for the kind of comprehensive Beatle library many (especially Americans) maintain. A tick but no gold stars. (*JT*)

CHUCK BERRY: THE AUTOBIOGRAPHY

(*Faber & Faber*)

One rock auto-biog which definitely *wasn't* ghosted, Chuck Berry's alliteratin' motorvatin' rock-and-tell memoir is more fun than anything the slimy old sod's recorded in the last 25 years. An account of 60 years' worth of chasing big bucks and hot sex in a guitar-powered, four-wheel-drive Cadillac of an ego, it's also an intensely revealing guided tour of working-class black life in the St Louis of the thirties, forties and fifties. Not surprisingly, it also functions as an anecdotal history of the early days of rock 'n' roll: Chess Records sent out carefully over-exposed publicity photos of Berry which, combined with his snappy rockabilly beats and careful diction, fooled quite a few promoters into thinking he was white. On at least one occasion, he was turned away from a white dance at which he was the featured attraction and as he drove away he heard a white band playing his hit. If his racial animosities are barely hidden, the reasons are scarcely surprising.

Berry is also more forthcoming in this book than he has ever been before when it comes to discussing his brushes with the law and his spells in jail: this is also scarcely surprising, because this way he gets to make the money from his revelations rather than some journalist whose only investment has been the cost of a TDK C-90. *Chuck Berry: The Autobiography* is hardly a nice story of a nice man, but it is – literally – not a whitewash of a difficult, greedy, suspicious man who was undoubtedly rock 'n' roll's first real genius. (*CSM*)

DAVID BOWIE: THE ARCHIVE

Chris Charlesworth (*Bobcat Books*)

DAVID BOWIE: GLASS IDOL (THE 1987 EUROPEAN TOUR)

David Currie (*Omnibus Press*)

Not exactly a vintage year for Bowie books: the repackaging of Chris Charlesworth's 1981 mini-biog-with-pictures hasn't stretched to any kind of revisions or updates from the author, with the result that everything crashes to a halt with *The Elephant Man* and the release of 1980's *Scary Monsters* album and we are even treated to Charlesworth's speculations as to whether Bowie is going to leave RCA and sign with another label, plus all the reasons why this should be a bad idea. Rule Number One of rock-book publishing is that if something is going to be flimsy and insubstantial it should at least be up-to-date, so whatever merit this book may have had in '81, it has precious little relevance now.

Since the 1987 *Glass Spider* tour wasn't exactly the greatest triumph of Bowie's career – and its accompanying album *Never Let Me Down* his least interesting album since the mid-sixties – omens are something less than positive for *Glass Idol*, a workmanlike and reasonably unsycophantic scissors-and-paste job by David Currie, editor of the long-running (if slightly occasional) Bowie fanzine *Starzone*. Currie was not granted anything even vaguely approaching access to Mr B, and devastating insights are correspondingly thin on the ground, but the book does, however, provide a wide variety of studies of what is probably Bowie's least impressive haircut for years. It is, by definition, aimed at the serious Bowie nut only; anybody else may feel somewhat left out. (*CSM*)

CELEBRATING BIRD: THE TRIUMPH OF CHARLIE PARKER

Gary Giddins (*Hodder & Stoughton*)

Charlie Parker's influence on post-war jazz cannot be under-estimated: he and his improvisory alto sax technique were the basis of what became known as bebop. That much is fairly common knowledge, as is Parker's fondness for sex, drugs and sharp suits. What Giddins has done is get behind all of this to use the excitement of a new development in the music to both contrast and offset the general lowlifeness that was very much a part of jazz at the time, and set it up as a background to the story of this extraordinary player. Through extensive interviews with the people who knew him best, and a fair amount of intelligent theorizing, he paints a vivid portrait of a mother-smothered young man who had no interest in music at an early age, then, as a teenager, taught himself sax with a tenacity bordering on obsession. A man who grew up utterly incapable of looking after himself – his wife, friends and fellow musicians all acted in a kind of nursemaid/money-lender capacity – provoked extreme personal reactions – people loved or hated Parker, but practically everyone he met was in awe of his music – and liked a good scoff. A genuinely interesting biography of one of music's true giants. (*LB*)

THE CURE: A VISUAL DOCUMENTARY

Dave Thompson & Jo-Ann Greene (*Omnibus*)

Scissors 'n' paste at heart, but upmarket in execution (i.e., heavyweight gloss stock, a £7.95 price tag), *A Visual Documentary* traces the career of Easy Cure (as they were known in the 8 June 1977 number of the *Crawley Advertiser*) month by month, through the release of 'Kiss Me, Kiss Me, Kiss Me'. Editorializing by the compilers is kept to a minimum; the story is told in pix and extracts from music-paper interviews. Sounds mondo cheap 'n' nasty, but a lot of attention has been lavished on this particular effort; I have no reservations about recommending it. And, so, see Robert Smith transmogrify from pert post-punkster to the tonsorial nightmare "Mad Bob"! Ponder his pronouncements on Morrissey ("I don't think I've read [a Morrissey interview] because he's such a boring bastard"), Simon Gallup ("My idea of hunkiness is Simon") and hair care ("I haven't washed it in three weeks")! Conclude that, despite the lipstick, Smith seems an okay sort of fellow. (*CS*)

THE DAMNED: THE LIGHT AT THE END OF THE TUNNEL

Carol Clerk (*Omnibus*)

After the appearance of The Damned's *Greatest Hits*-type double album earlier this year elevated them to almost institution status, it was obvious the "official" biography wouldn't be far behind. In keeping with the band that, over the past 12 years, has progressed from being a grubby little band to, er, a grubby little band that sells quite a lot of records, *Light At The End Of The Tunnel* is a grubby little book. Not that this should put anybody off, by steering clear of such niceties as the band's schooldays, what they did in cubs, family histories and so on, and going back no further than their formation, Carol Clerk captures the interminable squalor of punk as lived by this surly bunch of misfits. Indeed such is their saga of rows, walking outs, fights, brushes with the law and "practical" jokes – they once filled a drunken Elvis Costello's mouth with the contents of an ashtray and then set his shoes on fire, that sort of thing – that the reader wonders not how they've managed to remain a functioning pop band, but more how they've managed to stay alive. In spite of all this, though, the telling of this tale by the group, friends, associates and Clerk herself is done with good humour and considerable resilience of spirit. (*LB*)

BOOKS

DEF LEPPARD: ANIMAL INSTINCT

David Fricke (*Zomba*)

Almost as if to prove that this is indeed the official Lep biography, it opens with what appears to be a ringside seat at the car crash that removed drummer Rick Allen's arm and the rest of the group's reaction to the news. *Nobody* who didn't have considerable access to the band would know what Allen said before he went into shock, or that, because she's deaf, Joe Elliott's granny didn't know why he was crying. From there it goes back to school with the band – they began as a figment of 15-year-old Elliott's imagination, as he made posters for and wrote a review of Deaf Leopard's "triumphant homecoming gig" for a project – through a detailed account of the interminable recording of *Pyromania*, right up to their genuine "triumphant homecoming". Never the most straightforward rags-to-rock-'n'-roll-riches story, it seems littered with disasters both minor and major, but it's told here with wit and insight, which combine with Ross Halfin's photos to present a sparky account of five Sheffield lads who happen to be one of the biggest HM bands in the world. (*LB*)

DOLLY, HERE I COME AGAIN

Leonore Fleischer (*Star Books*)

The song says that "Dolly's got two big reasons why she's well known" and at times Leonore Fleischer labours the point. In the first two chapters she spends so much time telling us that Dolly is more than merely the owner of the most famous hour-glass figure in the West that you begin to wonder why she hasn't called the book *Dolly, Beyond The Boobs*. No matter, she soon gets down to business and unfolds the story and the truth – "Ah may look one way but I'm completely the other" – in a style that is chatty, informative but seldom condescending. It's the story of the mountain girl from the shotgun shack who rose to build a monument (musically and, with her Dollywood theme park, literally) for the people and place that she came from.

Dolly's a lady with more cutting, witty one-liners than Mae West, the writer of over 300 songs (many ranking with anything produced in country music – hell, in *any* music). In her time she's weathered starvation-level poverty, death threats, daunting legal wrangles, hormone and gynaecological problems and a weight-loss programme to rival that undertaken by Robert De Niro after *Raging Bull*. The book covers four main areas: her dreams and early struggle (back then Dolly would lie in bed with the little ones; the only warmth they got was, I kid you not, when one of the kids peed the bed); there's her early fame with Porter Wagonner and their bitter split when Dolly went her own way; her crossover and movie success; and then the personal midlife crisis and recuperation. Hollywood soap-opera writers would be hard-pushed to create a storyline as involved as Dolly's real-life dramas. So while Leonore shies away from anything in depth when it comes to Dolly's art or her views on South Africa (she's been blacklisted for playing Sun City) she accompanies the bare facts with just enough quotes from past interviews and well-chosen critical commentary to make *Here I Come Again* one of the punchiest biographies of the year. (*GM*)

THE DOORS

John Tobler & Andrew Doe (*Bobcat Books*)

A reprinting of the 1984 potted history of The Doors, whose iconic singer Jim Morrison mysteriously died into an odd kind of immortality in 1971. It's a tale, (over)simply told here, primarily of Jim – in fact always of Jim – and LSD and LA and gigs that were more ritual than concert, with Jim the snakeskin shaman. The whole, mostly grim, affair began to fall apart relatively quickly, with the notorious "indecent exposure" charge in Miami hovering over the release of the highly regarded *Morrison Hotel* album. *LA Woman*, The Doors' finest hour, just about closed the book on the band. Jim went to Paris, to die his young rock 'n' roll hero's death in the bathtub.

There's nothing much wrong with this book (though the "could-Jim-still-be-alive?" paragraphs are rather gratuitous), but it's more a "readable summary" rather than the claimed "searching study". Jerry Hopkins & Danny Sugerman's *No One Gets Out Of Here Alive* is to be preferred for the rock bookshelf, though. (*JB*)

BOB DYLAN: WRITINGS AND DRAWINGS

(*Grafton*)

At one time this year, there were no fewer than three different editions of Bob Dylan's lyrics on sale. This bright yellow paperback version of the original 1973 collection is the familiar best-seller, here in its eighth printing. However, the 1985 compendium of lyrics (available in Cape's large softback printing and in Paladin's pocket-sized paperback) surely represents better value, adding 12 years of Dylan's work to the original collection and losing only a few sketches in the process. As for the writings themselves, well they prove two things: one, that Dylan's art is multi-faceted and is as much dependent upon music and the singer's inimitable intonation as it is upon the words; but, two, that as a wordsmith alone Dylan's achievement is uniquely brilliant. He is the outstanding poetic voice of our age. (JB)

NO DIRECTION HOME: THE LIFE AND MUSIC OF BOB DYLAN

Robert Shelton (*Penguin*)

One might have hoped for a fascinating memoire from the *New York Times* critic who not only brought 20-year-old Bob Dylan to public attention by celebrating his talent in print for the first time, but who subsequently spent many hours watching that talent burgeon, the precocious coffee-house huckster becoming the most dazzling poet-troubadour of our times. And to express uneasy disappointment with a book which has 500 pages full of all manner of Dylan anecdote and assessment might seem churlish. But though the book has occasional but exceptional high points – tales of baby Bobby singing for his parents, or a marvellous speedy monologue delivered into Shelton's tape-recorder in the drug-dazed days of 1966 – the messed up confusion of chronology, the author's reluctance to cross certain taboo lines and the neglect of post-1974 Dylan mean that this big biography is far from being the last word on the matter. (*JB*)

PETER GABRIEL: AN AUTHORIZED BIOGRAPHY

Spencer Bright (*Sidgwick & Jackson*)

There is no doubt that Peter Gabriel has had an interesting time of it in rock 'n' roll: Charterhouse to Genesis to Africa; Charlie Drake (yes, Charlie "hallo my dar-lings" Drake) to Jimmy Pursey to WOMAD; and then to making prize-winning videos. Throughout this meandering career, Gabriel seems to have approached things with a single-minded resolve and a dry, occasionally self-deprecating humour – he was going to see things through until the bitter end, regardless of advice offered, but if they didn't work out then he wasn't that worried and would never blame anybody else. This much Bright gets over, communicating Gabriel's very likeable, down-to-earthness, just as his meticulous research leaves no stone unturned in detailing the artist's career. Unfortunately, what he fails to do is set it against any sort of background – you get the impression that Genesis and then Gabriel existed in some sort of rock-world vacuum – so it's hard to put the considerable achievements and the occasional mishaps into any form of context. A good book, but a far from great one. (*LB*)

IRON MAIDEN: A PHOTOGRAPHIC HISTORY

Ross Halfin (*Zomba*)

Ross Halfin has been ver Maiden's official photographer for nigh on a decade. This much you're made aware of pretty quickly, as page three is an attractive still-life composed entirely of his extensive collection of "Iron Maiden Access All Areas" laminates. By the end of this book (128 glossy pages), you're also aware that his job isn't that difficult: buy camera, learn to take three different photos – (a) the band performing feet astride, heads down (use of fish-eye lens optional); (b) the band lined up wearing civvies; (c) the band goofing around backstage ("funny" face pulling optional). All that changes are (a) the Satanic-type stage-prop in the background; (b) the recognizable landmark – Brooklyn Bridge, Japanese temple, Hungarian monastery, etc. – in the background; and (c) whether they have shirts on or not. At £8.95 this is for the serious fan only. (*LB*)

ELTON JOHN

Barry Tooberman (*Weidenfeld & Nicolson*)

This book opens with a chapter about Elton and *The Sun*. Neatly topical, at best it's a grand chance to tell the truth – much the same way the singer did on Parkinson – and at worst it could make for a "racy" opening chapter. But either way it would've been interesting and a controversy such as that, just in time to include in the book, must be a rare gift to the author. What does he do? He scratches about on the surface of it, not clearing anything up with hard facts or, by theorizing about it, throwing any light on Grub Street's fascination with "exposing" rock stars. After that you know this is going to be a work of little consequence. And it is, because the former Reg Dwight may have sold a lot of records, have a daft taste in clothes and like football so much he bought a team, but he's not the most interesting man in the world. About as dull, in fact, as Tooberman' wordily slavering text. (*DB*)

MADONNA: HER STORY

Michael McKenzie (*Bobcat*)

The back-jacket of this slim volume mentions the fact that author McKenzie has "known Madonna since she was an unknown artiste featured in his cabaret," but nowhere mentions that he has anything to do with her now. And from the text you can be pretty sure he doesn't, and that when he did he didn't realize she was anything too special. The book concentrates on her early days in New York, largely through interviews with her former associates, with scant attention to her childhood in Detroit, thus giving virtually no clues as to the whys and wherefores of the singer. Post-stardom it is even more at sea, cutting and pasting huge slabs of interviews and offering no insight into them, let alone their subject. It's a shameless piece of opportunism that even the often quite amusing early snapshots of the fledgling Madonna can't salvage. (*DB*)

BOOKS

MAKEBA: MY STORY

Miriam Makeba with James Hall (*Bloomsbury*)

They call Miriam Makeba "Mother Africa", and she holds passports from a host of African nations; the most notable exception being South Africa, the one in which she was born. This assisted autobiography takes her from her Xhosa childhood in the Sith Efrika of the thirties and forties through until just before her participation in Paul Simon's 1987 *Graceland Tour*, describing the humiliation and repression blacks in SA endure as a matter of course, her drift into a musical career, and how that musical career brought her to the attention of those – including Harry Belafonte, with whom she later fell out – who helped to make her an international attraction. However, simply escaping the apartheid regime did not free her from bigotry and racism: when she married Black Power leader Stokely Carmichael she found her adopted home of America no more hospitable than her native land. A woman who simply wanted to sing but whose life has led her to become a spokesperson for, and symbol of, African nationalism, Makeba is as inspiring in print as she is on stage, screen or record: this book is unhesitatingly recommended for its unselfconsciously affecting fusion of personal history, showbiz reminiscence and political fervour. It also emphasizes, tragically enough, that anybody who still believes that the South African regime will relinquish power or dismantle apartheid gracefully would do better to place their faith in something more tangible – like Father Christmas or the tooth-fairy. (*CSM*)

MOONWALK

Michael Jackson (*Heinemann*)

About halfway through this book, Michael Jackson makes the observation "I take some small pride in thinking that I've come out pretty well, all things considered." And, by his own standards, so he has – the Grammies, the album sales, the tour receipts and endorsement fees speak volumes. A chapter or so into *Moonwalk*, it becomes obvious that the only standards Jackson judges anything by, indeed the only standards he knows, are showbiz standards, measured in Grammies, album sales and so on. This much, and not much else, do you learn from the book, which talks of nothing other than performing or recording from as far back as he can remember. Even the photos follow this line: early family snapshots are posed affairs with stage suits and instruments and in the later ones the only time he shows any noticeable expression is when he has a mike in his hand.

However, the childish quality of the (presumably unedited) text, the impression given that everything that's happened to him is wonderful or it doesn't appear to have happened (there is practically no mention of his falling out with the Jehovah's Witnesses, the ill-fated Victory tour or the dismissal of his father as manager), and denials that he has had anything more than a nose job and chin cleft added, that verge on the stamping of little feet, are enough to convince that all is not what it should be for a healthy, wealthy 30-year-old. But there's no reason why it should be, when his childhood involved travelling to gigs, rehearsing and watching strippers and drag artists from the wings of shabby theatres instead of scrumping, playing "Knock Down Ginger" and discovering little girls.

All in all, it's a sad tale that adds or subtracts nothing from the myth that surrounds Michael Jackson, but that might be what it set out to do. I blame the parents. (*LB*)

NEVER STOP: THE ECHO & THE BUNNYMEN STORY

Tony Fletcher (*Omnibus*)

It was in late July '88 that grim-faced travellers, returning from Northern parts, brought reports to London of a split in that singular tribe that is called Echo & The Bunnymen. For the stories behind *that* story, however, you'd look in vain to the biog-book *Never Stop*. Indeed its very title seems unfortunate, now. Published just a couple of months before the group suspended their affairs, Tony Fletcher's dogged account of the Liverpool band's career leaves off at the point when they knew they'd have to break big, at last, or break up. For nearly a decade the cult quartet (actually a trio at first, with a drum machine called Echo) had built and nurtured a loyal legion of fans, attracted by the morbid grandeur of the music, the obscure poetry of Ian McCulloch's songs, and the wry, downbeat humour that the Bunnymen would wrap around themselves as if in self-protection.

It's a pity the book that bears their name has none of their quirky wit, nor any of their stubborn non-conformity. *Never Stop*, tells this unique group's story with due care and attention, but little flair. (*PDN*)

YOKO ONO: A BIOGRAHY

Jerry Hopkins (*Sidgwick & Jackson*)
Writing a book about Yoko Ono was never going to be the easiest task in the world: either she'd co-operate and, if her dealings with the press were anything to go by, not tell you anything; or she'd not co-operate and you're left to sort through cuttings in which she hasn't told anybody anything and interview people who once knew people who knew the subject. Here the author is lumbered with the latter option and writes some 250 pages that tell you very little about one of rock's favourite bogey-women. Judging from Hopkins' previous work on The Doors, levity would've been too much to expect, but the stodginess of much of this text, even accounting for the subject's reportedly dour disposition is quite remarkable. And while, like so much else that has been written about Ono, she only seems to exist relative to Lennon and the Fabs, it cops out of making any judgments on whether this really was the case – the one thing that could've made the work interesting. After finishing this book, I spent a long time wondering why Hopkins started it. (*LB*)

PRINCE: IMP OF THE PERVERSE

Barney Hoskyns (*Virgin*)
An unfortunate title that, while not actually saying anything about anything, gives the impression that this is some kind of super-cerebral think-piece about a performer who is impossible to define, let alone intellectualize over. Thankfully, it is exactly the opposite: a workmanlike account of Prince's recording/touring career (his childhood takes up less than a dozen pages) taking us through his different bands, styles and success levels with a keen eye for detail. More than a scissors-and-paste job, yet much less than a bona-fide biography, *Imp Of The Perverse* is ultimately frustrating. (This will come as a major disappointment to fans of Hoskyns' *Say It One Time For The Brokenhearted*, but I suppose it's asking too much to expect him to manage two works of that standard in the same year.) There is definitely a book to be written about Prince, and when it arrives this will be a worthy companion to it. (*DB*)

RUSH: VISIONS

Bill Banasiewicz (*Omnibus*)
Banasiewicz is a Rush fan. A major league Rush fan. If you were tempted to disbelieve the proclamation of such on the back-cover – well, I bet most of you have never met a Rush fan – then the text is more than enough to convince. With the aid of Geddy Lee's scrapbooks, he accurately chronicles the band's relentless rise from bar-rooms to stadiums, pausing only to let you know how much he admires and endorses them – even that pompous, quasi-classical period that saw them recording "suites" of 20-minute duration instead of catchy pop toons. In taking this all-approving stance, Banasiewicz skilfully avoids the one aspect of the group that would do something towards making them sound interesting: that, since their return to straightforward songs, they have been displaying a considerable self-deprecating sense of humour as they – especially Lee – look back on that period, admitting that segments now appear "self-indulgent", "a bit misguided" and "really quite funny". By taking it all so seriously, the author is as ripe for sending up as his subjects were. (*LB*)

SOLITARY STAR: A BIOGRAPHY OF NEIL DIAMOND

Rich Wiseman (*Sidgwick & Jackson*)
This saga of the life of Neil Diamond makes recurrent reference to the second verse of Diamond's melodramatic song 'I Am . . . I Said' – the one about the "frog who dreamed of being a king." "My story's the same one" sang Diamond. The first 20 years of the Diamond story – the tadpole days, if you will – occupy a mere eight pages. By page 37 he's written 'Solitary Man', and page 50 sees The Monkees have a number one hit with 'I'm A Believer'. The unseemly haste of all this leaves Wiseman, never an engaging storyteller, to fill 260 further pages with just about unstinting admiration for "Neil" – the chronicle of his success being plumped up with often inconsequential anecdotes by and about anybody who happened at any time to have anything to do with the erstwhile frog. The book falls down on two counts: one is its author's inability to make even the best stories vaguely interesting; the other is its subject's completely uninteresting life. (*JB*)

BOOKS

THE SMITHS: THE COMPLETE STORY

Mick Middles (*Omnibus*)

Originally published in 1985, *The Complete Story* has been updated to include full details of the group's split ("The blackest day in pop": an observer). Devotees of the Manchester miserablists undoubtedly own this tome – to date, the only comprehensive account in book form of Big Moz's transformation from Wilde-child recluse to angst-riddled millionaire – but, to recap: the moaners' tale is related with infinitesimal thoroughness, although the author tends to omit clarifying details like dates, causing, at times, a sense of fuzzy confusion. A fan's labour of love, it's full of decidedly idiosyncratic turns of phrase ("Alarming how a splash of fame can twist situations into reverse achievements") and, obviously, the viewpoint is highly partisan. To Middles' credit, though, when The Smiths act like schmucks (e.g. a spate of prima-donna-ish behaviour in mid-career), he gives them a roasting. Refreshingly unsycophantic, really. (*CS*)

U2: STORIES FOR BOYS

Dave Thomas (*Bobcat*)

A revised edition, but still only 64 pages long, of what is claimed to be the "first full length biography" (full length?). Many sneer at this type of quickie "cuttings book", but in the absence of anything more weighty at the time this book originally appeared (1986), it served the purpose of documenting (albeit sketchily) the rise and rise of a group which has subsequently scaled the heights of fame. However, remembering that U2's first record release hit the streets less than a decade ago, this slim volume is enough to contain much of the useful information those other than true disciples will be looking for. (*JT*)

U2: TOUCH THE FLAME. AN ILLUSTRATED DOCUMENTARY

Geoff Parkyn (*Omnibus*)

Parkyn started the U2 Information Service, and is now the distributor of the official U2 Fan Club magazine, so he should know his stuff, and he does. What this 96-page "lavishly illustrated" book lacks is much of a glimpse at U2 as people, although understandably this kind of gen can be found in *Unforgettable Fire* by Eamon Dunphy, which appears to be rather closer to the group's hearts than this undeniably useful and engaging mélange of fax 'n' info. Strong on chronology, only fair on personality, this isn't bad at all, and as a superior eighties version of the George Tremlett pop biogs of the seventies (which sold prodigiously and have become latterday collectables among fans of Bolan, Bowie, etc.) is a respectable enough read as well as containing minutiae like details of the venues and dates of group gigs, a Mother Records discography, etc. (*JT*)

UNFORGETTABLE FIRE – THE STORY OF U2

Eamon Dunphy (*Viking*)

What seemed the curious choice of an ex-Millwall soccer player to write the apparently definitive biog of the hottest act in the world last year was initially controversial, as various unsurprisingly envious writers vented their spleen at having been passed over. An exposé which was published in *Q* after having first appeared in that journal's Irish equivalent, *Hot Press*, was vociferous about inaccuracies and Dunphy's limited grasp of popular music, and to some extent was justified. However, for those who want to know something about U2's background and history, together with a smattering of contemporary Irish social history, this book could hardly be bettered. While it would have been justice if *Hot Press* sage Bill Graham had written the book (he recommended them to their manager, Paul McGuinness, and was their first influential fan), it might have been difficult to maintain objectivity, which Dunphy achieves effortlessly. Dunphy's unwillingness (or inability?) to comment on U2's music is also a plus factor – U2 appears to make music which obviously has much appeal, but is difficult, if not impossible, to verbalize with any precision, and this is probably the reason for their success. There may be better U2 books in future, but for now, this will do nicely. (*JT*)

MISCELLANEOUS

AFRICAN ALL-STARS

Chris Stapleton & Chris May (*Quartet*)

As African music continues to grow in popularity in the West, one of the factors holding back its development is the confusing amount of styles, jargon and names to be learned. It's too easy for the beginner to be put off for life by one sneering "What do you mean you want to hear some African music? What kind?" from a haughty record-shop assistant. Stapleton and May's book provides the ideal briefing for that first foray into the Dark Continent: it traces the history of urban African music, sketching out the roots but detailing it over the last 50 years; it breaks down and explains the different styles and provides portraits of their stars; and lastly it describes the African music business, with chapters on its expansion overseas and its assimilation of other styles. More than a tourist brochure – although it works well as a bluffer's phrase book – and far deeper than an Idiot's Guide To . . ., yet easily understood by novices. (*DB*)

BACK IN THE USSR – THE TRUE STORY OF ROCK IN RUSSIA

Artemy Troitsky (*Omnibus*)

It was inevitable that rock music (of a sort) should creep under the Iron Curtain, and equally inevitable that an earnest Russian should attempt to document its growth. However, the bottom line to all this has to be that while it's obligatory to acknowledge that this is an important item (at least in theory), without actually hearing any Russian rock, who knows if it has any real value in terms of emotion or the magic which The Lovin' Spoonful so eloquently described all those years ago? Probably the first in what will develop into a flood of books about Eastern block pop stars (if Gorbachev continues to be in charge), this one has the virtue of being the first – but without the music, it's ultimately a bit dull. Forward planners are recommended to invest now for the future, as this will probably become the *Sniffin' Glue* in its field. (*JT*)

FLASHING ON THE SIXTIES

Lisa Law (*Chronicle Books*)

This photographic scrapbook of hippy days in the USA is described in its foreword (by Baba Ram Dass) as "nostalgia, pure and simple". The photographer seems to have been born into vague affluence, to have been stolen – aged 22 – by music, cameras and the headiness of the days, and to have married into the heart of the times. Husband Tom Law, who worked in music (for Albert Grossman) and films (assistant to director Mike Nichols), moved with his new bride into the stately splendour of The Castle in LA – where they took in lodgers: Bob Dylan, Andy Warhol, The Velvet Underground, that sort of lodger.

All the while Lisa Law's camera was snapping away, and there's no shortage of rock 'n' roll celebrities in her photo album – Otis Redding, The Beatles, Janis Joplin, The Byrds and others – but by far the most interesting shots are those of the hippified tribes of California. There's plenty to smile and wonder at – geodesic domes, Kundalini yogists, teepees, and hair everywhere. It's often wonderfully silly, and always quite delightful. (*JB*)

GIANTS OF JAZZ

Dave Gelly & Weef (*Aurum*)

A dictionary of who's who in jazz, running chronologically from Dixieland monarch King Oliver to such present-day heroes as Wynton Marsalis and Bobby McFerrin and taking in 75 musicians from Lester Young to Benny Goodman to Herbie Hancock. Obviously there are omissions – Dexter Gordon and Fletcher Henderson being two that immediately spring to mind – but the style of the book makes up for that: it's not a textbook, and Gelly's essays are as lively as Weef's (cartoonist David Smith) illustrations, managing to inform without being turgid or falling into the train-spotter (endless lists of band line-ups and recording dates) mode that afflicts too many jazz books. The one complaint is that 'The Britons' section occupies a mere three pages. Perhaps it's because the majority of the book's sales are expected to be in America, but it's a fairly irritating state of affairs that there's no mention of either youngbloods like Courtney Pine and Andy Sheppard or old stalwarts such as John Stevens and George Melly. All the same, just as Miles Kington states in the introduction: "I wish I had this book to help me when I first discovered jazz." I'm glad I have. (*LB*)

BOOKS

HOW TO MAKE IT IN THE ROCK BUSINESS

Mary Wilson (*Columbus*)

Not to be confused with *How To Make It Big In The Rock Business* (reviewed in last year's book), this is for the less ambitious of you. And it's a pretty unambitious book, offering all sorts of theoretic advice about succeeding in the business – how to approach a record company, how to get on television, and good places to "gig". The problem is there's no mention of such variables as human nature, market forces and whether you're any good or not, thus it all sounds incredibly easy to "make it in the rock business", which anyone who has sense enough to be able to read this book will know it isn't. The £4.95 would be better off put towards hiring a decent lawyer. (*LB*)

HUNGRY FOR HEAVEN

Steve Turner (*Virgin*)

If you look hard enough for anything in an area as wide-reaching as rock/pop music, you'll be able to find it: racism, sexism, a social conscience, rebellion, violence, peace, Satanism, or, as in this case, the search for salvation. You'll be able to find definite examples and then, depending on how much time you have to theorize, tenuously rope in all sorts of illustrations. Turner sets out to reclaim rock from the devil, and in early instances – the gospel-based R&B that osmosed into rock 'n' roll – he's onto a winner. However, as time progresses, the connection becomes stretched beyond belief: U2's spirituality – not necessarily their search for conventional religion – is well known, but citing Stiv Bators of The Lords Of The New Church trotting out the familiar line about "The kids don't have much to believe in today . . . You can believe in rock 'n' roll with the fever of football or the fever of religion"as an example of "a renewed search for redemption" is contentious to say the least. Unfortunately, Turner is crusading rather than discussing; thus quotes are lifted from context and there is no other side presented. This area is an interesting issue, but needs to be approached in a way that sets out to convince a wider readership than the already committed author. (*LB*)

PHOTO PAST 1966–1986

Ray Stevenson (*Symbiosis*)

This collection of snaps and snarls is Ray Stevenson's memoir of two decades of not making money in the rock business. This is not so much a reflection on the quality of the pictures – though many of them have looked considerably better elsewhere – as a result of expecting rather more loyalty than he got from one-time buddies like Malcolm McLaren and David Bowie. Stevenson has certainly been in some right places at the right times, and his book has an impressively varied cast, including folkies (Sandy Denny, Roy Harper, Buffy Sainte-Marie, Bert Jansch), hippies (Hendrix, Joplin, Tyrannosaurus Rex, Syd Barrett-era Floyd, Fairports, Cream, Zappa, Young Bowie), punks (Pistols, Clash, Slits, Siouxsie, Damned, Gen X with Billy Idol; the entire cast of the Roxy and The Vortex, in short) and the avant-guarde (Brian Eno, Lydia Lunch, Karlheinz Stockhausen) . . . all leading up to "the best band I've seen this decade," Sigue Sigue Sputnik. The problem with *Photo Past* almost certainly lies with Stevenson's disdain of editors: it badly needed someone who could excise some of the more asinine captions ("Marsha Hunt – a beautiful reason for vasectomy") and spread the photos out a little so that the better ones would have the breathing space they deserve. That said , the book represents more than simply Stevenson's yesterdays: it's both amusing and alarming to study the effects of passing time sartorial revisionism on pop stars sublime and ridiculous, ancient and modern. (*CSM*)

ROCK OF AGES: THE ROLLING STONE HISTORY OF ROCK AND ROLL

Ed Ward, Geoffrey Stokes, Ken Tucker (*Penguin*)

A 620-page enthusiasts' guide to where the music came from, and where it's been in its 30- or 40-year journey. Like any such all-inclusive tome, the history is, from time to time, annoyingly potted – chunks of explanation and significance all-too-neatly pretending to be the definitive word on the matter. The enormous workload has been shared between three writers who take a decade each. Ed Ward's summary of the fifties and before is a credit to his industry and his erudition, though his complex weavings sometimes make great demands on the reader's powers of concentration. More accessible is Geoffrey Stokes' summary of the sixties. He's done a more basic job of stitching sources together, but with a welcome good humour. Unfortunately, in "The Seventies and Beyond" Ken Tucker decides to abandon objectivity to pass judgement on the artists and records he's supposed to be chronicling, and when such judgement is as wayward (or just plain wrong-headed) as is Tucker's, the text becomes more infuriating than informative. A useful slab of a book nevertheless. (*JB*)

ROCK ON COMPACT DISC: A CRITICAL GUIDE

David Prakel (*Salamander*)

Reviews of 350 rock CDs, awarding star ratings for desirability and recording quality. A worthy idea, but one that has come out about a year too late and, when selection relies so entirely on one man's opinion, not nearly enough titles included. The potted history of and technical guide to CD in the beginning highlights this first complaint – by now, there's been so much written elsewhere about CD that people either know or don't care. The latter beef becomes immediately apparent as soon as you flick through the reviews – if you really want Abba's *The Visitors* (number one in Prakel's top 100) or ZZ Top's *Afterburner* (number 99) in glorious digital sound, you're going to buy it no matter what anyone tells you. You end up simply finding out if you agree with him or not on the desirability quotient. (*DB*)

SHOWTIME AT THE APOLLO

Ted Fox (*Quartet*)

Harlem's Apollo Theatre (on 125th St, naturally) is not so much a building as an institution as far as the development of US jazz/R&B/soul music is concerned. Its nearest British equivalents would be what The Marquee was to UK R&B or The Vortex was to punk, but, in terms of the sheer volume of now world-status performers that used those places as a cradle, they are about as far away symbolically as they are physically. Quite rightly, Fox doesn't dwell on the building itself – shabby and badly equipped would be to put it mildly – but through the anecdotes and reminiscences of performers like James Brown, Sammy Davis Jr., Bill Cosby and Pearl Bailey, industry figures like Ahmet Ertugun and Berry Gordy and former stagehands and kiosk operators, he builds up a vivid and lively picture of the theatre's atmosphere, audience and (thoroughly deserved) place in black American music's history. The Apollo is shut now, a fact that makes this book even more vital, for anybody who's ever twitched an ear or shook a leg towards anything remotely funky. (*LB*)

STARMAKERS & SVENGALIS

Johnny Rogan (*Macdonald/Queen Anne Press*)

Any book on rock managers ought to be a bit of a hoot – full of ducking and diving, gold Amex cards, Crombie overcoats and any number of "porkie pies". A well-researched book on rock managers, as this is, ought to be a bloody good laugh, adding more than its fair share of wads of used fivers, "very heavy geezers" and the odd mercy dash to a private hospital to the mix. It should bring these characters, and the frequently unreal world they inhabit, alive for readers whose only brush with managers concern overdraft facilities. In spite of an interesting-sounding sub-dividing of managers into categories that include "The Concerned Parent", "The Neutered Lackey", "The Autocrat" and "The Overreacher", this book is tediously long on intellectual theorizing and painfully short on anecdote. And although chapters on a chronology of managers from Larry Parnes (Tommy Steele, Joe Brown, Bill Fury) to Gordon Mills (Tom Jones, Leapy Lee, Gilbert O'Sullivan) to Simon Napier-Bell (T-Rex, Japan, Wham!) to Stevo (Soft Cell, Yello, Test Department) are comprehensive enough, it inconclusively tells you what they did rather than give any clues as to why they did. A good reference book but hardly a gripping read, he should've given Peter Grant (Led Zep) a chapter. (*LB*)

TWENTY YEARS OF ROLLING STONE

(*Ebury Press*)

Born of the later, darker sixties, *Rolling Stone* magazine quickly poked its head out of the West Coast underground to become the firmly established organ of that decade's originally "alternative" society. Though pot-headed and political from the outset, it was primarily a music magazine, but faced with a patently untrustworthy and often frighteningly idiot "establishment" it became the clear-eyed chronicle of the often nasty times. In this weighty and glossy summary volume – subtitled "What a long, strange trip it's been" – founding editor and publisher Jann S. Wenner has culled interviews and profiles and investigations from his back pages. The social signposts are listed in the contents: Woodstock, Charles Manson, Kent State, Watergate, Vietnam, Karen Silkwood, Patty Hearst, Cocaine – the good old days. The musical colossi who bestride such pettinesses are not always predictable: Pete Townshend, The Grateful Dead, John Lennon, Sly Stone, Keith Moon, Alice Cooper – with Jagger, Springsteen, Wonder, Jackson, Dylan for better measure. Essentially a dippable coffee-table book, it will fill many an idle hour for the over-30s. Younger readers probably have better things to do. (*JB*)

IN MEMORIAM

JOE ALBANY
Died 12 January 1988, New York, aged 63

A legendary jazz figure, pianist Albany played with Charlie Parker in the early days of bebop. Born in Atlantic City, Albany was one of Parker's favourite pianists and worked both live and on record with Bird. He also played with Boyd Raeburn, Lester Young, Benny Carter and others, his life being the subject of a prize-winning documentary in 1980. Titled *Joe Albany – A Jazz Life*, it was screened on C4's *Late Shift* during 1988.

CHET BAKER
Died 13 May 1988, Amsterdam, aged 58

The Bix Beiderbecke of modern jazz, trumpeter Baker played briefly with Charlie Parker on club dates during the early fifties, then moved to become part of America's hottest cool combo, the pianoless Gerry Mulligan Quartet, an outfit that garnered the sort of acclaim normally afforded pop groups. A singer whose fragile, lyrical vocal style mirrored that of his trumpet playing, the Oklahoman formed his own quartet and became the darling of the pollsters, ousting Dizzy Gillespie in some listings. Visually a role model upon whom James Dean based his own image, Chet had it all but blew everything by moving into drugs. By 1959 he'd been busted seven times, eventually getting jailed not only in the States but also in Italy and Britain, from which country he was deported in 1963. In the late sixties, he was beaten up by thugs, injuring his mouth, after which he quit playing for a while, living on welfare payments. But, equipped with a set of false teeth and a methadone programme, he made a semi-successful comeback, sometimes playing in appalling, lack-lustre manner, sometimes re-shaping melodies in the pretty yet positive manner that had once made him a Downbeat New Star. Admired by Elvis Costello, he played on Costello's version of 'Shipbuilding' and also appeared in the *Round Midnight* movie. And when he appeared at London's Ronnie Scott's Club not long before his death, both Costello and Van Morrison participated in his set. Ill-fated to the last, he fell from an Amsterdam window on Friday 13.

BROOK BENTON
Died 9 April 1988, New York, aged 56

A warm-voiced baritone who was equally at home singing soul at the Apollo or Sinatra-styled standards in Vegas, Benton (real name Benjamin Peay), from South Carolina, began his musical career with the local Camden Jubilee Singers while holding down a day job as milk delivery boy, at 17, heading for New York where he worked with other groups, eventually joining Bill Landford's Spiritual Quartet. Later he joined The Sandmen, an R&B outfit, additionally working as a truck driver and as a session singer, cutting demos for others. In the wake of singles for Epic, he signed for Vik and gained a minor hit with 'A Million Miles From Nowhere', also teaming with songwriter Clyde Otis to write such hits as 'Looking Back' for Nat Cole and 'A Lover's Question' for Clyde McPhatter. In 1959 Benton signed for Mercury Records, where Otis was an A&R man, and began recording such million-sellers as 'It's Just A Matter Of Time', 'Endlessly' and 'Thank You Pretty Baby'. During the next four years he proved a virtual hit machine and was rarely out of the US charts thanks to records like 'So Many Ways', 'Kiddio', 'Think Twice', 'The Boll Weevil Song' and 'Hotel Happiness' plus such memorable duets with Dinah Washington as 'Baby (You've Got What it Takes)' and 'A Rockin' Good Way'. But in 1965 the hits dried up and he drifted from one record label to another, enjoying some sort of renaissance in 1970 when Cotillion released his soulful version of 'A Rainy Night In Georgia', briefly placing him on the charts worldwide. But it was just a brief respite. Before long he was back working mainly on nostalgia-linked tours with fellow members of the remember-when brigade.

★

JOHN BLISS
Died 7 July 1988, Los Angeles, aged 32

Drummer and founder member of Powertrip, regarded as one of the first American bands to fuse punk and heavy metal into speedmetal, Bliss died of a heart-attack. The Band's first album, *When We Cut We Bleed*, was reissued in recent months by PVC Records.

★

CLIFTON CHENIER
Died 12 December 1987, Lafayette, Louisiana, aged 62

The "King Of Zydeco", accordionist Chenier was undoubted ruler of the Cajun R&B genre, and displayed his authority by often performing with a crown on his head. Born on a farm near Opelousas, Louisiana, he cut his first record 'Clifton Blues' in 1954 and signed to Specialty, then a ground-breaking rock label, during the following year. He then label-hopped throughout the fifties, finding acceptance with a new record-buying audience after signing with specialist label Arhoolie in 1964. In the wake of this, he and his band – which included his brother Cleveland on washboard – made a hit at the 1966 Berkeley Folk Festival and became a regular on the US folk, blues and jazz festival circuit, appearing at the New Orleans Jazz and Heritage Festival each spring. Provider of a soundtrack to the French science-fiction movie *France société anonyme*, Chenier was also the subject of a *Les Blank* documentary, *Hot Pepper* (both 1973). A self-styled "black Cajun Frenchman", his music influenced many other zydeco musicians, including Rockin' Dopsie and Buckwheat Zydeco.

★

SADAY COURVILLE
Died 3 January 1988, Mamou, Louisiana, aged 82

A fiddle player who worked right up to the day before his death – he had his own weekly radio show originating at Fred's Lounge in Mamou, Courville was one of the two men who made the first known recording of Cajun music. His partner in that venture, lead fiddler Dennis McGee (Courville's brother-in-law) is still alive, aged 95, and recorded with Courville in New York only last year.

Divine

JESSE ED DAVIS
Died 22 June, Venice, California, aged 43

Another OD victim, guitarist Davis was, arguably, best known for his work with Taj Mahal, appearing on such albums as *Taj Mahal*, *The Natch'l Blues*, *Happy Just To Be Like I Am*, etc. An in-demand sessionman who worked with everyone, from The Monkees and Jackie DeShannon through to Jackson Browne and Rod Stewart. He recorded two solo albums for Atco, *Jesse Ed Davis* and *Ululu*, plus one for Epic, *Keep On Coming*, during the early seventies, and in 1971 appeared with George Harrison, Bob Dylan and a host of other stars at the Madison Square Garden Concert For Bangladesh. In more recent times, he played lead guitar for The Graffiti Band, headed by poet John Trudell.

DIVINE
Died 7 March 1988, Hollywood, aged 42

An obese female impersonator, he was born Harris Glenn Milstead, making his first appearance as the buxom, heavily made-up Divine in a John Waters movie, *Roman Candles*, during 1966. Star of several other Waters films, he achieved overnight notoriety in 1972 when he appeared in *Pink Flamingos* eating fresh poodle faeces – thus ensuring that the movie would become a cult sensation, running in LA for ten straight years. Apart from films, Divine appeared in several theatrical productions and countless disco productions around the world, gaining several hit records in the UK, the main contenders being 'You Think You're A Man' (1984) and 'Walk Like A Man' (1985). Just prior to his death, he had appeared in the movie *Hairspray*, portraying both a lower-class housewife and the racist owner of a Baltimore TV station.

★

JOHN DOPYERA
Died 1 January 1988, Grants Pass, Oregon, aged 94

A Czech-born violin-maker who emigrated to the US with his parents at the age of 15, he staked his place in musical history when, in 1925, he and his brothers took a standard Spanish guitar and fitted it with an aluminium cone to provide added sound amplification. The instrument became immediately popular, especially in the country and blues fields, and was dubbed the Dobro, a shortening of the name Dopyera Brothers.

★

GIL EVANS
Died 20 March 1988, Cuernavaca, Mexico, aged 75

Arguably the greatest jazz arranger since Duke Ellington, the Canadian-born Evans moved to California and formed his first band while in his early twenties. By 1941 he was chief arranger with the Claude Thornhill Orchestra, providing that aggregation with some of the finest scores ever to emerge from the dance-band world. He utilized French horn and tuba sounds to provide Thornhill with a multi-hued sound, powerful yet beautiful. Additionally, his charts enabled the band to operate almost like a bebop combo, with the ability to swing on such bop anthems as 'Donna Lee', 'Yardbird Suite' and 'Anthropology'. During 1949–50 Evans formed a liaison with Miles Davis contributing the nonet arrangements used on the trumpeter's ground-breaking *Birth Of The Cool* sessions. Later he was to back Davis on the CBS dates that provided such indispensable albums as *Miles Ahead* (1957), *Porgy And Bess* (1959) and *Sketches Of Spain* (1960). Less active for a while during the mid sixties, in 1969 Evans resumed occasional leadership of various ensembles, embracing electronic and rock sounds. In later years, he led a band that appeared each Monday at New York's Sweet Basil's and also embarked on regular tours of Europe and Japan. During 1985 Evans was invited to supply soundtrack music for the star-studded *Absolute Beginners* and two years later provided arrangements for Sting. In 1988 he planned to return to the UK yet again, lining up a Royal Festival Hall concert. But it was not to be, his death, from peritonitis, occurring in Mexico where he was recovering from prostate surgery

RAY "PABLO" FALCONER
Died 15 November 1987, Birmingham, aged 26

UB40's sound engineer and co-producer of most of the band's records, he was killed in a car-crash. Later, his brother Earl Falconer, the band's bass-guitarist, was deemed responsible and charged with drunken driving. Found guilty at a Birmingham Crown Court, he was jailed for 18 months with 12 months suspended.

CAROLYN FRANKLIN
Died 25 April 1988, Bloomfield Hills, Michigan, aged 43

Franklin was a singer-songwriter who wrote two major hits for her sister Aretha, 'Ain't No Way' (1968) and 'Angel' (1973). A superior soul-singer in her own right, she had UK album releases both on Joy and RCA and appeared, with her other sister Erma, on Aretha's *One Lord, One Faith, One Baptism* gospel album, in 1987.

ANDY GIBB
Died 10 March 1988, Oxford, aged 30

Always The Bee Gees' kid brother who somehow got lucky, Gibb was born in Manchester but grew up in Australia, where his family moved when he was six months old. The family returned to Britain in 1967, his brothers taking their first steps towards mega-stardom at this time. By 1975 Andy was back in Australia, eventually forming a band named Zenta and opening a tour featuring the Bay City Rollers. A few months later he visited impresario Robert Stigwood's home in Bermuda and was signed to the RSO label, notching his first major hit with 'I Just Want To Be Your Everything', penned by brother Barry. The single reached number one in the US charts during 1977. That same year, he attained another number one with '(Love Is) Thicker Than Water', completing a hat-trick with 'Shadow Dancing' during 1978, this third hit heading the US listings for seven weeks in a row. An almost overnight millionaire, Gibb did the whole rich-kid bit, living in a highly extravagant manner. But in the wake of 'Time Is Time' (1980), his flow of major hit singles dried up. His relationship with *Dallas* star Victoria Principal went sour and Gibb became a drug addict, eventually living on an allowance provided by his brothers. At the time of his death, in an Oxford hospital, he had filed for bankruptcy.

★

WILLIS "GATOR TAIL" JACKSON

Died 25 October 1987, New York, aged 59

A big-toned, stomping tenor sax man, best known for his work with tenor 'n' organ combos, Jackson began his professional career with the Cootie Williams big band during the forties and had his first hit record in 1949 with 'Gator Tail'. Later he moved on to work with small groups, recording for Prestige, Muse and other labels. He died following heart surgery.

"FAT LARRY" JAMES

Died 5 December 1987, Philadelphia, aged 38

Leader of the disco-funk oriented Fat Larry's Band, who had a number two hit in the UK charts with 'Zoom' during 1982. Along the way he worked for soft-soul groups The Delfonics and Blue Magic, leading the latter's backing band, and also managed Slick.

★

SCOTT LA ROCK

Died 25 August 1987, New York

Hip hop star La Rock was killed in a gangland shoot-out outside a club in the Bronx, just after the release of *Criminal Minded* a critically acclaimed debut album that saw him working with Blastmaster KRS One. A performer who retained a high profile in the "Bridge Wars" between rappers from the Bronx, Brooklyn and Queens areas. On the day of his death he'd signed a deal with Sleeping Bag/Fresh Records, who'd expected him to fill the gap left by the departing Mantronix.

JOE LIGGINS

Died 1 August 1987, Lynwood, California, aged 72

An R&B piano-player, singer-songwriter and bandleader, the Oklahoma-born Liggins first came to fame in 1945 when his recording of 'The Honeydripper' became a monster hit. Later he moved onto Specialty and again hit the jackpot in 1950 when Liggins And The Honeydrippers' recording of 'Pink Champagne' reached number one in the US R&B listings and remained in the charts for the next six months. He ultimately disbanded and then generally confined his activities to nightclubs, often using pick-up musicians to handle his stock of arrangements. In 1982, The Jets scored a mild UK hit with their version of 'The Honeydripper'.

IN MEMORIAM

MEMPHIS SLIM

Died 24 February 1988, Paris, France, aged 73

A piano-playing bluesman, Slim (real name was Peter Chatman) hailed from Memphis, Tennessee. At 16 he left home and jumped a freight train to Chicago but stayed only two weeks before returning home. During 1933 he replaced Roosevelt Sykes at a Memphis club, the gig leading to further bookings, first locally, then nationally. "I had to work at night and hide in my hotel room all day," he later claimed. "Because if a white farmer or landlord caught a negro not working by day, he used to take him by force to work on his plantation. I remember during the cotton season, they used to stop all the buses going to St Louis on Highway 61, pull the negroes out of the buses and force them at gun-point to pick cotton." Signed to Okeh, he first recorded as a soloist in 1940, working under the name "Peter Chatman And His Washboard Band". But it was as Memphis Slim that he recorded for RCA-Bluebird, logging his first hit with 'Beer Drinking Woman'. After working with Big Bill Broonzy and the first Sonny Boy Williamson, he formed a band known as The Houserockers, though it was while working as a duo with bassist Willie Dixon that he achieved most plaudits, storming New York before crossing to Europe. In the wake of a triumphant gig at the 1959 Newport Jazz Festival he toured Europe and paid his first visit to France in 1961, eventually settling down in Paris with his French wife and daughter. In later years he toured Europe, worked in Parisian clubs and often appeared on French TV, playing such material as 'Everyday I Have The Blues', a Slim original that was a huge hit for Joe Williams and The Count Basie Orchestra in the mid-fifties.

★

JACO PASTORIUS

Died 21 September 1987, Fort Lauderdale, Florida, aged 35

A formidable technician on electric bass, Pastorius first played clubs in South Florida with Wayne Cochran And The CC Riders but later gained much kudos from his work with Weather Report. He also recorded one eponymous solo album for CBS and acted as sideman with Blood, Sweat And Tears and Joni Mitchell. Nominated for three Grammys, his playing and writing talents earned him a reputation as one of the top men on his instrument. But he was a manic depressive and constant alcohol abuse worsened the disorder. On 12 September, Pastorius had jumped on stage at a Carlos Santana concert and had to be forcibly removed. Later that night he attempted to enter Fort Lauderdale's Midnight Club by kicking at the door, only to be beaten-up by club manager Luc Havan, receiving injuries from which he died some days later.

DAVID PRATER

Died 9 April 1988, Sycamore, Georgia, aged 50

Prater, who died when his car went off Interstate 75 and hit a tree, while he was travelling to Ocilla, Georgia, was one half of Sam And Dave, arguably the grittiest and most intense of all the sixties black music duos. He met Sam Moore in the late fifties, and the twosome began making records for Stax in 1965, their output including such hits as 'Hold On! I'm Coming' (1966), 'Soul Man' (1967) and 'I Thank You' (1968). When Stax was sold, Sam And Dave moved onto Atlantic but their records refused to sell in appreciable quantities and eventually the partnership went phut, Prater signing for Alston as a solo act. During the seventies, he and Moore got together again but couldn't recapture the old magic. By 1982, they'd once more gone their separate ways, Prater teaming with Sam Daniels to keep the Sam And Dave trademark intact. Just a few weeks after Prater's death, Atlantic announced that they would pay back-royalties on all their Sam And Dave releases, something they have neglected to do since the late sixties, even though 'Hold On I'm Coming' had formed part of the best-selling *Blues Brothers* soundtrack in 1980.

DANNIE RICHMOND
Died 16 March 1988, New York, aged 56

Regular drummer with Charlie Mingus, Richmond began his career as an R&B saxman but moved onto drums in 1956. At a jam session that year, he impressed Mingus, with whom he played until the bassist's death in 1979. When not working with Mingus, Richmond played with Mark Almond, Chet Baker and others, becoming part of Mingus Dynasty after Mingus' death. At the time of his own death, Richmond had just concluded a tour with the George Adams–Don Pullen Quartet, a group he helped found in 1979.

HILLEL SLOVAK
Died 27 June 1988, Hollywood, aged 25

Lead guitarist and founder member of the Red Hot Chilli Peppers, Slovak was initially believed to have OD'd but an autopsy proved inconclusive. Born in Haifa, Israel and taken to Hollywood at an early age, Slovak met the other members of the band while at Fairfax High School. At the time of his death, the Peppers were going into pre-production of a new album.

B.W. STEVENSON
Died 28 April 1988, Nashville, aged 38

An Austin-based singer-songwriter, Stevenson penned 'Shambala', a massive hit for Three Dog Night in 1973. Signed to RCA as a solo artist, he also achieved a breakthrough of his own in 1973, going Top 10 in the US pop charts with 'My Maria'.

SLAM STEWART
Died 9 December 1987, Binghamton, New York, aged 73

A scat singing jazz bassist, he was Slim Gaillard's partner in Slim and Slam, a duo that logged such zany hits as 'Flat Foot Floogie (With The Floy Floy)' and 'Tutti Frutti' during the late thirties. Along the way, Stewart also worked with Art Tatum, Benny Goodman and Fats Waller, appearing with Waller in the movie *Stormy Weather*. He was born Leroy Stewart but acquired his nickname from his habit of slapping the bass.

Peter Tosh

ABDUL RASHID TALHAH
Died 7 December 1987, aged 47

Born Richard Alonzo Taylor, was founder member of The Manhattans with whom he worked for 13 years before retiring in 1976.

TED TAYLOR
Died 22 October 1987, Louisiana, aged 50

An Oklahoma-born R&B singer, Taylor first sang with various gospel quartets then, while in his teens, gravitated to LA where he became a member of the Cadets/Jacks, recording for Modern in 1955–56. In 1957 he went solo, recording variously for Ebb, Duke, Top Rank, Laurie, Golden Eagle, Okeh and, during the seventies Ronn Records. A fine vocalist in Bobby Bland mould, he and his wife were killed in a car accident while touring Louisiana.

PETER TOSH
Died 11 September 1987, Jamaica, aged 42

Tosh and two friends were killed by gunmen during a robbery at the reggae star's home. Tosh – real name Winston Herbert MacIntosh – was born on a West Jamaican farm and made his first guitar out of board and tin, using plastic strings. His first concerts were in Kingston's slums during the early sixties and in 1963 he, together with Bob Marley and Bunny Livingstone, formed The Wailers, gaining hits with 'I Shot The Sheriff', 'Get Up, Stand Up' and 'Stir It Up'. He and Livingstone split with Marley in 1973, Tosh forming his own band, Word, Sound And Power. Highly political in his lyrical approach and ever-controversial, partly due to his insistence that the government legalize ganja, his anti-police song 'Mark Of The Beast' was banned from Jamaican radio in 1975. He supported The Rolling Stones on their 1978 tour of the US and was signed to the Rolling Stone label, recording such albums as *Bush Doctor* and *Mystic Man*. Signed to EMI in 1980, in 1985 he was nominated for a Grammy for Best Reggae Recording with *Captured Live*, his first album in four years. Tosh was finally hailed by Jamaican Prime Minister Edward P. G. Seaga as "the man who gave Jamaica and the world an unforgettable library of musical works which will be played and sung by many generations of people."

EDDIE "CLEANHEAD" VINSON
Died 2 July 1988, Los Angeles, aged 70

A hoarse-voiced blues singer and booting R&B saxman, Vinson started out with various big bands, becoming a sideman with The Cootie Williams Band in 1942 and recording his biggest hit, 'Cherry Red', during that period. After a stint leading his own big band, he returned to his hometown, Houston, in 1954 to teach music but, during the sixties, moved to LA to work with Johnny Otis. In later years he played many European jazz festivals, and in 1986 appeared at an LA Marla's Memory Lane Supper Club gig with Etta James that resulted in two live albums for Fantasy.

STEVE WALSH
Died 3 July 1988, London, aged 29

Heavyweight Radio London DJ, who had a hit with a cover of the Fatback Band's 'I Found Lovin''. His death followed a car-crash in Spain in which he suffered a broken leg. He was flown home to St Mary's Hospital for an essential operation on the damaged limb but suffered a fatal heart-attack during surgery.

THE BPI CERTIFIED AWARDS

The qualifying sales levels for BPI Gold and Platinum awards are, respectively, 500,000 units and 1,000,000 units (singles), and 100,000 units and 300,000 units (LPs). Sales of cassettes and compact discs are included.
To qualify for Double or Triple Platinum, a single or album must have been released since January 1985 or have appeared in the *Gallup* charts since then if it was released earlier. The Multi-Platinum category acknowledges sales over Triple Platinum.

MULTI-PLATINUM

(Over 900,000 units)

Rick Astley: Whenever You Need Somebody (RCA) *Jun 88* (×4, 1.2m)
Phil Collins: No Jacket Required (Virgin) *Jan 88* (×5, 1.5m)
Terence Trent D'Arby: The Hardline According To . . . (CBS) *Mar 88* (×4, 1.2m)
Dire Straits: Brothers In Arms (Phonogram) *Sep 87* (×9, 2.7m)
Dire Straits: Brothers In Arms (Phonogram) *Nov 87* (×10, 3.0m)
Fleetwood Mac: Tango In The Night (WEA) *Apr 88* (×4, 1.2m)
Fleetwood Mac: Tango In The Night (WEA) *Jun 88* (×5, 1.5m)
Whitney Houston: Whitney (Arista) *Jan 88* (×4, 1.2m)
Whitney Houston: Whitney (Arista) *May 88* (×5, 1.5m)
Michael Jackson: Bad (Epic) *Nov 87* (×4, 1.2m)
Michael Jackson: Bad (Epic) *Jan 88* (×5, 1.5m)
Michael Jackson: Bad (Epic) *Mar 88* (×6, 1.8m)
Michael Jackson: Thriller (Epic) *Nov 87* (×9, 2.7m)

Mike Oldfield: Tubular Bells (Virgin) *Jan 88* (×5, 1.5m)
Paul Simon: Graceland (WEA) *Jun 88* (×5, 1.5m)
U2: The Joshua Tree (Island) *Nov 87* (×4, 1.2m)
U2: The Joshua Tree (Island) *Jul 88* (×5, 1.5m)
Various Artists: Now That's What I Call Music 10 (EMI/Virgin/PolyGram) *Jan 88* (×4, 1.2m)
Wet Wet Wet: Popped In Souled Out (Phonogram) *Jun 88* (×4, 1.2m)

TRIPLE PLATINUM

(900,000 units)

Rick Astley: Whenever You Need Somebody (RCA) *Jan 88*
Terence Trent D'Arby: The Hardline According To . . . (CBS) *Jan 88*
Fleetwood Mac: Tango In The Night (WEA) *Jan 88*
Whitney Houston: Whitney (Arista) *Nov 87*
Michael Jackson: Bad (Epic) *Oct 87*
Paul McCartney: All The Best (EMI) *Feb 88*
Pet Shop Boys: Actually (EMI) *Apr 88*
Simon And Garfunkel: The Simon And Garfunkel Collection (CBS) *May 88*
T'Pau: Bridge Of Spies (Virgin) *Feb 88*
Various Artists: Hits 6 (CBS/WEA/BMG) *Sep 87*
Various Artists: Hits 7 (CBS/WEA/BMG) *Jan 88*
Various Artists: Now That's What I Call Music 10 (EMI/Virgin/PolyGram) *Dec 87*
Various Artists: Phantom Of The Opera (Phonogram) *Apr 88*
Wet Wet Wet: Popped In Souled Out (Phonogram) *May 88*

DOUBLE PLATINUM

(600,000 units)

Rick Astley: Whenever You Need Somebody (RCA) *Dec 87*
Bon Jovi: Slippery When Wet (Phonogram) *Aug 87*
The Christians: The Christians (Island) *Apr 88*
Terence Trent D'Arby: The Hardline According To . . . (CBS) *Dec 87*
Chris De Burgh: Into The Night (A&M) *Dec 87*
Fleetwood Mac: Tango In The Night (WEA) *Nov 87*
Genesis: Genesis (Virgin) *Oct 87*
Michael Jackson: Bad (Epic) *Sep 87*
Level 42: Running In The Family (Polydor) *Nov 87*
Huey Lewis And The News: Fore (Chrysalis) *Sep 87*
Paul McCartney: All The Best (EMI) *Dec 87*
George Michael: Faith (Epic) *Jan 88*
Alison Moyet: Raindancing (CBS) *Dec 87*
Pet Shop Boys: Actually (EMI) *Jan 88*
The Pretenders: The Singles (WEA) *Feb 88*
Lionel Ritchie: Dancing On The Ceiling (Motown) *Sep 87*
T'Pau: Bridge Of Spies (Virgin) *Jan 88*
UB40: The Best Of (Virgin) *Jan 88*
Luther Vandross: Give Me The Reason (CBS) *Mar 88*
Various Artists: Hits 6 (CBS/WEA/BMG) *Aug 87*
Various Artists: Hits 7 (CBS/WEA/BMG) *Dec 87*
Various Artists: Now That's What I Call Music 10 (EMI/Virgin/PolyGram) *Dec 87*
Various Artists: Now That's What I Call Music 11 (EMI/Virgin/PolyGram) *Apr 88*
Various Artists: Phantom Of The Opera (Phonogram) *Sep 87*
Wet Wet Wet: Popped In Souled Out (Phonogram) *Jan 88*

PLATINUM

(300,000 units)

Rick Astley: Whenever You Need Somebody (RCA) *Nov 87*
The Bee Gees: E.S.P. (WEA) *Jan 88*
Bros: Push (CBS) *Apr 88*
Belinda Carlisle: Heaven On Earth (Virgin) *Apr 88*
Tracy Chapman: Tracy Chapman (WEA) *Jul 88*
The Christians: The Christians (Island) *Jan 88*
Eric Clapton: The Cream Of Eric Clapton (Polydor) *Nov 87*
Richard Clayderman: The Music Of RC (London) *Dec 87*
The Communards: Red (London) *Jan 88*
Michael Crawford: Songs From The Stage And Screen (Telstar) *Jan 88*
Terence Trent D'Arby: The Hardline According To . . . (CBS) *Aug 87*
Def Leppard: Hysteria (Phonogram) *Dec 87*
Erasure: The Circus (Spartan) *Nov 87*
Eurythmics: Savage (RCA) *Nov 87*
Five Star: Between The Lines (RCA) *Sep 87*
Fleetwood Mac: Tango In The Night (WEA) *Oct 87*
Foster And Allen: Reflections (Stylus) *Jan 88*
Heart: Bad Animals (EMI) *Mar 88*
Billy Idol: Idol Songs (Chrysalis) *Jul 88*
Billy Idol: Vital Idol (Chrysalis) *Mar 88*
Michael Jackson: Bad (Epic) *Sep 87*
Michael Jackson/Diana Ross: Love Songs (Telstar) *Jan 88*
Johnny Hates Jazz: Turn Back The Clock (Virgin) *Feb 88*
Aled Jones: All Through The Night (BBC) *Nov 87*
Aled Jones: Voices From The Holyland (BBC) *Nov 87*
Andrew Lloyd Webber: Requiem (EMI) *Mar 88*
Madonna: Who's That Girl (WEA) *Dec 87*
Madonna: You Can Dance (WEA) *Nov 87*
Paul McCartney: All The Best (EMI) *Nov 87*
Mel & Kim: FLM (PRT) *Aug 87*
George Michael: Faith (Epic) *Nov 87*
OMD: The Best Of (Virgin) *Apr 88*
Alexander O'Neal: Hearsay (Epic) *Jan 88*
Pavarotti: The Pavarotti Collection (Stylus) *Jan 88*
Pet Shop Boys: Actually (EMI) *Sep 87*
Pet Shop Boys: Disco (EMI) *Jan 88*
The Pretenders: The Singles (WEA) *Dec 87*
Chris Rea: Dancing With Strangers (Magnet) *Nov 87*
Cliff Richard: Always Guaranteed (EMI) *Dec 87*
Sade: Stronger Than Pride (Epic) *Jul 88*
The Sex Pistols: Never Mind The Bollocks (Virgin) Jan 88
The Shadows: Simply Shadows (PolyGram) *Dec 87*
Simple Minds: Sparkle In The Rain (Virgin) *Feb 88*
The Smiths: Hatfull Of Hollow (Rough Trade) *Oct 87*
Bruce Springsteen: The Tunnel Of Love (CBS) *Oct 87*
Squeeze: 45s And Under (A&M) *Aug 87*
Sting: Nothing Like The Sun (A&M) *Jan 88*
Swing Out Sister: It's Better To Travel (Phonogram) *Sep 87*
T'Pau: Bridge Of Spies (Virgin) *Nov 87*
UB40: The Best Of (Virgin) *Nov 87*
Luther Vandross: Forever, For Always, For Love (CBS) *Oct 87*
Luther Vandross: Give Me The Reason (CBS) *Nov 87*
Various Artists: Dirty Dancing (RCA) *May 88*
Various Artists: From Motown With Love (K-Tel) *Jan 88*
Various Artists: Hits 6 (CBS/WEA/BMG) *Aug 87*
Various Artists: Hits 7 (CBS/WEA/BMG) *Nov 87*
Various Artists: Move Closer (CBS) *Aug 87*
Various Artists: Nite Flite (Epic) *Jun 88*
Various Artists: Now Smash Hits (EMI) *Oct 87*
Various Artists: Now That's What I Call Music 10 (EMI/Virgin/PolyGram) *Dec 87*
Various Artists: Now That's What I Call Music 11 (EMI/Virgin/PolyGram) *Apr 88*
Various Artists: The Sixties Mix (Stylus) *Oct 87*
Various Artists: The Greatest Love (Telstar) *Jul 88*
Wet Wet Wet: Popped In Souled Out (Phonogram) *Dec 87*
Whitesnake: Whitesnake 1987 (EMI) *Jan 88*

GOLD

(100,000 units)

ABC: Alphabet City (Phonogram) *Nov 87*
AC/DC: Blow Up Your Video (WEA) *Feb 88*
A-ha: Stay On These Roads (WEA) *May 88*
Rick Astley: Whenever You Need Somebody (RCA) *Nov 87*
Aswad: Distant Thunder (Island) *Jun 88*
Aztec Camera: Love (WEA) *Jun 88*
Bananarama: Wow! (London) *Feb 88*
The Bee Gees: E.S.P. (WEA) *Oct 87)*
Pat Benatar: Best Shots (Chrysalis) *Nov 87*
Black: Wonderful Life (A&M) *Sep 87*
James Brown: The Godfather Of Soul (K-Tel) *Nov 87*
Bros: Push (CBS) *Apr 88*
Jonathan Butler: Jonathan Butler (Jive) *Feb 88*
Belinda Carlisle: Heaven On Earth (Virgin) *Jan 88*
Tracy Chapman: Tracy Chapman (WEA) *Jun 88*
Cher: Cher (Geffen) *May 88*
The Christians: The Christians (Island) *Nov 87*
Eric Clapton: The Cream Of Eric Clapton (Polydor) *Sep 87*

Richard Clayderman: Songs Of Love (London) *Dec 87*
Climie Fisher: Everything (EMI) *May 88*
Lloyd Cole & The Commotions: Mainstream (Polydor) *Nov 87*
The Communards: Red (London) *Dec 87*
Elvis Costello: Blood & Chocolate (Demon) *Jan 88*
Michael Crawford: Songs From Stage & Screen (Telstar) *Nov 87*
Randy Crawford: Love Songs (Telstar) *Nov 87*

The Cure: Kiss Me, Kiss Me, Kiss Me (Polydor) *Aug 87*

Deacon Blue: Raintown (CBS) *Jun 88*

Def Leppard: Hysteria (Phonogram) *Sep 88*

Will Downing: Will Downing (Island) *Jul 88*

Erasure: The Innocents (Spartan) *Apr 88*

Eurhythmics: Savage (RCA) *Nov 87*

Everything But The Girl: Love Not Money (WEA) *May 88*

Fairground Attraction: The First Of A Million Kisses (RCA) *Jun 88*

Bryan Ferry: Bete Noire (Virgin) *Oct 87*

Five Star: Between The Lines (RCA) *Sep 87*

Foster & Allen: Reflections (Stylus) *Oct 87*

Foster & Allen: Remember You're Mine (Stylus) *May 88*

Debbie Gibson: Out Of The Blue (WEA) *May 88*

George Harrison: Cloud Nine (WEA) *Nov 87*

Heart: Bad Animals (EMI) *Aug 87*

Heart: Heart (EMI) *Mar 88*

Hothouse Flowers: People (London) *Jun 88*

The Housemartins: Now That's What I Call Quite Good (Chrysalis) *Jun 88*

The Housemartins: The People Who Grinned Themselves To Death (Chrysalis) *Sep 87*

The Human League: Reproduction (Virgin) *Feb 88*

Billy Idol: Idol Songs (Chrysalis) *Jun 88*

INXS: Kick (Phonogram) *Jan 88*

Iron Maiden: Seventh Son Of A Seventh Son (EMI) *Apr 88*

Janet Jackson: Control – The Remixes (A&M) *Nov 87*

Michael Jackson: Bad (Epic) *Sep 87*

Michael Jackson: The Michael Jackson Mix (Stylus) *Jan 88*

Michael Jackson/Diana Ross: Love Songs (Telstar) *Nov 87*

Japan: Oil On Canvas (Virgin) *Feb 88*

Jellybean: Just Visiting This Planet (Chrysalis) *Apr 88*

Johnny Hates Jazz: Turn Back The Clock (Virgin) *Jan 88*

Living In A Box: Living In A Box (Chrysalis) *Oct 87*

Phil Lynott/Thin Lizzy: Soldier Of Fortune (Telstar) *Jan 88*

Madonna: Who's That Girl (WEA) *Aug 87*

Madonna: You Can Dance (WEA) *Nov 87*

Rose Marie: Sentimentally Yours (Telstar) *Dec 87*

Paul McCartney: All The Best (EMI) *Nov 87*

Metallica: Master Of Puppets (MFN) *Dec 87*

George Michael: Faith (Epic) *Nov 87*

Mirage: In Full Effect (Stylus) *Jul 88*

Mirage: Jack Mix 88 – The Best Of (Stylus) *Jan 88*

The Mission: Children (Phonogram) *Mar 88*

Morrissey: Viva Hate (EMI) *Mar 88*

Billy Ocean: Tear Down These Walls (Jive) *Mar 88*

OMD: The Best Of (Virgin) *Mar 88*

Alexander O'Neal: Hearsay (Epic) *Nov 87*

Elaine Paige: Memories (Telstar) *Nov 87*

Pet Shop Boys: Actually (EMI) *Sep 87*

Pink Floyd: A Momentary Lapse of Reason (EMI) *Oct 87*

The Pogues: Rum, Sodomy & The Lash (Stiff) *Aug 87*

The Pogues: If I Should Fall From Grace With God (Stiff) *Mar 88*

Prefab Sprout: From Langley Park To Memphis (CBS) *Apr 88*

Elvis Presley: All Time Greatest Hits (RCA) *Sep 87*

The Pretenders: The Singles (WEA) *Nov 87*

Maxi Priest: Maxi (Virgin) *Jul 88*

Prince: Lovesexy (WEA) *May 88*

The Proclaimers: This Is The Story (Chrysalis) *Dec 87*

Chris Rea: Dancing With Strangers (Magnet) *Sep 87*

Cliff Richard: Always Guaranteed (EMI) *Sep 87*

Rondo Veneziano: Venice In Peril (Fanfare) *Jun 88*

Sade: Stronger Than Pride (Epic) *Apr 88*

Scritti Politti: Proviso (Virgin) *Jul 88*

The Shadows: Simply Shadows (PolyGram) *Nov 87*

Joyce Sims: Come Into My Life (London) *Feb 88*

Sinitta: Sinitta (Fanfare) *Jan 88*

Sisters Of Mercy: Floodland (WEA) *Mar 88*

The Smiths: Strangeways Here We Come (Rough Trade) *Oct 87*

Dusty Springfield: The Silver Collection (PolyGram) *Feb 88*

Status Quo: Ain't Complaining (Phonogram) *May 88*

Sting: Nothing Like The Sun (A&M) *Oct 87*

The Stranglers: All Live And All Of The Night (CBS) *Mar 88*

10 cc & Godley & Creme: Changing Faces (PolyGram) *Sep 87*

Talking Heads: Naked (EMI) *Mar 88*

Tiffany: Tiffany (MCA) *Mar 88*

T'Pau: Bridge Of Spies (Virgin) *Nov 87*

Tina Turner: Live In Europe (EMI) *Mar 88*

UB40: The Best Of UB40 (Virgin) *Nov 87*

UB40: UB40 (Virgin) *Jul 88*

Various Artists: Always And Forever (Telstar) *Nov 87*

Various Artists: A Very Special Christmas (A&M) *Nov 87*

Various Artists: Chart Show Rock The Nation (Chrysalis) *Mar 88*

Various Artists: Dance Mix (Telstar) *Nov 87*

Various Artists: Dirty Dancing (RCA) *Mar 88*

Various Artists: From Motown With Love (K-Tel) *Nov 87*

Various Artists: Greatest Hits (Telstar) *Dec 87*

Various Artists: Greatest Hits Of 1987 (Telstar) *Nov 87*

Various Artists: Hip Hop Rapping In The House (Stylus) *Apr 88*

Various Artists: Hit Mixs (Stylus) *Jan 88*

Various Artists: Hits 6 (WEA/CBS/BMG) *Aug 87*

Various Artists: Hits 7 (WEA/CBS/BMG) *Nov 87*

Various Artists: Horizons (K-Tel) *Apr 88*

Various Artists: My Fair Lady (PolyGram) *Nov 87*

Various Artists: La Bamba (London) *Dec 87*

Various Artists: Life In The Fast Lane (Telstar) *Jan 88*

Various Artists: More Dirty Dancing (RCA) *Jun 88*

Various Artists: Motown Dance Party (Motown) *Jun 88*

Various Artists: Nite Flite (Epic) *May 88*

Various Artists: Now That's What I Call Music 10 (EMI/Virgin/PolyGram) *Dec 87*

Various Artists: Now That's What I Call Music 11 (EMI/Virgin/PolyGram) *Apr 88*

Various Artists: Postman Pat (PRT) *Nov 87*

Various Artists: Sixties Mix (Stylus) *Aug 87*

Various Artists: Sixties Mix 2 (Stylus) *Apr 88*

Various Artists: Sixties Parties Mega Mix (Telstar) *Nov 87*

Various Artists: The Hit Factory (Stylus) *Oct 87*

Various Artists: The Hits Of House Are Here (K-Tel) *Jul 88*

Various Artists: The Hits Revival (K-Tel) *Aug 87*

Various Artists: Tracks Of My Tears (Telstar) *Jan 88*

Various Artists: Unforgettable (EMI) *May 88*

Wet Wet Wet: Popped In Souled Out (Phonogram) *Sep 87*

Barry White: The Collection (PolyGram) *Jul 88*

The Who: My Generation (Virgin) *Mar 88*

The Who: Who's Better, Who's Best (Polygram) *Mar 88*

Steve Windwood: Chronicles (Island) *Oct 87*

Steve Winwood: Roll With It (Virgin) *Jul 88*

Stevie Wonder: Characters (Motown) *Nov 87*

SINGLES ★

GOLD
(500,000 units)

Rick Astley: Never Gonna Give You Up (RCA) *Sep 87*

The Bee Gees: You Win Again (WEA) *Nov 87*

Phil Collins: Against All Odds (Virgin) *Jan 88*

Phil Collins: In The Air Tonight (Virgin) *Jul 88*

Whitney Houston: I Wanna Dance With Somebody (Arista) Aug 87

Kylie Minogue: I Should Be So Lucky (Pinnacle) *Mar 88*

Pet Shop Boys: Always On My Mind (EMI) *Jan 88*

Tiffany: I Think We're Alone Now (MCA) *Mar 88*

T'Pau: China In Your Hand (Virgin) *Dec 87*

NB There have been no singles selling more than gold status this year.

THE RIAA CERTIFIED AWARDS

Recording Industry Association Of America Inc, reprinted with permission. The qualifying levels for RIAA Gold and Platinum awards are, respectively, 1,000,000 units and 2,000,000 units (singles), and 500,000 units and 1,000,000 units (LPs). Sales of cassettes and compact discs are included. The figures at the end of the Multi-Platinum entries indicate the million level reached.

MULTI-PLATINUM

(2,000,000 units and above)

Aerosmith: Permanent Vacation (Geffen) *May 88* (2m)
Anita Baker: Rapture (Elektra) *Oct 87* (3m)
Beastie Boys Licensed To Ill (Columbia) *Oct 87* (4m)
Bon Jovi Slippery When Wet (Mercury) *Aug 87* (8m)
John Cougar Mellencamp: The Lonesome Jubilee (Mercury) *Jan 88* (2m)
Def Leppard: Hysteria (Mercury) *Nov 87* (2m)
Def Leppard: Hysteria (Mercury) *Jan 88* (3m)
Def Leppard: Hysteria (Mercury) *Jun 88* (4m)
Def Leppard: Hysteria (Mercury) *Jul 88* (5m)
Europe: The Final Countdown (Epic) *Oct 87* (2m)
Fleetwood Mac: Tango In The Night (Warner Bros) *Jan 88* (2m)
Genesis: ABACAB (Atlantic) *Feb 88* (2m)
Debbie Gibson: Out Of The Blue (Atlantic) *May 88* (2m)
Guns 'N Roses: Appetite For Destruction (Geffen) *Jul 88* (2m)
Heart: Bad Animals (Capitol) *Oct 87* (2m)
Whitney Houston: Whitney (Arista) *Aug 87* (3m)
Whitney Houston: Whitney (Arista) *Sep 87* (4m)
Whitney Houston: Whitney (Arista) *Nov 87* (5m)
Whitney Houston: Whitney (Arista) *Apr 88* (6m)
INXS: Kick (Atlantic) *Mar 88* (2m)

Michael Jackson: Bad (Epic) *Nov 87* (3m)
Michael Jackson: Bad (Epic) *Dec 87* (4m)
Michael Jackson: Bad (Epic) *Mar 88* (5m)
Michael Jackson: Bad (Epic) *Jun 88* (6m)
Michael Jackson: Off The Wall (Epic) *Jun 88* (6m)
Kenny G: Duotones (Arista) *Nov 87* (2m)
LL Cool J: Bigger And Deffer (Columbia) *Nov 87* (2m)
Huey Lewis & The News: Fore! (Chrysalis) *Jul 88* (3m)
Madonna: Madonna (Sire) *Mar 88* (4m)
Madonna: True Blue (Sire) *Aug 87* (5m)
Barry Manilow: Greatest Hits (Arista) *Sep 87* (3m)
Barry Manilow: This One's For You (Arista) *Sep 87* (2m)
Barry Manilow: Tryin' To Get The Feeling (Arista) *Sep 87* (2m)
Barry Manilow: Even Now (Arista) *Sep 87* (3m)
Barry Manilow: Barry Manilow Live (Arista) *Sep 87* (3m)
George Michael: Faith (Columbia) *Jan 88* (2m)
George Michael: Faith (Columbia) *Feb 88* (3m)
George Michael: Faith (Columbia) *May 88* (4m)
George Michael: Faith (Columbia) *Jul 88* (5m)
Mötley Crüe: Girls, Girls, Girls (Elektra) *Sep 87* (2m)
Anne Murray: Greatest Hits (Capitol) *Oct 87* (3m)
Pink Floyd: A Momentary Lapse Of Reason (Columbia) *Jan 88* (2m)
Poison: Look What The Cat Dragged In (Capitol) *Sep 87* (2m)
Elvis Presley: Elvis Sings The Wonderful World Of Christmas (RCA) *May 88* (2m)
Elvis Presley: Aloha From Hawaii Via Satellite (RCA) *May 88* (2m)
Paul Simon: Graceland (Warner Bros) *Jan 88* (3m)

Soundtrack: La Bamba (Warner Bros) *Dec 87* (2m)
Soundtrack: Dirty Dancing (RCA) *Dec 87* (2m)
Soundtrack: Dirty Dancing (RCA) *Dec 87* (3m)
Soundtrack: Dirty Dancing (RCA) *Feb 88* (4m)
Soundtrack: Dirty Dancing (RCA) *Feb 88* (5m)
Soundtrack: Dirty Dancing (RCA) *Mar 88* (6m)
Soundtrack: Dirty Dancing (RCA) *May 88* (7m)
Soundtrack: Dirty Dancing (RCA) *Jul 88* (8m)
Bruce Springsteen: Tunnel Of Love (Columbia) *Dec 87* (2m)
Bruce Springsteen: Tunnel Of Love (Columbia) *Apr 88* (3m)
Tiffany: Tiffany (MCA) *Dec 87* (2m)
Tiffany: Tiffany (MCA) *Feb 88* (3m)
Tiffany: Tiffany (MCA) *Apr 88* (4m)
Randy Travis: Always & Forever (Warner Bros) *Jan 88* (2m)
Randy Travis: Storms Of Life (Warner Bros) *Apr 88* (2m)

Tina Turner: Private Dancer (Capitol) *Sep 87* (5m)
U2: The Joshua Tree (Island) *Sep 87* (3m)
U2: The Joshua Tree (Island) *Dec 87* (4m)
Van Halen: OU812 (Warner Bros) *Jul 88* (2m)
Various: More Dirty Dancing (RCA) *May 88* (2m)
Various: More Dirty Dancing (RCA) *Jul 88* (3m)
Whitesnake: Whitesnake (Geffen) *Aug 87* (2m)
Whitesnake: Whitesnake (Geffen) *Sep 87* (3m)
Whitesnake: Whitesnake (Geffen) *Dec 87* (4m)
Whitesnake: Whitesnake (Geffen) *Jan 88* (5m)
Steve Winwood: Back In The High Life (Island) *Jan 88* (3m)

★

PLATINUM

(2,000,000 units)

AC/DC: Blow Up Your Video (Atlantic) *Apr 88*
Aerosmith: Permanent Vacation (Geffen) *Dec 87*
Rick Astley: Whenever You Need Somebody (RCA) *May 88*
Blue Oyster Cult: Some Enchanted Evening (Columbia) *Jul 88*
California Raisins: California Raisins (CBS) Jun 88
Belinda Carlisle: Heaven On Earth (MCA) *Jan 88*
Tracy Chapman: Tracy Chapman (Elektra) *Jul 88*
Patsy Cline: Greatest Hits (MCA) *Nov 87*
John Cougar Mellencamp: The Lonesome Jubilee (Mercury) *Oct 87*
Robert Cray: Strong Persuader (Mercury) *Feb 88*
Terence Trent D'Arby: Introducing The Hardline According To . . . (Columbia) *Apr 88*
Def Leppard: Hysteria (Mercury) *Oct 87*
Dokken: Back For The Attack (Elektra) *Jan 88*
Gloria Estefan, & Miami Sound Machine: Let It Loose (Epic) *May 88*
Europe: Final Countdown (Epic) *Aug 87*
Expose: Exposure (Arista) *Oct 87*
The Fabulous Thunderbirds: Tuff Enuff (CBS) *Jun 88*
Fat Boys: Crushin' (PolyGram) *Sep 87*
Fleetwood Mac: Bare Trees (Reprise) *Feb 88*
Foreigner: Inside Information (Atlantic) *Apr 88*
Genesis: And Then There Were Three (Atlantic) *Feb 88*
Genesis: Duke (Atlantic) *Feb 88*
Georgia Satellites: Georgia Satellites (Elektra) *Aug 87*
Debbie Gibson: Out Of The Blue (Atlantic) *Feb 88*
Grateful Dead: In The Dark (Arista) *Sep 87*
Great White: Once Bitten (Capitol) *Apr 88*
Guns 'N Roses: Appetite For Destruction (Geffen) *Apr 88*
George Harrison: Cloud Nine (Dark Horse) *Jan 88*
Bruce Hornsby & The Range: Scenes From The Southside (RCA) *Jul 88*
Billy Idol: Vital Idol (Chrysalis) *Jan 88*
INXS: Kick (Atlantic) *Dec 87*
INXS: Listen Like Thieves (Atlantic) *Jan 88*
Michael Jackson: Bad (Epic) *Nov 87*
DJ Jazzy Jeff & The Flesh Prince: He's The DJ, I'm The Rapper (Jive) *Jul 88*
Howard Jones: Dream Into Action (Elektra) *Mar 88*
Kiss: Crazy Nights (Mercury) *Feb 88*
L L Cool J: Bigger And Deffer (Columbia) *Aug 87*
L L Cool J: Radio (Columbia) *Apr 88*
Lisa Lisa And Cult Jam: Spanish Fly (Columbia) *Aug 87*
Madonna: Who's That Girl – Motion Picture Soundtrack (Sire) *Sep 87*
Barry Manilow: Barry Manilow II (Arista) *Sep 87*
Barry Manilow: Tryin' To Get The Feeling (Arista) *Sep 87*
Bob Marley & The Wailers: Legend (Island) *Jun 88*
Richard Marx: Richard Marx (EMI) *Feb 88*
Metallica: Masters Of Puppets (Elektra) *Jul 88*
George Michael: Faith (Columbia) *Jan 88*
Eddie Money: Can't Hold Back (Columbia) *Aug 87*
Eddie Money: No Control (Columbia) *Aug 87*
Anne Murray: Christmas Wishes (Capitol) *Aug 87*
Anne Murray: New Kind Of Feeling (Capitol) *Aug 87*
Billy Ocean: Tear Down These Walls (Arista) *Jul 88*
Pebbles: Pebbles (MCA) *Jul 88*
Pink Floyd: A Momentary Lapse Of Reason (Columbia) *Nov 87*
Robert Plant: Now And Zen (Atlantic) *May 88*
Poison: Open Up And Say . . . Ahh! (Capitol) *Jun 88*
Elvis Presley: Aloha From Hawaii Via Satellite (RCA) *May 88*
Elvis Presley: Elvis As Recorded At Madison Square Gardens (RCA) *May 88*
Elvis Presley: Elvis' Golden Records (RCA) *May 88*
Elvis Presley: Pure Gold (RCA) *May 88*
R.E.M.: Document (IRS) *Jan 88*
Run DMC: Tougher Than Leather (Profile) *Jul 88*
Rush: Exit . . . Stage Left (Mercury) *Nov 87*
Rush: Permanent Waves (Mercury) *Nov 87*
Salt 'N' Pepa: Hot, Cool & Vicious (Next Plateau Records) *Mar 88*
The Scorpions: Savage Amusement (Mercury) *Jun 88*
Carly Simon: Coming Around Again (Arista) *Feb 88*
Soundtrack: Beverly Hills Cop II (MCA) *Aug 87*
Soundtrack: Dirty Dancing (RCA) *Oct 87*

Soundtrack: La Bamba (Warner Bros) *Sep 87*
Bruce Springsteen: Tunnel Of Love (Columbia) *Dec 87*
Sting: Nothing Like The Sun (A&M) *Dec 87*
George Strait: Greatest Hits Vol. II (MCA) *Jun 88*
George Strait: Ocean Front Property (MCA) *Dec 87*
Barbra Streisand: One Voice (Columbia) *Feb 88*
Stryper: To Hell With The Devil (Enigma) *Jan 88*
Keith Sweat: Make It Last Forever (Elektra) *May 88*
Tiffany: Tiffany (MCA) *Dec 87*
Van Halen OU812 (Warner Bros) *Jul 88*
Various: Disney's Christmas Favorites (Disney) *Apr 88*
Various: Soundtrack – Good Morning Vietnam (A&M) *Jul 88*
Various: More Dirty Dancing (RCA) *May 88*
Various: Mousercise (Disney) *Apr 88*
Various: A Very Special Christmas (A&M) *Dec 87*
Jody Watley: Jody Watley (MCA) *Dec 87*
The Whispers Just Gets Better With Time (Slash Records) *Feb 88*
White Lion: Pride (Atlantic) *Jun 88*
Whitesnake: Slide It In (Geffen) *Nov 87*
Hank Williams Jr.: Born To Boogie (Warner Bros) *Feb 88*
George Winston: Autumn (Windham Hill) *Dec 87*

George Winston: Winter Into Spring (Windham Hill) *Dec 87*
Steve Winwood: Chronicles (Island) *May 88*
Stevie Wonder: Characters (Motown) *Jan 88*
Yes: Big Generator (Atlantic) *Apr 88*
Neil Young: Live Rust (Reprise) *Feb 88*

★

GOLD
(1,000,000 units)

AC/DC: Blow Up Your Video (Atlantic) *Apr 88*
Aerosmith: Permanent Vacation (Geffen) *Nov 87*
Al B Sure!: In Effect Mode (Warner Bros) *Jun 88*
Rick Astley: Whenever You Need Somebody (RCA) *Feb 88*
Bad Company: 10 From 6 (Atlantic) *Sep 87*
The Beach Boys: Made In The U.S.A. (Capitol) *May 88*
Earth, Wind & Fire: Touch The World (Columbia) *Jan 88*
Eric B & Rakim: Paid in Full (4th & Broadway) *Dec 87*
Gloria Estefan & Miami Sound Machine: Let It Loose (Epic) *Aug 87*
Lita Ford: Lita (Dreamland) *May 88*
Foreigner: Inside Information (Atlantic) *Feb 88*
Michael Franks: The Art Of Tea (Reprise) *Sep 87*
Debbie Gibson: Out Of The Blue (Atlantic) *Dec 87*
Grateful Dead: In The Dark (Arista) *Sep 87*
Grateful Dead: Shakedown Street (Arista) *Aug 87*
Grateful Dead: Terrapin Station (Arista) *Sep 87*
Great White: Once Bitten (Capitol) *Oct 87*
Guns 'N Roses: Appetite For Destruction (Geffen) *Feb 88*
Sammy Hagar: Sammy Hagar (Geffen) *Sep 87*
Hall & Oates: Ooh Yeah! (Arista) *Jun 88*
Emmylou Harris: Quarter Moon In A Ten Cent Town (Warner Bros) *Mar 88*
Madonna: You Can Dance (Sire) *Jan 88*
Manhattan Transfer: Best Of Manhattan Transfer (Atlantic) *Oct 87*
Manhattan Transfer: Manhattan Transfer (Atlantic) *Oct 87*
Barry Manilow: The Manilow Collection/Twenty Classic Hits (Arista) *Sep 87*
Mannheim Steamroller: Mannheim Steamroller Christmas (AMG) *Mar 88*
Bob Marley & The Wailers: Legend (Island) *Jun 88*
Ziggy Marley & The Melody Makers: Conscious Party (Virgin) *Jun 88*
Richard Marx: Richard Marx (EMI) *Nov 87*
Reba McEntire: Greatest Hits (MCA) *Dec 87*
Reba McEntire: The Last One To Know (MCA) *Apr 88*
Metallica: Garage Days Re-Visited (Elektra) *Dec 87*
Metallica: Ride The Lightning (Elektra) *Nov 87*
George Michael: Faith (Columbia) *Jan 88*
Midnight Oil: Diesel & Dust (Columbia) *Jul 88*
Stephanie Mills: If I Were Your Woman (MCA) *Aug 87*

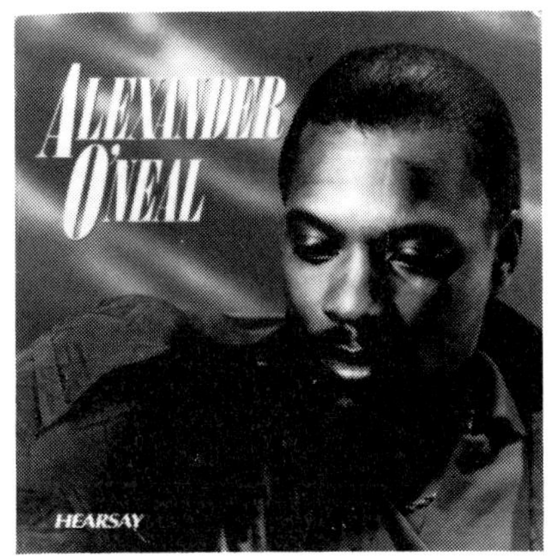

George Benson & Earl Klugh: Collaboration (Warner Bros) *Feb 88*
Jonathan Butler: Jonathan Butler (RCA) *Mar 88*
California Raisins: California Raisins (Priority) *Jan 88*
Belinda Carlisle: Heaven On Earth (MCA) *Dec 87*
The Cars: Door To Door (Elektra) *Oct 87*
Tracy Chapman: Tracy Chapman (Elektra) *Jun 88*
Cheap Trick: Lap Of Luxury (Epic) *Jul 88*
Cher: Cher (Geffen) *May 88*
Eric Clapton: Crossroads (Polydor) *Jun 88*
Natalie Cole: Everlasting (EMI) *Mar 88*
John Cougar Mellencamp: The Lonesome Jubilee (Mercury) *Oct 87*
The Cult: Electric (Sire) *Mar 88*
The Cure: Kiss Me, Kiss Me, Kiss Me (Elektra) *Aug 87*
Dana Dane: Dana Dane With Fame (Profile) *Jan 88*
Terence Trent D'Arby: Introducing The Hardline According To . . . (Columbia) *Mar 88*
Taylor Dayne: Tell It To My Heart (Arista) *May 88*
The Deele: Eyes Of A Stranger (Solar) *Jun 88*
Def Leppard: Hysteria (Mercury) *Oct 87*
Depeche Mode: Music For The Masses (Sire) *Mar 88*
DJ Jazzy Jeff & The Fresh Prince: He's The DJ I'm The Rapper (Jive) *May 88*
Dokken: Back For The Attack (Elektra) *Jan 88*
George Harrison: Cloud Nine (Dark Horse) *Jan 88*
The Hooters: One Way Home (Columbia) *Sep 87*
Bruce Hornsby & The Range: Scenes From The Southside (RCA) *Jul 88*
Billy Idol: Vital Idol (Chrysalis) *Nov 87*
Iron Maiden: Seventh Son Of A Seventh Son (Capitol) *Jun 88*
INXS: Kick (Atlantic) *Dec 87*
Michael Jackson: Bad (Epic) *Nov 87*
Jethro Tull: Crest Of A Knave (Chrysalis) *May 88*
The Jets: Magic (MCA) *Dec 87*
Billy Joel: Kohuept (Columbia) *Jan 88*
Elton John: Elton John Live In Australia (MCA) *Jan 88*
Judas Priest: Ram It Down (Columbia) *Jul 88*
Kingdom Come: Kingdom Come (PolyGram) *Apr 88*
Kiss: Crazy Nights (Mercury) *Nov 87*
Gladys Knight & The Pips: All Our Love (MCA) *Mar 88*
Kool Moe Dee: How Ya Like Me Now (Jive) *Apr 88*
L L Cool J: Bigger And Deffer (Columbia) *Aug 87*
Levert: The Big Throwdown (Atlantic) *Oct 87*
Lisa Lisa And Cult Jam: Spanish Fly (Columbia) *Aug 87*
Loverboy: Wildside (Columbia) *Nov 87*
Madonna: Who's That Girl – Motion Picture Soundtrack (Sire) *Sep 87*
Anne Murray: Something To Talk About (Capitol) *Sep 87*
Najee: Najee's Theme (EMI) *Feb 88*
Night Ranger: The Big Life (MCA) *Oct 87*
Billy Ocean: Tear Down These Walls (Arista) *Apr 88*
Alexander O'Neal: Hearsay (Tabu) *Oct 87*
Original Cast: Phantom Of The Opera (Polydor) *May 88*
Ozzy Osbourne/Randy Rhoads: Tribute (CBS) *Aug 87*
K.T. Oslin: '80's Ladies (RCA) *Mar 88*
The Outfield: Bangin' (Columbia) *Sep 87*
Pebbles: Pebbles (MCA) *Apr 88*
Pet Shop Boys: Actually (EMI) *Nov 87*
Tom Petty & The Heartbreakers: Tom Petty & The Heartbreakers (MCA) *Jan 88*
Pink Floyd: A Momentary Lapse of Reason (Columbia) *Nov 87*
Robert Plant: Now and Zen (Atlantic) *Apr 88*
Poison: Open Up And Say . . . Aah! (Capitol) *Jun 88*
Elvis Presley: Roustabout (RCA) *May 88*
R.E.M.: Document (IRS) *Nov 87*
R.E.O. Speedwagon: Life As We Know It (Epic) *Aug 87*
Restless Heart: Wheels (RCA) *Mar 88*
Smokey Robinson: One Heartbeat (Motown) *Sep 87*
Roger: Unlimited (Reprise) *Feb 88*
Linda Ronstadt: Canciones De Mi Padre (Elektra) *Feb 88*

Run DMC: Tougher Than Leather (Profile) *Jul 88*
Rush: Hold Your Fire (Mercury) *Nov 87*
Salt 'N' Pepa: Hot, Cool & Vicious (Next Plateau Records) *Jan 88*
David Sanborn: A Change Of Heart (Warner Bros) *Jan 88*
The Scorpions: Savage Amusement (Mercury) *Jun 88*
Sex Pistols: Never Mind The Bollocks Here's The Sex Pistols (Warner Bros) *Dec 87*
Ricky Van Shelton: Wild-Eyed Dream (Columbia) *Apr 88*
Carly Simon: Coming Around Again (Arista) *Aug 87*
Soundtrack: Beverly Hills Cop II (MCA) *Aug 87*
Soundtrack: Dirty Dancing (RCA) *Oct 87*
Soundtrack: La Bamba (Warner Bros) *Sep 87*
Soundtrack: Less Than Zero (Columbia) *Feb 88*
Soundtrack: The Lost Boys (Atlantic) *Sep 87*
Soundtrack: Somewhere In Time (MCA) *Dec 87*
Bruce Springsteen: Tunnel Of Love (Columbia) *Dec 87*

Squeeze: Singles 45's And Under (A&M) *Jan 88*
Starship: No Protection (RCA) *Nov 87*
Sting: Nothing Like The Sun (A&M) *Dec 87*
George Strait: Greatest Hits Volume II (MCA) *Nov 87*
George Strait: If You Ain't Lovin' (You Ain't Livin') (MCA) *Apr 88*
George Strait: Strait Country (MCA) *Apr 88*
Barbra Streisand: One Voice (Columbia) *Aug 87*

Stryper: Soldiers Under Command (Enigma) *Apr 88*
Keith Sweat: Make It Last Forever (Elektra) *Mar 88*
Swing Out Sister: It's Better To Travel (Mercury) *Apr 88*
Talking Heads: Naked (Sire) *May 88*
James Taylor: Never Die Young (Columbia) *Apr 88*
10,000 Maniacs: In My Tribe (Elektra) *Jul 88*
Tesla: Mechanical Resonance (Geffen) *Sep 87*
G. Thorogood & The Destroyers: Born To Be Bad (EMI) *Apr 88*
Tiffany: Tiffany (MCA) *Nov 87*
The 2 Live Crew: The 2 Live Crew Is What We Are (Luke Skywalker) *May 88*
Van Halen: OU812 (Warner Bros) *Jul 88*
Various: Chilling, Thrilling Sounds Of The Haunted House (Disney) *Apr 88*
Various: Soundtrack From Colors (Warner Bros) *Jul 88*
Various: More Dirty Dancing (RCA) *May 88*
Various: A Very Special Christmas (A&M) *Dec 87*
Various: A Winter's Solstice (Windham Hill) *Dec 87*

Stevie Ray Vaughn: Soul To Soul (Epic) *Aug 87*
Violent Femmes: Violent Femmes (SLS) *Dec 87*
White Lion: Pride (Atlantic) *Apr 88*
Whodini: Open Sesame (Jive) *Jan 88*
Wierd Al Yankovic: Even Worse (Rock 'N' Roll) *Jul 88*
Hank Williams Jr.: Hank Live (Warner Bros) *Aug 87*
Hank Williams Jr.: Born To Boogie (Cur) *Sep 87*

Steve Winwood: Chronicles (Island) *Jan 88*
Stevie Wonder: Characters (Motown) *Jan 88*
Yes: Big Generator (Atlantic) *Dec 87*
Dwight Yoakam: Hillbilly Deluxe (Reprise) *Oct 87*

SINGLES ★

GOLD
(1,000,000 units)

Michael Jackson: I Just Can't Stop Loving You (Epic) *Sep 87*
M/A/R/R/S: Pump Up The Volume (4th & Broadway) *Apr 88*
Salt 'N' Pepa: Push It (Next Plateau Records) *Mar 88*
Various: Alice In Wonderland (Disney) *Apr 88*
Various: Winnie The Pooh And The Honey Tree (Disney) *Apr 88*

PLATINUM
(2,000,000 units)

Various: Bambi (Disney) *Apr 88*
Various: Snow White (Disney) *Apr 88*

★

THE YEAR'S CHARTS

August 1987–July 1988

FEATURING THE MUSIC WEEK AND RADIO & RECORDS NEWS CHARTS

WEEK ENDING AUGUST 1 1987

UK

SINGLES		ALBUMS
LA BAMBA LOS LOBOS (SLASH/FFRR/LONDON)	1	HITS 6 VARIOUS (CBS/WEA/BMG)
WHO'S THAT GIRL MADONNA (SIRE)	2	INTRODUCING THE HARDLINE ACCORDING TO... TERENCE TRENT D'ARBY (CBS)
ALWAYS ATLANTIC STARR (WARNER BROS)	3	WHITNEY WHITNEY HOUSTON (ARISTA)
IT'S A SIN PET SHOP BOYS (PARLOPHONE/EMI)	4	ORIGINAL SOUNDTRACK 'WHO'S THAT GIRL' MADONNA/VARIOUS (SIRE)
ALONE HEART (CAPITOL)	5	THE JOSHUA TREE U2 (ISLAND)
UNDER THE BOARDWALK BRUCE WILLIS (MOTOWN)	6	SIXTIES MIX VARIOUS (STYLUS)
JIVE TALKIN' BOOGIE BOX HIGH (HARDBACK)	7	INVISIBLE TOUCH GENESIS (VIRGIN)
F.L.M. MEL & KIM (SUPREME)	8	THE RETURN OF BRUNO BRUCE WILLIS (MOTOWN)
JUST DON'T WANT TO BE LONELY FREDDIE McGREGOR (GERMAIN)	9	BAD ANIMALS HEART (CAPITOL)
SHE'S ON IT BEASTIE BOYS (DEF JAM)	10	F.L.M. MEL & KIM (SUPREME)
WISHING WELL TERENCE TRENT D'ARBY (CBS)	11	KEEP YOUR DISTANCE CURIOSITY KILLED THE CAT (MERCURY)
A LITTLE BOOGIE WOOGIE SHAKIN' STEVENS (EPIC)	12	TRUE BLUE MADONNA (SIRE)
LABOUR OF LOVE HUE & CRY (CIRCA/VIRGIN)	13	LICENSED TO ILL BEASTIE BOYS (DEF JAM)
I HEARD A RUMOUR BANANARAMA (LONDON)	14	IT'S BETTER TO TRAVEL SWING OUT SISTER (MERCURY/PHONOGRAM)
SWEETEST SMILE BLACK (A&M)	15	LIVE IN THE CITY OF LIGHT SIMPLE MINDS (VIRGIN)
I REALLY DIDN'T MEAN IT LUTHER VANDROSS (EPIC)	16	SOLITUDE STANDING SUZANNE VEGA (A&M)
THE LIVING DAYLIGHTS A-HA (WARNER BROS)	17	CLUTCHING AT STRAWS MARILLION (EMI)
YOU CAUGHT MY EYE JUDY BOUCHER (ORBITONE)	18	THE ISLAND STORY VARIOUS (ISLAND)
TRUE FAITH NEW ORDER (FACTORY)	19	CONTROL JANET JACKSON (A&M)
OOPS UPSIDE YOUR HEAD ('87 MIX) THE GAP BAND (CLUB/PHONOGRAM)	20	ATLANTIC SOUL CLASSICS VARIOUS (ATLANTIC)

US

SINGLES		ALBUMS
I STILL HAVEN'T FOUND WHAT I'M LOOKING FOR U2 (ISLAND)	1	IN THE DARK GRATEFUL DEAD (ARISTA)
WHO'S THAT GIRL MADONNA (SIRE/WARNER BROS)	2	SAMMY HAGAR SAMMY HAGAR (GEFFEN)
LUKA SUZANNE VEGA (A&M)	3	BAD ANIMALS HEART (CAPITOL)
SHAKEDOWN BOB SEGAR (MCA)	4	ONE WAY HOME HOOTERS (COLUMBIA)
HEART AND SOUL T'PAU (VIRGIN)	5	WHITESNAKE WHITESNAKE (GEFFEN)
CROSS MY BROKEN HEART JETS (MCA)	6	TANGO IN THE NIGHT FLEETWOOD MAC (WARNER BROS)
LA BAMBA LOS LOBOS (SLASH/WARNER BROS)	7	SOUNDTRACK LOST BOYS (ATLANTIC)
I WANT YOUR SEX GEORGE MICHAEL (COLUMBIA)	8	AFTER DARK CRUZADOS (ARISTA)
BACK IN THE HIGH LIFE AGAIN STEVE WINWOOD (ISLAND/WARNER BROS)	9	ROVER'S RETURN JOHN WAITE (EMI AMERICA)
DON'T MEAN NOTHING RICHARD MARX (EMI-MANHATTAN)	10	LET ME UP TOM PETTY & THE HEARTBREAKERS (MCA)
ROCK STEADY WHISPERS (SOLAR/CAPITOL)	11	NO PROTECTION STARSHIP (GRUNT/RCA)
RHYTHM IS GONNA GET YOU G. ESTEFAN & MIAMI SOUND MACHINE (EPIC)	12	THE JOSHUA TREE U2 (ISLAND)
ONLY IN MY DREAMS DEBBIE GIBSON (ATLANTIC)	13	HOT NUMBER FABULOUS THUNDERBIRDS (CBS ASSOCIATED)
THE PLEASURE PRINCIPLE JANET JACKSON (A&M)	14	BANGIN' OUTFIELD (COLUMBIA)
ALONE HEART (CAPITOL)	15	RADIO K.A.O.S. ROGER WATERS (COLUMBIA)
WOT'S IT TO YA ROBBIE NEVIL (MANHATTAN)	16	GOT ANY GUM? JOE WALSH (FULL MOON/WARNER BROS)
SEVEN WONDERS FLEETWOOD MAC (WARNER BROS)	17	ONCE BITTEN GREAT WHITE (CAPITOL)
I'D STILL SAY YES KLYMAXX (CONSTELLATION/MCA)	18	RICHARD MARX RICHARD MARX (MANHATTAN)
IT'S NOT OVER STARSHIP (GRUNT/RCA)	19	SOUNDTRACK LA BAMBA (SLASH/WARNER BROS)
LIVING IN A BOX LIVING IN A BOX (CHRYSALIS)	20	INTO THE FIRE BRYAN ADAMS (A&M)

WEEK ENDING AUGUST 8 1987

UK

SINGLES		ALBUMS
LA BAMBA LOS LOBOS (SLASH/FFRR/LONDON)	1	HITS 6 VARIOUS (CBS/WEA/BMG)
WHO'S THAT GIRL MADONNA (SIRE)	2	INTRODUCING THE HARDLINE ACCORDING TO... TERENCE TRENT D'ARBY (CBS)
ALONE HEART (CAPITOL)	3	THE JOSHUA TREE U2 (ISLAND)
ALWAYS ATLANTIC STARR (WARNER BROS)	4	SIXTIES MIX VARIOUS (STYLUS)
I JUST CAN'T STOP LOVING YOU MICHAEL JACKSON/SIEDAH GARRETT (EPIC)	5	ORIGINAL SOUNDTRACK 'WHO'S THAT GIRL' MADONNA/VARIOUS (SIRE)
LABOUR OF LOVE HUE & CRY (CIRCA/VIRGIN)	6	WHITNEY WHITNEY HOUSTON (ARISTA)
TRUE FAITH NEW ORDER (FACTORY)	7	BAD ANIMALS HEART (CAPITOL)
CALL ME SPAGNA (CBS)	8	INVISIBLE TOUCH GENESIS (VIRGIN)
JIVE TALKIN' BOOGIE BOX HIGH (HARDBACK)	9	F.L.M. MEL & KIM (SUPREME)
SHE'S ON IT BEASTIE BOYS (DEF JAM)	10	HEARSAY ALEXANDER O'NEAL (TABU)
IT'S A SIN PET SHOP BOYS (PARLOPHONE/EMI)	11	KEEP YOUR DISTANCE CURIOSITY KILLED THE CAT (MERCURY)
JUST DON'T WANT TO BE LONELY FREDDIE McGREGOR (GERMAIN)	12	THE RETURN OF BRUNO BRUCE WILLIS (MOTOWN)
UNDER THE BOARDWALK BRUCE WILLIS (MOTOWN)	13	LICENSED TO ILL BEASTIE BOYS (DEF JAM))
F.L.M. MEL & KIM (SUPREME)	14	TRUE BLUE MADONNA (SIRE)
I HEARD A RUMOUR BANANARAMA (LONDON)	15	LIVE IN THE CITY OF LIGHT SIMPLE MINDS (VIRGIN)
ANIMAL DEF LEPPARD (PHONOGRAM)	16	SOLITUDE STANDING SUZANNE VEGA (A&M)
ROADBLOCK STOCK AITKEN WATERMAN (BREAKOUT/A&M)	17	CLUTCHING AT STRAWS MARILLION (EMI)
I REALLY DIDN'T MEAN IT LUTHER VANDROSS (EPIC)	18	IT'S BETTER TO TRAVEL SWING OUT SISTER (MERCURY/PHONOGRAM)
A LITTLE BOOGIE WOOGIE SHAKIN' STEVENS (EPIC)	19	KICK IT – THE DEF JAM SAMPLER VOLUME 1 VARIOUS (DEF JAM)
YOU CAUGHT MY EYE JUDY BOUCHER (ORBITONE)	20	ATLANTIC SOUL CLASSICS VARIOUS (ATLANTIC)

US

SINGLES		ALBUMS
WHO'S THAT GIRL MADONNA (SIRE/WARNER BROS)	1	IN THE DARK GRATEFUL DEAD (ARISTA)
I STILL HAVEN'T FOUND WHAT I'M LOOKING FOR U2 (ISLAND)	2	SAMMY HAGAR SAMMY HAGAR (GEFFEN)
LUKA SUZANNE VEGA (A&M)	3	HYSTERIA DEF LEPPARD (MERCURY/PG)
LA BAMBA LOS LOBOS (SLASH/WARNER BROS)	4	ONE WAY HOME HOOTERS (COLUMBIA)
DON'T MEAN NOTHING RICHARD MARX (EMI-MANHATTAN)	5	WHITESNAKE WHITESNAKE (GEFFEN)
ROCK STEADY WHISPERS (SOLAR/CAPITOL)	6	BAD ANIMALS HEART (CAPITOL)
ONLY IN MY DREAMS DEBBIE GIBSON (ATLANTIC)	7	AFTER DARK CRUZADOS (ARISTA)
I WANT YOUR SEX GEORGE MICHAEL (COLUMBIA)	8	FLASHBACK 38 SPECIAL (A&M)
CROSS MY BROKEN HEART JETS (MCA)	9	SOUNDTRACK LOST BOYS (ATLANTIC)
HEART AND SOUL T'PAU (VIRGIN)	10	TANGO IN THE NIGHT FLEETWOOD MAC (WARNER BROS)
BACK IN THE HIGH LIFE AGAIN STEVE WINWOOD (ISLAND/WARNER BROS)	11	THE JOSHUA TREE U2 (ISLAND)
SHAKEDOWN BOB SEGAR (MCA)	12	LET ME UP TOM PETTY & THE HEARTBREAKERS (MCA)
RHYTHM IS GONNA GET YOU G. ESTEFAN & MIAMI SOUND MACHINE (EPIC)	13	SOUNDTRACK LA BAMBA (SLASH/WARNER BROS)
IT'S NOT OVER STARSHIP (GRUNT/RCA)	14	RADIO K.A.O.S. ROGER WATERS (COLUMBIA)
DOING IT ALL FOR MY BABY HUEY LEWIS & THE NEWS (CHRYSALIS)	15	ONCE BITTEN GREAT WHITE (CAPITOL)
CAN'T WE TRY? DAN HILL (COLUMBIA)	16	RICHARD MARX RICHARD MARX (MANHATTAN)
LIVING IN A BOX LIVING IN A BOX (CHRYSALIS)	17	GOT ANY GUM? JOE WALSH (FULL MOON/WARNER BROS)
I JUST CAN'T STOP LOVING YOU MICHAEL JACKSON/SIEDAH GARRETT (EPIC)	18	EVERYONE LOVES THE PILOT (EXCEPT THE CREW) JON ASTLEY (ATLANTIC)
DIDN'T WE ALMOST HAVE IT ALL WHITNEY HOUSTON (ARISTA)	19	INTO THE FIRE BRYAN ADAMS (A&M)
LOVE POWER DIONNE WARWICK & JEFFREY OSBORNE (ARISTA)	20	BANGIN' OUTFIELD (COLUMBIA)

WEEK ENDING AUGUST 15 1987

UK

Singles			Albums
I JUST CAN'T STOP LOVING YOU MICHAEL JACKSON/SIEDAH GARRETT (EPIC)	1		HITS 6 VARIOUS (CBS/WEA/BMG)
LA BAMBA LOS LOBOS (SLASH/FFRR/LONDON)	2		INTRODUCING THE HARDLINE ACCORDING TO... TERENCE TRENT D'ARBY (CBS)
CALL ME SPAGNA (CBS)	3		SIXTIES MIX VARIOUS (STYLUS)
TRUE FAITH NEW ORDER (FACTORY)	4		WHITNEY WHITNEY HOUSTON (ARISTA)
ALONE HEART (CAPITOL)	5		ORIGINAL SOUNDTRACK 'WHO'S THAT GIRL' MADONNA/VARIOUS (SIRE)
LABOUR OF LOVE HUE & CRY (CIRCA/VIRGIN)	6		THE JOSHUA TREE U2 (ISLAND)
ALWAYS ATLANTIC STARR (WARNER BROS)	7		BAD ANIMALS HEART (CAPITOL)
WHO'S THAT GIRL MADONNA (SIRE)	8		INVISIBLE TOUCH GENESIS (VIRGIN)
ANIMAL DEF LEPPARD (PHONOGRAM)	9		KEEP YOUR DISTANCE CURIOSITY KILLED THE CAT (MERCURY)
TOY BOY SINITTA (FANFARE)	10		F.L.M. MEL & KIM (SUPREME)
SOMEWHERE OUT THERE LINDA RONSTADT & JAMES INGRAM (MCA)	11		TRUE BLUE MADONNA (SIRE)
SWEET LITTLE MYSTERY WET WET WET (PHONOGRAM)	12		LICENSED TO ILL BEASTIE BOYS (DEF JAM)
ROADBLOCK STOCK AITKEN WATERMAN (BREAKOUT/A&M)	13		HEARSAY ALEXANDER O'NEAL (TABU)
NEVER GONNA GIVE YOU UP RICK ASTLEY (RCA)	14		THE RETURN OF BRUNO BRUCE WILLIS (MOTOWN)
JUST DON'T WANT TO BE LONELY FREDDIE McGREGOR (GERMAIN)	15		LIVE IN THE CITY OF LIGHT SIMPLE MINDS (VIRGIN)
I HEARD A RUMOUR BANANARAMA (LONDON)	16		SOLITUDE STANDING SUZANNE VEGA (A&M)
JIVE TALKIN' BOOGIE BOX HIGH (HARDBACK)	17		CLUTCHING AT STRAWS MARILLION (EMI)
SHE'S ON IT BEASTIE BOYS (DEF JAM)	18		IT'S BETTER TO TRAVEL SWING OUT SISTER (MERCURY/PHONOGRAM)
IT'S A SIN PET SHOP BOYS (PARLOPHONE/EMI)	19		GIVE ME THE REASON LUTHOR VANDROSS (EPIC)
UNDER THE BOARDWALK BRUCE WILLIS (MOTOWN)	20		ATLANTIC SOUL CLASSICS VARIOUS (ATLANTIC)

US

Singles			Albums
WHO'S THAT GIRL MADONNA (SIRE/WARNER BROS)	1		IN THE DARK GRATEFUL DEAD (ARISTA)
LA BAMBA LOS LOBOS (SLASH/WARNER BROS)	2		HYSTERIA DEF LEPPARD (MERCURY/PG)
LUKA SUZANNE VEGA (A&M)	3		ONE WAY HOME HOOTERS (COLUMBIA)
DON'T MEAN NOTHING RICHARD MARX (EMI-MANHATTAN)	4		I NEVER SAID GOODBYE SAMMY HAGAR (GEFFEN)
ONLY IN MY DREAMS DEBBIE GIBSON (ATLANTIC)	5		WHITESNAKE WHITESNAKE (GEFFEN)
ROCK STEADY WHISPERS (SOLAR/CAPITOL)	6		THE JOSHUA TREE U2 (ISLAND)
I STILL HAVEN'T FOUND WHAT I'M LOOKING FOR U2 (ISLAND)	7		BAD ANIMALS HEART (CAPITOL)
I JUST CAN'T STOP LOVING YOU MICHAEL JACKSON/SIEDAH GARRETT (EPIC)	8		AFTER DARK CRUZADOS (ARISTA)
DIDN'T WE ALMOST HAVE IT ALL WHITNEY HOUSTON (ARISTA)	9		RICHARD MARX RICHARD MARX (MANHATTAN)
DOING IT ALL FOR MY BABY HUEY LEWIS & THE NEWS (CHRYSALIS)	10		ONCE BITTEN GREAT WHITE (CAPITOL)
HERE I GO AGAIN WHITESNAKE (GEFFEN)	11		LET ME UP TOM PETTY & THE HEARTBREAKERS (MCA)
IT'S NOT OVER STARSHIP (GRUNT/RCA)	12		INTO THE FIRE BRYAN ADAMS (A&M)
CAN'T WE TRY? DAN HILL (COLUMBIA)	13		SOUNDTRACK LA BAMBA (SLASH/WARNER BROS)
I WANT YOUR SEX GEORGE MICHAEL (COLUMBIA)	14		RADIO K.A.O.S. ROGER WATERS (COLUMBIA)
HEART AND SOUL T'PAU (VIRGIN)	15		EVERYONE LOVES THE PILOT (EXCEPT THE CREW) JON ASTLEY (ATLANTIC)
LIVING IN A BOX LIVING IN A BOX (CHRYSALIS)	16		SOUNDTRACK LOST BOYS (ATLANTIC)
LOVE POWER DIONNE WARWICK & JEFFREY OSBORNE (ARISTA)	17		TANGO IN THE NIGHT FLEETWOOD MAC (WARNER BROS)
WHEN SMOKEY SINGS ABC (MERCURY/PG)	18		GOT ANY GUM? JOE WALSH (FULL MOON/WARNER BROS)
CROSS MY BROKEN HEART JETS (MCA)	19		FLASHBACK 38 SPECIAL (A&M)
GIVE TO LIVE SAMMY HAGAR (GEFFEN)	20		HOT NUMBER FABULOUS THUNDERBIRDS (CBS ASSOCIATED)

WEEK ENDING AUGUST 22 1987

UK

Singles			Albums
I JUST CAN'T STOP LOVING YOU MICHAEL JACKSON/SIEDAH GARRETT (EPIC)	1		HITS 6 VARIOUS (CBS/WEA/BMG)
CALL ME SPAGNA (CBS)	2		INTRODUCING THE HARDLINE ACCORDING TO... TERENCE TRENT D'ARBY (CBS)
NEVER GONNA GIVE YOU UP RICK ASTLEY (RCA)	3		SIXTIES MIX VARIOUS (STYLUS)
TOY BOY SINITTA (FANFARE)	4		WHITNEY WHITNEY HOUSTON (ARISTA)
TRUE FAITH NEW ORDER (FACTORY)	5		ORIGINAL SOUNDTRACK 'WHO'S THAT GIRL MADONNA/VARIOUS (SIRE)
ANIMAL DEF LEPPARD (PHONOGRAM)	6		THE JOSHUA TREE U2 (ISLAND)
LA BAMBA LOS LOBOS (SLASH/FFRR/LONDON)	7		BAD ANIMALS HEART (CAPITOL)
SOMEWHERE OUT THERE LINDA RONSTADT & JAMES INGRAM (MCA)	8		DREAM EVIL DIO (VERTIGO/PHONOGRAM)
SWEET LITTLE MYSTERY WET WET WET (PHONOGRAM)	9		TRUE BLUE MADONNA (SIRE)
WHAT HAVE I DONE TO DESERVE THIS? PET SHOP BOYS & D. SPRINGFIELD (PARLOPHONE)	10		INVISIBLE TOUCH GENESIS (VIRGIN)
FUNKY TOWN PSEUDO ECHO (RCA)	11		F.L.M. MEL & KIM (SUPREME)
LABOUR OF LOVE HUE & CRY (CIRCA/VIRGIN)	12		KEEP YOUR DISTANCE CURIOSITY KILLED THE CAT (MERCURY)
GIRLFRIEND IN A COMA THE SMITHS (ROUGH TRADE)	13		HEARSAY ALEXANDER O'NEAL (TABU)
ALONE HEART (CAPITOL)	14		LICENSED TO ILL BEASTIE BOYS (DEF JAM)
WHO'S THAT GIRL MADONNA (SIRE)	15		GIVE ME THE REASON LUTHER VANDROSS (EPIC)
ROADBLOCK STOCK AITKEN WATERMAN (BREAKOUT/A&M)	16		THE RETURN OF BRUNO BRUCE WILLIS (MOTOWN)
ALWAYS ATLANTIC STARR (WARNER BROS)	17		ATLANTIC SOUL CLASSICS VARIOUS (ATLANTIC)
WHENEVER YOU'RE READY FIVE STAR (TENT/RCA)	18		LIVE IN THE CITY OF LIGHT SIMPLE MINDS (VIRGIN)
U GOT THE LOOK PRINCE & SHEENA EASTON (PAISLEY PARK)	19		SLIPPERY WHEN WET BON JOVI (VERTIGO)
BRIDGE TO YOUR HEART WAX (RCA)	20		SOLITUDE STANDING SUZANNE VEGA (A&M)

US

Singles			Albums
LA BAMBA LOS LOBOS (SLASH/WARNER BROS)	1		IN THE DARK GRATEFUL DEAD (ARISTA)
WHO'S THAT GIRL MADONNA (SIRE/WARNER BROS)	2		HYSTERIA DEF LEPPARD (MERCURY/PG)
ONLY IN MY DREAMS DEBBIE GIBSON (ATLANTIC)	3		ONE WAY HOME HOOTERS (COLUMBIA)
DON'T MEAN NOTHING RICHARD MARX (EMI-MANHATTAN)	4		WHITESNAKE WHITESNAKE (GEFFEN)
I JUST CAN'T STOP LOVING YOU MICHAEL JACKSON/SIEDAH GARRETT (EPIC)	5		THE JOSHUA TREE U2 (ISLAND)
DIDN'T WE ALMOST HAVE IT ALL WHITNEY HOUSTON (ARISTA)	6		I NEVER SAID GOODBYE SAMMY HAGAR (GEFFEN)
HERE I GO AGAIN WHITESNAKE (GEFFEN)	7		RICHARD MARX RICHARD MARX (MANHATTAN)
DOING IT ALL FOR MY BABY HUEY LEWIS & THE NEWS (CHRYSALIS)	8		AFTER DARK CRUZADOS (ARISTA)
ROCK STEADY WHISPERS (SOLAR/CAPITOL)	9		ONCE BITTEN GREAT WHITE (CAPITOL)
LUKA SUZANNE VEGA (A&M)	10		BAD ANIMALS HEART (CAPITOL)
CAN'T WE TRY? DAN HILL (COLUMBIA)	11		INTO THE FIRE BRYAN ADAMS (A&M)
IT'S NOT OVER STARSHIP (GRUNT/RCA)	12		LET ME UP TOM PETTY & THE HEARTBREAKERS (MCA)
WHEN SMOKEY SINGS ABC (MERCURY/PG)	13		EVERYONE LOVES THE PILOT (EXCEPT THE CREW) JON ASTLEY (ATLANTIC)
I STILL HAVEN'T FOUND WHAT I'M LOOKING FOR U2 (ISLAND)	14		RADIO K.A.O.S. ROGER WATERS (COLUMBIA)
LOVE POWER DIONNE WARWICK & JEFFREY OSBORNE (ARISTA)	15		TANGO IN THE NIGHT FLEETWOOD MAC (WARNER BROS)
I WANT YOUR SEX GEORGE MICHAEL (COLUMBIA)	16		GOT ANY GUM? JOE WALSH (FULL MOON/WARNER BROS)
CARRIE EUROPE (EPIC)	17		GHOST ON THE BEACH INSIDERS (EPIC)
WHO FOUND WHO JELLYBEAN/ELISA FIORILLO (CHRYSALIS)	18		NEVER LET ME DOWN DAVID BOWIE (EMI-MANHATTEN)
I NEED LOVE LL COOL J (DEF JAM/COLUMBIA)	19		SOUNDTRACK LA BAMBA (SLASH/WARNER BROS)
GIVE TO LIVE SAMMY HAGAR (GEFFEN)	20		HOT NUMBER FABULOUS THUNDERBIRDS (CBS ASSOCIATED)

WEEK ENDING AUGUST 29 1987

UK

SINGLES	UK	ALBUMS
NEVER GONNA GIVE YOU UP RICK ASTLEY (RCA)	1	HYSTERIA DEF LEPPARD (PHONOGRAM)
WHAT HAVE I DONE TO DESERVE THIS? PET SHOP BOYS & D. SPRINGFIELD (PARLOPHONE)	2	HITS 6 VARIOUS (CBS/WEA/BMG)
I JUST CAN'T STOP LOVING YOU MICHAEL JACKSON/SIEDAH GARRETT (EPIC)	3	SUBSTANCE NEW ORDER (FACTORY)
TOY BOY SINITTA (FANFARE)	4	PRESLEY – THE ALL TIME GREATEST HITS ELVIS PRESLEY (RCA)
CALL ME SPAGNA (CBS)	5	ORIGINAL SOUNDTRACK 'WHO'S THAT GIRL' MADONNA/VARIOUS (SIRE)
SWEET LITTLE MYSTERY WET WET WET (PHONOGRAM)	6	WHITNEY WHITNEY HOUSTON (ARISTA)
TRUE FAITH NEW ORDER (FACTORY)	7	INTRODUCING THE HARDLINE ACCORDING TO… TERENCE TRENT D'ARBY (CBS)
FUNKY TOWN PSEUDO ECHO (RCA)	8	SIXTIES MIX VARIOUS (STYLUS)
ANIMAL DEF LEPPARD (PHONOGRAM)	9	THE JOSHUA TREE U2 (ISLAND)
SOMEWHERE OUT THERE LINDA RONSTADT & JAMES INGRAM (MCA)	10	TRUE BLUE MADONNA (SIRE)
WHENEVER YOUR READY FIVE STAR (TENT/RCA)	11	CHANGING FACES – THE VERY BEST OF… 10CC & GODLEY & CREME (PROTV/POLYGRAM)
BRIDGE TO YOUR HEART WAX (RCA)	12	INVISIBLE TOUCH GENESIS (VIRGIN)
U GOT THE LOOK PRINCE & SHEENA EASTON (PAISLEY PARK)	13	BAD ANIMALS HEART (CAPITOL)
DIDN'T WE ALMOST HAVE IT ALL WHITNEY HOUSTON (ARISTA)	14	F.L.M. MEL & KIM (SUPREME)
LA BAMBA LOS LOBOS (SLASH/FFRR/LONDON)	15	GIVE ME THE REASON LUTHER VANDROSS (EPIC)
GIRLFRIEND IN A COMA THE SMITHS (ROUGH TRADE)	16	HEARSAY ALEXANDER O'NEAL (TABU)
LABOUR OF LOVE HUE & CRY (CIRCA/VIRGIN)	17	KEEP YOUR DISTANCE CURIOSITY KILLED THE CAT (MERCURY)
WONDERFUL LIFE BLACK (A&M)	18	LICENSED TO ILL BEASTIE BOYS (DEF JAM)
WIPEOUT FAT BOYS/BEACH BOYS (POLYDOR)	19	THE RETURN OF BRUNO BRUCE WILLIS (MOTOWN)
WHO'S THAT GIRL MADONNA (SIRE)	20	LIVE IN THE CITY OF LIGHT SIMPLE MINDS (VIRGIN)

US

SINGLES	US	ALBUMS
LA BAMBA LOS LOBOS (SLASH/WARNER BROS)	1	THE LONESOME JUBILEE JOHN COUGAR MELLENCAMP (MERCURY/PG)
I JUST CAN'T STOP LOVING YOU MICHAEL JACKSON/SIEDAH GARRETT (EPIC)	2	IN THE DARK GRATEFUL DEAD (ARISTA)
DIDN'T WE ALMOST HAVE IT ALL WHITNEY HOUSTON (ARISTA)	3	DOOR TO DOOR CARS (ELEKTRA)
WHO'S THAT GIRL MADONNA (SIRE/WARNER BROS)	4	HYSTERIA DEF LEPPARD (MERCURY/PG)
HERE I GO AGAIN WHITESNAKE (GEFFEN)	5	THE JOSHUA TREE U2 (ISLAND)
ONLY IN MY DREAMS DEBBIE GIBSON (ATLANTIC)	6	ONE WAY HOME HOOTERS (COLUMBIA)
DOING IT ALL FOR MY BABY HUEY LEWIS & THE NEWS (CHRYSALIS)	7	WHITESNAKE WHITESNAKE (GEFFEN)
DON'T MEAN NOTHING RICHARD MARX (EMI-MANHATTAN)	8	RICHARD MARX RICHARD MARX (MANHATTAN)
WHEN SMOKEY SINGS ABC (MERCURY/PG)	9	INTO THE FIRE BRYAN ADAMS (A&M)
CAN'T WE TRY? DAN HILL (COLUMBIA)	10	I NEVER SAID GOODBYE SAMMY HAGAR (GEFFEN)
CARRIE EUROPE (EPIC)	11	ONCE BITTEN GREAT WHITE (CAPITOL)
ROCK STEADY WHISPERS (SOLAR/CAPITOL)	12	WILDSIDE LOVERBOY (COLUMBIA)
WHO FOUND WHO JELLYBEAN/ELISA FIORILLO (CHRYSALIS)	13	BAD ANIMALS HEART (CAPITOL)
I HEARD A RUMOUR BANANARAMA (LONDON/PG)	14	GHOST ON THE BEACH INSIDERS (EPIC)
LOVE POWER DIONNE WARWICK & JEFFREY OSBORNE (ARISTA)	15	TANGO IN THE NIGHT FLEETWOOD MAC (WARNER BROS)
I NEED LOVE LL COOL J (DEF JAM/COLUMBIA)	16	NEVER LET ME DOWN DAVID BOWIE (EMI-MANHATTEN)
IT'S NOT OVER STARSHIP (GRUNT/RCA)	17	RADIO K.A.O.S. ROGER WATERS (COLUMBIA)
LOST IN EMOTION LISA LISA (COLUMBIA)	18	EVERYONE LOVES THE PILOT (EXCEPT THE CREW) JON ASTLEY (ATLANTIC)
TOUCH OF GREY GRATEFUL DEAD (ARISTA)	19	HOT NUMBER FABULOUS THUNDERBIRDS (CBS ASSOCIATED)
ONE HEARTBEAT SMOKEY ROBINSON (MOTOWN)	20	A LETTER FROM ST PAUL SILENCERS (RCA)

WEEK ENDING SEPTEMBER 5 1987

UK

SINGLES	UK	ALBUMS
NEVER GONNA GIVE YOU UP RICK ASTLEY (RCA)	1	HITS 6 VARIOUS (CBS/WEA/BMG)
WHAT HAVE I DONE TO DESERVE THIS? PET SHOP BOYS & D. SPRINGFIELD (PARLOPHONE)	2	HYSTERIA DEF LEPPARD (PHONOGRAM)
WIPEOUT FAT BOYS/BEACH BOYS (POLYDOR)	3	SUBSTANCE NEW ORDER (FACTORY)
TOY BOY SINITTA (FANFARE)	4	WHITNEY WHITNEY HOUSTON (ARISTA)
SWEET LITTLE MYSTERY WET WET WET (PHONOGRAM)	5	PRESLEY – THE ALL TIME GREATEST HITS ELVIS PRESLEY (RCA)
CALL ME SPAGNA (CBS)	6	THE JOSHUA TREE U2 (ISLAND)
I JUST CAN'T STOP LOVING YOU MICHAEL JACKSON/SIEDAH GARRETT (EPIC)	7	ORIGINAL SOUNDTRACK 'WHO'S THAT GIRL' MADONNA/VARIOUS (SIRE)
WONDERFUL LIFE BLACK (A&M)	8	INTRODUCING THE HARDLINE ACCORDING TO… TERENCE TRENT D'ARBY (CBS)
HEART AND SOUL T'PAU (SIREN/VIRGIN)	9	CHANGING FACES – THE VERY BEST OF… 10CC & GODLEY & CREME (PROTV/POLYGRAM)
FUNKY TOWN PSEUDO ECHO (RCA)	10	GIVE ME THE REASON LUTHER VANDROSS (EPIC)
U GOT THE LOOK PRINCE & SHEENA EASTON (PAISLEY PARK)	11	SIXTIES MIX VARIOUS (STYLUS)
BRIDGE TO YOUR HEART WAX (RCA)	12	TRUE BLUE MADONNA (SIRE)
WHENEVER YOUR READY FIVE STAR (TENT/RCA)	13	HEARSAY ALEXANDER O'NEAL (TABU)
DIDN'T WE ALMOST HAVE IT ALL WHITNEY HOUSTON (ARISTA)	14	INVISIBLE TOUCH GENESIS (VIRGIN)
SOME PEOPLE CLIFF RICHARD (EMI)	15	BAD ANIMALS HEART (CAPITOL)
SOMEWHERE OUT THERE LINDA RONSTADT & JAMES INGRAM (MCA)	16	KEEP YOUR DISTANCE CURIOSITY KILLED THE CAT (MERCURY)
ANIMAL DEF LEPPARD (PHONOGRAM)	17	SLIPPERY WHEN WET BON JOVI (VERTIGO)
THE MOTIVE THEN JERICO (LONDON)	18	THE BEATLES THE BEATLES (PARLOPHONE)
TRUE FAITH NEW ORDER (FACTORY)	19	F.L.M. MEL & KIM (SUPREME)
CASANOVA LEVERT (ATLANTIC)	20	FRANKS WILD YEARS TOM WAITS (ISLAND)

US

SINGLES	US	ALBUMS
I JUST CAN'T STOP LOVING YOU MICHAEL JACKSON/SIEDAH GARRETT (EPIC)	1	THE LONESOME JUBILEE JOHN COUGAR MELLENCAMP (MERCURY/PG)
LA BAMBA LOS LOBOS (SLASH/WARNER BROS)	2	DOOR TO DOOR CARS (ELEKTRA)
DIDN'T WE ALMOST HAVE IT ALL WHITNEY HOUSTON (ARISTA)	3	IN THE DARK GRATEFUL DEAD (ARISTA)
HERE I GO AGAIN WHITESNAKE (GEFFEN)	4	HYSTERIA DEF LEPPARD (MERCURY/PG)
DOING IT ALL FOR MY BABY HUEY LEWIS & THE NEWS (CHRYSALIS)	5	PERMANENT VACATION AEROSMITH (GEFFEN)
WHEN SMOKEY SINGS ABC (MERCURY/PG)	6	WHITESNAKE WHITESNAKE (GEFFEN)
CARRIE EUROPE (EPIC)	7	THE JOSHUA TREE U2 (ISLAND)
CAN'T WE TRY? DAN HILL (COLUMBIA)	8	RICHARD MARX RICHARD MARX (MANHATTAN)
ONLY IN MY DREAMS DEBBIE GIBSON (ATLANTIC)	9	INTO THE FIRE BRYAN ADAMS (A&M)
I HEARD A RUMOUR BANANARAMA (LONDON/PG)	10	ONE WAY HOME HOOTERS (COLUMBIA)
LOST EMOTION LISA LISA (COLUMBIA)	11	WILDSIDE LOVERBOY (COLUMBIA)
WHO FOUND WHO JELLYBEAN/ELISA FIORILLO (CHRYSALIS)	12	DOCUMENT R.E.M. (IRS/MCA)
WHO'S THAT GIRL MADONNA (SIRE/WARNER BROS)	13	GHOST ON THE BEACH INSIDERS (EPIC)
I NEED LOVE LL COOL J (DEF JAM/COLUMBIA)	14	I NEVER SAID GOODBYE SAMMY HAGAR (GEFFEN)
TOUCH OF GREY GRATEFUL DEAD (ARISTA)	15	TANGO IN THE NIGHT FLEETWOOD MAC (WARNER BROS)
ONE HEARTBEAT SMOKEY ROBINSON (MOTOWN)	16	NEVER LET ME DOWN DAVID BOWIE (EMI-MANHATTEN)
DON'T MEAN NOTHING RICHARD MARX (EMI-MANHATTAN)	17	ONCE BITTEN GREAT WHITE (CAPITOL)
U GOT THE LOOK PRINCE & SHEENA EASTON (WARNER BROS)	18	BAD ANIMALS HEART (CAPITOL)
WHO WILL YOU RUN TO HEART (CAPITOL)	19	HOT NUMBER FABULOUS THUNDERBIRDS (CBS ASSOCIATED)
PAPER IN FIRE JOHN COUGAR MELLENCAMP (MERCURY/PG)	20	A LETTER FROM ST. PAUL SILENCERS (RCA)

WEEK ENDING SEPTEMBER 12 1987

SINGLES UK ALBUMS

Singles			Albums	
NEVER GONNA GIVE YOU UP	RICK ASTLEY (RCA)	1	BAD	MICHAEL JACKSON (EPIC)
WIPEOUT	FAT BOYS/BEACH BOYS (POLYDOR)	2	HITS 6	VARIOUS (CBS/WEA/BMG)
WHAT HAVE I DONE TO DESERVE THIS?	PET SHOP BOYS & D. SPRINGFIELD (PARLOPHONE)	3	HYSTERIA	DEF LEPPARD (PHONOGRAM)
WHERE THE STREETS HAVE NO NAME	U2 (ISLAND)	4	SUBSTANCE	NEW ORDER (FACTORY)
HEART AND SOUL	T'PAU (SIREN/VIRGIN)	5	DARKLANDS	JESUS AND MARY CHAIN (BLANCO Y NEGRO/WEA)
TOY BOY	SINITTA (FANFARE)	6	WHITNEY	WHITNEY HOUSTON (ARISTA)
SOME PEOPLE	CLIFF RICHARD (EMI)	7	CHANGING FACES – THE VERY BEST OF . . .	10CC & GODLEY & CREME (PROTV/POLYGRAM)
SWEET LITTLE MYSTERY	WET WET WET (PHONOGRAM)	8	PRESLEY – THE ALL TIME GREATEST HITS	ELVIS PRESLEY (RCA)
WONDERFUL LIFE	BLACK (A&M)	9	THE JOSHUA TREE	U2 (ISLAND)
CASANOVA	LEVERT (ATLANTIC)	10	INTRODUCING THE HARDLINE ACCORDING TO . . .	TERENCE TRENT D'ARBY (CBS)
PUMP UP THE VOLUME	M/A/R/R/S (4AD)	11	ORIGINAL SOUNDTRACK 'WHO'S THAT GIRL'	MADONNA/VARIOUS (SIRE)
BRIDGE TO YOUR HEART	WAX (RCA)	12	SIXTIES MIX	VARIOUS (STYLUS)
U GOT THE LOOK	PRINCE & SHEENA EASTON (PAISLEY PARK)	13	GIVE ME THE REASON	LUTHER VANDROSS (EPIC)
CALL ME	SPAGNA (CBS)	14	TRUE BLUE	MADONNA (SIRE)
ME AND THE FARMER	THE HOUSEMARTINS (GO! DISCS)	15	INVISIBLE TOUCH	GENESIS (VIRGIN)
HOURGLASS	SQUEEZE (A&M)	16	HEARSAY	ALEXANDER O'NEAL (TABU)
I JUST CAN'T STOP LOVING YOU	MICHAEL JACKSON/SIEDAH GARRETT (EPIC)	17	JONATHAN BUTLER	JONATHAN BUTLER (JIVE)
THE MOTIVE	THEN JERICO (LONDON)	18	THE RETURN OF BRUNO	BRUCE WILLIS (MOTOWN)
I DON'T WANT TO BE A HERO	JOHNNY HATES JAZZ (VIRGIN)	19	BAD ANIMALS	HEART (CAPITOL)
FUNKY TOWN	PSEUDO ECHO (RCA)	20	KEEP YOUR DISTANCE	CURIOSITY KILLED THE CAT (MERCURY)

SINGLES US ALBUMS

Singles			Albums	
I JUST CAN'T STOP LOVING YOU	MICHAEL JACKSON/SIEDAH GARRETT (EPIC)	1	THE LONESOME JUBILEE	JOHN COUGAR MELLENCAMP (MERCURY/PG)
DIDN'T WE ALMOST HAVE IT ALL	WHITNEY HOUSTON (ARISTA)	2	DOOR TO DOOR	CARS (ELEKTRA)
HERE I GO AGAIN	WHITESNAKE (GEFFEN)	3	A MOMENTARY LAPSE OF REASON	PINK FLOYD (COLUMBIA)
CARRIE	EUROPE (EPIC)	4	IN THE DARK	GRATEFUL DEAD (ARISTA)
WHEN SMOKEY SINGS	ABC (MERCURY/PG)	5	PERMANENT VACATION	AEROSMITH (GEFFEN)
LA BAMBA	LOS LOBOS (SLASH/WARNER BROS)	6	HYSTERIA	DEF LEPPARD (MERCURY/PG)
DOING IT ALL FOR MY BABY	HUEY LEWIS & THE NEWS (CHRYSALIS)	7	HOLD YOUR FIRE	RUSH (MERCURY/PG)
I HEARD A RUMOUR	BANANARAMA (LONDON/PG)	8	WHITESNAKE	WHITESNAKE (GEFFEN)
LOST IN EMOTION	LISA LISA (COLUMBIA)	9	DOCUMENT	R.E.M. (IRS/MCA)
CAN'T WE TRY?	DAN HILL (COLUMBIA)	10	THE JOSHUA TREE	U2 (ISLAND)
U GOT THE LOOK	PRINCE & SHEENA EASTON (WARNER BROS)	11	RICHARD MARX	RICHARD MARX (MANHATTAN)
WHO FOUND WHO	JELLYBEAN/ELISA FIORILLO (CHRYSALIS)	12	GHOST ON THE BEACH	INSIDERS (EPIC)
ONE HEARTBEAT	SMOKEY ROBINSON (MOTOWN)	13	WILDSIDE	LOVERBOY (COLUMBIA)
TOUCH OF GREY	GRATEFUL DEAD (ARISTA)	14	I NEVER SAID GOODBYE	SAMMY HAGAR (GEFFEN)
WHO WILL YOU RUN TO	HEART (CAPITOL)	15	ONE WAY HOME	HOOTERS (COLUMBIA)
PAPER IN FIRE	JOHN COUGAR MELLENCAMP (MERCURY/PG)	16	INTO THE FIRE	BRYAN ADAMS (A&M)
I NEED LOVE	LL COOL J (DEF JAM/COLUMBIA)	17	NEVER LET ME DOWN	DAVID BOWIE (EMI-MANHATTEN)
ONLY IN MY DREAMS	DEBBIE GIBSON (MANHATTAN)	18	TANGO IN THE NIGHT	FLEETWOOD MAC (WARNER BROS)
JUMP START	NATALIE COLE (EMI-MANHATTAN)	19	THE PASSENGER	MELVIN JAMES (MCA)
WIPE OUT	FAT BOYS/BEACH BOYS (TIN PAN APPLE/PG)	20	HOT NUMBER	FABULOUS THUNDERBIRDS (CBS ASSOCIATED)

WEEK ENDING SEPTEMBER 19 1987

SINGLES UK ALBUMS

Singles			Albums	
NEVER GONNA GIVE YOU UP	RICK ASTLEY (RCA)	1	BAD	MICHAEL JACKSON (EPIC)
PUMP UP THE VOLUME	M/A/R/R/S (4AD)	2	ACTUALLY	PET SHOP BOYS (PARLOPHONE)
WIPEOUT	FAT BOYS/BEACH BOYS (POLYDOR)	3	A MOMENTARY LAPSE OF REASON	PINK FLOYD (EMI)
HEART AND SOUL	T'PAU (SIREN/VIRGIN)	4	CHANGING FACES – THE VERY BEST OF . . .	10CC & GODLEY & CREME (PROTV/POLYGRAM)
WHERE THE STREETS HAVE NO NAME	U2 (ISLAND)	5	THE JOSHUA TREE	U2 (ISLAND)
SOME PEOPLE	CLIFF RICHARD (EMI)	6	HITS 6	VARIOUS (CBS/WEA/BMG)
CAUSING A COMMOTION	MADONNA (SIRE)	7	WHITNEY	WHITNEY HOUSTON (ARISTA)
WHAT HAVE I DONE TO DESERVE THIS?	PET SHOP BOYS & D. SPRINGFIELD (PARLOPHONE)	8	HYSTERIA	DEF LEPPARD (PHONOGRAM)
CASANOVA	LEVERT (ATLANTIC)	9	SUBSTANCE	NEW ORDER (FACTORY)
TOY BOY	SINITTA (FANFARE)	10	PRESLEY – THE ALL TIME GREATEST HITS	ELVIS PRESLEY (RCA)
IT'S OVER	LEVEL 42 (POLYDOR)	11	DARKLANDS	JESUS AND MARY CHAIN (BLANCO Y NEGRO/WEA)
HOUSE NATION	HOUSE MASTER/RUDE BOY (MAG. DANCE)	12	JONATHAN BUTLER	JONATHAN BUTLER (JIVE)
WONDERFUL LIFE	BLACK (A&M)	13	INTRODUCING THE HARDLINE ACCORDING TO . . .	TERENCE TRENT D'ARBY (CBS)
SWEET LITTLE MYSTERY	WET WET WET (PHONOGRAM)	14	BABYLON AND ON	SQUEEZE (A&M)
I DON'T WANT TO BE A HERO	JOHNNY HATES JAZZ (VIRGIN)	15	ORIGINAL SOUNDTRACK 'WHO'S THAT GIRL'	MADONNA/VARIOUS (SIRE)
BRIDGE TO YOUR HEART	WAX (RCA)	16	GIVE ME THE REASON	LUTHER VANDROSS (EPIC)
ME AND THE FARMER	THE HOUSEMARTINS (GO! DISCS)	17	ATLANTIC SOUL CLASSICS	VARIOUS (ATLANTIC)
LIES	JONATHAN BUTLER (JIVE)	18	SIXTIES MIX	VARIOUS (STYLUS)
HOURGLASS	SQUEEZE (A&M)	19	RUNNING IN THE FAMILY	LEVEL 42 (POLYDOR)
HEY MATTHEW	KAREL FIALKA (I.R.S./MCA)	20	CREST OF A KNAVE	JETHRO TULL (CHRYSALIS)

SINGLES US ALBUMS

Singles			Albums	
DIDN'T WE ALMOST HAVE IT ALL	WHITNEY HOUSTON (ARISTA)	1	THE LONESOME JUBILEE	JOHN COUGAR MELLENCAMP (MERCURY/PG)
HERE I GO AGAIN	WHITESNAKE (GEFFEN)	2	A MOMENTARY LAPSE OF REASON	PINK FLOYD (COLUMBIA)
CARRIE	EUROPE (EPIC)	3	DOOR TO DOOR	CARS (ELEKTRA)
I JUST CAN'T STOP LOVING YOU	MICHAEL JACKSON/SIEDAH GARRETT (EPIC)	4	PERMANENT VACATION	AEROSMITH (GEFFEN)
LOST IN EMOTION	LISA LISA (COLUMBIA)	5	HOLD YOUR FIRE	RUSH (MERCURY/PG)
I HEARD A RUMOUR	BANANARAMA (LONDON/PG)	6	IN THE DARK	GRATEFUL DEAD (ARISTA)
WHEN SMOKEY SINGS	ABC (MERCURY/PG)	7	HYSTERIA	DEF LEPPARD (MERCURY/PG)
U GOT THE LOOK	PRINCE & SHEENA EASTON (WARNER BROS)	8	PRIMITIVE COOL	MICK JAGGER (COLUMBIA)
ONE HEARTBEAT	SMOKEY ROBINSON (MOTOWN)	9	DOCUMENT	R.E.M. (IRS/MCA)
WHO WILL YOU RUN TO	HEART (CAPITOL)	10	WHITESNAKE	WHITESNAKE (GEFFEN)
PAPER IN FIRE	JOHN COUGAR MELLENCAMP (MERCURY/PG)	11	RICHARD MARX	RICHARD MARX (MANHATTAN)
TOUCH OF GREY	GRATEFUL DEAD (ARISTA)	12	GHOST ON THE BEACH	INSIDERS (EPIC)
LA BAMBA	LOS LOBOS (SLASH/WARNER BROS)	13	ONE WAY HOME	HOOTERS (COLUMBIA)
CASANOVA	LEVERT (ATLANTIC)	14	WILDSIDE	LOVERBOY (COLUMBIA)
CAUSING A COMMOTION	MADONNA (SIRE)	15	I NEVER SAID GOODBYE	SAMMY HAGAR (GEFFEN)
JUMP START	NATALIE COLE (EMI-MANHATTAN)	16	THE JOSHUA TREE	U2 (ISLAND)
DOING IT ALL FOR MY BABY	HUEY LEWIS & THE NEWS (CHRYSALIS)	17	CREST OF A KNAVE	JETHRO TULL (CHRYSALIS)
LET ME BE THE ONE	EXPOSE (ARISTA)	18	THE PASSENGER	MELVIN JAMES (MCA)
BAD	MICHAEL JACKSON (EPIC)	19	TANGO IN THE NIGHT	FLEETWOOD MAC (WARNER BROS)
LITTLE LIES	FLEETWOOD MAC (WARNER BROS)	20	TIMOTHY B	TIMOTHY B SCHMIDT (MCA)

WEEK ENDING SEPTEMBER 26 1987

SINGLES UK ALBUMS

Single	Artist (Label)	No.	Album	Artist (Label)
NEVER GONNA GIVE YOU UP	RICK ASTLEY (RCA)	1	BAD	MICHAEL JACKSON (EPIC)
PUMP UP THE VOLUME	M/A/R/R/S (4AD)	2	DANCING WITH STRANGERS	CHRIS REA (MAGNET)
SOME PEOPLE	CLIFF RICHARD (EMI)	3	WONDERFUL LIFE	BLACK (A&M)
CAUSING A COMMOTION	MADONNA (SIRE)	4	ACTUALLY	PET SHOP BOYS (PARLOPHONE)
BAD	MICHAEL JACKSON (EPIC)	5	ALWAYS GUARANTEED	CLIFF RICHARD (EMI)
HEART AND SOUL	T'PAU (SIREN/VIRGIN)	6	A MOMENTARY LAPSE OF REASON	PINK FLOYD (EMI)
WIPEOUT	FAT BOYS/BEACH BOYS (POLYDOR)	7	BETWEEN THE LINES	FIVE STAR (TENT/RCA)
HOUSE NATION	HOUSE MASTER/RUDE BOY (MAG. DANCE)	8	CHANGING FACES – THE VERY BEST OF . . .	10CC & GODLEY & CREME (PROTV/POLYGRAM)
HEY MATTHEW	KAREL FIALKA (IRS/MCA)	9	THE CREAM OF ERIC CLAPTON	ERIC CLAPTON (POLYDOR)
IT'S OVER	LEVEL 42 (POLYDOR)	10	THE JOSHUA TREE	U2 (ISLAND)
I DON'T WANT TO BE A HERO	JOHNNY HATES JAZZ (VIRGIN)	11	HYSTERIA	DEF LEPPARD (PHONOGRAM)
CASANOVA	LEVERT (ATLANTIC)	12	HITS 6	VARIOUS (CBS/WEA/BMG)
WHERE THE STREETS HAVE NO NAME	U2 (ISLAND)	13	WHITNEY	WHITNEY HOUSTON (ARISTA)
TOY BOY	SINITTA (FANFARE)	14	SUBSTANCE	NEW ORDER (FACTORY)
WHAT HAVE I DONE TO DESERVE THIS?	PET SHOP BOYS & D. SPRINGFIELD (PARLOPHONE)	15	PRESLEY – THE ALL TIME GREATEST HITS	ELVIS PRESLEY (RCA)
I NEED LOVE	LL COOL J (DEF JAM)	16	ORIGINAL SOUNDTRACK 'WHO'S THAT GIRL'	MADONNA/VARIOUS (SIRE)
WONDERFUL LIFE	BLACK (A&M)	17	JONATHAN BUTLER	JONATHAN BUTLER (JIVE)
LIES	JONATHAN BUTLER (JIVE)	18	GIVE ME THE REASON	LUTHER VANDROSS (EPIC)
CROCKETT'S THEME	JAN HAMMER (MCA)	19	CREST OF A KNAVE	JETHRO TULL (CHRYSALIS)
POUR SOME SUGAR ON ME	DEF LEPPARD (PHONOGRAM)	20	INTRODUCING THE HARDLINE ACCORDING TO . . .	TERENCE TRENT D'ARBY (CBS)

SINGLES US ALBUMS

Single	Artist (Label)	No.	Album	Artist (Label)
HERE I GO AGAIN	WHITESNAKE (GEFFEN)	1	A MOMENTARY LAPSE OF REASON	PINK FLOYD (COLUMBIA)
CARRIE	EUROPE (EPIC)	2	THE LONESOME JUBILEE	JOHN COUGAR MELLENCAMP (MERCURY/PG)
DIDN'T WE ALMOST HAVE IT ALL	WHITNEY HOUSTON (ARISTA)	3	DOOR TO DOOR	CARS (ELEKTRA)
LOST IN EMOTION	LISA LISA (COLUMBIA)	4	PERMANENT VACATION	AEROSMITH (GEFFEN)
U GOT THE LOOK	PRINCE & SHEENA EASTON (WARNER BROS)	5	HOLD YOUR FIRE	RUSH (MERCURY/PG)
I HEARD A RUMOUR	BANANARAMA (LONDON/PG)	6	PRIMITIVE COOL	MICK JAGGER (COLUMBIA)
WHO WILL YOU RUN TO	HEART (CAPITOL)	7	HYSTERIA	DEF LEPPARD (MERCURY/PG)
CAUSING A COMMOTION	MADONNA (SIRE)	8	DOCUMENT	R.E.M. (IRS/MCA)
PAPER IN FIRE	JOHN COUGAR MELLENCAMP (MERCURY/PG)	9	WHITESNAKE	WHITESNAKE (GEFFEN)
BAD	MICHAEL JACKSON (EPIC)	10	IN THE DARK	GRATEFUL DEAD (ARISTA)
CASANOVA	LEVERT (ATLANTIC)	11	CREST OF A KNAVE	JETHRO TULL (CHRYSALIS)
ONE HEARTBEAT	SMOKEY ROBINSON (MOTOWN)	12	GHOST ON THE BEACH	INSIDERS (EPIC)
LET ME BE THE ONE	EXPOSE (ARISTA)	13	ONE WAY HOME	HOOTERS (COLUMBIA)
JUMP START	NATALIE COLE (EMI-MANHATTAN)	14	LEGEND	LYNYRD SKYNYRD (MCA)
LITTLE LIES	FLEETWOOD MAC (WARNER BROS)	15	RICHARD MARX	RICHARD MARX (MANHATTAN)
I JUST CAN'T STOP LOVING YOU	MICHAEL JACKSON/SIEDAH GARRETT (EPIC)	16	THE PASSENGER	MELVIN JAMES (MCA)
WHEN SMOKEY SINGS	ABC (MERCURY/PG)	17	TIMOTHY B	TIMOTHY B SCHMIT (MCA)
TOUCH OF GREY	GRATEFUL DEAD (ARISTA)	18	I NEVER SAID GOODBYE	SAMMY HAGAR (GEFFEN)
I THINK WE'RE ALONE NOW	TIFFANY (MCA)	19	HEROES AND ZEROS	GLEN BURTNICK (A&M)
YOU ARE THE GIRL	CARS (ELEKTRA)	20	THE JOSHUA TREE	U2 (ISLAND)

WEEK ENDING OCTOBER 3 1987

SINGLES UK ALBUMS

Single	Artist (Label)	No.	Album	Artist (Label)
PUMP UP THE VOLUME	M/A/R/R/S (4AD)	1	BAD	MICHAEL JACKSON (EPIC)
NEVER GONNA GIVE YOU UP	RICK ASTLEY (RCA)	2	POPPED IN SOULED OUT	WET WET WET (PRECIOUS/PHONOGRAM)
BAD	MICHAEL JACKSON (EPIC)	3	WONDERFUL LIFE	BLACK (A&M)
SOME PEOPLE	CLIFF RICHARD (EMI)	4	DANCING WITH STRANGERS	CHRIS REA (MAGNET)
CAUSING A COMMOTION	MADONNA (SIRE)	5	ACTUALLY	PET SHOP BOYS (PARLOPHONE)
CROCKETT'S THEME	JAN HAMMER (MCA)	6	THE CREAM OF ERIC CLAPTON	ERIC CLAPTON (POLYDOR)
FULL METAL JACKET	ABIGAIL MEAD/NIGEL GOULDING (WARNER BROS)	7	NOW! SMASH HITS	VARIOUS (VIRGIN/EMI/POLYGRAM)
HOUSE NATION	HOUSE MASTER/RUDE BOY (MAG. DANCE)	8	ALWAYS GUARANTEED	CLIFF RICHARD (EMI)
I NEED LOVE	LL COOL J (DEF JAM)	9	THE PEOPLE WHO GRINNED	THE HOUSEMARTINS (GO! DISCS)
HEY MATTHEW	KAREL FIALKA (IRS/MCA)	10	CHANGING FACES – THE VERY BEST OF . . .	10CC & GODLEY & CREME (PROTV/POLYGRAM)
HEART AND SOUL	T'PAU (SIREN/VIRGIN)	11	HYSTERIA	DEF LEPPARD (PHONOGRAM)
WIPEOUT	FAT BOYS/BEACH BOYS (POLYDOR)	12	THE JOSHUA TREE	U2 (ISLAND)
THIS CORROSION	SISTERS OF MERCY (MERCIFUL RELEASE/WEA)	13	BETWEEN THE LINES	FIVE STAR (TENT/RCA)
I DON'T WANT TO BE A HERO	JOHNNY HATES JAZZ (VIRGIN)	14	A MOMENTARY LAPSE OF REASON	PINK FLOYD (EMI)
IT'S OVER	LEVEL 42 (POLYDOR)	15	WHITNEY	WHITNEY HOUSTON (ARISTA)
CARS ('E' REG MODEL)	GARY NUMAN (BEGGARS BANQUET)	16	HITS 6	VARIOUS (CBS/WEA/BMG)
CASANOVA	LEVERT (ATLANTIC)	17	GIVE ME THE REASON	LUTHER VANDROSS (EPIC)
POUR SOME SUGAR ON ME	DEF LEPPARD (PHONOGRAM)	18	SUBSTANCE	NEW ORDER (FACTORY)
JACK LE FREAK	CHIC (ATLANTIC)	19	ORIGINAL SOUNDTRACK 'WHO'S THAT GIRL'	MADONNA/VARIOUS (SIRE)
TOY BOY	SINITTA (FANFARE)	20	RUNNING IN THE FAMILY	LEVEL 42 (POLYDOR)

SINGLES US ALBUMS

Single	Artist (Label)	No.	Album	Artist (Label)
CARRIE	EUROPE (EPIC)	1	A MOMENTARY LAPSE OF REASON	PINK FLOYD (COLUMBIA)
LOST IN EMOTION	LISA LISA (COLUMBIA)	2	THE LONESOME JUBILEE	JOHN COUGAR MELLENCAMP (MERCURY/PG)
HERE I GO AGAIN	WHITESNAKE (GEFFEN)	3	BIG GENERATOR	YES (ATCO)
U GOT THE LOOK	PRINCE & SHEENA EASTON (WARNER BROS)	4	DOOR TO DOOR	CARS (ELEKTRA)
CAUSING A COMMOTION	MADONNA (SIRE)	5	HOLD YOUR FIRE	RUSH (MERCURY/PG)
BAD	MICHAEL JACKSON (EPIC)	6	PERMANENT VACATION	AEROSMITH (GEFFEN)
WHO WILL YOU RUN TO	HEART (CAPITOL)	7	DOCUMENT	R.E.M. (IRS/MCA)
CASANOVA	LEVERT (ATLANTIC)	8	PRIMITIVE COOL	MICK JAGGER (COLUMBIA)
PAPER IN FIRE	JOHN COUGAR MELLENCAMP (MERCURY/PG)	9	HYSTERIA	DEF LEPPARD (MERCURY/PG)
LET ME BE THE ONE	EXPOSE (ARISTA)	10	CREST OF A KNAVE	JETHRO TULL (CHRYSALIS)
I HEARD A RUMOUR	BANANARAMA (LONDON/PG)	11	WHITESNAKE	WHITESNAKE (GEFFEN)
LITTLE LIES	FLEETWOOD MAC (WARNER BROS)	12	LEGEND	LYNYRD SKYNYRD (MCA)
I THINK WE'RE ALONE NOW	TIFFANY (MCA)	13	ONE WAY HOME	HOOTERS (COLUMBIA)
JUMP START	NATALIE COLE (EMI-MANHATTAN)	14	IN THE DARK	GRATEFUL DEAD (ARISTA)
DIDN'T WE ALMOST HAVE IT ALL	WHITNEY HOUSTON (ARISTA)	15	THE PASSENGER	MELVIN JAMES (MCA)
MONY MONY	BILLY IDOL (CHRYSALIS)	16	TIMOTHY B	TIMOTHY B SCHMIT (MCA)
YOU ARE THE GIRL	CARS (ELEKTRA)	17	GHOST ON THE BEACH	INSIDERS (EPIC)
BREAKOUT	SWING OUT SISTER (MERCURY/PG)	18	A MAN OF COLOURS	ICEHOUSE (CHRYSALIS)
IN MY DREAMS	REO SPEEDWAGON (EPIC)	19	BABYLON AND ON	SQUEEZE (A&M)
IT'S A SIN	PET SHOP BOYS (EMI-MANHATTAN)	20	RICHARD MARX	RICHARD MARX (MANHATTAN)

WEEK ENDING OCTOBER 10 1987

SINGLES UK ALBUMS

Singles	Artist (Label)	Pos	Albums	Artist (Label)
PUMP UP THE VOLUME	M/A/R/R/S (4AD)	1	BAD	MICHAEL JACKSON (EPIC)
FULL METAL JACKET	ABIGAIL MEAD/NIGEL GOULDING (WARNER BROS)	2	STRANGEWAYS HERE WE COME	THE SMITHS (ROUGH TRADE)
BAD	MICHAEL JACKSON (EPIC)	3	POPPED IN SOULED OUT	WET WET WET (PRECIOUS/PHONOGRAM)
NEVER GONNA GIVE YOU UP	RICK ASTLEY (RCA)	4	THE CREAM OF ERIC CLAPTON	ERIC CLAPTON (POLYDOR)
CROCKETT'S THEME	JAN HAMMER (MCA)	5	NOW! SMASH HITS	VARIOUS (VIRGIN/EMI/POLYGRAM)
YOU WIN AGAIN	BEE GEES (WARNER BROS)	6	WONDERFUL LIFE	BLACK (A&M)
THIS CORROSION	SISTERS OF MERCY (MERCIFUL RELEASE/WEA)	7	DANCING WITH STRANGERS	CHRIS REA (MAGNET)
SOME PEOPLE	CLIFF RICHARD (EMI)	8	ACTUALLY	PET SHOP BOYS (PARLOPHONE)
I NEED LOVE	LL COOL J (DEF JAM)	9	ALWAYS GUARANTEED	CLIFF RICHARD (EMI)
CAUSING A COMMOTION	MADONNA (SIRE)	10	MUSIC FOR THE MASSES	DEPECHE MODE (MUTE)
HOUSE NATION	HOUSE MASTER/RUDE BOY (MAG. DANCE)	11	CHANGING FACES – THE VERY BEST OF . . .	10CC & GODLEY & CREME (PRO TV/POLYGRAM)
CRAZY CRAZY NIGHTS	KISS (VERTIGO/PHONOGRAM)	12	THE PEOPLE WHO GRINNED	THE HOUSEMARTINS (GO! DISCS)
I DON'T WANT TO BE A HERO	JOHNNY HATES JAZZ (VIRGIN)	13	BETWEEN THE LINES	FIVE STAR (TENT/RCA)
HEY MATTHEW	KAREL FIALKA (IRS/MCA)	14	THE JOSHUA TREE	U2 (ISLAND)
I FOUND LOVIN'	FATBACK BAND (MASTER MIX)	15	HYSTERIA	DEF LEPPARD (PHONOGRAM)
CARS ('E' REG MODEL)	GARY NUMAN (BEGGARS BANQUET)	16	WHITNEY	WHITNEY HOUSTON (ARISTA)
HEART AND SOUL	T'PAU (SIREN/VIRGIN)	17	BIG GENERATOR	YES (ATCO)
WIPEOUT	FAT BOYS/BEACH BOYS (POLYDOR)	18	A MOMENTARY LAPSE OF REASON	PINK FLOYD (EMI)
IT'S OVER	LEVEL 42 (POLYDOR)	19	HITS 6	VARIOUS (CBS/WEA/BMG)
BRILLIANT DISGUISE	BRUCE SPRINGSTEEN (CBS)	20	GIVE ME THE REASON	LUTHER VANDROSS (EPIC)

SINGLES US ALBUMS

Singles	Artist (Label)	Pos	Albums	Artist (Label)
LOST IN EMOTION	LISA LISA (COLUMBIA)	1	TUNNEL OF LOVE	BRUCE SPRINGSTEEN (COLUMBIA)
BAD	MICHAEL JACKSON (EPIC)	2	A MOMENTARY LAPSE OF REASON	PINK FLOYD (COLUMBIA)
U GOT THE LOOK	PRINCE & SHEENA EASTON (WARNER BROS)	3	BIG GENERATOR	YES (ATCO)
CAUSING A COMMOTION	MADONNA (SIRE)	4	THE LONESOME JUBILEE	JOHN COUGAR MELLENCAMP (MERCURY/PG)
CARRIE	EUROPE (EPIC)	5	DOOR TO DOOR	CARS (ELEKTRA)
CASANOVA	LEVERT (ATLANTIC)	6	DOCUMENT	R.E.M. (IRS/MCA)
WHO WILL YOU RUN TO	HEART (CAPITOL)	7	HOLD YOUR FIRE	RUSH (MERCURY/PG)
LITTLE LIES	FLEETWOOD MAC (WARNER BROS)	8	PERMANENT VACATION	AEROSMITH (GEFFEN)
LET ME BE THE ONE	EXPOSE (ARISTA)	9	HYSTERIA	DEF LEPPARD (MERCURY/PG)
I THINK WE'RE ALONE NOW	TIFFANY (MCA)	10	CREST OF A KNAVE	JETHRO TULL (CHRYSALIS)
HERE I GO AGAIN	WHITESNAKE (GEFFEN)	11	PRIMITIVE COOL	MICK JAGGER (COLUMBIA)
MONY MONY	BILLY IDOL (CHRYSALIS)	12	WHITESNAKE	WHITESNAKE (GEFFEN)
BREAKOUT	SWING OUT SISTER (MERCURY/PG)	13	LEGEND	LYNYRD SKYNYRD (MCA)
YOU ARE THE GIRL	CARS (ELEKTRA)	14	ONE WAY HOME	HOOTERS (COLUMBIA)
BRILLIANT DISGUISE	BRUCE SPRINGSTEEN (COLUMBIA)	15	A MAN OF COLOURS	ICEHOUSE (CHRYSALIS)
IT'S A SIN	PET SHOP BOYS (EMI-MANHATTAN)	16	TIMOTHY B	TIMOTHY B SCHMIT (MCA)
IN MY DREAMS	REO SPEEDWAGON (EPIC)	17	THE PASSENGER	MELVIN JAMES (MCA)
DON'T MAKE ME WAIT FOR LOVE	KENNY G/LENNY WILLIAMS (ARISTA)	18	BABYLON AND ON	SQUEEZE (A&M)
PAPER IN FIRE	JOHN COUGAR MELLENCAMP (MERCURY/PG)	19	IN THE DARK	GRATEFUL DEAD (ARISTA)
I'VE BEEN IN LOVE BEFORE	CUTTING CREW (VIRGIN)	20	I NEVER SAID GOODBYE	SAMMY HAGAR (GEFFEN)

WEEK ENDING OCTOBER 17 1987

SINGLES UK ALBUMS

Singles	Artist (Label)	Pos	Albums	Artist (Label)
YOU WIN AGAIN	BEE GEES (WARNER BROS)	1	TUNNEL OF LOVE	BRUCE SPRINGSTEEN (CBS)
FULL METAL JACKET	ABIGAIL MEAD/NIGEL GOULDING (WARNER BROS)	2	BAD	MICHAEL JACKSON (EPIC)
PUMP UP THE VOLUME	M/A/R/R/S (4AD)	3	THE CREAM OF ERIC CLAPTON	ERIC CLAPTON (POLYDOR)
CROCKETT'S THEME	JAN HAMMER (MCA)	4	RED	THE COMMUNARDS (LONDON)
CRAZY CRAZY NIGHTS	KISS (VERTIGO/PHONOGRAM)	5	STRANGEWAYS HERE WE COME	THE SMITHS (ROUGH TRADE)
BAD	MICHAEL JACKSON (EPIC)	6	POPPED IN SOULED OUT	WET WET WET (PRECIOUS/PHONOGRAM)
I FOUND LOVIN'	FATBACK BAND (MASTER MIX)	7	ACTUALLY	PET SHOP BOYS (PARLOPHONE)
I NEED LOVE	LL COOL J (DEF JAM)	8	DANCING WITH STRANGERS	CHRIS REA (MAGNET)
I FOUND LOVIN'	STEVE WALSH (A1)	9	WONDERFUL LIFE	BLACK (A&M)
NEVER GONNA GIVE YOU UP	RICK ASTLEY (RCA)	10	NOW! SMASH HITS	VARIOUS (VIRGIN/EMI/POLYGRAM)
THIS CORROSION	SISTERS OF MERCY (MERCIFUL RELEASE/WEA)	11	CHANGING FACES – THE VERY BEST OF . . .	10CC & GODLEY & CREME (PRO TV/POLYGRAM)
THE CIRCUS	ERASURE (MUTE)	12	TANGO IN THE NIGHT	FLEETWOOD MAC (WARNER BROS)
THE REAL THING	JELLYBEAN/STEVEN DANTE (CHRYSALIS)	13	BETWEEN THE LINES	FIVE STAR (TENT/RCA)
SOME PEOPLE	CLIFF RICHARD (EMI)	14	ALWAYS GUARANTEED	CLIFF RICHARD (EMI)
CAUSING A COMMOTION	MADONNA (SIRE)	15	E.S.P.	BEE GEES (WARNER BROS)
STRONG AS STEEL	FIVE STAR (TENT/RCA)	16	THE JOSHUA TREE	U2 (ISLAND)
MONY MONY	BILLY IDOL (CHRYSALIS)	17	WHITNEY	WHITNEY HOUSTON (ARISTA)
WALK THE DINOSAUR	WAS NOT WAS (FONTANA/PHONOGRAM)	18	INTRODUCING THE HARDLINE ACCORDING TO . . .	TERENCE TRENT D'ARBY (CBS)
VALERIE	STEVE WINWOOD (ISLAND)	19	HYSTERIA	DEF LEPPARD (PHONOGRAM)
RAIN IN THE SUMMERTIME	THE ALARM (IRS/MCA)	20	A MOMENTARY LAPSE OF REASON	PINK FLOYD (EMI)

SINGLES US ALBUMS

Singles	Artist (Label)	Pos	Albums	Artist (Label)
BAD	MICHAEL JACKSON (EPIC)	1	TUNNEL OF LOVE	BRUCE SPRINGSTEEN (COLUMBIA)
CAUSING A COMMOTION	MADONNA (SIRE)	2	BIG GENERATOR	YES (ATCO)
U GOT THE LOOK	PRINCE & SHEENA EASTON (WARNER BROS)	3	A MOMENTARY LAPSE OF REASON	PINK FLOYD (COLUMBIA)
I THINK WE'RE ALONE NOW	TIFFANY (MCA)	4	THE LONESOME JUBILEE	JOHN COUGAR MELLENCAMP (MERCURY/PG)
LITTLE LIES	FLEETWOOD MAC (WARNER BROS)	5	DOCUMENT	R.E.M. (IRS/MCA)
CASANOVA	LEVERT (ATLANTIC)	6	DOOR TO DOOR	CARS (ELEKTRA)
LOST IN EMOTION	LISA LISA (COLUMBIA)	7	HOLD YOUR FIRE	RUSH (MERCURY/PG)
LET ME BE THE ONE	EXPOSE (ARISTA)	8	CREST OF A KNAVE	JETHRO TULL (CHRYSALIS)
MONY MONY	BILLY IDOL (CHRYSALIS)	9	PERMANENT VACATION	AEROSMITH (GEFFEN)
BREAKOUT	SWING OUT SISTER (MERCURY/PG)	10	HYSTERIA	DEF LEPPARD (MERCURY/PG)
BRILLIANT DISGUISE	BRUCE SPRINGSTEEN (COLUMBIA)	11	PRIMITIVE COOL	MICK JAGGER (COLUMBIA)
IT'S A SIN	PET SHOP BOYS (EMI-MANHATTAN)	12	WHITESNAKE	WHITESNAKE (GEFFEN)
YOU ARE THE GIRL	CARS (ELEKTRA)	13	NOTHING LIKE THE SUN	STING (A&M)
CARRIE	EUROPE (EPIC)	14	LEGEND	LYNYRD SKYNYRD (MCA)
(I'VE HAD) THE TIME OF MY LIFE	BILL MEDLEY & JENNIFER WARNES (RCA)	15	A MAN OF COLOURS	ICEHOUSE (CHRYSALIS)
I'VE BEEN IN LOVE BEFORE	CUTTING CREW (VIRGIN)	16	TIMOTHY B	TIMOTHY B SCHMIT (MCA)
DON'T MAKE ME WAIT FOR LOVE	KENNY G/LENNY WILLIAMS (ARISTA)	17	BABYLON AND ON	SQUEEZE (A&M)
WHO WILL YOU RUN TO	HEART (CAPITOL)	18	I NEVER SAID GOODBYE	SAMMY HAGAR (GEFFEN)
WHERE THE STREETS HAVE NO NAME	U2 (ISLAND)	19	OUTSIDE LOOKING IN	BODEANS (SLASH/REPRISE)
HEAVEN IS A PLACE ON EARTH	BELINDA CARLISLE (MCA)	20	HAI HAI	ROGER HODGSON (A&M)

WEEK ENDING OCTOBER 24 1987

UK

SINGLES		UK	ALBUMS	
YOU WIN AGAIN	BEE GEES (WARNER BROS)	1	NOTHING LIKE THE SUN	STING (A&M)
CROCKETT'S THEME	JAN HAMMER (MCA)	2	TUNNEL OF LOVE	BRUCE SPRINGSTEEN (CBS)
FULL METAL JACKET	ABIGAIL MEAD/NIGEL GOULDING (WARNER BROS)	3	BAD	MICHAEL JACKSON (EPIC)
CRAZY CRAZY NIGHTS	KISS (VERTIGO/PHONOGRAM)	4	TANGO IN THE NIGHT	FLEETWOOD MAC (WARNER BROS)
LOVE IN THE FIRST DEGREE	BANANARAMA (LONDON)	5	E.S.P.	BEE GEES (WARNER BROS)
PUMP UP THE VOLUME	M/A/R/R/S (4AD)	6	THE CREAM OF ERIC CLAPTON	ERIC CLAPTON (POLYDOR)
THE CIRCUS	ERASURE (MUTE)	7	ALPHABET CITY	ABC (NEUTRON/PHONOGRAM)
MONY MONY	BILLY IDOL (CHRYSALIS)	8	ACTUALLY	PET SHOP BOYS (PARLOPHONE)
I FOUND LOVIN'	FATBACK BAND (MASTER MIX)	9	INTRODUCING THE HARDLINE ACCORDING TO...	TERENCE TRENT D'ARBY (CBS)
FAITH	GEORGE MICHAEL (EPIC)	10	BETWEEN THE LINES	FIVE STAR (TENT/RCA)
LITTLE LIES	FLEETWOOD MAC (WARNER BROS)	11	RED	THE COMMUNARDS (LONDON)
WALK THE DINOSAUR	WAS NOT WAS (FONTANA/PHONOGRAM)	12	DANCING WITH STRANGERS	CHRIS REA (MAGNET)
THE REAL THING	JELLYBEAN/STEVEN DANTE (CHRYSALIS)	13	POPPED IN SOULED OUT	WET WET WET (PRECIOUS/PHONOGRAM)
I FOUND LOVIN'	STEVE WALSH (A1)	14	WONDERFUL LIFE	BLACK (A&M)
MAYBE TOMORROW	UB40 (DEP INTERNATIONAL/VIRGIN)	15	NOW! SMASH HITS	VARIOUS (VIRGIN/EMI/POLYGRAM)
I NEED LOVE	LL COOL J (DEF JAM)	16	CHANGING FACES – THE VERY BEST OF...	10CC & GODLEY & CREME (PROTV/POLYGRAM)
RENT	PET SHOP BOYS (PARLOPHONE)	17	REFLECTIONS	FOSTER & ALLEN (STYLUS)
RAIN IN THE SUMMERTIME	THE ALARM (IRS/MCA)	18	STRANGEWAYS HERE WE COME	THE SMITHS (ROUGH TRADE)
STRONG AS STEEL	FIVE STAR (TENT/RCA)	19	THE JOSHUA TREE	U2 (ISLAND)
BAD	MICHAEL JACKSON (EPIC)	20	SIMPLY SHADOWS	THE SHADOWS (POLYDOR)

US

SINGLES		US	ALBUMS	
BAD	MICHAEL JACKSON (EPIC)	1	TUNNEL OF LOVE	BRUCE SPRINGSTEEN (COLUMBIA)
CAUSING A COMMOTION	MADONNA (SIRE)	2	BIG GENERATOR	YES (ATCO)
I THINK WE'RE ALONE NOW	TIFFANY (MCA)	3	A MOMENTARY LAPSE OF REASON	PINK FLOYD (COLUMBIA)
LITTLE LIES	FLEETWOOD MAC (WARNER BROS)	4	THE LONESOME JUBILEE	JOHN COUGAR MELLENCAMP (MERCURY/PG)
MONY MONY	BILLY IDOL (CHRYSALIS)	5	DOCUMENT	R.E.M. (IRS/MCA)
BREAKOUT	SWING OUT SISTER (MERCURY/PG)	6	HOLD YOUR FIRE	RUSH (MERCURY/PG)
BRILLIANT DISGUISE	BRUCE SPRINGSTEEN (COLUMBIA)	7	NOTHING LIKE THE SUN	STING (A&M)
LET ME BE THE ONE	EXPOSE (ARISTA)	8	CREST OF A KNAVE	JETHRO TULL (CHRYSALIS)
(I'VE HAD) THE TIME OF MY LIFE	BILL MEDLEY & JENNIFER WARNES (RCA)	9	PERMANENT VACATION	AEROSMITH (GEFFEN)
IT'S A SIN	PET SHOP BOYS (EMI-MANHATTAN)	10	DOOR TO DOOR	CARS (ELEKTRA)
CASANOVA	LEVERT (ATLANTIC)	11	PRIMITIVE COOL	MICK JAGGER (COLUMBIA)
HEAVEN IS A PLACE ON EARTH	BELINDA CARLISLE (MCA)	12	WHITESNAKE	WHITESNAKE (GEFFEN)
I'VE BEEN IN LOVE BEFORE	CUTTING CREW (VIRGIN)	13	HYSTERIA	DEF LEPPARD (MERCURY/PG)
U GOT THE LOOK	PRINCE & SHEENA EASTON (WARNER BROS)	14	A MAN OF COLOURS	ICEHOUSE (CHRYSALIS)
LOST IN EMOTION	LISA LISA (COLUMBIA)	15	OUTSIDE LOOKING IN	BODEANS (SLASH/REPRISE)
DON'T MAKE ME WAIT FOR LOVE	KENNY G/LENNY WILLIAMS (ARISTA)	16	I NEVER SAID GOODBYE	SAMMY HAGAR (GEFFEN)
WHERE THE STREETS HAVE NO NAME	U2 (ISLAND)	17	LEGEND	LYNYRD SKYNYRD (MCA)
SHOULD'VE KNOWN BETTER	RICHARD MARX (EMI-MANHATTAN)	18	BABYLON AND ON	SQUEEZE (A&M)
YOU ARE THE GIRL	CARS (ELEKTRA)	19	YO YO	BOURGEOIS TAGG (ISLAND)
I WON'T FORGET YOU	POISON (ENIGMA/CAPITOL)	20	TIMOTHY B	TIMOTHY B SCHMIT (MCA)

WEEK ENDING OCTOBER 31 1987

UK

SINGLES		UK	ALBUMS	
YOU WIN AGAIN	BEE GEES (WARNER BROS)	1	TANGO IN THE NIGHT	FLEETWOOD MAC (WARNER BROS)
FAITH	GEORGE MICHAEL (EPIC)	2	THE CHRISTIANS	THE CHRISTIANS (ISLAND)
LOVE IN THE FIRST DEGREE	BANANARAMA (LONDON)	3	NOTHING LIKE THE SUN	STING (A&M)
CROCKETT'S THEME	JAN HAMMER (MCA)	4	BAD	MICHAEL JACKSON (EPIC)
LITTLE LIES	FLEETWOOD MAC (WARNER BROS)	5	E.S.P.	BEE GEES (WARNER BROS)
THE CIRCUS	ERASURE (MUTE)	6	TUNNEL OF LOVE	BRUCE SPRINGSTEEN (CBS)
MONY MONY	BILLY IDOL (CHRYSALIS)	7	THE CREAM OF ERIC CLAPTON	ERIC CLAPTON (POLYDOR)
RENT	PET SHOP BOYS (PARLOPHONE)	8	ACTUALLY	PET SHOP BOYS (PARLOPHONE)
CRAZY CRAZY NIGHTS	KISS (VERTIGO/PHONOGRAM)	9	STRANGEWAYS HERE WE COME	THE SMITHS (ROUGH TRADE)
WALK THE DINOSAUR	WAS NOT WAS (FONTANA/PHONOGRAM)	10	DANCING WITH STRANGERS	CHRIS REA (MAGNET)
WHENEVER YOU NEED SOMEBODY	RICK ASTLEY (RCA)	11	INTRODUCING THE HARDLINE ACCORDING TO...	TERENCE TRENT D'ARBY (CBS)
FULL METAL JACKET	ABIGAIL MEAD/NIGEL GOULDING (WARNER BROS)	12	BRIDGE OF SPIES	T'PAU (SIREN)
THE REAL THING	JELLYBEAN/STEVEN DANTE (CHRYSALIS)	13	BETWEEN THE LINES	FIVE STAR (TENT/RCA)
MAYBE TOMORROW	UB40 (DEP INTERNATIONAL/VIRGIN)	14	SIMPLY SHADOWS	THE SHADOWS (POLYDOR)
I DON'T THINK THAT MAN SHOULD SLEEP...	RAY PARKER JR (GEFFEN)	15	ALPHABET CITY	ABC (NEUTRON/PHONOGRAM)
PUMP UP THE VOLUME	M/A/R/R/S (4AD)	16	REFLECTIONS	FOSTER & ALLEN (STYLUS)
I FOUND LOVIN'	FATBACK BAND (MASTER MIX)	17	THE BEST OF JAMES BROWN	JAMES BROWN (K-TEL)
COME ON, LET'S GO	LOS LOBOS (SLASH/LONDON)	18	NOW! SMASH HITS	VARIOUS (VIRGIN/EMI/POLYGRAM)
CHINA IN YOUR HAND	T'PAU (SIREN)	19	THE CIRCUS	ERASURE (MUTE)
DANCE LITTLE SISTER	TERENCE TRENT D'ARBY (CBS)	20	WONDERFUL LIFE	BLACK (A&M)

US

SINGLES		US	ALBUMS	
I THINK WE'RE ALONE NOW	TIFFANY (MCA)	1	TUNNEL OF LOVE	BRUCE SPRINGSTEEN (COLUMBIA)
CAUSING A COMMOTION	MADONNA (SIRE)	2	BIG GENERATOR	YES (ATCO)
MONY MONY	BILLY IDOL (CHRYSALIS)	3	A MOMENTARY LAPSE OF REASON	PINK FLOYD (COLUMBIA)
LITTLE LIES	FLEETWOOD MAC (WARNER BROS)	4	THE LONESOME JUBILEE	JOHN COUGAR MELLENCAMP (MERCURY/PG)
(I'VE HAD) THE TIME OF MY LIFE	BILL MEDLEY & JENNIFER WARNES (RCA)	5	NOTHING LIKE THE SUN	STING (A&M)
BREAKOUT	SWING OUT SISTER (MERCURY/PG)	6	DOCUMENT	R.E.M. (IRS/MCA)
BRILLIANT DISGUISE	BRUCE SPRINGSTEEN (COLUMBIA)	7	HOLD YOUR FIRE	RUSH (MERCURY/PG)
BAD	MICHAEL JACKSON (EPIC)	8	PERMANENT VACATION	AEROSMITH (GEFFEN)
HEAVEN IS A PLACE ON EARTH	BELINDA CARLISLE (MCA)	9	ROBBIE ROBERTSON	ROBBIE ROBERTSON (GEFFEN)
IT'S A SIN	PET SHOP BOYS (EMI-MANHATTAN)	10	CREST OF A KNAVE	JETHRO TULL (CHRYSALIS)
I'VE BEEN IN LOVE BEFORE	CUTTING CREW (VIRGIN)	11	PRIMITIVE COOL	MICK JAGGER (COLUMBIA)
SHOULD'VE KNOWN BETTER	RICHARD MARX (EMI-MANHATTAN)	12	WHITESNAKE	WHITESNAKE (GEFFEN)
LET ME BE THE ONE	EXPOSE (ARISTA)	13	DOOR TO DOOR	CARS (ELEKTRA)
CASANOVA	LEVERT (ATLANTIC)	14	A MAN OF COLOURS	ICEHOUSE (CHRYSALIS)
WHERE THE STREETS HAVE NO NAME	U2 (ISLAND)	15	HYSTERIA	DEF LEPPARD (MERCURY/PG)
DON'T MAKE ME WAIT FOR LOVE	KENNY G/LENNY WILLIAMS (ARISTA)	16	OUTSIDE LOOKING IN	BODEANS (SLASH/REPRISE)
I WON'T FORGET YOU	POISON (ENIGMA/CAPITOL)	17	I NEVER SAID GOODBYE	SAMMY HAGAR (GEFFEN)
COME ON, LET'S GO	LOS LOBOS (SLASH/WARNER BROS)	18	KICK	INXS (ATLANTIC)
WE'LL BE TOGETHER	STING (A&M)	19	YO YO	BOURGEOIS TAGG (ISLAND)
U GOT THE LOOK	PRINCE & SHEENA EASTON (WARNER BROS)	20	UNCHAIN MY HEART	JOE COCKER (CAPITOL)

WEEK ENDING NOVEMBER 7 1987

UK

SINGLES	ARTIST		ALBUMS	ARTIST
YOU WIN AGAIN	BEE GEES (WARNER BROS)	1	TANGO IN THE NIGHT	FLEETWOOD MAC (WARNER BROS)
FAITH	GEORGE MICHAEL (EPIC)	2	BRIDGE OF SPIES	T'PAU (SIREN)
WHENEVER YOU NEED SOMEBODY	RICK ASTLEY (RCA)	3	THE BEST OF UB40 VOL 1	UB40 (VIRGIN)
LOVE IN THE FIRST DEGREE	BANANARAMA (LONDON)	4	CRAZY CRAZY CRAZY	KISS (VERTIGO/PHONOGRAM)
CHINA IN YOUR HAND	T'PAU (SIREN)	5	NOTHING LIKE THE SUN	STING (A&M)
LITTLE LIES	FLEETWOOD MAC (WARNER BROS)	6	BEST SHOTS	PAT BENATAR (CHRYSALIS)
GOT MY MIND SET ON YOU	GEORGE HARRISON (DARK HORSE/WEA)	7	THE CHRISTIANS	THE CHRISTIANS (ISLAND)
MONY MONY	BILLY IDOL (CHRYSALIS)	8	E.S.P.	BEE GEES (WARNER BROS)
CROCKETT'S THEME	JAN HAMMER (MCA)	9	MAINSTREAM	LLOYD COLE & THE COMMOTIONS (POLYDOR)
WALK THE DINOSAUR	WAS NOT WAS (FONTANA/PHONOGRAM)	10	THE SINGLES	PRETENDERS (WEA)
THE CIRCUS	ERASURE (MUTE)	11	BAD	MICHAEL JACKSON (EPIC)
BARCELONA	F. MERCURY & M. CABALLE (POLYDOR)	12	CHRONICLES	STEVE WINWOOD (ISLAND)
I DON'T THINK THAT MAN SHOULD SLEEP . .	RAY PARKER JR (GEFFEN)	13	ACTUALLY	PET SHOP BOYS (PARLOPHONE)
RENT	PET SHOP BOYS (PARLOPHONE)	14	THE CREAM OF ERIC CLAPTON	ERIC CLAPTON (POLYDOR)
NEVER CAN SAY GOODBYE	THE COMMUNARDS (LONDON)	15	SIMPLY SHADOWS	THE SHADOWS (POLYDOR)
CRAZY CRAZY NIGHTS	KISS (VERTIGO/PHONOGRAM)	16	TUNNEL OF LOVE	BRUCE SPRINGSTEEN (CBS)
HERE I GO AGAIN	WHITESNAKE (EMI)	17	INTRODUCING THE HARDLINE ACCORDING TO . . .	TERENCE TRENT D'ARBY (CBS)
FULL METAL JACKET	ABIGAIL MEAD/NIGEL GOULDING (WARNER BROS)	18	REFLECTIONS	FOSTER & ALLEN (STYLUS)
THE REAL THING	JELLYBEAN/STEVEN DANTE (CHRYSALIS)	19	BETWEEN THE LINES	FIVE STAR (TENT/RCA)
WANTED	THE STYLE COUNCIL (POLYDOR)	20	HIT FACTORY	VARIOUS (STYLUS)

US

SINGLES	ARTIST		ALBUMS	ARTIST
I THINK WE'RE ALONE NOW	TIFFANY (MCA)	1	TUNNEL OF LOVE	BRUCE SPRINGSTEEN (COLUMBIA)
MONY MONY	BILLY IDOL (CHRYSALIS)	2	BIG GENERATOR	YES (ATCO)
(I'VE HAD) THE TIME OF MY LIFE	BILL MEDLEY & JENNIFER WARNES (RCA)	3	CLOUD NINE	GEORGE HARRISON (WARNER BROS)
HEAVEN IS A PLACE ON EARTH	BELINDA CARLISLE (MCA)	4	THE LONESOME JUBILEE	JOHN COUGAR MELLENCAMP (MERCURY/PG)
BRILLIANT DISGUISE	BRUCE SPRINGSTEEN (COLUMBIA)	5	A MOMENTARY LAPSE OF REASON	PINK FLOYD (COLUMBIA)
BREAKOUT	SWING OUT SISTER (MERCURY/PG)	6	NOTHING LIKE THE SUN	STING (A&M)
LITTLE LIES	FLEETWOOD MAC (WARNER BROS)	7	ROBBIE ROBERTSON	ROBBIE ROBERTSON (GEFFEN)
SHOULD'VE KNOWN BETTER	RICHARD MARX (EMI-MANHATTAN)	8	HOLD YOUR FIRE	RUSH (MERCURY/PG)
I'VE BEEN IN LOVE BEFORE	CUTTING CREW (VIRGIN)	9	PERMANENT VACATION	AEROSMITH (GEFFEN)
CAUSING A COMMOTION	MADONNA (SIRE)	10	DOCUMENT	R.E.M. (IRS/MCA)
IT'S A SIN	PET SHOP BOYS (EMI-MANHATTAN)	11	CREST OF A KNAVE	JETHRO TULL (CHRYSALIS)
FAITH	GEORGE MICHAEL (COLUMBIA)	12	PRIMITIVE COOL	MICK JAGGER (COLUMBIA)
I WON'T FORGET YOU	POISON (ENIGMA/CAPITOL)	13	A MAN OF COLOURS	ICEHOUSE (CHRYSALIS)
WE'LL BE TOGETHER	STING (A&M)	14	KICK	INXS (ATLANTIC)
COME ON, LET'S GO	LOS LOBOS (SLASH/WARNER BROS)	15	HYSTERIA	DEF LEPPARD (MERCURY/PG)
IS THIS LOVE	WHITESNAKE (GEFFEN)	16	OUTSIDE LOOKING IN	BODEANS (SLASH/REPRISE)
SHAKE YOUR LOVE	DEBBIE GIBSON (ATLANTIC)	17	CHRONICLES	STEVE WINWOOD (ISLAND/WARNER BROS)
HOURGLASS	SQUEEZE (A&M)	18	YO YO	BOURGEOIS TAGG (ISLAND)
BAD	MICHAEL JACKSON (EPIC)	19	WHITESNAKE	WHITESNAKE (GEFFEN)
THE ONE I LOVE	R.E.M. (IRS/MCA)	20	UNCHAIN MY HEART	JOE COCKER (CAPITOL)

WEEK ENDING NOVEMBER 14 1987

UK

SINGLES	ARTIST		ALBUMS	ARTIST
CHINA IN YOUR HAND	T'PAU (SIREN)	1	FAITH	GEORGE MICHAEL (EPIC)
GOT MY MIND SET ON YOU	GEORGE HARRISON (DARK HORSE/WEA)	2	ALL THE BEST!	PAUL McCARTNEY (PARLOPHONE)
YOU WIN AGAIN	BEE GEES (WARNER BROS)	3	TANGO IN THE NIGHT	FLEETWOOD MAC (WARNER BROS)
WHENEVER YOU NEED SOMEBODY	RICK ASTLEY (RCA)	4	BRIDGE OF SPIES	T'PAU (SIREN)
FAITH	GEORGE MICHAEL (EPIC)	5	THE BEST OF UB40 VOL 1	UB40 (VIRGIN)
NEVER CAN SAY GOODBYE	THE COMMUNARDS (LONDON)	6	THE SINGLES	PRETENDERS (WEA)
LOVE IN THE FIRST DEGREE/MR SLEAZE	BANANARAMA (LONDON)	7	BEST SHOTS	PAT BENATAR (CHRYSALIS)
BARCELONA	F. MERCURY & M. CABALLE (POLYDOR)	8	RUNNING IN THE FAMILY	LEVEL 42 (POLYDOR)
LITTLE LIES	FLEETWOOD MAC (WARNER BROS)	9	BETE NOIRE	BRYAN FERRY (VIRGIN)
(I'VE HAD) THE TIME OF MY LIFE	BILL MEDLEY & JENNIFER WARNES (RCA)	10	CLOUD NINE	GEORGE HARRISON (DARK HORSE/WEA)
MY BABY JUST CARES FOR ME	NINA SIMONE (CHARLY)	11	E.S.P.	BEE GEES (WARNER BROS)
HERE I GO AGAIN	WHITESNAKE (EMI)	12	FROM MOTOWN WITH LOVE	VARIOUS (K-TEL)
JACK MIX IV	MIRAGE (DEBUT/PASSION)	13	SIMPLY SHADOWS	THE SHADOWS (POLYDOR)
MONY MONY	BILLY IDOL (CHRYSALIS)	14	BAD	MICHAEL JACKSON (EPIC)
PAID IN FULL	ERIC B & RAKIM (4TH & B'WAY/ISLAND)	15	THE CHRISTIANS	THE CHRISTIANS (ISLAND)
I DON'T THINK THAT MAN SHOULD SLEEP . .	RAY PARKER JR (GEFFEN)	16	NOTHING LIKE THE SUN	STING (A&M)
CROCKETT'S THEME	JAN HAMMER (MCA)	17	ACTUALLY	PET SHOP BOYS (PARLOPHONE)
WALK THE DINOSAUR	WAS NOT WAS (FONTANA/PHONOGRAM)	18	MAINSTREAM	LLOYD COLE & THE COMMOTIONS (POLYDOR)
THE CIRCUS	ERASURE (MUTE)	19	CHRONICLES	STEVE WINWOOD (ISLAND)
SO EMOTIONAL	WHITNEY HOUSTON (ARISTA)	20	CONTROL – THE REMIXES	JANET JACKSON (BREAKOUT/A&M)

US

SINGLES	ARTIST		ALBUMS	ARTIST
MONY MONY	BILLY IDOL (CHRYSALIS)	1	TUNNEL OF LOVE	BRUCE SPRINGSTEEN (COLUMBIA)
(I'VE HAD) THE TIME OF MY LIFE	BILL MEDLEY & JENNIFER WARNES (RCA)	2	CLOUD NINE	GEORGE HARRISON (DARK HORSE)
HEAVEN IS A PLACE ON EARTH	BELINDA CARLISLE (MCA)	3	BIG GENERATOR	YES (ATCO)
I THINK WE'RE ALONE NOW	TIFFANY (MCA)	4	A MOMENTARY LAPSE OF REASON	PINK FLOYD (COLUMBIA)
BRILLIANT DISGUISE	BRUCE SPRINGSTEEN (COLUMBIA)	5	ROBBIE ROBERTSON	ROBBIE ROBERTSON (GEFFEN)
SHOULD'VE KNOWN BETTER	RICHARD MARX (EMI-MANHATTAN)	6	THE LONESOME JUBILEE	JOHN COUGAR MELLENCAMP (MERCURY/PG)
FAITH	GEORGE MICHAEL (COLUMBIA)	7	NOTHING LIKE THE SUN	STING (A&M)
I'VE BEEN IN LOVE BEFORE	CUTTING CREW (VIRGIN)	8	PERMANENT VACATION	AEROSMITH (GEFFEN)
BREAKOUT	SWING OUT SISTER (MERCURY/PG)	9	HOLD YOUR FIRE	RUSH (MERCURY/PG)
IS THIS LOVE	WHITESNAKE (GEFFEN)	10	CREST OF A KNAVE	JETHRO TULL (CHRYSALIS)
WE'LL BE TOGETHER	STING (A&M)	11	A MAN OF COLOURS	ICEHOUSE (CHRYSALIS)
I WON'T FORGET YOU	POISON (ENIGMA/CAPITOL)	12	KICK	INXS (ATLANTIC)
SHAKE YOUR LOVE	DEBBIE GIBSON (ATLANTIC)	13	DOCUMENT	R.E.M. (IRS/MCA)
SO EMOTIONAL	WHITNEY HOUSTON (ARISTA)	14	HYSTERIA	DEF LEPPARD (MERCURY/PG)
HOURGLASS	SQUEEZE (A&M)	15	YO YO	BOURGEOIS TAGG (ISLAND)
LITTLE LIES	FLEETWOOD MAC (WARNER BROS)	16	OUTSIDE LOOKING IN	BODEANS (SLASH/REPRISE)
THE ONE I LOVE	R.E.M. (IRS/MCA)	17	CHRONICLES	STEVE WINWOOD (ISLAND/WARNER BROS)
DON'T YOU WANT ME	JODY WATLEY (MCA)	18	PRIMITIVE COOL	MICK JAGGER (COLUMBIA)
VALERIE	STEVE WINWOOD (ISLAND/WARNER BROS)	19	UNCHAIN MY HEART	JOE COCKER (CAPITOL)
CATCH ME I'M FALLING	PRETTY POISON (VIRGIN)	20	EYE OF THE HURRICANE	ALARM (IRS/MCA)

WEEK ENDING NOVEMBER 21 1987

UK

SINGLES		ALBUMS
CHINA IN YOUR HAND T'PAU (SIREN)	1	BRIDGE OF SPIES T'PAU (SIREN)
GOT MY MIND SET ON YOU GEORGE HARRISON (DARK HORSE/WEA)	2	ALL THE BEST! PAUL McCARTNEY (PARLOPHONE)
WHENEVER YOU NEED SOMEBODY RICK ASTLEY (RCA)	3	THE BEST OF UB40 VOL 1 UB40 (VIRGIN)
NEVER CAN SAY GOODBYE THE COMMUNARDS (LONDON)	4	TANGO IN THE NIGHT FLEETWOOD MAC (WARNER BROS)
MY BABY JUST CARES FOR ME NINA SIMONE (CHARLY)	5	FAITH GEORGE MICHAEL (EPIC)
(I'VE HAD) THE TIME OF MY LIFE BILL MEDLEY & JENNIFER WARNES (RCA)	6	THE SINGLES PRETENDERS (WEA)
YOU WIN AGAIN BEE GEES (WARNER BROS)	7	SAVAGE EURYTHMICS (RCA)
JACK MIX IV MIRAGE (DEBUT/PASSION)	8	BEST SHOTS PAT BENATAR (CHRYSALIS)
SO EMOTIONAL WHITNEY HOUSTON (ARISTA)	9	FROM MOTOWN WITH LOVE VARIOUS (K-TEL)
BARCELONA F. MERCURY & M. CABALLE (POLYDOR)	10	HOLD YOUR FIRE RUSH (VERTIGO/PHONOGRAM)
HERE I GO AGAIN WHITESNAKE (EMI)	11	CLOUD NINE GEORGE HARRISON (DARK HORSE/WEA)
FAITH GEORGE MICHAEL (EPIC)	12	SIMPLY SHADOWS THE SHADOWS (POLYDOR)
LOVE IN THE FIRST DEGREE BANANARAMA (LONDON)	13	RUNNING IN THE FAMILY LEVEL 42 (POLYDOR)
CRITICIZE ALEXANDER O'NEAL (TABU)	14	E.S.P. BEE GEES (WARNER BROS)
LITTLE LIES FLEETWOOD MAC (WARNER BROS)	15	BAD MICHAEL JACKSON (EPIC)
PAID IN FULL ERIC B. & RAKIM (4TH & B'WAY/ISLAND)	16	ACTUALLY PET SHOP BOYS (PARLOPHONE)
DINNER WITH GERSHWIN DONNA SUMMER (WARNER BROS)	17	REFLECTIONS FOSTER & ALLEN (STYLUS)
SOME GUYS HAVE ALL THE LUCK MAXI PRIEST (10/VIRGIN)	18	HIT FACTORY VARIOUS (STYLUS)
MONY MONY BILLY IDOL (CHRYSALIS)	19	LOVE SONGS MICHAEL JACKSON & DIANA ROSS (TELSTAR)
SHO' YOU RIGHT BARRY WHITE (BREAKOUT/A&M)	20	THE CREAM OF ERIC CLAPTON ERIC CLAPTON (POLYDOR)

US

SINGLES		ALBUMS
(I'VE HAD) THE TIME OF MY LIFE BILL MEDLEY & JENNIFER WARNES (RCA)	1	CLOUD NINE GEORGE HARRISON (DARK HORSE)
HEAVEN IS A PLACE ON EARTH BELINDA CARLISLE (MCA)	2	TUNNEL OF LOVE BRUCE SPRINGSTEEN (COLUMBIA)
FAITH GEORGE MICHAEL (COLUMBIA)	3	BIG GENERATOR YES (ATCO)
SHOULD'VE KNOWN BETTER RICHARD MARX (EMI-MANHATTAN)	4	A MOMENTARY LAPSE OF REASON PINK FLOYD (COLUMBIA)
MONY MONY BILLY IDOL (CHRYSALIS)	5	ROBBIE ROBERTSON ROBBIE ROBERTSON (GEFFEN)
IS THIS LOVE WHITESNAKE (GEFFEN)	6	THE LONESOME JUBILEE JOHN COUGAR MELLENCAMP (MERCURY/PG)
SHAKE YOUR LOVE DEBBIE GIBSON (ATLANTIC)	7	NOTHING LIKE THE SUN STING (A&M)
SO EMOTIONAL WHITNEY HOUSTON (ARISTA)	8	PERMANENT VACATION AEROSMITH (GEFFEN)
WE'LL BE TOGETHER STING (A&M)	9	KICK INXS (ATLANTIC)
I'VE BEEN IN LOVE BEFORE CUTTING CREW (VIRGIN)	10	CREST OF A KNAVE JETHRO TULL (CHRYSALIS)
I THINK WE'RE ALONE NOW TIFFANY (MCA)	11	A MAN OF COLOURS ICEHOUSE (CHRYSALIS)
DON'T YOU WANT ME JODY WATLEY (MCA)	12	HOLD YOUR FIRE RUSH (MERCURY/PG)
HOURGLASS SQUEEZE (A&M)	13	HYSTERIA DEF LEPPARD (MERCURY/PG)
VALERIE STEVE WINWOOD (ISLAND/WARNER BROS)	14	YO YO BOURGEOIS TAGG (ISLAND)
THE ONE I LOVE R.E.M. (IRS/MCA)	15	DOCUMENT R.E.M. (IRS/MCA)
CATCH ME I'M FALLING PRETTY POISON (VIRGIN)	16	OUTSIDE LOOKING IN BODEANS (SLASH/REPRISE)
BRILLIANT DISGUISE BRUCE SPRINGSTEEN (COLUMBIA)	17	EYE OF THE HURRICANE ALARM (IRS/MCA)
GOT MY MIND SET ON YOU GEORGE HARRISON (DARK HORSE)	18	CHRONICLES STEVE WINWOOD (ISLAND/WARNER BROS)
I WON'T FORGET YOU POISON (ENIGMA/CAPITOL)	19	UNCHAIN MY HEART JOE COCKER (CAPITOL)
BREAKOUT SWING OUT SISTER (MERCURY/PG)	20	ONE GOOD REASON PAUL CARRACK (CHRYSALIS)

WEEK ENDING NOVEMBER 28 1987

UK

SINGLES		ALBUMS
CHINA IN YOUR HAND T'PAU (SIREN)	1	WHENEVER YOU NEED SOMEBODY RICK ASTLEY (RCA)
GOT MY MIND SET ON YOU GEORGE HARRISON (DARK HORSE/WEA)	2	BRIDGE OF SPIES T'PAU (SIREN)
WHENEVER YOU NEED SOMEBODY RICK ASTLEY (RCA)	3	THE BEST OF UB40 VOL 1 UB40 (VIRGIN)
NEVER CAN SAY GOODBYE THE COMMUNARDS (LONDON)	4	ALL THE BEST! PAUL McCARTNEY (PARLOPHONE)
SO EMOTIONAL WHITNEY HOUSTON (ARISTA)	5	YOU CAN DANCE MADONNA (SIRE)
(I'VE HAD) THE TIME OF MY LIFE BILL MEDLEY & JENNIFER WARNES (RCA)	6	TANGO IN THE NIGHT FLEETWOOD MAC (WARNER BROS)
MY BABY JUST CARES FOR ME NINA SIMONE (CHARLY)	7	THE SINGLES PRETENDERS (WEA)
CRITICIZE ALEXANDER O'NEAL (TABU)	8	FAITH GEORGE MICHAEL (EPIC)
HERE I GO AGAIN WHITESNAKE (EMI)	9	FLOODLAND THE SISTERS OF MERCY (MERCIFUL RELEASE)
LETTER FROM AMERICA THE PROCLAIMERS (CHRYSALIS)	10	BEST SHOTS PAT BENATAR (CHRYSALIS)
JACK MIX IV MIRAGE (DEBUT/PASSION)	11	FROM MOTOWN WITH LOVE VARIOUS (K-TEL)
SOME GUYS HAVE ALL THE LUCK MAXI PRIEST (10/VIRGIN)	12	THE GREATEST HITS OF 1987 VARIOUS (TELSTAR)
DINNER WITH GERSHWIN DONNA SUMMER (WARNER BROS)	13	SAVAGE EURYTHMICS (RCA)
SHO' YOU RIGHT BARRY WHITE (BREAKOUT/A&M)	14	BAD MICHAEL JACKSON (EPIC)
YOU WIN AGAIN BEE GEES (WARNER BROS)	15	LOVE SONGS MICHAEL JACKSON & DIANA ROSS (TELSTAR)
LOVE IN THE FIRST DEGREE BANANARAMA (LONDON)	16	ACTUALLY PET SHOP BOYS (PARLOPHONE)
BARCELONA F. MERCURY & M. CABALLE (POLYDOR)	17	SIMPLY SHADOWS THE SHADOWS (POLYDOR)
TO BE REBORN BOY GEORGE (VIRGIN)	18	WHITNEY WHITNEY HOUSTON (ARISTA)
BUILD THE HOUSEMARTINS (GO! DISCS)	19	CLOUD NINE GEORGE HARRISON (DARK HORSE/WEA)
PAID IN FULL ERIC B & RAKIM (4TH & B'WAY/ISLAND)	20	THE CREAM OF ERIC CLAPTON ERIC CLAPTON (POLYDOR)

US

SINGLES		ALBUMS
HEAVEN IS A PLACE ON EARTH BELINDA CARLISLE (MCA)	1	CLOUD NINE GEORGE HARRISON (DARK HORSE)
FAITH GEORGE MICHAEL (COLUMBIA)	2	TUNNEL OF LOVE BRUCE SPRINGSTEEN (COLUMBIA)
(I'VE HAD) THE TIME OF MY LIFE BILL MEDLEY & JENNIFER WARNES (RCA)	3	BIG GENERATOR YES (ATCO)
SHOULD'VE KNOWN BETTER RICHARD MARX (EMI-MANHATTAN)	4	A MOMENTARY LAPSE OF REASON PINK FLOYD (COLUMBIA)
IS THIS LOVE WHITESNAKE (GEFFEN)	5	ROBBIE ROBERTSON ROBBIE ROBERTSON (GEFFEN)
SHAKE YOUR LOVE DEBBIE GIBSON (ATLANTIC)	6	THE LONESOME JUBILEE JOHN COUGAR MELLENCAMP (MERCURY/PG)
SO EMOTIONAL WHITNEY HOUSTON (ARISTA)	7	NOTHING LIKE THE SUN STING (A&M)
WE'LL BE TOGETHER STING (A&M)	8	KICK INXS (ATLANTIC)
DON'T YOU WANT ME JODY WATLEY (MCA)	9	CREST OF A KNAVE JETHRO TULL (CHRYSALIS)
VALERIE STEVE WINWOOD (ISLAND/WARNER BROS)	10	PERMANENT VACATION AEROSMITH (GEFFEN)
GOT MY MIND SET ON YOU GEORGE HARRISON (DARK HORSE)	11	HYSTERIA DEF LEPPARD (MERCURY/PG)
CATCH ME I'M FALLING PRETTY POISON (VIRGIN)	12	YO YO BOURGEOIS TAGG (ISLAND)
THE ONE I LOVE R.E.M. (IRS/MCA)	13	A MAN OF COLOURS ICEHOUSE (CHRYSALIS)
MONY MONY BILLY IDOL (CHRYSALIS)	14	EYE OF THE HURRICANE ALARM (IRS/MCA)
HOURGLASS SQUEEZE (A&M)	15	DOCUMENT R.E.M. (IRS/MCA)
DUDE (LOOKS LIKE A LADY) AEROSMITH (GEFFEN)	16	UNCHAIN MY HEART JOE COCKER (CAPITOL)
I DO YOU JETS (MCA)	17	ONE GOOD REASON PAUL CARRACK (CHRYSALIS)
THAT'S WHAT LOVE IS ALL ABOUT MICHAEL BOLTON (COLUMBIA)	18	HOLD YOUR FIRE RUSH (MERCURY/PG)
TELL IT TO MY HEART TAYLOR DAYNE (ARISTA)	19	WHITESNAKE WHITESNAKE (GEFFEN)
CHERRY BOMB JOHN COUGAR MELLENCAMP (MERCURY/PG)	20	OUTSIDE LOOKING IN BODEANS (SLASH/REPRISE)

WEEK ENDING DECEMBER 5 1987

UK

Pos	Singles	Artist (Label)	Albums	Artist (Label)
1	CHINA IN YOUR HAND	T'PAU (SIREN)	NOW THAT'S WHAT I CALL MUSIC 10	VARIOUS (EMI/VIRGIN/POLYGRAM)
2	GOT MY MIND SET ON YOU	GEORGE HARRISON (DARK HORSE/WEA)	WHENEVER YOU NEED SOMEBODY	RICK ASTLEY (RCA)
3	LETTER FROM AMERICA	THE PROCLAIMERS (CHRYSALIS)	HITS 7	VARIOUS (CBS/WEA/ARISTA)
4	CRITICIZE	ALEXANDER O'NEAL (TABU)	BRIDGE OF SPIES	T'PAU (SIREN)
5	NEVER CAN SAY GOODBYE	THE COMMUNARDS (LONDON)	ALL THE BEST!	PAUL McCARTNEY (PARLOPHONE)
6	SO EMOTIONAL	WHITNEY HOUSTON (ARISTA)	THE BEST OF UB40 VOL 1	UB40 (VIRGIN)
7	WHAT DO YOU WANT TO MAKE THOSE . . .	SHAKIN' STEVENS (EPIC)	THE SINGLES	PRETENDERS (WEA)
8	WHENEVER YOU NEED SOMEBODY	RICK ASTLEY (RCA)	YOU CAN DANCE	MADONNA (SIRE)
9	(I'VE HAD) THE TIME OF MY LIFE	BILL MEDLEY & JENNIFER WARNES (RCA)	TANGO IN THE NIGHT	FLEETWOOD MAC (WARNER BROS)
10	HERE I GO AGAIN	WHITESNAKE (EMI)	FAITH	GEORGE MICHAEL (EPIC)
11	MY BABY JUST CARES FOR ME	NINA SIMONE (CHARLY)	SIMPLY SHADOWS	THE SHADOWS (POLYDOR)
12	SOME GUYS HAVE ALL THE LUCK	MAXI PRIEST (10/VIRGIN)	BAD	MICHAEL JACKSON (EPIC)
13	TO BE REBORN	BOY GEORGE (VIRGIN)	FROM MOTOWN WITH LOVE	VARIOUS (K-TEL)
14	ONCE UPON A LONG AGO	PAUL McCARTNEY (PARLOPHONE)	WHITNEY	WHITNEY HOUSTON (ARISTA)
15	BUILD	THE HOUSEMARTINS (GO! DISCS)	LOVE SONGS	MICHAEL JACKSON & DIANA ROSS (TELSTAR)
16	THE WAY YOU MAKE ME FEEL	MICHAEL JACKSON (EPIC)	BEST SHOTS	PAT BENATAR (CHRYSALIS)
17	SHO' YOU RIGHT	BARRY WHITE (BREAKOUT/A&M)	THE GREATEST HITS OF 1987	VARIOUS (TELSTAR)
18	WHO FOUND WHO	JELLYBEAN/ELISA FIORILLO (CHRYSALIS)	ACTUALLY	PET SHOP BOYS (PARLOPHONE)
19	JACK MIX IV	MIRAGE (DEBUT/PASSION)	ALWAYS GUARANTEED	CLIFF RICHARD (EMI)
20	DINNER WITH GERSHWIN	DONNA SUMMER (WARNER BROS)	SONGS FROM STAGE AND SCREEN	MICHAEL CRAWFORD/LSO (TELSTAR)

US

Pos	Singles	Artist (Label)	Albums	Artist (Label)
1	FAITH	GEORGE MICHAEL (COLUMBIA)	CLOUD NINE	GEORGE HARRISON (DARK HORSE)
2	HEAVEN IS A PLACE ON EARTH	BELINDA CARLISLE (MCA)	TUNNEL OF LOVE	BRUCE SPRINGSTEEN (COLUMBIA)
3	IS THIS LOVE	WHITESNAKE (GEFFEN)	BIG GENERATOR	YES (ATCO)
4	SO EMOTIONAL	WHITNEY HOUSTON (ARISTA)	ROBBIE ROBERTSON	ROBBIE ROBERTSON (GEFFEN)
5	SHAKE YOUR LOVE	DEBBIE GIBSON (ATLANTIC)	A MOMENTARY LAPSE OF REASON	PINK FLOYD (COLUMBIA)
6	DON'T YOU WANT ME	JODY WATLEY (MCA)	THE LONESOME JUBILEE	JOHN COUGAR MELLENCAMP (MERCURY/PG)
7	GOT MY MIND SET ON YOU	GEORGE HARRISON (DARK HORSE)	NOTHING LIKE THE SUN	STING (A&M)
8	WE'LL BE TOGETHER	STING (A&M)	KICK	INXS (ATLANTIC)
9	VALERIE	STEVE WINWOOD (ISLAND/WARNER BROS)	CREST OF A KNAVE	JETHRO TULL (CHRYSALIS)
10	CATCH ME I'M FALLING	PRETTY POISON (VIRGIN)	PERMANENT VACATION	AEROSMITH (GEFFEN)
11	SHOULD'VE KNOWN BETTER	RICHARD MARX (EMI-MANHATTAN)	HYSTERIA	DEF LEPPARD (MERCURY/PG)
12	(I'VE HAD) THE TIME OF MY LIFE	BILL MEDLEY & JENNIFER WARNES (RCA)	YO YO	BOURGEOIS TAGG (ISLAND)
13	THE WAY YOU MAKE ME FEEL	MICHAEL JACKSON (EPIC)	EYE OF THE HURRICANE	ALARM (IRS/MCA)
14	DUDE (LOOKS LIKE A LADY)	AEROSMITH (GEFFEN)	ONE GOOD REASON	PAUL CARRACK (CHRYSALIS)
15	NEED YOU TONIGHT	INXS (ATLANTIC)	DOCUMENT	R.E.M. (IRS/MCA)
16	TELL IT TO MY HEART	TAYLOR DAYNE (ARISTA)	UNCHAIN MY HEART	JOE COCKER (CAPITOL)
17	CHERRY BOMB	JOHN COUGAR MELLENCAMP (MERCURY/PG)	WHITESNAKE	WHITESNAKE (GEFFEN)
18	I DO YOU	JETS (MCA)	HOLD YOUR FIRE	RUSH (MERCURY/PG)
19	CANDLE IN THE WIND	ELTON JOHN (MCA)	A MAN OF COLOURS	ICEHOUSE (CHRYSALIS)
20	THE ONE I LOVE	R.E.M. (IRS/MCA)	THE JOSHUA TREE	U2 (ISLAND)

WEEK ENDING DECEMBER 12 1987

UK

Pos	Singles	Artist (Label)	Albums	Artist (Label)
1	CHINA IN YOUR HAND	T'PAU (SIREN)	NOW THAT'S WHAT I CALL MUSIC 10	VARIOUS (EMI/VIRGIN/POLYGRAM)
2	WHEN I FALL IN LOVE	RICK ASTLEY (RCA)	HITS 7	VARIOUS (CBS/WEA/ARISTA)
3	THE WAY YOU MAKE ME FEEL	MICHAEL JACKSON (EPIC)	WHENEVER YOU NEED SOMEBODY	RICK ASTLEY (RCA)
4	ALWAYS ON MY MIND	PET SHOP BOYS (PARLOPHONE)	ALL THE BEST!	PAUL McCARTNEY (PARLOPHONE)
5	WHAT DO YOU WANT TO MAKE THOSE . . .	SHAKIN' STEVENS (EPIC)	BRIDGE OF SPIES	T'PAU (SIREN)
6	LETTER FROM AMERICA	THE PROCLAIMERS (CHRYSALIS)	BAD	MICHAEL JACKSON (EPIC)
7	GOT MY MIND SET ON YOU	GEORGE HARRISON (DARK HORSE/WEA)	THE SINGLES	PRETENDERS (WEA)
8	CRITICIZE	ALEXANDER O'NEAL (TABU)	THE BEST OF UB40 VOL 1	UB40 (VIRGIN)
9	LOVE LETTERS	ALISON MOYET (CBS)	TANGO IN THE NIGHT	FLEETWOOD MAC (WARNER BROS)
10	ONCE UPON A LONG AGO	PAUL McCARTNEY (PARLOPHONE)	FAITH	GEORGE MICHAEL (EPIC)
11	WHO FOUND WHO	JELLYBEAN/ELISA FIORILLO (CHRYSALIS)	YOU CAN DANCE	MADONNA (SIRE)
12	SO EMOTIONAL	WHITNEY HOUSTON (ARISTA)	SIMPLY SHADOWS	THE SHADOWS (POLYDOR)
13	ROCKIN' AROUND THE CHRISTMAS TREE	KIM WILDE & MEL SMITH (10/VIRGIN)	SONGS FROM STAGE AND SCREEN	MICHAEL CRAWFORD/LSO (TELSTAR)
14	NEVER CAN SAY GOODBYE	THE COMMUNARDS (LONDON)	WHITNEY	WHITNEY HOUSTON (ARISTA)
15	THE LOOK OF LOVE	MADONNA (SIRE)	ALWAYS GUARANTEED	CLIFF RICHARD (EMI)
16	SOME GUYS HAVE ALL THE LUCK	MAXI PRIEST (10/VIRGIN)	LOVE SONGS	MICHAEL JACKSON & DIANA ROSS (TELSTAR)
17	BUILD	THE HOUSEMARTINS (GO! DISCS)	ACTUALLY	PET SHOP BOYS (PARLOPHONE)
18	TO BE REBORN	BOY GEORGE (VIRGIN)	FROM MOTOWN WITH LOVE	VARIOUS (K-TEL)
19	FAIRYTALE OF NEW YORK	POGUES/KIRSTY MACCALL (STIFF)	SONGS OF LOVE	RICHARD CLAYDERMAN (DECCA/LONDON)
20	I'M THE MAN	ANTHRAX (ISLAND)	BEST SHOTS	PAT BENATAR (CHRYSALIS)

US

Pos	Singles	Artist (Label)	Albums	Artist (Label)
1	FAITH	GEORGE MICHAEL (COLUMBIA)	CLOUD NINE	GEORGE HARRISON (DARK HORSE)
2	IS THIS LOVE	WHITESNAKE (GEFFEN)	ROBBIE ROBERTSON	ROBBIE ROBERTSON (GEFFEN)
3	SO EMOTIONAL	WHITNEY HOUSTON (ARISTA)	TUNNEL OF LOVE	BRUCE SPRINGSTEEN (COLUMBIA)
4	GOT MY MIND SET ON YOU	GEORGE HARRISON (DARK HORSE)	INSIDE INFORMATION	FOREIGNER (ATLANTIC)
5	SHAKE YOUR LOVE	DEBBIE GIBSON (ATLANTIC)	BIG GENERATOR	YES (ATCO)
6	DON'T YOU WANT ME	JODY WATLEY (MCA)	A MOMENTARY LAPSE OF REASON	PINK FLOYD (COLUMBIA)
7	VALERIE	STEVE WINWOOD (ISLAND/WARNER BROS)	THE LONESOME JUBILEE	JOHN COUGAR MELLENCAMP (MERCURY/PG)
8	HEAVEN IS A PLACE ON EARTH	BELINDA CARLISLE (MCA)	KICK	INXS (ATLANTIC)
9	CATCH ME I'M FALLING	PRETTY POISON (VIRGIN)	CREST OF A KNAVE	JETHRO TULL (CHRYSALIS)
10	THE WAY YOU MAKE ME FEEL	MICHAEL JACKSON (EPIC)	NOTHING LIKE THE SUN	STING (A&M)
11	NEED YOU TONIGHT	INXS (ATLANTIC)	HYSTERIA	DEF LEPPARD (MERCURY/PG)
12	TELL IT TO MY HEART	TAYLOR DAYNE (ARISTA)	PERMANENT VACATION	AEROSMITH (GEFFEN)
13	DUDE (LOOKS LIKE A LADY)	AEROSMITH (GEFFEN)	EYE OF THE HURRICANE	ALARM (IRS/MCA)
14	CHERRY BOMB	JOHN COUGAR MELLENCAMP (MERCURY/PG)	ONE GOOD REASON	PAUL CARRACK (CHRYSALIS)
15	CANDLE IN THE WIND	ELTON JOHN (MCA)	YO YO	BOURGEOIS TAGG (ISLAND)
16	WE'LL BE TOGETHER	STING (A&M)	DOCUMENT	R.E.M. (IRS/MCA)
17	SHOULD'VE KNOWN BETTER	RICHARD MARX (EMI-MANHATTAN)	THE JOSHUA TREE	U2 (ISLAND)
18	HAZY SHADE OF WINTER	BANGLES (DEF JAM/COLUMBIA)	HOLD YOUR FIRE	RUSH (MERCURY/PG)
19	THERE'S THE GIRL	HEART (CAPITOL)	WHITESNAKE	WHITESNAKE (GEFFEN)
20	COULD'VE BEEN	TIFFANY (MCA)	HEART	BAD ANIMALS (CAPITOL)

WEEK ENDING DECEMBER 19 1987

SINGLES UK ALBUMS

Singles	Pos	Albums
ALWAYS ON MY MIND PET SHOP BOYS (PARLOPHONE)	1	NOW THAT'S WHAT I CALL MUSIC 10 VARIOUS (EMI/VIRGIN/POLYGRAM)
WHEN I FALL IN LOVE RICK ASTLEY (RCA)	2	HITS 7 VARIOUS (CBS/WEA/ARISTA)
THE WAY YOU MAKE ME FEEL MICHAEL JACKSON (EPIC)	3	WHENEVER YOU NEED SOMEBODY RICK ASTLEY (RCA)
LOVE LETTERS ALISON MOYET (CBS)	4	BAD MICHAEL JACKSON (EPIC)
CHINA IN YOUR HAND T'PAU (SIREN)	5	ALL THE BEST! PAUL McCARTNEY (PARLOPHONE)
ROCKIN' AROUND THE CHRISTMAS TREE KIM WILDE & MEL SMITH (10/VIRGIN)	6	BRIDGE OF SPIES T'PAU (SIREN)
WHAT DO YOU WANT TO MAKE THOSE . . . SHAKIN' STEVENS (EPIC)	7	THE SINGLES PRETENDERS (WEA)
FAIRYTALE OF NEW YORK POGUES/KIRSTY MACCALL (STIFF)	8	TANGO IN THE NIGHT FLEETWOOD MAC (WARNER BROS)
THE LOOK OF LOVE MADONNA (SIRE)	9	ALWAYS GUARANTEED CLIFF RICHARD (EMI)
WHO FOUND WHO JELLYBEAN/ELISA FIORILLO (CHRYSALIS)	10	THE BEST OF UB40 VOL 1 UB40 (VIRGIN)
CRITICIZE ALEXANDER O'NEAL (TABU)	11	RAINDANCING ALISON MOYET (CBS)
LETTER FROM AMERICA THE PROCLAIMERS (CHRYSALIS)	12	SONGS FROM STAGE AND SCREEN MICHAEL CRAWFORD/LSO (TELSTAR)
GOT MY MIND SET ON YOU GEORGE HARRISON (DARK HORSE/WEA)	13	FAITH GEORGE MICHAEL (EPIC)
ONCE UPON A LONG AGO PAUL McCARTNEY (PARLOPHONE)	14	ACTUALLY PET SHOP BOYS (PARLOPHONE)
TURN BACK THE CLOCK JOHNNY HATES JAZZ (VIRGIN)	15	MEMORIES ELAINE PAIGE (TELSTAR)
SO EMOTIONAL WHITNEY HOUSTON (ARISTA)	16	NOW THE CHRISTMAS ALBUM VARIOUS (EMI/VIRGIN)
EV'RY TIME WE SAY GOODBYE SIMPLY RED (WEA)	17	LOVE SONGS MICHAEL JACKSON & DIANA ROSS (TELSTAR)
NEVER CAN SAY GOODBYE THE COMMUNARDS (LONDON)	18	SIMPLY SHADOWS THE SHADOWS (POLYDOR)
HEAVEN IS A PLACE ON EARTH BELINDA CARLISLE (VIRGIN)	19	YOU CAN DANCE MADONNA (SIRE)
WHEN I FALL IN LOVE NAT KING COLE (CAPITOL)	20	WHITNEY WHITNEY HOUSTON (ARISTA)

SINGLES US ALBUMS

Singles	Pos	Albums
FAITH GEORGE MICHAEL (COLUMBIA)	1	INSIDE INFORMATION FOREIGNER (ATLANTIC)
IS THIS LOVE WHITESNAKE (GEFFEN)	2	CLOUD NINE GEORGE HARRISON (DARK HORSE)
SO EMOTIONAL WHITNEY HOUSTON (ARISTA)	3	TUNNEL OF LOVE BRUCE SPRINGSTEEN (COLUMBIA)
GOT MY MIND SET ON YOU GEORGE HARRISON (DARK HORSE)	4	BIG GENERATOR YES (ATCO)
THE WAY YOU MAKE ME FEEL MICHAEL JACKSON (EPIC)	5	ROBBIE ROBERTSON ROBBIE ROBERTSON (GEFFEN)
SHAKE YOUR LOVE DEBBIE GIBSON (ATLANTIC)	6	A MOMENTARY LAPSE OF REASON PINK FLOYD (COLUMBIA)
DON'T YOU WANT ME JODY WATLEY (MCA)	7	THE LONESOME JUBILEE JOHN COUGAR MELLENCAMP (MERCURY/PG)
NEED YOU TONIGHT INXS (ATLANTIC)	8	HYSTERIA DEF LEPPARD (MERCURY/PG)
VALERIE STEVE WINWOOD (ISLAND/WARNER BROS)	9	KICK INXS (ATLANTIC)
TELL IT TO MY HEART TAYLOR DAYNE (ARISTA)	10	ONE GOOD REASON PAUL CARRACK (CHRYSALIS)
CATCH ME I'M FALLING PRETTY POISON (VIRGIN)	11	NOTHING LIKE THE SUN STING (A&M)
CANDLE IN THE WIND ELTON JOHN (MCA)	12	PERMANENT VACATION AEROSMITH (GEFFEN)
CHERRY BOMB JOHN COUGAR MELLENCAMP (MERCURY/PG)	13	EYE OF THE HURRICANE ALARM (IRS/MCA)
HAZY SHADE OF WINTER BANGLES (DEF JAM/COLUMBIA)	14	THE JOSHUA TREE U2 (ISLAND)
COULD'VE BEEN TIFFANY (MCA)	15	CREST OF A KNAVE JETHRO TULL (CHRYSALIS)
THERE'S THE GIRL HEART (CAPITOL)	16	DOCUMENT R.E.M. (IRS/MCA)
SEASONS CHANGE EXPOSE (ARISTA)	17	HOLD YOUR FIRE RUSH (MERCURY/PG)
I COULD NEVER TAKE THE PLACE OF YOUR MAN PRINCE (PAISLEY PARK/WARNER BROS)	18	HEART BAD ANIMALS (CAPITOL)
DUDE (LOOKS LIKE A LADY) AEROSMITH (GEFFEN)	19	WHITESNAKE WHITESNAKE (GEFFEN)
I WANT TO BE YOUR MAN ROGER (REPRISE)	20	VERY SPECIAL CHRISTMAS COMPILATION (A&M)

WEEK ENDING DECEMBER 26 1987

SINGLES UK ALBUMS

Singles	Pos	Albums
ALWAYS ON MY MIND PET SHOP BOYS (PARLOPHONE)	1	NOW THAT'S WHAT I CALL MUSIC 10 VARIOUS (EMI/VIRGIN/POLYGRAM)
FAIRYTALE OF NEW YORK POGUES/KIRSTY MACCALL (STIFF)	2	BAD MICHAEL JACKSON (EPIC)
ROCKIN' AROUND THE CHRISTMAS TREE KIM WILDE & MEL SMITH (10/VIRGIN)	3	WHENEVER YOU NEED SOMEBODY RICK ASTLEY (RCA)
WHEN I FALL IN LOVE RICK ASTLEY (RCA)	4	HITS 7 VARIOUS (CBS/WEA/ARISTA)
LOVE LETTERS ALISON MOYET (CBS)	5	BRIDGE OF SPIES T'PAU (SIREN)
THE WAY YOU MAKE ME FEEL MICHAEL JACKSON (EPIC)	6	ALL THE BEST! PAUL McCARTNEY (PARLOPHONE)
WHEN I FALL IN LOVE NAT KING COLE (CAPITOL)	7	RAINDANCING ALISON MOYET (CBS)
HEAVEN IS A PLACE ON EARTH BELINDA CARLISLE (VIRGIN)	8	TANGO IN THE NIGHT FLEETWOOD MAC (WARNER BROS)
CHINA IN YOUR HAND T'PAU (SIREN)	9	ACTUALLY PET SHOP BOYS (PARLOPHONE)
WHAT DO YOU WANT TO MAKE THOSE . . . SHAKIN' STEVENS (EPIC)	10	THE SINGLES PRETENDERS (WEA)
EV'RY TIME WE SAY GOODBYE SIMPLY RED (WEA)	11	ALWAYS GUARANTEED CLIFF RICHARD (EMI)
WHO FOUND WHO JELLYBEAN/ELISA FIORILLO (CHRYSALIS)	12	SONGS FROM STAGE AND SCREEN MICHAEL CRAWFORD/LSO (TELSTAR)
ANGEL EYES WET WET WET (PRECIOUS/PHONOGRAM)	13	LOVE SONGS MICHAEL JACKSON & DIANA ROSS (TELSTAR)
THE LOOK OF LOVE MADONNA (SIRE)	14	MEMORIES ELAINE PAIGE (TELSTAR)
TURN BACK THE CLOCK JOHNNY HATES JAZZ (VIRGIN)	15	THE BEST OF UB40 VOL 1 UB40 (VIRGIN)
LETTER FROM AMERICA THE PROCLAIMERS (CHRYSALIS)	16	WHITNEY WHITNEY HOUSTON (ARISTA)
CRITICIZE ALEXANDER O'NEAL (TABU)	17	FAITH GEORGE MICHAEL (EPIC)
GOT MY MIND SET ON YOU GEORGE HARRISON (DARK HORSE/WEA)	18	YOU CAN DANCE MADONNA (SIRE)
JINGO JELLYBEAN (CHRYSALIS)	19	THE CREAM OF ERIC CLAPTON ERIC CLAPTON/CREAM (POLYDOR)
TOUCHED BY THE HAND OF GOD NEW ORDER (FACTORY)	20	NOW THE CHRISTMAS ALBUM VARIOUS (EMI/VIRGIN)

SINGLES US ALBUMS

NO US CHARTS PUBLISHED

WEEK ENDING JANUARY 2 1988

UK — SINGLES / ALBUMS

Singles	Artist (Label)	Pos	Albums	Artist (Label)
ALWAYS ON MY MIND	PET SHOP BOYS (PARLOPHONE)	1	NOW THAT'S WHAT I CALL MUSIC 10	VARIOUS (EMI/VIRGIN/POLYGRAM)
FAIRYTALE OF NEW YORK	POGUES/KIRSTY MACCALL (STIFF)	2	BAD	MICHAEL JACKSON (EPIC)
ROCKIN' AROUND THE CHRISTMAS TREE	KIM WILDE & MEL SMITH (10/VIRGIN)	3	WHENEVER YOU NEED SOMEBODY	RICK ASTLEY (RCA)
WHEN I FALL IN LOVE	NAT KING COLE (CAPITOL)	4	HITS 7	VARIOUS (CBS/WEA/ARISTA)
HEAVEN IS A PLACE ON EARTH	BELINDA CARLISLE (VIRGIN)	5	BRIDGE OF SPIES	T'PAU (SIREN)
LOVE LETTERS	ALISON MOYET (CBS)	6	RAINDANCING	ALISON MOYET (CBS)
WHEN I FALL IN LOVE	RICK ASTLEY (RCA)	7	ALL THE BEST!	PAUL McCARTNEY (PARLOPHONE)
THE WAY YOU MAKE ME FEEL	MICHAEL JACKSON (EPIC)	8	ACTUALLY	PET SHOP BOYS (PARLOPHONE)
CHINA IN YOUR HAND	T'PAU (SIREN)	9	TANGO IN THE NIGHT	FLEETWOOD MAC (WARNER BROS)
ANGEL EYES	WET WET WET (PRECIOUS/PHONOGRAM)	10	THE SINGLES	PRETENDERS (WEA)
EV'RYTIME WE SAY GOODBYE	SIMPLY RED (WEA)	11	WHITNEY	WHITNEY HOUSTON (ARISTA)
WHAT DO YOU WANT TO MAKE THOSE . . .	SHAKIN' STEVENS (EPIC)	12	LOVE SONGS	MICHAEL JACKSON & DIANA ROSS (TELSTAR)
TURN BACK THE CLOCK	JOHNNY HATES JAZZ (VIRGIN)	13	POPPED IN SOULED OUT	WET WET WET (PRECIOUS/PHONOGRAM)
WHO FOUND WHO	JELLYBEAN/ELISA FIORILLO (CHRYSALIS)	14	THE BEST OF UB40 VOL 1	UB40 (VIRGIN)
LETTER FROM AMERICA	THE PROCLAIMERS (CHRYSALIS)	15	FAITH	GEORGE MICHAEL (EPIC)
THE LOOK OF LOVE	MADONNA (SIRE)	16	MEMORIES	ELAINE PAIGE (TELSTAR)
CRITICIZE	ALEXANDER O'NEAL (TABU)	17	ALWAYS GUARANTEED	CLIFF RICHARD (EMI)
GOT MY MIND SET ON YOU	GEORGE HARRISON (DARK HORSE/WEA)	18	YOU CAN DANCE	MADONNA (SIRE)
JINGO	JELLYBEAN (CHRYSALIS)	19	THE CREAM OF ERIC CLAPTON	ERIC CLAPTON/CREAM (POLYDOR)
HOUSE ARREST	KRUSH (CLUB/PHONOGRAM)	20	FROM MOTOWN WITH LOVE	VARIOUS (K-TEL)

US — SINGLES / ALBUMS

Singles	Artist (Label)	Pos	Albums	Artist (Label)
SO EMOTIONAL	WHITNEY HOUSTON (ARISTA)	1	INSIDE INFORMATION	FOREIGNER (ATLANTIC)
GOT MY MIND SET ON YOU	GEORGE HARRISON (DARK HORSE)	2	CLOUD NINE	GEORGE HARRISON (DARK HORSE)
FAITH	GEORGE MICHAEL (COLUMBIA)	3	TUNNEL OF LOVE	BRUCE SPRINGSTEEN (COLUMBIA)
THE WAY YOU MAKE ME FEEL	MICHAEL JACKSON (EPIC)	4	BIG GENERATOR	YES (ATCO)
IS THIS LOVE	WHITESNAKE (GEFFEN)	5	ROBBIE ROBERTSON	ROBBIE ROBERTSON (GEFFEN)
NEED YOU TONIGHT	INXS (ATLANTIC)	6	A MOMENTARY LAPSE OF REASON	PINK FLOYD (COLUMBIA)
COULD'VE BEEN	TIFFANY (MCA)	7	THE LONESOME JUBILEE	JOHN COUGAR MELLENCAMP (MERCURY/PG)
HAZY SHADE OF WINTER	BANGLES (DEF JAM/COLUMBIA)	8	HYSTERIA	DEF LEPPARD (MERCURY/PG)
TELL IT TO MY HEART	TAYLOR DAYNE (ARISTA)	9	ONE GOOD REASON	PAUL CARRACK (CHRYSALIS)
CANDLE IN THE WIND	ELTON JOHN (MCA)	10	KICK	INXS (ATLANTIC)
SHAKE YOUR LOVE	DEBBIE GIBSON (ATLANTIC)	11	NOTHING LIKE THE SUN	STING (A&M)
SEASONS CHANGE	EXPOSE (ARISTA)	12	THE JOSHUA TREE	U2 (ISLAND)
DON'T YOU WANT ME	JODY WATLEY (MCA)	13	PERMANENT VACATION	AEROSMITH (GEFFEN)
I COULD NEVER TAKE THE PLACE OF YOUR MAN	PRINCE (PAISLEY PARK/WARNER BROS)	14	EYE OF THE HURRICANE	ALARM (IRS/MCA)
THERE'S THE GIRL	HEART (CAPITOL)	15	CREST OF A KNAVE	JETHRO TULL (CHRYSALIS)
I WANT TO BE YOUR MAN	ROGER (REPRISE)	16	DOCUMENT	R.E.M. (IRS/MCA)
CHERRY BOMB	JOHN COUGAR MELLENCAMP (MERCURY/PG)	17	HOLD YOUR FIRE	RUSH (MERCURY/PG)
HUNGRY EYES	ERIC CARMEN (RCA)	18	HEART	BAD ANIMALS (CAPITOL)
CRAZY	ICEHOUSE (CHRYSALIS)	19	WHITESNAKE	WHITESNAKE (GEFFEN)
CATCH ME I'M FALLING	PRETTY POISON (VIRGIN)	20	BACK FOR THE ATTACK	DOKKEN (ELEKTRA)

WEEK ENDING JANUARY 9 1988

UK — SINGLES / ALBUMS

Singles	Artist (Label)	Pos	Albums	Artist (Label)
ALWAYS ON MY MIND	PET SHOP BOYS (PARLOPHONE)	1	NOW THAT'S WHAT I CALL MUSIC 10	VARIOUS (EMI/VIRGIN/POLYGRAM)
HEAVEN IS A PLACE ON EARTH	BELINDA CARLISLE (VIRGIN)	2	WHENEVER YOU NEED SOMEBODY	RICK ASTLEY (RCA)
THE WAY YOU MAKE ME FEEL	MICHAEL JACKSON (EPIC)	3	BAD	MICHAEL JACKSON (EPIC)
FAIRYTALE OF NEW YORK	POGUES/KIRSTY MACCALL (STIFF)	4	HITS 7	VARIOUS (CBS/WEA/ARISTA)
ANGEL EYES	WET WET WET (PRECIOUS/PHONOGRAM)	5	BRIDGE OF SPIES	T'PAU (SIREN)
LOVE LETTERS	ALISON MOYET (CBS)	6	ACTUALLY	PET SHOP BOYS (PARLOPHONE)
HOUSE ARREST	KRUSH (CLUB/PHONOGRAM)	7	TANGO IN THE NIGHT	FLEETWOOD MAC (WARNER BROS)
STUTTER RAP	MORRIS MINOR & THE MAJORS (10/VIRGIN)	8	POPPED IN SOULED OUT	WET WET WET (PRECIOUS/PHONOGRAM)
I FOUND SOMEONE	CHER (GEFFEN)	9	ALL THE BEST!	PAUL McCARTNEY (PARLOPHONE)
ROCKIN' AROUND THE CHRISTMAS TREE	KIM WILDE & MEL SMITH (10/VIRGIN)	10	WHITNEY	WHITNEY HOUSTON (ARISTA)
MY ARMS KEEP MISSING YOU	RICK ASTLEY (RCA)	11	THE SINGLES	PRETENDERS (WEA)
TURN BACK THE CLOCK	JOHNNY HATES JAZZ (VIRGIN)	12	YOU CAN DANCE	MADONNA (SIRE)
CHINA IN YOUR HAND	T'PAU (SIREN)	13	THE CHRISTIANS	THE CHRISTIANS (ISLAND)
WHEN I FALL IN LOVE	NAT KING COLE (CAPITOL)	14	THE BEST OF UB40 VOL 1	UB40 (VIRGIN)
THE LOOK OF LOVE	MADONNA (SIRE)	15	FAITH	GEORGE MICHAEL (EPIC)
WHO FOUND WHO	JELLYBEAN/ELISA FIORILLO (CHRYSALIS)	16	THE BEST OF MIRAGE JACK MIX '88	MIRAGE (STYLUS)
JINGO	JELLYBEAN (CHRYSALIS)	17	INTRODUCING THE HARDLINE ACCORDING TO . . .	TERENCE TRENT D'ARBY (CBS)
CRITICIZE	ALEXANDER O'NEAL (TABU)	18	THE CREAM OF ERIC CLAPTON	ERIC CLAPTON/CREAM (POLYDOR)
ALL DAY AND ALL OF THE NIGHT	THE STRANGLERS (EPIC)	19	RAINDANCING	ALISON MOYET (CBS)
G.T.O.	SINITTA (FANFARE)	20	HEARSAY	ALEXANDER O'NEAL (TABU)

US — SINGLES / ALBUMS

Singles	Artist (Label)	Pos	Albums	Artist (Label)
GOT MY MIND SET ON YOU	GEORGE HARRISON (DARK HORSE)	1	INSIDE INFORMATION	FOREIGNER (ATLANTIC)
THE WAY YOU MAKE ME FEEL	MICHAEL JACKSON (EPIC)	2	CLOUD NINE	GEORGE HARRISON (DARK HORSE)
NEED YOU TONIGHT	INXS (ATLANTIC)	3	TUNNEL OF LOVE	BRUCE SPRINGSTEEN (COLUMBIA)
SO EMOTIONAL	WHITNEY HOUSTON (ARISTA)	4	BIG GENERATOR	YES (ATCO)
COULD'VE BEEN	TIFFANY (MCA)	5	THE LONESOME JUBILEE	JOHN COUGAR MELLENCAMP (MERCURY/PG)
HAZY SHADE OF WINTER	BANGLES (DEF JAM/COLUMBIA)	6	A MOMENTARY LAPSE OF REASON	PINK FLOYD (COLUMBIA)
SEASONS CHANGE	EXPOSE (ARISTA)	7	ROBBIE ROBERTSON	ROBBIE ROBERTSON (GEFFEN)
CANDLE IN THE WIND	ELTON JOHN (MCA)	8	HYSTERIA	DEF LEPPARD (MERCURY/PG)
TELL IT TO MY HEART	TAYLOR DAYNE (ARISTA)	9	NOTHING LIKE THE SUN	STING (A&M)
I COULD NEVER TAKE THE PLACE OF YOUR MAN	PRINCE (PAISLEY PARK/WARNER BROS)	10	KICK	INXS (ATLANTIC)
I WANT TO BE YOUR MAN	ROGER (REPRISE)	11	ONE GOOD REASON	PAUL CARRACK (CHRYSALIS)
FAITH	GEORGE MICHAEL (COLUMBIA)	12	THE JOSHUA TREE	U2 (ISLAND)
HUNGRY EYES	ERIC CARMEN (RCA)	13	CREST OF A KNAVE	JETHRO TULL (CHRYSALIS)
THERE'S THE GIRL	HEART (CAPITOL)	14	PERMANENT VACATION	AEROSMITH (GEFFEN)
IS THIS LOVE	WHITESNAKE (GEFFEN)	15	HEART	BAD ANIMALS (CAPITOL)
CRAZY	ICEHOUSE (CHRYSALIS)	16	HOLD YOUR FIRE	RUSH (MERCURY/PG)
DON'T SHED A TEAR	PAUL CARRACK (CHRYSALIS)	17	EYE OF THE HURRICANE	ALARM (IRS/MCA)
WHAT HAVE I DONE TO DESERVE THIS?	PET SHOP BOYS/D. SPRINGFIELD (EMI-MAN.)	18	WHITESNAKE	WHITESNAKE (GEFFEN)
TUNNEL OF LOVE	BRUCE SPRINGSTEEN (COLUMBIA)	19	IN THE DARK	GRATEFUL DEAD (ARISTA)
SAY YOU WILL	FOREIGNER (ATLANTIC)	20	EARTH SUN MOON	LOVE & ROCKETS (BIG TIME/RCA)

WEEK ENDING JANUARY 16 1988

UK

SINGLES		ALBUMS
HEAVEN IS A PLACE ON EARTH BELINDA CARLISLE (VIRGIN)	1	POPPED IN SOULED OUT WET WET WET (PRECIOUS/PHONOGRAM)
ALWAYS ON MY MIND PET SHOP BOYS (PARLOPHONE)	2	BAD MICHAEL JACKSON (EPIC)
HOUSE ARREST KRUSH (CLUB/PHONOGRAM)	3	WHENEVER YOU NEED SOMEBODY RICK ASTLEY (RCA)
STUTTER RAP MORRIS MINOR & THE MAJORS (10/VIRGIN)	4	INTRODUCING THE HARDLINE ACCORDING TO... TERENCE TRENT D'ARBY (CBS)
I FOUND SOMEONE CHER (GEFFEN)	5	ACTUALLY PET SHOP BOYS (PARLOPHONE)
ANGEL EYES WET WET WET (PRECIOUS/PHONOGRAM)	6	NOW THAT'S WHAT I CALL MUSIC 10 VARIOUS (EMI/VIRGIN/POLYGRAM)
ALL DAY AND ALL OF THE NIGHT THE STRANGLERS (EPIC)	7	BRIDGE OF SPIES T'PAU (SIREN)
SIGN YOUR NAME TERENCE TRENT D'ARBY (CBS)	8	THE CHRISTIANS THE CHRISTIANS (ISLAND)
COME INTO MY LIFE JOYCE SIMS (FFRR/LONDON)	9	TANGO IN THE NIGHT FLEETWOOD MAC (WARNER BROS)
RISE TO THE OCCASION CLIMIE FISHER (EMI)	10	FAITH GEORGE MICHAEL (EPIC)
FATHER FIGURE GEORGE MICHAEL (EPIC)	11	THE BEST OF MIRAGE JACK MIX '88 MIRAGE (STYLUS)
JINGO JELLYBEAN (CHRYSALIS)	12	HITS 7 VARIOUS (CBS/WEA/ARISTA)
I THINK WE'RE ALONE NOW TIFFANY (MCA)	13	WHITNEY WHITNEY HOUSTON (ARISTA)
MY ARMS KEEP MISSING YOU RICK ASTLEY (RCA)	14	ALL THE BEST! PAUL McCARTNEY (PARLOPHONE)
G.T.O. SINITTA (FANFARE)	15	THE SINGLES PRETENDERS (WEA)
THE WAY YOU MAKE ME FEEL MICHAEL JACKSON (EPIC)	16	LIFE IN THE FAST LANE VARIOUS (TELSTAR)
HEATSEEKER AC/DC (ATLANTIC)	17	THE GREATEST LOVE VARIOUS (TELSTAR)
LOVE LETTERS ALISON MOYET (CBS)	18	THE JOSHUA TREE U2 (ISLAND)
FAIRYTALE OF NEW YORK POGUES/KIRSTY MACCALL (STIFF)	19	RAINDANCING ALISON MOYET (CBS)
TURN BACK THE CLOCK JOHNNY HATES JAZZ (VIRGIN)	20	HEARSAY ALEXANDER O'NEAL (TABU)

US

SINGLES		ALBUMS
THE WAY YOU MAKE ME FEEL MICHAEL JACKSON (EPIC)	1	INSIDE INFORMATION FOREIGNER (ATLANTIC)
NEED YOU TONIGHT INXS (ATLANTIC)	2	CLOUD NINE GEORGE HARRISON (DARK HORSE)
COULD'VE BEEN TIFFANY (MCA)	3	TUNNEL OF LOVE BRUCE SPRINGSTEEN (COLUMBIA)
HAZY SHADE OF WINTER BANGLES (DEF JAM/COLUMBIA)	4	BIG GENERATOR YES (ATCO)
SEASONS CHANGE EXPOSE (ARISTA)	5	THE LONESOME JUBILEE JOHN COUGAR MELLENCAMP (MERCURY/PG)
GOT MY MIND SET ON YOU GEORGE HARRISON (DARK HORSE)	6	A MOMENTARY LAPSE OF REASON PINK FLOYD (COLUMBIA)
I WANT TO BE YOUR MAN ROGER (REPRISE)	7	ROBBIE ROBERTSON ROBBIE ROBERTSON (GEFFEN)
CANDLE IN THE WIND ELTON JOHN (MCA)	8	HYSTERIA DEF LEPPARD (MERCURY/PG)
I COULD NEVER TAKE THE PLACE OF YOUR MAN PRINCE (PAISLEY PARK/WARNER BROS)	9	NOTHING LIKE THE SUN STING (A&M)
HUNGRY EYES ERIC CARMEN (RCA)	10	KICK INXS (ATLANTIC)
SO EMOTIONAL WHITNEY HOUSTON (ARISTA)	11	THE JOSHUA TREE U2 (ISLAND)
WHAT HAVE I DONE TO DESERVE THIS? PET SHOP BOYS/D. SPRINGFIELD (EMI-MAN.)	12	ONE GOOD REASON PAUL CARRACK (CHRYSALIS)
SAY YOU WILL FOREIGNER (ATLANTIC)	13	CREST OF A KNAVE JETHRO TULL (CHRYSALIS)
DON'T SHED A TEAR PAUL CARRACK (CHRYSALIS)	14	HOLD YOUR FIRE RUSH (MERCURY/PG)
TUNNEL OF LOVE BRUCE SPRINGSTEEN (COLUMBIA)	15	EARTH SUN MOON LOVE & ROCKETS (BIG TIME/RCA)
CRAZY ICEHOUSE (CHRYSALIS)	16	PERMANENT VACATION AEROSMITH (GEFFEN)
EVERYWHERE FLEETWOOD MAC (WARNER BROS)	17	HEART BAD ANIMALS (CAPITOL)
I LIVE FOR YOUR LOVE NATALIE COLE (EMI-MANHATTAN)	18	THE HUNGER MICHAEL BOLTON (COLUMBIA)
TELL IT TO MY HEART TAYLOR DAYNE (ARISTA)	19	IN THE DARK GRATEFUL DEAD (ARISTA)
THERE'S THE GIRL HEART (CAPITOL)	20	WHITESNAKE WHITESNAKE (GEFFEN)

WEEK ENDING JANUARY 23 1988

UK

SINGLES		ALBUMS
HEAVEN IS A PLACE ON EARTH BELINDA CARLISLE (VIRGIN)	1	TURN BACK THE CLOCK JOHNNY HATES JAZZ (VIRGIN)
SIGN YOUR NAME TERENCE TRENT D'ARBY (CBS)	2	POPPED IN SOULED OUT WET WET WET (PRECIOUS/PHONOGRAM)
I THINK WE'RE ALONE NOW TIFFANY (MCA)	3	INTRODUCING THE HARDLINE ACCORDING TO... TERENCE TRENT D'ARBY (CBS)
HOUSE ARREST KRUSH (CLUB/PHONOGRAM)	4	THE CHRISTIANS THE CHRISTIANS (ISLAND)
STUTTER RAP MORRIS MINOR & THE MAJORS (10/VIRGIN)	5	BAD MICHAEL JACKSON (EPIC)
I FOUND SOMEONE CHER (GEFFEN)	6	FAITH GEORGE MICHAEL (EPIC)
ALL DAY AND ALL OF THE NIGHT THE STRANGLERS (EPIC)	7	HEAVEN ON EARTH BELINDA CARLISLE (VIRGIN)
COME INTO MY LIFE JOYCE SIMS (FFRR/LONDON)	8	THE BEST OF MIRAGE JACK MIX '88 MIRAGE (STYLUS)
ANGEL EYES WET WET WET (PRECIOUS/PHONOGRAM)	9	WHENEVER YOU NEED SOMEBODY RICK ASTLEY (RCA)
RISE TO THE OCCASION CLIMIE FISHER (EMI)	10	LIFE IN THE FAST LANE VARIOUS (TELSTAR)
ALWAYS ON MY MIND PET SHOP BOYS (PARLOPHONE)	11	TANGO IN THE NIGHT FLEETWOOD MAC (WARNER BROS)
HEATSEEKER AC/DC (ATLANTIC)	12	BRIDGE OF SPIES T'PAU (SIREN)
FATHER FIGURE GEORGE MICHAEL (EPIC)	13	THE GREATEST LOVE VARIOUS (TELSTAR)
ROK DA HOUSE BEATMASTER/COOKIE CREW (MUTE)	14	ACTUALLY PET SHOP BOYS (PARLOPHONE)
IDEAL WORLD THE CHRISTIANS (ISLAND)	15	NOW THAT'S WHAT I CALL MUSIC 10 VARIOUS (EMI/VIRGIN/POLYGRAM)
WHEN WILL I BE FAMOUS? BROS (CBS)	16	COME INTO MY LIFE JOYCE SIMS (FFRR/LONDON)
JINGO JELLYBEAN (CHRYSALIS)	17	RAINDANCING ALISON MOYET (CBS)
O L'AMOUR DOLLAR (LONDON)	18	WHITNEY WHITNEY HOUSTON (ARISTA)
G.T.O. SINITTA (FANFARE)	19	THE SINGLES PRETENDERS (WEA)
I CAN'T HELP IT BANANARAMA (LONDON)	20	KICK INXS (MERCURY/PHONOGRAM)

US

SINGLES		ALBUMS
NEED YOU TONIGHT INXS (ATLANTIC)	1	INSIDE INFORMATION FOREIGNER (ATLANTIC)
COULD'VE BEEN TIFFANY (MCA)	2	CLOUD NINE GEORGE HARRISON (DARK HORSE)
HAZY SHADE OF WINTER BANGLES (DEF JAM/COLUMBIA)	3	TUNNEL OF LOVE BRUCE SPRINGSTEEN (COLUMBIA)
SEASONS CHANGE EXPOSE (ARISTA)	4	BIG GENERATOR YES (ATCO)
THE WAY YOU MAKE ME FEEL MICHAEL JACKSON (EPIC)	5	THE LONESOME JUBILEE JOHN COUGAR MELLENCAMP (MERCURY/PG)
I WANT TO BE YOUR MAN ROGER (REPRISE)	6	A MOMENTARY LAPSE OF REASON PINK FLOYD (COLUMBIA)
HUNGRY EYES ERIC CARMEN (RCA)	7	KICK INXS (ATLANTIC)
WHAT HAVE I DONE TO DESERVE THIS? PET SHOP BOYS/D. SPRINGFIELD (EMI-MAN.)	8	HYSTERIA DEF LEPPARD (MERCURY/PG)
I COULD NEVER TAKE THE PLACE OF YOUR MAN PRINCE (PAISLEY PARK/WARNER BROS)	9	NOTHING LIKE THE SUN STING (A&M)
SAY YOU WILL FOREIGNER (ATLANTIC)	10	ROBBIE ROBERTSON ROBBIE ROBERTSON (GEFFEN)
DON'T SHED A TEAR PAUL CARRACK (CHRYSALIS)	11	BORN TO BE BAD GEORGE THOROGOOD (EMI-MANHATTAN)
CANDLE IN THE WIND ELTON JOHN (MCA)	12	CREST OF A KNAVE JETHRO TULL (CHRYSALIS)
TUNNEL OF LOVE BRUCE SPRINGSTEEN (COLUMBIA)	13	PERMANENT VACATION AEROSMITH (GEFFEN)
EVERYWHERE FLEETWOOD MAC (WARNER BROS)	14	THE HUNGER MICHAEL BOLTON (COLUMBIA)
GOT MY MIND SET ON YOU GEORGE HARRISON (DARK HORSE)	15	HOLD YOUR FIRE RUSH (MERCURY/PG)
I LIVE FOR YOUR LOVE NATALIE COLE (EMI-MANHATTAN)	16	THE JOSHUA TREE U2 (ISLAND)
SHE'S LIKE THE WIND PATRICK SWAYZE (RCA)	17	ONE GOOD REASON PAUL CARRACK (CHRYSALIS)
FATHER FIGURE GEORGE MICHAEL (COLUMBIA)	18	ONCE BITTEN GREAT WHITE (CAPITOL)
CAN'T STAY AWAY FROM YOU G. ESTEFAN & MIAMI SOUND MACHINE (EPIC)	19	EARTH SUN MOON LOVE & ROCKETS (BIG TIME/RCA)
NEVER GONNA GIVE YOU UP RICK ASTLEY (RCA)	20	THE ROAD KINKS (MCA)

WEEK ENDING JANUARY 30 1988

UK

SINGLES			ALBUMS	
I THINK WE'RE ALONE NOW	TIFFANY (MCA)	1	INTRODUCING THE HARDLINE ACCORDING TO...	TERENCE TRENT D'ARBY (CBS)
HEAVEN IS A PLACE ON EARTH	BELINDA CARLISLE (VIRGIN)	2	TURN BACK THE CLOCK	JOHNNY HATES JAZZ (VIRGIN)
SIGN YOUR NAME	TERENCE TRENT D'ARBY (CBS)	3	IF I SHOULD FALL FROM GRACE WITH GOD	THE POGUES (POGUE MAHONE/STIFF)
HOUSE ARREST	KRUSH (CLUB/PHONOGRAM)	4	THE CHRISTIANS	THE CHRISTIANS (ISLAND)
STUTTER RAP	MORRIS MINOR & THE MAJORS (10/VIRGIN)	5	POPPED IN SOULED OUT	WET WET WET (PRECIOUS/PHONOGRAM)
WHEN WILL I BE FAMOUS?	BROS (CBS)	6	HEAVEN ON EARTH	BELINDA CARLISLE (VIRGIN)
COME INTO MY LIFE	JOYCE SIMS (FFRR/LONDON)	7	BAD	MICHAEL JACKSON (EPIC)
ROK DA HOUSE	BEATMASTER/COOKIE CREW (MUTE)	8	COME INTO MY LIFE	JOYCE SIMS (FFRR/LONDON)
OL' AMOUR	DOLLAR (LONDON)	9	FAITH	GEORGE MICHAEL (EPIC)
RISE TO THE OCCASION	CLIMIE FISHER (EMI)	10	THE BEST OF MIRAGE JACK MIX '88	MIRAGE (STYLUS)
I FOUND SOMEONE	CHER (GEFFEN)	11	TANGO IN THE NIGHT	FLEETWOOD MAC (WARNER BROS)
HEATSEEKER	AC/DC (ATLANTIC)	12	WHENEVER YOU NEED SOMEBODY	RICK ASTLEY (RCA)
ALL DAY AND ALL OF THE NIGHT	THE STRANGLERS (EPIC)	13	BRIDGE OF SPIES	T'PAU (SIREN)
IDEAL WORLD	THE CHRISTIANS (ISLAND)	14	THE GREATEST LOVE	VARIOUS (TELSTAR)
ANGEL EYES	WET WET WET (PRECIOUS/PHONOGRAM)	15	LIFE IN THE FAST LANE	VARIOUS (TELSTAR)
CANDLE IN THE WIND	ELTON JOHN (ROCKET/PHONOGRAM)	16	KICK	INXS (MERCURY/PHONOGRAM)
SHAKE YOUR LOVE	DEBBIE GIBSON (ATLANTIC)	17	ACTUALLY	PET SHOP BOYS (PARLOPHONE)
HOT IN THE CITY	BILLY IDOL (CHRYSALIS)	18	RAINDANCING	ALISON MOYET (CBS)
THE JACK THAT HOUSE BUILT	JACK 'N' CHILL (OVAL/10/VIRGIN)	19	WHITNEY	WHITNEY HOUSTON (ARISTA)
ALWAYS ON MY MIND	PET SHOP BOYS (PARLOPHONE)	20	NOW THAT'S WHAT I CALL MUSIC 10	VARIOUS (EMI/VIRGIN/POLYGRAM)

US

SINGLES			ALBUMS	
COULD'VE BEEN	TIFFANY (MCA)	1	SKYSCRAPER	DAVID LEE ROTH (WARNER BROS)
NEED YOU TONIGHT	INXS (ATLANTIC)	2	INSIDE INFORMATION	FOREIGNER (ATLANTIC)
SEASONS CHANGE	EXPOSE (ARISTA)	3	CLOUD NINE	GEORGE HARRISON (DARK HORSE)
HAZY SHADE OF WINTER	BANGLES (DEF JAM/COLUMBIA)	4	TUNNEL OF LOVE	BRUCE SPRINGSTEEN (COLUMBIA)
I WANT TO BE YOUR MAN	ROGER (REPRISE)	5	THE LONESOME JUBILEE	JOHN COUGAR MELLENCAMP (MERCURY/PG)
WHAT HAVE I DONE TO DESERVE THIS?	PET SHOP BOYS/D. SPRINGFIELD (EMI-MAN.)	6	NOTHING LIKE THE SUN	STING (A&M)
HUNGRY EYES	ERIC CARMEN (RCA)	7	KICK	INXS (ATLANTIC)
SAY YOU WILL	FOREIGNER (ATLANTIC)	8	BIG GENERATOR	YES (ATCO)
DON'T SHED A TEAR	PAUL CARRACK (CHRYSALIS)	9	BORN TO BE BAD	GEORGE THOROGOOD (EMI-MANHATTAN)
FATHER FIGURE	GEORGE MICHAEL (COLUMBIA)	10	HYSTERIA	DEF LEPPARD (MERCURY/PG)
SHE'S LIKE THE WIND	PATRICK SWAYZE (RCA)	11	A MOMENTARY LAPSE OF REASON	PINK FLOYD (COLUMBIA)
EVERYWHERE	FLEETWOOD MAC (WARNER BROS)	12	CREST OF A KNAVE	JETHRO TULL (CHRYSALIS)
TUNNEL OF LOVE	BRUCE SPRINGSTEEN (COLUMBIA)	13	PERMANENT VACATION	AEROSMITH (GEFFEN)
NEVER GONNA GIVE YOU UP	RICK ASTLEY (RCA)	14	THE HUNGER	MICHAEL BOLTON (COLUMBIA)
I LIVE FOR YOUR LOVE	NATALIE COLE (EMI-MANHATTAN)	15	ROBBIE ROBERTSON	ROBBIE ROBERTSON (GEFFEN)
CAN'T STAY AWAY FROM YOU	G. ESTEFAN & MIAMI SOUND MACHINE (EPIC)	16	ONCE BITTEN	GREAT WHITE (CAPITOL)
I COULD NEVER TAKE THE PLACE OF YOUR MAN	PRINCE (PAISLEY PARK/WARNER BROS)	17	THE ROAD	KINKS (MCA)
THE WAY YOU MAKE ME FEEL	MICHAEL JACKSON (EPIC)	18	HOLD YOUR FIRE	RUSH (MERCURY/PG)
I FOUND SOMEONE	CHER (GEFFEN)	19	UNCHAIN MY HEART	JOE COCKER (CAPITOL)
I GET WEAK	BELINDA CARLISLE (MCA)	20	CHRONICLES	STEVE WINWOOD (ISLAND/WARNER BROS)

WEEK ENDING FEBRUARY 6 1988

UK

SINGLES			ALBUMS	
I THINK WE'RE ALONE NOW	TIFFANY (MCA)	1	INTRODUCING THE HARDLINE ACCORDING TO...	TERENCE TRENT D'ARBY (CBS)
WHEN WILL I BE FAMOUS?	BROS (CBS)	2	THE CHRISTIANS	THE CHRISTIANS (ISLAND)
HEAVEN IS A PLACE ON EARTH	BELINDA CARLISLE (VIRGIN)	3	TURN BACK THE CLOCK	JOHNNY HATES JAZZ (VIRGIN)
SIGN YOUR NAME	TERENCE TRENT D'ARBY (CBS)	4	POPPED IN SOULED OUT	WET WET WET (PRECIOUS/PHONOGRAM)
ROK DA HOUSE	BEATMASTER/COOKIE CREW (MUTE)	5	IF I SHOULD FALL FROM GRACE WITH GOD	THE POGUES (POGUE MAHONE/STIFF)
HOUSE ARREST	KRUSH (CLUB/PHONOGRAM)	6	BRIDGE OF SPIES	T'PAU (SIREN)
OL' AMOUR	DOLLAR (LONDON)	7	THE BEST OF MIRAGE JACK MIX '88	MIRAGE (STYLUS)
TELL IT TO MY HEART	TAYLOR DAYNE (ARISTA)	8	HEAVEN ON EARTH	BELINDA CARLISLE (VIRGIN)
SHAKE YOUR LOVE	DEBBIE GIBSON (ATLANTIC)	9	KICK	INXS (MERCURY/PHONOGRAM)
CANDLE IN THE WIND	ELTON JOHN (ROCKET/PHONOGRAM)	10	COME INTO MY LIFE	JOYCE SIMS (FFRR/LONDON)
COME INTO MY LIFE	JOYCE SIMS (FFRR/LONDON)	11	SKYSCRAPER	DAVID LEE ROTH (WARNER BROS)
THE JACK THAT HOUSE BUILT	JACK 'N' CHILL (OVAL/10/VIRGIN)	12	BAD	MICHAEL JACKSON (EPIC)
HOT IN THE CITY	BILLY IDOL (CHRYSALIS)	13	TANGO IN THE NIGHT	FLEETWOOD MAC (WARNER BROS)
STUTTER RAP	MORRIS MINOR & THE MAJORS (10/VIRGIN)	14	FAITH	GEORGE MICHAEL (EPIC)
IDEAL WORLD	THE CHRISTIANS (ISLAND)	15	WHENEVER YOU NEED SOMEBODY	RICK ASTLEY (RCA)
I SHOULD BE SO LUCKY	KYLIE MINOGUE (PWL)	16	JUST VISITING THIS PLANET	JELLYBEAN (CHRYSALIS)
SAY IT AGAIN	JERMAINE STEWART (10/VIRGIN)	17	THE GREATEST LOVE	VARIOUS (TELSTAR)
TIRED OF GETTING PUSHED AROUND	2 MEN/DRUM MACHINE/TRUMPET (FFRR/LONDON)	18	ACTUALLY	PET SHOP BOYS (PARLOPHONE)
RISE TO THE OCCASION	CLIMIE FISHER (EMI)	19	RAINDANCING	ALISON MOYET (CBS)
VALENTINE	T'PAU (SIREN/VIRGIN)	20	LIFE IN THE FAST LANE	VARIOUS (TELSTAR)

US

SINGLES			ALBUMS	
COULD'VE BEEN	TIFFANY (MCA)	1	SKYSCRAPER	DAVID LEE ROTH (WARNER BROS)
SEASONS CHANGE	EXPOSE (ARISTA)	2	INSIDE INFORMATION	FOREIGNER (ATLANTIC)
WHAT HAVE I DONE TO DESERVE THIS?	PET SHOP BOYS/D. SPRINGFIELD (EMI-MAN.)	3	CLOUD NINE	GEORGE HARRISON (DARK HORSE)
FATHER FIGURE	GEORGE MICHAEL (COLUMBIA)	4	NOTHING LIKE THE SUN	STING (A&M)
I WANT TO BE YOUR MAN	ROGER (REPRISE)	5	THE LONESOME JUBILEE	JOHN COUGAR MELLENCAMP (MERCURY/PG)
HUNGRY EYES	ERIC CARMEN (RCA)	6	KICK	INXS (ATLANTIC)
SAY YOU WILL	FOREIGNER (ATLANTIC)	7	BORN TO BE BAD	GEORGE THOROGOOD (EMI-MANHATTAN)
SHE'S LIKE THE WIND	PATRICK SWAYZE (RCA)	8	TUNNEL OF LOVE	BRUCE SPRINGSTEEN (COLUMBIA)
DON'T SHED A TEAR	PAUL CARRACK (CHRYSALIS)	9	BIG GENERATOR	YES (ATCO)
NEVER GONNA GIVE YOU UP	RICK ASTLEY (RCA)	10	PERMANENT VACATION	AEROSMITH (GEFFEN)
NEED YOU TONIGHT	INXS (ATLANTIC)	11	HYSTERIA	DEF LEPPARD (MERCURY/PG)
HAZY SHADE OF WINTER	BANGLES (DEF JAM/COLUMBIA)	12	CREST OF A KNAVE	JETHRO TULL (CHRYSALIS)
CAN'T STAY AWAY FROM YOU	G. ESTEFAN & MIAMI SOUND MACHINE (EPIC)	13	THE HUNGER	MICHAEL BOLTON (COLUMBIA)
EVERYWHERE	FLEETWOOD MAC (WARNER BROS)	14	ONCE BITTEN	GREAT WHITE (CAPITOL)
I GET WEAK	BELINDA CARLISLE (MCA)	15	A MOMENTARY LAPSE OF REASON	PINK FLOYD (COLUMBIA)
I FOUND SOMEONE	CHER (GEFFEN)	16	UNCHAIN MY HEART	JOE COCKER (CAPITOL)
TUNNEL OF LOVE	BRUCE SPRINGSTEEN (COLUMBIA)	17	THE ROAD	KINKS (MCA)
I LIVE FOR YOUR LOVE	NATALIE COLE (EMI-MANHATTAN)	18	CHRONICLES	STEVE WINWOOD (ISLAND/WARNER BROS)
ENDLESS SUMMER NIGHTS	RICHARD MARX (EMI-MANHATTAN)	19	ROBBIE ROBERTSON	ROBBIE ROBERTSON (GEFFEN)
PUMP UP THE VOLUME	M/A/R/R/S (4th & BROADWAY/ISLAND)	20	ISLANDS	MIKE OLDFIELD (VIRGIN)

WEEK ENDING FEBRUARY 13 1988

SINGLES UK ALBUMS

Singles			Albums	
I THINK WE'RE ALONE NOW	TIFFANY (MCA)	1	INTRODUCING THE HARDLINE ACCORDING TO...	TERENCE TRENT D'ARBY (CBS)
I SHOULD BE SO LUCKY	KYLIE MINOGUE (PWL)	2	BLOW UP YOUR VIDEO	AC/DC (ATLANTIC/WEA)
WHEN WILL I BE FAMOUS?	BROS (CBS)	3	THE CHRISTIANS	THE CHRISTIANS (ISLAND)
TELL IT TO MY HEART	TAYLOR DAYNE (ARISTA)	4	BRIDGE OF SPIES	T'PAU (SIREN)
CANDLE IN THE WIND	ELTON JOHN (ROCKET/PHONOGRAM)	5	COME INTO MY LIFE	JOYCE SIMS (FFRR/LONDON)
THE JACK THAT HOUSE BUILT	JACK 'N' CHILL (OVAL/10/VIRGIN)	6	POPPED IN SOULED OUT	WET WET WET (PRECIOUS/PHONOGRAM)
SHAKE YOUR LOVE	DEBBIE GIBSON (ATLANTIC)	7	TURN BACK THE CLOCK	JOHNNY HATES JAZZ (VIRGIN)
GET OUTTA MY DREAMS, GET INTO MY CAR	BILLY OCEAN (JIVE)	8	THE BEST OF MIRAGE JACK MIX '88	MIRAGE (STYLUS)
ROK DA HOUSE	BEATMASTER/COOKIE CREW (MUTE)	9	KICK	INXS (MERCURY/PHONOGRAM)
SAY IT AGAIN	JERMAINE STEWART (10/VIRGIN)	10	BAD	MICHAEL JACKSON (EPIC)
OL' AMOUR	DOLLAR (LONDON)	11	IF I SHOULD FALL FROM GRACE WITH GOD	THE POGUES (POGUE MAHONE/STIFF)
SIGN YOUR NAME	TERENCE TRENT D'ARBY (CBS)	12	TANGO IN THE NIGHT	FLEETWOOD MAC (WARNER BROS)
HEAVEN IS A PLACE ON EARTH	BELINDA CARLISLE (VIRGIN)	13	HEAVEN ON EARTH	BELINDA CARLISLE (VIRGIN)
HOT IN THE CITY	BILLY IDOL (CHRYSALIS)	14	THE GREATEST LOVE	VARIOUS (TELSTAR)
VALENTINE	T'PAU (SIREN/VIRGIN)	15	JUST VISITING THIS PLANET	JELLYBEAN (CHRYSALIS)
HOUSE ARREST	KRUSH (CLUB/PHONOGRAM)	16	DUSTY – THE SILVER COLLECTION	DUSTY SPRINGFIELD (PHILIPS/PHONOGRAM)
COME INTO MY LIFE	JOYCE SIMS (FFRR/LONDON)	17	WHENEVER YOU NEED SOMEBODY	RICK ASTLEY (RCA)
GIVE ME ALL YOUR LOVE	WHITESNAKE (EMI)	18	FAITH	GEORGE MICHAEL (EPIC)
TIRED OF GETTING PUSHED AROUND	2 MEN/DRUM MACHINE/TRUMPET (FFRR/LONDON)	19	SKYSCRAPER	DAVID LEE ROTH (WARNER BROS)
TOWER OF STRENGTH	THE MISSION (MERCURY/PHONOGRAM)	20	ACTUALLY	PET SHOP BOYS (PARLOPHONE)

SINGLES US ALBUMS

Singles			Albums	
FATHER FIGURE	GEORGE MICHAEL (COLUMBIA)	1	SKYSCRAPER	DAVID LEE ROTH (WARNER BROS)
WHAT HAVE I DONE TO DESERVE THIS?	PET SHOP BOYS/D. SPRINGFIELD (EMI-MAN.)	2	INSIDE INFORMATION	FOREIGNER (ATLANTIC)
SEASONS CHANGE	EXPOSE (ARISTA)	3	NOTHING LIKE THE SUN	STING (A&M)
SHE'S LIKE THE WIND	PATRICK SWAYZE (RCA)	4	BORN TO BE BAD	GEORGE THOROGOOD (EMI-MANHATTAN)
COULD'VE BEEN	TIFFANY (MCA)	5	THE LONESOME JUBILEE	JOHN COUGAR MELLENCAMP (MERCURY/PG)
NEVER GONNA GIVE YOU UP	RICK ASTLEY (RCA)	6	KICK	INXS (ATLANTIC)
SAY YOU WILL	FOREIGNER (ATLANTIC)	7	CLOUD NINE	GEORGE HARRISON (DARK HORSE)
HUNGRY EYES	ERIC CARMEN (RCA)	8	PERMANENT VACATION	AEROSMITH (GEFFEN)
CAN'T STAY AWAY FROM YOU	G. ESTEFAN & MIAMI SOUND MACHINE (EPIC)	9	BIG GENERATOR	YES (ATCO)
I GET WEAK	BELINDA CARLISLE (MCA)	10	TUNNEL OF LOVE	BRUCE SPRINGSTEEN (COLUMBIA)
DON'T SHED A TEAR	PAUL CARRACK (CHRYSALIS)	11	HYSTERIA	DEF LEPPARD (MERCURY/PG)
I WANT TO BE YOUR MAN	ROGER (REPRISE)	12	ONCE BITTEN	GREAT WHITE (CAPITOL)
ENDLESS SUMMER NIGHTS	RICHARD MARX (EMI-MANHATTAN)	13	UNCHAIN MY HEART	JOE COCKER (CAPITOL)
I FOUND SOMEONE	CHER (GEFFEN)	14	CHRONICLES	STEVE WINWOOD (ISLAND/WARNER BROS)
NEED YOU TONIGHT	INXS (ATLANTIC)	15	ISLANDS	MIKE OLDFIELD (VIRGIN)
JUST LIKE PARADISE	DAVID LEE ROTH (WARNER BROS)	16	ROBBIE ROBERTSON	ROBBIE ROBERTSON (GEFFEN)
PUMP UP THE VOLUME	M/A/R/R/S (4th & BROADWAY/ISLAND)	17	THE ROAD	KINKS (MCA)
OUT OF THE BLUE	DEBBIE GIBSON (ATLANTIC)	18	CREST OF A KNAVE	JETHRO TULL (CHRYSALIS)
HAZY SHADE OF WINTER	BANGLES (DEF JAM/COLUMBIA)	19	THE HUNGER	MICHAEL BOLTON (COLUMBIA)
MAN IN THE MIRROR	MICHAEL JACKSON (EPIC)	20	PRIDE	WHITE LION (ATLANTIC)

WEEK ENDING FEBRUARY 20 1988

SINGLES UK ALBUMS

Singles			Albums	
I SHOULD BE SO LUCKY	KYLIE MINOGUE (PWL)	1	INTRODUCING THE HARDLINE ACCORDING TO...	TERENCE TRENT D'ARBY (CBS)
I THINK WE'RE ALONE NOW	TIFFANY (MCA)	2	BRIDGE OF SPIES	T'PAU (SIREN)
TELL IT TO MY HEART	TAYLOR DAYNE (ARISTA)	3	THE CHRISTIANS	THE CHRISTIANS (ISLAND)
GET OUTTA MY DREAMS, GET INTO MY CAR	BILLY OCEAN (JIVE)	4	POPPED IN SOULED OUT	WET WET WET (PRECIOUS/PHONOGRAM)
BEAT DIS	BOMB THE BASS (MUTE)	5	TURN BACK THE CLOCK	JOHNNY HATES JAZZ (VIRGIN)
WHEN WILL I BE FAMOUS?	BROS (CBS)	6	WHENEVER YOU NEED SOMEBODY	RICK ASTLEY (RCA)
CANDLE IN THE WIND	ELTON JOHN (ROCKET/PHONOGRAM)	7	COME INTO MY LIFE	JOYCE SIMS (FFRR/LONDON)
SAY IT AGAIN	JERMAINE STEWART (10/VIRGIN)	8	BLOW UP YOUR VIDEO	AC/DC (ATLANTIC/WEA)
VALENTINE	T'PAU (SIREN/VIRGIN)	9	BAD	MICHAEL JACKSON (EPIC)
SHAKE YOUR LOVE	DEBBIE GIBSON (ATLANTIC)	10	ACTUALLY	PET SHOP BOYS (PARLOPHONE)
THE JACK THAT HOUSE BUILT	JACK 'N' CHILL (OVAL/10/VIRGIN)	11	THE GREATEST LOVE	VARIOUS (TELSTAR)
GIMME HOPE JO'ANNA	EDDY GRANT (ICE)	12	ALL LIVE AND ALL OF THE NIGHT	THE STRANGLERS (EPIC)
TOWER OF STRENGTH	THE MISSION (MERCURY/PHONOGRAM)	13	THE JOSHUA TREE	U2 (ISLAND)
ROK DA HOUSE	BEATMASTER/COOKIE CREW (MUTE)	14	TANGO IN THE NIGHT	FLEETWOOD MAC (WARNER BROS)
SIGN YOUR NAME	TERENCE TRENT D'ARBY (CBS)	15	DUSTY – THE SILVER COLLECTION	DUSTY SPRINGFIELD (PHILIPS/PHONOGRAM)
HOT IN THE CITY	BILLY IDOL (CHRYSALIS)	16	FAITH	GEORGE MICHAEL (EPIC)
MANDINKA	SINEAD O'CONNOR (ENSIGN/CHRYSALIS)	17	RAINDANCING	ALISON MOYET (CBS)
GIVE ME ALL YOUR LOVE	WHITESNAKE (EMI)	18	GIVE ME THE REASON	LUTHER VANDROSS (EPIC)
OL' AMOUR	DOLLAR (LONDON)	19	IF I SHOULD FALL FROM GRACE WITH GOD	THE POGUES (POGUE MAHONE/STIFF)
HEAVEN IS A PLACE ON EARTH	BELINDA CARLISLE (VIRGIN)	20	KICK	INXS (MERCURY/PHONOGRAM)

SINGLES US ALBUMS

Singles			Albums	
FATHER FIGURE	GEORGE MICHAEL (COLUMBIA)	1	SKYSCRAPER	DAVID LEE ROTH (WARNER BROS)
SHE'S LIKE THE WIND	PATRICK SWAYZE (RCA)	2	NOTHING LIKE THE SUN	STING (A&M)
NEVER GONNA GIVE YOU UP	RICK ASTLEY (RCA)	3	BORN TO BE BAD	GEORGE THOROGOOD (EMI-MANHATTAN)
WHAT HAVE I DONE TO DESERVE THIS?	PET SHOP BOYS/D. SPRINGFIELD (EMI-MAN.)	4	INSIDE INFORMATION	FOREIGNER (ATLANTIC)
I GET WEAK	BELINDA CARLISLE (MCA)	5	THE LONESOME JUBILEE	JOHN COUGAR MELLENCAMP (MERCURY/PG)
CAN'T STAY AWAY FROM YOU	G. ESTEFAN & MIAMI SOUND MACHINE (EPIC)	6	KICK	INXS (ATLANTIC)
SEASONS CHANGE	EXPOSE (ARISTA)	7	CLOUD NINE	GEORGE HARRISON (DARK HORSE)
ENDLESS SUMMER NIGHTS	RICHARD MARX (EMI-MANHATTAN)	8	PERMANENT VACATION	AEROSMITH (GEFFEN)
SAY YOU WILL	FOREIGNER (ATLANTIC)	9	TUNNEL OF LOVE	BRUCE SPRINGSTEEN (COLUMBIA)
OUT OF THE BLUE	DEBBIE GIBSON (ATLANTIC)	10	ISLANDS	MIKE OLDFIELD (VIRGIN)
JUST LIKE PARADISE	DAVID LEE ROTH (WARNER BROS)	11	UNCHAIN MY HEART	JOE COCKER (CAPITOL)
MAN IN THE MIRROR	MICHAEL JACKSON (EPIC)	12	HYSTERIA	DEF LEPPARD (MERCURY/PG)
I FOUND SOMEONE	CHER (GEFFEN)	13	ONCE BITTEN	GREAT WHITE (CAPITOL)
HUNGRY EYES	ERIC CARMEN (RCA)	14	ROBBIE ROBERTSON	ROBBIE ROBERTSON (GEFFEN)
COULD'VE BEEN	TIFFANY (MCA)	15	A MAN OF COLOURS	ICEHOUSE (CHRYSALIS)
PUMP UP THE VOLUME	M/A/R/R/S (4th & BROADWAY/ISLAND)	16	CHRONICLES	STEVE WINWOOD (ISLAND/WARNER BROS)
DON'T SHED A TEAR	PAUL CARRACK (CHRYSALIS)	17	BIG GENERATOR	YES (ATCO)
BE STILL MY BEATING HEART	STING (A&M)	18	CASUAL GODS	JERRY HARRISON (SIRE/WARNER BROS)
HYSTERIA	DEF LEPPARD (MERCURY/PG)	19	HENRY LEE SUMMER	HENRY LEE SUMMER (CBS ASSOCIATED)
GET OUTTA MY DREAMS, GET INTO MY CAR	BILLY OCEAN (JIVE/ARISTA)	20	ANY MAN'S HUNGER	DANNY WILDE (GEFFEN)

WEEK ENDING FEBRUARY 27 1988

UK

SINGLES	UK	ALBUMS
I SHOULD BE SO LUCKY KYLIE MINOGUE (PWL)	1	INTRODUCING THE HARDLINE ACCORDING TO . . . TERENCE TRENT D'ARBY (CBS)
BEAT DIS BOMB THE BASS (MUTE)	2	BRIDGE OF SPIES T'PAU (SIREN)
GET OUTTA MY DREAMS, GET INTO MY CAR BILLY OCEAN (JIVE)	3	POPPED IN SOULED OUT WET WET WET (PRECIOUS/PHONOGRAM)
TELL IT TO MY HEART TAYLOR DAYNE (ARISTA)	4	THE CHRISTIANS THE CHRISTIANS (ISLAND)
I THINK WE'RE ALONE NOW TIFFANY (MCA)	5	TIFFANY TIFFANY (MCA)
SUEDEHEAD MORRISSEY (HIS MASTER'S VOICE)	6	TURN BACK THE CLOCK JOHNNY HATES JAZZ (VIRGIN)
SAY IT AGAIN JERMAINE STEWART (10/VIRGIN)	7	ALL ABOUT EVE ALL ABOUT EVE (MERCURY/PHONOGRAM)
GIMME HOPE JO'ANNA EDDY GRANT (ICE)	8	WHENEVER YOU NEED SOMEBODY RICK ASTLEY (RCA)
TOGETHER FOREVER RICK ASTLEY (RCA)	9	BAD MICHAEL JACKSON (EPIC)
DOCTORIN' THE HOUSE COLDCUT/YAZZ/PLAS. POP. (AHEAD OF OUR TIME)	10	COME INTO MY LIFE JOYCE SIMS (FFRR/LONDON)
WHEN WILL I BE FAMOUS? BROS (CBS)	11	ACTUALLY PET SHOP BOYS (PARLOPHONE)
TOWER OF STRENGTH THE MISSION (MERCURY/PHONOGRAM)	12	BLOW UP YOUR VIDEO AC/DC (ATLANTIC/WEA)
SHAKE YOUR LOVE DEBBIE GIBSON (ATLANTIC)	13	TANGO IN THE NIGHT FLEETWOOD MAC (WARNER BROS)
JOE LE TAXI VANESSA PARADIS (POLYDOR)	14	DUSTY – THE SILVER COLLECTION DUSTY SPRINGFIELD (PHILIPS/PHONOGRAM)
VALENTINE T'PAU (SIREN/VIRGIN)	15	THE JOSHUA TREE U2 (ISLAND)
CANDLE IN THE WIND ELTON JOHN (ROCKET/PHONOGRAM)	16	NOTHING LIKE THE SUN STING (A&M)
DOMINION SISTERS OF MERCY (MERCIFUL RELEASE/WEA)	17	THE GREATEST LOVE VARIOUS (TELSTAR)
THE JACK THAT HOUSE BUILT JACK 'N' CHILL (OVAL/10/VIRGIN)	18	GIVE ME THE REASON LUTHER VANDROSS (EPIC)
C'MON EVERYBODY EDDIE COCHRAN (LIBERTY)	19	HEAVEN ON EARTH BELINDA CARLISLE (VIRGIN)
HAZY SHADE OF WINTER BANGLES (DEF JAM)	20	KICK INXS (MERCURY/PHONOGRAM)

US

SINGLES	US	ALBUMS
FATHER FIGURE GEORGE MICHAEL (COLUMBIA)	1	NOW AND ZEN ROBERT PLANT (ES PARANZA/ATLANTIC)
SHE'S LIKE THE WIND PATRICK SWAYZE (RCA)	2	SKYSCRAPER DAVID LEE ROTH (WARNER BROS)
NEVER GONNA GIVE YOU UP RICK ASTLEY (RCA)	3	BORN TO BE BAD GEORGE THOROGOOD (EMI-MANHATTAN)
I GET WEAK BELINDA CARLISLE (MCA)	4	NOTHING LIKE THE SUN STING (A&M)
ENDLESS SUMMER NIGHTS RICHARD MARX (EMI-MANHATTAN)	5	THE LONESOME JUBILEE JOHN COUGAR MELLENCAMP (MERCURY/PG)
MAN IN THE MIRROR MICHAEL JACKSON (EPIC)	6	PERMANENT VACATION AEROSMITH (GEFFEN)
OUT OF THE BLUE DEBBIE GIBSON (ATLANTIC)	7	KICK INXS (ATLANTIC)
CAN'T STAY AWAY FROM YOU G. ESTEFAN & MIAMI SOUND MACHINE (EPIC)	8	CLOUD NINE GEORGE HARRISON (DARK HORSE)
JUST LIKE PARADISE DAVID LEE ROTH (WARNER BROS)	9	INSIDE INFORMATION FOREIGNER (ATLANTIC)
GET OUTTA MY DREAMS, GET INTO MY CAR BILLY OCEAN (JIVE/ARISTA)	10	TUNNEL OF LOVE BRUCE SPRINGSTEEN (COLUMBIA)
WHAT HAVE I DONE TO DESERVE THIS? PET SHOP BOYS/D. SPRINGFIELD (EMI-MAN.)	11	ISLANDS MIKE OLDFIELD (VIRGIN)
I FOUND SOMEONE CHER (GEFFEN)	12	HYSTERIA DEF LEPPARD (MERCURY/PG)
SEASONS CHANGE EXPOSE (ARISTA)	13	A MAN OF COLOURS ICEHOUSE (CHRYSALIS)
I WANT HER KEITH SWEAT (ELEKTRA)	14	HENRY LEE SUMMER HENRY LEE SUMMER (CBS ASSOCIATED)
BE STILL MY BEATING HEART STING (A&M)	15	CASUAL GODS JERRY HARRISON (SIRE/WARNER BROS)
HYSTERIA DEF LEPPARD (MERCURY/PG)	16	UNCHAIN MY HEART JOE COCKER (CAPITOL)
PUMP UP THE VOLUME M/A/R/R/S (4th & BROADWAY/ISLAND)	17	BIG GENERATOR YES (ATCO)
(SITTIN' ON) THE DOCK OF THE BAY MICHAEL BOLTON (COLUMBIA)	18	ONCE BITTEN GREAT WHITE (CAPITOL)
LOVE OVERBOARD GLADYS KNIGHT & THE PIPS (MCA)	19	ROBBIE ROBERTSON ROBBIE ROBERTSON (GEFFEN)
HUNGRY EYES ERIC CARMEN (RCA)	20	ANY MAN'S HUNGER DANNY WILDE (GEFFEN)

WEEK ENDING MARCH 5 1988

UK

SINGLES	UK	ALBUMS
I SHOULD BE SO LUCKY KYLIE MINOGUE (PWL)	1	INTRODUCING THE HARDLINE ACCORDING TO . . . TERENCE TRENT D'ARBY (CBS)
BEAT DIS BOMB THE BASS (MUTE)	2	BRIDGE OF SPIES T'PAU (SIREN)
GET OUTTA MY DREAMS, GET INTO MY CAR BILLY OCEAN (JIVE)	3	GIVE ME THE REASON LUTHER VANDROSS (EPIC)
TOGETHER FOREVER RICK ASTLEY (RCA)	4	POPPED IN SOULED OUT WET WET WET (PRECIOUS/PHONOGRAM)
SUEDEHEAD MORRISSEY (HIS MASTER'S VOICE)	5	WHENEVER YOU NEED SOMEBODY RICK ASTLEY (RCA)
TELL IT TO MY HEART TAYLOR DAYNE (ARISTA)	6	TURN BACK THE CLOCK JOHNNY HATES JAZZ (VIRGIN)
JOE LE TAXI VANESSA PARADIS (POLYDOR)	7	TIFFANY TIFFANY (MCA)
GIMME HOPE JO'ANNA EDDY GRANT (ICE)	8	THE CHRISTIANS THE CHRISTIANS (ISLAND)
DOCTORIN' THE HOUSE COLDCUT/YAZZ/PLAS. POP. (AHEAD OF OUR TIME)	9	BAD MICHAEL JACKSON (EPIC)
I THINK WE'RE ALONE NOW TIFFANY (MCA)	10	HEARSAY ALEXANDER O'NEAL (TABU)
SAY IT AGAIN JERMAINE STEWART (10/VIRGIN)	11	THE GREATEST LOVE VARIOUS (TELSTAR)
HAZY SHADE OF WINTER BANGLES (DEF JAM)	12	HEAVEN ON EARTH BELINDA CARLISLE (VIRGIN)
DOMINION SISTERS OF MERCY (MERCIFUL RELEASE/WEA)	13	ACTUALLY PET SHOP BOYS (PARLOPHONE)
C'MON EVERYBODY EDDIE COCHRAN (LIBERTY)	14	FAITH GEORGE MICHAEL (EPIC)
CRASH THE PRIMITIVES (RCA)	15	NOTHING LIKE THE SUN STING (A&M)
THAT'S THE WAY IT IS MEL & KIM (SUPREME)	16	ALL ABOUT EVE ALL ABOUT EVE (MERCURY/PHONOGRAM)
I GET WEAK BELINDA CARLISLE (VIRGIN)	17	TANGO IN THE NIGHT FLEETWOOD MAC (WARNER BROS)
TOWER OF STRENGTH THE MISSION (MERCURY/PHONOGRAM)	18	COME INTO MY LIFE JOYCE SIMS (FFRR/LONDON)
GOOD GROOVE DEREK B (MUSIC OF LIFE)	19	THE JOSHUA TREE U2 (ISLAND)
SHIP OF FOOLS ERASURE (MUTE)	20	TATTOOED BEAT MESSIAH ZODIAC MINDWARP (MERCURY/PHONOGRAM)

US

SINGLES	US	ALBUMS
FATHER FIGURE GEORGE MICHAEL (COLUMBIA)	1	NOW AND ZEN ROBERT PLANT (ES PARANZA/ATLANTIC)
NEVER GONNA GIVE YOU UP RICK ASTLEY (RCA)	2	SKYSCRAPER DAVID LEE ROTH (WARNER BROS)
I GET WEAK BELINDA CARLISLE (MCA)	3	THE LONESOME JUBILEE JOHN COUGAR MELLENCAMP (MERCURY/PG)
ENDLESS SUMMER NIGHTS RICHARD MARX (EMI-MANHATTAN)	4	PERMANENT VACATION AEROSMITH (GEFFEN)
MAN IN THE MIRROR MICHAEL JACKSON (EPIC)	5	BORN TO BE BAD GEORGE THOROGOOD (EMI-MANHATTAN)
OUT OF THE BLUE DEBBIE GIBSON (ATLANTIC)	6	CLOUD NINE GEORGE HARRISON (DARK HORSE)
SHE'S LIKE THE WIND PATRICK SWAYZE (RCA)	7	KICK INXS (ATLANTIC)
JUST LIKE PARADISE DAVID LEE ROTH (WARNER BROS)	8	NOTHING LIKE THE SUN STING (A&M)
GET OUTTA MY DREAMS, GET INTO MY CAR BILLY OCEAN (JIVE/ARISTA)	9	TUNNEL OF LOVE BRUCE SPRINGSTEEN (COLUMBIA)
I WANT HER KEITH SWEAT (ELEKTRA)	10	INSIDE INFORMATION FOREIGNER (ATLANTIC)
HYSTERIA DEF LEPPARD (MERCURY/PG)	11	KINGDOM COME KINGDOM COME (POLYDOR/PG)
(SITTIN' ON) THE DOCK OF THE BAY MICHAEL BOLTON (COLUMBIA)	12	HENRY LEE SUMMER HENRY LEE SUMMER (CBS ASSOCIATED)
BE STILL MY BEATING HEART STING (A&M)	13	A MAN OF COLOURS ICEHOUSE (CHRYSALIS)
I FOUND SOMEONE CHER (GEFFEN)	14	CASUAL GODS JERRY HARRISON (SIRE/WARNER BROS)
CAN'T STAY AWAY FROM YOU G. ESTEFAN & MIAMI SOUND MACHINE (EPIC)	15	ISLANDS MIKE OLDFIELD (VIRGIN)
ROCKET 2 U JETS (MCA)	16	HYSTERIA DEF LEPPARD (MERCURY/PG)
LOVE OVERBOARD GLADYS KNIGHT & THE PIPS (MCA)	17	ROBBIE ROBERTSON ROBBIE ROBERTSON (GEFFEN)
DEVIL INSIDE INXS (ATLANTIC)	18	TO THE POWER OF THREE 3 (GEFFEN)
WHAT HAVE I DONE TO DESERVE THIS? PET SHOP BOYS/D. SPRINGFIELD (EMI-MAN.)	19	ANY MAN'S HUNGER DANNY WILDE (GEFFEN)
WHERE DO BROKEN HEARTS GO? WHITNEY HOUSTON (ARISTA)	20	BIG GENERATOR YES (ATCO)

WEEK ENDING MARCH 12 1988

SINGLES UK ALBUMS

Singles		Albums
I SHOULD BE SO LUCKY KYLIE MINOGUE (PWL)	1	INTRODUCING THE HARDLINE ACCORDING TO... TERENCE TRENT D'ARBY (CBS)
TOGETHER FOREVER RICK ASTLEY (RCA)	2	CHILDREN THE MISSION (MERCURY/PHONOGRAM)
BEAT DIS BOMB THE BASS (MUTE)	3	GIVE ME THE REASON LUTHER VANDROSS (EPIC)
JOE LE TAXI VANESSA PARADIS (POLYDOR)	4	THE BEST OF OMD OMD (VIRGIN)
GET OUTTA MY DREAMS, GET INTO MY CAR BILLY OCEAN (JIVE)	5	WHENEVER YOU NEED SOMEBODY RICK ASTLEY (RCA)
DOCTORIN' THE HOUSE COLDCUT/YAZZ/PLAS. POP. (AHEAD OF OUR TIME)	6	POPPED IN SOULED OUT WET WET WET (PRECIOUS/PHONOGRAM)
GIMME HOPE JO'ANNA EDDY GRANT (ICE)	7	BRIDGE OF SPIES T'PAU (SIREN)
SUEDEHEAD MORRISSEY (HIS MASTER'S VOICE)	8	TURN BACK THE CLOCK JOHNNY HATES JAZZ (VIRGIN)
CRASH THE PRIMITIVES (RCA)	9	UNFORGETTABLE VARIOUS (EMI)
THAT'S THE WAY IT IS MEL & KIM (SUPREME)	10	NOW AND ZEN ROBERT PLANT (ESPARANZA/ATLANTIC)
HAZY SHADE OF WINTER BANGLES (DEF JAM)	11	HEAVEN ON EARTH BELINDA CARLISLE (VIRGIN)
SHIP OF FOOLS ERASURE (MUTE)	12	BAD MICHAEL JACKSON (EPIC)
I GET WEAK BELINDA CARLISLE (VIRGIN)	13	IDLEWILD EVERYTHING BUT THE GIRL (BLANCO Y NEGRO)
TELL IT TO MY HEART TAYLOR DAYNE (ARISTA)	14	TIFFANY TIFFANY (MCA)
DOMINION SISTERS OF MERCY (MERCIFUL RELEASE/WEA)	15	THE CHRISTIANS THE CHRISTIANS (ISLAND)
GOOD GROOVE DEREK B (MUSIC OF LIFE)	16	THE GREATEST LOVE VARIOUS (TELSTAR)
LOVE IS CONTAGIOUS TAJA SEVELLE (PAISLEY PARK/REPRISE/WEA)	17	THE JOSHUA TREE U2 (ISLAND)
C'MON EVERYBODY EDDIE COCHRAN (LIBERTY)	18	HEARSAY ALEXANDER O'NEAL (TABU)
I THINK WE'RE ALONE NOW TIFFANY (MCA)	19	THE FRENZ EXPERIMENT THE FALL (BEGGARS BANQUET)
NEVER/THESE DREAMS HEART (CAPITOL)	20	TANGO IN THE NIGHT FLEETWOOD MAC (WARNER BROS)

SINGLES US ALBUMS

Singles		Albums
NEVER GONNA GIVE YOU UP RICK ASTLEY (RCA)	1	NOW AND ZEN ROBERT PLANT (ES PARANZA/ATLANTIC)
MAN IN THE MIRROR MICHAEL JACKSON (EPIC)	2	SKYSCRAPER DAVID LEE ROTH (WARNER BROS)
ENDLESS SUMMER NIGHTS RICHARD MARX (EMI-MANHATTAN)	3	THE LONESOME JUBILEE JOHN COUGAR MELLENCAMP (MERCURY/PG)
I GET WEAK BELINDA CARLISLE (MCA)	4	PERMANENT VACATION AEROSMITH (GEFFEN)
OUT OF THE BLUE DEBBIE GIBSON (ATLANTIC)	5	CLOUD NINE GEORGE HARRISON (DARK HORSE)
FATHER FIGURE GEORGE MICHAEL (COLUMBIA)	6	BORN TO BE BAD GEORGE THOROGOOD (EMI-MANHATTAN)
GET OUTTA MY DREAMS, GET INTO MY CAR BILLY OCEAN (JIVE/ARISTA)	7	TUNNEL OF LOVE BRUCE SPRINGSTEEN (COLUMBIA)
I WANT HER KEITH SWEAT (ELEKTRA)	8	HENRY LEE SUMMER HENRY LEE SUMMER (CBS ASSOCIATED)
JUST LIKE PARADISE DAVID LEE ROTH (WARNER BROS)	9	KINGDOM COME KINGDOM COME (POLYDOR/PG)
HYSTERIA DEF LEPPARD (MERCURY/PG)	10	KICK INXS (ATLANTIC)
(SITTIN' ON) THE DOCK OF THE BAY MICHAEL BOLTON (COLUMBIA)	11	INSIDE INFORMATION FOREIGNER (ATLANTIC)
SHE'S LIKE THE WIND PATRICK SWAYZE (RCA)	12	NOTHING LIKE THE SUN STING (A&M)
ROCKET 2 U JETS (MCA)	13	A MAN OF COLOURS ICEHOUSE (CHRYSALIS)
DEVIL INSIDE INXS (ATLANTIC)	14	CASUAL GODS JERRY HARRISON (SIRE/WARNER BROS)
WHERE DO BROKEN HEARTS GO? WHITNEY HOUSTON (ARISTA)	15	HYSTERIA DEF LEPPARD (MERCURY/PG)
GIRLFRIEND PEBBLES (MCA)	16	TO THE POWER OF THREE 3 (GEFFEN)
BE STILL MY BEATING HEART STING (A&M)	17	ANY MAN'S HUNGER DANNY WILDE (GEFFEN)
WISHING WELL TERENCE TRENT D'ARBY (CBS)	18	ISLANDS MIKE OLDFIELD (VIRGIN)
SOME KIND OF LOVER JODY WATLEY (MCA)	19	ROBBIE ROBERTSON ROBBIE ROBERTSON (GEFFEN)
ROCK OF LIFE RICK SPRINGFIELD (RCA)	20	BIG GENERATOR YES (ATCO)

WEEK ENDING MARCH 19 1988

SINGLES UK ALBUMS

Singles		Albums
I SHOULD BE SO LUCKY KYLIE MINOGUE (PWL)	1	INTRODUCING THE HARDLINE ACCORDING TO... TERENCE TRENT D'ARBY (CBS)
TOGETHER FOREVER RICK ASTLEY (RCA)	2	THE BEST OF OMD OMD (VIRGIN)
JOE LE TAXI VANESSA PARADIS (POLYDOR)	3	TEAR DOWN THESE WALLS BILLY OCEAN (JIVE)
DON'T TURN AROUND ASWAD (MANGO/ISLAND)	4	WHENEVER YOU NEED SOMEBODY RICK ASTLEY (RCA)
CRASH THE PRIMITIVES (RCA)	5	UNFORGETTABLE VARIOUS (EMI)
SHIP OF FOOLS ERASURE (MUTE)	6	HEARSAY ALEXANDER O'NEAL (TABU)
LOVE IS CONTAGIOUS TAJA SEVELLE (PAISLEY PARK/REPRISE/WEA)	7	POPPED IN SOULED OUT WET WET WET (PRECIOUS/PHONOGRAM)
BEAT DIS BOMB THE BASS (MUTE)	8	TURN BACK THE CLOCK JOHNNY HATES JAZZ (VIRGIN)
DOCTORIN' THE HOUSE COLDCUT/YAZZ/PLAS. POP. (AHEAD OF OUR TIME)	9	GIVE ME THE REASON LUTHER VANDROSS (EPIC)
GET OUTTA MY DREAMS, GET INTO MY CAR BILLY OCEAN (JIVE)	10	WHO'S BETTER WHO'S BEST THE WHO (POLYDOR)
I GET WEAK BELINDA CARLISLE (VIRGIN)	11	BRIDGE OF SPIES T'PAU (SIREN)
NEVER/THESE DREAM HEART (CAPITOL)	12	HEAVEN ON EARTH BELINDA CARLISLE (VIRGIN)
I KNOW YOU GOT SOUL ERIC B & RAKIM (COOLTEMPO/CHRYSALIS)	13	CHILDREN THE MISSION (MERCURY/PHONOGRAM)
GIMME HOPE JO'ANNA EDDY GRANT (ICE)	14	THE GREATEST LOVE VARIOUS (TELSTAR)
THAT'S THE WAY IT IS MEL & KIM (SUPREME)	15	BAD MICHAEL JACKSON (EPIC)
WHERE DO BROKEN HEARTS GO WHITNEY HOUSTON (ARISTA)	16	WHITNEY WHITNEY HOUSTON (ARISTA)
DROP THE BOY BROS (CBS)	17	TANGO IN THE NIGHT FLEETWOOD MAC (WARNER BROS)
RECKLESS AFRIKA BAMBAATAA/UB40 (EMI)	18	THE CHRISTIANS THE CHRISTIANS (ISLAND)
HEART OF GOLD JOHNNY HATES JAZZ (VIRGIN)	19	NOTHING LIKE THE SUN STING (A&M)
.I'M NOT SCARED EIGHTH WONDER (CBS)	20	TIFFANY TIFFANY (MCA)

SINGLES US ALBUMS

Singles		Albums
MAN IN THE MIRROR MICHAEL JACKSON (EPIC)	1	NOW AND ZEN ROBERT PLANT (ES PARANZA/ATLANTIC)
ENDLESS SUMMER NIGHTS RICHARD MARX (EMI-MANHATTAN)	2	SKYSCRAPER DAVID LEE ROTH (WARNER BROS)
OUT OF THE BLUE DEBBIE GIBSON (ATLANTIC)	3	THE LONESOME JUBILEE JOHN COUGAR MELLENCAMP (MERCURY/PG)
GET OUTTA MY DREAMS, GET INTO MY CAR BILLY OCEAN (JIVE/ARISTA)	4	PERMANENT VACATION AEROSMITH (GEFFEN)
NEVER GONNA GIVE YOU UP RICK ASTLEY (RCA)	5	HENRY LEE SUMMER HENRY LEE SUMMER (CBS ASSOCIATED)
I WANT HER KEITH SWEAT (ELEKTRA)	6	KINGDOM COME KINGDOM COME (POLYDOR/PG)
I GET WEAK BELINDA CARLISLE (MCA)	7	TUNNEL OF LOVE BRUCE SPRINGSTEEN (COLUMBIA)
DEVIL INSIDE INXS (ATLANTIC)	8	CLOUD NINE GEORGE HARRISON (DARK HORSE)
WHERE DO BROKEN HEARTS GO? WHITNEY HOUSTON (ARISTA)	9	BORN TO BE BAD GEORGE THOROGOOD (EMI-MANHATTAN)
ROCKET 2 U JETS (MCA)	10	KICK INXS (ATLANTIC)
(SITTIN' ON) THE DOCK OF THE BAY MICHAEL BOLTON (COLUMBIA)	11	INSIDE INFORMATION FOREIGNER (ATLANTIC)
HYSTERIA DEF LEPPARD (MERCURY/PG)	12	A MAN OF COLOURS ICEHOUSE (CHRYSALIS)
GIRLFRIEND PEBBLES (MCA)	13	CASUAL GODS JERRY HARRISON (SIRE/WARNER BROS)
WISHING WELL TERENCE TRENT D'ARBY (CBS)	14	NAKED CITY TALKING HEADS (FLY/SIRE)
FATHER FIGURE GEORGE MICHAEL (COLUMBIA)	15	TO THE POWER OF THREE 3 (GEFFEN)
SOME KIND OF LOVER JODY WATLEY (MCA)	16	NOTHING LIKE THE SUN STING (A&M)
I SAW HIM STANDING THERE TIFFANY (MCA)	17	HYSTERIA DEF LEPPARD (MERCURY/PG)
ANGEL AEROSMITH (GEFFEN)	18	EYE OF THE HURRICANE ALARM (IRS/MCA)
ROCK OF LIFE RICK SPRINGFIELD (RCA)	19	ANY MAN'S HUNGER DANNY WILDE (GEFFEN)
JUST LIKE PARADISE DAVID LEE ROTH (WARNER BROS)	20	MIDNIGHT OIL DEISEL AND DUST (COLUMBIA)

WEEK ENDING MARCH 26 1988

UK

Singles		Albums
DON'T TURN AROUND ASWAD (MANGO/ISLAND)	1	VIVA HATE MORRISSEY (HIS MASTER'S VOICE)
DROP THE BOY BROS (CBS)	2	THE BEST OF OMD OMD (VIRGIN)
I SHOULD BE SO LUCKY KYLIE MINOGUE (PWL)	3	NAKED TALKING HEADS (EMI)
CAN I PLAY WITH MADNESS IRON MAIDEN (EMI)	4	HEARSAY ALEXANDER O'NEAL (TABU)
COULD'VE BEEN TIFFANY (MCA)	5	FROM LANGLEY PARK TO MEMPHIS PREFAB SPROUT (KITCHENWARE/CBS)
JOE LE TAXI VANESSA PARADIS (POLYDOR)	6	INTRODUCING THE HARDLINE ACCORDING TO... TERENCE TRENT D'ARBY (CBS)
CRASH THE PRIMITIVES (RCA)	7	UNFORGETTABLE VARIOUS (EMI)
NEVER/THESE DREAMS HEART (CAPITOL)	8	TEAR DOWN THESE WALLS BILLY OCEAN (JIVE)
SHIP OF FOOLS ERASURE (MUTE)	9	POPPED IN SOULED OUT WET WET WET (PRECIOUS/PHONOGRAM)
I GET WEAK BELINDA CARLISLE (VIRGIN)	10	WHENEVER YOU NEED SOMEBODY RICK ASTLEY (RCA)
TOGETHER FOREVER RICK ASTLEY (RCA)	11	TURN BACK THE CLOCK JOHNNY HATES JAZZ (VIRGIN)
LOVE IS CONTAGIOUS TAJA SEVELLE (PAISLEY PARK/REPRISE/WEA)	12	WHO'S BETTER WHO'S BEST THE WHO (POLYDOR)
I'M NOT SCARED EIGHTH WONDER (CBS)	13	HEAVEN ON EARTH BELINDA CARLISLE (VIRGIN)
CROSS MY BROKEN HEART SINITTA (FANFARE)	14	GIVE ME THE REASON LUTHER VANDROSS (EPIC)
WHERE DO BROKEN HEARTS GO WHITNEY HOUSTON (ARISTA)	15	WHITNEY WHITNEY HOUSTON (ARISTA)
BASS SIMON HARRIS (FFRR/LONDON)	16	TANGO IN THE NIGHT FLEETWOOD MAC (WARNER BROS)
RECKLESS AFRIKA BAMBAATAA/UB40 (EMI)	17	HORIZONS VARIOUS (K-TEL)
STAY ON THESE ROADS A-HA (WARNER BROS)	18	SO FAR, SO GOOD... SO WHAT! MEGADETH (CAPITOL)
I KNOW YOU GOT SOUL ERIC B & RAKIM (COALTEMPO/CHRYSALIS)	19	BRIDGE OF SPIES T'PAU (SIREN)
DOCTORIN' THE HOUSE COLDCUT/YAZZ/PLAS. POP. (AHEAD OF OUR TIME)	20	THE CHART SHOW ROCK THE NATION VARIOUS (DOVER/CHRYSALIS)

US

Singles		Albums
MAN IN THE MIRROR MICHAEL JACKSON (EPIC)	1	NOW AND ZEN ROBERT PLANT (ES PARANZA/ATLANTIC)
GET OUTTA MY DREAMS, GET INTO MY CAR BILLY OCEAN (JIVE/ARISTA)	2	SKYSCRAPER DAVID LEE ROTH (WARNER BROS)
OUT OF THE BLUE DEBBIE GIBSON (ATLANTIC)	3	HENRY LEE SUMMER HENRY LEE SUMMER (CBS ASSOCIATED)
ENDLESS SUMMER NIGHTS RICHARD MARX (EMI-MANHATTAN)	4	THE LONESOME JUBILEE JOHN COUGAR MELLENCAMP (MERCURY/PG)
I WANT HER KEITH SWEAT (ELEKTRA)	5	KINGDOM COME KINGDOM COME (POLYDOR/PG)
DEVIL INSIDE INXS (ATLANTIC)	6	TUNNEL OF LOVE BRUCE SPRINGSTEEN (COLUMBIA)
WHERE DO BROKEN HEARTS GO? WHITNEY HOUSTON (ARISTA)	7	INSIDE INFORMATION FOREIGNER (ATLANTIC)
ROCKET 2 U JETS (MCA)	8	BORN TO BE BAD GEORGE THOROGOOD (EMI-MANHATTAN)
GIRLFRIEND PEBBLES (MCA)	9	KICK INXS (ATLANTIC)
WISHING WELL TERENCE TRENT D'ARBY (CBS)	10	PERMANENT VACATION AEROSMITH (GEFFEN)
SOME KIND OF LOVER JODY WATLEY (MCA)	11	CLOUD NINE GEORGE HARRISON (DARK HORSE)
ANGEL AEROSMITH (GEFFEN)	12	CASUAL GODS JERRY HARRISON (SIRE/WARNER BROS)
I SAW HIM STANDING THERE TIFFANY (MCA)	13	A MAN OF COLOURS ICEHOUSE (CHRYSALIS)
NEVER GONNA GIVE YOU UP RICK ASTLEY (RCA)	14	NAKED TALKING HEADS (FLY/SIRE)
(SITTIN' ON) THE DOCK OF THE BAY MICHAEL BOLTON (COLUMBIA)	15	TO THE POWER OF THREE 3 (GEFFEN)
I GET WEAK BELINDA CARLISLE (MCA)	16	MIDNIGHT OIL DEISEL AND DUST (COLUMBIA)
HYSTERIA DEF LEPPARD (MERCURY/PG)	17	EYE OF THE HURRICANE ALARM (IRS/MCA)
PROVE YOUR LOVE TAYLOR DAYNE (ARISTA)	18	STARFISH CHURCH (ARISTA)
CHECK IT OUT JOHN COUGAR MELLENCAMP (MERCURY/PG)	19	NOTHING LIKE THE SUN STING (A&M)
YOU DON'T KNOW SCARLETT & BLACK (VIRGIN)	20	BIG GENERATOR YES (ATCO)

WEEK ENDING APRIL 2 1988

UK

Singles		Albums
DON'T TURN AROUND ASWAD (MANGO/ISLAND)	1	NOW! 11 VARIOUS (EMI/VIRGIN/POLYGRAM)
DROP THE BOY BROS (CBS)	2	THE BEST OF OMD OMD (VIRGIN)
CAN I PLAY WITH MADNESS IRON MAIDEN (EMI)	3	POPPED IN SOULED OUT WET WET WET (PRECIOUS/PHONOGRAM)
COULD'VE BEEN TIFFANY (MCA)	4	VIVA HATE MORRISSEY (HIS MASTER'S VOICE)
STAY ON THESE ROADS A-HA (WARNER BROS)	5	NAKED TALKING HEADS (EMI)
CROSS MY BROKEN HEART SINITTA (FANFARE)	6	INTRODUCING THE HARDLINE ACCORDING TO... TERENCE TRENT D'ARBY (CBS)
HEART PET SHOP BOYS (PARLOPHONE)	7	THE STORY OF THE CLASH THE CLASH (CBS)
I SHOULD BE SO LUCKY KYLIE MINOGUE (PWL)	8	LIVE IN EUROPE TINA TURNER (CAPITOL)
NEVER/THESE DREAMS HEART (CAPITOL)	9	HEARSAY ALEXANDER O'NEAL (TABU)
I'M NOT SCARED EIGHTH WONDER (CBS)	10	TURN BACK THE CLOCK JOHNNY HATES JAZZ (VIRGIN)
LOVE CHANGES CLIMIE FISHER (EMI)	11	WHENEVER YOU NEED SOMEBODY RICK ASTLEY (RCA)
BASS SIMON HARRIS (FFRR/LONDON)	12	TEAR DOWN THESE WALLS BILLY OCEAN (JIVE)
ONLY IN MY DREAMS DEBBIE GIBSON (ATLANTIC)	13	HORIZONS VARIOUS (K-TEL)
WHERE DO BROKEN HEARTS GO WHITNEY HOUSTON (ARISTA)	14	WHITNEY WHITNEY HOUSTON (ARISTA)
CRASH THE PRIMITIVES (RCA)	15	WHO'S BETTER WHO'S BEST THE WHO (POLYDOR)
I GET WEAK BELINDA CARLISLE (VIRGIN)	16	THE CHART SHOW ROCK THE NATION VARIOUS (DOVER/CHRYSALIS)
TEMPTATION WET WET WET (PRECIOUS/PHONOGRAM)	17	UNFORGETTABLE VARIOUS (EMI)
SHIP OF FOOLS ERASURE (MUTE)	18	FROM LANGLEY PARK TO MEMPHIS PREFAB SPROUT (KITCHENWARE/CBS)
RECKLESS AFRIKA BAMBAATAA/UB40 (EMI)	19	HEAVEN ON EARTH BELINDA CARLISLE (VIRGIN)
JOE LE TAXI VANESSA PARADIS (POLYDOR)	20	TANGO IN THE NIGHT FLEETWOOD MAC (WARNER BROS)

US

Singles		Albums
MAN IN THE MIRROR MICHAEL JACKSON (EPIC)	1	NOW AND ZEN ROBERT PLANT (ES PARANZA/ATLANTIC)
GET OUTTA MY DREAMS, GET INTO MY CAR BILLY OCEAN (JIVE/ARISTA)	2	SKYSCRAPER DAVID LEE ROTH (WARNER BROS)
DEVIL INSIDE INXS (ATLANTIC)	3	HENRY LEE SUMMER HENRY LEE SUMMER (CBS ASSOCIATED)
WHERE DO BROKEN HEARTS GO? WHITNEY HOUSTON (ARISTA)	4	KINGDOM COME KINGDOM COME (POLYDOR/PG)
OUT OF THE BLUE DEBBIE GIBSON (ATLANTIC)	5	INSIDE INFORMATION FOREIGNER (ATLANTIC)
WISHING WELL TERENCE TRENT D'ARBY (CBS)	6	KICK INXS (ATLANTIC)
ROCKET 2 U JETS (MCA)	7	TUNNEL OF LOVE BRUCE SPRINGSTEEN (COLUMBIA)
GIRLFRIEND PEBBLES (MCA)	8	NAKED TALKING HEADS (FLY/SIRE)
SOME KIND OF LOVER JODY WATLEY (MCA)	9	BORN TO BE BAD GEORGE THOROGOOD (EMI-MANHATTAN)
ANGEL AEROSMITH (GEFFEN)	10	CASUAL GODS JERRY HARRISON (SIRE/WARNER BROS)
I SAW HIM STANDING THERE TIFFANY (MCA)	11	MIDNIGHT OIL DEISEL AND DUST (COLUMBIA)
ENDLESS SUMMER NIGHTS RICHARD MARX (EMI-MANHATTAN)	12	THE LONESOME JUBILEE JOHN COUGAR MELLENCAMP (MERCURY/PG)
I WANT HER KEITH SWEAT (ELEKTRA)	13	TO THE POWER OF THREE 3 (GEFFEN)
PROVE YOUR LOVE TAYLOR DAYNE (ARISTA)	14	STARFISH CHURCH (ARISTA)
PINK CADILLAC NATALIE COLE (EMI-MANHATTAN)	15	SOUNDTRACK BRIGHT LIGHTS, BIG CITY (WARNER BROS)
ANYTHING FOR YOU G. ESTEFAN & MIAMI SOUND MACHINE (EPIC)	16	PERMANENT VACATION AEROSMITH (GEFFEN)
CHECK IT OUT JOHN COUGAR MELLENCAMP (MERCURY/PG)	17	EYE OF THE HURRICANE ALARM (IRS/MCA)
ELECTRIC BLUE ICEHOUSE (CHRYSALIS)	18	GREEN THOUGHTS SMITHEREENS (ENIGMA/CAPITOL)
YOU DON'T KNOW SCARLETT & BLACK (VIRGIN)	19	A MAN OF COLOURS ICEHOUSE (CHRYSALIS)
ONE STEP UP BRUCE SPRINGSTEEN (COLUMBIA)	20	CLOUD NINE GEORGE HARRISON (DARK HORSE)

WEEK ENDING APRIL 9 1988

SINGLES UK ALBUMS

		UK		
HEART	PET SHOP BOYS (PARLOPHONE)	1	NOW! 11	VARIOUS (EMI/VIRGIN/POLYGRAM)
DROP THE BOY	BROS (CBS)	2	PUSH	BROS (CBS)
DON'T TURN AROUND	ASWAD (MANGO/ISLAND)	3	THE BEST OF OMD	OMD (VIRGIN)
COULD'VE BEEN	TIFFANY (MCA)	4	POPPED IN SOULED OUT	WET WET WET (PRECIOUS/PHONOGRAM)
CAN I PLAY WITH MADNESS	IRON MAIDEN (EMI)	5	WINGS OF HEAVEN	MAGNUM (POLYDOR)
CROSS MY BROKEN HEART	SINITTA (FANFARE)	6	LOVELY	THE PRIMITIVES (RCA)
LOVE CHANGES	CLIMIE FISHER (EMI)	7	TANGO IN THE NIGHT	FLEETWOOD MAC (WARNER BROS)
STAY ON THESE ROADS	A-HA (WARNER BROS)	8	INTRODUCING THE HARDLINE ACCORDING TO . . .	TERENCE TRENT D'ARBY (CBS)
I'M NOT SCARED	EIGHTH WONDER (CBS)	9	LIVE IN EUROPE	TINA TURNER (CAPITOL)
I SHOULD BE SO LUCKY	KYLIE MINOGUE (PWL)	10	DISTANT THUNDER	ASWAD (MANGO/ISLAND)
ONLY IN MY DREAMS	DEBBIE GIBSON (ATLANTIC)	11	VIVA HATE	MORRISSEY (HIS MASTER'S VOICE)
TEMPTATION	WET WET WET (PRECIOUS/PHONOGRAM)	12	WHENEVER YOU NEED SOMEBODY	RICK ASTLEY (RCA)
EVERYWHERE	FLEETWOOD MAC (WARNER BROS)	13	WHITNEY	WHITNEY HOUSTON (ARISTA)
NEVER/THESE DREAMS	HEART (CAPITOL)	14	TURN BACK THE CLOCK	JOHNNY HATES JAZZ (VIRGIN)
PROVE YOUR LOVE	TAYLOR DAYNE (ARISTA)	15	DIRTY DANCING	ORIGINAL SOUNDTRACK (RCA)
DREAMING	GLEN GOLDSMITH (REPRODUCTIONS/RCA)	16	NAKED	TALKING HEADS (EMI)
WHERE DO BROKEN HEARTS GO	WHITNEY HOUSTON (ARISTA)	17	HEARSAY	ALEXANDER O'NEAL (TABU)
BASS	SIMON HARRIS (FFRR/LONDON)	18	UNFORGETTABLE	VARIOUS (EMI)
AIN'T COMPLAINING	STATUS QUO (VERTIGO/PHONOGRAM)	19	TIFFANY	TIFFANY (MCA)
WHO'S LEAVING WHO	HAZELL DEAN (EMI)	20	ACTUALLY	PET SHOP BOYS (PARLOPHONE)

SINGLES US ALBUMS

		US		
GET OUTTA MY DREAMS, GET INTO MY CAR	BILLY OCEAN (JIVE/ARISTA)	1	NOW AND ZEN	ROBERT PLANT (ES PARANZA/ATLANTIC)
WHERE DO BROKEN HEARTS GO?	WHITNEY HOUSTON (ARISTA)	2	SKYSCRAPER	DAVID LEE ROTH (WARNER BROS)
DEVIL INSIDE	INXS (ATLANTIC)	3	HENRY LEE SUMMER	HENRY LEE SUMMER (CBS ASSOCIATED)
MAN IN THE MIRROR	MICHAEL JACKSON (EPIC)	4	INSIDE INFORMATION	FOREIGNER (ATLANTIC)
WISHING WELL	TERENCE TRENT D'ARBY (CBS)	5	KINGDOM COME	KINGDOM COME (POLYDOR/PG)
GIRLFRIEND	PEBBLES (MCA)	6	KICK	INXS (ATLANTIC)
ROCKET 2 U	JETS (MCA)	7	NAKED	TALKING HEADS (FLY/SIRE)
ANGEL	AEROSMITH (GEFFEN)	8	TUNNEL OF LOVE	BRUCE SPRINGSTEEN (COLUMBIA)
SOME KIND OF LOVER	JODY WATLEY (MCA)	9	BORN TO BE BAD	GEORGE THOROGOOD (EMI-MANHATTAN)
ANYTHING FOR YOU	G. ESTEFAN & MIAMI SOUND MACHINE (EPIC)	10	CASUAL GODS	JERRY HARRISON (SIRE/WARNER BROS)
I SAW HIM STANDING THERE	TIFFANY (MCA)	11	MIDNIGHT OIL	DEISEL AND DUST (COLUMBIA)
PROVE YOUR LOVE	TAYLOR DAYNE (ARISTA)	12	STARFISH	CHURCH (ARISTA)
PINK CADILLAC	NATALIE COLE (EMI-MANHATTAN)	13	GREEN THOUGHTS	SMITHEREENS (ENIGMA/CAPITOL)
OUT OF THE BLUE	DEBBIE GIBSON (ATLANTIC)	14	SOUNDTRACK	BRIGHT LIGHTS, BIG CITY (WARNER BROS)
ELECTRIC BLUE	ICEHOUSE (CHRYSALIS)	15	TO THE POWER OF THREE	3 (GEFFEN)
ONE STEP UP	BRUCE SPRINGSTEEN (COLUMBIA)	16	LIVE FREE OR DIE	BALAAM & THE ANGEL (VIRGIN)
I WANT HER	KEITH SWEAT (ELEKTRA)	17	SOUTHERN BY THE GRACE OF GOD	LYNYRD SKYNYRD (MCA)
SHATTERED DREAMS	JOHNNY HATES JAZZ (VIRGIN)	18	EYE OF THE HURRICANE	ALARM (IRS/MCA)
I DON'T WANT TO LIVE WITHOUT YOU	FOREIGNER (ATLANTIC)	19	ONE GOOD REASON	PAUL CARRACK (CHRYSALIS)
PAMELA	TOTO (COLUMBIA)	20	NOTHING LIKE THE SUN	STING (A&M)

WEEK ENDING APRIL 16 1988

SINGLES UK ALBUMS

		UK		
HEART	PET SHOP BOYS (PARLOPHONE)	1	NOW! 11	VARIOUS (EMI/VIRGIN/POLYGRAM)
DROP THE BOY	BROS (CBS)	2	PUSH	BROS (CBS)
LOVE CHANGES	CLIMIE FISHER (EMI)	3	THE BEST OF OMD	OMD (VIRGIN)
COULD'VE BEEN	TIFFANY (MCA)	4	POPPED IN SOULED OUT	WET WET WET (PRECIOUS/PHONOGRAM)
EVERYWHERE	FLEETWOOD MAC (WARNER BROS)	5	TANGO IN THE NIGHT	FLEETWOOD MAC (WARNER BROS)
CROSS MY BROKEN HEART	SINITTA (FANFARE)	6	DIRTY DANCING	ORIGINAL SOUNDTRACK (RCA)
I'M NOT SCARED	EIGHTH WONDER (CBS)	7	ACTUALLY	PET SHOP BOYS (PARLOPHONE)
PROVE YOUR LOVE	TAYLOR DAYNE (ARISTA)	8	INTRODUCING THE HARDLINE ACCORDING TO . . .	TERENCE TRENT D'ARBY (CBS)
WHO'S LEAVING WHO	HAZELL DEAN (EMI)	9	HIP HOP AND RAPPING IN THE HOUSE	VARIOUS (STYLUS)
DON'T TURN AROUND	ASWAD (MANGO/ISLAND)	10	TURN BACK THE CLOCK	JOHNNY HATES JAZZ (VIRGIN)
PINK CADILLAC	NATALIE COLE (MANHATTAN/EMI)	11	WHITNEY	WHITNEY HOUSTON (ARISTA)
DREAMING	GLEN GOLDSMITH (REPRODUCTIONS/RCA)	12	LIVE IN EUROPE	TINA TURNER (CAPITOL)
GIRLFRIEND	PEBBLES (MCA)	13	LOVELY	THE PRIMITIVES (RCA)
I WANT YOU BACK	BANANARAMA (LONDON)	14	DISTANT THUNDER	ASWAD (MANGO/ISLAND)
JUST A MIRAGE	JELLYBEAN/ADELE BERTEI (CHRYSALIS)	15	TIFFANY	TIFFANY (MCA)
ONLY IN MY DREAMS	DEBBIE GIBSON (ATLANTIC)	16	BRIDGE OF SPIES	T'PAU (SIREN/VIRGIN)
STAY ON THESE ROADS	A-HA (WARNER BROS)	17	WHO'S BETTER WHO'S BEST	THE WHO (POLYDOR)
CAN I PLAY WITH MADNESS	IRON MAIDEN (EMI)	18	WINGS OF HEAVEN	MAGNUM (POLYDOR)
TEMPTATION	WET WET WET (PRECIOUS/PHONOGRAM)	19	VIVA HATE	MORRISSEY (HIS MASTER'S VOICE)
ARMAGEDDON IT	DEF LEPPARD (BLUDGEON RIFFOLA)	20	HEARSAY	ALEXANDER O'NEAL (TABU)

SINGLES US ALBUMS

		US		
GET OUTTA MY DREAMS, GET INTO MY CAR	BILLY OCEAN (JIVE/ARISTA)	1	NOW AND ZEN	ROBERT PLANT (ES PARANZA/ATLANTIC)
WHERE DO BROKEN HEARTS GO?	WHITNEY HOUSTON (ARISTA)	2	SKYSCRAPER	DAVID LEE ROTH (WARNER BROS)
DEVIL INSIDE	INXS (ATLANTIC)	3	NAKED	TALKING HEADS (FLY/SIRE)
WISHING WELL	TERENCE TRENT D'ARBY (CBS)	4	KICK	INXS (ATLANTIC)
ANGEL	AEROSMITH (GEFFEN)	5	HENRY LEE SUMMER	HENRY LEE SUMMER (CBS ASSOCIATED)
ANYTHING FOR YOU	G. ESTEFAN & MIAMI SOUND MACHINE (EPIC)	6	INSIDE INFORMATION	FOREIGNER (ATLANTIC)
GIRLFRIEND	PEBBLES (MCA)	7	MIDNIGHT OIL	DEISEL AND DUST (COLUMBIA)
PROVE YOUR LOVE	TAYLOR DAYNE (ARISTA)	8	CASUAL GODS	JERRY HARRISON (SIRE/WARNER BROS)
PINK CADILLAC	NATALIE COLE (EMI-MANHATTAN)	9	STARFISH	CHURCH (ARISTA)
MAN IN THE MIRROR	MICHAEL JACKSON (EPIC)	10	KINGDOM COME	KINGDOM COME (POLYDOR/PG)
SHATTERED DREAMS	JOHNNY HATES JAZZ (VIRGIN)	11	GREEN THOUGHTS	SMITHEREENS (ENIGMA/CAPITOL)
I SAW HIM STANDING THERE	TIFFANY (MCA)	12	TUNNEL OF LOVE	BRUCE SPRINGSTEEN (COLUMBIA)
ELECTRIC BLUE	ICEHOUSE (CHRYSALIS)	13	BORN TO BE BAD	GEORGE THOROGOOD (EMI-MANHATTAN)
I DON'T WANT TO LIVE WITHOUT YOU	FOREIGNER (ATLANTIC)	14	SOUNDTRACK	BRIGHT LIGHTS, BIG CITY (WARNER BROS)
ONE STEP UP	BRUCE SPRINGSTEEN (COLUMBIA)	15	THIS NOTE'S FOR YOU	NEIL YOUNG & THE BLUENOTES (REPRISE)
ALWAYS ON MY MIND	PET SHOP BOYS (EMI-MANHATTAN)	16	LIVE FREE OR DIE	BALAAM & THE ANGEL (VIRGIN)
SOME KIND OF LOVER	JODY WATLEY (MCA)	17	SOUTHERN BY THE GRACE OF GOD	LYNYRD SKYNYRD (MCA)
PAMELA	TOTO (COLUMBIA)	18	ONE GOOD REASON	PAUL CARRACK (CHRYSALIS)
NAUGHTY GIRLS	SAMANTHA FOX (JIVE/RCA)	19	CLOUD NINE	GEORGE HARRISON (DARK HORSE)
ROCKET 2 U	JETS (MCA)	20	CHALK MARK IN A RAINSTORM	JONI MITCHELL (GEFFEN)

WEEK ENDING APRIL 23 1988

UK

SINGLES		ALBUMS
HEART PET SHOP BOYS (PARLOPHONE)	1	SEVENTH SON OF A SEVENTH SON IRON MAIDEN (EMI)
LOVE CHANGES CLIMIE FISHER (EMI)	2	NOW! 11 VARIOUS (EMI/VIRGIN/POLYGRAM)
THEME FROM S'XPRESS S'EXPRESS (RHYTHM KING/MUTE)	3	PUSH BROS (CBS)
EVERYWHERE FLEETWOOD MAC (WARNER BROS)	4	TANGO IN THE NIGHT FLEETWOOD MAC (WARNER BROS)
PINK CADILLAC NATALIE COLE (MANHATTAN/EMI)	5	THE BEST OF OMD OMD (VIRGIN)
WHO'S LEAVING WHO HAZELL DEAN (EMI)	6	POPPED IN SOULED OUT WET WET WET (PRECIOUS/PHONOGRAM)
I WANT YOU BACK BANANARAMA (LONDON)	7	DIRTY DANCING ORIGINAL SOUNDTRACK (RCA)
GIRLFRIEND PEBBLES (MCA)	8	HIP HOP AND RAPPING IN THE HOUSE VARIOUS (STYLUS)
DROP THE BOY BROS (CBS)	9	ACTUALLY PET SHOP BOYS (PARLOPHONE)
I WANT YOU BACK '88 MICHAEL JACKSON/JACKSON 5 (MOTOWN)	10	BRIDGE OF SPIES T'PAU (SIREN/VIRGIN)
PROVE YOUR LOVE TAYLOR DAYNE (ARISTA)	11	INTRODUCING THE HARDLINE ACCORDING TO... TERENCE TRENT D'ARBY (CBS)
COULD'VE BEEN TIFFANY (MCA)	12	NAKED TALKING HEADS (EMI)
JUST A MIRAGE JELLYBEAN/ADELE BERTEI (CHRYSALIS)	13	HEAVEN ON EARTH BELINDA CARLISLE (VIRGIN)
ONE MORE TRY GEORGE MICHAEL (EPIC)	14	WHITNEY WHITNEY HOUSTON (ARISTA)
MARY'S PRAYER DANNY WILSON (VIRGIN)	15	THE CHRISTIANS THE CHRISTIANS (ISLAND)
DREAMING GLEN GOLDSMITH (REPRODUCTIONS/RCA)	16	TIFFANY TIFFANY (MCA)
GET LUCKY JERMAINE STEWART (SIREN/VIRGIN)	17	EVERYTHING CLIMIE FISHER (EMI)
I'M NOT SCARED EIGHTH WONDER (CBS)	18	TURN BACK THE CLOCK JOHNNY HATES JAZZ (VIRGIN)
LET'S ALL CHANT MICK AND PAT (PWL)	19	LOVELY THE PRIMITIVES (RCA)
CROSS MY BROKEN HEART SINITTA (FANFARE)	20	DISTANT THUNDER ASWAD (MANGO/ISLAND)

US

SINGLES		ALBUMS
WHERE DO BROKEN HEARTS GO? WHITNEY HOUSTON (ARISTA)	1	NOW AND ZEN ROBERT PLANT (ES PARANZA/ATLANTIC)
ANYTHING FOR YOU G. ESTEFAN & MIAMI SOUND MACHINE (EPIC)	2	SKYSCRAPER DAVID LEE ROTH (WARNER BROS)
WISHING WELL TERENCE TRENT D'ARBY (CBS)	3	KICK INXS (ATLANTIC)
ANGEL AEROSMITH (GEFFEN)	4	NAKED TALKING HEADS (FLY/SIRE)
DEVIL INSIDE INXS (ATLANTIC)	5	STARFISH CHURCH (ARISTA)
SHATTERED DREAMS JOHNNY HATES JAZZ (VIRGIN)	6	MIDNIGHT OIL DEISEL AND DUST (COLUMBIA)
PINK CADILLAC NATALIE COLE (EMI-MANHATTAN)	7	LAP OF LUXURY CHEAP TRICK (EPIC)
PROVE YOUR LOVE TAYLOR DAYNE (ARISTA)	8	THIS NOTE'S FOR YOU NEIL YOUNG & THE BLUENOTES (REPRISE)
GET OUTTA MY DREAMS, GET INTO MY CAR BILLY OCEAN (JIVE/ARISTA)	9	GREEN THOUGHTS SMITHEREENS (ENIGMA/CAPITOL)
I DON'T WANT TO LIVE WITHOUT YOU FOREIGNER (ATLANTIC)	10	INSIDE INFORMATION FOREIGNER (ATLANTIC)
ALWAYS ON MY MIND PET SHOP BOYS (EMI-MANHATTAN)	11	HENRY LEE SUMMER HENRY LEE SUMMER (CBS ASSOCIATED)
ELECTRIC BLUE ICEHOUSE (CHRYSALIS)	12	SAVAGE AMUSEMENT SCORPIONS (MERCURY/PG)
GIRLFRIEND PEBBLES (MCA)	13	SOUNDTRACK BRIGHT LIGHTS, BIG CITY (WARNER BROS)
ONE MORE TRY GEORGE MICHAEL (COLUMBIA)	14	LIVE FREE OR DIE BALAAM & THE ANGEL (VIRGIN)
NAUGHTY GIRLS SAMANTHA FOX (JIVE/RCA)	15	KINGDOM COME KINGDOM COME (POLYDOR/PG)
TWO OCCASIONS DEELE (SOLAR)	16	CROSSROADS ERIC CLAPTON (POLYDOR/PG)
WAIT WHITE LION (ATLANTIC)	17	DIAMOND SUN GLASS TIGER (EMI-MANHATTAN)
PAMELA TOTO (COLUMBIA)	18	CASUAL GODS JERRY HARRISON (SIRE/WARNER BROS)
ONE STEP UP BRUCE SPRINGSTEEN (COLUMBIA)	19	CLOUD NINE GEORGE HARRISON (DARK HORSE)
PIANO IN THE DARK BRENDA RUSSELL (A&M)	20	SOUTHERN BY THE GRACE OF GOD LYNYRD SKYNYRD (MCA)

WEEK ENDING APRIL 30 1988

UK

SINGLES		ALBUMS
THEME FROM S'XPRESS S'EXPRESS (RHYTHM KING/MUTE)	1	THE INNOCENTS ERASURE (MUTE)
HEART PET SHOP BOYS (PARLOPHONE)	2	NOW! 11 VARIOUS (EMI/VIRGIN/POLYGRAM)
MARY'S PRAYER DANNY WILSON (VIRGIN)	3	TANGO IN THE NIGHT FLEETWOOD MAC (WARNER BROS)
WHO'S LEAVING WHO HAZELL DEAN (EMI)	4	THE BEST OF OMD OMD (VIRGIN)
I WANT YOU BACK BANANARAMA (LONDON)	5	SEVENTH SON OF A SEVENTH SON IRON MAIDEN (EMI)
PINK CADILLAC NATALIE COLE (MANHATTAN/EMI)	6	HIP HOP AND RAPPING IN THE HOUSE VARIOUS (STYLUS)
LOVE CHANGES CLIMIE FISHER (EMI)	7	DIRTY DANCING ORIGINAL SOUNDTRACK (RCA)
ONE MORE TRY GEORGE MICHAEL (EPIC)	8	PUSH BROS (CBS)
I WANT YOU BACK '88 MICHAEL JACKSON/JACKSON 5 (MOTOWN)	9	BARBED WIRE KISSES JESUS AND MARY CHAIN (BLANCO Y NEGRO)
EVERYWHERE FLEETWOOD MAC (WARNER BROS)	10	POPPED IN SOULED OUT WET WET WET (PRECIOUS/PHONOGRAM)
GIRLFRIEND PEBBLES (MCA)	11	ACTUALLY PET SHOP BOYS (PARLOPHONE)
PERFECT FAIRGROUND ATTRACTION (RCA)	12	BRIDGE OF SPIES T'PAU (SIREN/VIRGIN)
GET LUCKY JERMAINE STEWART (SIREN/VIRGIN)	13	NITE FLITE VARIOUS (CBS)
THE PAYBACK MIX PART ONE JAMES BROWN (URBAN/POLYDOR)	14	EVERYTHING CLIMIE FISHER (EMI)
LET'S ALL CHANT MICK AND PAT (PWL)	15	INTRODUCING THE HARDLINE ACCORDING TO... TERENCE TRENT D'ARBY (CBS)
A LOVE SUPREME WILL DOWNING (4TH + BROADWAY/ISLAND)	16	FAITH GEORGE MICHAEL (EPIC)
SHE'S LIKE THE WIND PATRICK SWAYZE/WENDY FRASER (RCA)	17	THE CHRISTIANS THE CHRISTIANS (ISLAND)
JUST A MIRAGE JELLYBEAN/ADELE BERTEI (CHRYSALIS)	18	HEAVEN ON EARTH BELINDA CARLISLE (VIRGIN)
PROVE YOUR LOVE TAYLOR DAYNE (ARISTA)	19	WHITNEY WHITNEY HOUSTON (ARISTA)
DROP THE BOY BROS (CBS)	20	WILL DOWNING WILL DOWNING (4TH + BROADWAY/ISLAND)

US

SINGLES		ALBUMS
ANYTHING FOR YOU G. ESTEFAN & MIAMI SOUND MACHINE (EPIC)	1	NOW AND ZEN ROBERT PLANT (ES PARANZA/ATLANTIC)
WHERE DO BROKEN HEARTS GO? WHITNEY HOUSTON (ARISTA)	2	LAP OF LUXURY CHEAP TRICK (EPIC)
WISHING WELL TERENCE TRENT D'ARBY (CBS)	3	STARFISH CHURCH (ARISTA)
ANGEL AEROSMITH (GEFFEN)	4	GREEN THOUGHTS SMITHEREENS (ENIGMA/CAPITOL)
SHATTERED DREAMS JOHNNY HATES JAZZ (VIRGIN)	5	KICK INXS (ATLANTIC)
ONE MORE TRY GEORGE MICHAEL (COLUMBIA)	6	MIDNIGHT OIL DEISEL AND DUST (COLUMBIA)
PINK CADILLAC NATALIE COLE (EMI-MANHATTAN)	7	SKYSCRAPER DAVID LEE ROTH (WARNER BROS)
I DON'T WANT TO LIVE WITHOUT YOU FOREIGNER (ATLANTIC)	8	THIS NOTE'S FOR YOU NEIL YOUNG & THE BLUENOTES (REPRISE)
ALWAYS ON MY MIND PET SHOP BOYS (EMI-MANHATTAN)	9	CROSSROADS ERIC CLAPTON (POLYDOR/PG)
PROVE YOUR LOVE TAYLOR DAYNE (ARISTA)	10	NAKED TALKING HEADS (FLY/SIRE)
ELECTRIC BLUE ICEHOUSE (CHRYSALIS)	11	SAVAGE AMUSEMENT SCORPIONS (MERCURY/PG)
NAUGHTY GIRLS SAMANTHA FOX (JIVE/RCA)	12	HENRY LEE SUMMER HENRY LEE SUMMER (CBS ASSOCIATED)
TWO OCCASIONS DEELE (SOLAR)	13	DIAMOND SUN GLASS TIGER (EMI-MANHATTAN)
WAIT WHITE LION (ATLANTIC)	14	RACING AFTER MIDNIGHT HONEYMOON SUITE (WARNER BROS)
GET OUTTA MY DREAMS, GET INTO MY CAR BILLY OCEAN (JIVE/ARISTA)	15	INSIDE INFORMATION FOREIGNER (ATLANTIC)
DEVIL INSIDE INXS (ATLANTIC)	16	LIVE FREE OR DIE BALAAM & THE ANGEL (VIRGIN)
EVERYTHING YOUR HEART DESIRES DARYL HALL & JOHN OATES (ARISTA)	17	CLOUD NINE GEORGE HARRISON (DARK HORSE)
PIANO IN THE DARK BRENDA RUSSELL (A&M)	18	KINGDOM COME KINGDOM COME (POLYDOR/PG)
DREAMING OMD (VIRGIN/A&M)	19	TREAT HER RIGHT TREAT HER RIGHT (RCA)
PAMELA TOTO (COLUMBIA)	20	KINGS OF THE SUN KINGS OF THE SUN (RCA)

WEEK ENDING MAY 7 1988

UK

SINGLES		ALBUMS
THEME FROM S'XPRESS S'EXPRESS (RHYTHM KING/MUTE)	1	TANGO IN THE NIGHT FLEETWOOD MAC (WARNER BROS)
PERFECT FAIRGROUND ATTRACTION (RCA)	2	THE INNOCENTS ERASURE (MUTE)
MARY'S PRAYER DANNY WILSON (VIRGIN)	3	NOW! 11 VARIOUS (EMI/VIRGIN/POLYGRAM)
WHO'S LEAVING WHO HAZELL DEAN (EMI)	4	DIRTY DANCING ORIGINAL SOUNDTRACK (RCA)
I WANT YOU BACK BANANARAMA (LONDON)	5	HIP HOP AND RAPPING IN THE HOUSE VARIOUS (STYLUS)
PINK CADILLAC NATALIE COLE (MANHATTAN/EMI)	6	THE BEST OF OMD OMD (VIRGIN)
HEART PET SHOP BOYS (PARLOPHONE)	7	ACTUALLY PET SHOP BOYS (PARLOPHONE)
I WANT YOU BACK '88 MICHAEL JACKSON/JACKSON 5 (MOTOWN)	8	POPPED IN SOULED OUT WET WET WET (PRECIOUS/PHONOGRAM)
ONE MORE TRY GEORGE MICHAEL (EPIC)	9	PUSH BROS (CBS)
BLUE MONDAY 1988 NEW ORDER (FACTORY)	10	WHITNEY WHITNEY HOUSTON (ARISTA)
LET'S ALL CHANT MICK AND PAT (PWL)	11	SEVENTH SON OF A SEVENTH SON IRON MAIDEN (EMI)
THE PAYBACK MIX PART ONE JAMES BROWN (URBAN/POLYDOR)	12	BRIDGE OF SPIES T'PAU (SIREN/VIRGIN)
LOVE CHANGES CLIMIE FISHER (EMI)	13	NITE FLITE VARIOUS (CBS)
A LOVE SUPREME WILL DOWNING (4TH + BROADWAY/ISLAND)	14	LIFE'S TOO GOOD THE SUGARCUBES (ONE LITTLE INDIAN)
PUMP UP THE BITTER STAR TURN ON 45 PINTS (PACIFIC/IMMACULATE)	15	THE CHRISTIANS THE CHRISTIANS (ISLAND)
EVERYWHERE FLEETWOOD MAC (WARNER BROS)	16	BARBED WIRE KISSES JESUS AND MARY CHAIN (BLANCO Y NEGRO)
LOADSAMONEY HARRY ENFIELD (MERCURY/PHONOGRAM)	17	HEAVEN ON EARTH BELINDA CARLISLE (VIRGIN)
ALPHABET STREET PRINCE (PAISLEY PARK/WARNER BROS)	18	EVERYTHING CLIMIE FISHER (EMI)
GET LUCKY JERMAINE STEWART (SIREN/VIRGIN)	19	FAITH GEORGE MICHAEL (EPIC)
SHE'S LIKE THE WIND PATRICK SWAYZE/WENDY FRASER (RCA)	20	WILL DOWNING WILL DOWNING (4TH + BROADWAY/ISLAND)

US

SINGLES		ALBUMS
ANYTHING FOR YOU G. ESTEFAN & MIAMI SOUND MACHINE (EPIC)	1	NOW AND ZEN ROBERT PLANT (ES PARANZA/ATLANTIC)
ONE MORE TRY GEORGE MICHAEL (COLUMBIA)	2	SCENES FROM THE SOUTHSIDE BRUCE HORNSBY & THE RANGE (RCA)
SHATTERED DREAMS JOHNNY HATES JAZZ (VIRGIN)	3	LAP OF LUXURY CHEAP TRICK (EPIC)
I DON'T WANT TO LIVE WITHOUT YOU FOREIGNER (ATLANTIC)	4	GREEN THOUGHTS SMITHEREENS (ENIGMA/CAPITOL)
ALWAYS ON MY MIND PET SHOP BOYS (EMI-MANHATTAN)	5	CROSSROADS ERIC CLAPTON (POLYDOR/PG)
ANGEL AEROSMITH (GEFFEN)	6	STARFISH CHURCH (ARISTA)
WISHING WELL TERENCE TRENT D'ARBY (COLUMBIA)	7	THIS NOTE'S FOR YOU NEIL YOUNG & THE BLUENOTES (REPRISE)
NAUGHTY GIRLS SAMANTHA FOX (JIVE/RCA)	8	MIDNIGHT OIL DIESEL AND DUST (COLUMBIA)
TWO OCCASIONS DEELE (SOLAR)	9	SAVAGE AMUSEMENT SCORPIONS (MERCURY/PG)
ELECTRIC BLUE ICEHOUSE (CHRYSALIS)	10	SKYSCRAPER DAVID LEE ROTH (WARNER BROS)
WHERE DO BROKEN HEARTS GO? WHITNEY HOUSTON (ARISTA)	11	KICK INXS (ATLANTIC)
WAIT WHITE LION (ATLANTIC)	12	DIAMOND SUN GLASS TIGER (EMI-MANHATTAN)
EVERYTHING YOUR HEART DESIRES DARYL HALL & JOHN OATES (ARISTA)	13	NAKED TALKING HEADS (FLY/SIRE)
PINK CADILLAC NATALIE COLE (EMI-MANHATTAN)	14	RACING AFTER MIDNIGHT HONEYMOON SUITE (WARMER BROS)
TOGETHER FOREVER RICK ASTLEY (RCA)	15	CLOUD NINE GEORGE HARRISON (DARK HORSE)
PIANO IN THE DARK BRENDA RUSSELL (A&M)	16	TREAT HER RIGHT TREAT HER RIGHT (RCA)
DREAMING OMD (VIRGIN/A&M)	17	HENRY LEE SUMMER HENRY LEE SUMMER (CBS ASSOCIATED)
STRANGE BUT TRUE TIMES TWO (REPRISE)	18	KINGS OF THE SUN KINGS OF THE SUN (RCA)
FOOLISH BEAT DEBBIE GIBSON (ATLANTIC)	19	PRIDE WHITE LION (ATLANTIC)
MAKE IT REAL JETS (MCA)	20	INSIDE INFORMATION FOREIGNER (ATLANTIC)

WEEK ENDING MAY 14 1988

UK

SINGLES		ALBUMS
PERFECT FAIRGROUND ATTRACTION (RCA)	1	TANGO IN THE NIGHT FLEETWOOD MAC (WARNER BROS)
THEME FROM S'XPRESS S'EXPRESS (RHYTHM KING/MUTE)	2	STAY ON THESE ROADS A-HA (WARNER BROS)
BLUE MONDAY 1988 NEW ORDER (FACTORY)	3	STRONGER THAN PRIDE SADE (EPIC)
LOADSAMONEY HARRY ENFIELD (MERCURY/PHONOGRAM)	4	THE CHRISTIANS THE CHRISTIANS (ISLAND)
WITH A LITTLE . . ./SHE'S LEAVING HOME WET WET WET/BILLY BRAGG (CHILDLINE)	5	DIRTY DANCING ORIGINAL SOUNDTRACK (RCA)
I WANT YOU BACK BANANARAMA (LONDON)	6	NOW! 11 VARIOUS (EMI/VIRGIN/POLYGRAM)
MARY'S PRAYER DANNY WILSON (VIRGIN)	7	THE INNOCENTS ERASURE (MUTE)
WHO'S LEAVING WHO HAZELL DEAN (EMI)	8	POPPED IN SOULED OUT WET WET WET (PRECIOUS/PHONOGRAM)
ALPHABET STREET PRINCE (PAISLEY PARK/WARNER BROS)	9	MORE DIRTY DANCING VARIOUS (RCA)
I WANT YOU BACK '88 MICHAEL JACKSON/JACKSON 5 (MOTOWN)	10	WHITNEY WHITNEY HOUSTON (ARISTA)
PINK CADILLAC NATALIE COLE (MANHATTAN/EMI)	11	PUSH BROS (CBS)
PUMP UP THE BITTER STAR TURN ON 45 PINTS (PACIFIC/IMMACULATE)	12	THE BEST OF OMD OMD (VIRGIN)
ANFIELD RAP LIVERPOOL F.C. (VIRGIN)	13	NITE FLITE VARIOUS (CBS)
LET'S ALL CHANT MICK AND PAT (PWL)	14	HIP HOP AND RAPPING IN THE HOUSE VARIOUS (STYLUS)
GOT TO BE CERTAIN KYLIE MINOGUE (PWL)	15	ACTUALLY PET SHOP BOYS (PARLOPHONE)
DIVINE EMOTIONS NARADA (REPRISE/WARNER BROS)	16	SIXTIES MIX 2 VARIOUS (STYLUS)
A LOVE SUPREME WILL DOWNING (4TH + BROADWAY/ISLAND)	17	BRIDGE OF SPIES T'PAU (SIREN/VIRGIN)
HEART PET SHOP BOYS (PARLOPHONE)	18	SAVAGE AMUSEMENT SCORPIONS (HARVEST/EMI)
ONE MORE TRY GEORGE MICHAEL (EPIC)	19	HEAVEN ON EARTH BELINDA CARLISLE (VIRGIN)
THE PAYBACK MIX PART ONE JAMES BROWN (URBAN/POLYDOR)	20	SEVENTH SON OF A SEVENTH SON IRON MAIDEN (EMI)

US

SINGLES		ALBUMS
ONE MORE TRY GEORGE MICHAEL (COLUMBIA)	1	SCENES FROM THE SOUTHSIDE BRUCE HORNSBY & THE RANGE (RCA)
ANYTHING FOR YOU G. ESTEFAN & MIAMI SOUND MACHINE (EPIC)	2	NOW AND ZEN ROBERT PLANT (ES PARANZA/ATLANTIC)
SHATTERED DREAMS JOHNNY HATES JAZZ (VIRGIN)	3	LAP OF LUXURY CHEAP TRICK (EPIC)
I DON'T WANT TO LIVE WITHOUT YOU FOREIGNER (ATLANTIC)	4	GREEN THOUGHTS SMITHEREENS (ENIGMA/CAPITOL)
ALWAYS ON MY MIND PET SHOP BOYS (EMI-MANHATTAN)	5	CROSSROADS ERIC CLAPTON (POLYDOR/PG)
NAUGHTY GIRLS SAMANTHA FOX (JIVE/RCA)	6	THIS NOTE'S FOR YOU NEIL YOUNG & THE BLUENOTES (REPRISE)
EVERYTHING YOUR HEART DESIRES DARYL HALL & JOHN OATES (ARISTA)	7	SAVAGE AMUSEMENT SCORPIONS (MERCURY/PG)
TOGETHER FOREVER RICK ASTLEY (RCA)	8	STARFISH CHURCH (ARISTA)
TWO OCCASIONS DEELE (SOLAR)	9	MIDNIGHT OIL DIESEL AND DUST (COLUMBIA)
WAIT WHITE LION (ATLANTIC)	10	DIAMOND SUN GLASS TIGER (EMI-MANHATTAN)
ELECTRIC BLUE ICEHOUSE (CHRYSALIS)	11	RACING AFTER MIDNIGHT HONEYMOON SUITE (WARNER BROS)
PIANO IN THE DARK BRENDA RUSSELL (A&M)	12	KICK INXS (ATLANTIC)
FOOLISH BEAT DEBBIE GIBSON (ATLANTIC)	13	SKYSCRAPER DAVID LEE ROTH (WARNER BROS)
MAKE IT REAL JETS (MCA)	14	HENRY LEE SUMMER HENRY LEE SUMMER (CBS ASSOCIATED)
DREAMING OMD (VIRGIN/A&M)	15	TREAT HER RIGHT TREAT HER RIGHT (RCA)
STRANGE BUT TRUE TIMES TWO (REPRISE)	16	CLOUD NINE GEORGE HARRISON (DARK HORSE)
CIRCLE IN THE SAND BELINDA CARLISLE (MCA)	17	TAKE WHAT YOU NEED ROBIN TROWER (ATLANTIC)
ANGEL AEROSMITH (GEFFEN)	18	KINGS OF THE SUN KINGS OF THE SUN (RCA)
WE ALL SLEEP ALONE CHER (GEFFEN)	19	PRIDE WHITE LION (ATLANTIC)
WISHING WELL TERENCE TRENT D'ARBY (COLUMBIA)	20	THE LONESOME JUBILEE JOHN COUGAR MELLENCAMP (MERCURY/PG)

WEEK ENDING MAY 21 1988

SINGLES UK ALBUMS

WITH A LITTLE . . ./SHE'S LEAVING HOME	WET WET WET/BILLY BRAGG (CHILDLINE)	1	LOVESEXY	PRINCE (PAISLEY PARK)
PERFECT	FAIRGROUND ATTRACTION (RCA)	2	TANGO IN THE NIGHT	FLEETWOOD MAC (WARNER BROS)
ANFIELD RAP	LIVERPOOL F.C. (VIRGIN)	3	STRONGER THAN PRIDE	SADE (EPIC)
GOT TO BE CERTAIN	KYLIE MINOGUE (PWL)	4	THE CHRISTIANS	THE CHRISTIANS (ISLAND)
BLUE MONDAY 1988	NEW ORDER (FACTORY)	5	DIRTY DANCING	ORIGINAL SOUNDTRACK (RCA)
LOADSAMONEY	HARRY ENFIELD (MERCURY/PHONOGRAM)	6	POPPED IN SOULED OUT	WET WET WET (PRECIOUS/PHONOGRAM)
THEME FROM S'XPRESS	S'EXPRESS (RHYTHM KING/MUTE)	7	MORE DIRTY DANCING	VARIOUS (RCA)
DIVINE EMOTIONS	NARADA (REPRISE/WARNER BROS)	8	NOW THAT'S WHAT I CALL QUITE GOOD!	THE HOUSEMARTINS (GO! DISCS)
I WANT YOU BACK	BANANARAMA (LONDON)	9	WHITNEY	WHITNEY HOUSTON (ARISTA)
MARY'S PRAYER	DANNY WILSON (VIRGIN)	10	STAY ON THESE ROADS	A-HA (WARNER BROS)
ALPHABET STREET	PRINCE (PAISLEY PARK/WARNER BROS)	11	NOW! 11	VARIOUS (EMI/VIRGIN/POLYGRAM)
CIRCLE IN THE SAND	BELINDA CARLISLE (VIRGIN)	12	MOTOWN DANCE PARTY	VARIOUS (MOTOWN)
WHO'S LEAVING WHO	HAZELL DEAN (EMI)	13	THE INNOCENTS	ERASURE (MUTE)
KING OF ROCK 'N' ROLL	PREFAB SPROUT (KITCHENWARE/CBS)	14	SIXTIES MIX 2	VARIOUS (STYLUS)
PINK CADILLAC	NATALIE COLE (MANHATTAN/EMI)	15	HEAVEN ON EARTH	BELINDA CARLISLE (VIRGIN)
BAD YOUNG BROTHER	DEREK B (TUFF AUDIO/PHONOGRAM)	16	PUSH	BROS (CBS)
SOMEWHERE IN MY HEART	AZTEC CAMERA (WEA)	17	THE BEST OF OMD	OMD (VIRGIN)
I WANT YOU BACK '88	MICHAEL JACKSON/JACKSON 5 (MOTOWN)	18	OPEN UP AND SAY . . . AAH!	POISON (CAPITOL)
WHAT ABOUT LOVE	HEART (CAPITOL)	19	NITE FLITE	VARIOUS (CBS)
BROKEN LAND	THE ADVENTURES (ELEKTRA)	20	HIP HOP AND RAPPING IN THE HOUSE	VARIOUS (STYLUS)

SINGLES US ALBUMS

ONE MORE TRY	GEORGE MICHAEL (COLUMBIA)	1	SCENES FROM THE SOUTHSIDE	BRUCE HORNSBY & THE RANGE (RCA)
SHATTERED DREAMS	JOHNNY HATES JAZZ (VIRGIN)	2	NOW AND ZEN	ROBERT PLANT (ES PARANZA/ATLANTIC)
ANYTHING FOR YOU	G. ESTEFAN & MIAMI SOUND MACHINE (EPIC)	3	LAP OF LUXURY	CHEAP TRICK (EPIC)
TOGETHER FOREVER	RICK ASTLEY (RCA)	4	OUT OF ORDER	ROD STEWART (WARNER BROS)
EVERYTHING YOUR HEART DESIRES	DARYL HALL & JOHN OATES (ARISTA)	5	THIS NOTE'S FOR YOU	NEIL YOUNG & THE BLUENOTES (REPRISE)
NAUGHTY GIRLS	SAMANTHA FOX (JIVE/RCA)	6	GREEN THOUGHTS	SMITHEREENS (ENIGMA/CAPITOL)
I DON'T WANT TO LIVE WITHOUT YOU	FOREIGNER (ATLANTIC)	7	CROSSROADS	ERIC CLAPTON (POLYDOR/PG)
FOOLISH BEAT	DEBBIE GIBSON (ATLANTIC)	8	SAVAGE AMUSEMENT	SCORPIONS (MERCURY/PG)
MAKE IT REAL	JETS (MCA)	9	MIDNIGHT OIL	DIESEL AND DUST (COLUMBIA)
PIANO IN THE DARK	BRENDA RUSSELL (A&M)	10	STARFISH	CHURCH (ARISTA)
DIRTY DIANA	MICHAEL JACKSON (EPIC)	11	DIAMOND SUN	GLASS TIGER (EMI-MANHATTAN)
TWO OCCASIONS	DEELE (SOLAR)	12	RACING AFTER MIDNIGHT	HONEYMOON SUITE (WARNER BROS)
CIRCLE IN THE SAND	BELINDA CARLISLE (MCA)	13	THE LONESOME JUBILEE	JOHN COUGAR MELLENCAMP (MERCURY/PG)
WE ALL SLEEP ALONE	CHER (GEFFEN)	14	HENRY LEE SUMMER	HENRY LEE SUMMER (CBS ASSOCIATED)
STRANGE BUT TRUE	TIMES TWO (REPRISE)	15	TAKE WHAT YOU NEED	ROBIN TROWER (ATLANTIC)
WAIT	WHITE LION (ATLANTIC)	16	KICK	INXS (ATLANTIC)
THE VALLEY ROAD	BRUCE HORNSBY & THE RANGE (RCA)	17	TREAT HER RIGHT	TREAT HER RIGHT (RCA)
DREAMING	OMD (VIRGIN/A&M)	18	CONSCIOUS PARTY	ZIGGY MARLEY (VIRGIN)
ALWAYS ON MY MIND	PET SHOP BOYS (EMI-MANHATTAN)	19	KINGS OF THE SUN	KINGS OF THE SUN (RCA)
THE FLAME	CHEAP TRICK (EPIC)	20	ROBBIE ROBERTSON	ROBBIE ROBERTSON (GEFFEN)

WEEK ENDING MAY 28 1988

SINGLES UK ALBUMS

WITH A LITTLE . . ./SHE'S LEAVING HOME	WET WET WET/BILLY BRAGG (CHILDLINE)	1	TANGO IN THE NIGHT	FLEETWOOD MAC (WARNER BROS)
GOT TO BE CERTAIN	KYLIE MINOGUE (PWL)	2	NITE FLITE	VARIOUS (CBS)
PERFECT	FAIRGROUND ATTRACTION (RCA)	3	MORE DIRTY DANCING	VARIOUS (RCA)
ANFIELD RAP	LIVERPOOL F.C. (VIRGIN)	4	LOVESEXY	PRINCE (PAISLEY PARK)
BLUE MONDAY 1988	NEW ORDER (FACTORY)	5	DIRTY DANCING	ORIGINAL SOUNDTRACK (RCA)
CIRCLE IN THE SAND	BELINDA CARLISLE (VIRGIN)	6	WHITNEY	WHITNEY HOUSTON (ARISTA)
KING OF ROCK 'N' ROLL	PREFAB SPROUT (KITCHENWARE/CBS)	7	THE FIRST OF A MILLION KISSES	FAIRGROUND ATTRACTION (RCA)
SOMEWHERE IN MY HEART	AZTEC CAMERA (WEA)	8	POPPED IN SOULED OUT	WET WET WET (PRECIOUS/PHONOGRAM)
DIVINE EMOTIONS	NARADA (REPRISE/WARNER BROS)	9	HEAVEN ON EARTH	BELINDA CARLISLE (VIRGIN)
THEME FROM S'XPRESS	S'EXPRESS (RHYTHM KING/MUTE)	10	THE CHRISTIANS	THE CHRISTIANS (ISLAND)
DON'T GO	HOTHOUSE FLOWERS (FFRR/LONDON)	11	BULLET FROM A GUN	DEREK B (TUFF AUDIO/PHONOGRAM)
LOADSAMONEY	HARRY ENFIELD (MERCURY/PHONOGRAM)	12	STRONGER THAN PRIDE	SADE (EPIC)
CHECK THIS OUT	L.A. MIX (BREAKOUT/A&M)	13	MOTOWN DANCE PARTY	VARIOUS (MOTOWN)
WHAT ABOUT LOVE	HEART (CAPITOL)	14	NOW THAT'S WHAT I CALL QUITE GOOD!	THE HOUSEMARTINS (GO! DISCS)
IM NIN' ALU	OFRA HAZA (WEA)	15	NOW! 11	VARIOUS (EMI/VIRGIN/POLYGRAM)
BAD YOUNG BROTHER	DEREK B (TUFF AUDIO/PHONOGRAM)	16	SIXTIES MIX 2	VARIOUS (STYLUS)
MY ONE TEMPTATION	MICA PARIS (4TH + BROADWAY/ISLAND)	17	REMEMBER YOU'RE MINE	FOSTER & ALLEN (STYLUS)
OH PATTI	SCRITTI POLITTI (VIRGIN)	18	SCENES FROM THE SOUTHSIDE	BRUCE HORNSBY & THE RANGE (RCA)
OUT OF THE BLUE	DEBBIE GIBSON (ATLANTIC)	19	STAY ON THESE ROADS	A-HA (WARNER BROS)
MARY'S PRAYER	DANNY WILSON (VIRGIN)	20	THE BEST OF OMD	OMD (VIRGIN)

SINGLES US ALBUMS

ONE MORE TRY	GEORGE MICHAEL (COLUMBIA)	1	OU812	VAN HALEN (WARNER BROS)
SHATTERED DREAMS	JOHNNY HATES JAZZ (VIRGIN)	2	SCENES FROM THE SOUTHSIDE	BRUCE HORNSBY & THE RANGE (RCA)
TOGETHER FOREVER	RICK ASTLEY (RCA)	3	NOW AND ZEN	ROBERT PLANT (ES PARANZA/ATLANTIC)
EVERYTHING YOUR HEART DESIRES	DARYL HALL & JOHN OATES (ARISTA)	4	OUT OF ORDER	ROD STEWART (WARNER BROS)
FOOLISH BEAT	DEBBIE GIBSON (ATLANTIC)	5	LAP OF LUXURY	CHEAP TRICK (EPIC)
DIRTY DIANA	MICHAEL JACKSON (EPIC)	6	THIS NOTE'S FOR YOU	NEIL YOUNG & THE BLUENOTES (REPRISE)
MAKE IT REAL	JETS (MCA)	7	SAVAGE AMUSEMENT	SCORPIONS (MERCURY/PG)
NAUGHTY GIRLS	SAMANTHA FOX (JIVE/RCA)	8	GREEN THOUGHTS	SMITHEREENS (ENIGMA/CAPITOL)
CIRCLE IN THE SAND	BELINDA CARLISLE (MCA)	9	CROSSROADS	ERIC CLAPTON (POLYDOR/PG)
THE VALLEY ROAD	BRUCE HORNSBY & THE RANGE (RCA)	10	THE LONESOME JUBILEE	JOHN COUGAR MELLENCAMP (MERCURY/PG)
WE ALL SLEEP ALONE	CHER (GEFFEN)	11	HENRY LEE SUMMER	HENRY LEE SUMMER (CBS ASSOCIATED)
ANYTHING FOR YOU	G. ESTEFAN & MIAMI SOUND MACHINE (EPIC)	12	FREIGHT TRAIN HEART	JIMMY BARNES (GEFFEN)
THE FLAME	CHEAP TRICK (EPIC)	13	TAKE WHAT YOU NEED	ROBIN TROWER (ATLANTIC)
I DON'T WANT TO LIVE WITHOUT YOU	FOREIGNER (ATLANTIC)	14	MIDNIGHT OIL	DIESEL AND DUST (COLUMBIA)
PIANO IN THE DARK	BRENDA RUSSELL (A&M)	15	STARFISH	CHURCH (ARISTA)
ALPHABET STREET	PRINCE (PAISLEY PARK/WARNER BROS)	16	CONSCIOUS PARTY	ZIGGY MARLEY (VIRGIN)
KISS ME DEADLY	LITA FORD (RCA)	17	KICK	INXS (ATLANTIC)
TWO OCCASIONS	DEELE (SOLAR)	18	RACING AFTER MIDNIGHT	HONEYMOON SUITE (WARNER BROS)
MERCEDES BOY	PEBBLES (MCA)	19	DIAMOND SUN	GLASS TIGER (EMI-MANHATTAN)
NOTHIN' BUT A GOOD TIME	POISON (ENIGMA/CAPITOL)	20	OPEN UP AND SAY . . . AHH	POISON (ENIGMA/CAPITOL)

WEEK ENDING JUNE 4 1988

SINGLES UK ALBUMS

WITH A LITTLE . . ./SHE'S LEAVING HOME	WET WET WET/BILLY BRAGG (CHILDLINE)	1	NITE FLITE	VARIOUS (CBS)
GOT TO BE CERTAIN	KYLIE MINOGUE (PWL)	2	TANGO IN THE NIGHT	FLEETWOOD MAC (WARNER BROS)
PERFECT	FAIRGROUND ATTRACTION (RCA)	3	MOTOWN DANCE PARTY	VARIOUS (MOTOWN)
CIRCLE IN THE SAND	BELINDA CARLISLE (VIRGIN)	4	STRONGER THAN PRIDE	SADE (EPIC)
SOMEWHERE IN MY HEART	AZTEC CAMERA (WEA)	5	DIRTY DANCING	ORIGINAL SOUNDTRACK (RCA)
CHECK THIS OUT	L.A. MIX (BREAKOUT/A&M)	6	MORE DIRTY DANCING	VARIOUS (RCA)
KING OF ROCK 'N' ROLL	PREFAB SPROUT (KITCHENWARE/CBS)	7	POPPED IN SOULED OUT	WET WET WET (PRECIOUS/PHONOGRAM)
MY ONE TEMPTATION	MICA PARIS (4TH + BROADWAY/ISLAND)	8	HEAVEN ON EARTH	BELINDA CARLISLE (VIRGIN)
BLUE MONDAY 1988	NEW ORDER (FACTORY)	9	WHITNEY	WHITNEY HOUSTON (ARISTA)
LOVE WILL SAVE THE DAY	WHITNEY HOUSTON (ARISTA)	10	THE FIRST OF A MILLION KISSES	FAIRGROUND ATTRACTION (RCA)
DON'T GO	HOTHOUSE FLOWERS (FFRR/LONDON)	11	OUT OF ORDER	ROD STEWART (WARNER BROS)
ANFIELD RAP	LIVERPOOL F.C. (VIRGIN)	12	THE CHRISTIANS	THE CHRISTIANS (ISLAND)
OH PATTI	SCRITTI POLITTI (VIRGIN)	13	TOUGHER THAN LEATHER	RUN DMC (PROFILE/LONDON)
VOYAGE VOYAGE	DESIRELESS (CBS)	14	LOVESEXY	PRINCE (PAISLEY PARK)
WHAT ABOUT LOVE	HEART (CAPITOL)	15	SIXTIES MIX 2	VARIOUS (STYLUS)
IM NIN' ALU	OFRA HAZA (WEA)	16	OU812	VAN HALEN (WARNER BROS)
THEME FROM S'XPRESS	S'EXPRESS (RHYTHM KING/MUTE)	17	REMEMBER YOU'RE MINE	FOSTER & ALLEN (STYLUS)
GIVE A LITTLE LOVE	ASWAD (MANGO/ISLAND)	18	LOVE	AZTEC CAMERA (WARNER BROS)
OUT OF THE BLUE	DEBBIE GIBSON (ATLANTIC)	19	NOW! 11	VARIOUS (EMI/VIRGIN/POLYGRAM)
DIVINE EMOTIONS	NARADA (REPRISE/WARNER BROS)	20	THE INNOCENTS	ERASURE (MUTE)

SINGLES US ALBUMS

ONE MORE TRY	GEORGE MICHAEL (COLUMBIA)	1	OU812	VAN HALEN (WARNER BROS)
TOGETHER FOREVER	RICK ASTLEY (RCA)	2	SCENES FROM THE SOUTHSIDE	BRUCE HORNSBY & THE RANGE (RCA)
EVERYTHING YOUR HEART DESIRES	DARYL HALL & JOHN OATES (ARISTA)	3	NOW AND ZEN	ROBERT PLANT (ES PARANZA/ATLANTIC)
FOOLISH BEAT	DEBBIE GIBSON (ATLANTIC)	4	OUT OF ORDER	ROD STEWART (WARNER BROS)
DIRTY DIANA	MICHAEL JACKSON (EPIC)	5	SAVAGE AMUSEMENT	SCORPIONS (MERCURY/PG)
MAKE IT REAL	JETS (MCA)	6	LAP OF LUXURY	CHEAP TRICK (EPIC)
THE VALLEY ROAD	BRUCE HORNSBY & THE RANGE (RCA)	7	THIS NOTE'S FOR YOU	NEIL YOUNG & THE BLUENOTES (REPRISE)
CIRCLE IN THE SAND	BELINDA CARLISLE (MCA)	8	THE LONESOME JUBILEE	JOHN COUGAR MELLENCAMP (MERCURY/PG)
THE FLAME	CHEAP TRICK (EPIC)	9	FREIGHT TRAIN HEART	JIMMY BARNES (GEFFEN)
WE ALL SLEEP ALONE	CHER (GEFFEN)	10	HENRY LEE SUMMER	HENRY LEE SUMMER (CBS ASSOCIATED)
SHATTERED DREAMS	JOHNNY HATES JAZZ (VIRGIN)	11	TAKE WHAT YOU NEED	ROBIN TROWER (ATLANTIC)
ALPHABET STREET	PRINCE (PAISLEY PARK/WARNER BROS)	12	GREEN THOUGHTS	SMITHEREENS (ENIGMA/CAPITOL)
MERCEDES BOY	PEBBLES (MCA)	13	CONSCIOUS PARTY	ZIGGY MARLEY (VIRGIN)
KISS ME DEADLY	LITA FORD (RCA)	14	MIDNIGHT OIL	DIESEL AND DUST (COLUMBIA)
NAUGHTY GIRLS	SAMANTHA FOX (JIVE/RCA)	15	KICK	INXS (ATLANTIC)
NITE AND DAY	AL B SURE! (WARNER BROS)	16	OPEN UP AND SAY . . . AHH	POISON (ENIGMA/CAPITOL)
NOTHIN' BUT A GOOD TIME	POISON (ENIGMA/CAPITOL)	17	CROSSROADS	ERIC CLAPTON (POLYDOR/PG)
NEW SENSATION	INXS (ATLANTIC)	18	STARFISH	CHURCH (ARISTA)
I STILL BELIEVE	BRENDA K STARR (MCA)	19	MEMORY IN THE MAKING	JOHN KILZER (GEFFEN)
POUR SOME SUGAR ON ME	DEF LEPPARD (MERCURY/PG)	20	UP YOUR ALLEY	JOAN JET & THE BLACKHEARTS (CBS)

WEEK ENDING JUNE 11 1988

SINGLES UK ALBUMS

WITH A LITTLE . . ./SHE'S LEAVING HOME	WET WET WET/BILLY BRAGG (CHILDLINE)	1	NITE FLITE	VARIOUS (CBS)
GOT TO BE CERTAIN	KYLIE MINOGUE (PWL)	2	TANGO IN THE NIGHT	FLEETWOOD MAC (WARNER BROS)
SOMEWHERE IN MY HEART	AZTEC CAMERA (WEA)	3	POPPED IN SOULED OUT	WET WET WET (PRECIOUS/PHONOGRAM)
DOCTORIN' THE TARDIS	THE TIMELORDS (KLF COMMUNICATIONS)	4	MOTOWN DANCE PARTY	VARIOUS (MOTOWN)
VOYAGE VOYAGE	DESIRELESS (CBS)	5	HEAVEN ON EARTH	BELINDA CARLISLE (VIRGIN)
CIRCLE IN THE SAND	BELINDA CARLISLE (VIRGIN)	6	DIRTY DANCING	ORIGINAL SOUNDTRACK (RCA)
MY ONE TEMPTATION	MICA PARIS (4TH + BROADWAY/ISLAND)	7	MORE DIRTY DANCING	VARIOUS (RCA)
I SAW HIM STANDING THERE	TIFFANY (MCA)	8	STRONGER THAN PRIDE	SADE (EPIC)
CHECK THIS OUT	L.A. MIX (BREAKOUT/A&M)	9	WHITNEY	WHITNEY HOUSTON (ARISTA)
PERFECT	FAIRGROUND ATTRACTION (RCA)	10	LOVE	AZTEC CAMERA (WARNER BROS)
GIVE A LITTLE LOVE	ASWAD (MANGO/ISLAND)	11	PUSH	BROS (CBS)
EVERYDAY IS LIKE SUNDAY	MORRISSEY (HIS MASTER'S VOICE/EMI)	12	THE CHRISTIANS	THE CHRISTIANS (ISLAND)
KING OF ROCK 'N' ROLL	PREFAB SPROUT (KITCHENWARE/CBS)	13	OUT OF ORDER	ROD STEWART (WARNER BROS)
OH PATTI	SCRITTI POLITTI (VIRGIN)	14	THE FIRST OF A MILLION KISSES	FAIRGROUND ATTRACTION (RCA)
WILD WORLD	MAXI PRIEST (10/VIRGIN)	15	SIXTIES MIX 2	VARIOUS (STYLUS)
LOVE WILL SAVE THE DAY	WHITNEY HOUSTON (ARISTA)	16	REMEMBER YOU'RE MINE	FOSTER & ALLEN (STYLUS)
DON'T GO	HOTHOUSE FLOWERS (FFRR/LONDON)	17	HEARSAY	ALEXANDER O'NEAL (TABU)
ANOTHER WEEKEND	FIVE STAR (TENT/RCA)	18	LOVESEXY	PRINCE (PAISLEY PARK)
CHAINS OF LOVE	.ERASURE (MUTE)	19	HEART	HEART (CAPITOL)
BLUE MONDAY 1988	NEW ORDER (FACTORY)	20	OU812	VAN HALEN (WARNER BROS)

SINGLES US ALBUMS

TOGETHER FOREVER	RICK ASTLEY (RCA)	1	OU812	VAN HALEN (WARNER BROS)
ONE MORE TRY	GEORGE MICHAEL (COLUMBIA)	2	SCENES FROM THE SOUTHSIDE	BRUCE HORNSBY & THE RANGE (RCA)
FOOLISH BEAT	DEBBIE GIBSON (ATLANTIC)	3	NOW AND ZEN	ROBERT PLANT (ES PARANZA/ATLANTIC)
DIRTY DIANA	MICHAEL JACKSON (EPIC)	4	OUT OF ORDER	ROD STEWART (WARNER BROS)
MAKE IT REAL	JETS (MCA)	5	SUR LA MER	MOODY BLUES (POLYDOR/PG)
THE VALLEY ROAD	BRUCE HORNSBY & THE RANGE (RCA)	6	SAVAGE AMUSEMENT	SCORPIONS (MERCURY/PG)
THE FLAME	CHEAP TRICK (EPIC)	7	FREIGHT TRAIN HEART	JIMMY BARNES (GEFFEN)
CIRCLE IN THE SAND	BELINDA CARLISLE (MCA)	8	HENRY LEE SUMMER	HENRY LEE SUMMER (CBS ASSOCIATED)
EVERYTHING YOUR HEART DESIRES	DARYL HALL & JOHN OATES (ARISTA)	9	LAP OF LUXURY	CHEAP TRICK (EPIC)
MERCEDES BOY	PEBBLES (MCA)	10	THE LONESOME JUBILEE	JOHN COUGAR MELLENCAMP (MERCURY/PG)
ALPHABET STREET	PRINCE (PAISLEY PARK/WARNER BROS)	11	TAKE WHAT YOU NEED	ROBIN TROWER (ATLANTIC)
NEW SENSATION	INXS (ATLANTIC)	12	THIS NOTE'S FOR YOU	NEIL YOUNG & THE BLUENOTES (REPRISE)
KISS ME DEADLY	LITA FORD (RCA)	13	CONSCIOUS PARTY	ZIGGY MARLEY (VIRGIN)
NITE AND DAY	AL B SURE! (WARNER BROS)	14	DOWN IN THE GROOVE	BOB DYLAN (COLUMBIA)
NOTHIN' BUT A GOOD TIME	POISON (ENIGMA/CAPITOL)	15	MIDNIGHT OIL	DIESEL AND DUST (COLUMBIA)
POUR SOME SUGAR ON ME	DEF LEPPARD (MERCURY/PG)	16	KICK	INXS (ATLANTIC)
I STILL BELIEVE	BRENDA K STARR (MCA)	17	OPEN UP AND SAY . . . AHH	POISON (ENIGMA/CAPITOL)
WE ALL SLEEP ALONE	CHER (GEFFEN)	18	MEMORY IN THE MAKING	JOHN KILZER (GEFFEN)
SHATTERED DREAMS	JOHNNY HATES JAZZ (VIRGIN)	19	LOVE YOUR MAN	ROSSINGTON BAND (GOLD DUST/MCA)
HOLD ON TO THE NIGHTS	RICHARD MARX (EMI-MANHATTAN)	20	UP YOUR ALLEY	JOAN JET & THE BLACKHEARTS (CBS)

WEEK ENDING JUNE 18 1988

SINGLES UK ALBUMS

SINGLES	ARTIST	UK	ALBUMS	ARTIST
DOCTORIN' THE TARDIS	THE TIMELORDS (KLF COMMUNICATIONS)	1	NITE FLITE	VARIOUS (CBS)
I OWE YOU NOTHING	BROS (CBS)	2	PEOPLE	HOTHOUSE FLOWERS (LONDON)
WITH A LITTLE . . ./SHE'S LEAVING HOME	WET WET WET/BILLY BRAGG (CHILDLINE)	3	TANGO IN THE NIGHT	FLEETWOOD MAC (WARNER BROS)
BOYS	SABRINA (IBIZA/LONDON)	4	HEAVEN ON EARTH	BELINDA CARLISLE (VIRGIN)
VOYAGE VOYAGE	DESIRELESS (CBS)	5	MOTOWN DANCE PARTY	VARIOUS (MOTOWN)
GOT TO BE CERTAIN	KYLIE MINOGUE (PWL)	6	DIRTY DANCING	ORIGINAL SOUNDTRACK (RCA)
WILD WORLD	MAXI PRIEST (10/VIRGIN)	7	POPPED IN SOULED OUT	WET WET WET (PRECIOUS/PHONOGRAM)
SOMEWHERE IN MY HEART	AZTEC CAMERA (WEA)	8	PROVISION	SCRITTI POLITTI (VIRGIN)
EVERYDAY IS LIKE SUNDAY	MORRISSEY (HIS MASTER'S VOICE/EMI)	9	STRONGER THAN PRIDE	SADE (EPIC)
I SAW HIM STANDING THERE	TIFFANY (MCA)	10	MORE DIRTY DANCING	VARIOUS (RCA)
CHAINS OF LOVE	ERASURE (MUTE)	11	PUSH	BROS (CBS)
MY ONE TEMPTATION	MICA PARIS (4TH + BROADWAY/ISLAND)	12	AIN'T COMPLAINING	STATUS QUO (VERTIGO/PHONOGRAM)
CIRCLE IN THE SAND	BELINDA CARLISLE (VIRGIN)	13	WHITNEY	WHITNEY HOUSTON (ARISTA)
GIVE A LITTLE LOVE	ASWAD (MANGO/ISLAND)	14	LOVE	AZTEC CAMERA (WARNER BROS)
DON'T CALL ME BABY	VOICE OF THE BEEHIVE (FFRR/LONDON)	15	EVERYTHING	CLIMIE FISHER (EMI)
TRIBUTE	THE PASADENAS (CBS)	16	THE INNOCENTS	ERASURE (MUTE)
PERFECT	FAIRGROUND ATTRACTION (RCA)	17	THE HITS OF HOUSE ARE HERE	VARIOUS (K-TEL)
CHECK THIS OUT	L.A. MIX (BREAKOUT/A&M)	18	THE FIRST OF A MILLION KISSES	FAIRGROUND ATTRACTION (RCA)
THE TWIST	FAT BOYS/CHUBBY CHECKER (POLYDOR)	19	REMEMBER YOU'RE MINE	FOSTER & ALLEN (STYLUS)
LUCRETIA MY REFLECTION	SISTERS OF MERCY (MERCIFUL RELEASE/WEA)	20	HEART	HEART (CAPITOL)

SINGLES US ALBUMS

SINGLES	ARTIST	US	ALBUMS	ARTIST
FOOLISH BEAT	DEBBIE GIBSON (ATLANTIC)	1	OU812	VAN HALEN (WARNER BROS)
DIRTY DIANA	MICHAEL JACKSON (EPIC)	2	SCENES FROM THE SOUTHSIDE	BRUCE HORNSBY & THE RANGE (RCA)
TOGETHER FOREVER	RICK ASTLEY (RCA)	3	NOW AND ZEN	ROBERT PLANT (ES PARANZA/ATLANTIC)
THE FLAME	CHEAP TRICK (EPIC)	4	OUT OF ORDER	ROD STEWART (WARNER BROS)
MAKE IT REAL	JETS (MCA)	5	SUR LA MER	MOODY BLUES (POLYDOR/PG)
THE VALLEY ROAD	BRUCE HORNSBY & THE RANGE (RCA)	6	FREIGHT TRAIN HEART	JIMMY BARNES (GEFFEN)
MERCEDES BOY	PEBBLES (MCA)	7	SAVAGE AMUSEMENT	SCORPIONS (MERCURY/PG)
NEW SENSATION	INXS (ATLANTIC)	8	HENRY LEE SUMMER	HENRY LEE SUMMER (CBS ASSOCIATED)
POUR SOME SUGAR ON ME	DEF LEPPARD (MERCURY/PG)	9	DOWN IN THE GROOVE	BOB DYLAN (COLUMBIA)
ALPHABET STREET	PRINCE (PAISLEY PARK/WARNER BROS)	10	TAKE WHAT YOU NEED	ROBIN TROWER (ATLANTIC)
NITE AND DAY	AL B SURE! (WARNER BROS)	11	THIS NOTE'S FOR YOU	NEIL YOUNG & THE BLUENOTES (REPRISE)
ONE MORE TRY	GEORGE MICHAEL (COLUMBIA)	12	MIDNIGHT OIL	DIESEL AND DUST (COLUMBIA)
NOTHIN' BUT A GOOD TIME	POISON (ENIGMA/CAPITOL)	13	CONSCIOUS PARTY	ZIGGY MARLEY (VIRGIN)
CIRCLE IN THE SAND	BELINDA CARLISLE (MCA)	14	LAP OF LUXURY	CHEAP TRICK (EPIC)
HOLD ON TO THE NIGHTS	RICHARD MARX (EMI-MANHATTAN)	15	OPEN UP AND SAY . . . AHH	POISON (ENIGMA/CAPITOL)
I STILL BELIEVE	BRENDA K STARR (MCA)	16	MEMORY IN THE MAKING	JOHN KILZER (GEFFEN)
KISS ME DEADLY	LITA FORD (RCA)	17	KICK	INXS (ATLANTIC)
HANDS TO HEAVEN	BREATHE (A&M)	18	LOVE YOUR MAN	ROSSINGTON BAND (GOLD DUST/MCA)
RUSH HOUR	JANE WIEDLIN (EMI-MANHATTAN)	19	TRACY CHAPMAN	TRACY CHAPMAN (ELEKTRA)
EVERYTHING YOUR HEART DESIRES	DARYL HALL & JOHN OATES (ARISTA)	20	UP YOUR ALLEY	JOAN JET & THE BLACKHEARTS (CBS)

WEEK ENDING JUNE 25 1988

SINGLES UK ALBUMS

SINGLES	ARTIST	UK	ALBUMS	ARTIST
I OWE YOU NOTHING	BROS (CBS)	1	NITE FLITE	VARIOUS (CBS)
DOCTORIN' THE TARDIS	THE TIMELORDS (KLF COMMUNICATIONS)	2	TRACY CHAPMAN	TRACY CHAPMAN (ELEKTRA)
BOYS	SABRINA (IBIZA/LONDON)	3	TANGO IN THE NIGHT	FLEETWOOD MAC (WARNER BROS)
THE TWIST	FAT BOYS/CHUBBY CHECKER (POLYDOR)	4	WHITNEY	WHITNEY HOUSTON (ARISTA)
WILD WORLD	MAXI PRIEST (10/VIRGIN)	5	PUSH	BROS (CBS)
TRIBUTE	THE PASADENAS (CBS)	6	HEAVEN ON EARTH	BELINDA CARLISLE (VIRGIN)
VOYAGE VOYAGE	DESIRELESS (CBS)	7	POPPED IN SOULED OUT	WET WET WET (PRECIOUS/PHONOGRAM)
IN THE AIR TONIGHT	PHIL COLLINS (VIRGIN)	8	DIRTY DANCING	ORIGINAL SOUNDTRACK (RCA)
BREAKFAST IN BED	UB40/C. HYNDE (DEP INTERNATIONAL/VIRGIN)	9	STRONGER THAN PRIDE	SADE (EPIC)
WITH A LITTLE . . ./SHE'S LEAVING HOME	WET WET WET/BILLY BRAGG (CHILDLINE)	10	MOTOWN DANCE PARTY	VARIOUS (MOTOWN)
CHAINS OF LOVE	ERASURE (MUTE)	11	PEOPLE	HOTHOUSE FLOWERS (LONDON)
GOT TO BE CERTAIN	KYLIE MINOGUE (PWL)	12	THE HITS OF HOUSE ARE HERE	VARIOUS (K-TEL)
EVERYDAY IS LIKE SUNDAY	MORRISSEY (HIS MASTER'S VOICE/EMI)	13	BROTHERS IN ARMS	DIRE STRAITS (VERTIGO/PHONOGRAM)
SOMEWHERE IN MY HEART	AZTEC CAMERA (WEA)	14	PROVISION	SCRITTI POLITTI (VIRGIN)
I SAW HIM STANDING THERE	TIFFANY (MCA)	15	MORE DIRTY DANCING	VARIOUS (RCA)
DON'T CALL ME BABY	VOICE OF THE BEEHIVE (FFRR/LONDON)	16	REMEMBER YOU'RE MINE	FOSTER & ALLEN (STYLUS)
DON'T BLAME IT ON THAT GIRL	MATT BIANCO (WEA)	17	EVERYTHING	CLIMIE FISHER (EMI)
YOU HAVE PLACED A CHILL IN MY HEART	EURYTHMICS (RCA)	18	LOVE	AZTEC CAMERA (WARNER BROS)
MY ONE TEMPTATION	MICA PARIS (4TH + BROADWAY/ISLAND)	19	SIXTIES MIX 2	VARIOUS (STYLUS)
CAR WASH/IS IT LOVE YOU'RE AFTER	ROSE ROYCE (MCA)	20	THE INNOCENTS	ERASURE (MUTE)

SINGLES US ALBUMS

SINGLES	ARTIST	US	ALBUMS	ARTIST
DIRTY DIANA	MICHAEL JACKSON (EPIC)	1	OU812	VAN HALEN (WARNER BROS)
FOOLISH BEAT	DEBBIE GIBSON (ATLANTIC)	2	ROLL WITH IT	STEVE WINWOOD (VIRGIN)
THE FLAME	CHEAP TRICK (EPIC)	3	SCENES FROM THE SOUTHSIDE	BRUCE HORNSBY & THE RANGE (RCA)
MERCEDES BOY	PEBBLES (MCA)	4	SUR LA MER	MOODY BLUES (POLYDOR/PG)
NEW SENSATION	INXS (ATLANTIC)	5	OUTRIDER	JIMMY PAGE (GEFFEN)
MAKE IT REAL	JETS (MCA)	6	FREIGHT TRAIN HEART	JIMMY BARNES (GEFFEN)
POUR SOME SUGAR ON ME	DEF LEPPARD (MERCURY/PG)	7	NOW AND ZEN	ROBERT PLANT (ES PARANZA/ATLANTIC)
THE VALLEY ROAD	BRUCE HORNSBY & THE RANGE (RCA)	8	OUT OF ORDER	ROD STEWART (WARNER BROS)
NITE AND DAY	AL B SURE! (WARNER BROS)	9	DOWN IN THE GROOVE	BOB DYLAN (COLUMBIA)
HOLD ON TO THE NIGHTS	RICHARD MARX (EMI-MANHATTAN)	10	OPEN ALL NIGHT	GEORGIA SATELLITES (ELEKTRA)
NOTHIN' BUT A GOOD TIME	POISON (ENIGMA/CAPITOL)	11	MIDNIGHT OIL	DIESEL AND DUST (COLUMBIA)
TOGETHER FOREVER	RICK ASTLEY (RCA)	12	THIS NOTE'S FOR YOU	NEIL YOUNG & THE BLUENOTES (REPRISE)
ROLL WITH IT	STEVE WINWOOD (VIRGIN)	13	HENRY LEE SUMMER	HENRY LEE SUMMER (CBS ASSOCIATED)
HANDS TO HEAVEN	BREATHE (A&M)	14	LOVE YOUR MAN	ROSSINGTON BAND (GOLD DUST/MCA)
I STILL BELIEVE	BRENDA K STARR (MCA)	15	TRACY CHAPMAN	TRACY CHAPMAN (ELEKTRA)
RUSH HOUR	JANE WIEDLIN (EMI-MANHATTAN)	16	TAKE WHAT YOU NEED	ROBIN TROWER (ATLANTIC)
MAKE ME LOSE CONTROL	ERIC CARMEN (ARISTA)	17	REG STRIKES BACK	ELTON JOHN (MCA)
ALPHABET STREET	PRINCE (PAISLEY PARK/WARNER BROS)	18	SAVAGE AMUSEMENT	SCORPIONS (MERCURY/PG)
SIGN YOUR NAME	TERENCE TRENT D'ARBY (COLUMBIA)	19	MEMORY IN THE MAKING	JOHN KILZER (GEFFEN)
LOST IN YOU	ROD STEWART (WARNER BROS)	20	OPEN UP AND SAY . . . AHH	POISON (ENIGMA/CAPITOL)

WEEK ENDING JULY 2 1988

SINGLES UK ALBUMS

Singles			Albums	
I OWE YOU NOTHING	BROS (CBS)	1	TRACY CHAPMAN	TRACY CHAPMAN (ELEKTRA)
THE TWIST	FAT BOYS/CHUBBY CHECKER (POLYDOR)	2	PUSH	BROS (CBS)
BOYS	SABRINA (IBIZA/LONDON)	3	IDOL SONGS: 11 OF THE BEST	BILLY IDOL (CHRYSALIS)
IN THE AIR TONIGHT	PHIL COLLINS (VIRGIN)	4	ROLL WITH IT	STEVE WINWOOD (VIRGIN)
TRIBUTE	THE PASADENAS (CBS)	5	NITE FLITE	VARIOUS (CBS)
BREAKFAST IN BED	UB40/C. HYNDE (DEP INTERNATIONAL/VIRGIN)	6	TANGO IN THE NIGHT	FLEETWOOD MAC (WARNER BROS)
PUSH IT/TRAMP	SALT 'N PEPA (CHAMPION)	7	POPPED IN SOULED OUT	WET WET WET (PRECIOUS/PHONOGRAM)
DOCTORIN' THE TARDIS	THE TIMELORDS (KLF COMMUNICATIONS)	8	HEAVEN ON EARTH	BELINDA CARLISLE (VIRGIN)
WILD WORLD	MAXI PRIEST (10/VIRGIN)	9	DIRTY DANCING	ORIGINAL SOUNDTRACK (RCA)
FAST CAR	TRACY CHAPMAN (ELEKTRA)	10	STRONGER THAN PRIDE	SADE (EPIC)
NOTHING'S GONNA CHANGE MY LOVE FOR YOU	GLEN MEDEIROS (LONDON)	11	WHITNEY	WHITNEY HOUSTON (ARISTA)
VOYAGE VOYAGE	DESIRELESS (CBS)	12	PEOPLE	HOTHOUSE FLOWERS (LONDON)
CHAINS OF LOVE	ERASURE (MUTE)	13	LET IT BEE	VOICE OF THE BEEHIVE (LONDON)
DON'T BLAME IT ON THAT GIRL	MATT BIANCO (WEA)	14	THE HITS OF HOUSE ARE HERE	VARIOUS (K-TEL)
TOUGHER THAN THE REST	BRUCE SPRINGSTEEN (CBS)	15	CONFESSIONS OF A POP GROUP	THE STYLE COUNCIL (POLYDOR)
YOU HAVE PLACED A CHILL IN MY HEART	EURYTHMICS (RCA)	16	MORE DIRTY DANCING	VARIOUS (RCA)
I WILL BE WITH YOU	T'PAU (SIREN/VIRGIN)	17	MOTOWN DANCE PARTY	VARIOUS (MOTOWN)
MAYBE	HAZELL DEAN (EMI)	18	IRISH HEARTBEAT	VAN MORRISON/CHIEFTANS (MERCURY)
GOT TO BE CERTAIN	KYLIE MINOGUE (PWL)	19	THE COLLECTION	BARRY WHITE (MERCURY/PHONOGRAM)
CAR WASH/IS IT LOVE YOU'RE AFTER	ROSE ROYCE (MCA)	20	FAITH	GEORGE MICHAEL (EPIC)

SINGLES US ALBUMS

Singles			Albums	
THE FLAME	CHEAP TRICK (EPIC)	1	ROLL WITH IT	STEVE WINWOOD (VIRGIN)
MERCEDES BOY	PEBBLES (MCA)	2	OU812	VAN HALEN (WARNER BROS)
NEW SENSATION	INXS (ATLANTIC)	3	SCENES FROM THE SOUTHSIDE	BRUCE HORNSBY & THE RANGE (RCA)
POUR SOME SUGAR ON ME	DEF LEPPARD (MERCURY/PG)	4	OUTRIDER	JIMMY PAGE (GEFFEN)
FOOLISH BEAT	DEBBIE GIBSON (ATLANTIC)	5	SUR LA MER	MOODY BLUES (POLYDOR/PG)
HOLD ON TO THE NIGHTS	RICHARD MARX (EMI-MANHATTAN)	6	OUT OF ORDER	ROD STEWART (WARNER BROS)
ROLL WITH IT	STEVE WINWOOD (VIRGIN)	7	OPEN ALL NIGHT	GEORGIA SATELLITES (ELEKTRA)
NITE AND DAY	AL B SURE! (WARNER BROS)	8	NOW AND ZEN	ROBERT PLANT (ES PARANZA/ATLANTIC)
DIRTY DIANA	MICHAEL JACKSON (EPIC)	9	DOWN IN THE GROOVE	BOB DYLAN (COLUMBIA)
HANDS TO HEAVEN	BREATHE (A&M)	10	HEAVY NOVA	ROBERT PALMER (EMI-MANHATTAN)
MAKE IT REAL	JETS (MCA)	11	FREIGHT TRAIN HEART	JIMMY BARNES (GEFFEN)
MAKE ME LOSE CONTROL	ERIC CARMEN (ARISTA)	12	WIDE AWAKE IN DREAMLAND	PAT BENATAR (CHRYSALIS)
RUSH HOUR	JANE WIEDLIN (EMI-MANHATTAN)	13	REG STRIKES BACK	ELTON JOHN (MCA))
SIGN YOUR NAME	TERENCE TRENT D'ARBY (COLUMBIA)	14	MIDNIGHT OIL	DIESEL AND DUST (COLUMBIA)
THE VALLEY ROAD	BRUCE HORNSBY & THE RANGE (RCA)	15	TRACY CHAPMAN	TRACY CHAPMAN (ELEKTRA)
NOTHIN' BUT A GOOD TIME	POISON (ENIGMA/CAPITOL)	16	THIS NOTE'S FOR YOU	NEIL YOUNG & THE BLUENOTES (REPRISE)
1-2-3	G. ESTEFAN & MIAMI SOUND MACHINE (EPIC)	17	LOVE YOUR MAN	ROSSINGTON BAND (GOLD DUST/MCA)
LOST IN YOU	ROD STEWART (WARNER BROS)	18	APPETITE FOR DESTRUCTION	GUNS 'N' ROSES (GEFFEN)
I STILL BELIEVE	BRENDA K STARR (MCA)	19	MEMORY IN THE MAKING	JOHN KILZER (GEFFEN)
PARADISE	SADE (EPIC)	20	THE MONA LISA'S SISTER	GRAHAM PARKER (RCA)

WEEK ENDING JULY 9 1988

SINGLES UK ALBUMS

Singles			Albums	
NOTHING'S GONNA CHANGE MY LOVE FOR YOU	GLEN MEDEIROS (LONDON)	1	TRACY CHAPMAN	TRACY CHAPMAN (ELEKTRA)
THE TWIST	FAT BOYS/CHUBBY CHECKER (POLYDOR)	2	IDOL SONGS: 11 OF THE BEST	BILLY IDOL (CHRYSALIS)
PUSH IT/TRAMP	SALT 'N PEPA (CHAMPION)	3	PUSH	BROS (CBS)
I OWE YOU NOTHING	BROS (CBS)	4	ROLL WITH IT	STEVE WINWOOD (VIRGIN)
IN THE AIR TONIGHT	PHIL COLLINS (VIRGIN)	5	TANGO IN THE NIGHT	FLEETWOOD MAC (WARNER BROS)
BOYS	SABRINA (IBIZA/LONDON)	6	POPPED IN SOULED OUT	WET WET WET (PRECIOUS/PHONOGRAM)
FAST CAR	TRACY CHAPMAN (ELEKTRA)	7	DIRTY DANCING	ORIGINAL SOUNDTRACK (RCA)
BREAKFAST IN BED	UB40/C. HYNDE (DEP INTERNATIONAL/VIRGIN)	8	NITE FLITE	VARIOUS (CBS)
TRIBUTE	THE PASADENAS (CBS)	9	THE COLLECTION	BARRY WHITE (MERCURY/PHONOGRAM)
WILD WORLD	MAXI PRIEST (10/VIRGIN)	10	JACK MIX IN FULL EFFECT	MIRAGE (STYLUS)
DON'T BLAME IT ON THAT GIRL	MATT BIANCO (WEA)	11	HEAVEN ON EARTH	BELINDA CARLISLE (VIRGIN)
DOCTORIN' THE TARDIS	THE TIMELORDS (KLF COMMUNICATIONS)	12	STRONGER THAN PRIDE	SADE (EPIC)
TOUGHER THAN THE REST	BRUCE SPRINGSTEEN (CBS)	13	WHITNEY	WHITNEY HOUSTON (ARISTA)
I WILL BE WITH YOU	T'PAU (SIREN/VIRGIN)	14	THE HITS OF HOUSE ARE HERE	VARIOUS (K-TEL)
MAYBE	HAZELL DEAN (EMI)	15	TUNNEL OF LOVE	BRUCE SPRINGSTEEN (CBS)
ROSES ARE RED	MAC BAND/THE McCAMPBELL BROTHERS (MCA)	16	MORE DIRTY DANCING	VARIOUS (RCA)
VOYAGE VOYAGE	DESIRELESS (CBS)	17	HEAVY NOVA	ROBERT PALMER (EMI)
DON'T BELIEVE THE HYPE	PUBLIC ENEMY	18	BRIDGE OF SPIES	T'PAU (SIREN/VIRGIN)
YOU HAVE PLACED A CHILL IN MY HEART	EURYTHMICS (RCA)	19	LOVE	AZTEC CAMERA (WARNER BROS)
THERE'S MORE TO LOVE	COMMUNARDS (LONDON)	20	MOTOWN DANCE PARTY	VARIOUS (MOTOWN)

SINGLES US ALBUMS

Singles			Albums	
THE FLAME	CHEAP TRICK (EPIC)	1	ROLL WITH IT	STEVE WINWOOD (VIRGIN)
NEW SENSATION	INXS (ATLANTIC)	2	OU812	VAN HALEN (WARNER BROS)
POUR SOME SUGAR ON ME	DEF LEPPARD (MERCURY/PG)	3	OUTRIDER	JIMMY PAGE (GEFFEN)
MERCEDES BOY	PEBBLES (MCA)	4	SUR LA MER	MOODY BLUES (POLYDOR/PG)
HOLD ON TO THE NIGHTS	RICHARD MARX (EMI-MANHATTAN)	5	SCENES FROM THE SOUTHSIDE	BRUCE HORNSBY & THE RANGE (RCA)
ROLL WITH IT	STEVE WINWOOD (VIRGIN)	6	HEAVY NOVA	ROBERT PALMER (EMI-MANHATTAN)
HANDS TO HEAVEN	BREATHE (A&M)	7	WIDE AWAKE IN DREAMLAND	PAT BENATAR (CHRYSALIS)
MAKE ME LOSE CONTROL	ERIC CARMEN (ARISTA)	8	OPEN ALL NIGHT	GEORGIA SATELLITES (ELEKTRA)
NITE AND DAY	AL B SURE! (WARNER BROS)	9	OUT OF ORDER	ROD STEWART (WARNER BROS)
SIGN YOUR NAME	TERENCE TRENT D'ARBY (COLUMBIA)	10	DOWN IN THE GROOVE	BOB DYLAN (COLUMBIA)
RUSH HOUR	JANE WIEDLIN (EMI-MANHATTAN)	11	REG STRIKES BACK	ELTON JOHN (MCA)
1-2-3	G. ESTEFAN & MIAMI SOUND MACHINE (EPIC)	12	NOW AND ZEN	ROBERT PLANT (ES PARANZA/ATLANTIC)
DO YOU LOVE ME	CONTOURS (MOTOWN)	13	MIDNIGHT OIL	DIESEL AND DUST (COLUMBIA)
FOOLISH BEAT	DEBBIE GIBSON (ATLANTIC)	14	TRACY CHAPMAN	TRACY CHAPMAN (ELEKTRA)
I DON'T WANT TO LIVE WITHOUT YOU	CHICAGO (FULL MOON/REPRISE)	15	APPETITE FOR DESTRUCTION	GUNS 'N' ROSES (GEFFEN)
THE COLOUR OF LOVE	BILLY OCEAN (JIVE/ARISTA)	16	THIS NOTE'S FOR YOU	NEIL YOUNG & THE BLUENOTES (REPRISE)
I DON'T WANNA GO ON WITH YOU LIKE THAT	ELTON JOHN (MCA)	17	LOVE YOUR MAN	ROSSINGTON BAND (GOLD DUST/MCA)
PARENTS JUST DON'T UNDERSTAND	DJ JAZZY JEFF & FRESH PRINCE (JIVE/RCA)	18	FREIGHT TRAIN HEART	JIMMY BARNES (GEFFEN)
PARADISE	SADE (EPIC)	19	KICK	INXS (ATLANTIC)
LOST IN YOU	ROD STEWART (WARNER BROS)	20	SAVAGE AMUSEMENT	SCORPIONS (MERCURY/PG)

WEEK ENDING JULY 16 1988

UK

Singles			Albums	
NOTHING'S GONNA CHANGE MY LOVE FOR YOU	GLEN MEDEIROS (LONDON)	1	TRACY CHAPMAN	TRACY CHAPMAN (ELEKTRA)
PUSH IT/TRAMP	SALT 'N PEPA (CHAMPION)	2	KYLIE	KYLIE MINOGUE (PWL)
THE TWIST	FAT BOYS/CHUBBY CHECKER (POLYDOR)	3	IDOL SONGS: 11 OF THE BEST	BILLY IDOL (CHRYSALIS)
I OWE YOU NOTHING	BROS (CBS)	4	PUSH	BROS (CBS)
FAST CAR	TRACY CHAPMAN (ELEKTRA)	5	THE COLLECTION	BARRY WHITE (MERCURY/PHONOGRAM)
I DON'T WANT TO TALK ABOUT IT	EVERYTHING BUT THE GIRL (BLANCO Y NEGRO)	6	TANGO IN THE NIGHT	FLEETWOOD MAC (WARNER BROS)
BREAKFAST IN BED	UB40/C. HYNDE (DEP INTERNATIONAL/VIRGIN)	7	JACK MIX IN FULL EFFECT	MIRAGE (STYLUS)
BOYS	SABRINA (IBIZA/LONDON)	8	DIRTY DANCING	ORIGINAL SOUNDTRACK (RCA)
ROSES ARE RED	MAC BAND/THE McCAMPBELL BROTHERS (MCA)	9	POPPED IN SOULED OUT	WET WET WET (PRECIOUS/PHONOGRAM)
IN THE AIR TONIGHT	PHIL COLLINS (VIRGIN)	10	ROLL WITH IT	STEVE WINWOOD (VIRGIN)
TRIBUTE	THE PASADENAS (CBS)	11	WIDE AWAKE IN DREAMLAND	PAT BENATAR (CHRYSALIS)
DON'T BLAME IT ON THAT GIRL	MATT BIANCO (WEA)	12	TUNNEL OF LOVE	BRUCE SPRINGSTEEN (CBS)
CROSS MY HEART	EIGHTH WONDER (CBS)	13	HEAVEN ON EARTH	BELINDA CARLISLE (VIRGIN)
DIRTY DIANA	MICHAEL JACKSON (EPIC)	14	WHITNEY	WHITNEY HOUSTON (ARISTA)
I WANT YOUR LOVE	TRANSVISION VAMP (MCA)	15	NITE FLITE	VARIOUS (CBS)
TOUGHER THAN THE REST	BRUCE SPRINGSTEEN (CBS)	16	STRONGER THAN PRIDE	SADE (EPIC)
WILD WORLD	MAXI PRIEST (10/VIRGIN)	17	MORE DIRTY DANCING	VARIOUS (RCA)
FOOLISH BEAT	DEBBIE GIBSON (ATLANTIC)	18	REG STRIKES BACK	ELTON JOHN (ROCKET/PHONOGRAM)
MONKEY	GEORGE MICHAEL (EPIC)	19	THE HITS OF HOUSE ARE HERE	VARIOUS (K-TEL)
LOVE BITES	DEF LEPPARD (BLUDGEON RIFFOLA)	20	BAD	MICHAEL JACKSON (EPIC)

US

Singles			Albums	
POUR SOME SUGAR ON ME	DEF LEPPARD (MERCURY/PG)	1	ROLL WITH IT	STEVE WINWOOD (VIRGIN)
ROLL WITH IT	STEVE WINWOOD (VIRGIN)	2	OU812	VAN HALEN (WARNER BROS)
HOLD ON TO THE NIGHTS	RICHARD MARX (EMI-MANHATTAN)	3	OUTRIDER	JIMMY PAGE (GEFFEN)
NEW SENSATION	INXS (ATLANTIC)	4	HEAVY NOVA	ROBERT PALMER (EMI-MANHATTAN)
HANDS TO HEAVEN	BREATHE (A&M)	5	WIDE AWAKE IN DREAMLAND	PAT BENATAR (CHRYSALIS)
MAKE ME LOSE CONTROL	ERIC CARMEN (ARISTA)	6	JUST BEFORE THE BULLETS FLY	GREGG ALLMAN BAND (EPIC)
THE FLAME	CHEAP TRICK (EPIC)	7	SCENES FROM THE SOUTHSIDE	BRUCE HORNSBY & THE RANGE (RCA)
SIGN YOUR NAME	TERENCE TRENT D'ARBY (COLUMBIA)	8	SUR LA MER	MOODY BLUES (POLYDOR/PG)
1-2-3	G. ESTEFAN & MIAMI SOUND MACHINE (EPIC)	9	REG STRIKES BACK	ELTON JOHN (MCA)
RUSH HOUR	JANE WIEDLIN (EMI-MANHATTAN)	10	OUT OF ORDER	ROD STEWART (WARNER BROS)
DO YOU LOVE ME	CONTOURS (MOTOWN)	11	OPEN ALL NIGHT	GEORGIA SATELLITES (ELEKTRA)
I DON'T WANT TO LIVE WITHOUT YOU	CHICAGO (FULL MOON/REPRISE)	12	MIDNIGHT OIL	DIESEL AND DUST (COLUMBIA)
I DON'T WANNA GO ON WITH YOU LIKE THAT	ELTON JOHN (MCA)	13	NOW AND ZEN	ROBERT PLANT (ES PARANZA/ATLANTIC)
THE COLOUR OF LOVE	BILLY OCEAN (JIVE/ARISTA)	14	APPETITE FOR DESTRUCTION	GUNS 'N' ROSES (GEFFEN)
MERCEDES BOY	PEBBLES (MCA)	15	TRACY CHAPMAN	TRACY CHAPMAN (ELEKTRA)
MONKEY	GEORGE MICHAEL (COLUMBIA)	16	DOWN IN THE GROOVE	BOB DYLAN (COLUMBIA)
JUST GOT PAID	JOHNNY KEMP (COLUMBIA)	17	THIS NOTE'S FOR YOU	NEIL YOUNG & THE BLUENOTES (REPRISE)
PARENTS JUST DON'T UNDERSTAND	DJ JAZZY JEFF & FRESH PRINCE (JIVE/RCA)	18	DREAM OF LIFE	PATTI SMITH (ARISTA)
LOVE WILL SAVE THE DAY	WHITNEY HOUSTON (ARISTA)	19	SOUND ALARM	MICHAEL ANDERSON (A&M)
NITE AND DAY	AL B SURE! (WARNER BROS)	20	GREEN THOUGHTS	SMITHEREENS (ENIGMA/CAPITOL)

WEEK ENDING JULY 23 1988

UK

Singles			Albums	
NOTHING'S GONNA CHANGE MY LOVE FOR YOU	GLEN MEDEIROS (LONDON)	1	NOW! 12	VARIOUS EMI/VIRGIN/POLYGRAM)
PUSH IT/TRAMP	SALT 'N PEPA (CHAMPION)	2	TRACY CHAPMAN	TRACY CHAPMAN (ELEKTRA)
I DON'T WANT TO TALK ABOUT IT	EVERYTHING BUT THE GIRL (BLANCO Y NEGRO)	3	KYLIE	KYLIE MINOGUE (PWL)
DIRTY DIANA	MICHAEL JACKSON (EPIC)	4	IDOL SONGS: 11 OF THE BEST	BILLY IDOL (CHRYSALIS)
I WANT YOUR LOVE	TRANSVISION VAMP (MCA)	5	BAD	MICHAEL JACKSON (EPIC)
THE TWIST	FAT BOYS/CHUBBY CHECKER (POLYDOR)	6	PUSH	BROS (CBS)
FAST CAR	TRACY CHAPMAN (ELEKTRA)	7	1977-1980 SUBSTANCE	JOY DIVISION (FACTORY)
ROSES ARE RED	MAC BAND/THE McCAMPBELL BROTHERS (MCA)	8	THE COLLECTION	BARRY WHITE (MERCURY/PHONOGRAM)
FOOLISH BEAT	DEBBIE GIBSON (ATLANTIC)	9	DIRTY DANCING	ORIGINAL SOUNDTRACK (RCA)
BREAKFAST IN BED	UB40/C. HYNDE (DEP INTERNATIONAL/VIRGIN)	10	TANGO IN THE NIGHT	FLEETWOOD MAC (WARNER BROS)
I OWE YOU NOTHING	BROS (CBS)	11	POPPED IN SOULED OUT	WET WET WET (PRECIOUS/PHONOGRAM)
LOVE BITES	DEF LEPPARD (BLUDGEON RIFFOLA)	12	UB40	UB40 (VIRGIN)
MONKEY	GEORGE MICHAEL (EPIC)	13	TUNNEL OF LOVE	BRUCE SPRINGSTEEN (CBS)
CROSS MY HEART	EIGHTH WONDER (CBS)	14	WHAT YOU SEE IS WHAT YOU GET	GLEN GOLDSMITH (RCA)
BOYS	SABRINA (IBIZA/LONDON)	15	KICK	INXS (MERCURY/PHONOGRAM)
YOU CAME	KIM WILDE (MCA)	16	WHITNEY	WHITNEY HOUSTON (ARISTA)
DON'T BLAME IT ON THAT GIRL	MATT BIANCO (WEA)	17	HEAVEN ON EARTH	BELINDA CARLISLE (VIRGIN)
TRIBUTE	THE PASADENAS (CBS)	18	WIDE AWAKE IN DREAMLAND	PAT BENATAR (CHRYSALIS)
IN THE AIR TONIGHT	PHIL COLLINS (VIRGIN)	19	JACK MIX IN FULL EFFECT	MIRAGE (STYLUS)
SUPERFLY GUY	S-EXPRESS (RHYTHM KING/MUTE)	20	ROLL WITH IT	STEVE WINWOOD (VIRGIN))

US

Singles			Albums	
ROLL WITH IT	STEVE WINWOOD (VIRGIN)	1	OU812	VAN HALEN (WARNER BROS)
HOLD ON TO THE NIGHTS	RICHARD MARX (EMI-MANHATTAN)	2	ROLL WITH IT	STEVE WINWOOD (VIRGIN)
HANDS TO HEAVEN	BREATHE (A&M)	3	OUTRIDER	JIMMY PAGE (GEFFEN)
POUR SOME SUGAR ON ME	DEF LEPPARD (MERCURY/PG)	4	HEAVY NOVA	ROBERT PALMER (EMI-MANHATTAN)
MAKE ME LOSE CONTROL	ERIC CARMEN (ARISTA)	5	WIDE AWAKE IN DREAMLAND	PAT BENATAR (CHRYSALIS)
SIGN YOUR NAME	TERENCE TRENT D'ARBY (COLUMBIA)	6	JUST BEFORE THE BULLETS FLY	GREGG ALLMAN BAND (EPIC)
1-2-3	G. ESTEFAN & MIAMI SOUND MACHINE (EPIC)	7	SCENES FROM THE SOUTHSIDE	BRUCE HORNSBY & THE RANGE (RCA)
DO YOU LOVE ME	CONTOURS (MOTOWN)	8	APPETITE FOR DESTRUCTION	GUNS 'N' ROSES (GEFFEN)
I DON'T WANT TO LIVE WITHOUT YOU	CHICAGO (FULL MOON/REPRISE	9	REG STRIKES BACK	ELTON JOHN (MCA)
MONKEY	GEORGE MICHAEL (COLUMBIA)	10	MIDNIGHT OIL	DIESEL AND DUST (COLUMBIA)
I DON'T WANNA GO ON WITH YOU LIKE THAT	ELTON JOHN (MCA)	11	NOW AND ZEN	ROBERT PLANT (ES PARANZA/ATLANTIC)
LOVE WILL SAVE THE DAY	WHITNEY HOUSTON (ARISTA)	12	OUT OF ORDER	ROD STEWART (WARNER BROS)
JUST GOT PAID	JOHNNY KEMP (COLUMBIA)	13	COCKTAIL	SOUNDTRACK (ELEKTRA)
THE COLOUR OF LOVE	BILLY OCEAN (JIVE/ARISTA)	14	TRACY CHAPMAN	TRACY CHAPMAN (ELEKTRA)
NEW SENSATION	INXS (ATLANTIC)	15	GREEN THOUGHTS	SMITHEREENS (ENIGMA/CAPITOL)
RUSH HOUR	JANE WIEDLIN (EMI-MANHATTAN)	16	SUR LA MER	MOODY BLUES (POLYDOR/PG)
THE FLAME	CHEAP TRICK (EPIC)	17	SAVAGE AMUSEMENT	SCORPIONS (MERCURY/PG)
THE TWIST	FAT BOYS/CHUBBY CHECKER (PG)	18	DREAM OF LIFE	PATTI SMITH (ARISTA)
FAST CAR	TRACY CHAPMAN (ELEKTRA)	19	SOUND ALARM	MICHAEL ANDERSON (A&M)
PERFECT WORLD	HUEY LEWIS & THE NEWS (CHRYSALIS)	20	OPEN ALL NIGHT	GEORGIA SATELLITES (ELEKTRA)

UK MUSIC REFERENCE

RECORD COMPANIES

■ A&M Records
136-140 New Kings Road, London SW6 4LZ. Tel: (01) 736 3311 Tx: 916342
Labels: A&M,Breakout, Windham Hill

■ Abstract Sounds
10 Tiverton Road, London NW10 3HL.
Tel: (01) 969 4018
Labels: Abstract Dance, Abstract Records, TIM

■ Ace Records
45-50 Steele Road, London NW10.
Tel: (01) 453 1311 Tx: 893805 Acerec
Labels: Ace, Big Beat, Bluesville, Boplicity, Cascade, Contemporary, Debut, Del Rio, Fantasy, Globestyle, Impact, Jazzland, Kent, Milestone, Moodsville, Offbeat, Prestige, Riverside, Stax, Swingville

■ Arista Records
3 Cavendish Square, London W1.
Tel: (01) 580 5566 Tx: 298933
Labels: Arista

■ Backs Cartel
St Mary's Works, St Mary's Plain, Norwich NR6 3AF. Tel: (0603) 626221
Labels: Backs, Criminal Damage, Empire, Frank, Grunt-Grunt-A-Go-Go, Kick, Power Of Voice, Pure Trash, Ready To Eat, Re-Elect The President, Shellfish, Shelter, Small Wonder, Soul Supply, Vinyl Drip

■ Bam-Caruso Records
9 Ridgemont Road, St Albans, Herts
Tel: (0727) 32109
Labels: Bam-Caruso

■ BBC Records
Woodlands, 80 Wood Lane, London W12 0TT. Tel: (01) 576 0202 Tx: 934678
Labels: Artium, BBC Records

■ Beggar's Banquet
17-19 Alma Road, London SW18.
Tel: (01) 870 9912 Tx: 915733
Labels: Beggar's Banquet, Coda, 4AD

■ Carrere Records
PRT House, Bennett Street, London W4 2AH.
Tel: (01) 995 3031
Labels: Carrere

■ CBS Records
17-19 Soho Square, London W1.
Tel: (01) 734 8181 Tx: 24203
Labels: Blue Sky, Cameo, Caribou, CBS, Def Jam, Diamond, Epic, Monument, Portrait, Reformation, Tabu

■ Charly Records
156-166 Ilderton Road, London SE15 1NT.
Tel: (01) 639 8603/6 Tx: 8953184
Labels: Affinity, Atlantis, Caliente, Charly, Decal, Goldband, New Cross, Sun, Topline

■ Cherry Red Records
53 Kensington Gardens Square, London W2 4BA. Tel: (01) 229 8854 Tx: 943763 Chr
Labels: Anagram, Cherry Red, El, Time Stood Still, Virginia, Zebra

■ Chrysalis
12 Stratford Place, London W1N 9AF.
Tel: (01) 408 2355 Tx: 21753
Labels: Big Time, China, Chrysalis, Cooltempo, Ensign, Go! Discs, MAM, 2-Tone

■ Conifer Records
Horton Road, Wets Drayton, Middlesex UB7 8JL. Tel: (0895) 447707 Tx: 27492
Labels: Cambra, Conifer, DRG, EMI France/Germany/Holland/Italy/Sweden, Entertainers, Happy Days, Masters, MFP France, Moss Music, Muse, RCA Germany, Saville, Starjazz, Sunnyside

■ Creation Records
83 Clerkenwell Road, London EC1R 5AR.
Tel: (01) 831 7132
Labels: Creation Records, Elevation

■ Creole Records
Music House, 186 High Street, London NW10
Tel: (01) 965 9233 Tx: 28905
Labels: Blast From The Past, Cactus, Creole, Creole Classics, Dynamic, Ecstasy, 909, Replay, Review, Winner

■ Decca International
1 Rockley Road, London W14 0DL.
Tel: (01) 743 9111 Tx: 23533
Labels: Decca, Deram, Threshold

■ Demon Records
Canal House, Stars Estate, Transport Avenue, Brentford, Middlesex TW8 0QP.
Tel: (01) 847 2481 Tx: 894666
Labels: Demon, Edsel, HDH, Hi, Imp, Verbals, Zippo

■ DEP International
92 Fazeley Street, Digbeth, Birmingham B5 5RD. Tel: (021) 643 1321 Tx: 339447 Depint
Labels: DEP International

■ DJM Records
James House, Salisbury Place, Upper Montagu Street, London W1F 1FJ.
Tel: (01) 486 5838 Tx: 27135
Labels: DJM

■ EG Records
63 Kings Road, London SW3 4NT.
Tel: (01) 730 2162 Tx: 919205
Labels: Editions EG, EG Records

■ EMI Records
20 Manchester Square, London W1A 1ES.
Tel: (01) 486 4488 Tx: 22643
Labels: Blue Note, Capitol, Columbia, EMI, Harvest, HMV, Manhattan, Parlophone, Philadelphia International, RAK, Zonophone

■ Factory Communications
86 Palatine Road, Manchester 20.
Tel: (061) 434 3876 Tx: 669009 Facman
Labels: Factory Records

■ Fast Forward
21A Alva Street, Edinburgh EH2 4PS.
Tel: (031) 226 4616
Labels: Disposable, DDT, 53rd And 3rd

■ Flicknife
1st Floor, The Metrostore, 5/10 Eastman Road, The Vale, London W3 7YG.
Tel: (01) 743 9412
Labels: Flicknife

■ FM Revolver
152 Goldthorn Hill, Wolverhampton WV2 3JA. Tel: (0902) 345345 Tx: 335419 Rockson G
Labels: FM, FM Dance, Heavy Metal Worldwide, Revolver, Revolver Jazzmasters

■ Go! Discs
Son Of Go! Mansions, 320-322 King Street, London W6. Tel: (01) 748 7973 Tx: 923340
Labels: Go! Discs

■ Greensleeves Records
Unit 7, Goldhawk Industrial Estate, 2a Brackenbury Road, London W6.
Tel: (01) 749 3277/8 Tx: 8955504
Labels: Greensleeves, Ras, UK Bubblers, Unit 7

■ Hannibal Records
PO Box 742, London W11 3LZ.
Tel: (01) 727 7480 Tx: 8950511 Oneoneg
Labels: Hannibal

■ Illuminated Productions
46 Carter Lane, London EC4.
Tel: (01) 236 6668
Labels: Illuminated Records

■ (IRS) International Recording Syndicate
Bugle House, 21A Noel Street, London W1.
Tel: (01) 434 9513 Tx: 299338 Mcarec G
Labels: Illegal, IRS

■ Island Records
22 St Peter's Square, London W6 9NW.
Tel: (01) 741 1511 Tx: 934541
Labels: Antilles, Fourth & Broadway, Mango, Mother, Taxi, ZTT

■ K-Tel International
K-Tel House, 620 Western Avenue, London W3 0TL. Tel: (01) 992 8055 Tx: 934195
Labels: K-Tel, Lotus

■ London Records
1 Sussex Place, London W6 9SG.
Tel: (01) 846 8515 Tx: 263828
Labels: London, Slash

■ Magnet Records
Magnet House, 22 York Street, London W1H 1ED. Tel: (01) 486 8151 Tx: 25537
Labels: Magnet, Magnetic Dance

■ MCA Records
72-74 Brewer Street, London W1.
Tel: (01) 437 9797 Tx: 23158
Labels: MCA

■ Music For Nations
8 Carnaby Street, London W1 1PG.
Tel: (01) 437 4688 Tx: 296217
Labels: Food For Thought, Fun After All, Music For Nations, Rough Justice, Under One Flag

■ Music For Pleasure
1-3 Uxbridge Road, Hayes, Middlesex UB4 0SY. Tel: (01) 561 8722 Tx: 934614
Labels: Classics For Pleasure, Eminence, Fame, Golden Age, Hour Of, Listen For Pleasure, Music For Pleasure

■ Mute Records
429 Harrow Road, London W10 4RE.
Tel: (01) 969 8866 Tx: 268623
Labels: Blast First, Mute, Product Inc., Rhythm King

■ Neat Records
71 High Street, East Wallsend, Tyne and Wear NE28 7RJ. Tel: (091) 262 4999 Tx: 537681 Alwrld
Labels: Completely Different, Floating World, Neat

■ Nine Mile Records
Lower Avenue, Leamington Spa, Warwickshire. Tel: (0926) 881292
Labels: Chapter 22, Cooking Vinyl, Crammed Discs, Dojo, Fire, Glass, Moksha, One Little Indian, Red Flame, Ron Johnson, Wire

■ Old Gold Records
Unit 1, Langhedge Lane Industrial Estate, Edmonton N18 2TQ. Tel: (01) 884 2220
Tx: 264597 OldGol G
Labels: Decades, Old Gold, Start

■ Oval Records
11 Liston Road, London SW4. Tel: (01) 622 0111 Tx: 946240 Cweasy G Ref. 19017005
Labels: Oval

■ People Unite
50/52 King Street, Southall, Middlesex.
Tel: (01) 574 1718
Labels: People Unite

■ Phonogram Ltd
50 New Bond Street, London W1Y 9HA.
Tel: (01) 491 4600 Tx: 261583
Labels: Club, Fontana, Mercury, Neutron, Phillips, Phonogram, Rocket, Vertigo

■ Pickwick International
The Hyde Industrial Estate, The Hyde, London NW9 6JU. Tel: (01) 200 7000
Tx: 922170
Labels: Camden, Contour, Ditto, Hallmark, IMP Red, Pickwick, Spot

■ Polydor
1 Sussex Place, London W6 9XT.
Tel: (01) 846 8515 Tx: 263828
Labels: MGM, Polydor, RSO, Urban, Verve, Wonderland

■ President Records
Broadmead House, 21 Panton Street, London SW1 4DR. Tel: (01) 839 4672/5 Tx: 24158 Kassmu G
Labels: Bulldog, Energy, Enterprise, Joy, Max's Kansas City, New World, President, Rhapsody, Seville, Spiral, TBG

■ Probe Plus
8-12 Rainford Gardens, Liverpool 2.
Tel: (051) 236 6591
Labels: The Ark, Fat Wallet, Fend For Yourself, Galaxy, Moral Burro, Mother Africa, Snow Company, Swell Kitchen

■ PRT Records
PRT House, Bennett Street, London W4 2AH. Tel: (01) 995 3031
Labels: PRT

■ RCA/Ariola Records
1 Bedford Avenue, London WC1.
Tel: (01) 636 8311 Tx: 21349
Labels: Gordy, Inevitable, Morocco, Motown, Planet, Prelude, RCA, Salsoul, Tent, Total Experience, Victor

■ Red Rhino Records
The Coach House, Fetter Lane, York YO1 1EH.
Tel: (0904) 72828
Labels: Agit-Prop, All Or Nothing, American Activities, Batfish Inc., Black Lagoon, Dead Man's Curve, Dossier, Ediesta, Fundamental, In-Tape, Kaleidoscope Sounds, Media Burn, Medium Cool, Native, Play It Again Sam, Reception, Red Rhino, Roir UK, RRE, Ruska, Sever, Sharp, Sin, Skysaw, Sterile, Tanz, Technical, Uglyman, Volume, White Line

■ Revolver Records
The Old Malt House, Little Ann Street, Bristol 2. Tel: (0272) 541291/4
Labels: Antar, Bam Caruso, C.O.R., Disorder, Disque Afrique, Earrache, Five Hours Back, Get Ahead, Head, Heartland, ID, Manic Ears, Noise UK, One Big Guitar, RDL, Remorse, SS20, Subway, WOMAD, World Grant, Zap

■ Rocket Record Company
51 Holland Street, London W8 7JB.
Tel: (01) 938 1741 Tx: 265870
Labels: Rocket

■ Rough Trade Records
61-71 Collier Street, London N1.
Tel: (01) 833 2133/2561/3 Tx: 299579
Labels: All The Madmen, Alternative Tentacles, Bad, Big Life/Society, Burning Rome, Celluloid, Creation, Disc Chevalier, Dreamworld, Flying Nun, Fon, Food, Homestead, Hot, Lazy, Midnight, Nervous, NER, Own Up, Pink, Raw TV, Reflex, Rough Trade, Side Effects, Stuff, Sweatbox, Temple, Third Mind, United Dairies, Very Mouth, Vindaloo

■ See For Miles
PO Box 238, Maidenhead, Berks SL6 2NE.
Tel: (0628) 39790 or (01) 398 6143
Labels: See For Miles

■ Siren Records
61-63 Portobello Road, London W11 3DD.
Tel: (01) 221 7535 Tx: 295417 Siren G
Labels: Siren

■ Some Bizzare
166 New Cavendish Street, London W1M 7LJ.
Tel: (01) 631 3140 Tx: 8951182
Labels: Some Bizzare

■ Sonet Records
121 Ledbury Road, London W11.
Tel: (01) 229 7267 Tx: 25793
Labels: Gramavision, Red Stripe, Sonet, Stone, Titanic

■ Stiff Records
111 Talbot Road, London W11.
Tel: (01) 221 5101 Tx: 297314
Labels: Bluebird, Stiff

■ Ten Records
61-63 Portobello Road, London W11.
Tel: (01) 221 7535
Labels: MDM, Ten

■ Virgin Records
Kensal House, 533-579 Harrow Road, London W10. Tel: (01) 968 6688 Tx: 22542
Labels: Charisma, Circa, EG, Foundry, Linn, Red Eye, Venture, Virgin, Zarjazz

■ WEA Records
The Electric Lighting Station, 46 Kensington Court, London W8. Tel: (01) 938 2181
Tx: 261425
Labels: Asylum, Atco, Atlantic, blanco y negro, Cotillion, Duck, Elektra, Geffen, Korova, Megaforce, Nonesuch, Paisley Park, Q-West, Real, Reprise, Sire, Valentino, Warner Bros, WEA Int

■ Westside Records
Springbridge Mews, London W5 2AB.
Tel: (01) 840 4800 Tx: 935942
Labels: B-Boy, DJ International, Hardcore, Streetsounds, Westside

■ Zomba Productions
Zomba House, 165-167 Willesden High Road, London NW10 2SG. Tel: (01) 459 8899
Tx: 237316 Zomba
Labels: Jive, Jive Africa, Jive Electro, Lifestyle

■ ZTT Records
42/46 St Lukes Mews, London W11.
Tel: (01) 221 5101 Tx: 297314 Sarm G
Labels: ZTT

LABELS

Affinity – Charly
Agit-Prop – Red Rhino
All Or Nothing – Red Rhino
All The Madmen – Rough Trade
Alternative Tentacles – Rough Trade
American Activities – Red Rhino
Anagram – Cherry Red
Antar – Revolver
Antilles – Island
Artium – BBC
Asylum – WEA
Atco – WEA
Atlantic – WEA
Atlantis – Charly

B-Boy – Westside Records
Bad – Rough Trade
Batfish Inc – Red Rhino
Big Beat – Ace
Big Life/Society – Rough Trade
Big Time – Chrysalis
Black Lagoon – Red Rhino
blanco y negro – WEA
Blast First – Mute
Blast From The Past – Creole
Blue Note – EMI
Blue Sky – CBS
Bluebird – Stiff
Bluesville – Ace
Boplicity – Ace
Breakout – A&M
Bulldog – President
Burning Rome – Rough Trade

Cactus – Creole
Caliente – Charly
Cambra – Conifer
Camden – Pickwick
Cameo – CBS
Capitol – EMI
Caribou – CBS
Cascade – Ace
Celluloid – Rough Trade
Chapter 22 – Nine Mile
Charisma – Virgin
China – Chrysalis
Circa – Virgin
Classics For Pleasure – Music For Pleasure
Club – Phonogram
Coda – Beggar's Banquet
Columbia – EMI
Completely Different – Neat
Contemporary – Ace
Contour – Pickwick
Cool Tempo – Chrysalis
Cooking Vinyl – Nine Mile
C.O.R. – Revolver
Cotillion – WEA
Crammed Discs – Nine Mile
Criminal Damage – Backs
Crown – Ace

DDT – Fast Forward
Deadman's Curve – Red Rhino
Debut – Ace
Decades – Old Gold
Def Jam – CBS
Del Rio – Ace
Deram – Decca
Disc Chevalier – Rough Trade
Disorder – Revolver
Disposable – Fast Forward
Disqueafrique – Revolver
Ditto – Pickwick
DJ International – Westside Records
Dojo – Nine Mile
Dossier – Red Rhino
Dreamworld – Rough Trade
DRG – Conifer
Duck – WEA
Dynamic – Creole

Earache – Revolver
Ecstasy – Creole
Ediesta – Red Rhino
Edsel – Demon
El – Cherry Red
Elektra – WEA
Elevation – Creation
EMI France – Conifer
EMI Germany – Conifer
EMI Holland – Conifer
EMI Italy – Conifer
EMI Sweden – Conifer
Eminence – Music For Pleasure
Empire – Backs
Energy – President
Ensign – Chrysalis
Enterprise – President
Entertainers – Conifer
Epic – CBS

Fame – Music For Pleasure
Fantasy – Ace
Fat Wallet – Probe Plus
Fend For Yourself – Probe Plus
53rd And 3rd – Fast Forward
Fire – Nine Mile
Five Hours Back – Revolver
Floating World – Neat
Flying Nun – Rough Trade
Fon – Rough Trade
Fontana – Phonogram
Food – Rough Trade
Food For Thought – Music For Nations
Foundry – Virgin
4AD – Beggar's Banquet
Fourth And Broadway – Island
Frank – Backs
Fun After All – Music For Nations
Fundamental – Red Rhino

Galaxy – Probe Plus
Geffen – WEA
Get Ahead – Revolver
Glass – Nine Mile
Globestyle – Ace
Goldband – Charly
Golden Age – Music For Pleasure
Gordy – RCA/Ariola
Gramavision – Sonet
Grunt-Grunt-A-Go-Go – Backs

Hallmark – Pickwick
Happy Days – Conifer
Hardcore – Westside Records
Harvest – EMI
Head – Revolver
Heartland – Revolver
HDH – Demon
Heavy Metal Worldwide – FM Revolver
Hi – Demon
HMV – EMI
Homestead – Rough Trade
Hot – Rough Trade
Hour Of – Music For Pleasure

Ice – RCA/Ariola
ID – Revolver
Illegal – IRS
Imp – Demon
IMP Red – Pickwick
Impact – Ace
Inevitable – RCA/Ariola
In-Tape – Red Rhino

Jazzland – Ace
Jive – Zomba
Joy – President

Kaleidoscope Sounds – Red Rhino
Kent – Ace
Kick – Backs
Korova – WEA

Lazy – Rough Trade
Lifestyle – Zomba
Linn – Virgin
Listen For Pleasure – Music For Pleasure
Lotus – K-Tel

Magnetic Dance – Magnet
MAM – Chrysalis
Mango – Island
Manhattan – EMI
Manic Ears – Revolver
Masters – Conifer
Max's Kansas City – President
MDM – Ten
Media Burn – Red Rhino
Medium Cool – Red Rhino
Megaforce – WEA
Mercury – Phonogram
MFP France – Conifer
MGM – Polydor
Midnight – Rough Trade
Milestone – Ace
Moksha – Nine Mile
Monument – CBS
Moodsville – Ace
Moral Burro – Probe Plus
Morocco – RCA/Ariola
Moss Music – Conifer
Mother – Island
Mother Africa – Probe Plus
Motown – RCA/Ariola
Muse – Conifer

Native – Red Rhino
Neutron – Phonogram
Nervous – Rough Trade
NER – Rough Trade
New Cross – Charly
New World – President
909 – Creole
Noise UK – Revolver
Nonesuch – WEA

Off Beat – Ace
One Big Guitar – Revolver
One Little Indian – Nine Mile
Own Up – Rough Trade

Paisley Park – WEA
Parlophone – EMI
Philadelphia International – EMI
Phillips – Phonogram
Pink – Rough Trade
Planet – RCA/Ariola
Play It Again Sam – Red Rhino
Portrait – CBS
Power Of Voice – Backs
Prelude – RCA/Ariola
Prestige – Ace
Product Inc – Mute
Pure Trash – Backs

Q-West – WEA

RAK – EMI
Ras – Greensleeves
Raw TV – Rough Trade
RCA Germany – Conifer
RDL – Revolver
Ready To Eat – Backs
Real – WEA
Reception – Red Rhino
Red Eye – Virgin
Red Flame – Nine Mile
Red Stripe – Sonet
Re-Elect The President – Backs
Reflex – Rough Trade
Reformation – CBS
Remorse – Revolver
Replay – Creole
Reprise – WEA
Review – Creole
Revolver – FM Revolver
Rhapsody – President
Rhythm King – Mute
Riverside – Ace
Rocket – Phonogram
Roir UK – Red Rhino
Ron Johnson – Nine Mile
Rough Justice – Music For Nations
RRE – Red Rhino
RSO – Polydor
Ruska – Red Rhino

Salsoul – RCA/Ariola
Saville – Conifer
Sever – Red Rhino
Seville – President
Sharp – Red Rhino
Shellfish – Backs
Shelter – Backs
Side Effects – Rough Trade
Sin – Red Rhino
Sire – WEA
Skysaw – Red Rhino
Slash – London
Small Wonder – Backs
Snow Company – Probe Plus
Soul Supply – Backs
Spiral – President
Spot – Pickwick
SS20 – Revolver
Starjazz – Conifer
Start – Old Gold
Stax – Ace
Sterile – Red Rhino
Stone – Sonet
Streetsounds – Westside Records
Stuff – Rough Trade
Subway – Revolver
Sun – Charly
Sunnyside – Conifer
Sweatbox – Rough Trade
Swell Kitchen – Probe Plus
Swingville – Ace

Tabu – CBS
Tanz – Red Rhino
Taxi – Island
TBG – President
Technical – Red Rhino
Temple – Rough Trade
Tent – RCA/Ariola
The Ark – Probe Plus
Third Mind – Rough Trade
Threshold – Decca
TIM – Abstract
Time Stood Still – Abstract
Titanic – Sonet
Topline – Charly
Total Experience – RCA/Ariola
2-Tone – Chrysalis

Uglyman – Red Rhino
UK Bubblers – Greensleeves
Under One Flag – Music For Nations
Unit 7 – Greensleeves
United Dairies – Rough Trade
Urban – Polydor

Valentino – WEA
Venture – Virgin
Verbals – Demon
Vertigo – Phonogram
Verve – Polydor
Very Mouth – Rough Trade
Vindaloo – Rough Trade
Vinyl Drip – Backs
Virginia – Cherry Red
Volume – Red Rhino

Warner Bros – WEA
White Line – Red Rhino
Windham Hill – A&M
Winner – Creole
Wire – Nine Mile
WOMAD – Revolver
Wonderland – Polydor
World Grant – Revolver

Zap – Revolver
Zarjazz – Virgin
Zebra – Cherry Red
Zippo – Demon
Zonophone – EMI
ZTT – Island

MUSIC PUBLISHERS

- **Albion Music**
See Complete Music

- **All Boys Music**
4-7 The Vineyard, Sanctuary Street, London SE1. Tel: (01) 403 0007

- **Ambassador Music**
22 Denmark Street, London WC2. Tel:(01) 836 5996

- **APB Music**
28 Ivor Place, London NW1. Tel: (01) 723 9269

- **ATV Music**
See SBK Songs

- **Barn Publishing**
12 Thayer Street, London W1. Tel: (01) 935 8323 Tx: 22787 Thayer G

- **Belsize Music**
2nd Floor, 24 Baker Street, London W1. Tel: (01) 935 2076 Tx: 23840

- **Black Sheep Music**
Fulmer Gardens House, Fulmer, Bucks Tel: (02816) 2143/2109 Tx: 849208

- **Blue Mountain Music**
334-336 King Street, London W6 0RA. Tel: (01) 846 9566 Tx: 934541

- **Bocu Music**
1 Wyndham Yard, Wyndham Place, London W1H 1AR. Tel: (01) 402 7433/5 Tx: 298976

- **Margaret Brace Copyright Bureau**
7-9 Greenland Place, London NW1 0AT. Tel: (01) 482 4979 Tx: 94016170

- **Brampton Music**
9 Carnaby Street, London W1. Tel: (01) 437 1958

- **Burlington Music**
129 Park Street, London W1. Tel: (01) 499 0067 Tx: 268403

- **Carlin Music**
14 New Burlington Street, London W1X 2LR. Tel: (01) 734 3251 Tx: 267488

- **CBS Songs**
See SBK Songs

- **Chappell Music.**
129 Park Street, London W1Y 3FA. Tel: (01) 629 7600 Tx: 268403

- **Charisma Music**
Russell Chambers, Covent Garden, London WC2. Tel: (01) 240 9891

- **Charly Publishing.**
46-47 Pall Mall, London SW1 5JG. Tel: (01) 732 5647 Tx: 8953184

- **Chelsea Music Publishing**
184-186 Regent Street, London W1R 5DR. Tel: (01) 439 7731 Tx: 27557

- **Chrysalis Music**
12 Stratford Place, London W1N 9AF. Tel: (01) 408 2355 Tx: 21753

- **Complete Music**
49-53 Kensington Gardens Square, London W2 4BA. Tel: (01) 229 8854 Tx: 943763 Chr

- **Creole Music**
186 High Street, London NW10. Tel: (01) 965 9223 Tx: 28905

- **Eaton Music**
8 West Eaton Place, London SW1X 8LS. Tel: (01) 235 9046 Tx: 296133

- **EG Music**
63A King's Road, London SW3 4NT. Tel: (01) 730 2162 Tx: 919205

■ EMI Music Publishing
138-140 Charing Cross Road, London WC2H 0LD. Tel: (01) 836 6699 Tx: 269189 Emi Pub G

■ Empire Music
27 Queensdale Place, London W11.
Tel: (01) 602 5031

■ Faber Music
3 Queen Square, London WC1N 3AU.
Tel: (01) 278 6881 Tx: 299633

■ Filmtrax
7-9 Greenland Place, London NW1.
Tel: (01) 482 4979

■ Noel Gay Music
24 Denmark Street, London WC2H 8NJ.
Tel: (01) 836 3941 Tx: 21760

■ Go! Discs Music
Go! Mansions, 8 Wendell Road, London W12.
Tel: (01) 743 3845/3919

■ Handle Music
1 Derby Street, London W1. Tel: (01) 493 9637
Tx: 892756

■ Heath Levy Music
184-186 Regent Street, London W1.
Tel: (01) 439 7731

■ Hit And Run/Cleofine Music
81-83 Walton Street, London SW3 2HP.
Tel: (01) 581 0261

■ Illegal Music
Bugle House, 21A Noel Street, London W1.
Tel: (01) 734 3814 Tx: 268152

■ Intersong Music
129 Park Street, London W1Y 3FA.
Tel: (01) 499 0067 Tx: 268403

■ Island Music
Media House, 334-336 King Street
London W6 0RA. Tel: (01) 846 9141
Tx: 934541

■ Dick James Music
c/o PolyGram International, 45 Berkeley Square, London W1X 5DB. Tel: (01) 493 8800
Tx: 263872

■ Jobete Music
Tudor House, 35 Gresse Street, London W1P 1PN. Tel: (01) 631 0380 Tx: 8811658 G

■ Kassner Associated Publishers
21 Panton Street, London SW1.
Tel: (01) 839 4672 Tx: 24158

■ Leosong Copyright Service
7-8 Greenland Place, London NW1 0AT.
Tel: (01) 482 4979 Tx: 94016170

■ Magnet Music
22 York Street, London W1H 1FD.
Tel: (01) 486 8151 Tx: 25537

■ Bill Martin Music
11th Floor, Alembic House, 93 Albert Embankment, London SE1 7TY.
Tel: (01) 582 7622

■ Mautoglade
22 Denmark Street, London WC2.
Tel: (01) 836 5996

■ MCA Music
139 Piccadilly, London W1V 9FH.
Tel: (01) 629 7211 Tx: 22219

■ Minder Music
22 Bristol Gardens, London W9 2JQ.
Tel: (01) 289 7281 Tx: 923421 Wemsec G

■ Mood Music
35-37 Parkgate Road, London SW11.
Tel: (01) 228 4000

■ Morrison Leahy Music
1 Star Street, London W2.
Tel: (01) 402 9238 Tx: 266589 Mlm G

■ MPL Communications
1 Soho Square, LondonW1V 6BQ.
Tel: (01) 439 6621 Tx: 21294

■ Neptune Music
31 Old Burlington Street, London W1X 1LB.
Tel: (01) 437 2066/7 Tx: 8954748

■ Oval Music
326 Brixton Road, London SW9.
Tel: (01) 326 4907 Tx: 94012230

■ Pattern Music
22 Denmark Street, London WC2.
Tel: (01) 836 5996

■ Perfect Songs
111 Talbot Road, London W11.
Tel: (01) 221 5101

■ Pink Floyd Music Publishers
27 Noel Street, London W1V 3RD.
Tel: (01) 734 6892 Tx: 28905 Ref. 907

■ Plangent Visions
27 Noel Street, London W1V 3RD.
Tel: (01) 734 6892

■ Point Music
Studio 5, The Royal Victoria Patriotic Building, Trinity Road, London SW18.
Tel: (01) 871 4155 Tx: 265871Monres G
Attn. DGS1483

■ PolyGram Music
1 Sussex Place, London W6 9XS.
Tel: (01) 846 8515 Tx: 263828

■ RAK Publishing
42-48 Charlbert Street, London NW8 7BU.
Tel: (01) 586 2012 Tx: 299501

■ RCA Music
3 Cavendish Square, London W1.
Tel: (01) 580 5566 Tx: 298933

■ The Really Useful Company
20 Greek Street, London W1V 5LF.
Tel: (01) 734 2114 Tx: 8953151

■ Red Bus Music
Red Bus House, 48 Broadley Terrace, London NW1. Tel: (01) 258 0324/8
Tx: 25873 Red Bus

■ Reformation Music
Suite 7, 3rd Floor, 89 Great Portland Street, London W1. Tel: (01) 580 4007

■ Renegade Music
145 Oxford Street, London W1.
Tel: (01) 437 2777

■ Riva Music
45 Broadwick Street, London W1V 3LP.
Tel: (01) 734 3481 Tx: 28781 Glass G

■ Rock City Music
Shepperton Studio Centre, Shepperton, Middlesex. Tel: (09328) 66531/2

■ Rock Music
27 Noel Street, London W1V 3RD.
Tel: (01) 734 6892

■ Rondor Music
Rondor House, 10A Parsons Green, London SW6 4TW. Tel: (01) 731 4161/5

■ St Anne's Music
Kennedy House, 31 Stamford Street, Altrincham, Cheshire WA14 1ES.
Tel: (061) 941 5151 Tx: 666255

■ SBK Songs
3-5 Rathbone Place, London W1V 5DG.
Tel: (01) 637 5831

■ Sonet Music Publishing
121 Ledbury Road, London W11 2AQ.
Tel: (01) 229 7267 Tx: 25793

■ Sound Diagrams
21 Atholl Crescent, Edinburgh EH3 8HQ.
Tel: (031) 229 8946 Tx: 265871

■ Southern Music Publishing
8 Denmark Street, London WC2H 8LT.
Tel: (01) 836 4524 Tx: 23557

■ Ten Music
Advance House, 101-109 Ladbroke Grove, London W11 1PG. Tel: (01) 221 8585

■ Tritec Music
32 Marshall Street, London W1.
Tel: (01) 439 7100

■ Virgin Music Publishers
Advance House, 101-109 Ladbroke Grove, London W11 1PG. Tel: (01) 229 1282

■ Warner Brothers Music
17 Berners Street, London W1P 3DD.
Tel: (01) 637 3771 Tx: 25522

■ Westminster Music
19-20 Poland Street, London W1V 3DD.
Tel: (01) 734 8121 Tx: 22701

■ Zomba Music
165-167 Willesden High Road, London NW10. Tel: (01) 459 8899

INDEPENDENT DISTRIBUTORS

■ Arabesque Ltd
Swan Centre, Fisher's Lane, London W4 1RX.
Tel: (01) 747 0365 Tx: 291908

■ Backs Cartel
St Mary's Works, St Mary's Plain, Norwich
Tel: (0603) 626221

■ Caroline Exports
56 Standard Road, London NW10.
Tel: (01) 961 2919 Tx: 22164

■ Conifer Records
Horton Road, West Drayton, Middlesex
UB7 8LJ. Tel: (0895) 447707 Tx: 27492

■ Counterpoint Distribution
Wharf Road, London E15 2SU.
Tel: (01) 555 4321 Tx: 8951427

■ Discovery Records
107 Broad Street, Beechingstoke, Pewsey, Wilts. Tel: (067285) 406

■ Electronic Synthesizer Sound Projects (ESSP)
The Sound House, PO Box 37B, East Molesey, Surrey. Tel: (1) 979 9997/577 5818

■ Fast Forword
21A Alva Road, Edinburgh EH2 4PS.
Tel: (031) 226 4616

■ S. Gold and Son
Gold House, 69 Flempton Road, Leyton, London E10 7NL. Tel: (01) 539 3600
Tx: 894793

■ Greensleeves Records
Unit 7, Goldhawk Industrial Estate, 2a Brackenbury Road, London W6.
Tel: (01) 749 3277/8 Tx: 8955504

■ Hotshot Records
29 St Michael's Road, Headingly, Leeds, Yorkshire. Tel: (0532) 742106

■ Jazz Horizons
103 London Road, Sawbridgeworth, Herts CM1 9JJ. Tel: (0279) 724572

■ Jazz Music
12 Regent Street, Haslington, Lancs BB4 5HQ.
Tel: (0706) 228 722 Tx: 265871

■ Jungle Records
24 Gaskin Street, London N1 2RY.
Tel: (01) 359 8444 Tx: 896559
Gecoms G Attn. Jungle

■ Lasgo Exports
Unit 2, Chapman's Park Industrial Estate, 378-388 High Road, Willesden, London NW10 2DY. Tel: (01) 459 8800 Tx: 22111 Lasgo G

■ Lightning Distribution
Bashley Road, London NW10 6SD.
Tel: (01) 965 5555 Tx: 927813 Larrec

■ New Roots
61-71 Collier Street, London N1.
Tel: (01) 833 2133 Tx: 299579

■ Nine Mile Records
Lower Avenue, Leamington Spa, Warwickshire. Tel: (0926) 881292

■ Oldies Unlimited
Dukes Way, St George's, Telford, Shropshire.
Tel: (0952) 616911 Tx: 35493

■ Pickwick International
The Hyde Industrial Estate, The Hyde, London NW9 6JU. Tel: (01) 200 7000
Tx: 922170

■ Pinnacle Records
Unit 2, Orpington Trading Estate, Sevenoaks Way, Orpington, Kent BR5 3FR. Tel: (0689) 70622 Tx: 929053

■ Pizza Express Music Distribution
29 Romilly Street, London W1.
Tel: (01) 734 6112 Tx: 27950 Ref. 3396

■ Probe Plus
8-12 Rainford Gardens, Liverpool 2.
Tel: (051) 236 6591

■ PRT Distribution
105 Bond Road, Mitcham, Surrey CR4 3UT.
Tel: (01) 648 7000

■ Recommended Distribution
387 Wandsworth Road, London SW8.
Tel: (01) 622 8834 Tx: 8813271 Gecoms G

■ Red Lightnin' Records
The White House, North Lopham, Diss, Norfolk. Tel: (0379) 88693

■ Red Rhino Distribution
The Grain Store, 74 Eldon Street, York YO3 7NE. Tel: (0904) 611656

■ Revolver Distribution
The Old Malt House, Little Ann Street, Bristol 2. Tel: (0272) 541291/4

■ Rose Records
3 Ellington Street, London N7 8PP.
Tel: (01) 609 8288 Tx: 268048

■ Ross Record Distribution
29 Main Street, Turriff, Aberdeenshire
Tel: (0888) 62403

■ Rough Trade Distribution
61-71 Collier Street, London N1.
Tel: (01) 833 2133 Tx: 299579

■ Spartan Records
London Road, Wembley, Middlesex HA9 7HQ. Tel: (01) 903 4753 Tx: 923175

■ Wynd-Up Records
Turntable House, Guinness Road Trading Estate, Trafford Park, Manchester.
Tel: (061) 872 0170 Tx: 635363

■ World Service
61-71 Collier Street London N1.
Tel: (01) 833 2133 Tx: 299579

MUSIC MAGAZINES

■ Beatles Monthly
43 St Mary's Road, Ealing, London W5 5RQ.
Tel: (01) 579 1082

Beatlemania resurrected; monthly; 48pp; £1.25; circ. n/a

■ Blitz
40-42 Newman Street, London W1V 3PA.
Tel: (01) 436 5211

A stylish multi-media extravaganza; monthly; 116pp; £1.00; circ. 60,000

■ Blues and Rhythm
18 Maxwelton Close, London NW7 3NA.
Tel: (01) 906 0986

Blues, R&B, gospel, vintage, soul, cajun, tex-mex, news, updates, and latest albums; monthly (except January and August) in first fortnight; 36pp; £1.25; circ. 2,000

■ Blues and Soul
153 Praed Street, London W2.
Tel: (01) 402 6869

Covers all black music and dance music (except reggae); fortnightly; 48pp; £0.80; circ. 41,600

■ Brum Beat
195 Hagley Road, Edgbaston, Birmingham B16 6UT. Tel: (021) 454 7020

The Birmingham and West Midlands scene; monthly; 16pp; free; circ. 40,000

■ Country Music People
78 Grovelands Road, St Paul's Cray, Orpington, Kent. Tel: (01) 309 7606

Covers all country music; monthly; 42pp; £0.90; circ. 12,000 worldwide

■ The Cover
Nuvox House, 370 Coldharbour Lane, London SW9 8PL. Tel: (01) 737 7377

Music, film and television uncovered by a staff with a sense of humour; fortnightly; 36pp; £0.60; circ. n/a

■ Disco and Club Trade International
410 St John Street, London EC1.
Tel: (01) 278 3591/6 Tx: 24637 Wigmor

Trade magazine for discos, clubs, pubs etc; monthly; 86pp; £1.00; circ. 25,000

■ Echoes
Rococco House, 283 City Road, London EC1 1LA. Tel: (01) 253 6662/4

Covers all black music, especially funk, soul and reggae; every Wednesday; 24pp; £0.50; circ. 25,000

■ Electronics and Music Maker
Alexander House, 1 Milton Road, Cambridge CB4 1UY. Tel: (0223) 313722

Interviews and reviews of new equipment, for musicians and studio technicians; monthly; 112pp; £1.20; circ. 20,500

■ Elvis Monthly
41-47 Derby Road, Heanor, Derbyshire DE7 7QH. Tel: (0773) 712460

Elvis, Elvis . . . and more Elvis; monthly, last Tuesday; 56pp; £0.95; circ. 25,000

■ Elvisly Yours
107 Shoreditch High Street, London E1. Tel: (01) 739 2001

As above; bi-monthly; 32pp; £1.50; circ.n/a

■ The Face
The Old Laundry, Ossington Buildings, Off Moxon Street, London W1. Tel: (01) 935 8232

The magazine by which others are judged – the gazette of style in the UK; monthly, third Thursday; 116pp; £0.90; circ. 92,000 worldwide

■ Folk Roots
PO Box 73, Farnham, Surrey GU9 7UN. Tel: (0252) 724638

Across the board, traditional and modern folk from the UK, US, and around the world, plus blues, tex-mex, African, etc; monthly, third Thursday; 60pp; £1.20; circ. 12,000

■ Guitarist
Alexander House, 1 Milton Road, Cambridge CB4 1UY. Tel: (0223) 313722

For guitarists! Lots of interviews, reviews of new equipment; monthly, second Thursday; 72pp; £1.20; circ. 21,000

■ Home and Studio Recording
Alexander House, 1 Milton Road, Cambridge CB4 1UY. Tel: (0223) 313722

For anyone interested in music recording and how to do it; monthly, third Thursday; 80pp; £1.20; circ.18,500

■ Home Keyboard Review
Alexander House, 1 Milton Road, Cambridge CB4 1UY. Tel: (0223) 313722

For the domestic keyboard player; monthly, third Thursday; 64pp; £0.90; circ. 16,000

■ i-D
27-29 Macklin Street, London WC2. Tel: (01) 430 0871

Music of all descriptions, as well as fashion and features; monthly, third Tuesday; 100pp; £1.00; circ.47,000

■ International Country Music News
18 Burley Rise, Kegworth, Derby DE8 2DZ. Tel: (05097) 3224

British and American country music; monthly, fourth Thursday; 24pp; £0.50; circ. 25,000

■ International Musician and Recording World
PO Box 381, Mill Harbour, London E14. Tel: (01) 987 5090 Tx: 24676 Norshl G

Everything the modern musician needs to know about equipment, recordings, production, etc; monthly, in the last week; 148pp; £1.95; circ. 24,000

■ Jazz Journal International
35 Great Russell Street, London WC1 3PP. Tel: (01) 580 7244

Jazz enthusiasts' and record collectors' magazine; monthly, last Friday; 40pp; £1.20; circ. 11,500

■ Kerrang!
Greater London House, Hampstead Road, London NW1. Tel: (01) 387 6611

Heavy metal and heavy rock; fortnightly, Thursdays; 56pp; £0.85; circ. 90,000 worldwide

■ Mega Metal Kerrang!
Greater London House, Hampstead Road, London NW1. Tel: (01) 387 6611

Heavy, heavy metal; quarterly; 52pp; £1.25; circ. 45,000

■ Melody Maker
Berkshire House, 168-173 High Holborn, London WC1. Tel: (01) 379 3581

Music, trouble and fun for the older 'teenager'; every Wednesday; 52pp; £0.50; circ. 61,000

■ Music Week
Greater London House, Hampstead Road, London NW1. Tel: (01) 387 6611

Music trade magazine for record companies and retailers; every Wednesday; 36pp; £1.50; circ. 13,500

■ New Kommotion
3 Bowrons Avenue, Wembley, Middlesex. Tel: (01) 902 6417

Fifties rockabillity and rock 'n' roll for record collectors; quarterly; 50pp; £1.20; circ. 3,000

■ NME (New Musical Express)
Commonwealth House, 1-19 New Oxford Street, London WC1. Tel: (01) 404 0700

"What? You'll only give us twelve words to describe NME? It's *outrageous*!!!" – the editor; every Wednesday; 56pp; £0.50; circ. 105,000

■ No.1
Commonwealth House, 1-19 New Oxford Street, London WC1. Tel: (01) 404 0700

Teenage magazine covering the whole range of pop music; every Wednesday; 48pp; £0.45; circ. 171,000

■ Now Dig This
69 Quarry Lane, Simonside, South Shields, Tyne and Wear. Tel: (0632) 563213

Fifties US rock 'n' roll, roots; monthly, first week; 40pp; £1.25; circ. 2,000

■ One Two Testing/Zig Zag
PO Box 381, Mill Harbour, London E14. Tel: (01) 987 5090 Tx: 24676 Norshl G

Instrumental reviews, interviews, and features for the younger musician; monthly, third week; 100pp; £1.40; circ. 12,000

■ Q
42 Great Portland Street, London W1N 5AH. Tel: (01) 436 5430

A modern guide to music and more with features and reviews of albums, CDs, videos, books, films, etc; monthly; 100pp; £1,10; circ. n/a

■ Record Collector
43 St Mary's Road, London W5. Tel: (01) 579 1082

All kinds of music from the fifties to the present, with discographies of major artists, features etc. for the serious record collector; monthly; 116pp; £1.20; circ. 25,000

■ Rhythm
Alexander House, 1 Milton Road, Cambridge CB4 1UY. Tel: (0223) 313722

For drummers and drummer programmers. Interviews and reviews of new equipment; monthly; 72pp; £1.00; circ. 18,000

■ RM (Record Mirror)
Greater London House, Hampstead Road, London NW1. Tel: (01) 387 6611

Concentrates on up-and-coming bands, all types of music for the younger person; every Thursday; 48pp; £0.55; circ. 63,000

■ Sky
Rex House, 4-12 Lower Regent Street, London SW1 4PE. Tel: (01) 839 7799

Glossy, colour music, style and related issues magazine; fortnightly, Wednesdays; 76pp; £0.65; circ. n/a

■ Smash Hits
Lisa House, 52-55 Carnaby Street, London W1. Tel: (01) 437 8050

Chart hits, news and features for teenagers; "the biggest-selling music magazine in the world"; fortnightly, Wednesdays; 68pp; £0.45; circ. 515,000

■ Soul Underground
70-71 Wells Street, London W1P 3RD. Tel: (01) 637 4227

Enthusiastic and in depth coverage of non-mainstream soul and dance music; monthly; 36pp; £0.70; circ. 10,000

■ Sounds
Greater London House, Hampstead Road, London NW1. Tel: (01) 387 6611

Broad-based rock magazine for the under 25's; every Wednesday; 52pp; £0.55; circ. 77,000

■ Straight No Chaser
56 Clonmell Road, London N17 6JX. Tel: (01) 801 2534

World jazz and jive, a designer fanzine for those in tune with the freedom principle; bi-monthly; £1.00; circ. 7,500

■ Studio Sound and Broadcast Engineering
Link House, Dingwall Avenue, Croydon CR9 2TA. Tel: (01) 686 2599

Trade magazine for recording engineers, record producers, etc; monthly, second Friday; 140pp; £1.50 (free for professionals); circ. 16,000 worldwide

■ Swing 51
41 Bushey Road, Sutton, Surrey SM1 1QR.

Roots, rock and beyond . . . reviews of folk, ethnic, and rock music worldwide; every six months; 60pp; £1.50; circ. 1,500

■ The Wire
Unit G/H 115 Cleveland Street, London W1P 5PN.
Tel: (01) 580 7522

Jazz, improvised and new music etc; monthly, first week; 56pp; £1.20; circ. 15,000

MUSIC RELATED ASSOCIATIONS

■ American Society of Composers, Authors, and Publishers (ASCAP)
Suite 9, 52 Haymarket, London SW1Y 4RP.
Tel: (01) 930 1121 Tx: 25833

■ Association of Professional Recording Studios
23 Chestnut Avenue, Chorleywood, Herts WD3 4HA. Tel: (0923) 772907

■ British Academy of Songwriters, Composers and Authors
148 Charing Cross Road, London WC2H 0LB.
Tel: (01) 240 2823/4

■ The British Library National Sound Archive
29 Exhibition Road, London SW7 2AS.
Tel: (01) 589 6603/4

■ British Music Information Centre
10 Stratford Place, London W1N 9AE.
Tel: (01) 499 8567

■ British Phonographic Industry
4th Floor, Roxburghe House, 273/287 Regent Street, London W1R 7PB.
Tel: (01) 629 8642

■ British Tape Industry Association
7-15 Lansdowne Road, Croydon CR9 2PL.
Tel: (01) 688 4422 Tx: 917857 Binder G

■ Composers Guild of Great Britain
10 Stratford Place, London W1N 9AE.
Tel: (01) 499 4795

■ Country Music Association
Suite 3, 52 Haymarket, London SW1Y 4RP.
Tel: (01) 930 2445/6 Tx: 25833

■ International Federation of Phonogram and Videogram Producers
54 Regent Street, London W1R 5PJ.
Tel: (01) 434 3521 Tx: 919044 IFPI G

■ International Jazz Federation
13 Foulser Road, London SW17 8UE.
Tel: (01) 767 2213

■ Jazz Centre Society
5 Dryden Street, London WC2E 9NW.
Tel: (01) 240 2430

■ London Musicians' Collective
42A Gloucester Avenue, London NW1.
Tel: (01) 722 0456

■ Mechanical Copyright Protection Society
Elgar House, 41 Streatham High Road, London SW16 1ER. Tel: (01) 769 4400

■ Media Research and Information Bureau (MRIB)
12 Manchester Mews, London W1M 5PJ.
Tel: (01) 935 0346 Tx: 946240 Cweasy G

■ Music Publishers Association
7th Floor, 103 Kingsway, London WC2B 6QX.
Tel: (01) 831 7591

■ Musicians Benevolent Fund
16 Ogle Street, London W1P 7LG.
Tel: (01) 636 4481

■ Musicians' Union
60-62 Clapham Road, London SW9 0JJ.
Tel: (01) 582 5566 Tx: 881 4691

■ Performing Rights Society
29-33 Berners Street, London W1P 4AA.
Tel: (01) 580 5544 Tx: 892678

■ Record Labels Register
202 Finchley Road, London NW3 6BL.
Tel: (01) 794 0461 Tx: 261712

■ Royal Society of Musicians of Great Britain
10 Stratford Place, London W1N 9AE.
Tel: (01) 629 6137

■ Society for the Promotion of New Music
10 Stratford Place, London W1N 9AE.
Tel: (01) 491 8111

■ Variety Club of Great Britain
32 Welbeck Street, London W1M 7PG.
Tel: (01) 935 4466

US MUSIC REFERENCE

RECORD COMPANIES

■ **A&M Records**
1416 North LaBrea Avenue, Hollywood, CA 90068. Tel: (213) 469 2411 Tx: 691282
and
New York Office:
595 Madison Avenue, New York, NY 10022. Tel: (212) 826 0477
Tx: 961105
Labels: A&M

■ **Arista Records**
6 West 57th Street, New York, NY 10019.
Tel: (212) 489 7400 Tx: 666282
Labels: Arista

■ **Atlantic Recording Corp**
65 Rockerfeller Plaza, New York, NY 10019.
Tel: (212) 484 6000 Tx: 424602
and
LA office:
9229 Sunset Boulevard, Los Angeles, CA 90069. Tel: (213) 205 7450 Tx: 4720852
Labels: Atco, Atlantic, Cotillion, Elektra, Sire, 21

■ **Bearsville Records**
PO Box 135, Bearsville, NY 12409.
Tel: (914) 679 7303 Tx: 5102470848 Bearson G
Labels: Bearsville

■ **The Bensen Co**
365 Great Circle Road, Nashville, TN 37228.
Tel: (615) 259 9111
Labels: !Alarma!, Greentree, Heartwarming, Impact, Lifeline, NewPax, Onyx, Paragon

■ **Biograph Records**
Box 109, Caavaan, NY 12029. Tel: (518) 392 3400/1
Labels: Biograph, Center, Dawn, Historical, Melodeon, Waterfall

■ **Bomp Records**
2702 San Fernando Road, Los Angeles, CA 99065. Tel: (213) 227 4141
Labels: Bomp, Voxx

■ **Buddha Records**
1790 Broadway, New York, NY 10019.
Tel: (212) 582 6900 Tx: 422573
Labels: Buddah, Roulette, Streetwise, Sunnyview, Sutra

■ **Capitol/EMI Records**
1750 Vine Street, Hollywood, CA 90028.
Tel: (213) 462 6252 Tx: 674051
and
New York Office:
1370 Avenue of the Americas, New York, NY 10019. Tel: (212) 757 7470
Labels: Blue Note, Capitol, EMI-America, Manhattan

■ **CBS Records**
51 West 52nd Street, New York, NY 10019.
Tel: (212) 975 4321 Tx: 220561
and
LA Office:
1801 Century Park West, Los Angeles, CA 90067. Tel: (213) 556 4700
Labels: CBS, Columbia, Epic

■ **Celluloid Records**
330 Hudson Street, New York, NY 10013.
Tel: (212) 751 8310 Tx: 669253 Cell
Labels: Celluloid, OAO

■ **Chrysalis Records**
645 Madison Avenue, New York, NY 10022.
Tel: (212) 758 3555 Tx: 9718560
Labels: China, Chrysalis

■ **Def Jam Records**
594 Broadway (8th Floor), New York, NY 10012. Tel: (212) 925 0169

■ **Enigma Records**
1750 East Holly Avenue, PO Box 2428, El Segundo, CA 90245. Tel: (213) 640 6869
Tx: 503809
Labels: Attune, Enigma, Metal Blade, Pink Dust, Restless

■ **Fantasy Records**
2600 10th Street, Berkeley, CA 94710. Tel: (415) 549 2500 Tx: 171312 Universal Berk
Labels: Contemporary, Fantasy, Galaxy, Goodtime, Jazz, Milestone, Prestige, Riverside, Stax

■ **Flying Fish Records**
1304 West Schubert Street, Chicago, IL 60614.
Tel: (312) 528 5455 Tx: 297175
Labels: Flying Fish

■ **Folkways Records**
632 Broadway, New York, NY 10012.
Tel: (212) 6606 777 Tx: 220883 Tour
Labels: Folkways

■ **415 Records**
PO Box 14563, San Francisco, CA 94114.
Tel: (415) 621 3415
Labels: 415

■ **Geffen Records**
9130 Sunset Boulevard, Los Angeles, CA 90069. Tel: (213) 278 9010 Tx: 295854
and
New York Office:
75 Rockerfeller Plaza, New York, NY 10019.
Tel: (212) 474 7170 Tx: 424602
Labels: Geffen

■ **Hannibal Records**
3575 Cahuenga Boulevard West, Suite 470, Los Angeles, CA 90068. Tel: (213) 850 5660
Labels: Hannibal

■ **Homestead Records**
PO Box 570, Rockville Ctr, New York 11571.
Tel: (516) 764 6200

■ **Island Records**
14 East 4th Street, New York, NY 10012.
Tel: (212) 477 8000 Tx: 7105815292
Labels: Antilles, 4th and Broadway, Island, Mango

■ **Jem Records**
3619 Kennedy Road, South Plainfield, NJ 07080. Tel: (201) 753 6100 Tx: 275297 Jemur
and
West Coast Office:
18629 Topham Street, Reseda, CA 91335. Tel: (213) 996 6754 Tx: 674851 Jemrec wstreda
Labels: Audion, Coda, Editions EG, EG, EG Classics, Jem, Landscape, Ode, Passport, PVC, Visa

■ **MCA Records**
100 Universal City Plaza, Universal City, CA 91608. Tel: (818) 777 1000
and
New York Office:
445 Park Avenue, 6th Floor, New York, NY 10022. Tel: (212) 759 7500
Labels: Chess, Dot, Impulse, MCA, Zebra

■ **Motown Records**
6255 Sunset Boulevard, Los Angeles, CA 90028. Tel: (213) 468 3500. Tx: 4720916
Labels: Gordy, Motown, Tamla

■ **PolyGram Records**
810 Seventh Avenue, New York, NY 10019.
Tel: (212) 333 8000 Tx: 620985
and
LA Office:
8335 Sunset Boulevard, Los Angeles, CA 90069. Tel: (213) 656 3003
Labels: Casablanca, Mercury, Polydor

■ **Profile Records**
740 Broadway (7th Floor), New York, NY 10003. Tel: (212) 529 2600

■ **Ralph Records**
109 Minna Street, Suite 391, San Francisco, CA 94105. Tel: (415) 543 4085
Labels: Ralph

■ **RCA/Ariola Records**
1133 Avenue of the Americas, New York, NY 10036. Tel: (212) 930 4000 Tx: 234367
and
LA Office:
6363 Sunset Boulevard, Hollywood, CA 90028.
Tel: (213) 468 4000. Tx: 234367 Attn. Hollywood

■ **Reachout International Records**
611 Broadway, Suite 725, New York, NY 10012.
Tel: (212) 477 0563
Labels: Reachout

■ **Rhino Records**
1201 Olympic Boulevard, Santa Monica, CA 90404. Tel: (213) 450 6323 Tx: 4972305
Labels: Rhino

■ **Rough Trade Inc**
326 Sixth Street, San Francisco, CA 94103.
Tel: (415) 621 4045. Tx: 6771141
Labels: Factory-US, Pitch Attempt, Rough Trade, Silo

■ **Rounder Records**
1 Camp Street, Cambridge, MA 02142.
Tel: (617) 354 0700 Tx: 921724
Labels: Daring, Fretless, Heartbeat, Philo, Rounder, Varrick

■ **Shanachie Records**
1 Hollywood Avenue, Ho-Ho-Kus, NJ 07423.
Tel: (201) 445 5561 Tx: 247352
Labels: Herwin, Meadow Lark, Morning Star, Shanachie

■ **Slash Records**
7381 Beverly Boulevard, Los Angeles, CA 90036. Tel: (213) 937 4660
Labels: Slash

■ **Sugar Hill Records**
96 West Street, Englewood, NJ 07631.
Tel: (201) 569 5170 Tx: 429762
Labels: Sugar Hill

■ **Tommy Boy Records**
1747 First Avenue, New York, NY 10128
Tel: (212) 722 2211. Tx: 6971684 Funk
Labels: Tommy Boy

■ **Touch And Go Records**
PO Box 25520, Chicago, Illinois 60625.
Tel: (312) 463 4446

■ **Trax Records**
932 W. 38th Place, Chicago, Illinois 60629.
Tel: (312) 247 3033

■ **Vanguard Records**
71 West 23rd Street, New York, NY 10010.
Tel: (212) 255 7732 Tx: 469150
Labels: Terra, Vanguard

■ **Warner Brothers Records**
3300 Warner Boulevard, Burbank, CA 91510.
Tel: (818) 846 9090 Tx: 698512
and
New York Office:
3 East 54th Street, New York, NY 10022.
Tel: (212) 702 0318 Tx: 7105815718
Labels: Warner Brothers, Warner Nashville

■ **Wax Trax Records**
2445 N. Lincoln Ave, Chicago, Illinois 60614.
Tel: (312) 528 8753 Tx: 5106003326

■ **Windham Hill Records**
PO Box 9388, 247 High St, Paol Atto, CA 94305.
Tel: (415) 329 0647
Labels: Windham Hill

LABELS

!Alarma! – Benson
Antilles – Island
Atco – Atlantic
Attune – Enigma
Audion – Jem
Blue Note – Capitol/EMI
Casablanca – PolyGram
Center – Biograph
Chess – MCA
China – Chrysalis
Coda – Jem
Columbia – CBS
Contemporary – Fantasy
Cotillion – Atlantic
Daring – Rounder
Dawn – Biograph
Dot – MCA
Editions EG – Jem
EG – Jem
Elektra – Atlantic
EMI America – Capitol/EMI
Epic – CBS
Factory US – Rough Trade
4th and Broadway – Island
Fretless – Rounder
Galaxy – Fantasy
Goodtime Jazz – Fantasy
Gordy – Motown
Greentree – Benson
Heartbeat – Rounder
Heartwarming – Benson
Herwin – Shanachie
Hi – Cream
Historical – Biograph
Impact – Benson
Impulse – MCA
Landscape – Jem
Lifeline – Benson
Mango – Island
Manhattan – Capitol/EMI
Meadow Lark – Shanachie
Melodeon – Biograph
Mercury – PolyGram
Metal Blade – Enigma
Milestone – Fantasy
Morning Star – Shanachie
NewPax – Benson
Ode – Jem
Onyx – Benson
Paragon – Benson
Passport – Jem
Philo – Rounder
Pink Dust – Enigma
Pitch Attempt – Rough Trade
Polydor – PolyGram
Prestige – Fantasy
PVC – Jem
Restless – Enigma
Riverside – Fantasy
Roulette – Buddha
Silo – Rough Trade
Stax – Fantasy
Streetwise – Buddha
Sunnyview – Buddha
Sutra – Buddha
Tamla – Motown
Terra – Vanguard
21 – Atlantic
Varrick – Rounder
Visa – Jem
Voxx – Bomp
Waterfall – Biograph
Zebra – MCA

MUSIC PUBLISHERS

■ **Acuff-Rose Publications**
2510 Franklin Road, Nashville, TN 37204.
Tel: (615) 385 3031 Tx: 554366

■ **April/Blackwood Music**
49 East 52nd Street, New York, NY 10022.
Tel: (212) 975 4886 Tx: 220561

■ **Augsburg Publishing**
426 South Fifth Street, Minneapolis, MN 55415. Tel: (612) 330 3300

■ **Beserkely**
2054 University Avenue, Suite 400, Berkeley, CA 94704. Tel: (415) 848 6701

■ **Big Music**
10 George Street, Wallingford, CT 06492.
Tel: (203) 269 4465

■ **Big Seven Music**
1790 Broadway, 18th Floor, New York, NY 10019. Tel: (212) 582 4267 Tx: 422573

■ **Bourne Co**
437 Fifth Avenue, New York, NY 10016.
Tel: (212) 679 3700

■ **Buddha Music**
1790 Broadway, New York, NY 10019.
Tel: (212) 582 6900 Tx: 422573

■ **Bug Music**
6777 Hollywood Boulevard, 9th Floor, Hollywood, CA 90028. Tel: (213) 466 4352
Tx: 9103213926

■ Cameron Organisation
822 Hillgrove Avenue, Western Springs, IL 60558. Tel: (312) 246 8222

■ CBS Songs
49 East 52nd Street, New York, NY 10022. Tel: (212) 975 4886 Tx: 960213

■ Chappell/Intersong Music
810 Seventh Avenue, 32nd Floor, New York, NY 10019. Tel: (212) 399 6910 Tx: 421749

■ Chrysalis Music Group
645 Madison Avenue, New York, NY 10022. Tel: (212) 758 3555 Tx: 971860

■ Cotillion Music
75 Rockerfeller Plaza, New York, NY 10019. Tel: (212) 484 8132 Tx: 424602

■ Crazy Cajun Music
5626 Brock Street, Houston, TX 77023. Tel: (713) 926 4431

■ Cream Publishing
13107 Ventura Boulevard, Suite 102, Studio City, CA 91604. Tel: (818) 905 6344

■ Entertainment Company Music
1700 Broadway, 41st Floor, New York, NY 10019. Tel: (212) 265 2600 Tx: 6972989

■ Evansongs
1790 Broadway, New York, NY 10019. Tel: (212) 765 8450 Tx: 125609 Espnyk

■ Famous Music
1 Gulf and Western Plaza, New York, NY 10023. Tel: (212) 333 3433 Tx: 235260

■ Carl Fisher Inc
62 Cooper Square, New York, NY 10003. Tel: (212) 777 9000 Tx: 4774129

■ Flying Fish Music
1304 West Schubert Street, Chicago IL 60614. Tel: (312) 528 5455 Tx: 297175

■ Al Gallico Music
344 East 49th Street, New York, NY 10017. Tel: (212) 355 5980

■ Garrett Music
4121 Radford Avenue, Studio City, CA 91604. Tel: (818) 506 8964

■ Glad Music
3409 Brinkman Street, Houston, TX 77018. Tel: (713) 861 3630

■ Graph Music
34 Ratterman Road, Woodstock, New York, NY 12498. Tel: (914) 679 2458

■ Al Green Music
PO Box 456, Millington, TN 38053. Tel: (901) 794 6220

■ Hilaria Music
315 West Gorham Street, Madison, W1 53703. Tel: (608) 251 2644

■ Home Grown Music
4412 Whitsett Avenue, Studio City, CA 91604. Tel: (818) 763 6323

■ Hudson Bay Music
1619 Broadway 11th Floor, New York, NY 10019. Tel: (212) 489 8170 Tx: 62932

■ Intersong Music
6255 Sunset Boulevard, Suite 1904, Hollywood, CA 90028. Tel: (213) 469 5141 Tx: 4991128

■ Island Music
6525 Sunset Boulevard, 2nd Floor, Hollywood, CA 90028. Tel: (213) 469 1285 Tx: 691223 Ackeelsa

■ Jobete Music
6255 Sunset Boulevard, Hollywood, CA 90028. Tel: (213) 468 3500

■ Largo Music
425 Park Avenue, New York, NY 10022. Tel: (212) 371 9400 Tx: 8389487

■ Laurie Publishing
450 Livingston Street, Norwood, NJ 07648. Tel: (201) 767 5551

■ Hal Leonard Publishing
PO Box 13809, Milwaukee WI 53213. Tel: (414) 774 3630 Tx: 26668

■ Marsaint Music
3809 Clematis Avenue, New Orleans, LA 70122. Tel: (504) 949 8386

■ MCA Music
70 Universal City Plaza, Suite 425, Universal City CA 91608. Tel: (818) 777 4550 Tx: 677053 Universal City

■ Ivan Mogull Music
625 Madison Avenue, New York, NY 10022. Tel: (212) 355 5636 Tx: 236973

■ Neil Music
8400 Sunset Boulevard, Suite 4a, Los Angeles, CA 90069. Tel: (213) 656 2614 Tx: 5106000877

■ Pale Pachyderm Publishing
566 Folsom Street, San Francisco, CA 94105. Tel: (415) 543 8248

■ Peer-Southern Organisation
1740 Broadway, New York, NY 10019. Tel: (212) 265 3910 Tx: 424361

■ The Richmond Organisation (TRO)
10 Columbus Circle, New York, NY 10019. Tel: (212) 765 9889 Tx: 429359

■ SBK Songs
1290 Avenue of the Americas, 42nd Floor, NYC, NY 10019. Tel: (212) 975 4886

■ Screen Gems – EMI Music
6920 Sunset Boulevard, Hollywood, CA 90028. Tel: (213) 469 8371

■ Paul Simon Music
1619 Broadway, Room 500, New York, NY 10019. Tel: (212) 541 7571 Tx: 645 491

■ Special Rider Music
PO Box 860, Cooper Station, New York, NY 10276. Tel: (212) 473 5900 Tx: 661139

■ TRO
See the Richmond Organisation

■ 20th Century-Fox Music
PO Box 900, Beverly Hills, CA 90213. Tel: (213) 203 1487 Tx: 674895

■ Warner Brothers Music
9000 Sunset Boulevard, The Penthouse Suite, Los Angeles, CA 90069. Tel: (213) 273 3323 Tx: 9104902598

■ Welk Music
1299 Ocean Avenue, Suite 800, Santa Monica, CA 90401. Tel: (213) 870 1582

■ Word Music
PO Box 2790, Waco, TX 76796. Tel: (817) 772 7650 Tx: 530642

■ WPN Music
10 Swirl Lane, Levittown, NY 11756. Tel: (516) 796 3698

DISTRIBUTORS/IMPORTERS

■ Abbey Road Record Distributors
1721 Newport Circle, Santa Ana, CA 92705. Tel: (714) 546 7177

■ All South Distribution
1037 Broadway, New Orleans, LA 70118. Tel: (504) 861 2906

■ ARC Distributing Corp
580 Reading Road, Cincinnati, OH 45202. Tel: (513) 381 4237

■ Associated Distributors
3803 North 36th Avenue, Phoenix, AZ 85019. Tel: (602) 278 5584

■ Rick Ballard Imports
PO Box 24854, Oakland, CA 94623. Tel: (415) 832 1277

■ Bayside Record Distribution
10341 San Pablo Avenue, El Cerrito, CA 94530. Tel: (415) 525 4996

■ California Record Distributors
1242 Los Angeles Street, Glendale, CA 91204. Tel: (818) 246 8228

■ Dutch East India Trading
81 North Forest Avenue, Rockville Center, NY 11570. Tel: (516) 764 6200

■ Goldenrod Distribution
5505 Delta River Drive, Lansing, MI 48906. Tel: (517) 323 4325

■ Greenworld Distribution
20445 Gramercy Place, Torrance, CA 90501. Tel: (213) 533 8075 Tx: 4720103

■ Important Record Distribution
190-03 Guy R. Brewer Boulevard, Jamaica, NY 11434. Tel: (718) 995 9200

■ Jem Record Distributors
18629 Topham Street, Reseda, CA 91335. Tel: (818) 996 6754

■ MS Distributing Co
1050 Arthur Avenue, Elk Grove Village, IL 60007. Tel: (312) 364 2888

■ Music Town Record Distributors
830 Glastonbury Road, Suite 614, Nashville, TN 37217. Tel: (615) 327 4538

■ Rough Trade
326 Sixth Street, San Francisco, CA 94103. Tel: (415) 621 4045 Tx: 6771141

■ Rounder Distribution
1 Camp Street, Cambridge, MA 02142. Tel: (617) 345 0700 Tx: 921724

■ SDA Distribution
1109 Xerxes Avenue South, Minneapolis, MN 55405. Tel: (612) 0590

■ Sounds Good Import Co
3355 West El Segundo Avenue, Hawthorne, CA 90250. Tel: (213) 973 8800 Tx: 4990518

■ Southern Cross Record Distributors
1200 Newell Hill Place, Suite 302, Walnut Creek, CA 94596. Tel: (415) 945 1855

■ Spring Arbor Distribution
10885 Textile Road, Belleville, MI 48111. Tel: (313) 481 0900

■ Systematic Record Distributors
1331 Fulsom Street, San Francisco, CA 94103. Tel: (415) 431 9377

■ Twin Cities Imports
1451 University Avenue, St Paul, MN 55104. Tel: (612) 645 0227 Tx: 4940057

■ Universal Record Distribution
919 North Broad Street, Philadelphia, PA 19123. Tel: (215) 232 3333

MUSIC RELATED ASSOCIATIONS

■ Academy of Country Music
6255 Sunset Boulevard, Suite 915, Hollywood, CA 90028. Tel: (213) 462 2351

■ American Federation of Musicians
1501 Broadway, Suite 600, New York, NY 10036. Tel: (212) 869 1330

■ ASCAP
1 Lincoln Plaza, New York, NY 10023. Tel: (212) 585 3050 Tx: 7105812084

■ Association of Independent Music Publishers
c/o Harrison Music, 6253 Hollywood Boulevard, Hollywood, CA 90028. Tel: (213) 466 3834

■ Black Music Association
1500 Locust Street, Suite 1905, Philadelphia, PA 19102. Tel: (215) 545 8600

■ BMI
320 West 57th Street, New York, NY 10019. Tel: (212) 586 2000 Tx: 127823

■ Country Music Association
7 Music Circle North, Nashville, TN 37202. Tel: (615) 244 2840 Tx: 786528

■ Jazz Composers' Orchestra Association
500 Broadway, New York, NY 10012. Tel: (212) 925 2121. Tx: 291524

■ National Academy of Recording Arts and Sciences
303 North Gen Oaks Boulevard, Suite 140, Burbank, CA 91502. Tel: (818) 843 8233

■ National Association of Independent Record Distributors
c/o Richman Brothers Records, 6935 Airport Highway Lane, Pennsauken, NJ 08109. Tel: (609) 665 8085

■ National Association of Music Merchants
5240 Avenida Encinas, Carlsbad, CA 92008. Tel: (619) 438 8001

■ Recording Industry Association of America
888 Seventh Avenue, New York, NY 10106. Tel: (212) 765 4330

■ SESAC
10 Columbus Circle, 13th Floor, New York, NY 10019. Tel: (212) 586 3450

■ Songwriters Guild of America
276 5th Avenue, Room 306, New York, NY 10001. Tel: (212) 686 6820

MUSIC MAGAZINES

■ American Songwriter
5065 Lebanon Road, Old Hickory, Tennessee 37138. Tel: (615) 754 5200
Pop, R&B, country music, geared to the professional and amateur songwriter; bi-monthly; 32pp; $2.25; circ: 5,000 subscription only

■ BAM
5951 Canning Street, Oakland, CA 94609. Tel: (415) 652 3810
and
1800 North Highland, Suite 220, Hollywood CA 90028. Tel: (213) 467 7878
Covers US and international bands with the emphasis of commercial successes from mainstream rock to pop and progressive; also has features on up-and-coming bands (California edition covers mainly Californian artistes); national ed. bi-monthly, California ed. fortnightly; 64pp; national ed. $1.95, California ed. free; circ: 125,000 (each)

■ Billboard
1515 Broadway, New York, NY 10036. Tel: (212) 764 7300
Trade magazine covering most of the areas of rock music, also sells to the punter on the street; every Tuesday; 80pp; $3.50; circ: 48,000

■ Boston Rock
1318 Beacon Street, Suite 7, Brooklyme, MA 02146. Tel: (617) 734 7043
Alternative arts and lifestyle magazine, covering local and national underground acts as well as imports; monthly; 32pp; free in MA, $1.50 outside MA; circ: 30,000

■ Cash Box
330 West 58th Street, New York, NY 10019. Tel: (212) 586 2640
Trade magazine covering rock, pop, jazz, black contemporary and dance music; every Monday; 50pp; $3.50; circ: n/a

■ Circus
419 Park Avenue South, New York, NY 10016. Tel: (212) 685 5050
Hard rock and heavy metal superstars; monthly, last week; 90pp; $1.95/£1.50; circ: n/a

■ CMJ New Music Report
834 Willis Avenue, Albertson, NY 11507. Tel: (516) 248 9600
Magazine covering progressive rock, jazz, folk, country, reggae, selling primarily to younger musicians and record industry execs; 50% charts, 50% features; fortnightly; 60pp; $6.00; circ: 14,000

■ Country News
5065 Lebanon Road, Old Hickory, Tennessee 37138. Tel: (615) 754 5200
The latest country industry news for fans as well as record executives; monthly; 24pp; $1.50; circ: 160,000 subscription only

■ Country Rhythms
5065 Lebanon Road, Old Hickory, Tennessee 37138. Tel: (615) 754 5200
Features and interviews with prominent country artistes; monthly; 56pp; $2.50; circ: 120,000

■ Country Songs Round-up
Charlton Buildings, Division Street, Derby, CT 06418. Tel: (203) 735 3381
Lyrics of country music Top 40, reviews, features; monthly; 58pp; $1.75; circ: n/a

■ Country Sounds
700 East State Street, Iola, WI 54990. Tel: (715) 445 2214
Country record collectors' magazine; monthly; 60pp; $1.95; circ: n/a

■ CREEM
210 South Woodward Avenue, Birmingham, MI 48011. Tel: (313) 642 8833
Eclectic magazine that credits its readers with a sense of humour and the second longest-running US music magazine after *Rolling Stone*; monthly; 66pp; $2.25; circ: c. 100,000

■ Down Beat
180 West Park Avenue, Elmhurst, IL 60126. Tel: (312) 941 2030
Jazz magazine for contemporary musicians, also covering rock, blues and contemporary classical instrumentalists; monthly; 62pp; $1.75/£2.00; circ: 95,000

■ Flipside
PO Box 363, Whittier, CA 90608
Hardcore punk fanzine; irregular monthly; nothing else known

■ Frets
20625 Lazaneo, Cupertino, CA 95014. Tel: (408) 446 1105
Folk, classical, and bluegrass for acoustic stringed instrument players; monthly; 68pp; $1.95; circ: 70,000

■ Goldmine
700 East State Street, Iola, WI 54990. Tel: (715) 445 2214
Eclectic record collectors' magazine from hard rock to folk and country; fortnightly; 90pp; $1.95; circ: 15,000

■ Guitar Player
20605 Lazaneo, Cupertino, CA 95014. Tel: (408) 446 1105
Guitar magazine written by musicians for musicians, rock, jazz, classical; monthly; 156pp; $2.95; circ: 170,000

■ Guitar World
1115 Broadway, 8th Floor, New York, NY 10010. Tel: (212) 807 7100
Covers all kinds of guitar-based music, rock, jazz, blues, etc., except classical; bi-monthly; 102pp; $2.95; circ: 160,000

■ Hard Rock
475 Park Avenue South, New York, NY 10016. Tel: (212) 689 2830
Mainstream hard rock, hardcore and metal; lots of interviews and regular features; monthly; 80pp; $2.25/£1.45; circ: 200,000 worldwide

■ High Fidelity
825 Seventh Avenue, New York, NY 10019. Tel: (212) 887 8337
Reviews of the latest hi-fi equipment along with some features on pop and classical releases; monthly; 86pp; $2.25; circ: 350,000

■ Hit Parader
Charlton Building, Division Street, Derby, CT 06148. Tel: (203) 735 5381
and
New York Office:
441 Lexington Avenue, Suite 808, New York, NY 10017. Tel: (212) 370 0986
Looks at hard rock and heavy metal superstars, interviews, features, etc., for the teenager; monthly; 82pp; $2.25/£1.50; circ: 100,000

■ Illinois Entertainer
PO Box 356, Mount Prospect, IL 60056. Tel: (312) 298 9333
Entertainment magazine covering the music scene (among other things) in Illinois; monthly; 90pp; free in record stores, etc; circ: 80,000

■ International Musician and Recording World
1075 Easton Avenue, Suite 1, Tower 2, Somerset, NJ 08873. Tel: (201) 249 1600
Spans all types of contemporary music from pop, rock to avant-garde ethnic. Reviews latest equipment and releases primarily for musicians and recording executives, but also for the listener; monthly; 64pp; $2.50; circ: 65,000

■ Jazz Times
8055 13th Street, Silver Springs, MD 20910. Tel: (301) 558 4114
Straight-ahead traditional jazz, trade and fan magazine; news, reviews, artiste profiles, listings of radio airplay; monthly; 28pp; £1.50; circ: 58,000

■ Keyboard
20605 Lazaneo, Cupertino, CA 95014. Tel: (408) 446 1105
Features on equipment, techniques and artistes, for keyboard players; monthly; 140pp; $2.50/£2.00; circ: 85,000

■ Living Blues
The Center for the Study of Southern Culture, University of Mississippi, University, MS 38677. Tel: (601) 232 5993
Blues news, interviews, and record reviews; bi-monthly; 48pp; $3.00; circ: 5,000

■ Music Connection
6640 Sunset Boulevard, Suite 208, Hollywood, CA 90028. Tel: (213) 462 5772
An informed, amusing and often uncompromising rock musicians/industry magazine, devoting itself to the making of music rather than the making of

■ Musician
31 Commercial Street, Gloucester, MA 01930. Tel: (617) 281 3110
and
New York Office:
1515 Broadway, New York, NY 10036. Tel: (212) 764 7300
Up-market serious magazine covering the entire spectrum of the music-making process, creative and technological, for the professional and dedicated amateur; monthly; 116pp; $2.50/£1.50; circ: 116,000

■ Radio and Records
1930 Century Park West, Los Angeles, CA 90067. Tel: (213) 553 4330
Radio and record industry magazine with lots of charts, regular features on US radio, news, etc; every Friday; 96pp; $5.00; circ: n/a

■ Rock & Soul
Charlton Building, Division Street, Derby, CT 06418. Tel: (203) 735 3381
and
New York Office:
441 Lexington Avenue, Suite 808, New York, NY 10017. Tel: (212) 370 0986
Glossy magazine covering commercial black music, with news hotline, profiles, reviews; monthly; 50pp; $1.75; circ: 80,000

■ Rocket
Charlton Building, Division Street, Derby, CT 06418. Tel: (203) 735 3381
New superstar magazine; monthly; 50pp; $1.95; circ: n/a

■ The Rocket
2322 Second Avenue, Seattle, WA 98121. Tel: (206) 587 4001
Sardonic entertainments magazine covering local and national acts, music, arts, politics, cartoons and gossip columns; monthly; 38pp; $2.00; circ: 65,000

■ Rockpool Newsletter
83 Leonard Street, 2nd Floor, New York, NY 10013. Tel: (212) 219 0777
An alternative look at hip black music and new wave dance, playlists and charts from club DJs and US college radio scene; fortnightly; 30pp; $1.75; circ: 2,000

■ Rolling Stone
745 Fifth Avenue, New York, NY 10151. Tel: (212) 758 3800
The magazine for young American adults; much more than just a music magazine; looks at politics, popular culture, etc., etc; a national institution; fortnightly; 100pp; $1.95/£1.90; circ: 1,000,000 worldwide

■ Song Hits
Charlton Building, Division Street, Derby, CT 06418. Tel: (203) 735 3381
Song lyrics, concert and album reviews of Top 40 rock, soul and country musicians; for teenage girls; monthly, 66pp; $1.95; circ: 160,000

■ Spin
6 West 18th Street, New York, NY 10011. Tel: (212) 633 8200
A zany, humorous look at established, new, and underground acts; news and reviews from mainstream rock to ethnic sounds; also looks at topical issues of youth culture; monthly; 74pp; $2.50; circ: 20,000

■ Star Hits
25 W. 39th Street, New York, NY 10018. Tel: (212) 302 2626
Glossy teenage girls' magazine styled after the British *Smash Hits*; interviews and features on commercial successes; monthly; 64pp; $1.95; circ: 163,000

■ WAM
PO Box 356, Mount Prospect, IL 60056. Tel: (312) 298 9333

■ WAVELENGTH
PO Box 15667, New Orleans, LA 707175. Tel: (504) 895 2342
New Orleans jazz, R&B, blues, cajun, etc., and local culture; reviews independently released records; monthly; 40pp; free in LA, $1.50 outside LA; circ: 30,000